Tomáš Vojnar · Lijun Zhang (Eds.)

Tools and Algorithms for the Construction and Analysis of Systems

25th International Conference, TACAS 2019
Held as Part of the European Joint Conferences on Theory and Practice of Software, ETAPS 2019
Prague, Czech Republic, April 6–11, 2019
Proceedings, Part II

Editors
Tomáš Vojnar
Brno University of Technology
Brno, Czech Republic

Lijun Zhang
Chinese Academy of Sciences
Beijing, China

https://doi.org/10.1007/978-3-030-17465-1

LNCS Sublibrary: SL1 – Theoretical Computer Science and General Issues

ETAPS Foreword

Welcome to the 22nd ETAPS! This is the first time that ETAPS took place in the Czech Republic in its beautiful capital Prague.

ETAPS 2019 was the 22nd instance of the European Joint Conferences on Theory and Practice of Software. ETAPS is an annual federated conference established in 1998, and consists of five conferences: ESOP, FASE, FoSSaCS, TACAS, and POST. Each conference has its own Program Committee (PC) and its own Steering Committee (SC). The conferences cover various aspects of software systems, ranging from theoretical computer science to foundations to programming language developments, analysis tools, formal approaches to software engineering, and security.

Organizing these conferences in a coherent, highly synchronized conference program enables participation in an exciting event, offering the possibility to meet many researchers working in different directions in the field and to easily attend talks of different conferences. ETAPS 2019 featured a new program item: the Mentoring Workshop. This workshop is intended to help students early in the program with advice on research, career, and life in the fields of computing that are covered by the ETAPS conference. On the weekend before the main conference, numerous satellite workshops took place and attracted many researchers from all over the globe.

ETAPS 2019 received 436 submissions in total, 137 of which were accepted, yielding an overall acceptance rate of 31.4%. I thank all the authors for their interest in ETAPS, all the reviewers for their reviewing efforts, the PC members for their contributions, and in particular the PC (co-)chairs for their hard work in running this entire intensive process. Last but not least, my congratulations to all authors of the accepted papers!

ETAPS 2019 featured the unifying invited speakers Marsha Chechik (University of Toronto) and Kathleen Fisher (Tufts University) and the conference-specific invited speakers (FoSSaCS) Thomas Colcombet (IRIF, France) and (TACAS) Cormac Flanagan (University of California at Santa Cruz). Invited tutorials were provided by Dirk Beyer (Ludwig Maximilian University) on software verification and Cesare Tinelli (University of Iowa) on SMT and its applications. On behalf of the ETAPS 2019 attendants, I thank all the speakers for their inspiring and interesting talks!

ETAPS 2019 took place in Prague, Czech Republic, and was organized by Charles University. Charles University was founded in 1348 and was the first university in Central Europe. It currently hosts more than 50,000 students. ETAPS 2019 was further supported by the following associations and societies: ETAPS e.V., EATCS (European Association for Theoretical Computer Science), EAPLS (European Association for Programming Languages and Systems), and EASST (European Association of Software Science and Technology). The local organization team consisted of Jan Vitek and Jan Kofron (general chairs), Barbora Buhnova, Milan Ceska, Ryan Culpepper, Vojtech Horky, Paley Li, Petr Maj, Artem Pelenitsyn, and David Safranek.

The ETAPS SC consists of an Executive Board, and representatives of the individual ETAPS conferences, as well as representatives of EATCS, EAPLS, and EASST. The Executive Board consists of Gilles Barthe (Madrid), Holger Hermanns (Saarbrücken), Joost-Pieter Katoen (chair, Aachen and Twente), Gerald Lüttgen (Bamberg), Vladimiro Sassone (Southampton), Tarmo Uustalu (Reykjavik and Tallinn), and Lenore Zuck (Chicago). Other members of the SC are: Wil van der Aalst (Aachen), Dirk Beyer (Munich), Mikolaj Bojanczyk (Warsaw), Armin Biere (Linz), Luis Caires (Lisbon), Jordi Cabot (Barcelona), Jean Goubault-Larrecq (Cachan), Jurriaan Hage (Utrecht), Rainer Hähnle (Darmstadt), Reiko Heckel (Leicester), Panagiotis Katsaros (Thessaloniki), Barbara König (Duisburg), Kim G. Larsen (Aalborg), Matteo Maffei (Vienna), Tiziana Margaria (Limerick), Peter Müller (Zurich), Flemming Nielson (Copenhagen), Catuscia Palamidessi (Palaiseau), Dave Parker (Birmingham), Andrew M. Pitts (Cambridge), Dave Sands (Gothenburg), Don Sannella (Edinburgh), Alex Simpson (Ljubljana), Gabriele Taentzer (Marburg), Peter Thiemann (Freiburg), Jan Vitek (Prague), Tomas Vojnar (Brno), Heike Wehrheim (Paderborn), Anton Wijs (Eindhoven), and Lijun Zhang (Beijing).

I would like to take this opportunity to thank all speakers, attendants, organizers of the satellite workshops, and Springer for their support. I hope you all enjoy the proceedings of ETAPS 2019. Finally, a big thanks to Jan and Jan and their local organization team for all their enormous efforts enabling a fantastic ETAPS in Prague!

February 2019

Joost-Pieter Katoen
ETAPS SC Chair
ETAPS e.V. President

Preface

TACAS 2019 was the 25th edition of the International Conference on Tools and Algorithms for the Construction and Analysis of Systems conference series. TACAS 2019 was part of the 22nd European Joint Conferences on Theory and Practice of Software (ETAPS 2019). The conference was held at the Orea Hotel Pyramida in Prague, Czech Republic, during April 8–11, 2019.

Conference Description. TACAS is a forum for researchers, developers, and users interested in rigorously based tools and algorithms for the construction and analysis of systems. The conference aims to bridge the gaps between different communities with this common interest and to support them in their quest to improve the utility, reliability, flexibility, and efficiency of tools and algorithms for building systems. TACAS 2019 solicited four types of submissions:

- *Research papers*, identifying and justifying a principled advance to the theoretical foundations for the construction and analysis of systems, where applicable supported by experimental validation.
- *Case-study papers*, reporting on case studies and providing information about the system being studied, the goals of the study, the challenges the system poses to automated analysis, research methodologies and approaches used, the degree to which goals were attained, and how the results can be generalized to other problems and domains.
- *Regular tool papers*, presenting a new tool, a new tool component, or novel extensions to an existing tool, with an emphasis on design and implementation concerns, including software architecture and core data structures, practical applicability, and experimental evaluations.
- *Tool-demonstration papers* (short), focusing on the usage aspects of tools.

Paper Selection. This year, 164 papers were submitted to TACAS, among which 119 were research papers, 10 case-study papers, 24 regular tool papers, and 11 were tool-demonstration papers. After a rigorous review process, with each paper reviewed by at least three Program Committee members, followed by an online discussion, the Program Committee accepted 29 research papers, 2 case-study papers, 11 regular tool papers, and 8 tool-demonstration papers (50 papers in total).

Artifact-Evaluation Process. The main novelty of TACAS 2019 was that, for the first time, artifact evaluation was compulsory for all regular tool papers and tool demonstration papers. For research papers and case-study papers, artifact evaluation was optional. The artifact evaluation process was organized as follows:

- *Regular tool papers and tool demonstration papers.* The authors of the 35 submitted papers of these categories of papers were required to submit an artifact alongside their paper submission. Each artifact was evaluated independently by three reviewers. Out of the 35 artifact submissions, 28 were successfully evaluated, which corresponds to an acceptance rate of 80%. The AEC used a two-phase reviewing process: Reviewers first performed an initial check to see whether the artifact was technically usable and whether the accompanying instructions were consistent, followed by a full evaluation of the artifact. The main criterion for artifact acceptance was consistency with the paper, with completeness and documentation being handled in a more lenient manner as long as the artifact was useful overall. The reviewers were instructed to check whether results are consistent with what is described in the paper. Inconsistencies were to be clearly pointed out and explained by the authors. In addition to the textual reviews, reviewers also proposed a numeric value about (potentially weak) acceptance/rejection of the artifact. After the evaluation process, the results of the artifact evaluation were summarized and forwarded to the discussion of the papers, so as to enable the reviewers of the papers to take the evaluation into account. In all but three cases, tool papers whose artifacts did not pass the evaluation were rejected.

- *Research papers and case-study papers*. For this category of papers, artifact evaluation was voluntary. The authors of each of the 25 accepted papers were invited to submit an artifact immediately after the acceptance notification. Owing to the short time available for the process and acceptance of the artifact not being critical for paper acceptance, there was only one round of evaluation for this category, and every artifact was assigned to two reviewers. The artifacts were evaluated using the same criteria as for tool papers. Out of the 18 submitted artifacts of this phase, 15 were successfully evaluated (83% acceptance rate) and were awarded the TACAS 2019 AEC badge, which is added to the title page of the respective paper if desired by the authors.

TOOLympics. TOOLympics 2019 was part of the celebration of the 25th anniversary of the TACAS conference. The goal of TOOLympics is to acknowledge the achievements of the various competitions in the field of formal methods, and to understand their commonalities and differences. A total of 2^4 competitions joined TOOLympics and were presented at the event. An overview and competition reports of 11 competitions are included in the third volume of the TACAS 2019 proceedings, which are dedicated to the 25th anniversary of TACAS. The extra volume contains a review of the history of TACAS, the TOOLympics papers, and the papers of the annual Competition on Software Verification.

Competition on Software Verification. TACAS 2019 also hosted the 8th International Competition on Software Verification (SV-COMP), chaired and organized by Dirk Beyer. The competition again had high participation: 31 verification systems with developers from 14 countries were submitted for the systematic comparative evaluation, including three submissions from industry. The TACAS proceedings includes the competition report and short papers describing 11 of the participating verification systems. These papers were reviewed by a separate program committee (PC); each of the papers was assessed by four reviewers. Two sessions in the TACAS program (this year as part of the TOOLympics event) were reserved for the presentation of the results: the summary by the SV-COMP chair and the participating tools by the developer teams in the first session, and the open jury meeting in the second session.

Acknowledgments. We would like to thank everyone who helped to make TACAS 2019 successful. In particular, we would like to thank the authors for submitting their papers to TACAS 2019. We would also like to thank all PC members, additional reviewers, as well as all members of the artifact evaluation committee (AEC) for their detailed and informed reviews and, in the case of the PC and AEC members, also for their discussions during the virtual PC and AEC meetings. We also thank the Steering Committee for their advice. Special thanks go to the Organizing Committee of ETAPS 2019 and its general chairs, Jan Kofroň and Jan Vitek, to the chair of the ETAPS 2019 executive board, Joost-Pieter Katoen, and to the publication team at Springer.

March 2019

Tomáš Vojnar (PC Chair)
Lijun Zhang (PC Chair)
Marius Mikucionis (Tools Chair)
Radu Grosu (Use-Case Chair)
Dirk Beyer (SV-COMP Chair)
Ondřej Lengál (AEC Chair)
Ernst Moritz Hahn (AEC Chair)

Organization

Program Committee

Parosh Aziz Abdulla	Uppsala University, Sweden
Dirk Beyer	LMU Munich, Germany
Armin Biere	Johannes Kepler University Linz, Austria
Ahmed Bouajjani	IRIF, Paris Diderot University, France
Patricia Bouyer	LSV, CNRS/ENS Cachan, Université Paris Saclay, France
Yu-Fang Chen	Academia Sinica, Taiwan
Maria Christakis	MPI-SWS, Germany
Alessandro Cimatti	Fondazione Bruno Kessler, Italy
Rance Cleaveland	University of Maryland, USA
Leonardo de Moura	Microsoft Research, USA
Parasara Sridhar Duggirala	University of North Carolina at Chapel Hill, USA
Pierre Ganty	IMDEA Software Institute, Spain
Radu Grosu	Vienna University of Technology, Austria
Orna Grumberg	Technion – Israel Institute of Technology, Israel
Klaus Havelund	NASA/Caltech Jet Propulsion Laboratory, USA
Holger Hermanns	Saarland University, Germany
Falk Howar	TU Dortmund, Germany
Marieke Huisman	University of Twente, The Netherlands
Radu Iosif	Verimag, CNRS/University of Grenoble Alpes, France
Joxan Jaffar	National University of Singapore, Singapore
Stefan Kiefer	University of Oxford, UK
Jan Kretinsky	Technical University of Munich, Germany
Salvatore La Torre	Università degli studi di Salerno, Italy
Kim Guldstrand Larsen	Aalborg University, Denmark
Anabelle McIver	Macquarie University, Australia
Roland Meyer	TU Braunschweig, Germany
Marius Mikučionis	Aalborg University, Denmark
Sebastian A. Mödersheim	Technical University of Denmark, Denmark
David Parker	University of Birmingham, UK
Corina Pasareanu	CMU/NASA Ames Research Center, USA
Sanjit Seshia	University of California, Berkeley, USA
Bernhard Steffen	TU Dortmund, Germany
Jan Strejcek	Masaryk University, Czech Republic
Zhendong Su	ETH Zurich, Switzerland
Meng Sun	Peking University, China

Michael Tautschnig	Queen Mary University of London/Amazon Web Services, UK
Tomáš Vojnar (Co-chair)	Brno University of Technology, Czech Republic
Thomas Wies	New York University, USA
Lijun Zhang (Co-chair)	Institute of Software, Chinese Academy of Sciences, China
Florian Zuleger	Vienna University of Technology, Austria

Program Committee and Jury—SV-COMP

Dirk Beyer (Chair)	LMU Munich, Germany
Peter Schrammel (Representing 2LS)	University of Sussex, UK
Jera Hensel (Representing AProVE)	RWTH Aachen, Germany
Michael Tautschnig (Representing CBMC)	Amazon Web Services, UK
Kareem Khazem (Representing CBMC-Path)	University College London, UK
Vadim Mutilin (Representing CPA-BAM-BnB)	ISP RAS, Russia
Pavel Andrianov (Representing CPA-Lockator)	ISP RAS, Russia
Marie-Christine Jakobs (Representing CPA-Seq)	LMU Munich, Germany
Omar Alhawi (Representing DepthK)	University of Manchester, UK
Vladimír Štill (Representing DIVINE-Explicit)	Masaryk University, Czechia
Henrich Lauko (Representing DIVINE-SMT)	Masaryk University, Czechia
Mikhail R. Gadelha (Representing ESBMC-Kind)	University of Southampton, UK
Philipp Ruemmer (Representing JayHorn)	Uppsala University, Sweden
Lucas Cordeiro (Representing JBMC)	University of Manchester, UK
Cyrille Artho (Representing JPF)	KTH, Denmark
Omar Inverso (Representing Lazy-CSeq)	Gran Sasso Science Inst., Italy
Herbert Rocha (Representing Map2Check)	Federal University of Roraima, Brazil
Cedric Richter (Representing PeSCo)	University of Paderborn, Germany

Eti Chaudhary (Representing Pinaka)	IIT Hyderabad, India
Veronika Šoková (Representing PredatorHP)	BUT, Brno, Czechia
Franck Cassez (Representing Skink)	Macquarie University, Australia
Zvonimir Rakamaric (Representing SMACK)	University of Utah, USA
Willem Visser (Representing SPF)	Stellenbosch University, South Africa
Marek Chalupa (Representing Symbiotic)	Masaryk University, Czechia
Matthias Heizmann (Representing UAutomizer)	University of Freiburg, Germany
Alexander Nutz (Representing UKojak)	University of Freiburg, Germany
Daniel Dietsch (Representing UTaipan)	University of Freiburg, Germany
Priyanka Darke (Representing VeriAbs)	Tata Consultancy Services, India
R. K. Medicherla (Representing VeriFuzz)	Tata Consultancy Services, India
Pritom Rajkhowa (Representing VIAP)	Hong Kong UST, China
Liangze Yin (Representing Yogar-CBMC)	NUDT, China
Haining Feng (Representing Yogar-CBMC-Par.)	National University of Defense Technology, China

Artifact Evaluation Committee (AEC)

Pranav Ashok	TU Munich, Germany
Marek Chalupa	Masaryk University, Czech Republic
Gabriele Costa	IMT Lucca, Italy
Maryam Dabaghchian	University of Utah, USA
Bui Phi Diep	Uppsala, Sweden
Daniel Dietsch	University of Freiburg, Germany
Tom van Dijk	Johannes Kepler University, Austria
Tomáš Fiedor	Brno University of Technology, Czech Republic
Daniel Fremont	UC Berkeley, USA
Ondřej Lengál (Co-chair)	Brno University of Technology, Czech Republic
Ernst Moritz Hahn (Co-chair)	Queen's University Belfast, UK
Sam Huang	University of Maryland, USA
Martin Jonáš	Masaryk University, Czech Republic
Sean Kauffman	University of Waterloo, Canada
Yong Li	Chinese Academy of Sciences, China

Le Quang Loc	Teesside University, UK
Rasool Maghareh	National University of Singapore, Singapore
Tobias Meggendorfer	TU Munich, Germany
Malte Mues	TU Dortmund, Germany
Tuan Phong Ngo	Uppsala, Sweden
Chris Novakovic	University of Birmingham, UK
Thai M. Trinh	Advanced Digital Sciences Center, Illinois at Singapore, Singapore
Wytse Oortwijn	University of Twente, The Netherlands
Aleš Smrčka	Brno University of Technology, Czech Republic
Daniel Stan	Saarland University, Germany
Ilina Stoilkovska	TU Wien, Austria
Ming-Hsien Tsai	Academia Sinica, Taiwan
Jan Tušil	Masaryk University, Czech Republic
Pedro Valero	IMDEA, Spain
Maximilian Weininger	TU Munich, Germany

Additional Reviewers

Aiswarya, C.
Albarghouthi, Aws
Aminof, Benjamin
Américo, Arthur
Ashok, Pranav
Atig, Mohamed Faouzi
Bacci, Giovanni
Bainczyk, Alexander
Barringer, Howard
Basset, Nicolas
Bensalem, Saddek
Berard, Beatrice
Besson, Frédéric
Biewer, Sebastian
Bogomolov, Sergiy
Bollig, Benedikt
Bozga, Marius
Bozzano, Marco
Brazdil, Tomas
Caulfield, Benjamin
Chaudhuri, Swarat
Cheang, Kevin
Chechik, Marsha
Chen, Yu-Fang
Chin, Wei-Ngan
Chini, Peter
Ciardo, Gianfranco
Cohen, Liron
Cordeiro, Lucas
Cyranka, Jacek
Čadek, Pavel
Darulova, Eva
Degorre, Aldric
Delbianco, Germán Andrés
Delzanno, Giorgio
Devir, Nurit
Dierl, Simon
Dragoi, Cezara
Dreossi, Tommaso
Dutra, Rafael
Eilers, Marco
El-Hokayem, Antoine
Faella, Marco
Fahrenberg, Uli
Falcone, Ylies
Fox, Gereon
Freiberger, Felix
Fremont, Daniel
Frenkel, Hadar
Friedberger, Karlheinz
Frohme, Markus
Fu, Hongfei

Furbach, Florian
Garavel, Hubert
Ghosh, Bineet
Ghosh, Shromona
Gondron, Sebastien
Gopinath, Divya
Gossen, Frederik
Goyal, Manish
Graf-Brill, Alexander
Griggio, Alberto
Gu, Tianxiao
Guatto, Adrien
Gutiérrez, Elena
Hahn, Ernst Moritz
Hansen, Mikkel
Hartmanns, Arnd
Hasani, Ramin
Havlena, Vojtěch
He, Kangli
He, Pinjia
Hess, Andreas Viktor
Heule, Marijn
Ho, Mark
Ho, Nhut Minh
Holik, Lukas
Hsu, Hung-Wei
Inverso, Omar
Irfan, Ahmed
Islam, Md. Ariful
Itzhaky, Shachar
Jakobs, Marie-Christine
Jaksic, Stefan
Jasper, Marc
Jensen, Peter Gjøl
Jonas, Martin
Kaminski, Benjamin Lucien
Karimi, Abel
Katelaan, Jens
Kauffman, Sean
Kaufmann, Isabella
Khoo, Siau-Cheng
Kiesl, Benjamin
Kim, Eric
Klauck, Michaela
Kong, Hui
Kong, Zhaodan
Kopetzki, Dawid
Krishna, Siddharth
Krämer, Julia
Kukovec, Jure
Kumar, Rahul
Köpf, Boris
Lange, Martin
Le Coent, Adrien
Lemberger, Thomas
Lengal, Ondrej
Li, Yi
Lin, Hsin-Hung
Lluch Lafuente, Alberto
Lorber, Florian
Lu, Jianchao
Lukina, Anna
Lång, Magnus
Maghareh, Rasool
Mahyar, Hamidreza
Markey, Nicolas
Mathieson, Luke
Mauritz, Malte
Mayr, Richard
Mechtaev, Sergey
Meggendorfer, Tobias
Micheli, Andrea
Michelmore, Rhiannon
Monteiro, Pedro T.
Mover, Sergio
Mu, Chunyan
Mues, Malte
Muniz, Marco
Murano, Aniello
Murtovi, Alnis
Muskalla, Sebastian
Mutluergil, Suha Orhun
Neumann, Elisabeth
Ngo, Tuan Phong
Nickovic, Dejan
Nies, Gilles
Noller, Yannic
Norman, Gethin
Nowack, Martin
Olmedo, Federico
Pani, Thomas
Petri, Gustavo

Piazza, Carla
Poli, Federico
Poulsen, Danny Bøgsted
Prabhakar, Pavithra
Quang Trung, Ta
Ranzato, Francesco
Rasmussen, Cameron
Ratasich, Denise
Ravanbakhsh, Hadi
Ray, Rajarshi
Reger, Giles
Reynolds, Andrew
Rigger, Manuel
Rodriguez, Cesar
Rothenberg, Bat-Chen
Roveri, Marco
Rydhof Hansen, René
Rüthing, Oliver
Sadeh, Gal
Saivasan, Prakash
Sanchez, Cesar
Sangnier, Arnaud
Schlichtkrull, Anders
Schwoon, Stefan
Seidl, Martina
Shi, Xiaomu
Shirmohammadi, Mahsa
Shoukry, Yasser
Sighireanu, Mihaela
Soudjani, Sadegh
Spießl, Martin
Srba, Jiri
Srivas, Mandayam
Stan, Daniel
Stoilkovska, Ilina
Stojic, Ivan
Su, Ting
Summers, Alexander J.
Tabuada, Paulo
Tacchella, Armando
Tang, Enyi
Tian, Chun
Tonetta, Stefano
Trinh, Minh-Thai
Trtík, Marek
Tsai, Ming-Hsien
Valero, Pedro
van der Berg, Freark
Vandin, Andrea
Vazquez-Chanlatte, Marcell
Viganò, Luca
Villadsen, Jørgen
Wang, Shuai
Wang, Shuling
Weininger, Maximilian
Wendler, Philipp
Wolff, Sebastian
Wüstholz, Valentin
Xu, Xiao
Zeljić, Aleksandar
Zhang, Fuyuan
Zhang, Qirun
Zhang, Xiyue

Contents – Part II

Contents – Part I

Verification and Analysis

Model Checking

Tool Demos

Concurrent and Distributed Systems

Checking Deadlock-Freedom of Parametric Component-Based Systems

Marius Bozga, Radu Iosif(✉), and Joseph Sifakis

Univ. Grenoble Alpes, CNRS, Grenoble INP (Institute of Engineering Univ. Grenoble Alpes), VERIMAG, 38000 Grenoble, France
{Marius.Bozga,Radu.Iosif,Joseph.Sifakis}@univ-grenoble-alpes.fr

Abstract. We propose an automated method for computing inductive invariants used to proving deadlock freedom of parametric component-based systems. The method generalizes the approach for computing structural trap invariants from bounded to parametric systems with general architectures. It symbolically extracts trap invariants from interaction formulae defining the system architecture. The paper presents the theoretical foundations of the method, including new results for the first order monadic logic and proves its soundness. It also reports on a preliminary experimental evaluation on several textbook examples.

Modern computing systems exhibit dynamic and reconfigurable behavior. To tackle the complexity of such systems, engineers extensively use architectures that enforce, by construction, essential properties, such as fault tolerance or mutual exclusion. Architectures can be viewed as parametric operators that take as arguments instances of components of given types and enforce a characteristic property. For instance, client-server architectures enforce atomicity and resilience of transactions, for any numbers of clients and servers. Similarly, token-ring architectures enforce mutual exclusion between any number of components in the ring.

Parametric verification is an extremely relevant and challenging problem in systems engineering. In contrast to the verification of bounded systems, consisting of a known set of components, there exist no general methods and tools succesfully applied to parametric systems. Verification problems for very simple parametric systems, even with finite-state components, are typically intractable [10,16]. Most work in this area puts emphasis on limitations determined mainly by three criteria (1) the topology of the architecture, (2) the coordination primitives, and (3) the properties to be verified.

The main decidability results reduce parametric verification to the verification of a bounded number of instances of finite state components. Several methods try to determine a cut-off size of the system, i.e. the minimal size for which if a property holds, then it holds for any size, e.g. Suzuki [20], Emerson and Namjoshi [15]. Other methods identify systems with well-structured transition relations, for which symbolic enumeration

The research leading to these results has received funding from the European Union Horizon 2020 research and innovation programme under grant agreement no. 700665 CITADEL (Critical Infrastructure Protection using Adaptive MILS) and no. 730086 ERGO (European Robotic Goal-Oriented Autonomous Controller).

T. Vojnar and L. Zhang (Eds.): TACAS 2019, Part II, LNCS 11428, pp. 3–20, 2019.
https://doi.org/10.1007/978-3-030-17465-1_1

of reachable states is feasible [1] or reduce to known decidable problems, such as reachability in vector addition systems [16]. Typically, these methods apply to systems with global coordination. When theoretical decidability is not of concern, semi-algorithmic techniques such as *regular model checking* [2,17], SMT-based *bounded model checking* [3,14], *abstraction* [8,11] and *automata learning* [13] can be used to deal with more general classes of The interested reader can find a complete survey on parameterized model checking by Bloem et al. [10].

This paper takes a different angle of attack to the verification problem, seeking generality of the type of parametric systems and focusing on the verification of a particular but essential property: *deadlock-freedom*. The aim is to come up with effective methods for checking deadlock-freedom, by overcoming the complexity blowup stemming from the effective generation of reachability sets. We briefly describe our approach below.

A system is the composition of a finite number of component instances of given types, using interactions that follow the Behaviour-Interaction-Priorities (BIP) paradigm [7]. To simplify the technical part, we assume that components and interactions are finite abstractions of real-life systems. An instance is a finite-state transition system whose edges are labeled by ports. The instances communicate synchronously via a number of simultaneous interactions involving a set of ports each, such that no data is exchanged during interactions. If the number of instances in the system is fixed and known in advance, we say that the system is *bounded*, otherwise it is *parametric*.

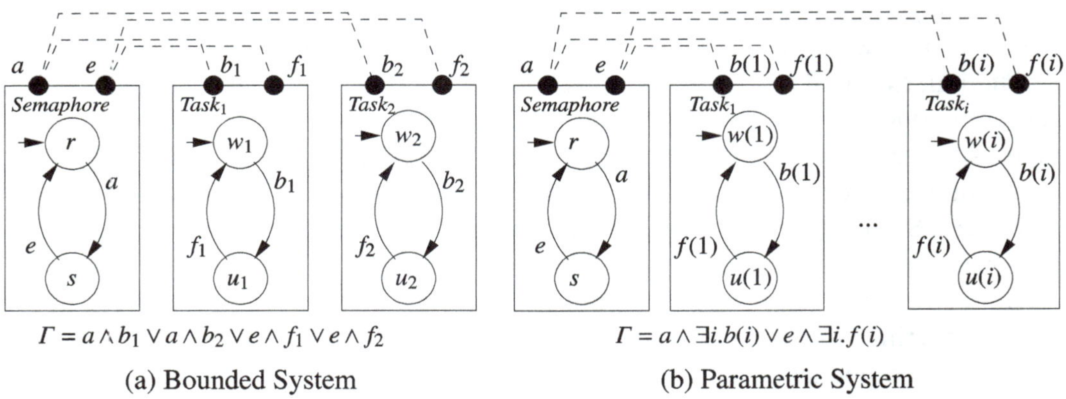

Fig. 1. Mutual exclusion example

For instance, the bounded system in Fig. 1a consist of component types *Semaphore*, with one instance, and *Task*, with two instances. A semaphore goes from the free state r to the taken state s by an acquire action a, and viceversa from s to r by a release action e. A task goes from waiting w to busy u by action b and viceversa, by action f. For the bounded system in Fig. 1a, the interactions are $\{a, b_1\}, \{a, b_2\}, \{e, f_1\}$ and $\{e, f_2\}$, depicted with dashed lines. Since the number of instances is known in advance, we can view an interaction as a minimal satisfying valuation of the boolean formula $\Gamma = (a \wedge b_1) \vee (a \wedge b_2) \vee (e \wedge f_1) \vee (e \wedge f_2)$, where the port symbols are propositional variables. Because every instance has finitely many states, we can write a boolean formula

$\Delta = [\neg r \vee \neg(w_1 \vee w_2)] \wedge [\neg s \vee \neg(u_1 \vee u_2)]$, this time over propositional state variables, which defines the configurations in which all interactions are disabled (deadlock). Proving that no deadlock configuration is reachable from the initial configuration $r \wedge w_1 \wedge w_2$, requires finding an over-approximation (invariant) I of the reachable configurations, such that the conjunction $I \wedge \Delta$ is not satisfiable.

The basic idea of our method, supported by the D-FINDER deadlock detection tool [9] for bounded component-based systems, is to compute an invariant straight from the interaction formula, without going through costly abstract fixpoint iterations. The invariants we are looking for are in fact solutions of a system of boolean constraints $\Theta(\Gamma)$, of size linear in the size of Γ (written in DNF). In our example, $\Theta(\Gamma) = \bigwedge_{i=1,2}(r \vee w_i) \leftrightarrow (s \vee u_i)$. Finding the (minimal) solutions of this constraint can be done, as currently implemented in D-FINDER, by exhaustive model enumeration using a SAT solver. Here we propose a more efficient solution, which consists in writing $\Theta(\Gamma)$ in DNF and remove the negative literals from each minterm. In our case, this gives the invariant $I = (r \vee s) \wedge \bigwedge_{i=1,2}(w_i \vee u_i) \wedge (r \vee u_1 \vee u_2) \wedge (s \vee w_1 \vee w_2)$ and $I \wedge \Delta$ is proved unsatisfiable using a SAT solver.

The main contribution of this paper is the generalization of this invariant generation method to the parametric case. To understand the problem, consider the parametric system from Fig. 1, in which a *Semaphore* interacts with n *Tasks*, where $n > 0$ is not known in advance. The interactions are described by a fragment of first order logic, in which the ports are either propositional or monadic predicate symbols, in our case $\Gamma = a \wedge \exists i \,.\, b(i) \vee e \wedge \exists i \,.\, f(i)$. This logic, called *Monadic Interaction Logic* (MIL), is also used to express the constraints $\Theta(\Gamma)$ and compute their solutions. In our case, we obtain $I = (r \vee s) \wedge [\forall i \,.\, w(i) \vee u(i)] \wedge [r \vee \exists i \,.\, u(i)] \wedge [s \vee \exists i \,.\, w(i)]$. As in the bounded case, we can give a parametric description of deadlock configurations $\Delta = [\neg r \vee \neg\exists i \,.\, w(i)] \wedge [\neg s \vee \neg\exists i \,.\, u(i)]$ and prove that $I \wedge \Delta$ is unsatisfiable, using the decidability of MIL, based on an early small model property result due to Löwenheim [19]. In practice, we avoid the model enumeration suggested by this result and check the satisfiability of such queries using a decidable theory of sets with cardinality constraints [18], available in the CVC4 SMT solver [4].

The paper is structured as follows: Sect. 1 presents existing results for checking deadlock-freedom of bounded systems using invariants, Sect. 2 formalizes the approach for computing invariants using MIL, Sect. 3 introduces cardinality constraints for invariant generation, Sect. 4 presents the integration of the above results within a verification technique for parametric systems and Sect. 5 reports on preliminary experiments carried out with a prototype tool. Finally, Sect. 6 presents concluding remarks and future work directions. For reasons of space, all proofs are given in [12].

1 Bounded Component-Based Systems

A *component* is a tuple $C = \langle \mathsf{P}, \mathsf{S}, s_0, \Delta \rangle$, where $\mathsf{P} = \{p, q, r, \ldots\}$ is a finite set of *ports*, S is a finite set of *states*, $s_0 \in \mathsf{S}$ is an initial state and $\Delta \subseteq \mathsf{S} \times \mathsf{P} \times \mathsf{S}$ is a set of *transitions* written $s \xrightarrow{p} s'$. To simplify the technical details, we assume there are *no two different transitions with the same port*, i.e. if $s_1 \xrightarrow{p_1} s'_1, s_2 \xrightarrow{p_2} s'_2 \in \Delta$ and $s_1 \neq s_2$ or

$s'_1 \neq s'_2$ then $p_1 \neq p_2$. In general, this restriction can be lifted, at the cost of cluttering the presentation.

A *bounded system* $\mathcal{S} = \langle C^1, \ldots, C^n, \Gamma \rangle$ consists of a fixed number (n) of components $C^k = \langle \mathsf{P}^k, \mathsf{S}^k, s_0{}^k, \Delta^k \rangle$ and an *interaction formula* Γ, describing the allowed interactions. Since the number of components is known in advance, we write interaction formulae using boolean logic over the set of propositional variables $\mathsf{BVar} \stackrel{\text{def}}{=} \bigcup_{k=1}^{n} (\mathsf{P}^k \cup \mathsf{S}^k)$. Here we intentionally use the names of states and ports as propositional variables.

A *boolean interaction formula* is either $a \in \mathsf{BVar}$, $f_1 \wedge f_2$ or $\neg f_1$, where f_i are formulae, for $i = 1, 2$, respectively. We define the usual shorthands $f_1 \vee f_2 \stackrel{\text{def}}{=} \neg(\neg f_1 \wedge \neg f_2)$, $f_1 \rightarrow f_2 \stackrel{\text{def}}{=} \neg f_1 \vee f_2$, $f_1 \leftrightarrow f_2 \stackrel{\text{def}}{=} (f_1 \rightarrow f_2) \wedge (f_2 \rightarrow f_1)$. A literal is either a variable or its negation and a minterm is a conjunction of literals. A formula is in disjunctive normal form (DNF) if it is written as $\bigvee_{i=1}^{n} \bigwedge_{j=1}^{m_i} \ell_{ij}$, where ℓ_{ij} is a literal. A formula is *positive* if and only if each variable occurs under an even number of negations, or, equivalently, its DNF forms contains no negative literals. We assume interaction formulae of bounded systems to be always positive.

A *Boolean Valuation* $\beta : \mathsf{BVar} \rightarrow \{\top, \bot\}$ maps each propositional variable to either true ($\top$) or false ($\bot$). We write $\beta \models f$ if and only if $f = \top$, when replacing each boolean variable a with $\beta(a)$ in f. We say that β is a *model* of f in this case and write $f \equiv g$ for $[\![f]\!] = [\![g]\!]$, where $[\![f]\!] \stackrel{\text{def}}{=} \{\beta \mid \beta \models f\}$. Given two valuations β_1 and β_2 we write $\beta_1 \subseteq \beta_2$ if and only if $\beta_1(a) = \top$ implies $\beta_2(a) = \top$, for each variable $a \in \mathsf{BVar}$. We write $f \equiv^\mu g$ for $[\![f]\!]^\mu = [\![g]\!]^\mu$, where $[\![f]\!]^\mu \stackrel{\text{def}}{=} \{\beta \in [\![f]\!] \mid \text{for all } \beta' : \beta' \subseteq \beta \text{ and } \beta' \neq \beta \text{ only if } \beta' \notin [\![f]\!]\}$ is the set of minimal models of f.

1.1 Execution Semantics of Bounded Systems

We use 1-safe marked Petri Nets to define the set of executions of a bounded system. A *Petri Net* (PN) is a tuple $N = \langle S, T, E \rangle$, where S is a set of *places*, T is a set of *transitions*, $S \cap T = \emptyset$, and $E \subseteq S \times T \cup T \times S$ is a set of *edges*. The elements of $S \cup T$ are called *nodes*. For a node n, let ${}^\bullet n \stackrel{\text{def}}{=} \{m \in S \cup T \mid E(m,n) = 1\}$, $n^\bullet \stackrel{\text{def}}{=} \{m \in S \cup T \mid E(n,m) = 1\}$ and lift these definitions to sets of nodes, as usual.

A *marking* for a PN $N = \langle S, T, E \rangle$ is a function $\mathrm{m} : S \rightarrow \mathbb{N}$. A *marked Petri net* is a pair $\mathcal{N} = (N, \mathrm{m}_0)$, where m_0 is the *initial marking* of $N = \langle S, T, E \rangle$. We consider that the reader is familiar with the standard execution semantics of a marked PN. A marking m is *reachable* in $\mathcal{N}$ if and only if there exists a sequence of transitions leading from m_0 to m. We denote by $\mathcal{R}(\mathcal{N})$ the set of reachable markings of $\mathcal{N}$. A set of markings $\mathcal{M}$ is an *invariant* of $\mathcal{N} = (N, \mathrm{m}_0)$ if and only if $\mathrm{m}_0 \in \mathcal{M}$ and $\mathcal{M}$ is closed under the transitions of N. A marked PN $\mathcal{N}$ is 1-*safe* if $\mathrm{m}(s) \leq 1$, for each $s \in S$ and each $\mathrm{m} \in \mathcal{R}(\mathcal{N})$. In the following, we consider only marked PNs that are 1-safe. In this case, any (necessarily finite) set of reachable markings can be defined by a boolean formula,

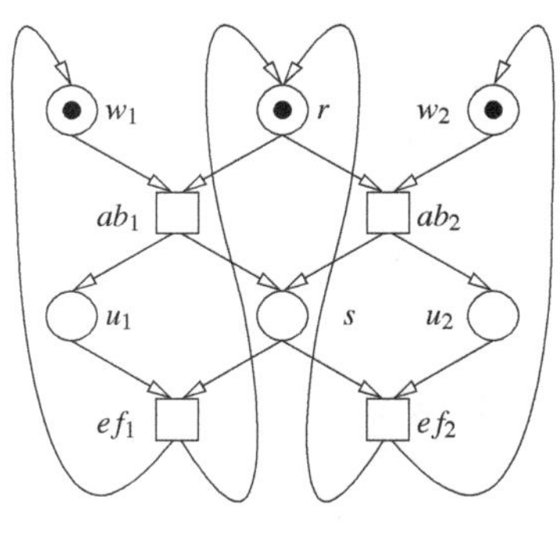

Fig. 2. PN for mutual exclusion

which identifies markings with the induced boolean valuations. A marking m is a *deadlock* if for no transition is enabled in m and let $\mathcal{D}(\mathcal{N})$ be the set of deadlocks of N. A marked PN $\mathcal{N}$ is *deadlock-free* if and only if $\mathcal{R}(\mathcal{N}) \cap \mathcal{D}(\mathcal{N}) = \emptyset$. A sufficient condition for deadlock freedom is $\mathcal{M} \cap \mathcal{D}(\mathcal{N}) = \emptyset$, for some invariant $\mathcal{M}$ of $\mathcal{N}$.

In the rest of this section, we fix a bounded system $\mathcal{S} = \langle C^1, \ldots, C^n, \Gamma \rangle$, where $C^k = \langle \mathsf{P}^k, \mathsf{S}^k, {s_0}^k, \Delta^k \rangle$, for all $k \in [1, n]$ and Γ is a positive boolean formula, over propositional variables denoting ports. The set of executions of $\mathcal{S}$ is given by the 1-safe marked PN $\mathcal{N}_\mathcal{S} = (N, \mathrm{m}_0)$, where $N = (\bigcup_{i=1}^n \mathsf{S}^i, T, E)$, $\mathrm{m}_0(s) = 1$ if and only if $s \in \{{s_0}^i \mid i \in [1, n]\}$ and T, E are as follows. For each minimal model $\beta \in [\![\Gamma]\!]^\mu$, we have a transition $\mathrm{t}_\beta \in T$ and edges $(s_i, \mathrm{t}_\beta), (\mathrm{t}_\beta, s_i') \in E$, for all $i \in [1, n]$ such that $s_i \xrightarrow{p_i} s_i' \in \Delta^i$ and $\beta(p_i) = \top$. Moreover, nothing else is in T or E.

For example, the marked PN from Fig. 2 describes the set of executions of the bounded system from Fig. 1a. Note that each transition of the PN corresponds to a minimal model of the interaction formula $\Gamma = a \wedge b_1 \vee a \wedge b_2 \vee e \wedge f_1 \vee e \wedge f_2$, or equivalently, to the set of (necessarily positive) literals of some minterm in the DNF of Γ.

1.2 Proving Deadlock Freedom of Bounded Systems

A bounded system $\mathcal{S}$ is deadlock-free if and only if its corresponding marked PN $\mathcal{N}_\mathcal{S}$ is deadlock-free. In the following, we prove deadlock-freedom of a bounded system, by defining a class of invariants that are particularly useful for excluding unreachable deadlock markings.

Given a Petri Net $N = (S, T, E)$, a set of places $W \subseteq S$ is called a *trap* if and only if $W^\bullet \subseteq {}^\bullet W$. A trap W of N is a *marked trap* of the marked PN $\mathcal{N} = (N, \mathrm{m}_0)$ if and only if $\mathrm{m}_0(s) = \top$ for some $s \in W$. A *minimal marked trap* is a marked trap such that none of its strict subsets is a marked trap. A marked trap defines an invariant of the PN because some place in the trap will always be marked, no matter which transition is fired. The *trap invariant* of $\mathcal{N}$ is the least set of markings that mark each trap of $\mathcal{N}$. Clearly, the trap invariant of $\mathcal{N}$ subsumes the set of reachable markings of $\mathcal{N}$, because the latter is the least invariant of $\mathcal{N}$ and invariants are closed under intersection[1].

Lemma 1. *Given a bounded system $\mathcal{S}$, the boolean formula:*

$$Trap(\mathcal{N}_\mathcal{S}) \stackrel{\mathsf{def}}{=} \bigwedge\{\textstyle\bigvee_{i=1}^k s_i \mid \{s_1, \ldots, s_k\} \text{ is a marked trap of } \mathcal{N}_\mathcal{S}\}$$

defines an invariant of $\mathcal{N}_\mathcal{S}$.

Next, we describe a method of computing trap invariants that does not explicitly enumerate all the marked traps of a marked PN. First, we consider a *trap constraint* $\Theta(\Gamma)$, derived from the interaction formula Γ, in linear time. By slight abuse of notation, we define, for a given port $p \in \mathsf{P}^i$ of the component C^i, for some $i \in [1, n]$, the pre- and post-state of p in C^i as ${}^\bullet p \stackrel{\mathsf{def}}{=} s$ and $p^\bullet \stackrel{\mathsf{def}}{=} s'$, where $s \xrightarrow{p} s'$ is the unique rule[2] involving

[1] The intersection of two or more invariants is again an invariant.

[2] We have assumed that each port is associated a unique transition rule.

p in Δ^i, and $^\bullet p = p^\bullet \stackrel{\text{def}}{=} \bot$ if there is no such rule. Assuming that the interaction formula is written in DNF as $\Gamma = \bigvee_{k=1}^{N} \bigwedge_{\ell=1}^{M_k} p_{k\ell}$, we define the trap constraint:

$$\Theta(\Gamma) \stackrel{\text{def}}{=} \bigwedge_{k=1}^{N} \left(\bigvee_{\ell=1}^{M_k} {}^\bullet p_{k\ell}\right) \rightarrow \left(\bigvee_{\ell=1}^{M_k} p_{k\ell}{}^\bullet\right)$$

It is not hard to show[3] that any satisfying valuation of $\Theta(\Gamma)$ defines a trap of $\mathcal{N}_\mathcal{S}$ and, moreover, any such trap is defined in this way. We also consider the formula $\mathit{Init}(\mathcal{S}) \stackrel{\text{def}}{=} \bigvee_{k=1}^{n} {s_0}^k$ defining the set of initially marked places of $\mathcal{S}$, and prove the following:

Lemma 2. *Let $\mathcal{S}$ be a bounded system with interaction formula Γ and β be a boolean valuation. Then $\beta \in [\![\Theta(\Gamma) \wedge \mathit{Init}(\mathcal{S})]\!]$ iff $\{s \mid \beta(s) = \top\}$ is a marked trap of $\mathcal{N}_\mathcal{S}$. Moreover, $\beta \in [\![\Theta(\Gamma) \wedge \mathit{Init}(\mathcal{S})]\!]^\mu$ iff $\{s \mid \beta(s) = \top\}$ is a minimal marked trap of $\mathcal{N}_\mathcal{S}$.*

Because $\Theta(\Gamma)$ and $\mathit{Init}(\mathcal{S})$ are boolean formulae, it is, in principle, possible to compute the trap invariant $\mathit{Trap}(\mathcal{N}_\mathcal{S})$ by enumerating the (minimal) models of $\Theta(\Gamma) \wedge \mathit{Init}(\mathcal{S})$ and applying the definition from Lemma 1. However, model enumeration is inefficient and, moreover, does not admit generalization for the parametric case, in which the size of the system is unknown. For these reasons, we prefer a computation of the trap invariant, based on two symbolic transformations of boolean formulae, described next.

For a formula f we denote by f^+ the positive formula obtained by deleting all negative literals from the DNF of f. We shall call this operation *positivation*. Second, for a positive boolean formula f, we define the *dual* formula $(f)^\sim$ recursively on the structure of f, as follows: $(f_1 \wedge f_2)^\sim \stackrel{\text{def}}{=} f_1{}^\sim \vee f_2{}^\sim$, $(f_1 \vee f_2)^\sim \stackrel{\text{def}}{=} f_1{}^\sim \wedge f_2{}^\sim$ and $a^\sim \stackrel{\text{def}}{=} a$, for any $a \in \mathsf{BVar}$. Note that $f^\sim$ is equivalent to the negation of the formula obtained from f by substituting each variable a with $\neg a$ in f.

The following theorem gives the main result of this section, the symbolic computation of the trap invariant of a bounded system, directly from its interaction formula.

Theorem 1. *For any bounded system $\mathcal{S}$, with interaction formula Γ, we have:*

$$\mathit{Trap}(\mathcal{N}_\mathcal{S}) \equiv ([\Theta(\Gamma) \wedge \mathit{Init}(\mathcal{S})]^+)^\sim$$

Intuitively, any satisfying valuation of $\Theta(\Gamma) \wedge \mathit{Init}(\mathcal{S})$ defines an initially marked trap of $\mathcal{N}_\mathcal{S}$ and a minimal such valuation defines a minimal such trap (Lemma 2). Instead of computing the minimal satisfying valuations by model enumeration, we directly cast the above formula in DNF and remove the negative literals. This is essentially because the negative literals do not occur in the propositional definition of a set of places[4]. Then the dualization of this positive formula yields the trap invariants in CNF, as a conjunction over disjunctions of propositional variables corresponding to the places inside a minimal initially marked trap.

Just as any invariants, trap invariants can be used to prove absence of deadlocks in a bounded system. Assuming, as before, that the interaction formula is given in DNF

[3] See [5] for a proof.

[4] If the DNF is $(p \wedge q) \vee (p \wedge \neg r)$, the dualization would give $(p \vee q) \wedge (p \vee \neg r)$. The first clause corresponds to the trap $\{p, q\}$ (either p or q is marked), but the second does not directly define a trap. However, by first removing the negative literals, we obtain the traps $\{p, q\}$ and $\{r\}$.

as $\Gamma = \bigvee_{k=1}^{N} \bigwedge_{\ell=1}^{M_k} p_{k\ell}$, we define the set of deadlock markings of $\mathcal{N}_S$ by the formula $\Delta(\Gamma) \stackrel{\text{def}}{=} \bigwedge_{k=1}^{N} \bigvee_{\ell=1}^{M_k} \neg({}^{\bullet}p_{k\ell})$. This is the set of configurations in which all interactions are disabled. With this definition, proving deadlock freedom amounts to proving unsatisfiability of a boolean formula.

Corollary 1. *A bounded system $\mathcal{S}$ with interaction formula Γ is deadlock-free if the boolean formula $([\Theta(\Gamma) \wedge Init(\mathcal{S})]^{+})^{\sim} \wedge \Delta(\Gamma)$ is unsatisfiable.*

2 Parametric Component-Based Systems

From now on we shall focus on parametric systems, consisting of a fixed set of component types $C^1, \ldots, C^n$, such that the number of instances of each type is not known in advance. These numbers are given by a function $\mathsf{M} : [1, n] \rightarrow \mathbb{N}$, where $\mathsf{M}(k)$ denotes the number of components of type C^k that are active in the system. To simplify the technical presentation of the results, we assume that all instances of a component type are created at once, before the system is started[5]. For the rest of this section, we fix a parametric system $\mathcal{S} = \langle C^1, \ldots, C^n, \mathsf{M}, \Gamma \rangle$, where each component type $C^k = \langle \mathsf{P}^k, \mathsf{S}^k, {s_0}^k, \Delta^k \rangle$ has the same definition as a component in a bounded system and Γ is an interaction formula, written in the fragment of first order logic, defined next.

2.1 Monadic Interaction Logic

For each component type C^k, where $k \in [1, n]$, we assume a set of index variables Var^k and a set of predicate symbols $\mathsf{Pred}^k \stackrel{\text{def}}{=} \mathsf{P}^k \cup \mathsf{S}^k$. Similar to the bounded case, we use state and ports names as monadic (unary) predicate symbols. We also define the sets $\mathsf{Var} \stackrel{\text{def}}{=} \bigcup_{k=1}^{n} \mathsf{Var}^k$ and $\mathsf{Pred} \stackrel{\text{def}}{=} \bigcup_{k=1}^{n} \mathsf{Pred}^k$. Moreover, we consider that $\mathsf{Var}^k \cap \mathsf{Var}^\ell = \emptyset$ and $\mathsf{Pred}^k \cap \mathsf{Pred}^\ell = \emptyset$, for all $1 \leq k < \ell \leq n$. For simplicity's sake, we assume that all predicate symbols in Pred are of arity one. For component types C^k, such that $\mathsf{M}(k) = 1$ and predicate symbols $\mathsf{pr} \in \mathsf{Pred}^k$, we shall write pr instead of $\mathsf{pr}(1)$, as in the interaction formula of the system from Fig. 1b. The syntax of the *monadic interaction logic* (MIL) is given below:

$$i, j \in \mathsf{Var} \ \text{ index variables}$$
$$\phi := i = j \mid \mathsf{pr}(i) \mid \phi_1 \wedge \phi_2 \mid \neg\phi_1 \mid \exists i \,.\, \phi_1$$

where, for each predicate atom $\mathsf{pr}(i)$, if $\mathsf{pr} \in \mathsf{Pred}^k$ and $i \in \mathsf{Var}^\ell$ then $k = \ell$. We use the shorthands $\forall i \,.\, \phi_1 \stackrel{\text{def}}{=} \neg(\exists i \,.\, \neg\phi_1)$ and $\mathrm{distinct}(i_1, \ldots, i_m) \stackrel{\text{def}}{=} \bigwedge_{1 \leq j < \ell \leq m} \neg i_j = i_\ell$[6]. A *sentence* is a formula in which all variables are in the scope of a quantifier. A formula is *positive* if each predicate symbol occurs under an even number of negations. The semantics of MIL is given in terms of structures $\mathcal{I} = (\mathfrak{U}, \nu, \iota)$, where:

- $\mathfrak{U} \stackrel{\text{def}}{=} [1, \max_{k=1}^{n} \mathsf{M}(k)]$ is the *universe* of instances, over which variables range,

[5] This is not a limitation, since dynamic instance creation can be simulated by considering that all instances are initially in a waiting state, which is left as result of an interaction involving a designated "spawn" port.

[6] Throughout this paper, we consider that $\bigwedge_{i \in I} \phi_i = \top$ if $I = \emptyset$.

- $\nu : \mathsf{Var} \rightarrow \mathfrak{U}$ is a *valuation* mapping variables to elements of the universe,
- $\iota : \mathsf{Pred} \rightarrow 2^{\mathfrak{U}}$ is an *interpretation* of predicates as subsets of the universe.

For a structure $\mathcal{I} = (\mathfrak{U}, \nu, \iota)$ and a formula ϕ, the satisfaction relation $\mathcal{I} \models \phi$ is defined as:

$$\begin{array}{llll} \mathcal{I} \models \bot \Leftrightarrow \text{never} & \mathcal{I} \models i = j & \Leftrightarrow \nu(i) = \nu(j) & \\ \mathcal{I} \models p(i) \Leftrightarrow \nu(i) \in \iota(p) & \mathcal{I} \models \exists i \,.\, \phi_1 & \Leftrightarrow (\mathfrak{U}, \nu[i \leftarrow m], \iota) \models \phi_1 & \text{for some } m \in [1, \mathsf{M}(k)] \\ & & & \text{provided that } i \in \mathsf{Var}^k \end{array}$$

where $\nu[i \leftarrow m]$ is the valuation that acts as ν, except for i, which is assigned to m. Whenever $\mathcal{I} \models \phi$, we say that $\mathcal{I}$ is a *model* of ϕ. It is known that, if a MIL formula has a model, then it has a model with universe of cardinality at most exponential in the size (number of symbols) of the formula [19]. This result, due to Löwenheim, is among the first decidability results for a fragment of first order logic.

Structures are partially ordered by pointwise inclusion, i.e. for $\mathcal{I}_i = (\mathfrak{U}, \nu_i, \iota_i)$, for $i = 1, 2$, we write $\mathcal{I}_1 \subseteq \mathcal{I}_2$ iff $\iota_1(p) \subseteq \iota_2(p)$, for all $p \in \mathsf{Pred}$ and $\mathcal{I}_1 \subset \mathcal{I}_2$ iff $\mathcal{I}_1 \subseteq \mathcal{I}_2$ and $\mathcal{I}_1 \neq \mathcal{I}_2$. As before, we define the sets $[\![\phi]\!] = \{\mathcal{I} \mid \mathcal{I} \models \phi\}$ and $[\![\phi]\!]^\mu = \{\mathcal{I} \in [\![\phi]\!] \mid \forall \mathcal{I}' \,.\, \mathcal{I}' \subset \mathcal{I} \rightarrow \mathcal{I}' \notin [\![\phi]\!]\}$ of models and minimal models of a MIL formula, respectively. Given formulae ϕ_1 and ϕ_2, we write $\phi_1 \equiv \phi_2$ for $[\![\phi_1]\!] = [\![\phi_2]\!]$ and $\phi_1 \equiv^\mu \phi_2$ for $[\![\phi_1]\!]^\mu = [\![\phi_2]\!]^\mu$.

2.2 Execution Semantics of Parametric Systems

We consider the interaction formulae of parametric systems to be finite disjunctions of formulae of the form below:

$$\exists i_1 \ldots \exists i_\ell \wedge \varphi \wedge \bigwedge_{j=1}^{\ell} p_j(i_j) \wedge \bigwedge_{j=\ell+1}^{\ell+m} \forall i_j \,.\, \psi_j \rightarrow p_j(i_j) \qquad (1)$$

where $\varphi, \psi_{\ell+1}, \ldots, \psi_{\ell+m}$ are conjunctions of equalities and disequalities involving index variables. Intuitively, the formulae (1) state that there are at most ℓ component instances that engage in a multiparty rendez-vous interaction on ports $p_1(i_1), \ldots, p_\ell(i_\ell)$, together with a broadcast to the ports $p_{\ell+1}(i_{\ell+1}), \ldots, p_{\ell+m}(i_{\ell+m})$ of the instances that fulfill the constraints $\psi_{\ell+1}, \ldots, \psi_{\ell+m}$. Observe that, if $m = 0$, the above formula corresponds to a multiparty (generalized) rendez-vous interaction $\exists i_1 \ldots \exists i_\ell \wedge \varphi \wedge \bigwedge_{j=1}^{\ell} p_j(i_j)$. An example of peer-to-peer rendez-vous is the parametric system from Fig. 1. Another example of broadcast is given below.

Example 1. Consider the parametric system obtained from an arbitrary number of *Worker* components (Fig. 3), where $C^1 = Worker$, $\mathsf{Var}^1 = \{i, i_1, i_2, j\}$ and $\mathsf{Pred}^1 = \{a, b, f, u, w\}$. Any pair of instances can jointly execute the b (*begin*) action provided *all* others are taking the a (*await*) action. Any instance can also execute alone the f (*finish*) action.

The execution semantics of a parametric system $\mathcal{S}$ is the marked PN $\mathcal{N}_\mathcal{S} = (N, \mathrm{m}_0)$, where $N = (\bigcup_{k=1}^{n} \mathsf{S}^k \times [1, \mathsf{M}(k)], T, E)$, $\mathrm{m}_0((s_0{}^k, i)) = 1$, for all $k \in [1, n]$ and $i \in [1, \mathsf{M}(k)]$, and the sets of transitions T and edges E are defined next. For each minimal model $\mathcal{I} = (\mathfrak{U}, \nu, \iota) \in [\![\Gamma]\!]^\mu$, we have a transition $\mathrm{t}_\mathcal{I} \in T$ and the edges $((s_i, k), \mathrm{t}_\mathcal{I}), (\mathrm{t}_\mathcal{I}, (s_i', k)) \in E$

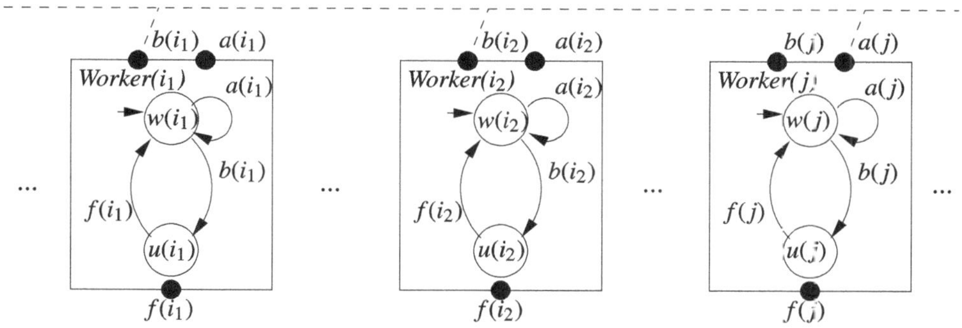

$$\Gamma = [\exists i_1 \exists i_2 \,.\, i_1 \neq i_2 \wedge b(i_1) \wedge b(i_2) \wedge \forall j \,.\, j \neq i_1 \wedge j \neq i_2 \rightarrow a(j)] \;\vee\; \exists i. f(i)$$

Fig. 3. Parametric system with broadcast

for all $i \in [1, n]$ such that $s_i \xrightarrow{p_i} s_i' \in \Delta^i$ and $k \in \iota(p_i)$. Moreover, nothing else is in T or E.

As a remark, unlike in the case of bounded systems, the size of the marked PN $\mathcal{N}_\mathcal{S}$, that describes the execution semantics of a parametric system $\mathcal{S}$, depends on the maximum number of instances of each component type. The definition of the trap invariant $Trap(\mathcal{N}_\mathcal{S})$ is the same as in the bounded case, except that, in this case, the size of the boolean formula depends on the (unbounded) number of instances in the system. The challenge, addressed in the following, is to define trap invariants using MIL formulae of a fixed size.

2.3 Computing Parametric Trap Invariants

To start with, we define the trap constraint of an interaction formula Γ consisting of a finite disjunction of (1) formulae, as a finite conjunction of formulae of the form below:

$$\forall i_1 \ldots \forall i_\ell \,.\, \left[\varphi \wedge \left(\bigvee_{j=1}^{\ell} {}^{\bullet}p_j(i_j) \vee \bigvee_{j=\ell+1}^{\ell+m} \exists i_j \,.\, \psi_j \wedge {}^{\bullet}p_j(i_j)\right)\right] \rightarrow$$
$$\left[\bigvee_{j=1}^{\ell} p_j{}^{\bullet}(i_j) \vee \bigvee_{j=\ell+1}^{\ell+m} \exists i_j \,.\, \psi_j \wedge p_j{}^{\bullet}(i_j)\right]$$

where, for a port $p \in \mathsf{P}^k$ of some component type C^k, ${}^{\bullet}p(i)$ and $p(i)^{\bullet}$ denote the unique predicate atoms $s(i)$ and $s'(i)$, such that $s \xrightarrow{p} s' \in \Delta^k$ is the (unique) transition involving p in T^k, or $\perp$ if there is no such rule.

Example 2. For example, the trap constraint for the parametric (rendez-vous) system in Fig. 1b is $\forall i.[r \vee w(i)] \rightarrow [s \vee u(i)] \;\wedge\; \forall i.[s \vee u(i)] \rightarrow [r \vee u(i)]$. Analogously, the trap constraint for the parametric (broadcast) system in Fig. 3 is:

$$\forall i_1 . \forall i_2 . \; [i_1 \neq i_2 \wedge (w(i_1) \vee w(i_2) \vee \exists j.(j \neq i_1 \wedge j \neq i_2 \wedge w(j)))] \rightarrow$$
$$[i_1 \neq i_2 \wedge (u(i_1) \vee u(i_2) \vee \exists j.(j \neq i_1 \wedge j \neq i_2 \wedge w(j)))]$$
$$\wedge \; \forall i. \; u(i) \rightarrow w(i)$$

We define a translation of MIL formulae into boolean formulae of unbounded size. Given a function $\mathsf{M} : [1, n] \rightarrow \mathbb{N}$, the *unfolding* of a MIL sentence ϕ is the boolean formula $\mathrm{B_M}(\phi)$ obtained by replacing each existential [universal] quantifier $\exists i \,.\, \psi(i)$ [$\forall i \,.\, \psi(i)$], for $i \in \mathsf{Var}^k$, by a finite disjunction [conjunction] $\bigvee_{\ell=1}^{\mathsf{M}(k)} \psi[\ell/i]$ [$\bigwedge_{\ell=1}^{\mathsf{M}(k)} \psi[\ell/i]$], where the substitution of the constant $\ell \in \mathsf{M}(k)$ for the variable i is defined recursively as usual, except for $\mathsf{pr}(i)[\ell/i] \stackrel{\mathsf{def}}{=} (\mathsf{pr}, \ell)$, which is a propositional variable. Further, we relate structures to boolean valuations of unbounded sizes. For a structure $\mathcal{I} = (\mathfrak{U}, \nu, \iota)$ we define the boolean valuation $\beta_{\mathcal{I}}((\mathsf{pr}, \ell)) = \top$ if and only if $\ell \in \iota(\mathsf{pr})$, for each predicate symbol pr and each integer constant ℓ. Conversely, for each valuation β of the propositional variables (pr, ℓ), there exists a structure $\mathcal{I}_\beta = (\mathfrak{U}, \nu, \iota)$ such that $\iota(\mathsf{pr}) \stackrel{\mathsf{def}}{=} \{\ell \mid \beta((\mathsf{pr}, \ell)) = \top\}$, for each $\mathsf{pr} \in \mathsf{Pred}$. The following lemma relates the semantics of MIL formulae with that of their boolean unfoldings:

Lemma 3. *Given a* MIL *sentence* ϕ *and a function* $\mathsf{M} : [1, n] \to \mathbb{N}$, *the following hold:*

1. *for each structure* $\mathcal{I} \in [\![\phi]\!]$, *we have* $\beta_{\mathcal{I}} \in [\![\mathrm{B_M}(\phi)]\!]$ *and conversely, for each valuation* $\beta \in [\![\mathrm{B_M}(\phi)]\!]$, *we have* $\mathcal{I}_\beta \in [\![\phi]\!]$.
2. *for each structure* $\mathcal{I} \in [\![\phi]\!]^\mu$, *we have* $\beta_{\mathcal{I}} \in [\![\mathrm{B_M}(\phi)]\!]^\mu$ *and conversely, for each valuation* $\beta \in [\![\mathrm{B_M}(\phi)]\!]^\mu$, *we have* $\mathcal{I}_\beta \in [\![\phi]\!]^\mu$.

Considering the MIL formula $\mathit{Init}(\mathcal{S}) \stackrel{\mathsf{def}}{=} \bigvee_{k=1}^{n} \exists i_k \,.\, s_0{}^k(i_k)$, that defines the set of initial configurations of a parametric system $\mathcal{S}$, the following lemma formalizes the intuition behind the definition of parametric trap constraints:

Lemma 4. *Let* $\mathcal{S}$ *be a parametric system with interaction formula* Γ *and* $\mathcal{I}$ *be a structure. Then* $\mathcal{I} \models \Theta(\Gamma) \wedge \mathit{Init}(\mathcal{S})$ *iff* $\{(s, k) \mid k \in \iota(s)\}$ *is a marked trap of* $\mathcal{N}_{\mathcal{S}}$. *Moreover,* $\mathcal{I} \in [\![\Theta(\Gamma) \wedge \mathit{Init}(\mathcal{S})]\!]^\mu$ *iff* $\{(s, k) \mid k \in \iota(s)\}$ *is a minimal marked trap of* $\mathcal{N}_{\mathcal{S}}$.

We are currently left with the task of computing a MIL formula which defines the trap invariant $\mathit{Trap}(\mathcal{N}_{\mathcal{S}})$ of a parametric component-based system $\mathcal{S} = \langle C^1, \ldots, C^n, \mathsf{M}, \Gamma \rangle$. The difficulty lies in the fact that the size of $\mathcal{N}_{\mathcal{S}}$ and thus, that of the boolean formula $\mathit{Trap}(\mathcal{N}_{\mathcal{S}})$ depends on the number $\mathsf{M}(k)$ of instances of each component type $k \in [1, n]$. As we aim at computing an invariant able to prove safety properties, such as deadlock freedom, independently of how many components are present in the system, we must define the trap invariant using a formula depending exclusively on Γ, i.e. not on M.

Observe first that $\mathit{Trap}(\mathcal{N}_{\mathcal{S}})$ can be equivalently defined using only the minimal marked traps of $\mathcal{N}_{\mathcal{S}}$, which, by Lemma 4, are exactly the sets $\{(s, k) \mid k \in \iota(s)\}$, defined by some structure $(\mathfrak{U}, \nu, \iota) \in [\![\Theta(\Gamma) \wedge \mathit{Init}(\mathcal{S})]\!]^\mu$. Assuming that the set of structures $[\![\Theta(\Gamma) \wedge \mathit{Init}(\mathcal{S})]\!]^\mu$, or an over-approximation of it, can be defined by a positive MIL formula, the trap invariant is defined using a generalization of boolean dualisation to predicate logic, defined recursively, as follows:

$$(i = j)^{\sim} \stackrel{\mathsf{def}}{=} \neg i = j \quad (\phi_1 \vee \phi_2)^{\sim} \stackrel{\mathsf{def}}{=} \phi_1{}^{\sim} \wedge \phi_2{}^{\sim} \quad (\exists i \,.\, \phi_1)^{\sim} \stackrel{\mathsf{def}}{=} \forall i \,.\, \phi_1{}^{\sim} \quad p(i)^{\sim} \stackrel{\mathsf{def}}{=} p(i)$$
$$(\neg i = j)^{\sim} \stackrel{\mathsf{def}}{=} i = j \quad (\phi_1 \wedge \phi_2)^{\sim} \stackrel{\mathsf{def}}{=} \phi_1{}^{\sim} \vee \phi_2{}^{\sim} \quad (\forall i \,.\, \phi_1)^{\sim} \stackrel{\mathsf{def}}{=} \exists i \,.\, \phi_1{}^{\sim}$$

The crux of the method is the ability of defining, given an arbitrary MIL formula ϕ, a positive MIL formula $\phi^{\oplus}$ that preserve its minimal models, formally $\phi \equiv^\mu \phi^{\oplus}$. Because of quantification over unbounded domains, a MIL formula ϕ does not have a disjunctive normal form and thus one cannot define $\phi^{\oplus}$ by simply deleting the negative literals in DNF, as was done for the definition of the positivation operation $(.)^{+}$, in the propositional case. For now we assume that the transformation $(.)^{\oplus}$ of monadic predicate formulae into positive formulae preserving minimal models is defined (a detailed presentation of this step is given next in Sect. 3) and close this section with a parametric counterpart of Theorem 1.

Theorem 2. *For any parametric system $\mathcal{S} = \langle C^1, \ldots, C^n, \mathsf{M}, \Gamma\rangle$, we have*

$$Trap(\mathcal{N}_{\mathcal{S}}) \equiv \mathsf{B}_{\mathsf{M}}\left(\left((\Theta(\Gamma) \wedge Init(\mathcal{S}))^{\oplus}\right)^{\sim}\right)$$

3 Cardinality Constraints

This section is concerned with the definition of a *positivation* operator $(.)^{\oplus}$ for MIL sentences, whose only requirements are that $\phi^{\oplus}$ is positive and $\phi \equiv^{\mu} \phi^{\oplus}$. For this purpose, we use a logic of quantifier-free *boolean cardinality constraints* [4, 18] as an intermediate language, on which the positive formulae are defined. The translation of MIL into cardinality constraints is done by an equivalence-preserving quantifier elimination procedure, described in Sect. 3.1. As a byproduct, since the satisfiability of quantifier-free cardinality constraints is NP-complete [18] and integrated with SMT [4], we obtain a practical decision procedure for MIL that does not use model enumeration, as suggested by the small model property [19]. Finally, the definition of a positive MIL formula from a boolean combination of quantifier-free cardinality constraints is given in Sect. 3.2.

We start by giving the definition of cardinality constraints. Given the set of monadic predicate symbols Pred, a *boolean term* is generated by the syntax:

$$t := \mathsf{pr} \in \mathsf{Pred} \mid \neg t_1 \mid t_1 \wedge t_2 \mid t_1 \vee t_2$$

When there is no risk of confusion, we borrow the terminology of propositional logic and say that a term is in DNF if it is a disjunction of conjunctions (minterms). We also write $t_1 \rightarrow t_2$ if and only if the implication is valid when t_1 and t_2 are interpreted as boolean formulae, with each predicate symbol viewed as a propositional variable. Two boolean terms t_1 and t_2 are said to be *compatible* if and only if $t_1 \wedge t_2$ is satisfiable, when viewed as a boolean formula.

For a boolean term t and a first-order variable $i \in \mathsf{Var}$, we define the shorthand $t(i)$ recursively, as $(\neg t_1)(i) \stackrel{\text{def}}{=} \neg t_1(i)$, $(t_1 \wedge t_2)(i) \stackrel{\text{def}}{=} t_1(i) \wedge t_2(i)$ and $(t_1 \vee t_2)(i) \stackrel{\text{def}}{=} t_1(i) \vee t_2(i)$. Given a positive integer $n \in \mathbb{N}$ and t a boolean term, we define the following *cardinality constraints*, by MIL formulae:

$$|t| \geq n \stackrel{\text{def}}{=} \exists i_1 \ldots \exists i_n \,.\, \mathrm{distinct}(i_1, \ldots, i_n) \wedge \bigwedge_{j=1}^{n} t(i_j) \qquad |t| \leq n \stackrel{\text{def}}{=} \neg(|t| \geq n+1)$$

We shall further use cardinality constraints with $n = \infty$, by defining $|t| \geq \infty \stackrel{\text{def}}{=} \bot$ and $|t| \leq \infty \stackrel{\text{def}}{=} \top$. The intuitive semantics of cardinality constraints is formally defined in terms of structures $\mathcal{I} = (\mathfrak{U}, \nu, \iota)$ by the semantics of monadic predicate logic, given in the previous. For instance, $|p \wedge q| \geq 1$ means that the intersection of the sets p and q is not empty, whereas $|\neg p| \leq 0$ means that p contains all elements from the universe.

3.1 Quantifier Elimination

Given a sentence ϕ, written in MIL, we build an equivalent boolean combination of cardinality constraints $\mathrm{qe}(\phi)$, using quantifier elimination. We describe the elimination of a single existential quantifier and the generalization to several existential or universal quantifiers is immediate. Assume that $\phi = \exists i_1 \,.\, \bigvee_{k\in K} \psi_k(i_1,\ldots,i_m)$, where K is a finite set of indices and, for each $k \in K$, ψ_k is a quantifier-free conjunction of atomic propositions of the form $i_j = i_\ell$, $\mathsf{pr}(i_j)$ and their negations, for some $j,\ell \in [1,m]$. We write, equivalently, $\phi \equiv \bigvee_{k\in K} \varphi_k \wedge \exists i_1 \,.\, \theta_k(i_1,\ldots,i_m)$, where φ_k does not contain occurrences of i_1 and θ_k is a conjunction of literals of the form $\mathsf{pr}(i_1)$, $\neg\mathsf{pr}(i_1)$, $i_1 = i_j$ and $\neg i_1 = i_j$, for some $j \in [2,m]$. For each $k \in K$, we distinguish the following cases:

1. if $i_1 = i_j$ is a consequence of θ_k, for some $j > 1$, let $\mathrm{qe}(\exists i_1 \,.\, \theta_k) \stackrel{\mathrm{def}}{=} \theta_k[i_j/i_1]$.
2. else, $\theta_k = \bigwedge_{j\in J_k} \neg i_1 = i_j \wedge t_k(i_1)$ for some $J_k \subseteq [2,m]$ and boolean term t_k, and let:

$$\mathrm{qe}(\exists i_1 \,.\, \theta_k) \stackrel{\mathrm{def}}{=} \bigwedge_{J\subseteq J_k} \left[\mathrm{distinct}(\{i_j\}_{j\in J}) \wedge \bigwedge_{j\in J} t_k(i_j)\right] \rightarrow |t_k| \geq ||J|| + 1$$
$$\mathrm{qe}(\phi) \stackrel{\mathrm{def}}{=} \bigvee_{k\in K} \varphi_k \wedge \mathrm{qe}(\exists i_1 \,.\, \theta_k)$$

Universal quantification is dealt with using the duality $\mathrm{qe}(\forall i_1 \,.\, \psi) \stackrel{\mathrm{def}}{=} \neg\mathrm{qe}(\exists i_1 \,.\, \neg\psi)$. For a prenex formula $\phi = Q_n i_n \ldots Q_1 i_1 \,.\, \psi$, where $Q_1,\ldots,Q_n \in \{\exists,\forall\}$ and ψ is quantifier-free, we define, recursively $\mathrm{qe}(\phi) \stackrel{\mathrm{def}}{=} \mathrm{qe}(Q_n i_n \,.\, \mathrm{qe}(Q_{n-1} i_{n-1} \ldots Q_1 i_1 \,.\, \psi))$. It is easy to see that, if ϕ is a sentence, $\mathrm{qe}(\phi)$ is a boolean combination of cardinality constraints. The correctness of the construction is a consequence of the following lemma:

Lemma 5. *Given a* MIL *formula $\phi = Q_n i_n \ldots Q_i i_1 \,.\, \psi$, where $Q_1,\ldots,Q_n \in \{\forall,\exists\}$ and ψ is a quantifier-free conjunction of equality and predicate atoms, we have $\phi \equiv \mathrm{qe}(\phi)$.*

Example 3. (contd. from Example 2) Below we show the results of quantifier elimination applied to the conjunction $\Theta(\Gamma) \wedge \mathit{Init}(\mathcal{S})$ for the system in Fig. 1b:

$$(\neg r \wedge \neg s \wedge |w \wedge \neg u| \leq 0 \wedge |u \wedge \neg w| \leq 0 \wedge 1 \leq |w|) \vee$$
$$(\neg r \wedge |w \wedge \neg u| \leq 0 \wedge |\neg w| \leq 0 \wedge 1 \leq |w|) \vee (s \wedge r) \vee (s \wedge |\neg w| \leq 0 \wedge 1 \leq |w|) \vee$$
$$(\neg s \wedge |\neg u| \leq 0 \wedge |u \wedge \neg w| \leq 0 \wedge 1 \leq |w|) \vee (|\neg u| \leq 0 \wedge |\neg w| \leq 0 \wedge 1 \leq |w|).$$

Similarly, for the system in Fig. 3, we obtain the following cardinality constraints:

$$(3 \leq |w| \wedge |u \wedge \neg w| \leq 0) \vee (2 \leq |w| \wedge |w \wedge \neg u| \leq 1 \wedge |u \wedge \neg w| \leq 0) \vee$$
$$(|\neg u| \leq 1 \wedge |\neg u \wedge \neg w| \leq 0 \wedge |u \wedge \neg w| \leq 0 \wedge 1 \leq |w|) \vee (|w \wedge \neg u| \leq 0 \wedge |u \wedge \neg w| \leq 0 \wedge 1 \leq |w|).$$

3.2 Building Positive Formulae that Preserve Minimal Models

Let ϕ be a MIL formula, not necessarily positive. We shall build a positive formula $\phi^\oplus$, such that $\phi \equiv^\mu \phi^\oplus$. By the result of the last section, ϕ is equivalent to a boolean combination of cardinality constraints $\mathrm{qe}(\phi)$, obtained by quantifier elimination. Thus we assume w.l.o.g. that the DNF of ϕ is a disjunction of conjunctions of the form $\bigwedge_{i\in L} |t_i| \geq \ell_i \wedge \bigwedge_{j\in U} |t_j| \leq u_j$, for some sets of indices L, U and some positive integers $\{\ell_i\}_{i\in L}$ and $\{u_j\}_{j\in U}$.

For a boolean combination of cardinality constraints ψ, we denote by $\mathrm{P}(\psi)$ the set of predicate symbols that occur in a boolean term of ψ and by $\mathrm{P}^+(\psi)$ ($\mathrm{P}^-(\psi)$) the set of predicate symbols that occur under an even (odd) number of negations in ψ. The following proposition allows to restrict the form of ϕ even further, without losing generality:

Proposition 1. *Given* MIL *formulae ϕ_1 and ϕ_2, for any positivation operator $(.)^\oplus$, the following hold:*

1. $(\phi_1 \vee \phi_2)^\oplus \equiv^\mu {\phi_1}^\oplus \vee {\phi_2}^\oplus$,
2. $(\phi_1 \wedge \phi_2)^\oplus \equiv^\mu {\phi_1}^\oplus \wedge {\phi_2}^\oplus$, *provided that* $\mathrm{P}(\phi_1) \cap \mathrm{P}(\phi_2) = \emptyset$.

From now on, we assume that ϕ is a conjunction of cardinality constraints that cannot be split as $\phi = \phi_1 \wedge \phi_2$, such that $\mathrm{P}(\phi_1) \cap \mathrm{P}(\phi_2) = \emptyset$.

Let us consider a cardinality constraint $|t| \geq \ell$ that occurs in ϕ. Given a set $\mathcal{P}$ of predicate symbols, for a set of predicates $S \subseteq \mathcal{P}$, the *complete* boolean minterm corresponding to S with respect to $\mathcal{P}$ is $t_S^{\mathcal{P}} \stackrel{\text{def}}{=} \bigwedge_{p \in S} p \wedge \bigwedge_{p \in \mathcal{P} \setminus S} \neg p$. Moreover, let $\mathcal{S}_t \stackrel{\text{def}}{=} \{S \subseteq \mathrm{P}(\phi) \mid t_S \rightarrow t\}$ be the set of sets S of predicate symbols for which the complete minterm t_S implies t. Finally, each cardinality constraint $|t| \geq \ell$ is replaced by the equivalent disjunction[7], in which each boolean term is complete with respect to $\mathrm{P}(\phi)$:

$$|t| \geq \ell \equiv \bigvee \Big\{ \bigwedge_{S \in \mathcal{S}_t} \left|t_S^{\mathrm{P}(\phi)}\right| \geq \ell_S \mid \text{ for some constants } \{\ell_S \in \mathbb{N}\}_{S \in \mathcal{S}_t} \text{ such that } \sum_{S \in \mathcal{S}_t} \ell_S = \ell \Big\}$$

Note that because any two complete minterms t_S and t_T, for $S \neq T$, are incompatible, then necessarily $|t_S \vee t_T| = |t_S| + |t_T|$. Thus $|t_S \vee t_T| \geq \ell$ if and only if there exist $\ell_1, \ell_2 \in \mathbb{N}$ such that $\ell_1 + \ell_2 = \ell$ and $|t_S| \geq \ell_1$, $|t_T| \geq \ell_2$, respectively.

Notice that, restricting the sets of predicates in $\mathcal{S}_t$ to subsets of $\mathrm{P}(\phi)$, instead of the entire set of predicates, allows to apply Proposition 1 and reduce the number of complete minterm to be considered. That is, whenever possible, we write each minterm $\bigwedge_{i \in L} |t_i| \geq \ell_i \wedge \bigwedge_{j \in U} \left|t_j\right| \leq u_j$ in the DNF of ϕ as $\psi_1 \wedge \ldots \wedge \psi_k$, such that $\mathrm{P}(\psi_i) \cap \mathrm{P}(\psi_j) = \emptyset$ for all $1 \leq i < j \leq k$. In practice, this optimisation turns out to be quite effective, as shown by the small execution times of our test cases, reported in Sect. 5.

The second step is building, for each conjunction $C = \bigwedge\{\ell_S \leq \left|t_S^{\mathrm{P}(\phi)}\right| \wedge \left|t_S^{\mathrm{P}(\phi)}\right| \leq u_S \mid S \subseteq \mathrm{P}(\phi)\}$[8], as above, a positive formula $C^\oplus$, that preserves its set of minimal models $[\![C]\!]^\mu$. The generalization to arbitrary boolean combinations of cardinality constraints is a direct consequence of Proposition 1. Let $\mathcal{L}^+(\phi)$ (resp. $\mathcal{L}^-(\phi)$) be the set of positive boolean combinations of predicate symbols $p \in \mathrm{P}^+(\phi)$ (resp. $\neg p$, where $p \in \mathrm{P}^-(\phi)$). Further, for a complete minterm $t_S^{\mathcal{P}}$, we write $t_S^{\mathcal{P}+}$ ($t_S^{\mathcal{P}-}$) for the conjunction of the positive (negative) literals in $t_S^{\mathcal{P}}$. Then, we define:

$$C^\oplus \stackrel{\text{def}}{=} \bigwedge \Big\{|\tau| \geq \textstyle\sum_{t_S^{\mathrm{P}(\phi)+} \rightarrow \tau} \ell_S \mid \tau \in \mathcal{L}^+(\phi)\Big\} \wedge \bigwedge \Big\{|\tau| \leq \textstyle\sum_{t_S^{\mathrm{P}(\phi)-} \rightarrow \tau} u_S \mid \tau \in \mathcal{L}^-(\phi)\}$$

It is not hard to see that $C^\oplus$ is a positive MIL formula, because:

[7] The constraints $|t| \leq u$ are dealt with as $\neg(|t| \geq u + 1)$.

[8] Missing lower bounds ℓ_S are replaced with 0 and missing upper bounds u_S with ∞.

- for each $\tau \in \mathcal{L}^+(\phi)$, we have $|\tau| \geq k \equiv \exists i_1 \ldots \exists i_k \,.\, \mathrm{distinct}(i_1, \ldots, i_k) \wedge \bigwedge_{j=1}^{k} \tau(j)$ and
- for each $\tau \in \mathcal{L}^-(\phi)$, we have $|\tau| \leq k \equiv \forall i_1 \ldots \forall i_{k+1} \,.\, \mathrm{distinct}(i_1, \ldots, i_{k+1}) \rightarrow \bigvee_{j=1}^{k+1} \neg\tau(i_j)$.

The following lemma proves that the above definition meets the second requirement of positivation operators, concerning the preservation of minimal models.

Lemma 6. *Given $\mathcal{P}$ a finite set of monadic predicate symbols, $\{\ell_S \in \mathbb{N}\}_{S \subseteq \mathcal{P}}$ and $\{u_S \in \mathbb{N} \cup \{\infty\}\}_{S \subseteq \mathcal{P}}$ sets of constants, for any conjunction $C = \bigwedge\{\ell_S \leq |t_S^{\mathcal{P}}| \wedge |t_S^{\mathcal{P}}| \leq u_S \mid S \subseteq \mathcal{P}\}$, we have $C \equiv^{\mu} C^{\oplus}$.*

Example 4 (contd. from Example 3).

Consider the first minterm of the DNF of the cardinality constraint obtained by quantifier elimination in Example 3, from the system in Fig. 1b. The result of positivation for this minterm is given below:

$$(\neg r \wedge \neg s \wedge |w \wedge \neg u| \leq 0 \wedge |u \wedge \neg w| \leq 0 \wedge 1 \leq |w|)^{\oplus} = 1 \leq |u \wedge w|$$

Intuitively, the negative literals $\neg r$ and $\neg s$ may safely disappear, because no minimal model will assign r or s to true. Further, the constraints $|w \wedge \neg u| \leq 0$ and $|u \wedge \neg w| \leq 0$ are equivalent to the fact that, in any structure $\mathcal{I} = (\mathfrak{U}, \nu, \iota)$, we must have $\iota(u) = \iota(w)$. Finally, because $|w| \geq 1$, then necessarily $|u \wedge w| \geq 1$.

Similarly, the result of positivation applied to the second conjunct of the DNF cardinality constraint corresponding to the system in Fig. 3 is given below:

$$(2 \leq |w| \wedge |w \wedge \neg u| \leq 1 \wedge |u \wedge \neg w| \leq 0)^{\oplus} = 2 \leq |w| \wedge 1 \leq |u \wedge w|$$

Here, the number of elements in w is at least 2 and, in any structure $\mathcal{I} = (\mathfrak{U}, \nu, \iota)$, we must have $\iota(u) \subseteq \iota(w)$ and at most one element in $\iota(w) \setminus \iota(u)$. Consequently, the intersection of the sets $\iota(u)$ and $\iota(w)$ must contain at least one element, i.e. $|u \wedge w| \geq 1$.

4 Proving Deadlock Freedom of Parametric Systems

We have gathered all the ingredients necessary for checking deadlock freedom of parametric systems, using our method based on trap invariant generation (Fig. 4). In particular, we derive a trap constraint $\Theta(\Gamma)$ directly from the interaction formula Γ, both of which are written in MIL. Second, we compute a positive formula that preserves the set of minimal models of $\Theta(\Gamma) \wedge \mathit{Init}(\mathcal{S})$, by first converting the MIL formula into a quantifier-free cardinality constraint, using quantifier elimination, and deriving a positive MIL formula from the latter.

The conjunction between the dual of this positive formula and the formula $\Delta(\Gamma)$ that defines the deadlock states is then checked for satisfiability. Formally, given a parametric system $\mathcal{S}$, with an interaction formula Γ written in the form (1), the MIL formula characterizing the deadlock states of the system is the following:

$$\Delta(\Gamma) \stackrel{\text{def}}{=} \forall i_1 \ldots \forall i_\ell \,.\, \varphi \rightarrow \left[\bigvee_{j=1}^{\ell} \neg^{\bullet} p_j(i_j) \vee \bigvee_{j=\ell+1}^{\ell+m} \exists i_j \,.\, \psi_j \wedge \neg^{\bullet} p_j(i_j)\right]$$

We state a sufficient verification condition for deadlock freedom in the parametric case:

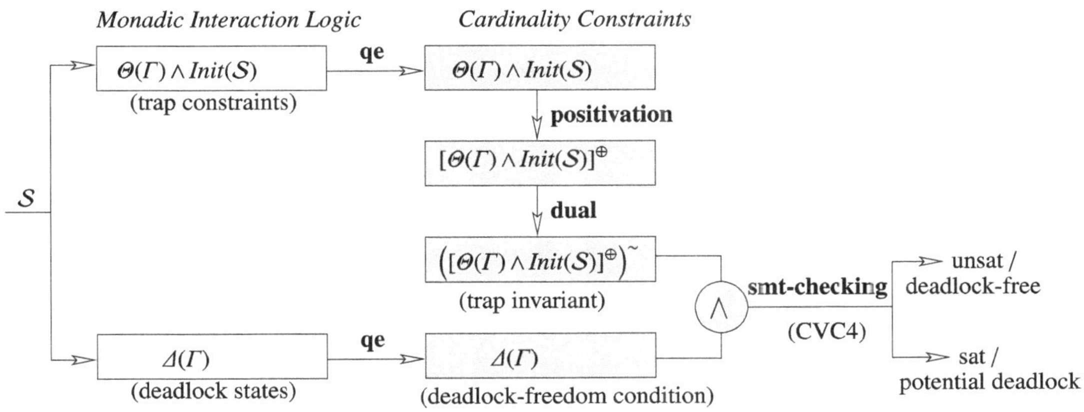

Fig. 4. Verification of parametric component-based systems

Corollary 2. *A parametric system* $\mathcal{S} = \langle C^1, \ldots, C^n, \mathsf{M}, \Gamma\rangle$ *is deadlock-free if*

$$\left((\Theta(\Gamma) \wedge Init(\mathcal{S}))^{\oplus}\right)^{\sim} \wedge \Delta(\Gamma) \rightarrow \bot$$

The satisfiability check is carried out using the conversion to cardinality constraints via quantifier elimination Sect. 3.1 and an effective set theory solver for cardinality constraints, implemented in the CVC4 SMT solver [6].

5 Experimental Results

To assess our method for proving deadlock freedom of parametric component-based system, we ran a number of experiments on systems with a small numbers of rather simple component types, but with nontrivial interaction patterns, given by MIL formulae. The `task-sem` *i/n* examples, $i = 1, 2, 3$, are generalizations of the parametric *Task-Semaphore* example depicted in Fig. 1b, in which n *Tasks* synchronize using n *Semaphores*, such that i *Tasks* interact with a single *Semaphore* at once, in a multiparty rendez-vous. In a similar vein, the `broadcast` *i/n* examples, $i = 2, 3$ are generalizations of the system in Fig. 3, in which i out of n *Workers* engage in rendez-vous on the b port, whereas all the other stay idle—here idling is modeled as a broadcast on the a ports. Finally, in the `sync` i/n examples, $i = 1, 2, 3$, we consider systems composed of n *Workers* (Fig. 1b) such that either i out of n instances simultaneously interact on the b ports, or all interact on the f ports. Notice that, for $i = 2, 3$, these systems have a deadlock if and only if $n \neq 0 \mod i$. This is because, if $n = m \mod i$, for some $0 < m < i$, there will be be m instances that cannot synchronize on their b port, in order to move from w to u, in order to engage in the f broadcast.

All experiments were carried out on a Intel(R) Xeon(R) CPU @ 2.00 GHz virtual machine with 4 GB of RAM. Table 1 shows separately the times needed to generate the proof obligations (trap invariants and deadlock states) from the interaction formulae and the times needed by CVC4 1.7 to show unsatisfiabilty or come up with a model. All systems considered, for which deadlock freedom could not be shown using our method, have a real deadlock scenario that manifests only under certain modulo constraints on

Table 1. Benchmarks

example	interaction formula	t-gen	t-smt	result
task-sem $1/n$	$\exists i \exists j_1 .\ a(i) \wedge b(j_1) \bigvee \exists i \exists j_1 .\ e(i) \wedge f(j_1)$	22 ms	20 ms	unsat
task-sem $2/n$	$\exists i \exists j_1 \exists j_2 .\ j_1 \neq j_2 \wedge a(i) \wedge b(j_1) \wedge b(j_2) \bigvee$ $\exists i \exists j_1 \exists j_2 .\ j_1 \neq j_2 \wedge e(i) \wedge f(j_1) \wedge f(j_2)$	34 ms	40 ms	unsat
task-sem $3/n$	$\exists i \exists j_1 \exists j_2 \exists j_3 .\ \mathrm{distinct}(j_1, j_2, j_3) \wedge a(i) \wedge b(j_1) \wedge b(j_2) \wedge b(j_3) \bigvee$ $\exists i \exists j_1 \exists j_2 \exists j_3 .\ \mathrm{distinct}(j_1, j_2, j_3) \wedge e(i) \wedge f(j_1) \wedge f(j_2) \wedge f(j_3)$	73 ms	40 ms	unsat
broadcast $2/n$	$\exists i_1 \exists i_2 . i_1 \neq i_2 \wedge b(i_1) \wedge b(i_2) \wedge$ $\forall j.\ j \neq i_1 \wedge j \neq i_2 \rightarrow a(j) \bigvee \exists i. f(i)$	14 ms	20 ms	unsat
broadcast $3/n$	$\exists i_1 \exists i_2 \exists i_3 . \mathrm{distinct}(i_1, i_2, i_3) \wedge b(i_1) \wedge b(i_2) \wedge b(i_3) \wedge$ $\forall j.\ j \neq i_1 \wedge j \neq i_2 \wedge j \neq i_3 \rightarrow a(j) \bigvee \exists i. f(i)$	409 ms	20 ms	unsat
sync $1/n$	$\exists i. b(i) \bigvee \forall i. f(i)$	5 ms	20 ms	unsat
sync $2/n$	$\exists i_1 \exists i_2 .\ i_1 \neq i_2 \wedge b(i_1) \wedge b(i_2) \bigvee \forall i. f(i)$	7 ms	50 ms	sat
sync $3/n$	$\exists i_1 \exists i_2 \exists i_3 . \mathrm{distinct}(i_1, i_2, i_3) \wedge b(i_1) \wedge b(i_2) \wedge b(i_3) \bigvee \forall i. f(i)$	11 ms	40 ms	sat

the number n of instances. These constraints cannot be captured by MIL formulae, or, equivalently by cardinality constraints, and would require cardinality constraints of the form $|t| = n \mod m$, for some constants $n, m \in \mathbb{N}$.

6 Conclusions

This work is part of a lasting research program on BIP linking two work directions: (1) recent work on modeling architectures using interaction logics, and (2) older work on verification by using invariants. Its rationale is to overcome as much as possible complexity and undecidability issues by proposing methods which are adequate for the verification of essential system properties.

The presented results are applicable to a large class of architectures characterized by the MIL. A key technical result is the translation of MIL formulas into cardinality constraints. This allows on the one hand the computation of the MIL formula characterizing the minimal trap invariant. On the other hand, it provides a decision procedure for MIL, that leverages from recent advances in SMT, implemented in the CVC4 solver [6].

References

1. Abdulla, P.A.: Well (and better) quasi-ordered transition systems. Bull. Symb. Log. **16**(4), 457–515 (2010)
2. Abdulla, P.A., Delzanno, G., Henda, N.B., Rezine, A.: Regular model checking without transducers (on efficient verification of parameterized systems). In: Grumberg, O., Huth, M. (eds.) TACAS 2007. LNCS, vol. 4424, pp. 721–736. Springer, Heidelberg (2007). https://doi.org/10.1007/978-3-540-71209-1_56
3. Alberti, F., Ghilardi, S., Sharygina, N.: A framework for the verification of parameterized infinite-state systems*. In: CEUR Workshop Proceedings, vol. 1195, pp. 302–308, January 2014

4. Bansal, K., Reynolds, A., Barrett, C.W., Tinelli, C.: A new decision procedure for finite sets and cardinality constraints in SMT. In: Olivetti, N., Tiwari, A. (eds.) IJCAR 2016. LNCS (LNAI), vol. 9706, pp. 82–98. Springer, Cham (2016). https://doi.org/10.1007/978-3-319-40229-1_7
5. Barkaoui, K., Lemaire, B.: An effective characterization of minimal deadlocks and traps in petri nets based on graph theory. In: 10th International Conference on Application and Theory of Petri Nets, ICATPN 1989, pp. 1–21 (1989)
6. Barrett, C., et al.: CVC4. In: Gopalakrishnan, G., Qadeer, S. (eds.) CAV 2011. LNCS, vol. 6806, pp. 171–177. Springer, Heidelberg (2011). https://doi.org/10.1007/978-3-642-22110-1_14
7. Basu, A., et al.: Rigorous component-based system design using the BIP framework. IEEE Softw. **28**(3), 41–48 (2011)
8. Baukus, K., Bensalem, S., Lakhnech, Y., Stahl, K.: Abstracting WS1S systems to verify parameterized networks. In: Graf, S., Schwartzbach, M. (eds.) TACAS 2000. LNCS, vol. 1785, pp. 188–203. Springer, Heidelberg (2000). https://doi.org/10.1007/3-540-46419-0_14
9. Bensalem, S., Bozga, M., Nguyen, T., Sifakis, J.: D-finder: a tool for compositional deadlock detection and verification. In: Bouajjani, A., Maler, O. (eds.) CAV 2009. LNCS, vol. 5643, pp. 614–619. Springer, Heidelberg (2009). https://doi.org/10.1007/978-3-642-02658-4_45
10. Bloem, R., et al.: Decidability of Parameterized Verification: Synthesis Lectures on Distributed Computing Theory. Morgan & Claypool Publishers, San Rafael (2015)
11. Bouajjani, A., Habermehl, P., Vojnar, T.: Abstract regular model checking. In: Alur, R., Peled, D.A. (eds.) CAV 2004. LNCS, vol. 3114, pp. 372–386. Springer, Heidelberg (2004). https://doi.org/10.1007/978-3-540-27813-9_29
12. Bozga, M., Iosif, R., Sifakis, J.: Checking deadlock-freedom of parametric component-based systems (2018). Technical report. arXiv:1805.10073
13. Chen, Y., Hong, C., Lin, A.W., Rümmer, P.: Learning to prove safety over parameterised concurrent systems. In: 2017 Formal Methods in Computer Aided Design, FMCAD 2017, Vienna, Austria, 2–6 October 2017, pp. 76–83 (2017)
14. Conchon, S., Goel, A., Krstić, S., Mebsout, A., Zaïdi, F.: Cubicle: a parallel smt-based model checker for parameterized systems. In: Madhusudan, P., Seshia, S.A. (eds.) Computer Aided Verification, pp. 718–724 (2012)
15. Emerson, E.A., Namjoshi, K.S.: Reasoning about rings. In: POPL 1995 Proceedings, pp. 85–94 (1995)
16. German, S.M., Sistla, A.P.: Reasoning about systems with many processes. J. ACM **39**(3), 675–735 (1992)
17. Kesten, Y., Maler, O., Marcus, M., Pnueli, A., Shahar, E.: Symbolic model checking with rich assertional languages. Theor. Comput. Sci. **256**(1), 93–112 (2001)
18. Kuncak, V., Nguyen, H.H., Rinard, M.C.: Deciding Boolean algebra with Presburger arithmetic. J. Autom. Reason. **36**(3), 213–239 (2006)
19. Löwenheim, L.: Über Möglichkeiten im Relativkalkül. Math. Ann. **470**, 76–447 (1915)
20. Suzuki, I.: Proving properties of a ring of finite-state machines. Inf. Process. Lett. **28**(4), 213–214 (1988)

The mCRL2 Toolset for Analysing Concurrent Systems

Improvements in Expressivity and Usability

Olav Bunte[1], Jan Friso Groote[1](✉), Jeroen J. A. Keiren[1,2], Maurice Laveaux[1], Thomas Neele[1], Erik P. de Vink[1], Wieger Wesselink[1], Anton Wijs[1], and Tim A. C. Willemse[1]

[1] Eindhoven University of Technology, Eindhoven, The Netherlands
j.f.groote@tue.nl

[2] Open University of the Netherlands, Heerlen, The Netherlands

Abstract. Reasoning about the correctness of parallel and distributed systems requires automated tools. By now, the mCRL2 toolset and language have been developed over a course of more than fifteen years. In this paper, we report on the progress and advancements over the past six years. Firstly, the mCRL2 language has been extended to support the modelling of probabilistic behaviour. Furthermore, the usability has been improved with the addition of refinement checking, counterexample generation and a user-friendly GUI. Finally, several performance improvements have been made in the treatment of behavioural equivalences. Besides the changes to the toolset itself, we cover recent applications of mCRL2 in software product line engineering and the use of domain specific languages (DSLs).

1 Introduction

Parallel programs and distributed systems become increasingly common. This is driven by the fact that Dennard's scaling theory [17], stating that every new processor core is expected to provide a performance gain over older cores, does not hold any more, and instead performance is to be gained from exploiting multiple cores. Consequently, distributed system paradigms such as cloud computing have grown popular. However, designing parallel and distributed systems correctly is notoriously difficult. Unfortunately, it is all too common to observe flaws such as data loss and hanging systems. Although these may be acceptable for many non-critical applications, the occasional hiccup may be impermissible for critical applications, *e.g.*, when giving rise to increased safety risks or financial loss.

The mCRL2 toolset is designed to reason about concurrent and distributed systems. Its language [27] is based on a rich, ACP-style process algebra and has an axiomatic view on processes. The data theory is rooted in the theory of abstract data types (ADTs). The toolset consists of over sixty tools supporting visualisation, simulation, minimisation and model checking of complex systems.

T. Vojnar and L. Zhang (Eds.): TACAS 2019, Part II, LNCS 11428, pp. 21–39, 2019.
https://doi.org/10.1007/978-3-030-17465-1_2

In this paper, we present an overview of the mCRL2 toolset in general, focussing on the developments from the past six years. We first present a cursory overview of the mCRL2 language, and discuss the recent addition of support for modelling and analysing *probabilistic processes.*

Behavioural equivalences such as strong and branching bisimulation are used to reduce and compare state spaces of complex systems. Recently, the complexity of branching bisimulation has been significantly improved from $O(mn)$ to $O(m(\log|Act| + \log n))$, where m is the number of transitions, n the number of states, and Act the set of actions. This was achieved by implementing the new algorithm by Groote *et al.* [24]. Additionally, support for checking (weak) failures refinement and failures divergence refinement has been added.

Model checking in mCRL2 is based on parameterised boolean equation systems (PBES) [33] that combine information from a given mCRL2 specification and a property in the modal μ-calculus. Solving the PBES answers the encoded model checking problem. Recent developments include improved static analysis of PBESs using liveness analysis, and solving PBESs for infinite-state systems using symbolic quotienting algorithms and abstraction. One of the major features recently introduced is the ability to generate comprehensive counterexamples in the form of a subgraph of the original system.

To aid novice users of mCRL2, an alternative graphical user-interface (GUI), `mcrl2ide`, has been added, that contains a text editor to create mCRL2 specifications, and provides access to the core functionality of mCRL2 without requiring the user to know the interface of each of the sixty tools. The use of the language and tools is illustrated by means of a selection of case studies conducted with mCRL2. We focus on the application of the tools as a verification back-end for domain specific languages (DSLs), and the verification of software product lines.

The mCRL2 toolset can be downloaded from the website www.mcrl2.org. This includes binaries as well as source code packages[1]. To promote external contributions, the source code of mCRL2 and the corresponding issue tracker have been moved to GitHub.[2] The mCRL2 toolset is open source under the permissive Boost license, that allows free use for any purpose. Technical documentation and a user manual of the mCRL2 toolset, including a tutorial, can be found on the website. An extensive introduction to the mCRL2 language can be found in the textbook *Modeling and analysis of communicating systems* [27].

The rest of the paper is structured as follows. Section 2 introduces the basics of the mCRL2 language and Sect. 3 its probabilistic extension. In Sect. 4, we discuss several new and improved tools for various behavioural relations. Section 5 gives an overview of novel analysis techniques for PBESs, while Sect. 6 introduces mCRL2's improved GUI and Sect. 7 discusses a number of applications. Related work is discussed in Sects. 8 and 9 presents a conclusion and future plans.

[1] The source code is also archived on https://doi.org/10.5281/zenodo.2555054.

[2] https://github.com/mCRL2org/mCRL2.

2 The mCRL2 Language and Workflow

The behavioural specification language mCRL2 [27] is the successor of μCRL (micro Common Representation Language [28]) that was in turn a response to a language called CRL (Common Representation Language) that became so complex that it would not serve a useful purpose.

$$
\begin{array}{l}
\textbf{sort}\ \mathit{Content} = \textbf{struct}\ \mathit{bad\_data} \mid \mathit{data}_1 \mid \mathit{data}_2\,; \\[1em]
\textbf{act}\ \mathit{read}, \mathit{deliver}, \mathit{get}, \mathit{put}, \mathit{pass\_on} : \mathit{Content}\,; \\[1em]
\textbf{proc}\ \mathit{Filter} = \\
\qquad\qquad \sum_{c:\mathit{Content}} \mathit{get}(c)\cdot(c \approx \mathit{bad\_data} \rightarrow \mathit{Filter} \diamond \mathit{put}(c)\cdot\mathit{Filter})\,; \\
\qquad \mathit{Queue}(q : \mathit{List}(\mathit{Content})) = \\
\qquad\qquad \sum_{c:\mathit{Content}} \mathit{read}(c)\cdot\mathit{Queue}(c \triangleright q) + \\
\qquad\qquad\qquad q \not\approx [\,] \rightarrow \mathit{deliver}(\mathit{rhead}(q))\cdot\mathit{Queue}(\mathit{rtail}(q))\,; \\[1em]
\textbf{init}\ \nabla_{\{\mathit{get},\mathit{deliver},\mathit{pass\_on}\}}(\Gamma_{\{\mathit{put}|\mathit{read}\rightarrow\mathit{pass\_on}\}}(\mathit{Filter} \,||\, \mathit{Queue}([\,])))\,;
\end{array}
$$

Fig. 1. A filter process communicating with an infinite queue in mCRL2.

The languages μCRL and mCRL2 are quite similar combinations of process algebra in the style of ACP [8] together with equational abstract data types [19]. A typical example illustrating most of the language features of mCRL2 is given in Fig. 1, which shows a filter process (*Filter*) that iteratively reads data via an action *get* and forwards it to a queue using the action *put* if the data is not bad. The queue (*Queue*) is infinitely sized, reading data via the action *read* and delivering data via the action *deliver*. The processes are put in parallel using the parallel operator $\|$. The actions *put* and *read* are forced to synchronise into the action *pass_on* using the communication operator Γ and the allow operator ∇.

The language mCRL2 only contains a minimal set of primitives to express behaviour, but this set is well chosen such that behaviour of communicating systems can be easily expressed. Both μCRL and mCRL2 allow to express systems with time, using positive real time tags to indicate when an action takes place. Recently the possibility has been added to express probabilistic behaviour in mCRL2, which will be explained in Sect. 3.

The differences between μCRL and mCRL2 are minor but significant. In mCRL2 the if-then-else is written as $c \rightarrow p \diamond q$ (was $p \triangleleft c \triangleright q$). mCRL2 allows for multi-actions, e.g., $a|b|c$ expresses that the actions a, b and c happen at the same time. mCRL2 does not allow multiple actions with the same time tag to happen consecutively (μCRL does, as do most other process specification formalisms with time). Finally, mCRL2 has built-in standard datatypes, mechanisms to allow to specify datatypes far more compactly, and it allows for function datatypes, including lambda expressions, as well as arbitrary sets and bags.

The initial purpose of μCRL was to have a mathematical language to model realistic protocols and distributed systems of which the correctness could be proven manually using process algebraic axioms and rules, as well as the equations for the equational data types. The result of this is that mCRL2 is equipped with a nice fundamental theory as well as highly effective proof methods [29,30], which have been used, for instance, to provide a concise, computer checked proof of the correctness of Tanenbaum's most complex sliding window protocol [1].

When the language μCRL began to be used for specifying actual systems [20], it became obvious that such behavioural specifications are too large to analyse by hand and tools were required, a toolset was developed. It also became clear that specifications of actual systems are hard to give without flaws, and verification is needed to eliminate those flaws. In the early days verification had the form of proving that an implementation and a specification were (branching) bisimilar.

Often it is more convenient to prove properties about aspects of the behaviour. For this purpose mCRL2 was extended with a modal logic, in the form of the modal μ-calculus with data and time. A typical example of a formula in modal logic is the following:

$$\begin{aligned}\nu X(n{:}\mathbb{N}=0).\forall m:\mathbb{N}.[\mathit{enter}(m)]X(n{+}m)\wedge\\ \forall m:\mathbb{N}.[\mathit{extract}(m)](m\leq n\wedge X(n{-}m))\end{aligned}$$

which says that the amount extracted using actions *extract* can never exceed the cumulative amount entered via the action *enter*. The modal μ-calculus with data is far more expressive than languages such as LTL and CTL*, which can be mapped into it [13].

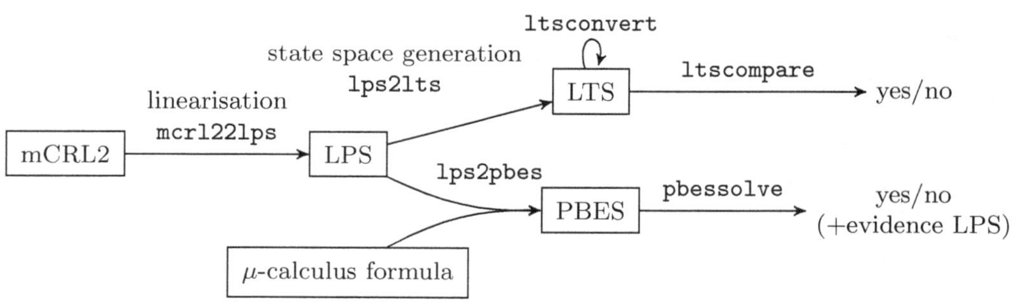

Fig. 2. The mCRL2 model checking workflow

Verification of modal formulae is performed through transformations to *linear process specifications* (LPSs) and *parameterised boolean equation systems* (PBESs) [25,33]. See Fig. 2 for the typical model checking workflow. An LPS is a process in normal form, where all state behaviour is translated into data parameters. An LPS essentially consists of a set of condition-action-effect rules saying which action can be done in which state, and as such is a symbolic representation of a state space. A PBES is constructed using a modal formula and a linear process. It consists of a parameterised sequence of boolean fixed point equations. A PBES can be solved to obtain an answer to the question whether the mCRL2 specification satisfies the supplied formula. For more details on PBESs and the generation of evidence, refer to Sect. 5.

Whereas an LPS is a symbolic description of the behaviour of a system, a *labelled transition system* (LTS), makes this behaviour explicit. An LTS can be defined in the context of a set of action labels. The LTS itself consists of a set of states, an initial state, and a transition relation between states where each transition is labelled by an action. The mCRL2 toolset contains the `lps2lts` tool to obtain the LTS from a given LPS by means of state space exploration. The resulting LTS contains all reachable states of this LPS and the transition relation defining the possible actions in each state. The mCRL2 toolset provides tools for visualising and reducing LTSs and also for comparing LTSs in a pairwise manner. For more details on reducing and comparing LTSs, refer to Sect. 4.

3 Probabilistic Extensions to mCRL2

A recent addition to the mCRL2 language is the possibility to specify probabilistic processes using the construct **dist** $x{:}D[\, dist(x)\,].p(x)$ which behaves as the process $p(x)$ with probability $dist(x)$. The distribution *dist* may be discrete or continuous. For example, a process describing a light bulb that fails according to a negative exponential distribution of rate λ is described as

$$\textbf{dist}\ r{:}\mathbb{R}.[\, if(r{\geq}0,\ \lambda e^{-\lambda r},\ 0)\,].fail^{\varsigma}r$$

where $fail^{\varsigma}r$ is the notation for the action *fail* that takes place at time r.

The modelling of probabilistic behaviour with the probabilistic extension of mCRL2 can be rather insightful as advocated in [32]. There it is illustrated for the Monty Hall problem and the so-called "problem of the lost boarding pass" how strong probabilistic bisimulation and reduction modulo probabilistic weak trace equivalence can be applied to visualise the *probabilistic LTS* (PLTS) of the underlying probabilistic process as well as to establish the probability of reaching a target state (or set of states). We illustrate this by providing the description and state space of the Monty Hall problem here.

In the Monty Hall problem, there are three doors, one of which is hiding a prize. A player can select a door. Then one of the remaining doors that does not hide the prize is opened. The player can then decide to select the other door. If he does so, he will get the prize with probability $\frac{2}{3}$. The action `prize`(*true*) indicates that a prize is won. The action `prize`(*false*) is an indication that no prize is obtained. A possible model in mCRL2 is given below. In this model the player switches doors. So, the prize is won if the initially selected door was not the door with the prize.

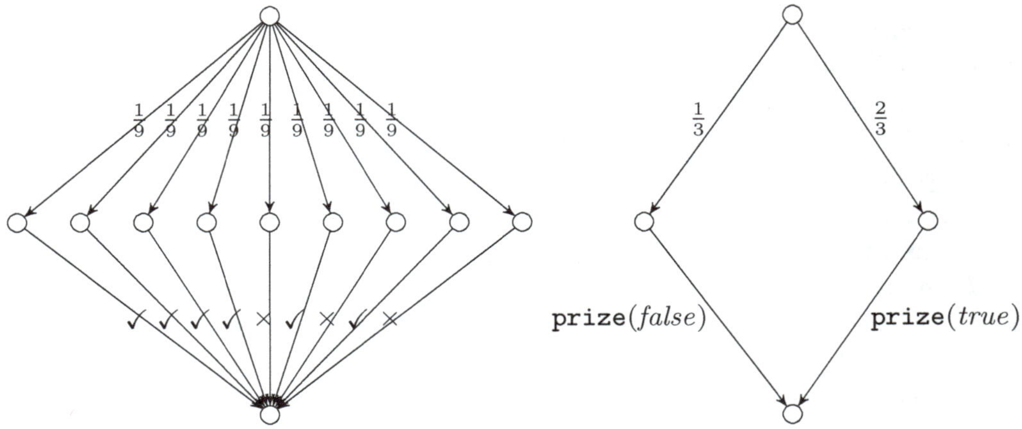

Fig. 3. The non-reduced and reduced state space of the Monty Hall problem. At the left the label ✓ abbreviates `prize`(*true*) and × stands for `prize`(*false*)

$$\begin{array}{l}\textbf{sort}\ \ \mathit{Doors} = \textbf{struct}\ \mathit{door}_1 \mid \mathit{door}_2 \mid \mathit{door}_3\,;\\ \textbf{init}\ \ \textbf{dist}\ \mathit{door\_with\_prize} : \mathit{Doors}\,[1/3]\,.\\ \qquad\qquad \textbf{dist}\ \mathit{initially\_selected\_door} : \mathit{Doors}\,[1/3]\,.\\ \qquad\qquad\quad \mathtt{prize}(\mathit{initially\_selected\_door} \not\approx \mathit{door\_with\_prize})\cdot\delta\,;\end{array}$$

The generated state space for this model is given in Fig. 3 at the left. From probabilistic mCRL2 processes probabilistic transition systems can be generated, which can be reduced modulo strong probabilistic bisimulation [26] (see the next section). The reduced transition system is provided at the right, and clearly shows that the prize is won with probability $\frac{2}{3}$.

Moreover, modal mu-calculus formulae yielding a probability, *i.e.* a real number, can be evaluated invoking probabilistic counterparts of the central tools in the toolset. For the Monty Hall model the modal formula $\langle \mathtt{prize}(\mathit{true})\rangle \mathit{true}$ will evaluate to the probability $\frac{2}{3}$. The tool that verified this modal formula is presented in [10]. Although the initial results are promising, the semantic and axiomatic underpinning of the process theory for probabilities is demanding.

4 Behavioural Relations

Given two LTSs, the `ltscompare` tool can check whether they are related according to one of a number of equivalence and refinement relations. Additionally, the `ltsconvert` tool can reduce a given LTS modulo an equivalence relation. In the following subsections the recently added implementations of several equivalence and refinement relations are described.

4.1 Equivalences

The `ltscompare` tool can check simulation equivalence, and (weak) trace equivalence between LTSs. In the latest release an algorithm for checking ready simulation was implemented and integrated into the toolset [23]. Regarding bisimulations, the tool can furthermore check strong, branching and weak bisimulation between LTSs. The latter two are sensitive to so-called *internal* behaviour, represented by the action τ. *Divergence-preserving* variants of these bisimulations are supported, which take the ability to perform infinite sequences of internal behaviour into account. The above mentioned equivalences can also be used by the `ltsconvert` tool.

Recently, the Groote/Jansen/Keiren/Wijs algorithm (GJKW) for branching bisimulation [24], with complexity $O(m(\log|Act| + \log n))$, was implemented. When tested in practice, it frequently demonstrates performance improvements by a factor of 10, and occasionally by a factor of 100 over the previous algorithm by Groote and Vaandrager [31].

The improved complexity is the result of combining the *process the smaller half* principle [35] with the key observations made by Groote and Vaandrager regarding internal transitions [31]. GJKW uses partition refinement to identify all classes of equivalent states. Repeatedly, one class (or *block*) B is selected to be the so-called *splitter*, and each block B' is checked for the reachability of B, where internal behaviour should be skipped over. In case B is reachable from some states in B' but not from others, B' needs to be split into two subblocks, separating the states from which B can and cannot be reached. Whenever a fixed-point is reached, the obtained partition defines the equivalence relation.

GJKW applies *process the smaller half* in two ways. First of all, it is ensured that each time a state s is part of a splitter B, the size of B, in terms of number of states, is at most half the size of the previous splitter in which s resided. To do this, blocks are partitioned in *constellations*. A block is selected as splitter iff its size is at most half the number of states in the constellation in which it resides. When a splitter is selected, it is moved into its own, new, constellation, and when a block is split, the resulting subblocks remain in the same constellation.

Second of all, it has to be ensured that splitting a block B' takes time proportional to the smallest resulting subblock. To achieve this, two state selection procedures are executed in lockstep, one identifying the states in B' that can reach the splitter, and one detecting the other states. Once one of these procedures has identified all its states, those states can be split off from B'.

Reachability checking is performed efficiently by using the notion of *bottom state* [31], which is a state that has no outgoing internal transitions leading to a state in the same block. It suffices to check whether any bottom state in B' can reach B. Hence, it is crucial that for each block, the set of bottom states is maintained during execution of the algorithm.

GJKW is very complicated due to the amount of book keeping needed to achieve the complexity. Among others, a data structure by Valmari, called *refinable partition* [46] is used, together with three copies of all transitions, structured in different ways to allow fast retrieval in the various stages of the algorithm.

Besides checking for branching bisimulation, GJKW is used as a basis for checking strong bisimulation (in which case it corresponds to the Paige-Tarjan algorithm [41]) and as a preprocessing step for checking weak bisimulation.

For the support of the analysis of probabilistic systems, a number of preliminary extensions have been made to the mCRL2 toolset. In particular, a new algorithm has been added to reduce PLTSs – containing both non-deterministic and probabilistic choice [44] – modulo strong probabilistic bisimulation. This new Paige-Tarjan style algorithm, called GRV [26] and implemented in the tool `ltspbisim`, improves upon the complexity of the best known algorithm so far by Baier *et al.* [2]. The GRV algorithm was inspired by work on lumping of Markov Chains by Valmari and Franceschinis [47] to limit the number of times a probabilistic transition needs to be sorted. Under the assumption of a bounded fan-out for probabilistic states, the time complexity of GRV is $O(n_p \log n_a)$ with n_p equal to the number of probabilistic transitions and n_a being the number of non-deterministic states in a PLTS.

4.2 Refinement

In model checking there is typically a single model on which properties, defined in another language, are verified. An alternative approach that can be employed is *refinement* checking. Here, the correctness of the model is verified by establishing a refinement relation between an implementation LTS and a specification LTS. The chosen refinement relation must be strong enough to preserve the desired properties of the model, but also weak enough to allow many valid implementations.

For refinement relations the `ltscompare` tool can check the asymmetric variants of simulation, ready simulation and (weak) trace equivalence between LTSs. In the latest release, several algorithms have been added to check (weak) trace, (weak) failures and failures-divergences refinement relations based on the algorithms introduced in [48]. We remark that weak failures refinement is known as stable failures refinement in the literature. Several improvements have been made to the reference algorithms and the resulting implementation has been successfully used in practice, as described in Sect. 7.1.

The newly introduced algorithms are based on the notion of *antichains*. These algorithms try to find a witness to show that no refinement relation exists. The antichain data structure keeps track of the explored part of the state space and assists in pruning other parts based on an ordering. If no refinement relation exists, the tool provides a counterexample trace to a violating state. To further speed up refinement checking, the tool applies divergence-preserving branching bisimulation reduction as a preprocessing step.

5 Model Checking

Behavioural properties can be specified in a first-order extension of the modal μ-calculus. The problem of deciding whether a μ-calculus property holds for a given mCRL2 specification is converted to a problem of (partially) solving a PBES. Such an equation system consists of a sequence of parameterised fixpoint equations of the form $(\sigma X(d_1{:}D_1, \ldots, d_n{:}D_n) = \phi)$, where σ is either a least (μ) or greatest (ν) fixpoint, X is an n-ary typed second-order recursion variable, each d_i is a parameter of type D_i and ϕ is a predicate formula (technically, a first-order formula with second-order recursion variables). The entire translation is syntax-driven, *i.e.*, linear in the size of the linear process specification and the property. We remark that mCRL2 also comes with tools that encode decision problems for behavioural equivalences as equation system solving problems; moreover, mCRL2 offers similar translations operating on labelled transition systems instead of linear process specifications.

5.1 Improved Static Analysis of Equation Systems

The parameters occurring in an equation system are derived from the parameters present in process specifications and first-order variables present in μ-calculus formulae. Such parameters typically determine the set of second-order variables on which another second-order variable in an equation system depends. Most equation system solving techniques rely on explicitly computing these dependencies. Obviously, such techniques fail when the set of dependencies is infinite. Consider, for instance the equation system depicted below:

$$\nu X(i,k{:}N) = (i \neq 1 \vee X(1,k+1)) \wedge \forall m{:}N.\ Y(2,k+m)$$
$$\mu Y(i,k{:}N) = (k < 10 \vee i = 2) \wedge (i \neq 2 \vee Y(1,1))$$

Observe that the solution to $X(1,1)$, which is *true*, depends on the solution to $X(1,2)$, but also on the solution to $Y(2,1+m)$ for all m, see Fig. 4. Consequently, techniques that rely on explicitly computing the dependencies will fail to compute the solution to $X(1,1)$.

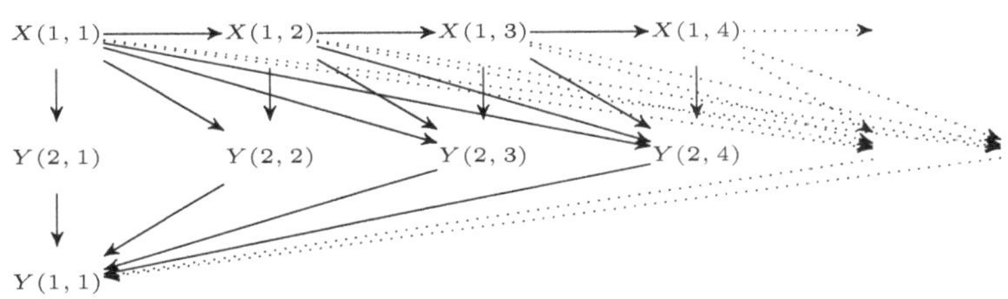

Fig. 4. Dependencies of second-order recursion variables on other second-order recursion variables in an equation system.

Not all parameters are 'used' equally in an equation system: some parameters may only influence the truth-value of a second-order variable, whereas others may also influence whether an equation depends on second-order variables. For instance, in our example, the parameter i of X determines when there is a dependency of X on X, and in the equation for Y, parameter i determines when there is a dependency of Y on Y. The value for parameter k, however, is only of interest in the equation for Y, where it immediately determines its solution when $i \neq 2$: it will be *true* when $k < 10$ and *false* otherwise. For $i = 2$, the value of k is immaterial. As suggested by the dependency graph in Fig. 4, for $X(1,1)$, the only dependency that is ultimately of consequence is the dependency on $Y(1,1)$, *i.e.*, $k = 1$; other values for k cannot be reached.

The techniques implemented in the `pbesstategraph` tool, and which are described in [37], perform a *liveness analysis* for data variables, such as k in our example, and reset these values to default values when their actual value no longer matters. To this end, a static analysis determines a set of *control flow parameters* in an equation system. Intuitively, a control flow parameter is a parameter in an equation for which we can statically detect that it can assume only a finite number of distinct values, and that its values determine which occurrences of recursion variables in an equation are relevant. Such control flow parameters are subsequently used to approximate the dependencies of an equation system, and compute the set of data variables that are still *live*. As soon as a data variable switches from live to not live, it can be set to a default, pre-determined value.

In our example, parameter i in equations X and Y is a control flow parameter that can take on value 1 or 2. Based on a liveness analysis one can conclude that the second argument in both occurrences of the recursion variable X in the equation for X can be reset, leading to an equation system that has the same solution as the original one:

$$\begin{aligned}\nu X(i,k{:}N) &= (i \neq 1 \vee X(1,1)) \wedge \forall m{:}N.\ Y(2,1)\\ \mu Y(i,k{:}N) &= (k < 10 \vee i = 2) \wedge (i \neq 2 \vee Y(1,1))\end{aligned}$$

Observe that there are only a finite number of dependencies in the above equation system, as the universally quantified variable m no longer induces an infinite set of dependencies. Consequently, it can be solved using techniques that rely on computing the dependencies in an equation system. The experiments in [37] show that `pbesstategraph` in general speeds up solving when it is able to reduce the underlying set of dependencies in an equation system, and when it is not able to do so, the overhead caused by the analysis is typically small.

5.2 Infinite-State Model Checking

Two new experimental tools, `pbessymbolicbisim` [40] and `pbesabsinthe` [16], support model checking of infinite-state systems. These are two of the few symbolic tools in the toolset. Regular PBES solving techniques, such as those implemented in `pbessolve`, store each state explicitly, which prohibits the analysis of infinite-state systems. In `pbessymbolicbisim`, (infinite) sets of states are represented using first-order logic expressions. Instead of straightforward exploration, it performs symbolic partition refinement based on the information about the underlying state space that is contained in the PBES. The approximation of the state space is iteratively refined, until it equals the bisimulation quotient of that state space. Moreover, since the only goal of this tool is to solve a PBES, *i.e.* give the answer *true* or *false*, additional abstraction techniques can be very coarse. As a result, the tool often terminates before the bisimulation quotient has been fully computed.

The second tool, `pbesabsinthe`, requires the user to specify an abstraction mapping manually. If the abstraction mapping satisfies certain criteria, it will be used to generate a finite underlying graph structure. By solving the graph structure, the tool obtains a solution to the PBES under consideration.

The theoretical foundations of `pbessymbolicbisim` and `pbesabsinthe` are similar: `pbessymbolicbisim` computes an abstraction based on an equivalence relation and `pbesabsinthe` works with preorder-based abstractions. Both approaches have their own strengths and weaknesses: `pbesabsinthe` requires the user to specify an abstraction manually, whereas `pbessymbolicbisim` runs fully automatically. However, the analysis of `pbessymbolicbisim` can be very costly for larger models. A prime application of `pbessymbolicbisim` and `pbesabsinthe` is the verification of real-time systems.

5.3 Evidence Extraction

One of the major new features of the mCRL2 toolset that, until recently, was lacking is the ability to generate informative counterexamples (resp. witnesses) from a failed (resp. successful) verification. The theory of evidence generation that is implemented is based on that of [15], which explains how to extract diagnostic evidence for μ-calculus formulae via the *Least Fixed-Point* (LFP) logic. The diagnostic evidence that is extracted is a subgraph of the original labelled transition system that permits to reconstruct the same proof of a failing (or successful) verification. Note that since the input language for properties can encode branching-time and linear-time properties, diagnostic evidence cannot always be presented in terms of traces or lassos; for linear-time properties, however, the theory permits to generate trace- and lasso-shaped evidence.

A straightforward implementation of the ideas of [15] in the setting of equation systems is, however, hampered by the fact that the original evidence theory builds on a notion of *proof graph* that is different from the one developed in [14] for equation systems. In [49], we show that these differences can be overcome by modifying the translation of the model checking problem as an equation system solving problem. This new translation is invoked by passing the flag '-c' to the tool `lps2pbes`. The new equation system solver `pbessolve` can be directed to extract and store the diagnostic evidence from an equation system by passing the linear process specification along with this equation system; the resulting evidence, which is stored as a linear process specification, can subsequently be simulated, minimised or visualised for further inspection.

Figure 5, taken from [49], gives an impression of the shape of diagnostic evidence that can be generated using the new tooling. The labelled transition system that is depicted presents the counterexample to a formula for the CERN job storage management system [43] that states that invariantly, each task that is terminated is inevitably removed. Note that this counterexample is obtained by minimising the original 142-state large evidence produced by our tools modulo branching bisimulation.

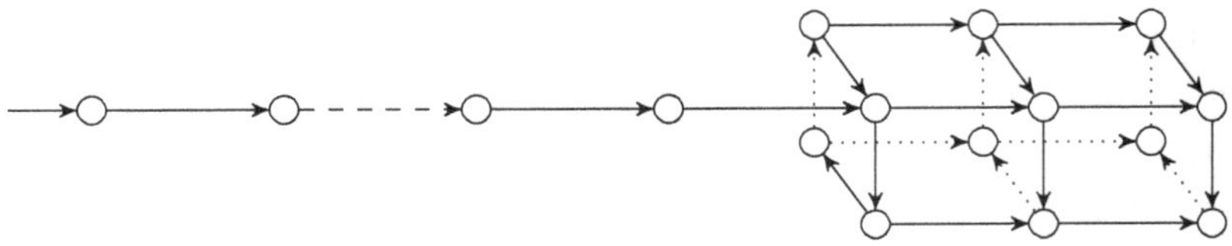

Fig. 5. Counterexamples for the requirement that *each task in a terminating state is eventually removed* for the Storage Management Systems. We omitted all edge labels, and the dashed line indicates a lengthy path through a number of other states (not depicted), whereas the dotted transitions are 3D artefacts.

6 User-Friendly GUI

The techniques explained in this paper may not be easily accessible to users that are new to the mCRL2 toolset. This is because the toolset is mostly intended for scientific purposes; at least initially, not much attention had been spent on user friendliness. As the toolset started to get used in workshops and academic courses however, the need for this user friendliness increased. This gave rise to the tools `mcrl2-gui`, a graphical alternative to the command line usage of the toolset, and `mcrl2xi`, an editor for mCRL2 specifications. However, to use the functionality of the toolset it was still required to know about the individual tools. For instance, to visualise the state space of an mCRL2 specification, one needed to manually run the tools `mcrl22lps`, `lps2lts` and `ltsgraph`.

As an alternative, the tool `mcrl2ide` has been added to the mCRL2 toolset. This tool provides a graphical user interface with a text editor to create and edit mCRL2 specifications and it provides the core functionality of the toolset such as visualising the (reduced) state space and verifying properties. The tools that correspond to this functionality are abstracted away from the user; only one or a few button clicks are needed.

See Fig. 6 for an instance of `mcrl2ide` with an open project, consisting of an mCRL2 specification and a number of properties. The UI consists of an editor for mCRL2 specifications, a toolbar at the top, a dock listing defined properties on the right and a dock with console output at the bottom. The toolbar contains buttons for creating, opening and saving a project and buttons for running tools. The properties dock allows verifying each single property on the given mCRL2 specification, editing/removing properties and showing the witness/counterexample after verification.

7 Applications

The mCRL2 toolset and its capabilities have not gone unnoticed. Over the years numerous initiatives and collaborations have sprouted to apply its functionality.

7.1 mCRL2 as a Verification Back-End

The mCRL2 toolset enjoys a sustained application in industry, often in the context of case studies carried out by MSc or PhD students. Moreover, the mCRL2

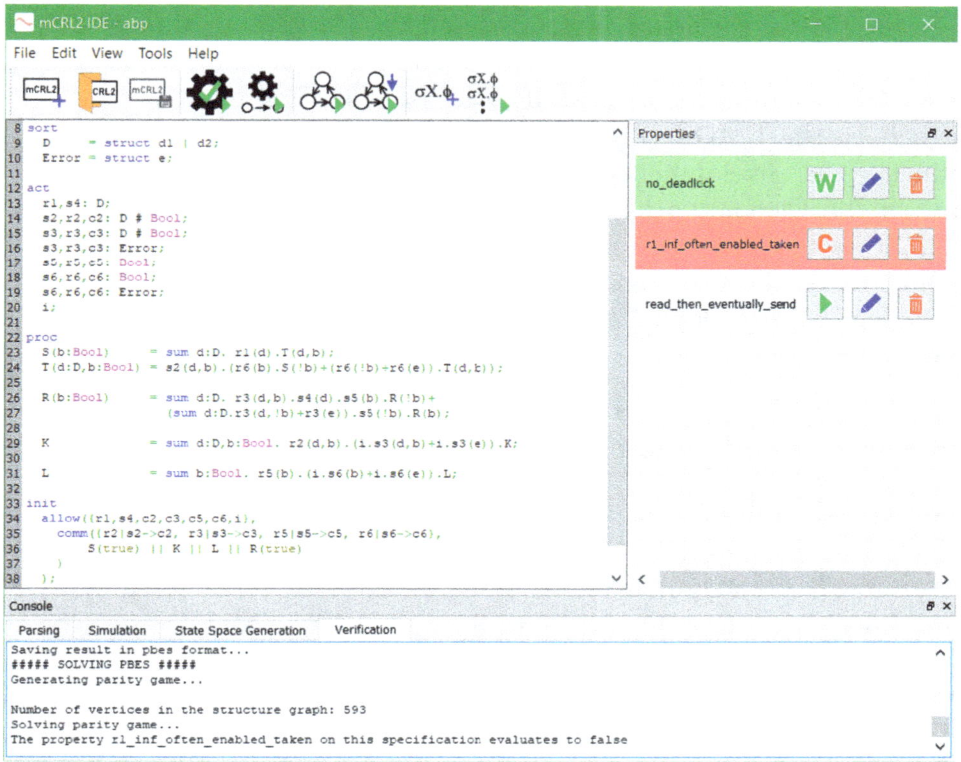

Fig. 6. An instance of `mcrl2ide` in Windows 10 with an mCRL2 specification of the alternating bit protocol. The properties in the dock on the right are (from top to bottom) *true*, *false* and not checked yet.

toolset is increasingly used as a back-end aiming at verification of higher-level languages. Some of these applications are built on academic languages; *e.g.*, in [22] the Algebra for Wireless Networks is translated to mCRL2, enabling the verification of protocols for Mobile Ad hoc Networks and Wireless Mesh Networks. Models written in the state-machine based Simple Language of Communicating Objects (SLCO) are translated to mCRL2 to verify shared-memory concurrent systems and reason about the sequential consistency of automatically generated multi-threaded software [42]. Others are targeting more broadly used languages; *e.g.*, in [39], Go programs are translated to mCRL2 and the mCRL2 toolset is used for model checking Go programs.

The use of mCRL2 in industry is furthermore driven by the current *Formal Model-Driven Engineering* (FMDE) trend. In the FMDE paradigm, programs written in a Domain-Specific Language (DSL) are used to generate both executable code and verifiable models. A recent example is the commercial FMDE toolset *Dezyne* developed by Verum, see [9], which uses mCRL2 to check for livelocks and deadlocks, and which relies on mCRL2's facilities to check for refinement relations (see Sect. 4.2) to check for *interface compliance*. Similar languages and methodologies are under development at other companies. For instance, ASML, one of the world's leading manufacturers of chip-making equipment, is developing the *Alias* language, and Océ, a global leading company in digital imaging, industrial printing and collaborative business services, is developing the *OIL* language. Both FMDE solutions build on mCRL2.

We believe the FMDE trend will continue in the coming years and that it will influence the development of the toolset. For example, the use of refinement checking in the Dezyne back-end has forced us to implement several optimisations (*cf.* Sect. 4.2). Furthermore, machine-generated specifications are typically longer and more verbose than handwritten specifications. This will require a more efficient implementation of the lineariser – as implemented in `mcrl22lps` – in the coming years.

7.2 Software Product Lines

A software product line (SPL) is a collection of systems, individually called products, sharing a common core. However, at specific points the products may show slightly different behaviour dependent on the presence or absence of so-called features. The overall system can be concisely represented as a featured transition system (FTS), an LTS with both actions and boolean expressions over a set of features decorating the transitions (see [12]). If a product, given its features, fulfils the boolean expression guarding the transition the transition may be taken by the product. Basically, there are two ways to analyse SPLs: product-based and family-based. In product-based analysis each product is verified separately; in family-based model checking one seeks to verify a property for a group of products, referred to as a family, as a whole.

Traditionally, dedicated model checkers are exploited for the verification of SPLs. Examples of such SPL model checkers are SNIP and ProVeLines by the team of [12] that are derived from SPIN. However, the mCRL2 toolset as-is, without specific modifications, has also been used to compare product-based vs. family-based model checking [3,5,7]. For this, the extension of the modal μ-calculus for the analysis of FTSes proposed in [4], that combines actions and feature expressions for its modalities, was translated into the first-order μ-calculus [25], the property language of the mCRL2 toolset. As a result, verification of SPLs can be done using the standard workflow for mCRL2, achieving family-based model checking without a family-based model checker [18], with running times slightly worse than, but comparable to those of dedicated tools.

8 Related Work

Among the many model checkers available, the CADP toolset [21] is the closest related to mCRL2. In CADP, specifications are written in the LOTOS NT language, which has been derived from the E-LOTOS ISO standard. Similar to mCRL2, CADP relies on *action-based* semantics, *i.e.*, state spaces are stored as an LTS. Furthermore, the verification engine in CADP takes a μ-calculus formula as input and encodes it in a BES or PBES. However, CADP has limited support for μ-calculus formulae with fixpoint alternation and, unlike mCRL2, does not support arbitrary nesting of fixpoints. Whereas the probabilistic analysis tools for mCRL2 are still in their infancy, CADP offers more advanced analysis techniques for Markovian probabilistic systems. The user-license of CADP is restrictive: CADP is not open source and a free license is only available for academic use.

Another toolset that is based on process algebra is PAT [45]. This toolset has native support for the verification of real-time specifications and implements on-the-fly reduction techniques, in particular partial-order reduction and symmetry reduction. PAT can perform model checking of LTL properties.

The toolset LTSMIN [36] has a unique architecture in the sense that it is language-independent. One of the supported input languages is mCRL2. Thus, the state space of an mCRL2 specification can also be generated using LTSMIN's high-performance multi-core and symbolic back-ends.

Well-known tools that have less in common with mCRL2 are SPIN [34], NUSMV [11], PRISM [38] and UPPAAL [6]. Each of these tools has its own strengths. First of all, SPIN is an explicit-state model checker that incorporates advanced techniques to reduce the size of the state space (partial-order reduction and symmetry reduction) or the amount of memory required (bit hashing). SPIN supports the checking of assertions and LTL formulae. Secondly, NUSMV is a powerful symbolic model checker that offers model checking algorithms such as bounded model checking and counterexample guided abstraction refinement (CEGAR). The tools PRISM and UPPAAL focus on quantitative aspects of model checking. The main goal of PRISM is to analyse probabilistic systems, whereas UPPAAL focusses on systems that involve real-time behaviour.

9 Conclusion

In the past six years many additions and changes have been made to the mCRL2 toolset and language to improve its expressivity, usability and performance. Firstly, the mCRL2 language has been extended to enable modelling of probabilistic behaviour. Secondly, by adding the ability to check refinement and to do infinite-state model checking the mCRL2 toolset has become applicable in a wider range of situations. Also, the introduction of the generation of counterexamples and witnesses for model checking problems and the introduction of an enhanced GUI has improved the experience of users of the mCRL2 toolset. Lastly, refinements to underlying algorithms, such as those for equivalence reductions and static analyses of PBESs, have resulted in lowered running times when applying the corresponding tools.

For the future, we aim to further strengthen several basic building blocks of the toolset, in particular the term library and the rewriter. The term library is responsible for storage and retrieval of terms that underlie mCRL2 data expressions. The rewriter manipulates data expressions based on rewrite rules specified by the user. Currently, these two components have evolved over time but are rather limitedly documented. It has proven to be difficult to revitalise the current implementation or to make amendments to experiment with new ideas.

For this, one of the aims is to investigate the benefits of multi-core algorithms, expecting a subsequent speed-up for many other algorithms in the toolset.

References

1. Badban, B., et al.: Verification of a sliding window protocol in μCRL and PVS. Formal Aspects Comput. **17**(3), 342–388 (2005)
2. Baier, C., Engelen, B., Majster-Cederbaum, M.E.: Deciding bisimilarity and similarity for probabilistic processes. JCSS **60**(1), 187–231 (2000)
3. ter Beek, M.H., de Vink, E.P.: Using mCRL2 for the analysis of software product lines. In: Proceedings of the FormaliSE 2014, pp. 31–37. ACM (2014)
4. ter Beek, M.H., de Vink, E.P., Willemse, T.A.C.: Towards a feature mu-calculus targeting SPL verification. In: Proceedings of the FMSPLE 2016, EPTCS, p. 15 (2016)
5. ter Beek, M.H., de Vink, E.P., Willemse, T.A.C.: Family-based model checking with mCRL2. In: Huisman, M., Rubin, J. (eds.) FASE 2017. LNCS, vol. 10202, pp. 387–405. Springer, Heidelberg (2017). https://doi.org/10.1007/978-3-662-54494-5_23
6. Behrmann, G., David, A., Larsen, K.G.: A tutorial on UPPAAL. In: Bernardo, M., Corradini, F. (eds.) SFM-RT 2004. LNCS, vol. 3185, pp. 200–236. Springer, Heidelberg (2004). https://doi.org/10.1007/978-3-540-30080-9_7
7. Ben Snaiba, Z., de Vink, E.P., Willemse, T.A.C.: Family-based model checking of SPL based on mCRL2. In: Proceedings of the SPLC 2017, vol. B, pp. 13–16. ACM (2017)
8. Bergstra, J.A., Klop, J.W.: The algebra of recursively defined processes and the algebra of regular processes. In: Paredaens, J. (ed.) ICALP 1984. LNCS, vol. 172, pp. 82–94. Springer, Heidelberg (1984). https://doi.org/10.1007/3-540-13345-3_7
9. van Beusekom, R., et al.: Formalising the Dezyne modelling language in mCRL2. In: Petrucci, L., Seceleanu, C., Cavalcanti, A. (eds.) FMICS/AVoCS-2017. LNCS, vol. 10471, pp. 217–233. Springer, Cham (2017). https://doi.org/10.1007/978-3-319-67113-0_14
10. Bunte, O.: Quantitative model checking on probabilistic systems using pLμ. Master's thesis, Eindhoven University of Technology (2017)
11. Cimatti, A., et al.: NuSMV 2: an opensource tool for symbolic model checking. In: Brinksma, E., Larsen, K.G. (eds.) CAV 2002. LNCS, vol. 2404, pp. 359–364. Springer, Heidelberg (2002). https://doi.org/10.1007/3-540-45657-0_29
12. Classen, A., et al.: Model checking lots of systems. In: Proceedings of ICSE 2010, pp. 335–344. ACM (2010)
13. Cranen, S., Groote, J.F., Reniers, M.A.: A linear translation from CTL* to the first-order modal μ-calculus. Theoret. Comput. Sci. **412**, 3129–3139 (2011)
14. Cranen, S., Luttik, B., Willemse, T.A.C.: Proof graphs for parameterised Boolean equation systems. In: D'Argenio, P.R., Melgratti, H. (eds.) CONCUR 2013. LNCS, vol. 8052, pp. 470–484. Springer, Heidelberg (2013). https://doi.org/10.1007/978-3-642-40184-8_33
15. Cranen, S., Luttik, B., Willemse, T.A.C.: Evidence for fixpoint logic. In: Proceedings of CSL, LIPIcs, vol. 41, pp. 78–93 (2015)
16. Cranen, S., et al.: Abstraction in fixpoint logic. ACM Trans. Computat. Logic **16**(4), 29 (2015)
17. Dennard, R., et al.: Design of ion-implanted MOSFET's with very small physical dimensions. IEEE J. Solid-State Circ. **9**(5), 256–268 (1974)

18. Dimovski, A., Al-Sibahi, A.S., Brabrand, C., Wąsowski, A.: Family-based model checking without a family-based model checker. In: Fischer, B., Geldenhuys, J. (eds.) SPIN 2015. LNCS, vol. 9232, pp. 282–299. Springer, Cham (2015). https://doi.org/10.1007/978-3-319-23404-5_18
19. Ehrig, H., Mahr, B.: Fundamentals of Algebraic Specification 1: Equations und Initial Semantics. Springer, Heidelberg (1985). https://doi.org/10.1007/978-3-642-69962-7
20. Engel, A.J.P.M., et al.: Specification, design and simulation of services and protocols for a PDA using the infra red medium. Report RWB-510-re-95012, Philips (1995)
21. Garavel, H., Lang, F., Mateescu, R., Serwe, W.: CADP 2011: a toolbox for the construction and analysis of distributed processes. STTT **15**(2), 89–107 (2013)
22. van Glabbeek, R.J., Höfner, P., van der Wal, D.: Analysing AWN-specifications using mCRL2 (Extended Abstract). In: Furia, C.A., Winter, K. (eds.) IFM 2018. LNCS, vol. 11023, pp. 398–418. Springer, Cham (2018). https://doi.org/10.1007/978-3-319-98938-9_23
23. Gregorio-Rodríguez, C., Llana, L., Martínez-Torres, R.: Extending mCRL2 with ready simulation and Iocos input-output conformance simulation. In: SAC 2015, pp. 1781–1788. ACM (2015)
24. Groote, J.F., Jansen, D.N., Keiren, J.J.A., Wijs, A.J.: An $O(m \log n)$ algorithm for computing stuttering equivalence and branching bisimulation. ACM Trans. Comput. Logic **18**(2), 13:1–13:34 (2017)
25. Groote, J.F., Mateescu, R.: Verification of temporal properties of processes in a setting with data. In: Haeberer, A.M. (ed.) AMAST 1999. LNCS, vol. 1548, pp. 74–90. Springer, Heidelberg (1998). https://doi.org/10.1007/3-540-49253-4_8
26. Groote, J.F., Rivera Verduzco, J., de Vink, E.P.: An efficient algorithm to determine probabilistic bisimulation. Algorithms **11**(9), 131, 1–22 (2018)
27. Groote, J.F., Mousavi, M.R.: Modeling and Analysis of Communicating Systems. The MIT Press, Cambridge (2014)
28. Groote, J.F., Ponse, A.: The syntax and semantics of mCRL. In: Ponse, A., Verhoef, C., van Vlijmen, S.F.M. (eds.) Algebra of Communicating Processes. Workshops in Computing, pp. 26–62. Springer, London (1994). https://doi.org/10.1007/978-1-4471-2120-6_2
29. Groote, J.F., Sellink, M.P.A.: Confluence for process verification. Theoret. Comput. Sci. **170**(1–2), 47–81 (1996)
30. Groote, J.F., Springintveld, J.: Focus points and convergent process operators: a proof strategy for protocol verification. J. Logic Algebraic Program. **49**(1–2), 31–60 (2001)
31. Groote, J.F., Vaandrager, F.W.: An efficient algorithm for branching bisimulation and stuttering equivalence. In: Paterson, M.S. (ed.) ICALP 1990. LNCS, vol. 443, pp. 626–638. Springer, Heidelberg (1990). https://doi.org/10.1007/BFb0032063
32. Groote, J.F., de Vink, E.P.: Problem solving using process algebra considered insightful. In: Katoen, J.-P., Langerak, R., Rensink, A. (eds.) ModelEd, TestEd, TrustEd. LNCS, vol. 10500, pp. 48–63. Springer, Cham (2017). https://doi.org/10.1007/978-3-319-68270-9_3
33. Groote, J.F., Willemse, T.A.C.: Parameterised boolean equation systems. Theoret. Comput. Sci. **343**(3), 332–369 (2005)
34. Holzmann, G.J.: The SPIN Model Checker: Primer and Reference Manual. Addison-Wesley, Boston (2004)
35. Hopcroft, J.: An $n \log n$ algorithm for minimizing states in a finite automaton. In: Proceedings of TMC, pp. 189–196. Academic Press (1971)

36. Kant, G., Laarman, A., Meijer, J., van de Pol, J., Blom, S., van Dijk, T.: LTSmin: high-performance language-independent model checking. In: Baier, C., Tinelli, C. (eds.) TACAS 2015. LNCS, vol. 9035, pp. 692–707. Springer, Heidelberg (2015). https://doi.org/10.1007/978-3-662-46681-0_61
37. Keiren, J.J.A., Wesselink, W., Willemse, T.A.C.: Liveness analysis for parameterised boolean equation systems. In: Cassez, F., Raskin, J.-F. (eds.) ATVA 2014. LNCS, vol. 8837, pp. 219–234. Springer, Cham (2014). https://doi.org/10.1007/978-3-319-11936-6_16
38. Kwiatkowska, M., Norman, G., Parker, D.: PRISM 4.0: verification of probabilistic real-time systems. In: Gopalakrishnan, G., Qadeer, S. (eds.) CAV 2011. LNCS, vol. 6806, pp. 585–591. Springer, Heidelberg (2011). https://doi.org/10.1007/978-3-642-22110-1_47
39. Lange, J., et al.: A static verification framework for message passing in go using behavioural types. In: Proceedings of ICSE, pp. 1137–1148. ACM (2018)
40. Neele, T., Willemse, T.A.C., Groote, J.F.: Solving parameterised boolean equation systems with infinite data through quotienting. In: Bae, K., Ölveczky, P.C. (eds.) FACS 2018. LNCS, vol. 11222, pp. 216–236. Springer, Cham (2018). https://doi.org/10.1007/978-3-030-02146-7_11
41. Paige, R., Tarjan, R.E.: Three partition refinement algorithms. SIAM J. Comput. **16**(6), 973–989 (1987)
42. de Putter, S.M.J., Wijs, A.J., Zhang, D.: The SLCO framework for verified, model-driven construction of component software. In: Bae, K., Ölveczky, P.C. (eds.) FACS 2018. LNCS, vol. 11222, pp. 288–296. Springer, Cham (2018). https://doi.org/10.1007/978-3-030-02146-7_15
43. Remenska, D., et al.: Using model checking to analyze the system behavior of the LHC production grid. FGCS **29**(8), 2239–2251 (2013)
44. Segala, R.: Modeling and verification of randomized distributed real-time systems. Ph.D. thesis, MIT (1995)
45. Sun, J., Liu, Y., Dong, J.S., Pang, J.: PAT: towards flexible verification under fairness. In: Bouajjani, A., Maler, O. (eds.) CAV 2009. LNCS, vol. 5643, pp. 709–714. Springer, Heidelberg (2009). https://doi.org/10.1007/978-3-642-02658-4_59
46. Valmari, A., Lehtinen, P.: Efficient minimization of DFAs with partial transition functions. In: Proceedings of STACS, LIPIcs, vol. 1, pp. 645–656 (2008)
47. Valmari, A., Franceschinis, G.: Simple $O(m \log n)$ time Markov chain lumping. In: Esparza, J., Majumdar, R. (eds.) TACAS 2010. LNCS, vol. 6015, pp. 38–52. Springer, Heidelberg (2010). https://doi.org/10.1007/978-3-642-12002-2_4
48. Wang, T., et al.: More anti-chain based refinement checking. In: Aoki, T., Taguchi, K. (eds.) ICFEM 2012. LNCS, vol. 7635, pp. 364–380. Springer, Heidelberg (2012). https://doi.org/10.1007/978-3-642-34281-3_26
49. Wesselink, W., Willemse, T.A.C.: Evidence extraction from parameterised boolean equation systems. In: Proceedings of ARQNL, CEUR 2095, pp. 86–100 (2018)

Automatic Analysis of Consistency Properties of Distributed Transaction Systems in Maude

Si Liu[1(✉)], Peter Csaba Ölveczky[2(✉)], Min Zhang[3(✉)], Qi Wang[1], and José Meseguer[1]

[1] University of Illinois, Urbana-Champaign, USA
siliu3@illinois.edu
[2] University of Oslo, Oslo, Norway
peterol@ifi.uio.no
[3] Shanghai Key Laboratory of Trustworthy Computing, ECNU, Shanghai, China
zhangmin@sei.ecnu.edu.cn

Abstract. Many transaction systems distribute, partition, and replicate their data for scalability, availability, and fault tolerance. However, observing and maintaining strong consistency of distributed and partially replicated data leads to high transaction latencies. Since different applications require different consistency guarantees, there is a plethora of consistency properties—from weak ones such as read atomicity through various forms of snapshot isolation to stronger serializability properties—and distributed transaction systems (DTSs) guaranteeing such properties. This paper presents a general framework for formally specifying a DTS in Maude, and formalizes in Maude nine common consistency properties for DTSs so defined. Furthermore, we provide a fully automated method for analyzing whether the DTS satisfies the desired property for all initial states up to given bounds on system parameters. This is based on automatically recording relevant history during a Maude run and defining the consistency properties on such histories. To the best of our knowledge, this is the first time that model checking of all these properties in a unified, systematic manner is investigated. We have implemented a tool that automates our method, and use it to model check state-of-the-art DTSs such as P-Store, RAMP, Walter, Jessy, and ROLA.

1 Introduction

Applications handling large amounts of data need to partition their data for scalability and elasticity, and need to replicate their data across widely distributed sites for high availability and fault and disaster tolerance. However, guaranteeing strong consistency properties for transactions over partially replicated

This work has been partially supported by NRL contract N00173-17-1-G002, and NSFC Project No. 61872146.

T. Vojnar and L. Zhang (Eds.): TACAS 2019, Part II, LNCS 11428, pp. 40–57, 2019.
https://doi.org/10.1007/978-3-030-17465-1_3

distributed data requires lot of costly coordination that results in long transaction delays. Different applications require different consistency guarantees, and balancing well the trade-off between performance and consistency guarantees is key to designing distributed transaction systems (DTSs). There is therefore a plethora of consistency properties for DTSs over partially replicated data—from weak properties such as read atomicity through various forms of snapshot isolation to strong serializability guarantees—and DTSs providing such guarantees.

DTSs and their consistency guarantees are typically specified informally and validated only by testing; there is very little work on their automated formal analysis (see Section 8). We have previously formally modeled and analyzed single state-of-the-art industrial and academic DTSs, such as Google's Megastore, Apache Cassandra, Walter, P-Store, Jessy, ROLA, and RAMP, in Maude [14].

In this paper we present a *generic* framework for formalizing both DTSs and their consistency properties in Maude. The modeling framework is very general and should allow us to naturally model most DTSs. We formalize nine popular consistency models in this framework and provide a fully automated method—and a tool which automates this method—for analyzing whether a DTS specified in our framework satisfies the desired consistency property for all initial states with the user-given number of transactions, data items, sites, and so on.

In particular, we show how one can automatically add a monitoring mechanism which records relevant history during a run of a DTS specified in our framework, and we define the consistency properties on such histories so that the DTS can be directly model checked in Maude. We have implemented a tool that uses Maude's meta-programming features to automatically add the monitoring mechanism, that automatically generates all the desired initial states, and that performs the Maude model checking. We have applied our tool to model check state-of-the-art DTSs such as variants of RAMP, P-Store, ROLA, Walter, and Jessy. To the best of our knowledge, this is the first time that model checking of all these properties in a unified, systematic manner is investigated.

This paper is organized as follows. Section 2 provides background on rewriting and Maude. Section 3 gives an overview of the consistency properties that we formalize. Section 4 presents our framework for modeling DTSs in Maude, and Section 5 explains how to record the history in such models. Section 6 formally defines consistency models as Maude functions on such recorded histories. Section 7 briefly introduces our tool which automates the entire process. Finally, Section 8 discusses related work and Section 9 gives some concluding remarks.

2 Rewriting Logic and Maude

Maude [14] is a rewriting-logic-based executable formal specification language and high-performance analysis tool for object-based distributed systems.

A Maude module specifies a *rewrite theory* $(\Sigma, E \cup A, R)$, where:

- Σ is an algebraic *signature*; i.e., a set of *sorts*, *subsorts*, and *function symbols*.
- $(\Sigma, E \cup A)$ is a *membership equational logic theory* [14], with E a set of possibly conditional equations and membership axioms, and A a set of equational

axioms such as associativity, commutativity, and identity, so that equational deduction is performed *modulo* the axioms A. The theory $(\Sigma, E \cup A)$ specifies the system's states as members of an algebraic data type.

- R is a collection of *labeled conditional rewrite rules* $[l] : t \longrightarrow t'$ **if** *cond*, specifying the system's local transitions.

Equations and rewrite rules are introduced with, respectively, keywords `eq`, or `ceq` for conditional equations, and `rl` and `crl`. The mathematical variables in such statements are declared with the keywords `var` and `vars`, or can have the form *var*:*sort* and be introduced on the fly. An equation $f(t_1, \ldots, t_n) = t$ with the `owise` ("otherwise") attribute can be applied to a subterm $f(\ldots)$ only if no other equation with left-hand side $f(u_1, \ldots, u_n)$ can be applied. Maude also provides standard parameterized data types (sets, maps, etc.) that can be instantiated (and renamed); for example, `pr SET{Nat} * (sort Set{Nat} to Nats)` defines a sort `Nats` of *sets* of natural numbers.

A *class* declaration `class` C `|` att_1 `:` s_1`,` `...`, att_n `:` s_n declares a class C of objects with attributes att_1 to att_n of sorts s_1 to s_n. An *object instance* of class C is represented as a term `<` $O : C \mid att_1 : val_1, \ldots, att_n : val_n$ `>`, where O, of sort `Oid`, is the object's *identifier*, and where val_1 to val_n are the current values of the attributes att_1 to att_n. A *message* is a term of sort `Msg`. A system state is modeled as a term of the sort `Configuration`, and has the structure of a *multiset* made up of objects and messages.

The dynamic behavior of a system is axiomatized by specifying each of its transition patterns by a rewrite rule. For example, the rule (with label `l`)

```
rl [l] :  m(O,w)
          < O : C | a1 : x, a2 : O', a3 : z >
         =>
          < O : C | a1 : x + w, a2 : O', a3 : z >
          m'(O',x) .
```

defines a family of transitions in which a message `m(O, w)` is read and consumed by an object `O` of class `C`, whose attribute `a1` is changed to `x + w`, and a new message `m'(O',x)` is generated. Attributes whose values do not change and do not affect the next state, such as `a3` and `a2`, need not be mentioned in a rule.

Maude also supports *metaprogramming* in the sense that a Maude specification M can be represented as a *term* $\overline{M}$ (of sort `Module`), so that a module transformation can be defined as a Maude function f : `Module` $\rightarrow$ `Module`.

Reachability Analysis in Maude. Maude provides a number of analysis methods, including rewriting for simulation purposes, reachability analysis, and linear temporal logic (LTL) model checking. In this paper, we use reachability analysis. Given an initial state *init*, a state pattern *pattern* and an (optional) condition *cond*, Maude's `search` command searches the reachable state space from *init* in a breadth-first manner for states that match *pattern* such that *cond* holds:

`search` [*bound*] *init* `=>!` *pattern* `such that` *cond* `.`

where *bound* is an upper bound on the number of solutions to look for. The arrow `=>!` means that Maude only searches for *final* states (i.e., states that cannot be further rewritten) that match *pattern* and satisfies *cond*. If the arrow is instead `=>*` then Maude searches for all reachable states satisfying the search condition.

3 Transactional Consistency

Different applications require different consistency guarantees. There are therefore many consistency properties for DTSs on partially replicated distributed data stores. This paper focuses on the following nine, which span a spectrum from weak consistency such as read committed to strong consistency like serializability:

- *Read committed* (*RC*) [6] disallows a transaction[1] from seeing any uncommitted or aborted data.
- *Cursor stability* (*CS*) [16], widely implemented by commercial SQL systems (e.g., IBM DB2 [1]) and academic prototypes (e.g., MDCC [21]), guarantees *RC* and in addition prevents the *lost update* anomaly.
- *Read atomicity* (*RA*) [5] guarantees that either *all* or *none* of a (distributed) transaction's updates are visible to other transactions. For example, if Alice and Bob become friends on social media, then Charlie should not see that Alice is a friend of Bob's, and that Bob is not a friend of Alice's.
- *Update atomicity* (*UA*) [12,25] guarantees read atomicity and prevents the lost update anomaly.
- *Snapshot isolation* (*SI*) [6] requires a multi-partition transaction to read from a snapshot of a distributed data store that reflects a single commit order of transactions across sites, even if they are independent of each other: Alice sees Charlie's post before seeing David's post if and only if Bob sees the two posts in the same order. Charlie and David must therefore coordinate the order of committing their posts even if they do not know each other.
- *Parallel snapshot isolation* (*PSI*) [36] weakens *SI* by allowing different commit orders at different sites, while guaranteeing that a transaction reads the most recent version committed at the transaction execution site, as of the time when the transaction begins. For example, Alice may see Charlie's post before seeing David's post, even though Bob sees David's post before Charlie's post, as long as the two posts are independent of each other. Charlie and David can therefore commit their posts without waiting for each other.
- *Non-monotonic snapshot isolation* (*NMSI*) [4] weakens *PSI* by allowing a transaction to read a version committed after the transaction begins: Alice may see Bob's post that committed after her transaction started executing.
- *Serializability* (*SER*) [33] ensures that the execution of concurrent transactions is equivalent to one where the transactions are run one at a time.
- Strict Serializability (*SSER*) strengthens *SER* by enforcing the serial order to follow real time.

[1] A transaction is a user application request, typically consisting of a sequence of read and/or write operations on data items, that is submitted to a (distributed) database.

4 Modeling Distributed Transaction Systems in Maude

This section presents a framework for modeling in Maude DTSs that satisfy the following general assumptions:

- We can identify and record "when"[2] a transaction starts executing at its server/proxy and "when" the transaction is committed and aborted at the different sites involved in its validation.
- The transactions record their read and write sets.

If a such a DTS is modeled in this framework, our tool can automatically model check whether it satisfies the above consistency properties, as long as it can detect the read and write sets and the above events: start of transaction execution, and abort/commit of a transaction at a certain site. This section explains how the system should be modeled so that our tool automatically discovers these events.

We make the following additional assumptions about the DTSs we target:

- The database is distributed across of a number of *sites*, or *servers* or *replicas*, that communicate by asynchronous *message passing*. Data are *partially replicated* across these sites: a data item may be replicated/stored at more than one site. The sites replicating a data item are called that item's *replicas*.
- Systems evolve by message passing or local computations. Servers communicate by asynchronous message passing with arbitrary but finite delays.
- A client forwards a transaction to be executed to some server (called the transaction's *executing server* or *proxy*), which executes the transaction.
- Transaction execution should terminate in commit or abort.

4.1 Modeling DTSs in Maude

A DTS is modeled in an object-oriented style, where the state consists of a number of *replica* objects, each modeling a local database/server/site, and a number of messages traveling between the replica objects. A transaction is modeled as an object which resides inside the replica object executing the transaction.

Basic Data Types. There are user-defined sorts `Key` for data items (or keys) and `Version` for versions of data items, with a partial order `<` on versions, with $v < v'$ denoting that v' is a later version of v in `<`. We then define key-version pairs `<`*key*`,`*version*`>` and sets of such pairs, that model a transaction's read and write sets, as follows:

```
sorts Key Version KeyVersion .
op <_,_> : Key Version -> KeyVersion .
pr SET{KeyVersion} * (sort Set{KeyVersion} to KeyVersions) .
```

[2] Since we do not necessarily deal with real-time systems, this "when" may not denote the real time, but when the event takes place *relative* to other events.

To track the status of a transaction (on non-proxies, or remote servers) we define a sort `TxnStatus` consisting of some transaction's identifier and its status; this is used to indicate whether a remote transaction (one executed on another server) is committed on this server:

```
op [_,_] : Oid Bool -> TxnStatus [ctor] .
pr SET{TxnStatus} * (sort Set{TxnStatus} to TxnStatusSet) .
```

Modeling Replicas. A *replica* (or *site*) stores parts of the database, executes the transactions for which it is the proxy, helps validating other transactions, and is formalized as an object instance of a subclass of the following class `Replica`:

```
class Replica | executing : Configuration,   committed : Configuration,
                aborted : Configuration,     decided : TxnStatusSet .
```

The attributes `executing`, `committed`, and `aborted` contain, respectively, transactions that are being executed, and have been committed or aborted on the executing server; `decided` is the status of transactions executed on other servers.

To model a system-specific replica a user should specify it as an object instance of a subclass of the class `Replica` with new attributes.

Example 1. A replica in our Maude model of Walter [26] is modeled as an object instance of the following subclass `Walter-Replica` of class `Replica` that adds 14 new attributes (only 4 shown below):

```
class Walter-Replica | store : Datastore,     sqn : Nat,
                       locked : Locks,        votes : Vote, ...
subclass Walter-Replica < Replica .
```

Modeling Transactions. A *transaction* should be modeled as an object of a subclass of the following class `Txn`:

```
class Txn | readSet : KeyVersions, writeSet : KeyVersions .
```

where `readSet` and `writeSet` denote the key/version pairs read and written by the transaction, respectively.

Example 2. Walter transactions can be modeled as object instances of the subclass `Walter-Txn` with four new attributes:

```
class Walter-Txn | operations : OperationList,  localVars : LocalVars,
                   startVTS : VectorTimestamp,  txnSQN : Nat .
subclass Walter-Txn < Txn .
```

Modeling System Dynamics. We describe how the rewrite rules defining the start of a transaction execution and aborts and commits at different sites should be defined so that our tool can detect these events.

– The start of a transaction execution must be modeled by a rewrite rule where the transaction object appears in the proxy server's `executing` attribute in the right-hand side, but not in the left-hand side, of the rewrite rule.

Example 3. A Walter replica starts executing a transaction `TID` by moving `TID` in `gotTxns` (buffering transactions from clients) to `executing`:[3]

```
rl [start-txn] :
   < RID : Walter-Replica | executing : TRANSES, committedVTS : VTS,
           gotTxns :  < TID : Txn | startVTS : empty > ;; TXNS >
 =>
   < RID : Walter-Replica | gotTxns : TXNS,
           executing : TRANSES < TID : Txn | startVTS : VTS > > .
```

– When a transaction is *committed* on the executing server, the transaction object must appear in the `committed` attribute in the right-hand side—but not in the left-hand side—of the rewrite rule. Furthermore, the `readSet` and `writeSet` attributes must be explicitly given in the transaction object.

Example 4. In Walter, when all operations of an executing read-only transaction have been performed, the proxy commits the transaction directly:

```
rl [commit-read-only-txn] :
   < RID : Walter-Replica | committed : TRANSES',
                            executing : TRANSES
      < TID : Txn | operations : nil, writeSet : empty, readSet : RS > >
 =>
   < RID : Walter-Replica | committed : (TRANSES' < TID : Txn | >),
                            executing : TRANSES > .
```

– When a transaction is aborted by the executing server, the transaction object must appear in the `aborted` attribute in the right-hand side, but not in the left-hand side, of a rewrite rule. Again, the transaction should present its attributes `writeSet` and `readSet` (to be able to record relevant history). See our longer report [27] for an example of such a rule.
– A rewrite rule that models when a transaction's status is decided remotely (i.e., not on the executing server) must contain in the right-hand side (only) the transaction's identifier and its status in the replica's `decided` attribute.

These requirements are not very strict. The Maude models of the DTSs RAMP [29], Faster [24], Walter [26], ROLA [25], Jessy [28], and P-Store [32] can all be seen as instantiations of our modeling framework, with very small syntactic changes, such as defining transaction and replica objects as subclasses of `Txn` and `Replica`, changing the names of the attributes and sorts, etc. The Apache Cassandra NoSQL key-value store can be seen as a transaction system where each transaction is a single operation; the Maude model of Cassandra in [30] can also be easily modified to fit within our modeling framework.

[3] We do not give variable declarations, but follow the convention that variables are written in (all) capital letters.

5 Adding Execution Logs

To formalize and analyze consistency properties of distributed transaction systems we add an "execution log" that records the *history* of relevant events during a system execution. This section explains how this history recording can be added *automatically* to a model of a DTS that is specified as explained in Section 4.

5.1 Execution Log

To capture the total order of relevant events in a run, we use a "logical global clock" to order all key events (i.e., transaction starts, commits, and aborts). This clock is incremented by one each time such an event takes place.

A transaction in a replicated DTS is typically committed both locally (at its executing server) and remotely at different times. To capture this, we define a "time vector" using Maude's map data type that maps replica identifiers (of sort `Oid`) to (typically "logical") clock values (of sort `Time`, which here are the natural numbers: `subsort Nat < Time`):

```
pr MAP{Oid,Time} * (sort Map{Oid,Time} to VectorTime) .
```

where each element in the mapping has the form `replica-id |-> time`.

An execution log (of sort `Log`) maps each transaction (identifier) to a record <*proxy*, *issueTime*, *finishTime*, *committed*, *reads*, *writes*>, with *proxy* its proxy server, *issueTime* the starting time at its proxy server, *finishTime* the commit/abort times at each relevant server, *committed* a flag indicating whether the transaction is committed at its proxy, *reads* the key-version pairs read by the transaction, and *writes* the key-version pairs written:

```
sort Record .
op <_,_,_,_,_,_> : Oid Time VectorTime
                   Bool KeyVersions KeyVersions -> Record .
pr MAP{Oid,Record} * (sort Map{Oid,Record} to Log) .
```

5.2 Logging Execution History

We show how the relevant history of an execution can be recorded during a run of our Maude model by transforming the original Maude model into one which also records this history.

First, we add to the state a `Monitor` object that stores the current logical global time in the `clock` attribute and the current log in the `log` attribute:

```
< M : Monitor | clock : Time, log : Log >.
```

The log is updated each time an interesting event (see Section 4.1) happens. Our tool identifies those events and *automatically* transforms the corresponding rewrite rules by adding and updating the monitor object.

Executing. A transaction starts executing when the transaction object appears in a Replica's executing attribute in the right-hand side, but not in the left-hand side, of a rewrite rule. The monitor then adds a record for this transaction, with the proxy and start time, to the log, and increments the logical global clock.

Example 5. The rewrite rule in Example 3 where a Walter replica is served a transaction is modified by adding and updating the monitor object (in blue):

```
rl [start-txn] :
   < O@M : Monitor | clock : GT@M, log : LOG@M >
   < RID : Walter-Replica | executing : TRANSES,   committedVTS : VTS,
               gotTxns : < TID : Txn | startVTS : empty > ;; TXNS >
 =>
   < O@M : Monitor | clock : GT@M + 1 , log : LOG@M,
                     (TID |-> < RID, GT@M, empty, false, empty, empty >) >
   < RID : Walter-Replica | gotTxns : TXNS,
               executing : TRANSES < TID : Txn | startVTS : VTS > > .
```

where the monitor O@M adds a new record for the transaction TID in the log, with starting time (i.e., the current logical global time) GT@M at its executing server RID, finish time (empty), flag (false), read set (empty), and write set (empty). The monitor also increments the global clock by one.

Commit. A transaction commits at its proxy when the transaction object appears in the proxy's committed attribute in the right-hand side, but not in the left-hand side, of a rewrite rule. The record for that transaction is updated with commit status, versions read and written, and commit time, and the global logical clock is incremented.

Example 6. The monitor object is added to the rewrite rule in Example 4 for committing a read-only transaction:

```
rl [commit-read-only-txn] :
   < O@M : Monitor | clock : GT@M, log : LOG@M ,
          (TID |-> < RID, T@M, VTS@M, FLAG@M, READS@M, WRITES@M)) >
   < RID : Walter-Replica | committed : TRANSES',
                            executing : TRANSES
          < TID : Txn | operations : nil, writeSet : empty, readSet : RS > >
 =>
   < O@M : Monitor | clock : GT@M + 1 , log : LOG@M ,
          (TID |-> < RID, T@M, insert(RID,GT@M,VTS@M), true, RS, empty >)
   < RID : Walter-Replica | committed : (TRANSES' < TID : Txn | >),
                            executing : TRANSES > .
```

The monitor updates the log for the transaction TID by setting its finish time at the executing server RID to GT@M (insert(RID,GT@M,VTS@M)), setting the committed flag to true, setting the read set to RS and write set to empty (this is a read-only transaction), and increments the global clock.

ABORT. Abort is treated as commit, but the commit flag remains `false`.

DECIDED. When a transaction's status is decided remotely, the record for that transaction's decision time at the remote replica is updated with the current global time. See [27] for an example.

We have formalized/implemented the transformation from a Maude specification of a DTS into one with a monitor as a meta-level function `monitorRules : Module -> Module` in Maude. See our longer report [27] for details.

6 Formalizing Consistency Models in Maude

This section formalizes the consistency properties in Section 3 as functions on the "history log" of a *completed* run. The entire Maude specification of these functions is available at https://github.com/siliunobi/cat. Due to space restrictions, we only show the formalization of four of the consistency models, and refer to our report [27] for the formalization of the other properties.

Read Committed (RC). (A transaction cannot read any writes by uncommitted transactions.) Note that standard definitions for single-version databases disallow reading versions that are not committed at the time of the read. We follow the definition for multi-versioned systems by Adya, summarized by Bailis et al. [5], that defines the RC property as follows: (i) a committed transaction cannot read a version that was written by an aborted transaction; and (ii) a transaction cannot read *intermediate values*: that is, if T writes two versions `< X,V >` and `< X,V' >` with `V < V'`, then no $T' \neq T$ can read `< X,V >`.

The first equation defining the function `rc`, specifying when RC holds, checks whether some (committed) transaction `TID1` read version `V` of key `X` (i.e., `< X,V >` is in `TID`'s read set `< X,V > , RS`, where `RS` matches the rest of `TID`'s read set), and this version `V` was written by some transaction `TID2` that was never committed (i.e., `TID2`'s commit flag is `false`, and its write set is `< X,V > , WS'`). The second equation checks whether there was an *intermediate* read of a version `< X,V >` that was overwritten by the same transaction `TID2` that wrote the version:[4]

```
op rc : Log -> Bool .
eq rc(TID1 |-> < O, T, VT, true, (< X,V >, RS), WS >,
      TID2 |-> < O', T', VT', false, RS', (< X,V >, WS') >, LOG) = false .
eq rc(TID1 |-> < O, T, VT, true, (< X,V >, RS), WS >,
      TID2 |-> < O', T', VT', true, RS', (< X,V >, < X,V' >,WS') >,
      LOG)  = false if V < V' .
eq rc(LOG) = true [owise] .
```

[4] The configuration union and the union operator ',' for maps and sets are declared *associative* and *commutative*. The first equation therefore matches *any* log where some committed transaction read a key-version pair written by some aborted transaction.

Read Atomicity (RA). A system guarantees *RA* if it prevents fractured reads and prevents transactions from reading uncommitted or aborted data. A transaction T_j exhibits *fractured reads* if transaction T_i writes versions x_m and y_n, T_j reads version x_m and version y_k, and $k < n$ [5]. The function `fracRead` checks whether there are fractured reads in the log. There is a fractured read if a transaction `TID2` reads `X` and `Y`, transaction `TID1` writes `X` and `Y`, `TID2` reads the version `VX` of `X` written by `TID1`, and reads a version `VY'` of `Y` written *before* `VY` (`VY' < VY`):

```
 op fracRead : Log -> Bool .
ceq fracRead(TID1 |-> < O, T, VT, true, (< X,VX > , < Y,VY' >, RS), WS >,
             TID2 |-> < O', T', VT', true, RS', (< X,VX > , < Y,VY >, WS') >, LOG)
    = true if VY' < VY .
eq fracRead(LOG) = false [owise] .
```

We define *RA* as the combination of *RC* and no fractured reads:

```
op ra : Log -> Bool .
eq ra(LOG) = rc(LOG) and not fracRead(LOG) .
```

Parallel snapshot isolation (PSI) is given by three properties [36]:

- PSI-1 (site snapshot read): All operations read the most recent committed version at the transaction's site as of time when the transaction began.
- PSI-2 (no write-write conflicts): The write sets of each pair of committed *somewhere-concurrent*[5] transactions must be disjoint.
- PSI-3 (commit causality across sites): If a transaction T_1 commits at a site S before a transaction T_2 starts at site S, then T_1 cannot commit after T_2 at any site.

The function `notSiteSnapshotRead` checks whether the system log satisfies PSI-1 by returning `true` if there is a transaction that did not read the most recent committed version at its executing site when it began:

```
 op notSiteSnapshotRead : Log -> Bool .
ceq notSiteSnapshotRead(
       TID1 |-> < RID1, T, VT1, true, (< X,V > , RS1), WS1 >,
       TID2 |-> < RID2, T', (RID1 |-> T2 , VT2), true, RS2, (< X,V > , WS2) >,
       TID3 |-> < RID3, T'', (RID1 |-> T3 , VT3), true, RS3, (< X,V' > , WS3) >,
       LOG) = true if V =/= V' /\ T3 < T /\ T3 > T2 .
ceq notSiteSnapshotRead(
       TID1 |-> < RID1, T, VT1, true, (< X,V > , RS1), WS1 >,
       TID2 |-> < RID2, T', (RID1 |-> T2 , VT2), true, RS2, (< X,V > , WS2) >,
       LOG) = true if T < T2 .
 eq notSiteSnapshotRead(LOG) = false [owise] .
```

[5] Two transactions are *somewhere-concurrent* if they are concurrent at one of their sites.

In the first equation, the transaction TID1, hosted at site RID1, has in its read set a version < X,V > written by TID2. Some transaction TID3 wrote version < X,V' > and was committed at RID1 after TID2 was committed at RID1 (T3 > T2) and before TID1 started executing (T3 < T). Hence, the version read by TID1 was stale. The second equation checks if TID1 read some version that was committed at RID1 after TID1 started (T < T2).

The function someWhereConflict checks whether PSI-2 holds by looking for a write-write conflict between any pair of committed *somewhere-concurrent transactions* in the system log:

```
 op someWhereConflict : Log -> Bool .
ceq someWhereConflict(
       TID1 |-> < RID1,T,(RID1 |-> T1 , VT1),true,RS,(< X,V > , WS) >,
       TID2 |-> < RID2,T',(RID1 |-> T2 , VT2),true,RS',(< X,V' > , WS') >,
       LOG) = true if T2 > T /\ T2 < T1 .
 eq someWhereConflict(LOG) = false [owise] .
```

The above function checks whether the transactions with the write conflict are concurrent at the transaction TID1's proxy RID1. Here, TID2 commits at RID1 at time T2, which is between TID1's start time T and its commit time T1 at RID1.

The function notCausality analyzes PSI-3 by checking whether there was a "bad situation" in which a transaction TID1 committed at site RID2 *before* a transaction TID2 started at site RID2 (T1 < T2), while TID1 committed at site RID *after* TID2 committed at site RID (T3 > T4):

```
 op notCausality : Log -> Bool .
ceq notCausality(
        TID1 |-> < RID1,T,(RID2 |-> T1 , RID |-> T3 , VT2),true,RS,WS >,
        TID2 |-> < RID2,T2,(RID |-> T4 , VT4),true,RS',WS' >,
        LOG) = true if T1 < T2 /\ T3 > T4 .
 eq notCausality(LOG) = false [owise] .
```

PSI can then be defined by combining the above three properties:

```
op psi : Log -> Bool .
eq psi(LOG) = not notSiteSnapshotRead(LOG) and
              not someWhereConflict(LOG) and not notCausality(LOG) .
```

Non-monotonic snapshot isolation (NMSI) is the same as *PSI* except that a transaction may read a version committed even after the transaction begins [3]. *NMSI* can therefore be defined as the conjunction of PSI-2 and PSI-3:

```
op nmsi : Log -> Bool .
eq nmsi(LOG) = not someWhereConflict(LOG) and not notCausality(LOG) .
```

Serializability (SER) means that the concurrent execution of transactions is equivalent to executing them in some (non-overlapping in time) sequence [33].

A formal definition of *SER* is based on *direct serialization graphs* (DSGs): an execution is serializable if and only if the corresponding DSG is acyclic. Each node in a DSG corresponds to a committed transaction, and directed edges in a DSG correspond to the following types of direct dependencies [2]:

- Read dependency: Transaction T_j *directly read-depends* on transaction T_i if T_i writes some version x_i and T_j reads that version x_i.
- Write dependency: Transaction T_j *directly write-depends* on transaction T_i if T_i writes some version x_i and T_j writes x's next version after x_i in the version order.
- Antidependency: Transaction T_j *directly antidepends* on transaction T_i if T_i reads some version x_k and T_j writes x's next version after x_k.

There is a directed edge from a node T_i to another node T_j if transaction T_j directly read-/write-/antidepends on transaction T_i.

The dependencies/edges can easily be extracted from the our log as follows:

- If there is a key-version pair <X , V> both in T2's read set and in T1's write set, then T2 read-depends on T1.
- If T1 writes <X, V1> and T2 writes <X, V2>, and V1 < V2, and there *no* version <X, V> with V1 < V < V2, then T2 write-depends on T1.
- T2 antidepends on T1 if <X, V1> is in T1's read set, <X, V2> is in T2's write set with V1 < V2 and there is no version <X, V> such that V1 < V < V2.

We have defined a data type Dsg for DSGs, a function dsg : Log -> Dsg that constructs the DSG from a log, and a function cycle : Dsg -> Bool that checks whether a DSG has cycles. We refer to [27] for their definition in Maude.

SER then holds if there is no cycle in the constructed DSG:

```
op ser : Log -> Bool .
eq ser(LOG) = not cycle(dsg(LOG)) .
```

7 Formal Analysis of Consistency Properties of DTSs

We have implemented the *Consistency Analysis Tool* (CAT) that automates the method in this paper. CAT takes as input:

- A Maude model of the DTS specified as explained in Section 4.
- The *number* of each of the following parameters: read-only, write-only, and read-write transactions; operations for each type of transaction; keys; replicas per key; clients; and servers. The tool analyzes the desired property for *all* initial states with the number of each of these parameters.
- The consistency property to be analyzed.

Given these inputs, CAT performs the following steps:

1. adds the monitoring mechanism to the user-provided system model;
2. generates all possible initial states with the user-provided number of the different parameters; and
3. executes the following command to search, from all generated initial states, for *one* reachable *final* state where the consistency property does *not* hold:

```
search [1] init =>! C:Configuration
     < M:Oid : Monitor | log: LOG:Log clock: N:Nat >
          such that not consistency-property(LOG:Log) .
```

where the underlined functions are parametric, and are instantiated by the user inputs; e.g., *consistency-property* is replaced by the corresponding function `rc`, `psi`, `nmsi`, ..., or `ser`, depending on which property to analyze.

CAT outputs either "`No solution`," meaning that all runs from all the given initial states satisfy the desired consistency property, or a counterexample (in Maude at the moment) showing a behavior that violates the property.

Table 1. Model checking results w.r.t. consistency properties. "✓", "×", and "-" refer to satisfying and violating the property, and "not applicable," respectively.

Maude Model	LOC	Consistency Property								
		RC	RA	CS	UA	NMSI	PSI	SI	SER	SSER
RAMP-F [29]	330	✓	✓	×	×	-	-	×	×	×
Faster [24]	300	✓	×	×	×	-	-	×	×	×
ROLA [25]	410	✓	✓	✓	✓	-	-	×	×	×
Jessy [28]	490	✓	✓	✓	✓	✓	×	×	×	×
Walter [26]	830	✓	✓	✓	✓	✓	✓	×	×	×
P-Store [32]	440	✓	✓	✓	✓	✓	✓	✓	✓	×

We have applied our tool to 14 Maude models of state-of-the-art academic DTSs (different variants of RAMP and Walter, ROLA, Jessy, and P-Store) against all nine properties. Table 1 only shows six case studies due to space limitations. All model checking results are as expected It is worth remarking that our automatic analysis found all the violations of properties that the respective systems should violate. There are also some cases where model checking is not applicable ("-" in Table 1): some system models do not include a mechanism for committing a transaction on remote servers (i.e., no commit time on any remote server is recorded by the monitor). Thus, model checking *NMSI* or *PSI* is not applicable.

We have performed our analysis with different initial states, with up to 4 transactions, 4 operations per transaction, 2 clients, 2 servers, 2 keys, and 2 replicas per key. Each analysis command took about 15 minutes (worst case) to execute on a 2.9 GHz Intel 4-Core i7-3520M CPU with 3.6 GB memory.

8 Related Work

Formalizing Consistency Properties in a Single Framework. Adya [2] uses dependencies between reads and writes to define different isolation models in database systems. Bailis et al. [5] adopts this model to define read atomicity. Burckhardt et al. [11] and Cerone et al. [12] propose axiomatic specifications of consistency models for transaction systems using visibility and arbitration relationships. Shapiro et al. [35] propose a classification along three dimensions (total order, visibility, and transaction composition) for transactional consistency models. Crooks et al. [15] formalizes transactional consistency properties in terms of observable states from a client's perspective. On the non-transactional side, Burckhardt [10] focuses on session and eventual consistency models. Viotti *et al.* [38] expands his work by covering more than 50 non-transactional consistency properties. Szekeres *et al.* [37] propose a unified model based on result visibility to formalize both transactional and non-transactional consistency properties.

All of these studies propose semantic models of consistency properties suitable for theoretical analysis. In contrast, we aim at algorithmic methods for automatically verifying consistency properties based on executable specifications of both the systems and their consistency models. Furthermore, none of the studies covered all of the transactional consistency models considered in this paper.

Model Checking Distributed Transaction Systems. There is very little work on model checking state-of-the-art DTSs, maybe because the complexity of these systems requires expressive formalisms. Engineers at Amazon Web Services successfully used TLA+ to model check key algorithms in Amazon's Simple Storage Systems and DynamoDB database [31]; however, they do not state which consistency properties, if any, were model checked. The designers of the TAPIR transaction protocol have specified and model checked correctness properties of their design using TLA+ [41]. The IronFleet framework [20] combines TLA+ analysis and Floyd-Hoare-style imperative verification to reason about protocol-level concurrency and implementation complexities, respectively. Their methodology requires "considerable assistance from the developer" to perform the proofs.

Distributed model checkers [22,40] are used to model check *implementations* of distributed systems such as Cassandra, ZooKeeper, the BerkeleyDB database and a replication protocol implementation.

Our previous work [8,18,19,24–26,28,29,32] specifies and model checks *single* DTSs and consistency properties in different ways, as opposed to in a single framework that, furthermore, automates the "monitoring" and analysis process.

Other Formal Reasoning about Distributed Database Systems. Cerone et al. [13] develop a new characterization of *SI* and apply it to the static analysis of DTSs. Bernardi et al. [7] propose criteria for checking the robustness of transactional programs against consistency models. Bouajjani et al. [9] propose a formal definition of eventual consistency, and reduce the problem of checking eventual consistency to reachability and model checking problems. Gotsman *et al.* [17] propose a proof rule for reasoning about non-transactional consistency choices.

There is also work [23,34,39] that focuses on specifying, implementing and verifying distributed systems using the Coq proof assistant. Their executable Coq "implementations" can be seen as executable high-level formal specifications, but the theorem proving requires nontrivial user interaction.

9 Concluding Remarks

In this paper we have provided an object-based framework for formally modeling distributed transaction systems (DTSs) in Maude, have explained how such models can be automatically instrumented to record relevant events during a run, and have formally defined a wide range of consistency properties on such histories of events. We have implemented a tool which automates the entire instrumentation and model checking process. Our framework is very general: we could easily adapt previous Maude models of state-of-the-art DTSs such as Apache Cassandra, P-Store, RAMP, Walter, Jessy, and ROLA to our framework.

We then model checked the DTSs w.r.t. all the consistency properties for all initial states with 4 transactions, 2 sites, and so on. This analysis was sufficient to differentiate the DTSs according to which consistency properties they satisfy.

In future work we should formally relate our definitions of the consistency properties to other (non-executable) formalizations of consistency properties. We should also extend our work to formalizing and model checking non-transactional consistency properties for key-value stores such as Cassandra.

References

1. IBM DB2. https://www.ibm.com/analytics/us/en/db2/
2. Adya, A.: Weak Consistency: A Generalized Theory and Optimistic Implementations for Distributed Transactions. MIT, Cambridge (1999)
3. Ardekani, M.S., Sutra, P., Preguiça, N.M., Shapiro, M.: Non-monotonic snapshot isolation. CoRR abs/1306.3906 (2013). http://arxiv.org/abs/1306.3906
4. Ardekani, M.S., Sutra, P., Shapiro, M.: Non-monotonic snapshot isolation: scalable and strong consistency for geo-replicated transactional systems. In: SRDS, pp. 163–172 (2013)
5. Bailis, P., Fekete, A., Ghodsi, A., Hellerstein, J.M., Stoica, I.: Scalable atomic visibility with RAMP transactions. ACM Trans. Database Syst. **41**(3), 15:1–15:45 (2016)
6. Berenson, H., Bernstein, P.A., Gray, J., Melton, J., O'Neil, E.J., O'Neil, P.E.: A critique of ANSI SQL isolation levels. In: SIGMOD, pp. 1–10. ACM (1995)
7. Bernardi, G., Gotsman, A.: Robustness against consistency models with atomic visibility. In: CONCUR. LIPIcs, vol. 59, pp. 7:1–7:15. Schloss Dagstuhl - Leibniz-Zentrum fuer Informatik (2016)
8. Bobba, R., et al.: Survivability: design, formal modeling, and validation of cloud storage systems using Maude. In: Assured Cloud Computing. Wiley/IEEE (2018)
9. Bouajjani, A., Enea, C., Hamza, J.: Verifying eventual consistency of optimistic replication systems. In: POPL, pp. 285–296. ACM (2014)
10. Burckhardt, S.: Principles of Eventual Consistency. Foundations and Trends in Programming Languages, vol. 1. Now Publishers, Delft (2014)

11. Burckhardt, S., Leijen, D., Fähndrich, M., Sagiv, M.: Eventually Consistent Transactions. In: Seidl, H. (ed.) ESOP 2012. LNCS, vol. 7211, pp. 67–86. Springer, Heidelberg (2012). https://doi.org/10.1007/978-3-642-28869-2_4
12. Cerone, A., Bernardi, G., Gotsman, A.: A framework for transactional consistency models with atomic visibility. In: CONCUR. Schloss Dagstuhl - Leibniz-Zentrum fuer Informatik (2015)
13. Cerone, A., Gotsman, A.: Analysing snapshot isolation. In: PODC, pp. 55–64. ACM (2016)
14. Clavel, M., et al.: All About Maude - A High-Performance Logical Framework. LNCS, vol. 4350. Springer, Heidelberg (2007). https://doi.org/10.1007/978-3-540-71999-1
15. Crooks, N., Pu, Y., Alvisi, L., Clement, A.: Seeing is believing: a client-centric specification of database isolation. In: PODC, pp. 73–82. ACM (2017)
16. Date, C.: An Introduction to Database Systems, 5th edn. Addison-Wesley, Reading (1990)
17. Gotsman, A., Yang, H., Ferreira, C., Najafzadeh, M., Shapiro, M.: 'Cause I'm strong enough: reasoning about consistency choices in distributed systems. In: POPL, pp. 371–384. ACM (2016)
18. Grov, J., Ölveczky, P.C.: Formal modeling and analysis of Google's Megastore in Real-Time Maude. In: Iida, S., Meseguer, J., Ogata, K. (eds.) Specification, Algebra, and Software. LNCS, vol. 8373, pp. 494–519. Springer, Heidelberg (2014). https://doi.org/10.1007/978-3-642-54624-2_25
19. Grov, J., Ölveczky, P.C.: Increasing consistency in multi-site data stores: Megastore-CGC and its formal analysis. In: Giannakopoulou, D., Salaün, G. (eds.) SEFM 2014. LNCS, vol. 8702, pp. 159–174. Springer, Cham (2014). https://doi.org/10.1007/978-3-319-10431-7_12
20. Hawblitzel, C., et al.: IronFleet: proving practical distributed systems correct. In: SOSP. ACM (2015)
21. Kraska, T., Pang, G., Franklin, M.J., Madden, S., Fekete, A.: MDCC: multi-data center consistency. In: EuroSys, pp. 113–126. ACM (2013)
22. Leesatapornwongsa, T., Hao, M., Joshi, P., Lukman, J.F., Gunawi, H.S.: SAMC: semantic-aware model checking for fast discovery of deep bugs in cloud systems. In: OSDI. USENIX Association (2014)
23. Lesani, M., Bell, C.J., Chlipala, A.: Chapar: certified causally consistent distributed key-value stores. In: POPL, pp. 357–370. ACM (2016)
24. Liu, S., Ölveczky, P.C., Ganhotra, J., Gupta, I., Meseguer, J.: Exploring design alternatives for RAMP transactions through statistical model checking. In: Duan, Z., Ong, L. (eds.) ICFEM 2017. LNCS, vol. 10610, pp. 298–314. Springer, Cham (2017). https://doi.org/10.1007/978-3-319-68690-5_18
25. Liu, S., Ölveczky, P.C., Santhanam, K., Wang, Q., Gupta, I., Meseguer, J.: ROLA: a new distributed transaction protocol and its formal analysis. In: Russo, A., Schürr, A. (eds.) FASE 2018. LNCS, vol. 10802, pp. 77–93. Springer, Cham (2018). https://doi.org/10.1007/978-3-319-89363-1_5
26. Liu, S., Ölveczky, P.C., Wang, Q., Meseguer, J.: Formal modeling and analysis of the Walter transactional data store. In: Rusu, V. (ed.) WRLA 2018. LNCS, vol. 11152, pp. 136–152. Springer, Cham (2018). https://doi.org/10.1007/978-3-319-99840-4_8
27. Liu, S., Ölveczky, P., Zhang, M., Wang, Q., Meseguer, J.: Automatic analysis of consistency properties of distributed transaction systems in Maude. Technical report, University of Illinois at Urbana-Champaign (2019). http://hdl.handle.net/2142/102291

28. Liu, S., Ölveczky, P., Wang, Q., Gupta, I., Meseguer, J.: Read atomic transactions with prevention of lost updates: ROLA and its formal analysis. Technical report, University of Illinois at Urbana-Champaign (2018). http://hdl.handle.net/2142/101836
29. Liu, S., Ölveczky, P.C., Rahman, M.R., Ganhotra, J., Gupta, I., Meseguer, J.: Formal modeling and analysis of RAMP transaction systems. In: SAC. ACM (2016)
30. Liu, S., Rahman, M.R., Skeirik, S., Gupta, I., Meseguer, J.: Formal modeling and analysis of Cassandra in Maude. In: Merz, S., Pang, J. (eds.) ICFEM 2014. LNCS, vol. 8829, pp. 332–347. Springer, Cham (2014). https://doi.org/10.1007/978-3-319-11737-9_22
31. Newcombe, C., Rath, T., Zhang, F., Munteanu, B., Brooker, M., Deardeuff, M.: How Amazon Web Services uses formal methods. Commun. ACM **58**(4), 66–73 (2015)
32. Ölveczky, P.C.: Formalizing and validating the P-Store replicated data store in Maude. In: James, P., Roggenbach, M. (eds.) WADT 2016. LNCS, vol. 10644, pp. 189–207. Springer, Cham (2017). https://doi.org/10.1007/978-3-319-72044-9_13
33. Papadimitriou, C.H.: The serializability of concurrent database updates. J. ACM **26**(4), 631–653 (1979)
34. Sergey, I., Wilcox, J.R., Tatlock, Z.: Programming and proving with distributed protocols. Proc. ACM Program. Lang. **2**(POPL), 28:1–28:30 (2017)
35. Shapiro, M., Ardekani, M.S., Petri, G.: Consistency in 3D. In: CONCUR. LIPIcs, vol. 59, pp. 3:1–3:14. Schloss Dagstuhl - Leibniz-Zentrum fuer Informatik (2016)
36. Sovran, Y., Power, R., Aguilera, M.K., Li, J.: Transactional storage for geo-replicated systems. In: SOSP. ACM (2011)
37. Szekeres, A., Zhang, I.: Making consistency more consistent: a unified model for coherence, consistency and isolation. In: PaPoC. ACM (2018)
38. Viotti, P., Vukolić, M.: Consistency in non-transactional distributed storage systems. ACM Comput. Surv. **49**(1), 19:1–19:34 (2016)
39. Wilcox, J.R., et al.: Verdi: a framework for implementing and formally verifying distributed systems. In: PLDI, pp. 357–368. ACM (2015)
40. Yang, J., et al.: MODIST: transparent model checking of unmodified distributed systems. In: NSDI, pp. 213–228. USENIX Association (2009)
41. Zhang, I., Sharma, N.K., Szekeres, A., Krishnamurthy, A., Ports, D.R.K.: Building consistent transactions with inconsistent replication. In: SOSP 2015, pp. 263–278. ACM (2015)

Multi-core On-The-Fly Saturation

Tom van Dijk[1,2(✉)], Jeroen Meijer[1], and Jaco van de Pol[1,3]

[1] Formal Methods and Tools, University of Twente, Enschede, The Netherlands
t.vandijk@utwente.nl

[2] Formal Models and Verification, Johannes Kepler University, Linz, Austria

[3] Department of Computer Science, University of Aarhus, Aarhus, Denmark

Abstract. Saturation is an efficient exploration order for computing the set of reachable states symbolically. Attempts to parallelize saturation have so far resulted in limited speedup. We demonstrate for the first time that on-the-fly symbolic saturation can be successfully parallelized at a large scale. To this end, we implemented saturation in Sylvan's multi-core decision diagrams used by the LTSmin model checker.

We report extensive experiments, measuring the speedup of parallel symbolic saturation on a 48-core machine, and compare it with the speedup of parallel symbolic BFS and chaining. We find that the parallel scalability varies from quite modest to excellent. We also compared the speedup of on-the-fly saturation and saturation for pre-learned transition relations. Finally, we compared our implementation of saturation with the existing sequential implementation based on Meddly.

The empirical evaluation uses Petri nets from the model checking contest, but thanks to the architecture of LTSmin, parallel on-the-fly saturation is now available to multiple specification languages. Data or code related to this paper is available at: [34].

1 Introduction

Model checking is an exhaustive algorithm to verify that a finite model of a concurrent system satisfies certain temporal properties. The main challenge is to handle the large state space, resulting from the combination of parallel components. Symbolic model checking exploits regularities in the set of reachable states, by storing this set concisely in a decision diagram. In asynchronous systems, transitions have locality, i.e. they affect only a small part of the state vector. This locality is exploited in the saturation strategy, which is probably the most efficient strategy to compute the set of reachable states.

T. van Dijk—Supported by FWF, NFN Grant S11408-N23 (RiSE).
J. Meijer—Supported by STW SUMBAT Grant 13859.

T. Vojnar and L. Zhang (Eds.): TACAS 2019, Part II, LNCS 11428, pp. 58–75, 2019.
https://doi.org/10.1007/978-3-030-17465-1_4

In this paper, we investigate the efficiency and speedup of a new parallel implementation of saturation, aiming at a multi-core, shared-memory implementation. The implementation is carried out in the parallel decision diagram framework Sylvan [16], in the language-independent model checker LTSmin [22]. We empirically evaluate the speedup of parallel saturation on Petri nets from the Model Checking Contest [24], running the algorithm on up to 48 cores.

1.1 Related Work

The saturation strategy has been developed and improved by Ciardo et al. We refer to [13] for an extensive description of the algorithm. Saturation derives its efficiency from firing all local transitions that apply at a certain level of the decision diagram, before proceeding to the next higher level. An important step in the development of the saturation algorithm allows on-the-fly generation of the transition relations, without knowing the cardinality of the state variable domains in advance [12]. This is essential to implement saturation in LTSmin, which is based on the PINS interface to discover transitions on-the-fly.

Since saturation obtains its efficiency from a restrictive firing order, it seems inherently sequential. Yet the problem of parallelising saturation has been studied intensively. The first attempt, Saturation NOW [9], used a network of PCs. This version could exploit the collective memory of all PCs, but due to the sequential procedure, no speedup was achieved. By firing local transitions speculatively (but with care to avoid memory waste), some speedup has been achieved [10]. More relevant to our work is the parallelisation of saturation for a shared memory architecture [20]. The authors used CILK to schedule parallel work originating from firing multiple transitions at the same level. They reported some speedup on a dual-core machine, at the expense of a serious memory increase. Their method also required to precompute the transition relation. An improvement of the parallel synchronisation mechanism was provided in [31]. They reported a parallel speedup of 2× on 4 CPUs. Moreover, their implementation supports learning the transition relation on-the-fly. Still, the successful parallelisation of saturation remained widely open, as indicated by Ciardo [14]: "Parallel symbolic state-space exploration is difficult, but what is the alternative?"

For an extensive overview of parallel decision diagrams on various hardware architectures, see [15]. Here we mention some other approaches to parallel symbolic model checking, different from saturation for reachability analysis. First, Grumberg and her team [21] designed a parallel BDD package based on vertical partitioning. Each worker maintains its own sub-BDD. Workers exchange BDD nodes over the network. They reported some speedup on 32 PCs for BDD based model checking under the BFS strategy. The Sylvan [16] multi-core decision diagram package supports symbolic on-the-fly reachability analysis, as well as bisimulation minimisation [17]. Oortwijn [28] experimented with a heterogeneous distributed/multi-core architecture, by porting Sylvan's architecture to RDMA over MPI, running symbolic reachability on 480 cores spread over 32 PCs and reporting speedups of BFS symbolic reachability up to 50. Finally, we mention some applications of saturation beyond reachability, such as model checking CTL [32] and detecting strongly connected components to detect fair cycles [33].

1.2 Contribution

Here we show that implementing saturation on top of the multi-core decision diagram framework Sylvan [16] yields a considerable speedup in a shared-memory setting of up to 32.5× on 48 cores with pre-learned transition relations, and 52.2× with on-the-fly transition learning.

By design decision, our implementation reuses several features provided by Sylvan, such as: its own fine-grained, work-stealing framework Lace [18], its implementation of both BDDs (Binary Decision Diagrams) and LDDs (a List-implementation of Multiway Decision Diagrams), its concurrent unique table and operations cache, and finally, its parallel operations like set union and relational product. As a consequence, the pseudocode of the algorithm and additional code for saturation is quite small, and orthogonal to other BDD features. To improve orthogonality with the existing decision diagrams, we deviated from the standard presentation of saturation [13]: we never update BDD nodes in situ, and we eliminated the mutual recursion between saturation and the BDD operations for relational product to fire transitions.

The implementation is available in the open-source high-performance model checking tool LTSmin [22], with its language-agnostic interface, Partitioned Next-State Interface (PINS) [5,22,25]. Here, a specification basically provides a next-state function equipped with dependency information, from which LTSmin can derive locality information. We fully support the flexible method of learning the transition relation on-the-fly during saturation [12]. As a consequence, our contribution extends the tool LTSmin with saturation for various specification languages, like Promela, DVE, Petri nets, mCRL2, and languages supported by the ProB model checker. See Sect. 4 on how to use saturation in LTSmin.

The experiments with saturation in Sylvan are carried out in LTSmin as well. We used Petri nets from the MCC competition. Our experimental design has been carefully set up in order to facilitate fair comparisons. Besides learning the transition relation on-the-fly, we also pre-learned them in order to measure the overhead of learning, and eliminating its effect in comparisons. It is well known that the variable ordering has a large effect on the BDD sizes [29]. Hence, our experiments are based on two of the best static variable orderings known, Sloan [26] and Force [1]. In particular, our experiments measure and compare:

- The performance of our parallel algorithm with one worker, compared to a state-of-the art sequential implementation of saturation in Meddly [4].
- The parallel speedup of our algorithm on 16 cores, and for specific examples up to 48 cores.
- The efficiency and speedup of saturation compared to the BFS and chaining strategies for reachability analysis.
- The effect of choosing Binary Decision Diagrams or List Decision Diagrams.
- The effect of choosing Sloan or Force to compute static variable orders.

2 Preliminaries

This paper proposes an algorithm for decision diagrams to perform the fixed point application of multiple transition relations according to the saturation strategy, combined with on-the-fly transition learning as implemented in LTSMIN. We briefly review these concepts in the following.

2.1 Partitioned Transition Systems

A transition system (TS) is a tuple $(S, \rightarrow, s^0)$, where S is a set of states, $\rightarrow \subseteq S \times S$ is a transition relation and $s^0 \in S$ is the initial state. We define $\rightarrow^*$ to be the reflexive and transitive closure of $\rightarrow$. The set of reachable states is $R = \{s \in S \mid s^0 \rightarrow^* s\}$. The goal of this work is to compute R via a novel multi-core saturation strategy.

In this paper, we evaluate multi-core saturation using Petri nets. Figure 1 shows an example of a (safe) Petri net. We show its initial marking, which is the initial state. A Petri net transition can fire if there is a token in each of its source places. On firing, these tokens are consumed and tokens in each target place are generated. For example, t_1 will produce one token in both p_2 and p_5, if there is a token in p_4. Transition t_6 requires a token in both p_3 and p_1 to fire. The markings of this Petri net form the states of the corresponding TS, so here $|S| = 2^5 = 32$. From the initial marking shown, four more markings are reachable, connected by 10 enabled transition firings. This means $|R| = 5$, and $|\rightarrow| = 10$.

Notice that transitions in Petri nets are quite local; transitions consume from, and produce into relatively few places. The firing of a Petri net transition is called an event and the number of involved places is known as the *degree of event locality*. This notion is easily defined for other asynchronous specification languages and can be computed by a simple control flow graph analysis.

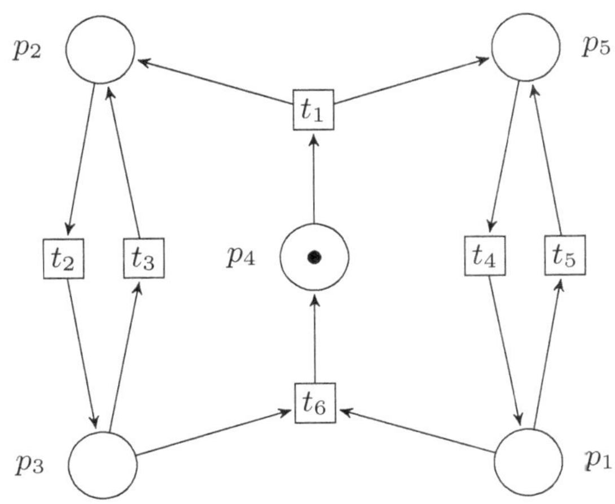

Fig. 1. Example Petri net

To exploit event locality, saturation requires a disjunctive partitioning of the transition relation $\rightarrow$, giving rise to a Partitioned Transition System (PTS). In a PTS, states are vectors of length N, and $\rightarrow$ is partitioned as a union of M transition groups. A natural way to partition a Petri net is by viewing each transition as a transition group. For Fig. 1 this means we have $N = 5$ and $M = 6$. After disjunctive partitioning, each transition group depends on very few entries of the state vector. This allows for efficiently computing the reachable state space for the large class of asynchronous specification languages. LTSMIN supports commonly used specification languages, like DVE, mCRL2, Promela, PNML for Petri nets, and languages supported by ProB.

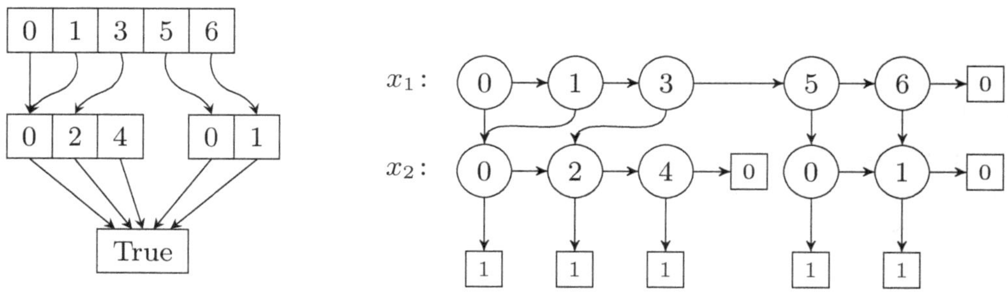

(a) LDD as array (b) Same LDD, internal linked-list representation

Fig. 2. LDD for $\{\langle 0,0\rangle,\langle 0,2\rangle,\langle 0,4\rangle,\langle 1,0\rangle,\langle 1,2\rangle,\langle 1,4\rangle,\langle 3,2\rangle,\langle 3,4\rangle,\langle 5,0\rangle,\langle 5,1\rangle,\langle 6,1\rangle\}$.

2.2 Decision Diagrams

Binary decision diagrams (BDDs) are a concise and canonical representation of Boolean functions $\mathbb{B}^N \rightarrow \mathbb{B}$ [7]. A BDD is a rooted directed acyclic graph with leaves 0 and 1. Each internal node v has a variable label x_i, denoted by $\text{var}(v)$, and two outgoing edges labeled 0 and 1, denoted by $\text{low}(v)$ and $\text{high}(v)$. The efficiency of *reduced, ordered* BDDs is achieved by minimizing the structure with some invariants: The BDD may neither contain *equivalent nodes*, with the same $\text{var}(v)$, $\text{low}(v)$ and $\text{high}(v)$, nor *redundant nodes*, with $\text{low}(v) = \mathit{high}(v)$. Also, the variables must occur according to a fixed ordering along each path.

Multi-valued or multiway decision diagrams (MDDs) generalize BDDs to finite domains ($\mathbb{N}^N \rightarrow \mathbb{B}$). Each internal MDD node with variable x_i now has n_i outgoing edges, labeled 0 to $n_i - 1$. We use quasi-reduced MDDs with sparse nodes. In the sparse representation, values with edges to leaf 0 are skipped from MDD nodes, so outgoing edges must be explicitly labeled with remaining domain values. Contrary to BDDs, MDDs are usually "quasi-reduced", meaning that variables are never skipped. In that case, the variable x_i can be derived from the depth of the MDD, so it is not stored.

A variation of MDDs are list decision diagrams (LDDs) [5,16], where sparse MDD nodes are represented as a linked list. See Fig. 2 for two visual representations of the same LDD. Each LDD node contains a value, a "down" edge for the corresponding child, and a "right" edge pointing to the next element in the list. Each list ends with the leaf 0 and each path from the root downwards ends with the leaf 1. The values in an LDD are strictly ordered, i.e., the values must increase to the "right".

LDD nodes have the advantage that common suffixes can be shared: The MDD for Fig. 2a requires two more nodes, one for [2, 4] and one for [1], because edges can only point to an entire MDD node. LDDs suffer from an increased memory footprint and inferior memory locality, but their memory management is simpler, since each LDD node has a fixed small size.

	p_1	p_2	p_3	p_4	p_5
t_1	0	1	0	1	1
t_2	0	1	1	0	0
t_3	0	1	1	0	0
t_4	1	0	0	0	1
t_5	1	0	0	0	1
t_6	1	0	1	1	0

(a) Natural order

	p_2	p_3	p_4	p_5	p_1
t_2	1	1	0	0	0
t_3	1	1	0	0	0
t_1	1	0	1	1	0
t_6	0	1	1	0	1
t_4	0	0	0	1	1
t_5	0	0	0	1	1

(b) Optimized order

Fig. 3. Dependency matrices of Fig. 1.

2.3 Variable Orders and Event Locality

Good variable orders are crucial for efficient operations on decision diagrams. The syntactic variable order from the specification is often inadequate for the saturation algorithm to perform well. Hence, finding a good variable order is necessary. Variable reordering algorithms use heuristics based on event locality. The locality of events can be illustrated with dependency matrices. The size of those matrices is $M \times N$, where M is the number of transition groups, and N is the length of the state vector. The order of columns in dependency matrices determines the order of variables in the DD. Figure 3a shows the natural order on places in Fig. 1. A measure of event locality is called *event span* [29]. Lower event span is correlated to a lower number of nodes in decision diagrams. This can be seen in LDDs in Figs. 4a and b that are ordered according to columns in Figs. 3a and b respectively.

Event span is defined as the sum over all rows of the distance from the leftmost non-zero column to the rightmost non-zero column. The event span of Fig. 3a is 22 (= 4+2+2+5+5+4); the event span of Fig. 3b is 16, which is better. Optimizing the event span and thus variable order of DDs is NP-complete [6], yet there are heuristic approaches that run in subquadratic time and provide good enough orders. Commonly used algorithms are Noack [27], Force [1] and Sloan [30]. Noack creates a permutation of variables by iteratively minimizing some objective function. The Force algorithm acts as if there are springs in between nonzeros in the dependency matrix, and tries to minimize the average tension among them. Sloan tries to minimize the profile of matrices. In short, profile is

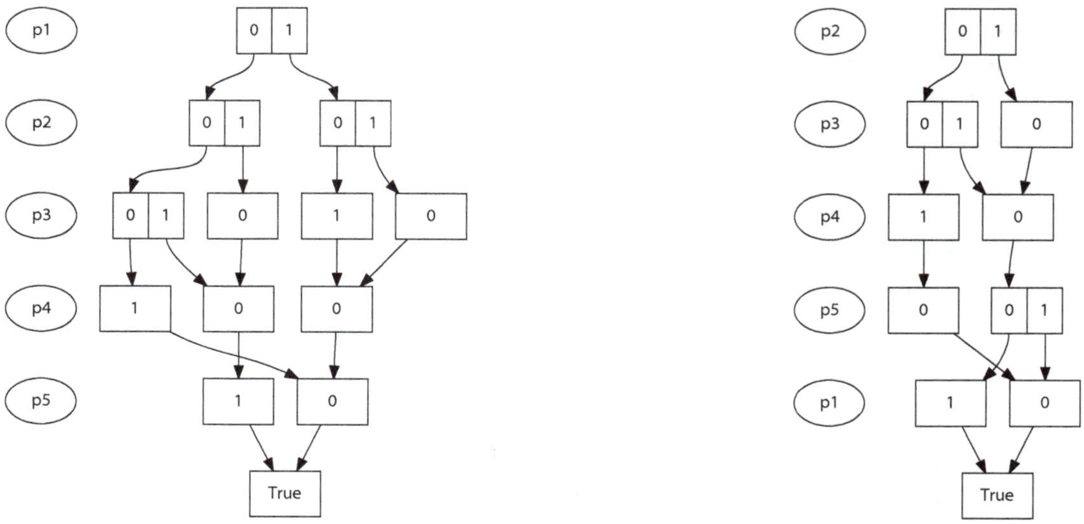

(a) Natural order (b) Optimized order

Fig. 4. Reachable states as LDDs with different orders on places

the symmetric counterpart to event span. For a more detailed overview of these algorithms see [3]. In our empirical evaluation we use both Sloan and Force, because these have been shown to give the best results [2,26].

2.4 The Saturation Strategy

The saturation strategy for reachability analysis, i.e., the transitive closure of transition relations applied to some set of states, was first proposed by Ciardo et al. See for an overview [11,13]. Saturation was combined with on-the-fly transition learning in [12]. Besides reachability, saturation has also been applied to CTL model checking [32] and in checking fairness constraints with strongly connected components [33].

Saturation is well-studied. The core idea is to always fire enabled transitions at the lower levels in the decision diagram, before proceeding to the next level. This tends to keep the intermediate BDD sizes much smaller than for instance the breadth-first exploration strategy. This is in particular the case for asynchronous systems, where transitions exhibit locality. There is also a major influence from the variable reordering: if the variables involved in a transition are grouped together, then this transition only affects adjacent levels in the decision diagram.

We refer to [13] for a precise description of saturation. Our implementation deviates from the standard presentation in three ways. First, we implemented saturation for LDDs and BDDs, instead of MDDs. Next, we never update nodes in the LDD forest in situ; instead, we always create new nodes. Finally, the standard representation has a mutual recursion between *saturation* and *firing transitions*. Instead, we fire transition using the existing function for relational product, which is called from our saturation algorithm. As a consequence, the extension with saturation becomes more orthogonal to the specific decision diagram implementation. We refer to Sect. 3 for a detailed description of our algorithm. We show in Sect. 5 that these design decisions do not introduce computational overhead.

3 Multi-core Saturation Algorithm

To access the three elements of an LDD node x, Sylvan [16] provides the functions `value`(x), `down`(x), `right`(x). To create or retrieve a unique LDD node using the hash table, Sylvan provides `LookupLDDNode`(*value*, *down*, *right*).

Furthermore, Sylvan provides several operations on LDDs that we use to implement reachability algorithms, such as `union`(A, B) to compute the set union $A \cup B$ and `minus`(A, B) to compute the set difference $A \setminus B$. For transition relations, Sylvan provides an operation `relprod`(S, R) to compute the successors of S with transition relation R, and an operation `relprodunion`(S, R) that computes `union`$(S,$ `relprod`$(S, R))$, i.e., computing the successors and adding them to the given set of states, in one operation. All these operations are internally parallelized, as described in [16].

We implement multi-core saturation as in Algorithm 1. We have a transition relation disjunctively partitioned into M relations $R_0 \dots R_{M-1}$. These relations are sorted by the level (depth) of the decision diagram where they are applied, which is the first level touched by the relation. We say that relation R_i is applied

```
global: M transition relations R_0 ... R_{M-1} starting at depths d_0 .. d_{M-1}
def saturate(S, k, d):
    if S = 0 ∨ S = 1 : return S
    if k = M : return S
    if result ← cache[(S, k, d)] : return result
    if d = d_k :
        k' ← next relation k < k' < M where d_{k'} ≠ d, or M
        while S changes :
            S ← saturate(S, k', d)
            for i ∈ [k, k') : S ← relprodunion(S, R_i)
        result ← S
    else:
        do in parallel:
            right ← saturate(right(S), k, d)
            down ← saturate(down(S), k, d + 1)
        result ← LookupLDDNode(value(S), down, right)
    cache[(S, k, d)] ← result
    return result
```

Algorithm 1: The multi-core saturation algorithm, which, given a set of states S and next transition relation k and current decision diagram depth d, exhaustively applies all transition relations $R_k \dots R_{M-1}$ using the saturation strategy.

at depth d_i. We identify the current next relation with a number k, $0 \leq k \leq M$, where $k = M$ denotes "no next relation". Decision diagram levels are sequentially numbered with 0 for the root level.

The `saturate` algorithm is given the initial set of states S and the initial next transition relation $k = 0$ and the initial decision diagram level $d = 0$. The algorithm is a straightforward implementation of saturation. First we check the easy cases where we reach either the end of an LDD list, where $S = 0$, or the bottom of the decision diagram, where $S = 1$. If there are no more transition relations to apply, then $k = M$ and we can simply return S. When we arrive at line 4, the operation is not trivial and we consult the operation cache.

If the result of this operation was not already in the cache, then we check whether we have relations at the current level. Since the relations are sorted by the level where they must be applied, we compare the current level d with the level d_k of the next relation k. If we have relations at the current level, then we perform the fixed point computation where we first saturate S for the remaining relations, starting at relation k', which is the first relation that must be applied on a deeper level than d, and then apply the relations of the current level, that is, all R_i where $k \leq i < k'$. If no relations match the current level, then we compute in parallel the results of the suboperations for the LDD of successor "right" and for the LDD of successor "down". After obtaining these sub results, we use `LookupLDDNode` to compute the final result for this LDD node. Finally, we store this result in the operation cache and return it.

The **do in parallel** keyword is implemented with the work-stealing framework Lace [18], which is embedded in Sylvan [16] and offers the primitives `spawn` and `sync` to create subtasks and wait for their completion. The implementation using `spawn` and `sync` of lines 12–14 is as follows.

```
12 spawn(saturate(right(S), k, d))
13 down ← saturate(down(S), k, d + 1)
14 right ← sync()
```

The implementation of multi-core saturation for BDDs is identical, except that we parallelize on the "then" and "else" successors of a BDD node, instead of on the "down" and "right" successors of an LDD node.

To add on-the-fly transition relation learning to this algorithm, we simply modify the loop at line 9 as follows:

```
 9 for i ∈ [k, k′) :
10     learn-transitions(S, i, d)
11     S ← relprodunion(S, Ri)
```

The `learn-transitions` function provided by LTSmin updates relation i given a set of states S. The function first restricts S to so-called short states S^i, which is the projection of S on the state variables that are touched by relation i. Then it calls the `next-state` function of the PINS interface for each new short state and it updates R_i with the new transitions.

Updating transition relations from multiple threads is not completely trivial. LTSmin solves this using lock-free programming with the compare-and-swap operation. After collecting all new transitions, LTSMIN computes the union with the known transitions and uses compare-and-swap to update the global relation; if this fails, the union is repeated with the new known transitions.

4 Contributed Tools

We present several new tools and extensions to existing tools produced in this work. The new tools support experiments and comparisons between various DD formats. The extension to Sylvan and LTSMIN provides end-users with multi-core saturation for reachability analysis.

4.1 Tools for Experimental Purposes

For the empirical evaluation, we need to isolate the reachability analysis of a given LDD (or BDD or MDD). To that end, we implemented three small tools that only compute the set of reachable states, namely `lddmc` for LDDs, `bddmc` for BDDs and `medmc` for MDDs using the library Meddly. These tools are given an input file representing the model, compute the set of reachable states, and report the number of states and the required time to compute all reachable states. Additionally we provide the tools `ldd2bdd` and `ldd2meddly` that convert an LDD file to a BDD file and to an MDD file. The LDD input files are generated using LTSMIN (see below). These tools can all be found online[1].

4.2 Tools for On-The-Fly Multi-core Saturation

On-the-fly multi-core saturation is implemented in the LTSMIN toolset, which can be found online[2]. The examples in this section are also online[3]. On-the-fly multi-core saturation for Petri nets is available in LTSMIN's tool `pnml2lts-sym`. This tool computes all reachable markings with parallel saturation. The command line to run it on Fig. 1 is `pnml2lts-sym pnml/example.pnml --saturation=sat`. The tool reports: `pnml2lts-sym: state space has 5 states, 16 nodes`. Additionally, it appears the final LDD has 16 nodes.

Here the syntactic variable order of the places in `pnml/example.pnml` is used. To use a better variable order, the option `-r` is added to the command line. For instance adding `-rf` runs *Force*, while `-rbs` runs *Sloan*'s algorithm (as implemented in the well-known Boost library). Running `pnml2lts-sym pnml/example.pnml --saturation=sat -rf` reports that the final LDD has only 12 nodes.

The naming convention of LTSMIN's binaries follows the Partitioned Next-State Interface (PINS) architecture [5,22,25]. PINS forms a bridge between several language front-ends and algorithmic back-ends. Consequently, besides

[1] https://github.com/trolando/sylvan.
[2] https://github.com/utwente-fmt/ltsmin.
[3] https://github.com/trolando/ParallelSaturationExperiments.

pnml2lts-sym, LTSMIN also provides {**pnml,dve,prom**}**2lts-**{**dist,mc,sym**} and several other combinations. These binaries generate the state space for the languages PNML, DVE and Promela, by means of distributed explicit-state, multi-core explicit-state and multi-core symbolic algorithms, respectively. Additionally, LTSMIN supports checking for deadlocks and invariants, and verifying LTL properties and μ-calculus formulas. In this work we focus on state space generation with the symbolic back-end only.

We now demonstrate multi-core saturation for Promela models. Consider the file `Promela/garp_1b2a.prm` which is an implementation of the GARP protocol [23]. To compute the reachable state space with the proposed algorithm and Force order, run: `prom2lts-sym --saturation=sat Promela/garp_1b2a.prm -rf`. On a consumer laptop with 8 hardware threads, LTSMIN reports 385,000,995,634 reachable states within 1 min. To run the example with a single worker, run `prom2lts-sym –saturation=sat Promela/garp_1b2a.prm -rf --lace-workers=1`. On the same laptop, the algorithm runs in 4 min with 1 worker. We thus have a speedup of 4× with 8 workers for symbolic saturation on a Promela model.

5 Empirical Evaluation

Our goal with the empirical study is five-fold. *First*, we compare our parallel implementation with only 1 core to the purely sequential implementation of the MDD library Meddly [4], in order to determine whether our implementation is competitive with the state-of-the-art. *Second*, we study parallel scalability up to 16 cores for all models and up to 48 cores with a small selection of models. *Third*, we compare parallel saturation with LDDs to parallel saturation with ordinary BDDs, to see if we get similar results with BDDs. *Fourth*, we compare parallel saturation without on-the-fly transition learning to on-the-fly parallel saturation, to see the effects of on-the-fly transition learning on the performance of the algorithm. *Fifth*, we compare parallel saturation with other reachability strategies, namely chaining and BFS, to confirm whether saturation is indeed a better strategy than chaining and BFS.

To perform this evaluation, we use the P/T Petri net benchmarks obtained from the Model Checking Contest 2016 [24]. These are 491 models in total, stored in PNML files. We use parallel on-the-fly saturation (in LTSMIN) with a generous timeout of 1 hour to obtain LDD files of the models, using the Force variable ordering and using the Sloan variable ordering. In total, 413 of potentially 982 LDD files were generated. These LDD files simply store the list decision diagrams of the initial states and of all transition relations. We convert the LDD files to BDD files (binary decision diagrams) with an optimal number of binary variables. We also convert the LDD files to MDD files for the experiments using Meddly. This ensures that all solvers have *the same input model with the same variable order.*

Table 1. The six solving methods that we use in the empirical evaluation. Five methods are parallelized and one method is on-the-fly.

Method	Tool	Description	Input	Parallel	OTF
otf-ldd-sat	`pnml2lts-sym`	saturation	PNML	✓	✓
ldd-sat	`lddmc`	saturation	LDD	✓	
ldd-chaining	`lddmc`	chaining	LDD	✓	
ldd-bfs	`lddmc`	BFS	LDD	✓	
bdd-sat	`bddmc`	saturation	BDD	✓	
mdd-sat	`medmc`	saturation in Meddly	MDD		

Table 2. Number of benchmarks (out of 413) solved within 20 min with each method with the given number of workers.

Method	Number of solved models with # workers					
	1	2	4	8	16	Any
otf-ldd-sat	387	397	399	404	407	408
ldd-sat	388	393	399	402	402	404
ldd-chaining	351	354	360	367	371	371
ldd-bfs	325	331	347	360	362	362
bdd-sat	395	396	401	402	403	405
mdd-sat	375	–	–	–	–	375

See Table 1 for the list of solving methods. As described in Sect. 4, we implement the tools `lddmc`, `bddmc` and `medmc` to isolate reachability computation for the purposes of this comparison, using respectively the LDDs and BDDs of Sylvan and the MDDs of Meddly. The on-the-fly parallel saturation using LDDs is performed with the `pnml2lts-sym` tool of LTSmin. We use the command line `pnml2lts-sym ORDER --lace-workers=WORKERS --saturation=sat FILE`, where `ORDER` is `-rf` for Force and `-rbs` for Sloan and `WORKERS` is a number from the set $\{1, 2, 4, 8, 16\}$.

All experimental scripts, input files and log files are available online (see footnote 3). The experiments are performed on a cluster of Dell PowerEdge M610 servers with two Xeon E5520 processors and 24 GB internal memory each. The tools are compiled with gcc 5.4.0 on Ubuntu 16.04. The experiments for up to 48 cores are performed on a single computer with 4 AMD Opteron 6168 processors with 12 cores each and 128 GB internal memory.

When reporting on parallel executions, we use *the number of workers* for how many hardware threads (cores) were used.

Overview. After running all experiments, we obtain the results for 413 models in total, of which 196 models with the Force variable ordering and 217 models with the Sloan variable ordering. In the remainder of this section, we study these

Table 3. Cumulative time and parallel speedups for each method-#workers combination on the models where all methods solved the model in time. These are 301 models in total: 151 models with Force, 150 models with Sloan.

Method	Order	Total time (sec) with # workers					Total speedup			
		1	2	4	8	16	2	4	8	16
otf-ldd-sat	Sloan	1850	1546	698	398	313	1.2	2.7	4.6	5.9
ldd-sat	Sloan	932	609	311	194	151	1.5	3.0	4.8	6.2
ldd-chaining	Sloan	4156	3019	1916	1121	863	1.4	2.2	3.7	4.8
ldd-bfs	Sloan	9030	5585	2990	1652	1219	1.6	3.0	5.5	7.4
bdd-sat	Sloan	708	419	212	139	115	1.7	3.3	5.1	6.1
mdd-sat	Sloan	572	–	–	–	–	–	–	–	–
otf-ldd-sat	Force	2704	1162	712	401	343	2.3	3.8	6.8	7.9
ldd-sat	Force	856	602	348	216	180	1.4	2.5	4.0	4.7
ldd-chaining	Force	3149	2560	1835	1160	1024	1.2	1.7	2.7	3.1
ldd-bfs	Force	4696	2951	1556	859	633	1.6	3.0	5.5	7.4
bdd-sat	Force	1041	733	384	253	206	1.4	2.7	4.1	5.1
mdd-sat	Force	1738	–	–	–	–	–	–	–	–

413 benchmarks. See Table 2, which shows the number of models for which each method could compute the set of reachable states within 20 min.

To correctly compare all runtimes, we restrict the set of models to those where all methods finish within 20 min with any number of workers. We retain in total 301 models where no solver hit the timeout. See Table 3 for the cumulative times for each method and number of workers and the parallel speedup. Notice that this is the speedup for the *entire* set of 301 models and not for individual models.

Comparing LDD saturation with Meddly's saturation. We evaluate how ldd-sat with just 1 worker compares to the sequential saturation of Meddly. The goal is not to directly measure whether there is a parallel overhead from using parallelism in Sylvan, as the algorithm in `lddmc` is fundamentally different because it uses LDDs instead of MDDs and the algorithm does not in-place saturate nodes, as also explained in Sect. 3. The low parallel overheads of Sylvan are already demonstrated elsewhere [15,16,18]. Rather, the goal is to see how our version of saturation compares to the state-of-the-art.

Table 2 shows that Meddly's implementation (mdd-sat) and our implementation (ldd-sat 1) are quite similar in the number of solved models. Meddly solves 375 benchmarks and our implementation solves 388 within 20 min.

See Table 3 for a comparison of runtimes. Meddly solves the 150 models with Sloan almost 2× as fast as our implementation in Sylvan, but is slower than our implementation for the 151 models with Force. We observe for individual models that the difference between the two solvers is within an order of magnitude for

Table 4. Parallel speedup for a selection of benchmarks on the 48-core machine (only top 5 shown)

Model (with ldd-sat)	Order	Time (sec)			Speedup	
		1	24	48	24	48
Dekker-PT-015	Sloan	77.3	4.7	2.4	16.3	32.5
PhilosophersDyn-PT-10	Force	273.8	16.8	12.4	16.3	22.1
Angiogenesis-PT-10	Sloan	333.2	28.5	16.5	11.7	20.2
SwimmingPool-PT-02	Force	25.0	2.1	1.4	11.6	17.8
BridgeAndVehicles-PT-V20P10N20	Force	1035.8	101.8	60.7	10.2	17.1
Model (with otf-ldd-sat)						
Dekker-PT-015	Sloan	174.5	7.4	3.3	23.6	52.2
SwimmingPool-PT-07	Sloan	1008.0	69.2	42.0	14.6	24.0
SmallOperatingSystem-PT-MT0256DC0064	Sloan	957.3	52.9	40.0	18.1	23.9
Kanban-PT-0050	Sloan	940.6	78.7	48.9	11.9	19.2
TCPcondis-PT-10	Force	68.4	5.7	3.8	11.9	17.8

most models, although there are some exceptions. Our implementation quickly overtakes Meddly with additional workers.

Parallel Scalability. As shown in Table 3, using 16 workers, we obtain a modest parallel speedup for saturation of 6.2× (with Sloan) and 4.7× (with Force). On individual models, the differences are large. The average speedup of the individual benchmarks is only 1.8× with 16 workers, but there are many slowdowns for models that take less than a second with 1 worker. We take an arbitrary selection of models with a high parallel speedup and run these on a dedicated 48-core machine. Table 4 shows that even up to 48 cores, parallel speedup keeps improving. We even see a speedup of 52.2×. For this superlinear speedup we have two possible explanations. One is that there is some nondeterminism inherent in any parallel computation; another is already noted in [20] and is related to the "chaining" in saturation, see further [20].

Comparing LDD saturation with BDD saturation. As Table 3 shows, the ldd-sat and bdd-sat method have a similar performance and similar parallel speedups.

On-the-fly LDD saturation. Comparing the performance of offline saturation with on-the-fly saturation, we observe the same scalability with the Sloan variable order, but on-the-fly saturation requires roughly 2× as much time. With the Force variable order, on-the-fly saturation is slower but has a higher parallel speedup of 7.9×.

Comparing saturation, chaining and BFS. We also compare the saturation algorithm with other popular strategies to compute the set of reachable states,

```
global: N transition relations R_0 ... R_{M-1}
def bfs(S):
    U ← S
    while U ≠ ∅ :
        U ← par-next(U, 0, M)
        U ← minus(U, S)
        S ← union(U, S)
    return S
def par-next(S, i, k):
    if k = 1 : return relprod(S, R_i)
    do in parallel:
        left ← par-next(S, i, k/2)
        right ← par-next(S, i + k/2, k − k/2)
    return union(left, right)
```

```
def chaining(S):
    U ← S
    while U ≠ ∅ :
        for i ∈ [0, M) :
            U ← relprodunion(U, R_i)
        U ← minus(U, S)
        S ← union(U, S)
    return S
```

Fig. 5. Algorithms `bfs` and `chaining` implement the Parallel BFS and Chaining strategies for reachability.

namely standard (parallelized) BFS and chaining, given in Fig. 5. As Tables 2 and 3 show, chaining is significantly faster than BFS and saturation is again significantly faster than chaining. In terms of parallel scalability, we see that parallelized BFS scales better than the others, because it can already parallelize in the main loop by computing successors for all relations in parallel, which chaining and saturation cannot do. For the entire set of benchmarks, saturation is the superior method, however there are individual differences and for some models, saturation is not the fastest method.

6 Conclusion

We presented a multi-core implementation of saturation for the efficient computation of the set of reachable states. Based on Sylvan's multi-core decision diagram framework, the design of the saturation algorithm is mostly orthogonal to the type of decision diagram. We showed the implementation for BDDs and LDDs; the translation relation can be learned on-the-fly. The functionality is accessible through the LTSmin high-performance model checker. This makes parallel saturation available for a whole collection of asynchronous specification languages. We demonstrated multi-core saturation for Promela and for Petri nets in PNML representation.

We carried out extensive experiments on a benchmark of Petri nets from the Model Checking Contest. The total speedup of on-the-fly saturation is 5.9× on 16 cores with the Sloan variable ordering and 7.9× with the Force variable ordering. However, there are many small models (computed in less than a second) in this benchmark. For some larger models we showed an impressive 52× speedup on a 48-core machine. From our measurements, we further conclude that the efficiency and parallel speedup for the BDD variant is just as good as the speedup for

LDDs. We compared efficiency and speedup of saturation versus other popular exploration strategies, BFS and chaining. As expected, saturation is significantly faster than chaining, which is faster than BFS; this trend is maintained in the parallel setting. Our measurements show that the variable ordering (Sloan versus Force), and the model representation (pre-computed transition relations versus learned on-the-fly) do have an impact on efficiency and speedup. Parallel speedup should not come at the price of reduced efficiency. To this end, we compared our parallel saturation algorithm for one worker to saturation in Meddly. Meddly solves fewer models within the timeout, but is slightly faster in other cases, but parallel saturation quickly overtakes Meddly with multiple workers.

Future work could include the study of parallel saturation on exciting new BDD types, like tagged BDDs and chained BDDs [8,19]. The results on tagged BDDs showed a significant speedup compared to ordinary BDDs on experiments in LTSmin with the BEEM benchmark database. Another direction would be to investigate the efficiency and speedup of parallel saturation in other applications, like CTL model checking, SCC decomposition, and bisimulation reduction.

References

1. Aloul, F.A., Markov, I.L., Sakallah, K.A.: FORCE: a fast and easy-to-implement variable-ordering heuristic. In: VLSI 2003, pp. 116–119. ACM (2003)
2. Amparore, E.G., Beccuti, M., Donatelli, S.: Gradient-based variable ordering of decision diagrams for systems with structural units. In: D'Souza, D., Narayan Kumar, K. (eds.) ATVA 2017. LNCS, vol. 10482, pp. 184–200. Springer, Cham (2017). https://doi.org/10.1007/978-3-319-68167-2_13
3. Amparore, E.G., Donatelli, S., Beccuti, M., Garbi, G., Miner, A.S.: Decision diagrams for Petri nets: which variable ordering? In: PNSE @ Petri Nets. CEUR Workshop Proceedings, vol. 1846, pp. 31–50. CEUR-WS.org (2017)
4. Babar, J., Miner, A.S.: Meddly: multi-terminal and edge-valued decision diagram library. In: QEST, pp. 195–196. IEEE Computer Society (2010)
5. Blom, S., van de Pol, J., Weber, M.: LTSmin: distributed and symbolic reachability. In: Touili, T., Cook, B., Jackson, P. (eds.) CAV 2010. LNCS, vol. 6174, pp. 354–359. Springer, Heidelberg (2010). https://doi.org/10.1007/978-3-642-14295-6_31
6. Bollig, B., Wegener, I.: Improving the variable ordering of OBDDs is NP-complete. IEEE Trans. Comput. **45**(9), 993–1002 (1996)
7. Bryant, R.E.: Graph-based algorithms for Boolean function manipulation. IEEE Trans. Comput. **C–35**(8), 677–691 (1986)
8. Bryant, R.E.: Chain reduction for binary and zero-suppressed decision diagrams. In: Beyer, D., Huisman, M. (eds.) TACAS 2018. LNCS, vol. 10805, pp. 81–98. Springer, Cham (2018). https://doi.org/10.1007/978-3-319-89960-2_5
9. Chung, M., Ciardo, G.: Saturation NOW. In: QEST, pp. 272–281. IEEE Computer Society (2004)
10. Chung, M., Ciardo, G.: Speculative image computation for distributed symbolic reachability analysis. J. Logic Comput. **21**(1), 63–83 (2011)
11. Ciardo, G., Lüttgen, G., Siminiceanu, R.: Saturation: an efficient iteration strategy for symbolic state—space generation. In: Margaria, T., Yi, W. (eds.) TACAS 2001. LNCS, vol. 2031, pp. 328–342. Springer, Heidelberg (2001). https://doi.org/10.1007/3-540-45319-9_23

12. Ciardo, G., Marmorstein, R.M., Siminiceanu, R.: Saturation unbound. In: Garavel, H., Hatcliff, J. (eds.) TACAS 2003. LNCS, vol. 2619, pp. 379–393. Springer, Heidelberg (2003). https://doi.org/10.1007/3-540-36577-X_27
13. Ciardo, G., Marmorstein, R.M., Siminiceanu, R.: The saturation algorithm for symbolic state-space exploration. STTT **8**(1), 4–25 (2006)
14. Ciardo, G., Zhao, Y., Jin, X.: Parallel symbolic state-space exploration is difficult, but what is the alternative? In: PDMC, EPTCS, vol. 14, pp. 1–17 (2009)
15. van Dijk, T.: Sylvan: multi-core decision diagrams. Ph.D. thesis, University of Twente, July 2016
16. van Dijk, T., van de Pol, J.: Sylvan: multi-core framework for decision diagrams. STTT **19**(6), 675–696 (2017)
17. van Dijk, T., van de Pol, J.: Multi-core symbolic bisimulation minimisation. STTT **20**(2), 157–177 (2018)
18. van Dijk, T., van de Pol, J.C.: Lace: non-blocking split deque for work-stealing. In: Lopes, L., et al. (eds.) Euro-Par 2014. LNCS, vol. 8806, pp. 206–217. Springer, Cham (2014). https://doi.org/10.1007/978-3-319-14313-2_18
19. van Dijk, T., Wille, R., Meolic, R.: Tagged BDDs: combining reduction rules from different decision diagram types. In: FMCAD, pp. 108–115. IEEE (2017)
20. Ezekiel, J., Lüttgen, G., Ciardo, G.: Parallelising symbolic state-space generators. In: Damm, W., Hermanns, H. (eds.) CAV 2007. LNCS, vol. 4590, pp. 268–280. Springer, Heidelberg (2007). https://doi.org/10.1007/978-3-540-73368-3_31
21. Heyman, T., Geist, D., Grumberg, O., Schuster, A.: A scalable parallel algorithm for reachability analysis of very large circuits. Formal Methods Syst. Des. **21**(3), 317–338 (2002)
22. Kant, G., Laarman, A., Meijer, J., van de Pol, J., Blom, S., van Dijk, T.: LTSmin: high-performance language-independent model checking. In: Baier, C., Tinelli, C. (eds.) TACAS 2015. LNCS, vol. 9035, pp. 692–707. Springer, Heidelberg (2015). https://doi.org/10.1007/978-3-662-46681-0_61
23. Konnov, I., Letichevsky, O.: Model checking GARP protocol using Spin and VRS. In: IW on Automata, Algorithms, and Information Technology (2010)
24. Kordon, F., et al.: Complete Results for the 2016 Edition of the Model Checking Contest, June 2016. http://mcc.lip6.fr/2016/results.php
25. Meijer, J., Kant, G., Blom, S., van de Pol, J.: Read, write and copy dependencies for symbolic model checking. In: Yahav, E. (ed.) HVC 2014. LNCS, vol. 8855, pp. 204–219. Springer, Cham (2014). https://doi.org/10.1007/978-3-319-13338-6_16
26. Meijer, J., van de Pol, J.: Bandwidth and wavefront reduction for static variable ordering in symbolic reachability analysis. In: Rayadurgam, S., Tkachuk, O. (eds.) NFM 2016. LNCS, vol. 9690, pp. 255–271. Springer, Cham (2016). https://doi.org/10.1007/978-3-319-40648-0_20
27. Noack, A.: A ZBDD package for efficient model checking of Petri nets. Forschungsbericht, Branderburgische Technische Uinversität Cottbus (1999)
28. Oortwijn, W., van Dijk, T., van de Pol, J.: Distributed binary decision diagrams for symbolic reachability. In: 24th ACM SIGSOFT International SPIN Symposium on Model Checking of Software, pp. 21–30 (2017)
29. Siminiceanu, R., Ciardo, G.: New metrics for static variable ordering in decision diagrams. In: Hermanns, H., Palsberg, J. (eds.) TACAS 2006. LNCS, vol. 3920, pp. 90–104. Springer, Heidelberg (2006). https://doi.org/10.1007/11691372_6
30. Sloan, S.W.: A FORTRAN program for profile and wavefront reduction. Int. J. Numer. Methods Eng. **28**(11), 2651–2679 (1989)

31. Vörös, A., Szabó, T., Jámbor, A., Darvas, D., Horváth, Á., Bartha, T.: Parallel saturation based model checking. In: ISPDC, pp. 94–101. IEEE Computer Society (2011)
32. Zhao, Y., Ciardo, G.: Symbolic CTL model checking of asynchronous systems using constrained saturation. In: Liu, Z., Ravn, A.P. (eds.) ATVA 2009. LNCS, vol. 5799, pp. 368–381. Springer, Heidelberg (2009). https://doi.org/10.1007/978-3-642-04761-9_27
33. Zhao, Y., Ciardo, G.: Symbolic computation of strongly connected components and fair cycles using saturation. ISSE **7**(2), 141–150 (2011)
34. van Dijk, T., van de Pol, J., Meijer, J.: Artifact and instructions to generate experimental results for TACAS 2019 paper: Multi-core On-The-Fly Saturation (artifact). Figshare (2019). https://doi.org/10.6084/m9.figshare.7825406.v1

Monitoring and Runtime Verification

Specification and Efficient Monitoring Beyond STL

Alexey Bakhirkin(✉) and Nicolas Basset

Univ. Grenoble Alpes, CNRS, Grenoble INP, VERIMAG, 38000 Grenoble, France
abakhirkin@gmail.com

Abstract. An appealing feature of Signal Temporal Logic (STL) is the existence of efficient monitoring algorithms both for Boolean and real-valued robustness semantics, which are based on computing an aggregate function (conjunction, disjunction, min, or max) over a sliding window. On the other hand, there are properties that can be monitored with the same algorithms, but that cannot be directly expressed in STL due to syntactic restrictions. In this paper, we define a new specification language that extends STL with the ability to produce and manipulate real-valued output signals and with a new form of until operator. The new language still admits efficient offline monitoring, but also allows to express some properties that in the past motivated researchers to extend STL with existential quantification, freeze quantification, and other features that increase the complexity of monitoring.

1 Introduction

Signal Temporal Logic (STL [16,17]) is a temporal logic designed to specify properties of real-valued dense-time signals. It gained popularity due to the rigour and the ability to reason about analog and mixed signals; and it found use in such domains as analog circuits, systems biology, cyber-physical control systems (see [3] for a survey). A major use of STL is in monitoring: given a signal and an STL formula, an automated procedure can decide whether the formula holds at a given time point.

Monitoring of STL is reliably efficient. A monitoring procedure typically traverses the formula bottom up, and for every sub-formula computes a satisfaction signal, based on satisfaction signals of its operands. Boolean monitoring is based on the computation of conjunctions and disjunctions over a sliding window ("until" is implemented using a specialized version of running conjunction), and robustness monitoring (computing how well a signal satisfies a formula [9,10]) is based on the computation of minimum and maximum over a sliding window. The complexity of both Boolean and robustness monitoring is linear in the length of the signal and does not depend on the width of temporal windows appearing in

This work was partially supported by the European Research Council under the European Union's Seventh Framework Programme (FP/2007-2013)/ERC Grant Agreement nr. 306595 "STATOR".

T. Vojnar and L. Zhang (Eds.): TACAS 2019, Part II, LNCS 11428, pp. 79–97, 2019.
https://doi.org/10.1007/978-3-030-17465-1_5

the formula. At the same time, for a range of applications, pure STL is either not expressive enough or difficult to use, and specifying a desired property often becomes a puzzle of its own. The existence of robustness and other real-valued semantics does not always help, since a monitor can perform a limited set of operations that the semantics assigns to Boolean operators. For example, for robustness semantics, min and max are the only operations beyond the atomic proposition level.

One way to work around the expressiveness issues of STL is pre-processing: a computation that cannot be performed by an STL monitor can be performed by a pre-processor and supplied as an extra input signal. For a number of reasons, this is not always satisfactory. First, for monitoring of continuous-time signals, there is a big gap between the logical definitions of properties and the implementation of monitors. In continuous-time setting, properties are defined using quantification, upper and lower bounds, and similar mathematical tools for dense sets, while a monitor works with a finite piecewise representation of a signal and performs a computation that is based on induction and other tools for discrete sets. Leaving this gap exposed to the user, who has to implement the pre-processing step, is not very user-friendly. Second, monitoring of some properties cannot be cleanly decomposed into a pre-processing step followed by standard STL monitoring. Later, we give a concrete example using an extended "until" operator, and for now, notice that "until" instructs the monitor to compute a conjunction over the window that is not fixed in advance, but is defined by its second operand. Because of that, multiple researches have been motivated to search for a more expressive superset of STL that would allow to specify the properties they were interested in.

One direction for extension is to add to the original quantifier-free logic (MTL, STL) a form of variable binding: a freeze quantifier as in STL* [6], a clock reset as in TPTL [1], or even first order quantification [2]. Unfortunately, such extensions are detrimental to complexity of monitoring. When monitoring logics with quantifiers using standard bottom-up approach, subformulas containing free variables evaluate not to Boolean- or real-valued signals, but to maps from time to non-convex sets, and they cannot in general be efficiently manipulated (although for some classes of formulas monitoring of logics with quantifiers works well [4,13]). Perhaps the most benign in this respect but also least expressive extension is 1-TPTL (TPTL with one active clock), which is as expressive as MITL, but is easier to use and admits a reasonably efficient monitoring procedure [11].

An alternative direction is to define a quantifier-free specification language with more flexible syntax and sliding window operations. For example, Signal Convolution Logic (SCL [20]) allows to specify properties using convolution with a set of select kernels. In particular, it can express properties of the form "statement φ holds on an interval for at least X% of the time". In SCL, every formula has a Boolean satisfaction signal, but some works go further and allow a formula to produce a real-valued output signal based on the real-valued signals of its subformulas. This already happens for robustness of STL in a very limited way, and can be extended. For example, [19] presents temporal logic monitoring as filtering, which allows to derive multiple different real-valued semantics. Another work [7] focuses on the practical application of robustness in falsification and allows to choose between different possible robust semantics for "eventually" and "always", in particular to replace min or max with integration where necessary.

This paper is our take on extending STL in the latter direction. We define a specification language that is more expressive than STL, but not less efficient to monitor offline, i.e., the complexity of monitoring is linear in the length of the signal and does not depend on the width of temporal windows in the formula (the latter property tends to be missing from the STL extensions, even when the authors can achieve linear complexity for a fixed formula). The most important features of the new language are as follows.

1. We remove several syntactic constrains from STL: we allow a formula to have a real-valued output signal; we allow these signals to be combined in a pointwise way with arithmetic operations, comparisons, etc. This distinguishes us from the works that use standard MTL or STL syntax and assign them new semantics [10,19].
2. We allow to apply an efficiently computable aggregate function over a sliding window. We currently focus on min and max, which are enough to specify properties that motivated the development of more expressive and hard to monitor logics.
3. We offer a version of "until" operator that performs aggregation over a sliding window of dynamic width, that depends on satisfaction of some formula. This distinguishes us from the works that focus on aggregation over a fixed window [20].

Finally, we focus our attention on continuous-time piecewise-constant and piecewise linear signals; we describe the algorithms and prepare an implementation only for piecewise-constant.

2 Motivating Examples

Before formally defining the new language, let us look at some examples of properties that we would like to express. In particular, we look at properties that motivated the development of more expressive and harder to monitor logics.

Example 1 (Stabilization). The first interesting property is stabilization around a value that is not known in advance, e.g., "x stays within 0.05 units of some value for at least 200 time units". It is tempting, to formalize this property using existential quantification "there exists a threshold v, such that…", which is possible with first-order logic of signals (and was one of its motivational properties [2]), but it is actually not necessary. Instead, we can compute the minimum and maximum of x over the next 200 time units and compare their distance to $0.1 = 2 \cdot 0.05$. In some imaginary language, we could write

$\max_{[0,200]} x - \min_{[0,200]} x \leq 0.1$. At this point we propose to separate the aggregate operators from the operator that defines the temporal window, which will be useful later, when the "until" operator will define a window of variable width. We use the operator $\text{On}_{[a,b]}$ to define the temporal window of constant width and the operators Min and Max (capitalized) to denote the minimum and maximum over the previously defined window. *Signal x stabilizes within* 0.05 *units of an unknown value for* 200 *time units:*

$$\text{On}_{[0,200]}\, \text{Max}\, x - \text{On}_{[0,200]}\, \text{Min}\, x \leq 0.1$$

Figure 1 shows an example of a signal $x(t)$ (red) performing damped oscillation with the period of 250 time units. Blue and green curves are the maximum and the minimum of x over a siding window $[t, t + 200]$. Finally, the orange Boolean signal (its y scale is on the right) evaluates to true (i.e., $y = 1$) when the maximum and minimum of x over the next 200 time units are within 0.1.

Example 2 (Local Maximum). Consider the property: "the current value of x is a minimum or maximum in some neighbourhood of current time point". Previously, a similar property became a motivation to extend STL with freeze quantifiers [6], but we can also express it by comparing the value of a signal with some aggregate information about its neighbourhood, which we can do similarly to the previous example.
Current value of x is a local maximum on the interval [0, 85] *relative to the current time.*

$$x \geq \text{On}_{[0,85]}\, \text{Max}\, x$$

Figure 2 shows an example of a sine wave $x(t)$ (red) with the period of 250 time units. Blue curve is the maximum x over a siding window $[t, t + 85]$. The orange Boolean signal evaluates to true when the current value of x is a maximum for the next 85 time units.

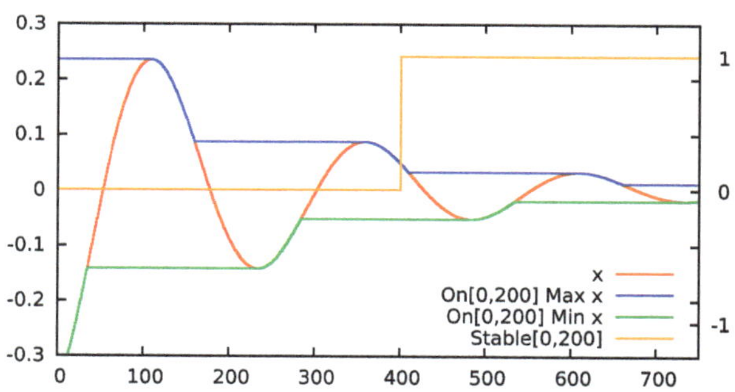

Fig. 1. Damped oscillation $x(t)$ and its maximum and minimum over the window $[t, t + 200]$. (Color figure online)

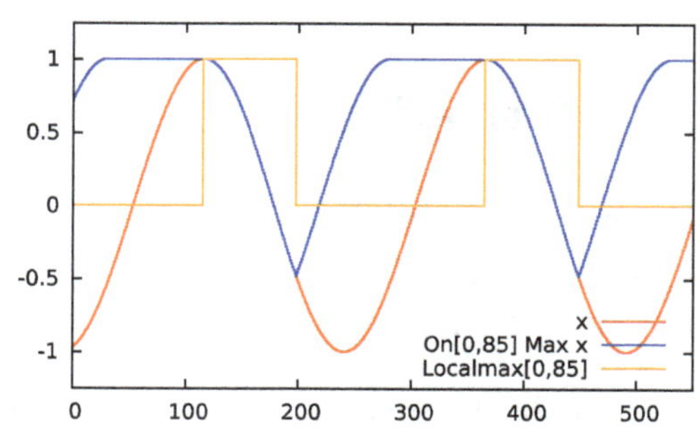

Fig. 2. Sine wave $x(t)$, its maximum over the window $[t, t + 200]$, and whether $x(t)$ is a local maximum on the interval $[t, t + 200]$. (Color figure online)

Example 3 (Stabilization Contd.). We want to be able to assert that x becomes stable around some value not for a fixed duration, but until some signal q becomes true. We will be able to do this with our version of "until" operator. *Signal x is stable within* 0.05 *units of an unknown value until q becomes true:*

$$(\mathrm{Max}\, x \ \mathrm{U}\ q) - (\mathrm{Min}\, x \ \mathrm{U}\ q) \leq 0.1$$

Intuitively, for a given time point, we want the monitor to find the closest future time point, where q holds and compute Min and Max of x over the resulting interval. Note that this property cannot be easily monitored in the framework of "STL with pre-processing", since it requires the monitor to compute Min and Max over a sliding window of variable width, which depends on the satisfaction signal of q.

Example 4 (Linear Increase). At this point, we can assert x to follow a more complex shape, for example, to increase or decrease with a given slope. Let T denote an auxiliary signal that linearly increases with rate 1 (like a clock of a timed automaton), i.e. we define $T(t) = t$; this example works as well for $T(t) = t + c$, where c is a constant. To specify that x increases with the rate 2.5, we assert that the distance from x to $2.5 \cdot \mathrm{T}$ stays within some bounds.
Signal x increases approximately with slope 2.5 *during the next* 100 *time units:*

$$\mathrm{On}_{[0,100]}\, \mathrm{Max}\, |x - 2.5\mathrm{T}| - \mathrm{On}_{[0,100]}\, \mathrm{Min}\, |x - 2.5\mathrm{T}| \leq 0.1$$

3 Syntax and Semantics

From the examples above we can foresee how the new language looks like. Formally, an *(input) signal* is a function $w : \mathbb{T} \to \mathbb{R}^n$, where the time domain $\mathbb{T}$ is a closed real interval $[0, |w|] \subseteq \mathbb{R}$, and the number $|w|$ is the *duration* of the signal. We refer to signal components using their own letters: $x, y, \dots \in \mathbb{T} \to \mathbb{R}$. We assume that every signal component is piecewise-constant or piecewise-linear.

The semantics of a formula is a piecewise-constant or piecewise-linear function from real time (thus, has real-valued switching points) to a dual number (rather than a real). We defer the discussion of dual numbers until Sect. 3.2; for now we note that they extend reals, and a dual number can be written in the form $a + b\varepsilon$, which, when $b \neq 0$, denotes a point infinitely close to a. We denote the set of dual numbers as $\mathbb{R}_\varepsilon$. Our primary use of a dual number is to represent a time point strictly after an event (switching point, threshold crossing, etc.) but before any other event can happen; as a result we have to allow an output signal to have a dual value, denoting a value that is attained at this dual time point.

Syntax. We can write the abstract syntax of our language as follows:

$$\begin{aligned} \varphi &::= c \mid x \mid f(\varphi_1 \cdots \varphi_n) \mid \mathrm{On}_{[a,b]}\, \psi \mid \psi\ \mathrm{U}^d_{[a,b]}\ \varphi \mid \varphi_1 {\downarrow}\ \mathrm{U}^d_{[a,b]} \varphi_2 \\ \psi &::= \mathrm{Min}\, \varphi \mid \mathrm{Max}\, \varphi \end{aligned} \tag{1}$$

where c is a real-valued constant; x refers to an input signal; f is a real-valued function symbol (e.g., sum, absolute value, etc.); for the On-operator, a and b can be real numbers or (with some abuse of notation) $\pm\infty$, i.e., the interval may refer to both past and future, bounded or unbounded; for the U-operator, d is a real value, and a, b are non-negative, and b can be ∞, i.e., the interval refers to bounded or unbounded future. Let us go over some of the features of the new language and then formally write down its semantics.

Point-wise Functions. Function symbol f ranges over real-valued functions $\mathbb{R}^n \to \mathbb{R}$ that preserve the chosen shape of signals (and can be lifted to dual numbers). In this paper, we focus on piecewise-constant and piecewise-linear signals, so when f is applied point-wise to a piecewise-constant input, we want the result to be piecewise-constant; when f is applied point-wise to a piecewise-linear input, we want the result to be piecewise-linear. Examples of such functions are addition, subtraction, min and max of finitely many operands (we use lowercase min and max to denote a real-valued n-ary function), multiplication by a constant, absolute value, etc.

Boolean Output Signals. Output signals of some formulas can informally be interpreted as Boolean-valued. In Example 2, "x" and "$\mathrm{On}_{[0,85]}\,\mathrm{Max}\, x$" are dual-valued, but the result of their comparison, "$x \geq \mathrm{On}_{[0,85]}\,\mathrm{Max}\, x$" should be interpreted as Boolean. Here, we take the more simple path and treat a Boolean signal as a special case of a real-valued signal that can take the value of 0 or 1. We expect comparison operators to produce a value in $\{0, 1\}$, e.g., $\varphi_1 \leq \varphi_2$ is a shortcut for "if $\varphi_1 \leq \varphi_2$ then 1 else 0". Standard Boolean connectives can then be defined as follows:

$$\varphi_1 \wedge \varphi_2 = \min\{\varphi_1, \varphi_2\} \qquad \varphi_1 \vee \varphi_2 = \max\{\varphi_1, \varphi_2\} \qquad \neg\varphi = 1 - \varphi$$

Another option would be to distinguish Boolean-valued formulas on the syntactic level.

Temporal φ-Formulas. Symbol φ denotes a temporal formula that has a dual-valued output signal. In other words, it can be evaluated at a time point and produces a dual value. A φ-formula may:

1. refer to an input signal x;
2. apply a real-valued function f pointwise to the outputs its φ-subformulas;
3. apply an aggregate function over the sliding window $[a, b]$ (with some abuse of notation a can be $-\infty$, and b can be ∞);
4. be an "until" formula, which is described in Sect. 3.3.

Interval ψ-Formulas. A ψ-formula is evaluated on an interval and does not have an output signal by itself. Instead, it supplies an aggregate operation that will be computed when evaluating the containing On-formula or "until"-formula. It should be possible to efficiently compute this aggregate operation over a sliding window, and it should preserve the chosen shape of signals. Since we focus on piecewise-constant and piecewise-linear signals, the two operations that we can immediately offer are Min and Max, which can be efficiently computed over a sliding window using the algorithm of Lemire [9,15], and preserve the piecewise-constant and piecewise-linear shapes. In discrete time or for piecewise-polynomial signals, we could use more aggregate operations, e.g., integration.

"Eventually" and "Always". Standard STL "eventually" and "always" operators can be expressed in the new language as follows:

$$\mathrm{F}_{[a,b]}\,\varphi = \mathrm{On}_{[a,b]}\,\mathrm{Max}\,\varphi \qquad\qquad \mathrm{G}_{[a,b]}\,\varphi = \mathrm{On}_{[a,b]}\,\mathrm{Min}\,\varphi$$

3.1 Semantics of Until-Free Fragment

The semantics of the until-free fragment is straightforward. The semantics of a φ-formula is a function $[\![\varphi]\!] : \mathbb{T} \to \mathbb{R}_\varepsilon$ mapping real time to a dual value. We define it as:

$$\begin{aligned} &[\![x]\!](t) = x(t) \qquad\qquad [\![\mathrm{On}_{[a,b]}\,\psi]\!](t) = [\![\psi]\!]([t+a, t+b]) \\ &[\![f(\varphi_1 \dots \varphi_n)]\!](t) = f([\![\varphi_1]\!](t) \dots [\![\varphi_n]\!](t)) \end{aligned} \tag{2}$$

We abuse the notation so that x is both a symbol referring to a component of an input signal and the corresponding real-valued function; similarly, f is both a function symbol and the corresponding function.

The semantics of a ψ-formula is a function $[\![\psi]\!] : (\mathbb{R} \cup -\infty) \times (\mathbb{R}_\varepsilon \cup \infty) \to \mathbb{R}_\varepsilon$ from an interval of time with real lower bound to a dual value. The upper bound of the interval can be dual-valued, which will be used by the "until" operation (see Sect. 3.3).

$$[\![\mathrm{Min}\,\varphi]\!][a,b] = \min_{[a,b]}[\![\varphi]\!] \qquad [\![\mathrm{Max}\,\varphi]\!][a,b] = \max_{[a,b]}[\![\varphi]\!] \tag{3}$$

The way we define min and max over an interval for a discontinuous piecewise-linear function relies on dual numbers, which we explain just below.

3.2 Dual Numbers

Dual numbers extend reals with a new element ε that has a property $\varepsilon^2 = 0$. A dual number can be written in a form $a + b\varepsilon$, where $a, b \in \mathbb{R}$. We denote the set of dual numbers as $\mathbb{R}_\varepsilon$. Dual numbers were proposed by the English mathematician W. Clifford in 1873 and later applied in geometry by the German mathematician E. Study. One of modern applications of dual numbers and their extensions is in automatic differentiation [12]: one can exactly compute the value of the first derivative at a given point using the identity $f(x+\varepsilon) = f(x) + f'(x)\varepsilon$. Intuitively, ε can be understood as an infinitesimal value, and $a + b\varepsilon$ (for $b \neq 0$) is a point that is infinitely close to a. Polynomial functions can be extended to dual numbers, and via Taylor expansion, so can exponents, logarithms, and trigonometric functions. We work with piecewise-constant and piecewise-linear functions with real switching points, and we only make use of basic arithmetic. For example, if on the interval (b_1, b_2) the signal x is defined as $x(t) = a_1 t + a_0$, then $x(b_1 + \varepsilon) = a_1 b_1 + a_0 + a_1\varepsilon$ and $x(b_2 - \varepsilon) = a_1 b_2 + a_0 - a_1\varepsilon$.

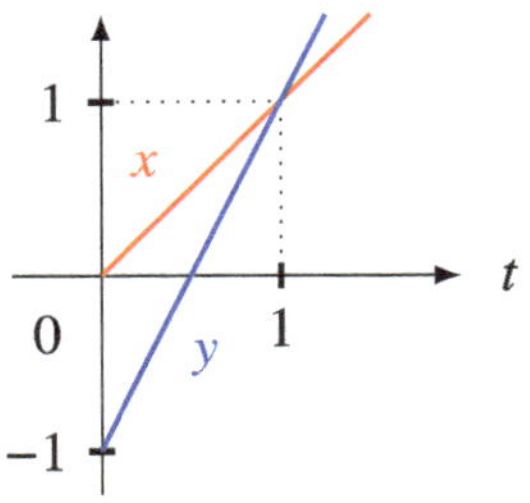

Fig. 3. Signals x and y for Example 8.

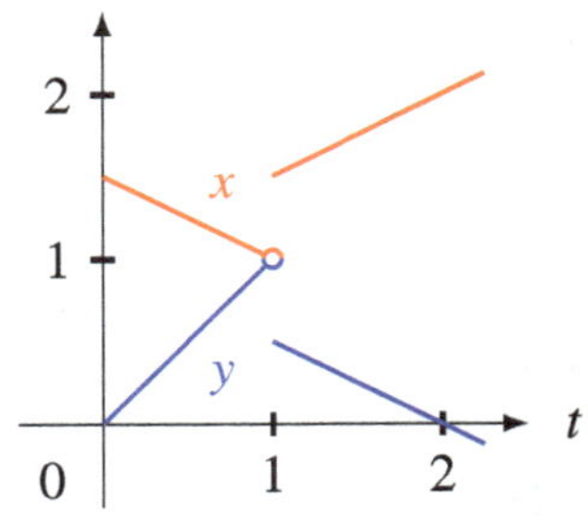

Fig. 4. Signals x and y for Examples 5 and 6.

Our primary use of a dual number is to represent a time point strictly after an event (a switching point, a threshold crossing, etc.) but before any other event can happen, i.e., we use $t' + \varepsilon$ to represent the time point that happens right after t'. The coefficient 1 at ε denotes that time advances with the rate of 1 (although another consistently used coefficient works as well). Consequently, we also allow an output signal to produce a dual value, denoting a value that is attained at this dual time point. On the other hand, we require that signals are defined over real time, switching points of piecewise signals are reals, and time constants in formulas are reals. That is, dual-valued time is only used internally by the temporal operators and cannot be directly observed.

Minimum and Maximum of a Discontinuous Function. We also use dual-valued time to define the result of Min and Max for a discontinuous piecewise-linear function. The standard way to compute minimum and maximum of a continuous piecewise-linear function on a closed interval is based on the fact that they are attained at the endpoints of the interval or at the endpoints of the segments on which the function is defined. Using dual numbers, we extend it to discontinuous functions: if for $t \in (b_1, b_2)$, $x(t) = a_1 t + a_2$ then we consider time points $b_1 + \varepsilon$ and $b_2 - \varepsilon$ as the candidates for reaching the minimum or maximum. Let us demonstrate this with an example.

Example 5. Consider the signal x defined as: "$x(t) = -0.5t + 1.5$ if $t \in [0, 1)$; $x(t) = 0.5t + 1$ if $t \geq 1$", as shown in Fig. 4. Let us find the minimum of x on the interval $[0, 2+\varepsilon]$. By our definition, $\min_{t \in [0,2+\varepsilon]} x(t) = \min\{x(0), x(1-\varepsilon), x(1), x(2+\varepsilon)\} = x(1-\varepsilon) = 1+0.5\varepsilon$. This result should be understood as follows: $x(t)$ approaches the value of 1 from the above with derivative -0.5, but never reaches it.

Example 6. Our definition of minimum and maximum allows to correctly compare values of piecewise-linear functions around their discontinuity points. In Example 5, x never reaches the value of its lower bound, and our definition of minimum produces a dual number that reflects this fact and also specifies the rate at which x approaches its lower bound. This information would be lost if we computed the infimum of x. Again consider the signals in Fig. 4, with x defined as before, and "$y(t) = t$, if $t \in [0, 1)$, $y(t) = -0.5t + 1$, if $t \geq 1$". Let us evaluate at time $t = 0$ the formula $\mathrm{On}_{[0,2]}\,\mathrm{Min}\,x > \mathrm{On}_{[0,2]}\,\mathrm{Max}\,y$, which denotes the property $\forall t, t' \in [0,2].\ x(t) > y(t')$. From the previous example, we have that $[\![\mathrm{On}_{[0,2]}\,\mathrm{Min}\,x]\!](0) = 1 + 0.5\varepsilon$. By a similar argument, $[\![\mathrm{On}_{[0,2]}\,\mathrm{Max}\,y]\!](0) = y(1-\varepsilon) = 1 - \varepsilon$, which means that y approaches 1 from below with the rate of 1. Since, $1 + 0.5\varepsilon > 1 - \varepsilon$, our property holds at time 0, as expected.

We want to emphasize that while an output signal can take a dual value, its domain is considered to be a subset of reals. The semantics of temporal operators are allowed to internally use dual-valued time points, but has to produce an output signal that is defined over real time. This ensures that a piecewise signal always has real-valued switching points and that no event can happen at a dual-valued time point.

Example 7. Consider a formula $\varphi = \mathrm{F}_{[0,2]}(x = \mathrm{On}_{(-\mathrm{inf},\mathrm{inf})}\,\mathrm{Min}\,x)$, where x is as in Fig. 4. The meaning of φ is that within 2 time units x reaches its global minimum. In our semantics, this formula does not hold at time 0. By our definition, the global minimum of x is $1 + 0.5\varepsilon$, so the semantics of the formula at time 0 is equivalent to:

$$\begin{aligned}[\![\varphi]\!](0) &= [\![\mathrm{F}_{[0,2]}(x = 1 + 0.5\varepsilon)]\!](0)\\ &= \text{ if } \exists t \in \mathbb{T}.\ t \in [0,2] \wedge x(t) = 1 + 0.5\varepsilon \text{ then } 1 \text{ else } 0\end{aligned}$$

where $\mathbb{T} = [0, |w|] \subseteq \mathbb{R}$. There is no real value of time, where $x(t)$ yields a dual value, so the formula does not hold.

3.3 Semantics of Until

The On-operator allowed us to compute minima and maxima over a sliding window of fixed width. In this section, we introduce a new version of "until" operator that allows the window to have variable width that depends on the output signal of some formula.

Reinterpreting the Classical Until as "Find First". Let us explain how we extend the "until" operator to work in the new setting. There already exists real-valued robust semantics of "until", but we do not believe it to be a good specification primitive. Instead, re-state standard the Boolean semantics and based on the re-stated version introduce the new real-(actually, dual-)valued semantics. Let us recall a possible semantics of untimed until in STL. Informally, "until" computes a conjunction of the values of the first operand over an interval that is not fixed, but defined by the second operand. Formally,

$$[\![p\ \mathrm{U}^{\mathrm{STL}}\ q]\!](t) = \exists t' \geq t.\ q(t') \wedge \forall s \in [t, t'].\ p(s)$$

To denote the STL version of "until" we write it with the superscript: $\mathrm{U}^{\mathrm{STL}}$, to distinguish from the new version that we define for our language. The version of "until" that we use in this paper is non-strict in the sense of [17]; it requites that p holds both at t and t'.

Efficient monitoring of STL "until" relies on instantiating the existential quantifier. The monitor scans the signal backwards and instantiates t' based on the earliest time point where q is true. The monitor needs to consider three cases shown in Figs. 5, 6 and 7.

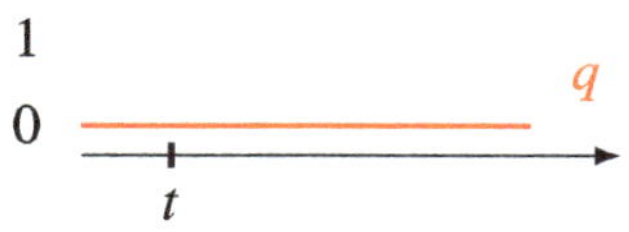

Fig. 5. Case 1: q is never true in the future.

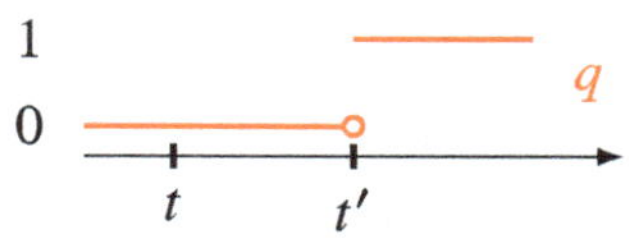

Fig. 6. Case 2: q there exists the earliest time point, where q becomes true.

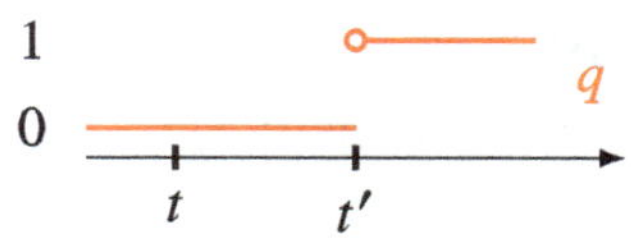

Fig. 7. Case 3: q becomes true, but there is no earliest time point.

1. Figure 5: q is false for every $t' \geq t$. Then the value of $p\ \mathrm{U}^{\mathrm{STL}}\ q$ at t is false.
2. Figure 6: there exists the smallest $t' \geq t$, where q is true (this includes the case, where $t' = t$). Then the value of $p \mathrm{U}^{\mathrm{STL}} q$ at t is $\forall s \in [t, t'].\ p(s)$ (predicate p is not shown in the figure). The monitor needs not consider time points after t', since if "forall" produces false on a smaller interval, it will produce false on a larger one.
3. Figure 7: q becomes true in the future, but there is no earliest time point. In this case, the monitor needs to take the universal quantification over an interval that ends just after t' (the switching point of q), but before any other event occurs. We can formalize this reasoning using dual numbers and say that the value of $p\ \mathrm{U}^{\mathrm{STL}}\ q$ at t is $\forall s \in [t, t' + \varepsilon].\ p(s)$, where $t' + \varepsilon$ can be intuitively understood as a time point that happens after t', but before any other event can occur.

Below is the equivalent semantics of STL until that resolves the existential quantifier:

$$[\![p\ \mathrm{U}^{\mathrm{STL}}\ q]\!](t) = \begin{cases} \forall s \in [t, t'].\ p(s), & \text{if there exists the smallest } t' \geq t, \text{ s.t. } q(t') \\ \forall s \in [t, t' + \varepsilon].\ p(s), & \text{where } t' = \inf\{t' | t' \geq t \wedge q(t')\}, \\ & \text{if } \exists t' \geq t.\ q(t'), \text{ but there is no smallest } t' \\ \mathit{false}, & \text{otherwise} \end{cases}$$

Then, a monitor evaluates the universal quantifier via a finite conjunction, since in practice the signal p has finite variability, i.e. every interval is intersected by a finite number of constant segments.

Example 8. Let us consider two linear input signals: $x(t) = t$ and $y(t) = 2t - 1$ (see Fig. 3), and let us evaluate the formula $(y \leq x)\ \mathrm{U}^{\mathrm{STL}}\ (x > 1)$ at time 0 using non-strict "until" semantics. We define the earliest time point where $x > 1$ becomes true to be $1 + \varepsilon$, thus we need to evaluate the expression $\forall t \in [0, 1 + \varepsilon].\ y(t) \leq x(t)$. At time $1 + \varepsilon$, we get $y(1 + \varepsilon) = 1 + 2\varepsilon > 1 + \varepsilon = x(1 + \varepsilon)$, thus the "until" formula does not hold. Informally, we can interpret the result as follows: when x becomes greater than 1, y becomes greater than x, while non-strict "until" requires that there exists a point, where both its left- and right-hand operands hold at the same time.

New Until as "Find First". At this point, extending "until" to produce a dual value is straightforward. With every time point, "until" possibly associates an interval, and we can compute an arbitrary aggregate function over it, instead of just conjunction. In fact, we introduce two flavors of "until". The first version: $\psi \ \mathrm{U}^{d}_{[a,b]} \ \varphi$ – works as follows. For every time point t, we either associate an interval ending when φ becomes non-zero (i.e., starts holding); or we report that no suitable end point was found. When such interval exists, we evaluate ψ on it. When the interval does not exist, we produce d. Formally,

$$[\![\psi \mathrm{U}^{d}_{[a,b]} \varphi]\!](t) = \begin{cases} [\![\psi]\!][t,t'], & \text{if } \exists \text{ the smallest } t' \in [t+a, t+b], \text{ s.t. } [\![\varphi]\!](t') \neq 0 \\ [\![\psi]\!][t,t'+\varepsilon], & \text{where } t' = \inf\{t' | t' \in [t+a, t+b] \wedge [\![\varphi]\!](t')\}, \\ & \quad \text{if } \exists t' \in [t+a, t+b].\ [\![\varphi]\!](t') \neq 0, \text{ but there is no smallest } t' \\ d, & \text{otherwise} \end{cases}$$

The second version: $\varphi_1 \downarrow \mathrm{U}^{d}_{[a,b]} \varphi_2$ does not perform aggregation, but evaluates φ_1 at the time point where φ_2 becomes non-zero, or produces d if such time point does not exist:

$$[\![\varphi_1 \downarrow \mathrm{U}^{d}_{[a,b]} \varphi_2]\!](t) = \begin{cases} [\![\varphi_1]\!](t'), & \text{if } \exists \text{ the smallest } t' \in [t+a, t+b], \text{ s.t. } [\![\varphi_2]\!](t') \neq 0 \\ [\![\varphi_1]\!](t'+\varepsilon), & \text{where } t' = \inf\{t' | t' \in [t+a, t+b] \wedge [\![\varphi_2]\!](t')\}, \\ & \quad \text{if } \exists t' \in [t+a, t+b].\ [\![\varphi_2]\!](t') \neq 0, \text{ but there is no smallest } t' \\ d, & \text{otherwise} \end{cases}$$

In a similar way, we could define past versions "until", where the interval $[a, b]$ refers to the past; we do not discuss them here due to space constraints.

STL Until. The standard STL "until" can be expressed in the new language as follows:

$$\varphi_1 \ \mathrm{U}^{\mathrm{STL}}_{[a,b]} \ \varphi_2 = (\mathrm{Min}\, \varphi_1) \ \mathrm{U}^{0}_{[a,b]} \ \varphi_2$$

Lookup. Using "until", we can express the "lookup" operator that queries the value of a signal at a point in the future, or returns some default value if the point does not exist.

$$\mathrm{D}^{d}_{a} \varphi = \varphi \downarrow \mathrm{U}^{d}_{[a,a]} 1$$

Example 9 (Spike). The ST-Lib library [14] uses the following formula to define a start point of a spike: $x' > m \wedge \mathrm{F}_{[0,d]}(x' < -m)$, where x' is the approximation of the right derivative $x'(t) = (x(t+\delta) - x(t))/\delta$, m is the magnitude of the spike, and d is the width. Using the lookup operator, we can include the definition of x' in the property itself:

$$(\mathrm{D}^{y}_{\delta}\, x - x)/\delta \geq m \wedge \mathrm{F}_{[0,d]}((\mathrm{D}^{y}_{\delta}\, x - x)/\delta \leq -m)$$

where y gives the value of the signal outside of its original domain.

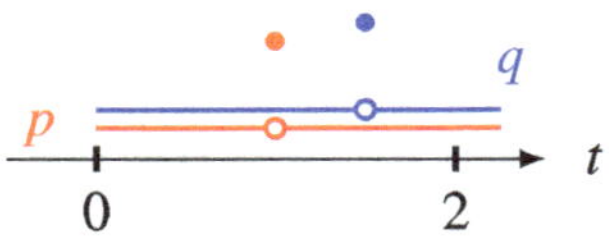

Fig. 8. Before time 2, an event p is followed by an event q.

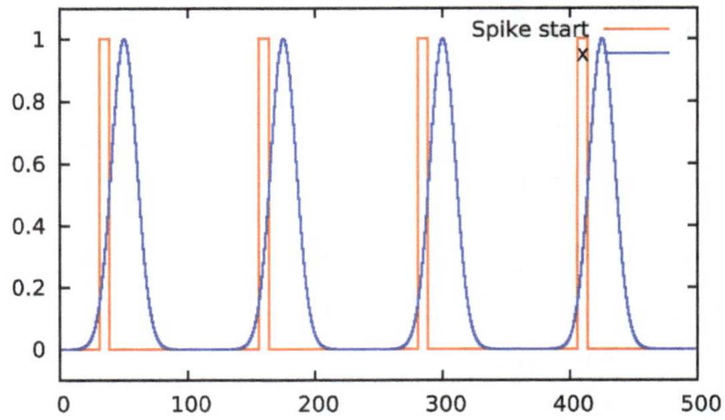

Fig. 9. A sequence of spikes and a Boolean signal marking the detected start times of spikes. (Color figure online)

Example 10 (Spike of Given Width and Height). Our language offers several alternative ways to define a spike. We can define a (start point of a) spike by composing two ramps: an increasing one, where the signal x increases by at least m withing w time units, and a decreasing one, where x decreases by at least m within w time units; the two ramps should be at most w units apart. The parameter w is the half-width of the spike.

$$(\mathrm{On}_{[0,w]} \operatorname{Max} x \geq x + m) \wedge \mathrm{F}_{[0,w]}(\mathrm{On}_{[0,w]} \operatorname{Min} x \leq x - m)$$

Figure 9 shows an example of a series of spikes (blue) and a Boolean signal (red) that marks the detected start times of spikes.

Example 11 (TPTL-like Assertion). The second form of "until" allows to reason explicitly about time points and durations, somewhat similarly to TPTL. Consider the property "within 2 time units, we should observe an event p followed by an event q" (Fig. 8 shows an example of a satisfying signal). With some case analysis, this property can be expressed in MTL [5], but probably the best way to express it is offered by TPTL, that allows to assert "$c.\,\mathrm{F}(p \wedge \mathrm{F}(q \wedge c \leq 2))$", meaning "reset a clock c, eventually, we should observe p and from that point, eventually we should observe q, while the clock value will be at most 2". To express the property in our language, we introduce three auxiliary signals: $T(t) = t$ (which we use in some other examples as well), $pdelay = (T \downarrow \mathrm{U}^{\infty} p) - T$, which denotes the duration until the next occurrence of p and similarly $qdelay = (T \downarrow \mathrm{U}^{\infty} q) - T$, the duration until the next occurrence of q. Then, the property can be expressed as: $pdelay + (qdelay \downarrow \mathrm{U}^{\infty} p) \leq 2$.

4 Monitoring

Similarly to other works on STL monitoring (e.g., [9]), we implement the algorithms for a subset of the language, and support the remaining operators via rewriting rules.

Rewriting of Until. Similarly to STL, the timed "until" operator in our language can be expressed in terms of "eventually" (which is expressed using On), "lookup", and untimed "until".

$$(\mathrm{Min}\,\varphi_1)\,\mathrm{U}^d_{[a,b]}\,\varphi_2 = \text{ if } \neg\,\mathrm{F}_{[a,b]}\,\varphi_2 \text{ then } d \text{ else } \mathrm{On}_{[0,a]}\,\mathrm{Min}((\mathrm{Min}\,\varphi_1)\,\mathrm{U}\,\varphi_2)$$
$$(\mathrm{Max}\,\varphi_1)\,\mathrm{U}^d_{[a,b]}\,\varphi_2 = \text{ if } \neg\,\mathrm{F}_{[a,b]}\,\varphi_2 \text{ then } d \text{ else } \mathrm{On}_{[0,a]}\,\mathrm{Max}((\mathrm{Max}\,\varphi_1)\,\mathrm{U}\,\varphi_2)$$
$$\varphi_1\!\downarrow \mathrm{U}^d_{[a,b]}\varphi_2 = \text{ if } \neg\,\mathrm{F}_{[a,b]}\,\varphi_2 \text{ then } d \text{ else } \mathrm{D}_a(\varphi_1\!\downarrow \mathrm{U}\varphi_2)$$

Let us prove that the first equivalence is true, and for the other two the proof idea is similar. Let t be the time point where we evaluate $(\mathrm{Min}\,\varphi_1)\mathrm{U}^d_{[a,b]}\varphi_2$ and its rewriting. If there is no time point $s \in [t+a, t+b]$ where φ_2 holds, both the original formula and its rewriting evaluate to d. Otherwise, let s be the earliest time point in $[t+a, t+b]$, where φ_2 holds, which can be a real or dual value, as explained in Sect. 3.3. Then the original formula evaluates to $\min\{[\![\varphi_1]\!](t') \mid t' \in [t, s]\}$. The rewritten formula at t evaluates to $\min\{[\![(\mathrm{Min}\,\varphi_1)\ \mathrm{U}\ \varphi_2]\!] \mid t' \in [t, t+a]\}$. Notice that for every t' there is a time point in the future, which we denote $g(t')$ where φ_2 holds, which is at most s, and for $t' = t + a$ it is exactly s. That is, the rewritten formula evaluates to $\min\{\min\{[\![\varphi_1]\!](t'') \mid t'' \in [t', g(t')]\} \mid t' \in [t, t+a]\} = \min\{[\![\varphi_1]\!](t'') \mid t'' \in \bigcup\{[t', g(t')] \mid t' \in [t, t+a]\}\}$. Notice that since $g(t') \in [t', s]$ and $g(t+a) = s$, then $\bigcup\{[t', g(t')] \mid t' \in [t, t+a]\} = [t, s]$, and thus the rewritten formula evaluates to the same value as the original one.

Referring to Both Future and Past. In the syntax, we allow the $\mathrm{On}_{[a,b]}$ operator to refer to both future and past, i.e., we allow the case when $a < 0$ and $b > 0$. Algorithms for Min/Max over a running window typically cannot work with this situation directly, and we need to apply the following rewriting: if $a < 0$ and $b > 0$,

$$\mathrm{On}_{[a,b]}\,\mathrm{Min}\,\varphi = \min\{\mathrm{On}_{[a,0]}\,\mathrm{Min}\,\varphi,\ \mathrm{On}_{[0,b]}\,\mathrm{Min}\,\varphi\}$$
$$\mathrm{On}_{[a,b]}\,\mathrm{Max}\,\varphi = \max\{\mathrm{On}_{[a,0]}\,\mathrm{Max}\,\varphi,\ \mathrm{On}_{[0,b]}\,\mathrm{Max}\,\varphi\}$$

Language of the Monitor. The following subset of the language is equally expressive as the full language presented in (1). We implement the monitoring algorithms for this language, and the full syntax of (1) we support via rewriting.

$$\varphi ::= c \mid x \mid f(\varphi_1 \cdots \varphi_n) \mid \mathrm{On}_{[a,b]}\,\psi \mid \psi\ \mathrm{U}^d\ \varphi \mid \varphi_1\!\downarrow \mathrm{U}^d\varphi_2 \mid \mathrm{D}^d_a\,\varphi$$
$$\psi ::= \mathrm{Min}\,\varphi \mid \mathrm{Max}\,\varphi$$

where either $a \geq 0$ or $b \leq 0$, i.e., the interval $[a, b]$ cannot refer to both future and past.

All operators in the language of the monitor admit efficient offline monitoring. Minimum and maximum over a sliding window required by the On-operator can be computed using a variation of Lemire's algorithm [9,15]; "lookup" operator D shifts its input signal by a constant distance; and for untimed "until" we can scan the input signal backwards and perform a special case of running minimum or maximum.

4.1 Monitoring Algorithms

In this section, we briefly describe monitoring algorithms for piecewise-constant signals.

Representation of Signals. We represent a piecewise-constant function $\mathbb{T} \to \mathbb{R}$ or $\mathbb{T} \to \mathbb{R}_\varepsilon$ as a sequence of segments: $\langle s_0, s_1, \ldots, s_{m-1} \rangle$, where every segment $s_i = J_i \mapsto v_i$ maps an interval J_i to a real or dual value v_i. The intervals J_i form a partition the domain of the signal and are ordered in ascending time order, i.e., $\sup J_i = \inf J_{i+1}$ and $J_i \cap J_{i+1} = \varnothing$. The domain of the signal corresponding to the sequence $u = \langle J_0 \mapsto v_o, \ldots, J_{m-1} \mapsto v_{m-1} \rangle$ is denoted by $dom(u) = J_0 \cup \ldots \cup J_{m-1}$. For example, if the function $x(t)$ is defined as $x(t) = 0$, if $t \in [0, 1)$, and $x(t) = 1$, if $t \in [1, 2]$, then $x(t)$ is represented by the sequence $u_x = \langle [0, 1) \mapsto 0, [1, 2] \mapsto 1 \rangle$, and $dom(u_x) = [0, 2]$.

Empty brackets $\langle\rangle$ denote an empty sequence that does not represent a valid signal, but can be used by algorithms as an intermediate value. We manipulate the sequences with two main operations. The function *append* adds a segment to the end of a sequence: $append(\langle s_0, \ldots, s_{m-1} \rangle, s') = \langle s_0, \ldots, s_{m-1}, s' \rangle$. The function *prepend* adds a segment to the start of a sequence: $prepend(\langle s_0, \ldots, s_{m-1} \rangle, s') = \langle s', s_0, \ldots, s_{m-1} \rangle$. This may produce a sequence where the first segment does not start time at time 0. While such a sequence does not represent a valid signal, it can be used by the algorithms as an intermediate value. The function *removeLast* removes the last segment of a sequence, assuming it was non-empty: $removeLast(\langle s_0, \ldots, s_{m-1} \rangle) = \langle s_0, \ldots, s_{m-2} \rangle$.

An output signal of a formula is scalar-valued and is represented by one such sequence. An input signal usually has multiple components, i.e., it is a function $\mathbb{T} \to \mathbb{R}^n$, and is represented by a set of n sequences.

On-Formulas. For $\mathrm{On}_{[a,b]} \mathrm{Min}\, \varphi$ and $\mathrm{On}_{[a,b]} \mathrm{Max}\, \varphi$, a monitor needs to compute the minimum or maximum of the output signal of φ over the sliding window. The corresponding algorithm was developed for discrete time by Lemire [15] and later adapted for continuous time [9].

Lookup-Formulas. Computing the output signal for $\mathrm{D}^d_a\, \varphi$ is straightforward. We need to shift every segment of u_φ (the representation of the output signal of φ) to the left by a truncating at 0 and append a padding segment with the value of d.

Until-Formulas. Informally, monitoring the "until"-formulas, $\mathrm{Min}\, \varphi_1 \mathrm{U}^d\, \varphi_2$, $\mathrm{Max}\, \varphi_1 \mathrm{U}^d\, \varphi_2$, and $\varphi_1 \downarrow \mathrm{U}^d \varphi_2$, works as follows. The monitor scans the output signals of φ_1 and φ_2 backwards. While φ_2 evaluates to a non-zero value, the monitor outputs the value of φ_1. When φ_2 evaluates to 0, the monitor outputs either the default value (if the monitor did not yet encounter a non-zero value of φ_2), or the running minimum or maximum of φ_1, or the value that φ_1 had at the last time point where φ_2 was non-zero.

The function *until* and *untilAnd* in Fig. 10 implement this idea. The inputs to the function *until* are: sequences u_1 and u_2 representing the output signals of φ_1 and φ_2 (with $dom(u_1) = dom(u_2)$), default value d, and the function f used for aggregation; it can be min, max, or the special function $\lambda x, y.\ x$ which

```
function until(u_1, u_2, f, d)
  let u_1 = ⟨J^1_0 ↦ v^1_0, ..., J^1_{m-1} ↦ v^1_{m-1}⟩
  let u_2 = ⟨J^2_0 ↦ v^2_0, ..., J^2_{k-1} ↦ v^2_{k-1}⟩
  i ← m − 1, j ← k − 1
  (u_r, s, v′) ← (⟨⟩, 0, d)
  while i ≥ 0 ∧ j ≥ 0 do
    J ← J^1_i ∩ J^2_j
    (u_r, s, v′) ← untilAdd(u_r, s, v′, J, v^1_i, v^2_j)
    if ∃t_1 ∈ J^1_i. ∀t_2 ∈ J^2_j. t_1 > t_2 then
      j ← j + 1
    else if ∃t_2 ∈ J^2_j. ∀t_1 ∈ J^1_i. t_2 > t_1
    then
      i ← i + 1
    else
      i ← i + 1, j ← j + 1
    end
  end
  return u_r
end
```

```
function untilAdd(u_r, s, v′, J, v_1, v_2)
  if v_2 ≠ 0 then
    v′ ← v_1
    s ← 1
  else if s ≠ 0 then
    v′ ← f(v′, v_1)
  end
  prepend(u_r, J ↦ v′)
  return (u_r, s, v′)
end
```

Fig. 10. Algorithm for monitoring "until"-formulas.

returns the value of its first argument and which we use to monitor the formula $\varphi_1 \downarrow \mathrm{U}^d \varphi_2$. The function *until* scans the input sequences backwards and iterates over intervals where both input signals maintain a constant value (J). Each such interval is passed to the function *untilAdd*, which updates the state of the algorithm (v', s) and constructs the output signal (u_r).

5 Implementation and Experiments

We implemented the monitoring algorithm in a prototype tool that is available at https://gitlab.com/abakhirkin/StlEval. The tool has a number of limitations, notably it can only use piecewise-constant interpolation (so we cannot evaluate examples that use the auxiliary signal $T(t) = t$) and does not support past-time operators. It is written in C++ and uses double-precision floating point numbers for time points and signal values. We evaluate the tool using a number of synthetic signals and a number of properties based on the ones described earlier in the paper.

Signals. We use the following signals discretized with time step 1.

- x_{sin} – sine wave with amplitude 1 and period 250; see red curve in Fig. 2.
- x_{decay} – damped oscillation with period 250. For $t \in [0, 1000)$, x defined as $x_{\text{decay}}(t) = \frac{1}{e}\sin(250t + 250)e^{-\frac{1}{250}x}$, see red curve in Fig. 1; for $t \geq 1000$, the pattern repeats;

- x_{spike} – series of spikes; a single spike is defined for $t \in [0, 125)$ as: $x_{\text{spike}}(t) = e^{\frac{(t-50)^2}{2 \cdot 10^2}}$, and after that the pattern repeats; see blue curve in Fig. 9.

Properties. We use the following properties:

- $\varphi_{\text{stab}} = \mathrm{G}\,\mathrm{F}\,(\mathrm{On}_{[0,200]}\,\mathrm{Max}\,x - \mathrm{On}_{[0,200]}\,\mathrm{Min}\,x \le 0.1)$, x always eventually becomes stable around some value for 200 time units.
- $\varphi_{\text{stab-0}} = \mathrm{G}\,\mathrm{F}\,\mathrm{G}_{[0,200]}(|x| \le 0.05)$: x always eventually becomes stable around 0 for 200 time units.
- $\varphi_{\text{until}} = \mathrm{G}_{[0,20k]}\,\mathrm{F}\,\big((\mathrm{Max}\,x)\mathrm{U}^{\infty}_{[200,\infty)}(|x'| \ge 0.1)\big) - \big((\mathrm{Min}\,x)\mathrm{U}^{-\infty}_{[200,\infty)}(|x'| \ge 0.1)\big) \le 0.1$, where $x' = (\mathrm{D}^0_1\,x - x)$, x always eventually becomes stable for at least 200 time units and then starts changing with derivative of at least 0.1.
- $\varphi_{\text{max-min}} = \mathrm{G}\,\big((x \ge \mathrm{On}_{[0,85]}\,\mathrm{Max}\,x) \Rightarrow \mathrm{F}(x \le \mathrm{On}_{[0,85]}\,\mathrm{Min}\,x)\big)$, every local maximum is followed by a local minimum.
- $\varphi_{\text{above-below}} = \mathrm{G}\,\big(x \ge 0.85 \Rightarrow (\mathrm{F}\,x \le -0.85)\big)$, if x is above 0.85, it should eventually become below −0.85.
- $\varphi_{\text{spike}} = (\mathrm{On}_{[0,16]}\,\mathrm{Max}\,x \ge x + 0.5) \wedge \mathrm{F}_{[0,16]}(\mathrm{On}_{[0,16]}\,\mathrm{Min}\,x \le x - 0.5)$, spike of half-width 16 and height at least 0.5.
- $\varphi_{\text{spike-stlib}} = \mathrm{F}\,\big(x' \ge 0.04 \wedge \mathrm{F}_{[0,25]}(x' \le -0.04)\big)$, where $x' = (\mathrm{D}^0_1\,x - x)$, spike of width at most 25 and magnitude 0.04.

Some properties are expressed in our language using On- and "until"-operators, and some are STL properties. This allows us to see how much time it takes to monitor a more complicated property in our language (e.g., φ_{stab}, stabilization around an unknown value) compared to a similar but more simple STL property (e.g., $\varphi_{\text{stab-0}}$, stabilization around a known value). In our experiments we see a constant factor between 2 and 5.

Table 1 shows the evaluation results. A row gives a formula and a signal shape; a column gives the number of samples in the input signal, and a table cell gives two time figures in seconds: the monitoring time excluding the time required to read the input data, and the total runtime of an executable. We note that for our tool, the total runtime is dominated by the time required to read the input signal from a text file. For the three STL properties we include the time it took AMT 2.0 (a monitoring tool written in Java [18]) and Breach (a Matlab toolbox partially written in C++ [8]; Breach does not have a standalone executable, so the we leave the corresponding columns empty) to evaluate the formula. This way we show that our implementation of STL monitoring has good enough performance to be used as a baseline when evaluating the cost of the added expressiveness in the new language. Time figures were obtained using a PC with a Core i3-2120 CPU and 8 GB RAM running 64-bit Debian 8.

Table 1. Monitoring time for different formulas and signals.

		This paper				AMT 2.0				Breach			
		100k		1M		100k		1M		100k		1M	
φ_{stab}	x_{decay}	0.004	0.05	0.048	0.39								
$\varphi_{\text{stab-0}}$	x_{decay}	0.003	0.04	0.023	0.38	0.59	4.0	2.4	7.3	0.053	-	0.42	-
φ_{until}	x_{decay}	0.01	0.05	0.097	0.43								
$\varphi_{\text{max-min}}$	x_{sin}	0.007	0.04	0.07	0.4								
$\varphi_{\text{above-below}}$	x_{sin}	0.002	0.04	0.02	0.36	0.6	3.1	2.4	7.5	0.05	-	0.4	-
φ_{spike}	x_{spike}	0.01	0.05	0.1	0.45								
$\varphi_{\text{spike-stlib}}$	x_{spike}	0.006	0.05	0.05	0.43	1.0	4.0	5.0	13	0.058	-	0.47	-

6 Conclusion and Future Work

We describe a new specification language that extends STL with the ability to produce and manipulate real-valued output signals (while in STL, every formula has a Boolean output signal). Properties in the new language are specified in terms of minima and maxima over a sliding window, which can have fixed width, when using a generalization of F- and G-operators, or variable width, when using a new version "until". We show how the new language can express properties that motivated the creation of more expressive and harder to monitor logics. Offline monitoring for the new language is almost as efficient as STL monitoring; the complexity is linear in the length of the input signal and does not depend on the constants appearing in the formula.

There are multiple directions for future work; perhaps more interesting one is adding integration over a sliding window (in addition to minimum and maximum). This is already allowed by some formalisms [7], and when added to our language will allow to assert that a signal approximates the behaviour of a system defined by a given differential equation (since we will be able to assert $y(t) \approx \int_0^t x(t)dt$). Before making integration available, we wish to investigate how to better deal in a specification language with approximation errors. Finally, we wish to make our language usable in falsification, which means that for every formula with Boolean output signal we wish to be able to compute a real-valued robustness measure.

Acknowledgements. The authors thank T. Ferrére, D. Nickovic, E. Asarin for comments on the draft of this paper, and O. Lebeltel for providing a version of AMT for the experiments.

References

1. Alur, R., Henzinger, T.A.: A really temporal logic. J. ACM **41**(1), 181–204 (1994)
2. Bakhirkin, A., Ferrère, T., Henzinger, T.A., Nickovic, D.: The first-order logic of signals: keynote. In: Brandenburg, B.B., Sankaranarayanan, S. (eds.) International Conference on Embedded Software (EMSOFT), pp. 1:1–1:10. ACM (2018)

3. Bartocci, E., et al.: Specification-based monitoring of cyber-physical systems: a survey on theory, tools and applications. In: Bartocci, E., Falcone, Y. (eds.) Lectures on Runtime Verification. LNCS, vol. 10457, pp. 135–175. Springer, Cham (2018). https://doi.org/10.1007/978-3-319-75632-5_5
4. Basin, D.A., Klaedtke, F., Müller, S., Zalinescu, E.: Monitoring metric first-order temporal properties. J. ACM **62**(2), 15:1–15:45 (2015)
5. Bouyer, P., Chevalier, F., Markey, N.: On the expressiveness of TPTL and MTL. Inf. Comput. **208**(2), 97–116 (2010)
6. Brim, L., Dluhos, P., Safránek, D., Vejpustek, T.: STL*: extending signal temporal logic with signal-value freezing operator. Inf. Comput. **236**, 52–67 (2014)
7. Claessen, K., Smallbone, N., Eddeland, J., Ramezani, Z., Akesson, K.: Using valued Booleans to find simpler counterexamples in random testing of cyber-physical systems. In: Workshop on Discrete Event Systems (WODES) (2018)
8. Donzé, A.: Breach, a toolbox for verification and parameter synthesis of hybrid systems. In: Touili, T., Cook, B., Jackson, P. (eds.) CAV 2010. LNCS, vol. 6174, pp. 167–170. Springer, Heidelberg (2010). https://doi.org/10.1007/978-3-642-14295-6_17
9. Donzé, A., Ferrère, T., Maler, O.: Efficient robust monitoring for STL. In: Sharygina, N., Veith, H. (eds.) CAV 2013. LNCS, vol. 8044, pp. 264–279. Springer, Heidelberg (2013). https://doi.org/10.1007/978-3-642-39799-8_19
10. Donzé, A., Maler, O.: Robust satisfaction of temporal logic over real-valued signals. In: Chatterjee, K., Henzinger, T.A. (eds.) FORMATS 2010. LNCS, vol. 6246, pp. 92–106. Springer, Heidelberg (2010). https://doi.org/10.1007/978-3-642-15297-9_9
11. Elgyütt, A., Ferrère, T., Henzinger, T.A.: Monitoring temporal logic with clock variables. In: Jansen, D.N., Prabhakar, P. (eds.) FORMATS 2018. LNCS, vol. 11022, pp. 53–70. Springer, Cham (2018). https://doi.org/10.1007/978-3-030-00151-3_4
12. Fike, J.A., Alonso, J.J.: Automatic differentiation through the use of hyper-dual numbers for second derivatives. In: Forth, S., Hovland, P., Phipps, E., Utke, J., Walther, A. (eds.) Recent Advances in Algorithmic Differentiation, vol. 87, pp. 163–173. Springer, Heidelberg (2012). https://doi.org/10.1007/978-3-642-30023-3_15
13. Havelund, K., Peled, D.: Efficient runtime verification of first-order temporal properties. In: Gallardo, M.M., Merino, P. (eds.) SPIN 2018. LNCS, vol. 10869, pp. 26–47. Springer, Cham (2018). https://doi.org/10.1007/978-3-319-94111-0_2
14. Kapinski, J., et al.: ST-Lib: a library for specifying and classifying model behaviors. In: SAE Technical Paper. SAE International, April 2016
15. Lemire, D.: Streaming maximum-minimum filter using no more than three comparisons per element. Nordic J. Comput. **13**(4), 328–339 (2006)
16. Maler, O., Nickovic, D.: Monitoring temporal properties of continuous signals. In: Lakhnech, Y., Yovine, S. (eds.) FORMATS/FTRTFT -2004. LNCS, vol. 3253, pp. 152–166. Springer, Heidelberg (2004). https://doi.org/10.1007/978-3-540-30206-3_12
17. Nickovic, D.: Checking timed and hybrid properties: theory and applications. (Vérification de propriétés temporisées et hybrides: théorie et applications). Ph.D. thesis, Joseph Fourier University, Grenoble, France (2008)
18. Nickovic, D., Lebeltel, O., Maler, O., Ferrère, T., Ulus, D.: AMT 2.0: qualitative and quantitative trace analysis with extended signal temporal logic. In: Beyer, D., Huisman, M. (eds.) TACAS 2018. LNCS, vol. 10806, pp. 303–319. Springer, Heidelberg (2018). https://doi.org/10.1007/978-3-319-89963-3_18

19. Rodionova, A., Bartocci, E., Nickovic, D., Grosu, R.: Temporal logic as filtering. In: Dependable Software Systems Engineering, pp. 164–185 (2017)
20. Silvetti, S., Nenzi, L., Bartocci, E., Bortolussi, L.: Signal convolution logic. In: Lahiri, S.K., Wang, C. (eds.) ATVA 2018. LNCS, vol. 11138, pp. 267–283. Springer, Cham (2018). https://doi.org/10.1007/978-3-030-01090-4_16

VyPR2: A Framework for Runtime Verification of Python Web Services

Joshua Heneage Dawes[1,2(✉)], Giles Reger[1], Giovanni Franzoni[2], Andreas Pfeiffer[2], and Giacomo Govi[3]

[1] University of Manchester, Manchester, UK
[2] CERN, Geneva, Switzerland
joshua.dawes@cern.ch
[3] Fermi National Accelerator Laboratory, Batavia, IL, USA

Abstract. Runtime Verification (RV) is the process of checking whether a run of a system holds a given property. In order to perform such a check online, the algorithm used to monitor the property must induce minimal overhead. This paper focuses on two areas that have received little attention from the RV community: Python programs and web services. Our first contribution is the VyPR runtime verification tool for single-threaded Python programs. The tool handles specifications in our, previously introduced, Control-Flow Temporal Logic (CFTL), which supports the specification of state and time constraints over runs of functions. VyPR minimally (in terms of reachability) instruments the input program with respect to a CFTL specification and then uses instrumentation information to optimise the monitoring algorithm. Our second contribution is the lifting of VyPR to the web service setting, resulting in the VyPR2 tool. We first describe the necessary modifications to the architecture of VyPR, and then describe our experience applying VyPR2 to a service that is critical to the physics reconstruction pipeline on the CMS Experiment at CERN.

1 Introduction

Runtime Verification [1] is the process of checking whether a run of a system holds a given property (often written in a temporal logic). This can be checked while the system is running (*online*) or after it has run (*post-mortem* or *offline*). Often this is presented abstractly as checking an abstraction of behaviour, captured by a *trace*. This abstract setting often ignores the practicalities of instrumentation and deployment. This paper presents a tool for the runtime verification of Python-based web services that efficiently handles the instrumentation problem and integrates with the widely used web-framework Flask [2]. This work is carried out within the context of verifying web-services used at the CMS Experiment at CERN.

Despite the wealth of existing logics [3–9], in our work [10,11] performing verification of state and time constraints over Python-based web services on the

T. Vojnar and L. Zhang (Eds.): TACAS 2019, Part II, LNCS 11428, pp. 98–114, 2019.
https://doi.org/10.1007/978-3-030-17465-1_6

CMS Experiment at CERN we have found that, in most cases, the existing logics operate at a high level of abstraction in relation to the program under scrutiny. This leads to (1) a less straightforward specification process for engineers, who have to think indirectly about their programs; and (2) difficulty writing specifications about behaviour inside functions themselves. These observations led us to develop Control-Flow Temporal Logic [10,11] (CFTL), a logic that has a tight-coupling with the control flow of the program under scrutiny (so operates at a lower level of abstraction which, in our experience, makes writing specifications with it easier for engineers) and is easy to use to specify state and time constraints over single runs of functions.

After the introduction of CFTL (Sect. 2), the first contribution of this paper is a description of the VyPR tool (Sect. 3), which verifies single-threaded Python programs with respect to CFTL specifications. It does this by (1) providing PyCFTL, the Python binding for CFTL, for writing specifications; (2) instrumenting the input program minimally with respect to reachability; and (3) using the resulting instrumentation information to make its online monitoring algorithm more efficient.

Since the development of VyPR as a prototype verification tool for CFTL, we have found that there are, to the best of our knowledge, no frameworks for fully-automated instrumentation and verification of multiple functions in web services with respect to low-level properties. Therefore, the second contribution of this paper is the lifting of CFTL and VyPR to the web service setting in a tool we call VyPR2 (Sect. 4). We present a general infrastructure for the runtime verification of Python-based web services with respect to CFTL specifications. Moving from VyPR to VyPR2 presents a number of challenges, which we discuss in detail. For the moment, we focus on web services that use the Flask framework, a Python framework that allows one to write a web service by writing Python functions to serve as end-points. VyPR2 admits a simple specification process using PyCFTL, performs automatic and optimised instrumentation of the web service under scrutiny, and provides a separate verdict server for collection of verdicts obtained by monitoring CFTL specifications.

Our final contribution is a case study (Sect. 5) applying VyPR2 to the CMS Conditions Upload Service [12], a single-threaded Python-based web service used on the CMS Experiment at CERN. We find that our verification infrastructure induces minimal overhead on Conditions uploads, with experiments showing an overhead of approximately 4.7%. We also find unexpected violations of the specification, one of which has triggered investigations into a mechanism that was designed to be an optimisation but is in danger of adding unnecessary latency. Ultimately, VyPR2 has made analysis of the performance of a critical part of CMS' physics reconstruction pipeline much more straightforward.

2 Control-Flow Temporal Logic (CFTL)

Both of the tools presented in this paper make use of the CFTL specification language [10,11]. We briefly describe this language, focusing on the kinds of

$$
\begin{aligned}
\phi &:= \forall q \in \Gamma_S : \phi \mid \forall t \in \Gamma_T : \phi \mid \phi \vee \phi \mid \neg\phi \mid \mathit{true} \mid \phi_A \\
\phi_A &:= S(x) = v \mid S(x) = S(x) \mid S(x) \in (n, m) \mid S(x) \in [n, m] \\
&\quad \mid \mathsf{duration}(T) \in (n, m) \mid \mathsf{duration}(T) \in [n, m] \\
\Gamma_S &:= \mathsf{changes}(x) \mid \mathsf{future}_S(q, \mathsf{changes}(x)) \mid \mathsf{future}_S(t, \mathsf{changes}(x)) \\
\Gamma_T &:= \mathsf{calls}(f) \mid \mathsf{future}_T(q, \mathsf{calls}(f)) \mid \mathsf{future}_T(t, \mathsf{calls}(f)) \\
S &:= q \mid \mathsf{source}(T) \mid \mathsf{dest}(T) \mid \mathsf{next}_S(S, \mathsf{changes}(x)) \mid \mathsf{next}_S(T, \mathsf{changes}(x)) \\
T &:= t \mid \mathsf{incident}(S) \mid \mathsf{next}_T(S, \mathsf{calls}(f)) \mid \mathsf{next}_T(T, \mathsf{calls}(f))
\end{aligned}
$$

Fig. 1. Syntax of CFTL.

properties it can capture. CFTL is a linear-time temporal logic whose formulas reason over two central types of objects: *states*, instantaneous *checkpoints* in a program's runtime; and *transitions*, the computation that must happen to move between states.

Consider the following property, taken from the case study in Sect. 5:

> *Whenever* `authenticated` *is changed, if it is set to* `True`, *then all future calls to* `execute` *should take no more than 1 second.*

This can be expressed in CFTL as

$$
\begin{aligned}
&\forall q \in \mathsf{changes}(\text{authenticated}) : \\
&\forall t \in \mathsf{future}(q, \mathsf{calls}(\text{execute})) : \\
&\qquad q(\text{authenticated}) = \text{True} \implies \mathsf{duration}(t) \in [0, 1]
\end{aligned} \tag{1}
$$

This first quantifies over the states q in which the program variable `authenticated` is changed and then over the transitions t occurring after that state that correspond to a call of a program function called `execute`. Given this pair of q and t, the specification then states that if `authenticated` is mapped to `True` by q then the duration of the transition t is within the given range.

Syntax. Figure 1 gives the syntax of CFTL. CFTL specifications take prenex form consisting of a list of quantifiers followed by a quantifier-free part. The quantification domains are defined by Γ_S (for states) and Γ_T (for transitions). Terms produced by the S and T cases denote states and transitions respectively. We often drop the S and T subscripts from future and next when the meaning is clear from the context. The quantifier-free part of CFTL formulas is a boolean combination of *atoms* generated by ϕ_A. Let $A(\varphi)$ be the set of atoms of a CFTL formula φ and, for $\alpha \in A(\varphi)$, let $\mathsf{var}(\alpha)$ be the variable on which α is based. In the above example $A(\varphi) = \{q(\text{authenticated}) = \text{True}, \mathsf{duration}(t) \in [0, 1]\}$, $\mathsf{var}(q(\text{authenticated}) = \text{True}) = q$, and $\mathsf{var}(\mathsf{duration}(t) \in [0, 1]) = t$. A CFTL formula is well-formed if it does not contain any free variables (those not captured by a quantifier) and every nested quantifier depends on the previously quantified variable.

```
Forall(q = changes('authenticated')).\
Forall(t = calls('execute', after='q')).\
Check(lambda q, t : (
  If(q('authenticated').equals(True)).then(
    t.duration()._in([0, 1])
  )
))
```

Fig. 2. An example of a CFTL specification written in Python using PyCFTL.

Semantics. The semantics of CFTL is defined over a *dynamic run* of the program. A dynamic run is a sequence of *states* $\tau = \langle \sigma, t \rangle$, where σ is a map (partial functions with finite domain) from program variables/functions to values and $t \in \mathbb{R}^{\geq}$ is a timestamp. Transitions are then pairs $\langle \tau_i, \tau_j \rangle$ for states τ_i and τ_j. The *product quantification domain* over which a CFTL formula is evaluated is derived from the dynamic run using the quantifier list e.g. by extracting all states where some variable changes. Elements of the product quantification domain are maps from specification variables to concrete states/transitions and will be referred to as *concrete bindings*.

3 VyPR

We now present VyPR, which can perform runtime verification on a single Python function with respect to some CFTL specification φ. Further details can be found in a paper [11] and technical report [10], and the tool is available online at http://cern.ch/vypr/.

Tool Workflow. To runtime verify a Python function we follow the following steps. Firstly the property is captured as a CFTL specification using a Python binding called PyCFTL. Given this specification, VyPR instruments the input program so that the monitoring algorithm receives data from any points in the program that could contribute to a verdict. Finally, the modified program will communicate with the monitor at runtime, which will process the observations to produce a verdict.

3.1 Writing CFTL Specifications with PyCFTL

The first step is to write a CFTL specification. Note that such a specification is specific to a particular function being verified as it refers directly to the symbols in that function. For specification we provide PyCFTL, a Python binding for CFTL. Figure 2 shows the PyCFTL specification for the CFTL specification in Eq. 1. A CFTL specification is defined in PyCFTL in two parts:

1. The first part is the quantification sequence. For example, the quantification $\forall q \in \mathsf{changes}(x)$ is given as `Forall(q = changes('x'))`.

2. The second part, the argument to `Check()`, gives the property to be evaluated for each concrete binding in the quantification domain. This is done by specifying a *template* for the specification with a lambda expression (an anonymous function in Python) whose arguments match the variables in the quantification sequence.

3.2 Instrumenting for CFTL

VyPR instruments a Python program for a CFTL specification φ by building up the set Inst containing all points in the program that could contribute to the verdict of φ. VyPR works at the level of the *abstract syntax tree* (AST) of the program and the program points of interest are nodes in the AST. Once this set of nodes has been computed, the AST is modified to add instruments at each of these points.

During runtime monitoring the most expensive operation is usually the lookup of the relevant monitor state that needs to be modified. To make monitoring more efficient, our instrumentation algorithm computes Inst by computing a direct lookup structure that allows the monitoring algorithm to go directly to this state. This structure can be abstractly viewed as a tree, $\mathcal{H}_\varphi$, whose leaves are sets that form a partition of Inst and whose intermediate nodes contain the information required to identify the relevant monitoring state.

The first step in computing $\mathcal{H}_\varphi$ is to construct the *Symbolic Control-Flow Graph* (SCFG) of the body of a (Python) function f.

Definition 1. *A symbolic control-flow graph (SCFG) is a directed graph $\langle V, E, v_s\rangle$ where V is a finite set of symbolic states (maps from all program symbols, e.g. program variables/functions, to a status in {changed, unchanged, called, undefined}), $E \subseteq V \times V$ is a finite set of edges, and $v_s \in V$ is the initial symbolic state.*

The SCFG of a function f is independent of any property φ being checked. Our construction of the SCFG of a program encodes information about state changes (by symbolic states) and reachability (by edges being generated for each state-changing instruction in code), making it an ideal structure from which to derive candidate points for state changes. The SCFG is used to find all symbolic states or edges that *could* generate concrete bindings in the product quantification domain of a formula. For example, if the CFTL specification is $\forall q \in \mathsf{changes}(x) : q(x) < 10$, all symbolic states representing changes to x will be identified as having potential to generate concrete bindings. From this, we construct a set of *static* bindings, which are maps from specification variables to candidate symbolic states/edges in the SCFG. The key distinction between *concrete* and *static* bindings is that static bindings are computed from the SCFG before runtime, and can correspond to zero or more concrete bindings during runtime. We call the set of static bindings the *binding space* for φ with respect to the SCFG and denote it by $\mathcal{B}_\varphi$ with the SCFG implicit. Elements β of $\mathcal{B}_\varphi$ form the top level of the tree $\mathcal{H}_\varphi$.

```
Data: φ and the SCFG ⟨V, E, v_s⟩ of function f
Result: Lookup tree H_φ
// Construct B_φ
B_φ = {∅};
foreach quantified variable (x_i ∈ predicate) in φ in order do
    for v ∈ V do
        if v is a candidate for predicate then
        B_φ = {β ∪ [x_i ↦ v] | β ∈ B_φ ∧ i > 1 → reaches(β(x_{i−1}), v)};
    end
end
// Construct H_φ
H_φ = ∅;
for β ∈ B_φ with index i_β do
    for quantified variable x_i in φ with index i_q do
        foreach α ∈ {α ∈ A(φ) | var(α) = x_i} with index i_α do
            H_φ⟨i_β, i_q, i_α⟩ ← lift(α, β(x_i));
        end
    end
end
```

Algorithm 1: VyPR's algorithm for construction of the tree $\mathcal{H}_\varphi$.

Once $\mathcal{B}_\varphi$ is constructed, for each $\beta \in \mathcal{B}_\varphi$, VyPR lifts each $\alpha \in A(\varphi)$ (the atoms of φ) from the dynamic context to the SCFG in order to find the relevant symbolic states/edges around the symbolic state/edge $\beta(\mathsf{var}(\alpha))$. This process constructs the second and third levels of the tree $\mathcal{H}_\varphi$: the second level consisting of variables, and the third level of atoms in $A(\varphi)$. The leaves on the fourth level of the tree $\mathcal{H}_\varphi$ are then the subsets of Inst; sets of symbolic states or edges from the SCFG.

Whilst we can abstractly view $\mathcal{H}_\varphi$ as a tree, in practice we represent it as a map from triples $\langle i_\mathcal{B}, i_\forall, i_\alpha \rangle$ to symbolic states/edges of the SCFG where $i_\mathcal{B}$, $i_\forall$ and i_α are indices into the binding space, quantifier list, and set of atoms respectively. An instrument placed in the input program for an atom α, using $\mathcal{H}_\varphi$, contains a triple to identify a subset of Inst and a value obs which is whatever code is required to obtain the value necessary to compute a truth value for α. For example, if the instrument is being placed to record the value of a program variable, obs is the name of the variable which, at runtime, is evaluated to give the value the variable holds. Such an instrument, which pushes its triple and evaluated obs value to a queue to be consumed by the monitoring thread, is placed by modifying the Abstract Syntax Tree (AST) of the program.

Our algorithm for construction of $\mathcal{H}_\varphi$ is Algorithm 1. This makes use of a predicate reaches which checks whether one symbolic state is reachable from another in the SCFG; and a function $\mathsf{lift}(\alpha, v)$ for $\alpha \in A(\varphi)$ and $v \in V$ which gives the symbolic states reachable from v obtained by lifting α to the static context. With the tree $\mathcal{H}_\varphi$ and binding space $\mathcal{B}_\varphi$ defined, in the next section we present our monitoring approach.

3.3 Monitoring for CFTL

The modified version of the body of f resulting from instrumentation is run alongside VyPR's monitoring algorithm, which consumes data from instruments via a consumption queue populated by the main program thread. Monitoring is performed asynchronously. VyPR's monitoring algorithm involves instantiating a formula tree (an and-or tree) for each binding in the quantification domain of a formula. This algorithm uses the triple $\langle i_{\mathcal{B}}, i_{\forall}, i_{\alpha} \rangle$ and evaluated obs value given by each instrument to perform lookup (to find in which formula trees to update the truth value of a specific atom), decide if new formula trees should be instantiated and compute the truth value of the atom at index i_α in $A(\varphi)$.

Given a CFTL formula $\forall q_1 \in \Gamma_1, \ldots, \forall q_n \in \Gamma_n : \psi(q_1, \ldots, q_n)$, when monitoring one can interpret multiple quantification as single quantification over a product space $\Gamma_1 \times \cdots \times \Gamma_n$. Such a space contains concrete bindings $[q_1 \mapsto v_1, \ldots, q_n \mapsto v_n]$ for states or transitions v_i. Each of these concrete bindings generated at runtime corresponds to a single static binding $\beta \in \mathcal{B}_\varphi$. Using this correspondence, we say that each concrete binding has a *supporting static binding* $\beta \in \mathcal{B}_\varphi$.

Given that monitoring is performed by instantiating a formula tree for each concrete binding in the product quantification domain, the speed of lookup of relevant formula trees is greatly increased by grouping them by the indices of supporting static bindings (determined by $i_{\mathcal{B}}$). Hence, to either update or instantiate formula trees, when information is observed from an instrument that helps to evaluate ψ at some concrete binding, the supporting static binding must be found, giving rise to the requirement for static information during monitoring. During monitoring, lookup of which set of formula trees to use is straightforward since the index $i_{\mathcal{B}}$ is given by the instrument.

Once lookup has been performed, the result is a set of formula trees corresponding to the static binding index $i_{\mathcal{B}}$ received from the instrument. From here, the index i_α is used to determine the atom in $A(\varphi)$ whose truth value (computed using the value given by obs) must be updated in each formula tree.

3.4 Verdict Reports

Once execution has finished, a verdict report is generated, which VyPR keeps in memory. Since each formula tree corresponds to a single concrete binding, verdicts share concrete bindings' correspondence with static bindings. Hence, verdicts can be grouped by the supporting static bindings. Given the binding space $\mathcal{B}_\varphi$ computed during instrumentation, a verdict report $\mathcal{V}$ from a single run of a function can be seen as a partial function

$$\mathcal{V} : \mathcal{B}_\varphi \rightarrow (\{\top, \bot\} \times \mathbb{R}_{\geq})^*,$$

sending a static binding $\beta \in \mathcal{B}_\varphi$ to a sequence of pairs containing a verdict from $\{\top, \bot\}$ and a timestamp (the time at which the verdict was obtained). The map $\mathcal{V}$ sends static bindings to sequences of pairs, rather than single pairs, because single static bindings can support multiple concrete bindings, generating multiple verdicts. This is the case if, for example, the static binding is inside a loop that iterates more than once at runtime.

4 An Architecture for Web Service Verification

We begin our description of the architecture of VyPR2, the extension of VyPR to web services, by isolating a number of requirements imposed by web service deployment environments, and production software environments in general, that must be met.

The environment at CERN inside which our verification infrastructure must function is similar to most production environments. It consists of machines for development and production, with each machine automatically pulling the relevant tags from a central repository once engineers have pushed their (locally-tested) code. Based on this deployment architecture, and the architecture of web services, requirements for our Runtime Verification framework include:

Centralised specifications over multiple functions with multiple properties. It should be possible to verify each function in a web service with respect to multiple properties. Further, specifications for the whole web service should be written in a single file, to minimise intrusion into the web service's code.

Making instrumentation data persistent. Web services' code can be pulled from a repository onto a production server and, once launched, be restarted multiple times between successive deployments of different code versions. Therefore, instrumentation data must be persistent between processes.

Persistent verdict data. Similarly, verdict data must be persistent and, furthermore, engineers must be able to perform offline analysis of the verdicts reached by web services at runtime.

An architecture that meets these requirements is illustrated in Fig. 3, and described in the following sections. The resulting tool, VyPR2, will soon be publicly available from http://cern.ch/vypr.

4.1 Specifying Multiple Function, Multiple Property Specifications

For simplicity of use, we have opted to have engineers write their entire specification in a central configuration file, in the root directory of their web service. This is a file written in Python, specifying CFTL properties over the service using the PyCFTL library.

Part of such a configuration file, using the PyCFTL specification given in Fig. 2, is shown in Fig. 4: one must first give the fully-qualified name of the module in the service in standard Python *dot* notation and then, for each function, the list of properties built up using PyCFTL.

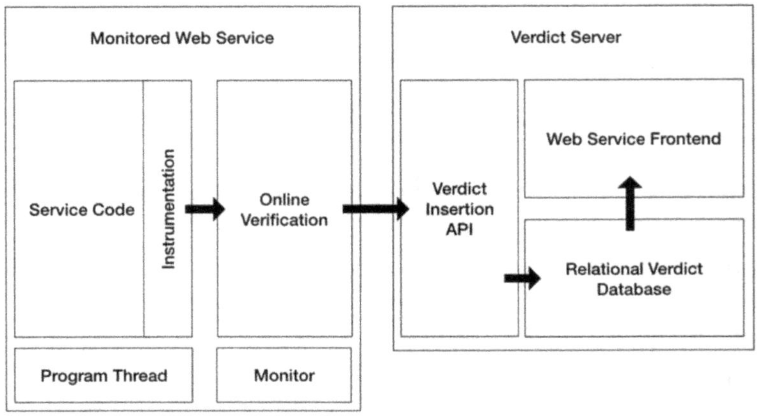

Fig. 3. The architecture of VyPR extended to web services.

$$\varphi_{\mathsf{auth}} \equiv \left(\begin{array}{l} \forall q \in \mathsf{changes}(\text{authenticated}) : \\ \forall t \in \mathsf{future}(q, \mathsf{calls}(\text{execute})) : \\ \qquad q(\text{authenticated}) = \text{True} \implies \mathsf{duration}(t) \in [0, 1] \end{array} \right)$$

```
"app.metadata_handler" : {
  "MetadataHandler.__init__" : [
    Forall(q = changes('authenticated')).\
    Forall(t = calls('execute', after='q')).\
    Check(lambda q, t : (
      If(q('authenticated').equals(True)).then(
        t.duration()._in([0, 1])
      )
    ))
  ]
}
```

Fig. 4. A CFTL specification and its PyCFTL equivalent.

4.2 Instrumentation

Given a specification such as that in Fig. 4, VyPR's strategy must be extended to the multiple function, multiple property context. Multiple functions are dealt with by constructing the SCFG for each function found in the specification and performing instrumentation for each property.

Instrumentation for each property over the same function is performed sequentially: VyPR2 instruments using the AST of the input code, and so instrumentation for each property progressively modifies the AST.

We now describe the modifications required to the actual instruments. In VyPR's simplified setting, instruments need only send the $\langle i_{\mathcal{B}}, i_{\forall}, i_{\alpha} \rangle$ triple along with the obs value relevant to the atom for which the instrument was placed. The multiple function, multiple property setting yields several problems that are solved by modifying existing instruments and adding a new kind.

In our architecture, monitoring is performed by a single thread, which means that this thread must have a way to distinguish between instruments received from different functions. We accomplish this by adding the name of the function to all instruments added to code. By adding the name of the function to all instruments, we deal not only with multiple functions, but with monitored functions calling other monitored functions, in which case monitor states for multiple functions must be maintained at the same time.

We deal with multiple properties over the same function by adding a unique identifier of a property to each of its instruments. We compute a uniquely identifying string for each property by taking the SHA1 hash of the combination of the quantification sequence and the template. We add this unique identifier to each instrument, giving the monitoring algorithm a way to distinguish properties.

Taking the original triple $\langle i_{\mathcal{B}}, i_{\forall}, i_{\alpha} \rangle$, the appropriate obs code, and the new requirements for the function name and the property hash, the new form of instruments that are placed by VyPR2 is $\langle \mathsf{function}, \mathsf{hash}, \mathsf{obs}, i_{\mathcal{B}}, i_{\forall}, i_{\alpha} \rangle$.

4.3 Making Instrumentation Data Persistent

The tree $\mathcal{H}_{\varphi}$ is dependent on the CFTL formula φ for which it has been computed. Hence, if the specification for a given function in the web service consists of a set $\bar{\varphi} = \{\varphi_1, \ldots, \varphi_n\}$ of CFTL formulas, the data required to monitor each property at the same time over the same execution of the given function consists of the set of maps $\mathcal{H}_{\varphi_i}$ which can be identified by φ_i. In particular, when data is received from an instrument by the monitoring algorithm, we can assume from Sect. 4.2 that it will contain a unique identifier for the formula for which it was placed. Therefore, the correct tree $\mathcal{H}_{\varphi_i}$ can be determined for each instrument.

We make such instrumentation data persistent by creating new directories in the root of the web service called `binding_spaces` and `instrumentation_maps` to hold the binding spaces and trees, respectively, computed for each function/CFTL property combination. To dump the binding spaces and hierarchy functions in files in these directories, we use Python's `pickle` [13] module.

4.4 Activating Verification in a Web Service

Our infrastructure is designed to minimise intrusion, both by minimising the amount of instrumentation performed and by minimising the amount of code engineers must add to their services for verification to be performed.

With the Flask-based implementation of VyPR2 that we present here, one can *activate* verification by adding the lines `from vypr import Verification` and `verification = Verification(app)` where app is the Flask application object required when building a web service with the Flask framework.

Running `verification = Verification(app)` will start up the separate monitoring thread, similar to VyPR, and will also read the serialised binding spaces and trees from the directories described in Sect. 4.3. It will subsequently place them in a map $\mathcal{G}$ from $\langle \text{module.function}, \text{property hash} \rangle$ pairs to objects containing the unserialised forms of the binding spaces and trees.

4.5 A Modified Monitoring Algorithm

VyPR's algorithm uses the tuple $\langle i_{\mathcal{B}}, i_{\forall}, i_{\alpha} \rangle$ with $\mathcal{H}_{\varphi}$ to determine the set of formula trees to update. In this case, $\mathcal{H}_{\varphi}$ is fixed. However, in the web service setting, the additional information regarding the current function that has control and the property to update is present and required to find the correct binding space and tree given by $\mathcal{G}$. From here the process is the same as that used by VyPR, since the monitoring problem has once again collapsed to monitoring a single property over a single function.

4.6 A Verdict Server

For a CFTL formula $\forall q_1 \in \Gamma_1, \ldots, \forall q_n \in \Gamma_n : \psi(q_1, \ldots, q_n)$ over a function f, we use *verdicts* to refer to the sequence of truth values in $(\{\top, \bot\} \times \mathbb{R}^{\geq})^*$, where $\psi(q_1, \ldots, q_n)$ generates a truth value in $\{\top, \bot\}$ for each binding in $\Gamma_1 \times \cdots \times \Gamma_n$ at a time $t \in \mathbb{R}^{\geq}$. To store such verdicts from a specification written over a web service, we now present the most substantial modification to VyPR's architecture: a central server to collect verdicts. This is, in itself, a separate system; communication with it takes place via HTTP. It consists of two major components:

- The server, a Python program that provides an API both for verdict insertion by the monitoring algorithm and for querying by a front-end for verdict visualisation.
- A relational database whose schema is derived from that of the tree $\mathcal{H}_{\varphi}$.

We omit further discussion of the server and first state some facts regarding our relational schema. Functions and properties are paired, so multiple properties over a single function yield multiple pairs; HTTP requests are used to group function calls; function calls correspond to function/property pairs; and verdicts are organised into bindings belonging to a function/property pair. With these facts in mind, one can answer questions such as:

- "For a given HTTP request, function and property φ combination, what were the verdicts generated by monitoring φ across all calls?"
- "For a given verdict and subsystem, which function/property pairs generated the verdict?"
- "For a given function call and verdict, which lines were part of bindings that generated this verdict while monitoring some property φ?"

5 An Application: The CMS Conditions Uploader

We now present the details of the application of VyPR2 to the CMS Conditions Upload Service. We begin by introducing the data with which the CMS Conditions Upload Service works. We then give a brief overview of the existing performance analysis approaches taken at CERN, before describing our approach for replaying real data from LHC runs. Finally, we give our specification and present an analysis of the verdicts derived by monitoring the Conditions Uploader with input taken from our test data, consisting of in the order of 10^4 inputs recorded during LHC runs.

5.1 Conditions Data, Their Computation and Upload

CERN is home to the Large Hadron Collider (LHC) [14], the largest and most powerful particle accelerator ever built. At one of the interaction points on the LHC beamline lies the Compact Muon Solenoid (CMS) [15], a general purpose detector which is a composite of sub-detector systems. Physics analysis at CERN requires reconstruction; a process whose input consists of both Event (collisions) and Non-Event (alignment and calibrations, or Conditions) data. The lifecycle of Conditions data begins with its computation during LHC runs, and ends with its upload to a central Conditions database. The service responsible for this upload is the CMS Conditions Upload service, a precise understanding of the performance of which is vital given planned upgrades to the LHC that will increase the amount of data taken.

The Conditions data used in reconstruction by CMS must define (1) the alignment and calibrations constants associated with a particular subdetector of CMS and (2) the time (run of the LHC) during which those constants are valid. The atomic unit of Conditions is the *Payload*, which is a serialised C++ class whose fields are specific to the subdetector of CMS to which the class corresponds. We define when a Payload applies to the subdetector by associating with it an *Interval of Validity* (IOV). We then group IOVs into sequences by defining *Tags*, which define to which subdetector each Payload associated with the IOVs it contains applies.

The CMS Conditions Uploader is used for release of Conditions by the automated Conditions computation that takes place at Tier 0 [16] (CERN's local computing grid) and detector experts who require their own Conditions. The Uploader is responsible for checking whether the Conditions proposed are valid before inserting the Conditions into the central database.

5.2 A Specification

We now give the specification with which we tested the Upload service on the upload data we collected, along with an interpretation for each property. These were written in collaboration with engineers working on the service.

1. app.usage.Usage.new_upload_session

$$\forall q \in \mathsf{changes}(\text{authenticated}) : \forall t \in \mathsf{future}(q, \mathsf{calls}(\text{execute})) : \begin{pmatrix} q(\text{authenticated}) = \text{True} \\ \implies \mathsf{duration}(t) \in [0, 1] \end{pmatrix}$$

Whenever `authenticated` *is changed, if it is set to* `True`*, then all future calls to* `execute` *should take no more than 1 second.*

2. app.routes.check_hashes

$$\forall q \in \mathsf{changes}(\text{hashes}) : \mathsf{duration}(\mathsf{next}(q, \mathsf{calls}(\text{find\_new\_hashes}))) \in [0, 0.3]$$

When the variable `hashes` *is assigned, the next call to* `find_new_hashes` *should take no more than 0.3 seconds.*

3. app.routes.store_blobs

$$\forall t \in \mathsf{calls}(\text{con.execute}) : \mathsf{duration}(t) \in [0, 2]$$

Every call to the `con.execute` *method on the current database connection should take no more than 2 seconds.*

4. app.metadata_handler.MetadataHandler.__init__

$$\forall t \in \mathsf{calls}(\text{insert\_iovs}) : \mathsf{duration}\left(\begin{array}{l}\mathsf{next}(t,\\ \quad \mathsf{calls}(\text{commit}))\end{array}\right) \in [0, 1]$$

Every time the method `insert_iovs` *is called, the next commit after the insertion should take no more than 1 second.*

5. app.routes.upload_metadata

$$\forall t \in \mathsf{calls}(\text{MetadataHandler}) : \mathsf{duration}(t) \in [0, 1]$$

Every time `MetadataHandler` *is instantiated, the instantiation should take no more than 1 second.*

5.3 Analysis of Verdicts

We present our analysis of the Conditions uploader with respect to the specification in Sect. 5.2. The analysis is performed in two parts:

1. *Complete Replay* - performing a complete upload replay of 14,610 uploads collected over a period of 7 months. The time between uploads in this part is fixed.
2. *Single Tag Replay* - performing a smaller upload replay of ≈ 900 uploads based on a single Tag. This part is a subset of the first, but where the time between uploads is varied.

Complete Replay. Figure 5 shows the results of monitoring our specification over a dataset of 14,610 uploads. The x axis is function/property pair IDs from the verdict database snapshot used to generate the plot. The ID to property correspondence is such that ID 99 refers to property 1; ID 100 to property 2; ID 101 to property 3; ID 102 to property 4; and ID 103 to property 5. Clearly, from this plot, the violations of property 2 exceed those caused by other properties by an order of magnitude. The `check_hashes` function carries out an optimisation that we call *hash checking*, used to make sure that a Conditions upload only sends the Payloads that are not already in the target Conditions database. This

Fig. 5. A plot of number of violations vs properties in the specification, monitored over 14,610 uploads.

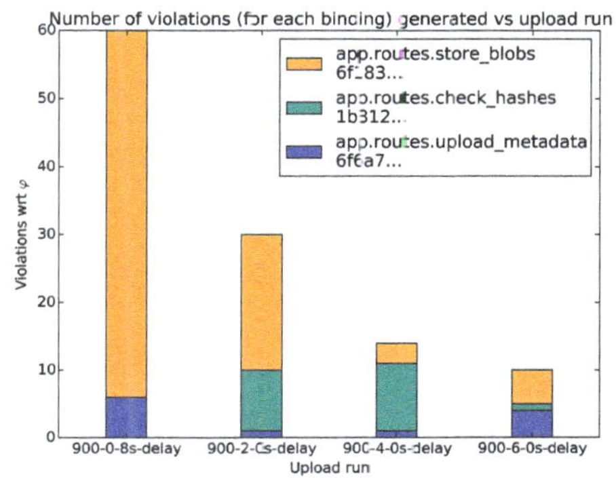

Fig. 6. A plot of violations of parts of our specification vs the replay of the 900 upload dataset. (Color figure online)

is possible because Payloads are uniquely identifiable by their hashes. This optimisation reduces the time spent on Payload uploads by an order of magnitude [12], but the frequency of violation in Fig. 5 suggests that the optimisation itself may be causing unacceptable latency.

Single Tag Replay. Figure 6 shows the results of monitoring a subset of our specification over a dataset of ≈ 900 uploads from a single Tag in the Conditions database. In this case, the x axis is runs of this upload dataset performed with varying delays between uploads, and the y axis is the number of violations based on a specification with 3 properties. This plot is of interest because, for the ≈ 300 Payloads inserted during this replay, it shows that the latency experienced by those insertions (in terms of violations of property 3, shown in orange) decreases as the delay between uploads increases.

5.4 Resulting Investigation

Based on the observations presented in Sect. 5.3, we have made investigation of the number of violations caused by *hash checking* a priority. It is recognised that this process is required, and its addition to the Conditions Uploader was a significant optimisation, but the optimisation can only be considered as such if it does not introduce unacceptable overhead to the upload process.

It is also clear that we should understand the pattern of violations in Fig. 6 more precisely. Given that the Conditions Uploader must operate successfully with both the current and upgraded LHC, it is a priority to understand the behaviour of the Uploader under varying frequencies of uploads. We suspect that investigation into the pattern seen in Fig. 6 will result in modification of either the Conditions Uploader's code, or the way in which Conditions are sent for upload during LHC runs.

5.5 Performance

We now describe the time and space overhead induced by using VyPR2 to monitor the specification in Sect. 5.2 over the Conditions Uploader. We consider both the time overhead on a single upload, and the space required to store intermediate instrumentation data.

To measure the time overhead induced over a single upload, we found that measuring overhead by running our complete upload dataset in a small period of time resulted in erratic database latency (the dataset was recorded over 7 months), so we opted to run a single upload 10 times with and without monitoring. This provided a more realistic upload scenario, and allowed us to see the overhead induced with respect to a single upload process (the process varies depending on the Conditions being uploaded). The result, from 10 runs of the same upload, was an average time overhead of 4.7%. Uploads are performed by a client sending the Conditions to the upload server over multiple HTTP requests, so this overhead is measured starting from when the first request is received by the upload server to when the last response is sent.

The space required to store all of the necessary instrumentation data for the specification in Sect. 5.2 is divided into space for *binding spaces* ($\mathcal{B}_\varphi$), *instrumentation maps* ($\mathcal{H}_\varphi$) and indices (a map from property hashes to the position in the specification at which they are found). The binding spaces took up 170 KB, the instrumentation maps 173 KB and the index map 4.3 KB, giving a total space overhead for instrumentation data storage of 347.3 KB.

6 Related Work

To the best of our knowledge, there is no existing work on Runtime Verification of web services. We are also unaware of other (available and maintained) RV tools for Python (there is Nagini [17], but this focuses on static verification) as most either operate offline (on log files) or focus on other languages such as Java [5,7,18] using AspectJ for instrumentation, C [19], or Erlang [20]. Few RV tools consider the instrumentation problem within the tool. The main exception is Java-MaC [3] who also use the specification to rewrite the Java code directly.

High-Energy Physics. In High Energy Physics, any form of monitoring concentrates on instrumentation in order to carry out manual inspection. For example, the instrumentation and subsequent monitoring of CMS' PhEDEx system for transfer of physics data was performed [21] and resulted in the identification of areas in which latency could be improved. Closer to the case study we present here, CMS uses the pclMon tool to monitor Conditions computation [22]. Finally, the Frontier query caching system performs offline monitoring by analysing logs [23]. None of these approaches uses a formal specification language, and they all collect a single type of statistics for a single defined use case. On the contrary, VyPR2 is *configurable* in the sense that one can change the specification being checked using our formal specification language, CFTL.

7 Conclusion

We have introduced the VyPR tool for monitoring single-threaded Python programs with respect to CFTL specifications, expressed using the PyCFTL library for Python. We then highlighted the problems that one must solve to extend VyPR's architecture to the web service setting, and presented the VyPR2 framework which implements our solutions. VyPR2 is a complete Runtime Verification framework for Flask-based web services written in Python; it provides the PyCFTL library for writing CFTL specifications over an entire web service, automatic minimal (with respect to reachability) instrumentation and efficient monitoring. Finally, we have described our experience using VyPR2 to analyse performance of the CMS Conditions Uploader, a critical part of the physics reconstruction pipeline of the CMS Experiment at CERN.

With the large amount of test data we have at CERN, we plan to extend VyPR2 to address explanation of violations of any part of a specification. This has been agreed within the CMS Experiment as being a significant step in developing the necessary software analysis tools ready for the upgraded LHC.

References

1. Bartocci, E., Falcone, Y., Francalanza, A., Reger, G.: Introduction to runtime verification. In: Bartocci, E., Falcone, Y. (eds.) Lectures on Runtime Verification. LNCS, vol. 10457, pp. 1–33. Springer, Cham (2018). https://doi.org/10.1007/978-3-319-75632-5_1
2. Flask for Python. http://flask.pocoo.org
3. Kim, M., Viswanathan, M., Kannan, S., Lee, I., Sokolsky, O.: Java-MaC: a run-time assurance approach for Java programs. Form. Methods Syst. Des. **24**(2), 129–155 (2004)
4. Havelund, K., Reger, G.: Runtime verification logics a language design perspective. In: Aceto, L., Bacci, G., Bacci, G., Ingólfsdóttir, A., Legay, A., Mardare, R. (eds.) Models, Algorithms, Logics and Tools. LNCS, vol. 10460, pp. 310–338. Springer, Cham (2017). https://doi.org/10.1007/978-3-319-63121-9_16
5. Meredith, P.O.N., Jin, D., Griffith, D., Chen, F., Rosu, G.: An overview of the MOP runtime verification framework. STTT **14**(3), 249–289 (2012)
6. Havelund, K.: Rule-based runtime verification revisited. STTT **17**(2), 143–170 (2015)
7. Colombo, C., Pace, G.J.: Industrial experiences with runtime verification of financial transaction systems: lessons learnt and standing challenges. In: Bartocci, E., Falcone, Y. (eds.) Lectures on Runtime Verification. LNCS, vol. 10457, pp. 211–232. Springer, Cham (2018). https://doi.org/10.1007/978-3-319-75632-5_7
8. Alur, R., Etessami, K., Madhusudan, P.: A temporal logic of nested calls and returns. In: Jensen, K., Podelski, A. (eds.) TACAS 2004. LNCS, vol. 2988, pp. 467–481. Springer, Heidelberg (2004). https://doi.org/10.1007/978-3-540-24730-2_35
9. Basin, D., Krstić, S., Traytel, D.: Almost event-rate independent monitoring of metric dynamic logic. In: Lahiri, S., Reger, G. (eds.) RV 2017. LNCS, vol. 10548, pp. 85–102. Springer, Cham (2017). https://doi.org/10.1007/978-3-319-67531-2_6

10. Dawes, J.H., Reger, G.: Specification of State and Time Constraints for Runtime Verification of Functions (2018). arXiv:1806.02621
11. Dawes, J.H., Reger, G.: Specification of temporal properties of functions for runtime verification. In: The 34th ACM/SIGAPP Symposium on Applied Computing (2019)
12. Dawes, J.H., CMS Collaboration: A Python object-oriented framework for the CMS alignment and calibration data. J. Phys.: Conf. Ser. **898**(4), 042059 (2017)
13. `Pickle` for Python. https://docs.python.org/2/library/pickle.html
14. Evans, L., Bryant, P.: LHC machine. J. Instrum. **3**(08), S08001 (2008)
15. The CMS Collaboration: The CMS experiment at the CERN LHC. J. Instrum. **3**(08), S08004 (2008)
16. Britton, D., Lloyd, S.L.: How to deal with petabytes of data: the LHC Grid project. Rep. Progress Phys. **77**(6), 065902 (2014)
17. Eilers, M., Müller, P.: Nagini: a static verifier for python. In: Chockler, H., Weissenbacher, G. (eds.) CAV 2018. LNCS, vol. 10981, pp. 596–603. Springer, Cham (2018). https://doi.org/10.1007/978-3-319-96145-3_33
18. Reger, G., Cruz, H.C., Rydeheard, D.: MarQ: monitoring at runtime with QEA. In: Baier, C., Tinelli, C. (eds.) TACAS 2015. LNCS, vol. 9035, pp. 596–610. Springer, Heidelberg (2015). https://doi.org/10.1007/978-3-662-46681-0_55
19. Signoles, J.: E-ACSL: Executable ANSI/ISO C Specification Language, version 1.5-4, March 2014. frama-c.com/download/e-acsl/e-acsl.pdf
20. Cassar, I., Francalanza, A., Attard, D.P., Aceto, L., Ingólfsdóttir, A.: A suite of monitoring tools for Erlang. In: An International Workshop on Competitions, Usability, Benchmarks, Evaluation, and Standardisation for Runtime Verification Tools, RV-CuBES 2017, 15 September 2017, Seattle, WA, USA, pp. 41–47 (2017)
21. Bonacorsi, D., Diotalevi, T., Magini, N., Sartirana, A., Taze, M., Wildish, T.: Monitoring data transfer latency in CMS computing operations. J. Phys.: Conf. Ser. **664**(3), 032033 (2015)
22. Oramus, P., et al.: Continuous and fast calibration of the CMS experiment: design of the automated workflows and operational experience. J. Phys.: Conf. Ser. **898**(3), 032041 (2017)
23. Blumenfeld, B., Dykstra, D., Kreuzer, P., Ran, D., Wang, W.: Operational experience with the frontier system in CMS. J. Phys.: Conf. Ser. **396**(5), 052014 (2012)

Constraint-Based Monitoring of Hyperproperties

Christopher Hahn, Marvin Stenger(✉), and Leander Tentrup

Reactive Systems Group, Saarland University, Saarbrücken, Germany
{hahn,stenger,tentrup}@react.uni-saarland.de

Abstract. Verifying hyperproperties at runtime is a challenging problem as hyperproperties, such as non-interference and observational determinism, relate multiple computation traces with each other. It is necessary to store previously seen traces, because every new incoming trace needs to be compatible with every run of the system observed so far. Furthermore, the new incoming trace poses requirements on *future* traces. In our monitoring approach, we focus on those requirements by rewriting a hyperproperty in the temporal logic HyperLTL to a Boolean constraint system. A hyperproperty is then violated by multiple runs of the system if the constraint system becomes unsatisfiable. We compare our implementation, which utilizes either BDDs or a SAT solver to store and evaluate constraints, to the automata-based monitoring tool RVHyper.

Keywords: Monitoring · Rewriting · Constraint-based · Hyperproperties

1 Introduction

As today's complex and large-scale systems are usually far beyond the scope of classic verification techniques like model checking or theorem proving, we are in the need of light-weight monitors for controlling the flow of information. By instrumenting efficient monitoring techniques in such systems that operate in an unpredictable privacy-critical environment, countermeasures will be enacted before irreparable information leaks happen. Information-flow policies, however, cannot be monitored with standard runtime verification techniques as they relate *multiple* runs of a system. For example, *observational determinism* [19,21,24] is a policy stating that altering non-observable input has no impact on the observable behavior. Hyperproperties [7] are a generalization of trace properties and are thus capable of expressing information-flow policies. HyperLTL [6] is a recently introduced temporal logic for hyperproperties,

This work was partially supported by the German Research Foundation (DFG) as part of the Collaborative Research Center "Methods and Tools for Understanding and Controlling Privacy" (CRC 1223) and the Collaborative Research Center "Foundations of Perspicuous Software Systems" (CRC 248), and by the European Research Council (ERC) Grant OSARES (No. 683300).

T. Vojnar and L. Zhang (Eds.): TACAS 2019, Part II, LNCS 11428, pp. 115–131, 2019.
https://doi.org/10.1007/978-3-030-17465-1_7

which extends Linear-time Temporal Logic (LTL) [20] with trace variables and explicit trace quantification. Observational determinism is expressed as the formula $\forall \pi, \pi'. (out_\pi \leftrightarrow out_{\pi'}) \mathcal{W} (in_\pi \not\leftrightarrow in_{\pi'})$, stating that all traces π, π' should agree on the output as long as they agree on the inputs.

In contrast to classic trace property monitoring, where a single run suffices to determine a violation, in runtime verification of HyperLTL formulas, we are concerned whether a *set* of runs through a system violates a given specification. In the common setting, those runs are given sequentially to the runtime monitor [1,2,12,13], which determines if the given set of runs violates the specification. An alternative view on HyperLTL monitoring is that every new incoming trace poses requirements on future traces. For example, the event $\{in, out\}$ in the observational determinism example above asserts that for every other trace, the output out has to be enabled if in is enabled. Approaches based on static automata constructions [1,12,13] perform very well on this type of specifications, although their scalability is intrinsically limited by certain parameters: The automaton construction becomes a bottleneck for more complex specifications, especially with respect to the number of atomic propositions. Furthermore, the computational workload grows steadily with the number of incoming traces, as every trace seen so far has to be checked against every new trace. Even optimizations [12], which minimize the amount of traces that must be stored, turn out to be too coarse grained as the following example shows. Consider the monitoring of the HyperLTL formula $\forall \pi, \pi'. \square(a_\pi \rightarrow \neg b_{\pi'})$, which states that globally if a occurs on any trace π, then b is not allowed to hold on any trace π', on the following incoming traces:

$\{a\}$	$\{\}$	$\{\}$	$\{\}$	$\neg b$ *is enforced on the 1st pos.*	(1)
{a}	$\{a\}$	$\{\}$	$\{\}$	$\neg b$ *is enforced on the 1st and 2nd pos.*	(2)
{a}	$\{\}$	$\{a\}$	$\{\}$	$\neg b$ *is enforced on the 1st and 3rd pos.*	(3)

In prior work [12], we observed that traces, which pose *less requirements* on future traces, can safely be discarded from the monitoring process. In the example above, the requirements of trace 1 are dominated by the requirements of trace 2, namely that b is not allowed to hold on the first and second position of new incoming traces. Hence, trace 1 must not longer be stored in order to detect a violation. But with the proposed language inclusion check in [12], neither trace 2 nor trace 3 can be discarded, as they pose incomparable requirements. They have, however, overlapping constraints, that is, they both enforce $\neg b$ in the first step.

To further improve the conciseness of the stored traces information, we use *rewriting*, which is a more fine-grained monitoring approach. The basic idea is to track the requirements that future traces have to fulfill, instead of storing a set of traces. In the example above, we would track the requirement that b is not allowed to hold on the first three positions of every freshly incoming trace. Rewriting has been applied successfully to trace properties, namely LTL formulas [17]. The idea is to partially evaluate a given LTL specification φ on an incoming event by unrolling φ according to the expansion laws of the temporal operators. The result of a single rewrite is again an LTL formula representing the updated specification, which the continuing execution has to satisfy. We use rewriting techniques to reduce $\forall^2$HyperLTL formulas to LTL constraints and check those constraints for inconsistencies corresponding to violations.

In this paper, we introduce a complete and provably correct rewriting-based monitoring approach for $\forall^2$HyperLTL formulas. Our algorithm rewrites a HyperLTL formula and a single event into a constraint composed of plain LTL and HyperLTL. For example, assume the event $\{in, out\}$ while monitoring observational determinism formalized above. The first step of the rewriting applies the expansion laws for the temporal operators, which results in $(in_\pi \nleftrightarrow in_{\pi'}) \vee (out_\pi \leftrightarrow out_{\pi'}) \wedge \bigcirc((out_\pi \leftrightarrow out_{\pi'})\,\mathcal{W}(in_\pi \nleftrightarrow in_{\pi'}))$. The event $\{in, out\}$ is rewritten for atomic propositions indexed by the trace variable π. This means replacing each occurrence of in or out in the current expansion step, i.e., before the $\bigcirc$ operator, with $\top$. Additionally, we strip the π' trace quantifier in the current expansion step from all other atomic propositions. This leaves us with $(\top \nleftrightarrow in) \vee (\top \leftrightarrow out) \wedge \bigcirc((out_\pi \leftrightarrow out_{\pi'})\,\mathcal{W}(in_\pi \nleftrightarrow in_{\pi'}))$. After simplification we have $\neg in \vee out \wedge \bigcirc((out_\pi \leftrightarrow out_{\pi'})\,\mathcal{W}(in_\pi \nleftrightarrow in_{\pi'}))$ as the new specification, which consists of a plain LTL part and a HyperLTL part. Based on this, we incrementally build a Boolean constraint system: we start by encoding the constraints corresponding to the LTL part and encode the HyperLTL part as variables. Those variables will then be incrementally defined when more elements of the trace become available. With this approach, we solely store the necessary information needed to detect violations of a given hyperproperty.

We evaluate two implementations of our approach, based on BDDs and SAT-solving, against RVHyper [13], a highly optimized automaton-based monitoring tool for temporal hyperproperties. Our experiments show that the rewriting approach performs equally well in general and better on a class of formulas which we call *guarded invariants*, i.e., formulas that define a certain invariant relation between two traces.

Related Work. With the need to express temporal hyperproperties in a succinct and formal manner, the above mentioned temporal logics HyperLTL and HyperCTL* [6] have been proposed. The model-checking [6, 14, 15], satisfiability [9], and realizability problem [10] of HyperLTL has been studied before.

Runtime verification of HyperLTL formulas was first considered for (co-)k-safety hyperproperties [1]. In the same paper, the notion of monitorability for HyperLTL was introduced. The authors have also identified syntactic classes of HyperLTL formulas that are monitorable and they proposed a monitoring algorithm based on a progression logic expressing trace interdependencies and the composition of an LTL$_3$ monitor.

Another automata-based approach for monitoring HyperLTL formulas was proposed in [12]. Given a HyperLTL specification, the algorithm starts by creating a deterministic monitor automaton. For every incoming trace it is then checked that all combinations with the already seen traces are accepted by the automaton. In order to minimize the number of stored traces, a language-inclusion-based algorithm is proposed, which allows to prune traces with redundant information. Furthermore, a method to reduce the number of combination of traces which have to get checked by analyzing the specification for relations such as reflexivity, symmetry, and transitivity with a HyperLTL-SAT solver [9,11], is proposed. The algorithm is implemented in the tool RVHyper [13], which was used to monitor information-flow policies and to detect spurious dependencies in hardware designs.

Another rewriting-based monitoring approach for HyperLTL is outlined in [5]. The idea is to identify a set of propositions of interest and aggregate constraints such that inconsistencies in the constraints indicate a violation of the HyperLTL formula. While the paper describes the building blocks for such a monitoring approach with a number of examples, we have, unfortunately, not been successful in applying the algorithm to other hyperproperties of interest, such as observational determinism.

In [3], the authors study the complexity of monitoring hyperproperties. They show that the form and size of the input, as well as the formula have a significant impact on the feasibility of the monitoring process. They differentiate between several input forms and study their complexity: a set of linear traces, tree-shaped Kripke structures, and acyclic Kripke structures. For acyclic structures and alternation-free HyperLTL formulas, the problems complexity gets as low as NC.

In [4], the authors discuss examples where static analysis can be combined with runtime verification techniques to monitor HyperLTL formulas beyond the alternation-free fragment. They discuss the challenges in monitoring formulas beyond this fragment and lay the foundations towards a general method.

2 Preliminaries

Let AP be a finite set of *atomic propositions* and let $\Sigma = 2^{AP}$ be the corresponding *alphabet*. An infinite *trace* $t \in \Sigma^\omega$ is an infinite sequence over the alphabet. A subset $T \subseteq \Sigma^\omega$ is called a *trace property*. A *hyperproperty* $H \subseteq 2^{(\Sigma^\omega)}$ is a generalization of a trace property. A finite trace $t \in \Sigma^+$ is a finite sequence over Σ. In the case of finite traces, $|t|$ denotes the length of a trace. We use the following notation to access and manipulate traces: Let t be a trace and i be a natural number. $t[i]$ denotes the i-th element of t. Therefore, $t[0]$ represents the first element of the trace. Let j be natural number. If $j \geq i$ and $i \geq |t|$, then $t[i,j]$ denotes the sequence $t[i]t[i+1]\cdots t[min(j,|t|-1)]$. Otherwise it denotes the empty trace ϵ. $t[i\rangle$ denotes the suffix of t starting at position i. For two finite traces s and t, we denote their concatenation by $s \cdot t$.

HyperLTL Syntax. HyperLTL [6] extends LTL with trace variables and trace quantifiers. Let $\mathcal{V}$ be a finite set of trace variables. The syntax of HyperLTL is given by the grammar

$$\varphi := \forall\pi.\ \varphi \mid \exists\pi.\ \varphi \mid \psi$$
$$\psi := a_\pi \mid \psi \wedge \psi \mid \neg\psi \mid \bigcirc\psi \mid \psi\ \mathcal{U}\ \psi,$$

where $a \in AP$ is an atomic proposition and $\pi \in \mathcal{V}$ is a trace variable. Atomic propositions are indexed by trace variables. The explicit trace quantification enables us to express properties like "on all traces φ must hold", expressed by $\forall\pi.\,\varphi$. Dually, we can express "there exists a trace such that φ holds", expressed by $\exists\pi.\,\varphi$. We use the standard derived operators *release* $\varphi\,\mathcal{R}\,\psi := \neg(\neg\varphi\,\mathcal{U}\,\neg\psi)$, *eventually* $\Diamond\varphi := \mathit{true}\,\mathcal{U}\,\varphi$, *globally* $\Box\varphi := \neg\Diamond\neg\varphi$, and *weak until* $\varphi_1\,\mathcal{W}\,\varphi_2 := (\varphi_1\,\mathcal{U}\,\varphi_2) \vee \Box\varphi_1$. As we use the finite trace semantics, $\bigcirc\varphi$ denotes the *strong* version of the next operator, i.e., if a trace ends before the satisfaction of φ can be determined, the satisfaction relation, defined below, evaluates to false. To enable duality in the finite trace setting, we additionally use the *weak* next operator $\tilde{\bigcirc}\varphi$ which evaluates to true if a trace ends before the satisfaction of φ can be determined and is defined as $\tilde{\bigcirc}\varphi := \neg\bigcirc\neg\varphi$. We call ψ of a HyperLTL formula $\boldsymbol{Q}.\psi$, with an arbitrary quantifier prefix $\boldsymbol{Q}$, the *body* of the formula. A HyperLTL formula $\boldsymbol{Q}.\psi$ is in the *alternation-free fragment* if either $\boldsymbol{Q}$ consists solely of universal quantifiers or solely of existential quantifiers. We also denote the respective alternation-free fragments as the $\forall^n$ fragment and the $\exists^n$ fragment, with n being the number of quantifiers in the prefix.

Finite Trace Semantics. We recap the finite trace semantics for HyperLTL [5] which is itself based on the finite trace semantics of LTL [18]. In the following, when using $\mathcal{L}(\varphi)$ we refer to the finite trace semantics of a HyperLTL formula φ. Let $\Pi_{\mathit{fin}} : \mathcal{V} \to \Sigma^+$ be a partial function mapping trace variables to finite traces. We define $\epsilon[0]$ as the empty set. $\Pi_{\mathit{fin}}[i\rangle$ denotes the trace assignment that is equal to $\Pi_{\mathit{fin}}(\pi)[i\rangle$ for all $\pi \in \mathrm{dom}(\Pi_{\mathit{fin}})$. By slight abuse of notation, we write $t \in \Pi_{\mathit{fin}}$ to access traces t in the image of Π_{fin}. The satisfaction of a HyperLTL formula φ over a finite trace assignment Π_{fin} and a set of finite traces T, denoted by $\Pi_{\mathit{fin}} \models_T \varphi$, is defined as follows:

$$
\begin{array}{ll}
\Pi_{\mathit{fin}} \models_T a_\pi & \text{if } a \in \Pi_{\mathit{fin}}(\pi)[0] \\
\Pi_{\mathit{fin}} \models_T \neg\varphi & \text{if } \Pi_{\mathit{fin}} \not\models_T \varphi \\
\Pi_{\mathit{fin}} \models_T \varphi \vee \psi & \text{if } \Pi_{\mathit{fin}} \models_T \varphi \text{ or } \Pi_{\mathit{fin}} \models_T \psi \\
\Pi_{\mathit{fin}} \models_T \bigcirc\varphi & \text{if } \forall t \in \Pi_{\mathit{fin}}.\, |t| > 1 \text{ and } \Pi_{\mathit{fin}}[1\rangle \models_T \varphi \\
\Pi_{\mathit{fin}} \models_T \varphi\,\mathcal{U}\,\psi & \text{if } \exists i < \min_{t \in \Pi_{\mathit{fin}}} |t|.\, \Pi_{\mathit{fin}}[i\rangle \models_T \psi \wedge \forall j < i.\, \Pi_{\mathit{fin}}[j\rangle \models_T \varphi \\
\Pi_{\mathit{fin}} \models_T \exists\pi.\,\varphi & \text{if there is some } t \in T \text{ such that } \Pi_{\mathit{fin}}[\pi \mapsto t] \models_T \varphi \\
\Pi_{\mathit{fin}} \models_T \forall\pi.\,\varphi & \text{if for all } t \in T \text{ such that } \Pi_{\mathit{fin}}[\pi \mapsto t] \models_T \varphi
\end{array}
$$

Due to duality of $\mathcal{U}\,/\,\mathcal{R}$, $\bigcirc\,/\,\tilde{\bigcirc}$, $\exists/\forall$, and the standard Boolean operators, every HyperLTL formula φ can be transformed into negation normal form (NNF), i.e., for every φ there is some ψ in negation normal form such that for all Π_{fin} and T it holds that $\Pi_{\mathit{fin}} \models_T \varphi$ if, and only if, $\Pi_{\mathit{fin}} \models_T \psi$. The standard LTL semantic, written $t \models_{\mathrm{LTL}_{\mathit{fin}}} \varphi$, for some LTL formula φ is equal to $\{\pi \mapsto t\}_{\mathit{fin}} \models_\emptyset \varphi'$, where φ' is derived from φ by replacing every proposition $p \in AP$ by p_π.

3 Rewriting HyperLTL

Given the body φ of a $\forall^2$HyperLTL formula $\forall\pi,\pi'.\,\varphi$, and a finite trace $t \in \Sigma^+$, we define alternative language characterizations. These capture the intuitive idea that, if one fixes a finite trace t, the language of $\forall\pi,\pi'.\,\varphi$ includes exactly those traces t' that satisfy φ in conjunction with t.

$$\begin{aligned}
\mathcal{L}_t^{\pi}(\varphi) &:= \left\{t' \in \Sigma^+ \mid \{\pi \mapsto t, \pi' \mapsto t'\}_{\mathit{fin}} \models \varphi\right\}\\
\mathcal{L}_t^{\pi'}(\varphi) &:= \left\{t' \in \Sigma^+ \mid \{\pi \mapsto t', \pi' \mapsto t\}_{\mathit{fin}} \models \varphi\right\}\\
\mathcal{L}_t(\varphi) &:= \mathcal{L}_t^{\pi}(\varphi) \cap \mathcal{L}_t^{\pi'}(\varphi)
\end{aligned}$$

We call $\hat{\varphi} := \varphi \wedge \varphi[\pi'/\pi, \pi/\pi']$ the symmetric closure of φ, where $\varphi[\pi'/\pi, \pi/\pi']$ represents the expression φ in which the trace variables π, π' are swapped. The language of the symmetric closure, when fixing one trace variable, is equivalent to the language of φ.

Lemma 1. *Given the body φ of a $\forall^2$HyperLTL formula $\forall\pi,\pi'.\,\varphi$, and a finite trace $t \in \Sigma^+$, it holds that $\mathcal{L}_t^{\pi}(\hat{\varphi}) = \mathcal{L}_t(\varphi)$.*

Proof.

$$\begin{aligned}
\mathcal{L}_t^{\pi}(\hat{\varphi}) &= \left\{t' \in \Sigma^+ \mid \{\pi \mapsto t, \pi' \mapsto t'\}_{\mathit{fin}} \models \hat{\varphi}\right\}\\
&= \left\{t' \in \Sigma^+ \mid \{\pi \mapsto t, \pi' \mapsto t'\}_{\mathit{fin}} \models \varphi \wedge \varphi[\pi'/\pi, \pi/\pi']\right\}\\
&= \left\{t' \in \Sigma^+ \mid \{\pi \mapsto t, \pi' \mapsto t'\}_{\mathit{fin}} \models \varphi, \{\pi \mapsto t, \pi' \mapsto t'\}_{\mathit{fin}} \models \varphi[\pi'/\pi, \pi/\pi']\right\}\\
&= \left\{t' \in \Sigma^+ \mid \{\pi \mapsto t, \pi' \mapsto t'\}_{\mathit{fin}} \models \varphi, \{\pi \mapsto t', \pi' \mapsto t\}_{\mathit{fin}} \models \varphi\right\} = \mathcal{L}_t(\varphi)
\end{aligned}$$

We exploit this to rewrite a $\forall^2$HyperLTL formula into an LTL formula. We define the projection $\varphi|_t^{\pi}$ of the body φ of a $\forall^2$HyperLTL formula $\forall\pi,\pi'.\,\varphi$ in NNF and a finite trace $t \in \Sigma^+$ to an LTL formula recursively on the structure of φ:

$$\begin{aligned}
a_\pi|_t^{\pi} &:= \begin{cases}\top & \text{if } a \in t[0]\\ \bot & \text{otherwise}\end{cases} &
\neg a_\pi|_t^{\pi} &:= \begin{cases}\top & \text{if } a \notin t[0]\\ \bot & \text{otherwise}\end{cases}\\
a_{\pi'}|_t^{\pi} &:= a & \neg a_{\pi'}|_t^{\pi} &:= \neg a\\
(\varphi \vee \psi)|_t^{\pi} &:= \varphi|_t^{\pi} \vee \psi|_t^{\pi} & (\varphi \wedge \psi)|_t^{\pi} &:= \varphi|_t^{\pi} \wedge \psi|_t^{\pi}
\end{aligned}$$

$$\begin{aligned}
(\bigcirc\varphi)|_t^{\pi} &:= \begin{cases}\bot & \text{if } |t| \leq 1\\ \bigcirc\varphi|_{t[1\rangle}^{\pi} & \text{otherwise}\end{cases}\\
(\tilde{\bigcirc}\varphi)|_t^{\pi} &:= \begin{cases}\top & \text{if } |t| \leq 1\\ \tilde{\bigcirc}\varphi|_{t[1\rangle}^{\pi} & \text{otherwise}\end{cases}\\
(\varphi\,\mathcal{U}\,\psi)|_t^{\pi} &:= \begin{cases}\psi|_t^{\pi} & \text{if } |t| \leq 1\\ \psi|_t^{\pi} \vee (\varphi|_t^{\pi} \wedge \bigcirc((\varphi\,\mathcal{U}\,\psi)|_{t[1\rangle}^{\pi})) & \text{otherwise}\end{cases}\\
(\varphi\,\mathcal{R}\,\psi)|_t^{\pi} &:= \begin{cases}\psi|_t^{\pi} & \text{if } |t| \leq 1\\ \psi|_t^{\pi} \wedge (\varphi|_t^{\pi} \vee \tilde{\bigcirc}((\varphi\,\mathcal{R}\,\psi)|_{t[1\rangle}^{\pi})) & \text{otherwise}\end{cases}
\end{aligned}$$

Theorem 1. *Given a $\forall^2$HyperLTL formula $\forall\pi,\pi'.\varphi$ and any two finite traces $t,t' \in \Sigma^+$ it holds that $t' \in \mathcal{L}_t^\pi(\varphi)$ if, and only if $t' \vDash_{LTL_{fin}} \varphi|_t^\pi$.*

Proof. By induction on the size of t. Induction Base ($t = e$, where $e \in \Sigma$): Let $t' \in \Sigma^+$ be arbitrarily chosen. We distinguish by structural induction the following cases over the formula φ. We begin with the base cases.

- a_π: we know by definition that $a_\pi|_t^\pi$ equals $\top$ if $a \in t[0]$ and $\bot$ otherwise, so it follows that $t' \vDash_{\mathrm{LTL}_{fin}} a_\pi|_t^\pi \Leftrightarrow a \in t[0] \Leftrightarrow t' \in \mathcal{L}_t^\pi(a_\pi)$.
- $a_{\pi'}$: $t' \in \mathcal{L}_t^\pi(a_{\pi'}) \Leftrightarrow a \in t'[0] \Leftrightarrow t' \vDash_{\mathrm{LTL}_{fin}} a \Leftrightarrow t' \vDash_{\mathrm{LTL}_{fin}} a_{\pi'}|_t^\pi$.
- $\neg a_\pi$ and $\neg a_{\pi'}$ are proven analogously.

The structural induction hypothesis states that $\forall t' \in \Sigma^+ . t' \in \mathcal{L}_t^\pi(\psi) \Leftrightarrow t' \vDash_{\mathrm{LTL}_{fin}} \psi|_t^\pi$ (SIH1), where ψ is a strict subformula of φ.

- $\varphi \vee \psi$: $t' \in \mathcal{L}_t^\pi(\varphi \vee \psi) \Leftrightarrow (t' \in \mathcal{L}_t^\pi(\varphi)) \vee (t' \in \mathcal{L}_t^\pi(\psi)) \overset{\text{SIH1}}{\Longleftrightarrow} (t' \vDash_{\mathrm{LTL}_{fin}} \varphi|_t^\pi) \vee (t' \vDash_{\mathrm{LTL}_{fin}} \psi|_t^\pi) \Leftrightarrow t' \vDash_{\mathrm{LTL}_{fin}} (\varphi \vee \psi)|_t^\pi$.
- $\bigcirc\varphi$: $t' \in \mathcal{L}_t^\pi(\bigcirc\varphi) \overset{|t|=1}{\Longleftrightarrow} \bot \overset{|t|=1}{\Longleftrightarrow} t' \vDash_{\mathrm{LTL}_{fin}} (\bigcirc\varphi)|_t^\pi$.
- $\varphi\,\mathcal{U}\,\psi$: $t' \in \mathcal{L}_t^\pi(\varphi\,\mathcal{U}\,\psi) \overset{|t|=1}{\Longleftrightarrow} t' \in \mathcal{L}_t^\pi(\psi) \overset{\text{SIH1}}{\Longleftrightarrow} t' \vDash_{\mathrm{LTL}_{fin}} \psi|_t^\pi \overset{|t|=1}{\Longleftrightarrow} t' \vDash_{\mathrm{LTL}_{fin}} (\varphi\,\mathcal{U}\,\psi)|_t^\pi$.
- $\varphi \wedge \psi$, $\tilde{\bigcirc}\varphi$ and $\varphi\,\mathcal{R}\,\psi$ are proven analogously.

Induction Step ($t = e{\cdot}t^*$, where $e \in \Sigma, t^* \in \Sigma^+$): The induction hypothesis states that $\forall t' \in \Sigma^+ . t' \in \mathcal{L}_{t^*}^\pi(\varphi) \Leftrightarrow t' \vDash_{\mathrm{LTL}_{fin}} \varphi|_{t^*}^\pi$ (IH). We make use of structural induction over φ. All cases without temporal operators are covered as their proofs above were independent of $|t|$. The structural induction hypothesis states for all strict subformulas ψ that $\forall t' \in \Sigma^+ . t' \in \mathcal{L}_t^\pi(\psi) \Leftrightarrow t' \vDash_{\mathrm{LTL}_{fin}} \psi|_t^\pi$ (SIH2).

- $\bigcirc\varphi$: $t' \in \mathcal{L}_{t^*}^\pi(\bigcirc\varphi) \overset{|t^*|\geq 2}{\Longleftrightarrow} t'[1\rangle \in \mathcal{L}_t^\pi(\varphi) \overset{\text{IH}}{\Leftrightarrow} t'[1\rangle \vDash_{\mathrm{LTL}_{fin}} \varphi|_t^\pi \Leftrightarrow t' \vDash_{\mathrm{LTL}_{fin}} \bigcirc(\varphi|_t^\pi) \overset{t^*=e\cdot t}{\Longleftrightarrow} t' \vDash_{\mathrm{LTL}_{fin}} (\bigcirc\varphi)|_{t^*}^\pi$.
- $\varphi\,\mathcal{U}\,\psi$: $t' \in \mathcal{L}_{t^*}^\pi(\varphi\,\mathcal{U}\,\psi) \overset{|t^*|\geq 2}{\Longleftrightarrow} (t' \in \mathcal{L}_{t^*}^\pi(\psi)) \vee (t' \in \mathcal{L}_{t^*}^\pi(\varphi)) \wedge (t'[1\rangle \in \mathcal{L}_t^\pi(\varphi\,\mathcal{U}\,\psi)) \overset{\text{SIH2+IH}}{\Longleftrightarrow} (t' \vDash_{\mathrm{LTL}_{fin}} \psi|_{t^*}^\pi) \vee (t' \vDash \varphi|_{t^*}^\pi) \wedge (t'[1\rangle \vDash_{\mathrm{LTL}_{fin}} (\varphi\,\mathcal{U}\,\psi)|_t^\pi) \Leftrightarrow (t' \vDash_{\mathrm{LTL}_{fin}} \psi|_{t^*}^\pi) \vee (t' \vDash \varphi|_{t^*}^\pi) \wedge (t' \vDash_{\mathrm{LTL}_{fin}} \bigcirc((\varphi\,\mathcal{U}\,\psi)|_t^\pi)) \Leftrightarrow t' \vDash_{\mathrm{LTL}_{fin}} (\varphi\,\mathcal{U}\,\psi)|_{t^*}^\pi$.
- $\tilde{\bigcirc}\varphi$ and $\varphi\,\mathcal{R}\,\psi$ are proven analogously.

4 Constraint-Based Monitoring

For monitoring, we need to define an *incremental* rewriting that accurately models the semantics of $\varphi|_t^\pi$ while still being able to detect violations early. To this end, we define an operation $\varphi[\pi, e, i]$, where $e \in \Sigma$ is an event and i is the current position in the trace. $\varphi[\pi, e, i]$ transforms φ into a propositional formula, where the variables are either indexed atomic propositions p_i for $p \in AP$, or a variable $v_{\varphi',i+1}^-$ and $v_{\varphi',i+1}^+$ that act as placeholders until new information about the trace comes in. Whenever the next event e' occurs, the variables are defined with the result of $\varphi'[\pi, e', i+1]$. If the trace ends, the variables are set to *true* and *false* for v^+ and v^-, respectively. We define $\varphi[\pi, e, i]$ of a $\forall^2$HyperLTL formula $\forall\pi,\pi'.\varphi$ in NNF, event $e \in \Sigma$, and $i \geq 0$ recursively on the structure of the body φ:

$$\begin{array}{llll}
a_\pi[\pi,e,i] & := \begin{cases} \top & \text{if } a \in e \\ \bot & \text{otherwise} \end{cases} & (\neg a_\pi)[\pi,e,i] & := \begin{cases} \top & \text{if } a \notin e \\ \bot & \text{otherwise} \end{cases} \\
a_{\pi'}[\pi,e,i] & := a_i & (\neg a_{\pi'})[\pi,e,i] & := \neg a_i \\
(\varphi \vee \psi)[\pi,e,i] & := \varphi[\pi,e,i] \vee \psi[\pi,e,i] & (\varphi \wedge \psi)[\pi,e,i] & := \varphi[\pi,e,i] \wedge \psi[\pi,e,i] \\
(\bigcirc \varphi)[\pi,e,i] & := v^-_{\varphi,i+1} & (\tilde{\bigcirc} \varphi)[\pi,e,i] & := v^+_{\varphi,i+1}
\end{array}$$

$$\begin{aligned}
(\varphi\,\mathcal{U}\,\psi)[\pi,e,i] &:= \psi[\pi,e,i] \vee (\varphi[\pi,e,i] \wedge v^-_{\varphi\mathcal{U}\psi,i+1}) \\
(\varphi\,\mathcal{R}\,\psi)[\pi,e,i] &:= \psi[\pi,e,i] \wedge (\varphi[\pi,e,i] \vee v^+_{\varphi\mathcal{R}\psi,i+1})
\end{aligned}$$

We encode a $\forall^2$HyperLTL formula and finite traces into a constraint system, which, as we will show, is satisfiable if and only if the given traces satisfy the formula w.r.t. the finite semantics of HyperLTL. We write $v_{\varphi,i}$ to denote either $v^-_{\varphi,i}$ or $v^+_{\varphi,i}$. For $e \in \Sigma$ and $t \in \Sigma^*$, we define

$$\begin{aligned}
constr(v^+_{\varphi,i}, \epsilon) &:= \top \\
constr(v^-_{\varphi,i}, \epsilon) &:= \bot \\
constr(v_{\varphi,i}, e \cdot t) &:= \varphi[\pi,e,i] \wedge \bigwedge_{v_{\psi,i+1} \in \varphi[\pi,e,i]} \Big(v_{\psi,i+1} \rightarrow constr(v_{\psi,i+1}, t)\Big) \\
enc^i_{\mathrm{AP}}(\epsilon) &:= \top \\
enc^i_{\mathrm{AP}}(e \cdot t) &:= \bigwedge_{a \in \mathrm{AP} \cap e} a_i \wedge \bigwedge_{a \in \mathrm{AP} \setminus e} \neg a_i \wedge enc^{i+1}_{\mathrm{AP}}(t),
\end{aligned}$$

where we use $v_{\psi,i+1} \in \varphi[\pi,e,i]$ to denote variables $v_{\psi,i+1}$ occurring in the propositional formula $\varphi[\pi,e,i]$. *enc* is used to transform a trace into a propositional formula, e.g., $enc^0_{\{a,b\}}(\{a\}\{a,b\}) = a_0 \wedge \neg b_0 \wedge a_1 \wedge b_1$. For $n = 0$ we omit the annotation, i.e., we write $enc_{\mathrm{AP}}(t)$ instead of $enc^0_{\mathrm{AP}}(t)$. Also we omit the index AP if it is clear from the context. By slight abuse of notation, we use $constr^n(\varphi, t)$ for some quantifier free HyperLTL formula φ to denote $constr(v_{\varphi,n}, t)$ if $|t| > 0$. For a trace $t' \in \Sigma^+$, we use the notation $enc(t') \vDash constr(\varphi, t)$, which evaluates to *true* if, and only if $enc(t') \wedge constr(\varphi, t)$ is satisfiable.

4.1 Algorithm

Figure 1 depicts our constraint-based algorithm. Note that this algorithm can be used in an offline and online fashion. Before we give algorithmic details, consider again, the observational determinism example from the introduction, which is expressed as $\forall^2$HyperLTL formula $\forall\pi,\pi'.(out_\pi \leftrightarrow out_{\pi'})\,\mathcal{W}(in_\pi \not\leftrightarrow in_{\pi'})$. The basic idea of the algorithm is to transform the HyperLTL formula to a formula consisting partially of LTL, which expresses the requirements of the incoming trace in the current step, and partially of HyperLTL. Assuming the event $\{in, out\}$, we transform the observational determinism formula to the following formula: $\neg in \vee out \wedge \bigcirc((out_\pi \leftrightarrow out_{\pi'})\,\mathcal{W}(in_\pi \not\leftrightarrow in_{\pi'}))$.

```
   Input  : ∀π, π′. φ, T ⊆ Σ⁺
   Output: violation or no violation
1  ψ := nnf(φ̂)
2  C := ⊤
3  foreach t ∈ T do
4  │  C_t := v_{ψ,0}
5  │  t_enc := ⊤
6  │  while e_i := getNextEvent(t) do
7  │  │  t_enc := t_enc ∧ enc^i(e_i)
8  │  │  foreach v_{φ,i} ∈ C_t do
9  │  │  │  c := φ[π, e_i, i]
10 │  │  └  C_t := C_t ∧ (v_{φ,i} → c)
11 │  │  if ¬sat(C ∧ C_t ∧ t_enc) then
12 │  └  └  return violation
13 │  foreach v⁺_{φ,i+1} ∈ C_t do
14 │  └  C_t := C_t ∧ v⁺_{φ,i+1}
15 │  foreach v⁻_{φ,i+1} ∈ C_t do
16 │  └  C_t := C_t ∧ ¬v⁻_{φ,i+1}
17 └  C := C ∧ C_t
18 return no violation
```

Fig. 1. Constraint-based algorithm for monitoring $\forall^2$HyperLTL formulas.

A Boolean constraint system is then build incrementally: we start encoding the constraints corresponding to the LTL part (in front of the next-operator) and encode the HyperLTL part (after the next-operator) as variables that are defined when more events of the trace come in. We continue by explaining the algorithm in detail. In line 1, we construct ψ as the negation normal form of the symmetric closure of the original formula. We build two constraint systems: C containing constraints of previous traces and C_t (built incrementally) containing the constraints for the current trace t. Consequently, we initialize C with $\top$ and C_t with $v_{\psi,0}$ (lines 2 and 4). If the trace ends, we define the remaining v variables according to their polarities and add C_t to C. For each new event e_i in the trace t, and each "open" constraint in C_t corresponding to step i, i.e., $v_{\phi,i} \in C_t$, we rewrite the formula ϕ (line 9) and define $v_{\phi,i}$ with the rewriting result, which, potentially introduced new open constraints $v_{\phi',i+1}$ for the next step $i+1$. The constraint encoding of the current trace is aggregated in constraint t_{enc} (line 7). If the constraint system given the encoding of the current trace turns out to be unsatisfiable, a violation to the specification is detected, which is then returned.

In the following, we sketch two algorithmic improvements. First, instead of storing the constraints corresponding to traces individually, we use a new data structure, which is a *tree maintaining nodes* of formulas, their corresponding variables and also child nodes. Such a node corresponds to already seen rewrites. The initial node captures the (transformed) specification (similar to line 4) and it is also the root of the tree structure, representing all the generated constraints which replaces C in Fig. 1. Whenever a trace deviates in its rewrite result a new child or branch is added to the tree. If a rewrite result is already present in the node tree structure there is no need to create any new constraints nor new variables. This is crucial in case we observe many equal traces or traces behaving effectively the same. In case no new constraints were added to the constraint system, we omit a superfluous check for satisfiability.

Second, we use *conjunct splitting* to utilize the node tree optimization even more. We illustrate the basic idea on an example. Consider $\forall \pi, \pi'. \varphi$ with $\varphi =$

$\square((a_\pi \leftrightarrow a'_\pi) \vee (b_\pi \leftrightarrow b'_\pi))$, which demands that on all executions on each position at least on of propositions a or b agree in its evaluation. Consider the two traces $t_1 = \{a\}\{a\}\{a\}$, $t_2 = \{a\}\{a,b\}\{a\}$ that satisfy the specification. As both traces feature the same first event, they also share the same rewrite result for the first position. Interestingly, on the second position, we get $(a \vee \neg b) \wedge s_\varphi$ for t_1 and $(a \vee b) \wedge s_\varphi$ for t_2 as the rewrite results. While these constraints are no longer equal, by the nature of invariants, both feature the same subterm on the right hand side of the conjunction. We split the resulting constraint on its syntactic structure, such that we would no longer have to introduce a branch in the tree.

4.2 Correctness

In this technical subsection, we will formally prove correctness of our algorithm by showing that our incremental construction of the Boolean constraints is equisatisfiable to the HyperLTL rewriting presented in Sect. 3. We begin by showing that satisfiability is preserved when shifting the indices, as stated by the following lemma.

Lemma 2. *For any $\forall^2$HyperLTL formula $\forall \pi, \pi'. \varphi$ over atomic propositions AP, any finite traces $t, t' \in \Sigma^+$ and $n \geq 0$ it holds that $enc_{AP}(t') \vDash constr(\varphi, t) \Leftrightarrow enc^n_{AP}(t') \vDash constr^n(\varphi, t)$.*

Proof. By renaming of the positional indices.

In the following lemma and corollary, we show that the semantics of the next operators matches the finite LTL semantics.

Lemma 3. *For any $\forall^2$HyperLTL formula $\forall \pi, \pi'. \varphi$ over atomic propositions AP and any finite traces $t, t' \in \Sigma^+$ it holds that $enc(t') \vDash constr(\bigcirc \varphi, t) \Leftrightarrow enc(t') \vDash constr(v^-_{\varphi,1}, t[1\rangle) \Leftrightarrow enc(t'[1\rangle) \vDash constr(v^-_{\varphi,0}, t[1\rangle)$.*

Proof. Let φ, t, t' be given. It holds that $constr(\bigcirc \varphi, t) = constr(v^-_{\varphi,1}, t[1\rangle)$ by definition. As $constr(v^-_{\varphi,1}, t[1\rangle)$ by construction does not contain any variables with positional index 0, we only need to check satisfiability with respect to $enc(t'[1\rangle)$. Thus $enc(t') \vDash constr(\bigcirc \varphi, t) \Leftrightarrow enc(t') \vDash constr(v^-_{\psi,1}, t[1\rangle) \Leftrightarrow enc^1(t'[1\rangle) \vDash constr(v^-_{\varphi,1}, t[1\rangle) \overset{\text{Lem2}}{\Longleftrightarrow} enc(t'[1\rangle) \vDash constr(v^-_{\varphi,0}, t[1\rangle)$.

Corollary 1. *For any $\forall^2$HyperLTL formula $\forall \pi, \pi'. \varphi$ over atomic propositions AP and any finite traces $t, t' \in \Sigma^+$ it holds that $enc(t') \vDash constr(\tilde{\bigcirc} \varphi, t) \Leftrightarrow enc(t') \vDash constr(v^+_{\varphi,1}, t[1\rangle) \Leftrightarrow enc(t'[1\rangle) \vDash constr(v^+_{\varphi,0}, t[1\rangle)$.*

We will now state the correctness theorem, namely that our algorithm preserves the HyperLTL rewriting semantics.

Theorem 2. *For every $\forall^2$HyperLTL formula $\forall \pi, \pi'. \varphi$ in negation normal form over atomic propositions AP and any finite trace $t \in \Sigma^+$ it holds that $\forall t' \in \Sigma^+. t' \vDash_{LTL_{fin}} \varphi|^\pi_t \Leftrightarrow enc_{AP}(t') \vDash constr(\varphi, t)$.*

Proof. By induction over the size of t. Induction Base ($t = e$, where $e \in \Sigma$): We choose $t' \in \Sigma^+$ arbitrarily. We distinguish by structural induction the following cases over the formula φ:

- a_π: $constr(a_\pi, e) = (a_\pi)[\pi, e, 0] = \top$ if, and only if, $a \in e$. Thus $enc(t') \vDash constr(a_\pi, e) \Leftrightarrow a \in e \Leftrightarrow t' \vDash_{\mathrm{LTL}_{fin}} a_\pi|_e^\pi$.
- $a_{\pi'}$: $constr(a_{\pi'}, e) = (a_{\pi'})[\pi, e, 0] = a_0$ Thus $enc(t') \vDash constr(a_{\pi'}, e) \Leftrightarrow enc(t') \vDash a_0 \overset{\text{def } enc}{\Longleftrightarrow} a \in t'[0] \Leftrightarrow t' \vDash_{\mathrm{LTL}_{fin}} a \overset{\text{def } |^\pi}{\Longleftrightarrow} t' \vDash_{\mathrm{LTL}_{fin}} a_{\pi'}|_e^\pi$.
- $\neg a_\pi$ and $\neg a_{\pi'}$ are proven analogously.

The structural induction hypothesis states that $\forall t' \in \Sigma^+ . t' \vDash_{\mathrm{LTL}_{fin}} \psi|_t^\pi \Leftrightarrow enc(t') \vDash constr(\psi, t)$ (SIH1), where ψ is a strict subformula of φ.

- $\varphi \vee \psi$: $t' \vDash_{\mathrm{LTL}_{fin}} (\varphi \vee \psi)|_e^\pi \Leftrightarrow (t' \vDash_{\mathrm{LTL}_{fin}} \varphi|_e^\pi) \vee (t' \vDash_{\mathrm{LTL}_{fin}} \psi|_e^\pi) \overset{\text{SIH1}}{\Longleftrightarrow} (enc(t') \vDash constr(\varphi, e)) \vee (enc(t') \vDash constr(\psi, e)) \Leftrightarrow (enc(t') \vDash \varphi[\pi, e, 0]) \vee (enc(t') \vDash \psi[\pi, e, 0]) \Leftrightarrow enc(t') \vDash \varphi[\pi, e, 0] \vee \psi[\pi, e, 0] \overset{\text{def } enc}{\Longleftrightarrow} enc(t') \vDash (\varphi \vee \psi)[\pi, e, 0] \Leftrightarrow enc(t') \vDash constr(\varphi \vee \psi, e)$.
- $\bigcirc \varphi$: $constr(\bigcirc \varphi, e) = (\bigcirc \varphi)[\pi, e, 0] = v_{\varphi,0}^- \wedge (v_{\varphi,0}^- \rightarrow constr(v_{\varphi,0}^-, \epsilon)) = \bot$. Thus $t' \vDash_{\mathrm{LTL}_{fin}} (\bigcirc \varphi)|_e^\pi = \bot \Leftrightarrow enc(t') \vDash \bot$.
- $\varphi \mathcal{U} \psi$: $constr(\varphi \mathcal{U} \psi, e) = (\varphi \mathcal{U} \psi)[\pi, e, 0] = \psi[\pi, e, 0] \vee (\varphi[\pi, e, 0] \wedge constr(v_{\varphi \mathcal{U} \psi,0}^-, \epsilon)) = \psi[\pi, e, 0] = constr(\psi, e)$. Thus $t' \vDash_{\mathrm{LTL}_{fin}} (\varphi \mathcal{U} \psi)|_e^\pi \vDash_{\mathrm{LTL}_{fin}} \psi|_e^\pi \overset{\text{SIH1}}{\Longleftrightarrow} enc(t') \vDash constr(\psi, e)$.
- $\varphi \wedge \psi$, $\tilde{\bigcirc} \varphi$, and $\varphi \mathcal{R} \psi$ are proven analogously.

Induction Step ($t = e \cdot t^*$, where $e \in \Sigma$ and $t^* \in \Sigma^+$): The induction hypothesis states that $\forall t' \in \Sigma^+ . t' \vDash_{\mathrm{LTL}_{fin}} \varphi|_{t^*}^\pi \Leftrightarrow enc(t') \vDash constr(\varphi, t^*)$ (IH). We make use of structural induction over φ. All base cases are covered as their proofs above are independent of $|t|$. The structural induction hypothesis states for all strict subformulas ψ that $\forall t' \in \Sigma^+ . t' \vDash_{\mathrm{LTL}_{fin}} \psi|_t^\pi \Leftrightarrow enc(t') \vDash constr(\psi, t)$.

- $\varphi \vee \psi$:

$$
\begin{aligned}
& t' \vDash_{\mathrm{LTL}_{fin}} (\varphi \vee \psi)|_t^\pi \Leftrightarrow t' \vDash_{\mathrm{LTL}_{fin}} \varphi|_t^\pi \ \vee \ t' \vDash_{\mathrm{LTL}_{fin}} \psi|_t^\pi \\
\overset{\text{SIH1}}{\Longleftrightarrow} \quad & enc(t') \vDash constr(\varphi, t) \ \vee \ enc(t') \vDash constr(\psi, t) \\
\overset{t=e\cdot t^*}{\Longleftrightarrow} \quad & enc(t') \vDash (\varphi[\pi, e, 0] \wedge \bigwedge_{v_{\varphi',1} \in \varphi[\pi,e,0]} v_{\varphi',1} \rightarrow constr(v_{\varphi',1}, t^*)) \\
& \vee enc(t') \vDash (\psi[\pi, e, 0] \wedge \bigwedge_{v_{\psi',1} \in \varphi[\pi,e,0]} v_{\psi',1} \rightarrow constr(v_{\psi',1}, t^*)) \\
\overset{\dagger}{\Leftrightarrow} \quad & enc(t') \vDash (\varphi[\pi, e, 0] \vee \psi[\pi, e, 0]) \\
& \wedge \bigwedge_{v_{\varphi',1} \in \varphi[\pi,e,0]} v_{\varphi',1} \rightarrow constr(v_{\varphi',1}, t^*) \\
& \wedge \bigwedge_{v_{\psi',1} \in \varphi[\pi,e,0]} v_{\psi',1} \rightarrow constr(v_{\psi',1}, t^*) \\
\Leftrightarrow \quad & enc(t') \vDash (\varphi \vee \psi)[\pi, e, 0] \\
& \wedge \bigwedge_{v_{\phi,1} \in (\varphi \vee \psi)[\pi,e,0]} v_{\phi,1} \rightarrow constr(v_{\phi,1}, t^*) \\
\overset{t=e\cdot t^*}{\Longleftrightarrow} \quad & enc(t') \vDash constr(\varphi \vee \psi, t)
\end{aligned}
$$

†: ⇐: trivial, ⇒: Assume a model M_φ for $enc(t') \vDash \varphi[\pi, e, 0] \wedge A$. By construction, constraints by φ do not share variable with constraints by ψ. We extend the model by assigning $v_{\psi',1}$ with $\bot$, for all $v_{\psi',1} \in \psi[\pi, e, 0]$ and assigning the rest of the variables in $\psi[\pi, e, 0]$ arbitrarily.

- $\bigcirc\varphi$: $t' \vDash_{\mathrm{LTL}_{fin}} (\bigcirc\varphi)|_t^\pi \Leftrightarrow t' \vDash_{\mathrm{LTL}_{fin}} \bigcirc\varphi|_{t^*}^\pi \Leftrightarrow t'[1\rangle \vDash_{\mathrm{LTL}_{fin}} \varphi|_{t^*}^\pi \overset{\mathrm{IH}}{\Leftrightarrow}$ $enc(t'[1\rangle) \vDash constr(\varphi, t^*) \overset{\mathrm{Lem3}}{\Longleftrightarrow} enc(t') \vDash constr(\bigcirc\varphi, t)$.
- $\varphi\,\mathcal{U}\,\psi$:

$$
\begin{aligned}
& t' \vDash_{\mathrm{LTL}_{fin}} (\varphi\,\mathcal{U}\,\psi)|_t^\pi \\
\Leftrightarrow\quad & t' \vDash_{\mathrm{LTL}_{fin}} \psi|_t^\pi \vee \left[t' \vDash_{\mathrm{LTL}_{fin}} \varphi|_t^\pi \wedge t'[1\rangle \vDash_{\mathrm{LTL}_{fin}} (\varphi\,\mathcal{U}\,\psi)|_{t^*}^\pi\right] \\
\overset{\mathrm{SIH1+IH,L3}}{\Longleftrightarrow}\quad & enc(t') \vDash constr(\psi, t) \\
& \vee \left[enc(t') \vDash constr(\varphi, t) \wedge enc(t') \vDash constr(v^-_{\varphi\,\mathcal{U}\,\psi,1}, t^*)\right] \\
\Leftrightarrow\quad & enc(t') \vDash (\psi[\pi, e, 0] \wedge \bigwedge_{v_{\psi',1} \in \psi[\pi,e,0]} v_{\psi',1} \rightarrow constr(v_{\psi',1}, t^*)) \\
& \vee \begin{pmatrix} enc(t') \vDash (\varphi[\pi, e, 0] \wedge \bigwedge_{v_{\varphi',1} \in \varphi[\pi,e,0]} v_{\varphi',1} \rightarrow constr(v_{\varphi',1}, t^*)) \\ \wedge\, enc(t') \vDash (v^-_{\varphi\,\mathcal{U}\,\psi,1} \wedge v^-_{\varphi\,\mathcal{U}\,\psi,1} \rightarrow constr(v^-_{\varphi\,\mathcal{U}\,\psi,1}, t^*)) \end{pmatrix} \\
\overset{\text{same as } \dagger}{\Longleftrightarrow}\quad & enc(t') \vDash (\psi[\pi, e, 0] \vee (\varphi[\pi, e, 0] \wedge v^-_{\varphi\,\mathcal{U}\,\psi,1})) \\
& \wedge \bigwedge_{v_{\psi',1} \in \psi[\pi,e,0]} v_{\psi',1} \rightarrow constr(v_{\psi,1}, t^*) \\
& \wedge \bigwedge_{v_{\varphi',1} \in \varphi[\pi,e,0]} v_{\varphi',1} \rightarrow constr(v_{\varphi',1}, t^*) \\
& \wedge\, v^-_{\varphi\,\mathcal{U}\,\psi,1} \rightarrow constr(v^-_{\varphi\,\mathcal{U}\,\psi,1}, t^*) \\
\Leftrightarrow\quad & enc(t') \vDash \varphi\,\mathcal{U}\,\psi[\pi, e, 0] \\
& \wedge \bigwedge_{v_{\phi,1} \in \varphi\,\mathcal{U}\,\psi[\pi,e,0]} v_{\phi,1} \rightarrow constr(v_{\phi,1}, t^*) \\
\Leftrightarrow\quad & enc(t') \vDash constr(\varphi\,\mathcal{U}\,\psi, t)
\end{aligned}
$$

- $\varphi \wedge \psi$, $\tilde{\bigcirc}\varphi$, and $\varphi\,\mathcal{R}\,\psi$ are proven analogously.

Corollary 2. *For any $\forall^2$HyperLTL formula $\forall\pi,\pi'.\varphi$ in negation normal form over atomic propositions AP and any finite traces $t, t' \in \Sigma^+$ it holds that $t' \in \mathcal{L}_t(\varphi) \Leftrightarrow enc_{AP}(t') \vDash constr(\hat{\varphi}, t)$.*

Proof. $t' \in \mathcal{L}_t(\varphi) \overset{\mathrm{Thm1}}{\Longleftrightarrow} t' \vDash_{\mathrm{LTL}_{fin}} \hat{\varphi}|_t^\pi \overset{\mathrm{Lem2}}{\Longleftrightarrow} enc(t') \vDash constr(\hat{\varphi}, t)$.

Lemma 4. *For any $\forall^2$HyperLTL formula $\forall\pi,\pi'.\varphi$ in negation normal form over atomic propositions AP and any finite traces $t, t' \in \Sigma^+$ it holds that $enc_{AP}(t') \nvDash constr(\varphi, t) \Rightarrow \forall t'' \in \Sigma^+. t' \leq t'' \rightarrow enc_{AP}(t'') \nvDash constr(\varphi, t)$.*

Proof. We proof this via contradiction. We choose t, t' as well as φ arbitrarily, but in a way such that $enc(t') \nvDash constr(\varphi, t)$ holds. Assume that there exists a continuation of t', that we call t'', for which $enc(t'') \vDash constr(\varphi, t)$ holds. So there has to exist a model assigning truth values to the variables in $constr(\varphi, t)$, such that the constraint system is consistent. From this model we extract all assigned truths values for positional variables for position $|t'|$ to $|t''| - 1$. As t' is a prefix of t'', we can use these truth values to construct a valid model for $enc(t') \vDash constr(\varphi, t)$, which is a contradiction.

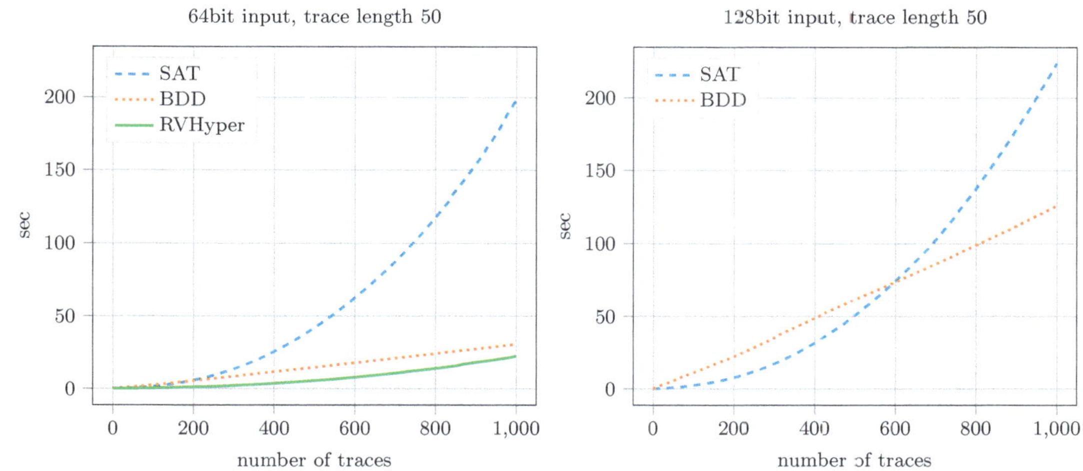

Fig. 2. Runtime comparison between RVHyper and our constraint-based monitor on a non-interference specification with traces of varying input size.

Corollary 3. *For any $\forall^2$HyperLTL formula $\forall\pi,\pi'.\varphi$ in negation normal form over atomic propositions AP and any finite set of finite traces $T \in \mathcal{P}(\Sigma^+)$ and finite trace $t' \in \Sigma^+$ it holds that*

$$t' \in \bigcap_{t\in T} \mathcal{L}_t(\varphi) \iff enc_{AP}(t') \vDash \bigwedge_{t\in T} constr(\hat{\varphi}, t).$$

Proof. It holds that $\forall t, t' \in \Sigma^+ . t \neq t' \rightarrow constr(\varphi, t) \neq constr(\varphi, t')$. Follows with same reasoning as in earlier proofs combined with Corollary 2.

5 Experimental Evaluation

We implemented two versions of the algorithm presented in this paper. The first implementation encodes the constraint system as a Boolean satisfiability problem (SAT), whereas the second one represents it as a (reduced ordered) binary decision diagram (BDD). The formula rewriting is implemented in a Maude [8] script. The constraint system is solved by either CryptoMiniSat [23] or CUDD [22]. All benchmarks were executed on an Intel Core i5-6200U CPU @2.30 GHz with 8 GB of RAM. The set of benchmarks chosen for our evaluation is composed out of two benchmarks presented in earlier publications [12,13] plus instances of *guarded invariants* at which our implementations excels.

Non-interference. Non-interference [16,19] is an important information flow policy demanding that an observer of a system cannot infer any high security input of a system by observing only low security input and output. Reformulated we could also say that all low security outputs $\boldsymbol{o}^{low}$ have to be equal on all system executions as long as the low security inputs $\boldsymbol{i}^{low}$ of those executions are the same: $\forall\pi,\pi'.\,(\boldsymbol{o}^{low}_\pi \leftrightarrow \boldsymbol{o}^{low}_{\pi'})\,\mathcal{W}(\boldsymbol{i}^{low}_\pi \not\leftrightarrow \boldsymbol{i}^{low}_{\pi'})$. This class of benchmarks was used to evaluated RVHyper [13], an automata-based runtime verification tool

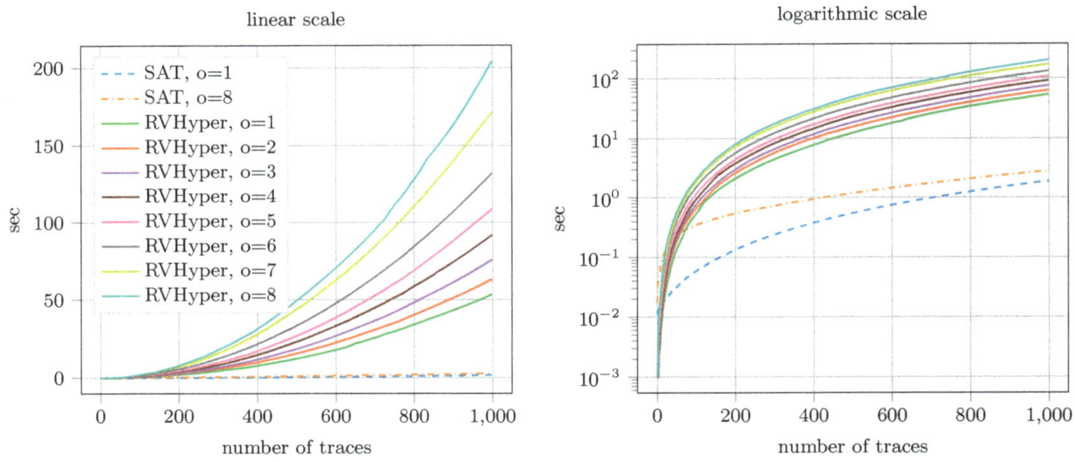

Fig. 3. Runtime comparison between RVHyper and our constraint-based monitor on the guarded invariant benchmark with trace lengths 20, 20 bit input size.

Table 1. Average results of our implementation compared to RVHyper on traces generated from circuit instances. Every instance was run 10 times.

instance	# traces	length	time RVHyper	time SAT	time BDD
XOR1	19	5	12 ms	47 ms	49 ms
XOR2	1000	5	16913 ms	996 ms	1666 ms
counter1	961	20	9610 ms	8274 ms	303 ms
counter2	1353	20	19041 ms	13772 ms	437 ms
MUX1	1000	5	14924 ms	693 ms	647 ms
MUX2	80	5	121 ms	79 ms	81 ms

for HyperLTL formulas. We repeated the experiments and depict the results in Fig. 2. We choose a trace length of 50 and monitored non-interference on 1000 randomly generated traces, where we distinguish between a 64 bit input (left) and an 128 bit input (right). For 64 bit input, our BDD implementation performs comparably well to RVHyper, which statically constructs a monitor automaton. For 128 bit input, RVHyper was not able to construct the automaton in reasonable time. Our implementation, however, shows promising results for this benchmark class that puts the automata-based construction to its limit.

Detecting Spurious Dependencies in Hardware Designs. The problem whether input signals influence output signals in hardware designs, was considered in [13]. Formally, we specify this property as the following HyperLTL formula: $\forall \pi_1 \forall \pi_2 . (\boldsymbol{o}_{\pi_1} \leftrightarrow \boldsymbol{o}_{\pi_2}) \mathcal{W} (\overline{\boldsymbol{i}}_{\pi_1} \not\leftrightarrow \overline{\boldsymbol{i}}_{\pi_2})$, where $\overline{\boldsymbol{i}}$ denotes all inputs except $\boldsymbol{i}$. Intuitively, the formula asserts that for every two pairs of execution traces (π_1, π_2) the value of $\boldsymbol{o}$ has to be the same until there is a difference between π_1 and π_2 in the input vector $\overline{\boldsymbol{i}}$, i.e., the inputs on which $\boldsymbol{o}$ may depend. We consider the same hardware and specifications as in [13]. The results are depicted in Table 1. Again, the BDD implementation handles this set of benchmarks well.

The biggest difference can be seen between the runtimes for counter2. This is explained by the fact that this benchmark demands the highest number of observed traces, and therefore the impact of the quadratic runtime costs in the number of traces dominates the result. We can, in fact, clearly observe this correlation between the number of traces and the runtime on RVHyper's performance over all benchmarks. On the other hand our constraint-based implementations do not show this behavior.

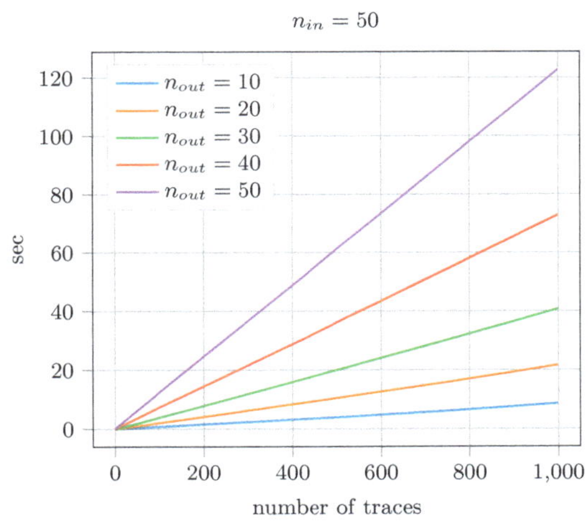

Fig. 4. Runtime of the SAT-based algorithm on the guarded invariant benchmark with a varying number of atomic propositions.

Guarded Invariants. We consider a new class of benchmarks, called *guarded invariants*, which express a certain invariant relation between two traces, which are, additionally, guarded by a precondition. Figure 3 shows the results of monitoring an arbitrary invariant $P : \Sigma \rightarrow \mathbb{B}$ of the following form: $\forall \pi, \pi'. \Diamond(\vee_{i \in I} i_\pi \nleftrightarrow i_{\pi'}) \rightarrow \Box(P(\pi) \leftrightarrow P(\pi'))$. Our approach significantly outperforms RVHyper on this benchmark class, as the conjunct splitting optimization, described in Sect. 4.1, synergizes well with SAT-solver implementations.

Atomic Proposition Scalability. While RVHyper is inherently limited in its scalability concerning formula size as the construction of the deterministic monitor automaton gets increasingly hard, the rewrite-based solution is not affected by this limitation. To put it to the test we have ran the SAT-based implementation on guarded invariant formulas with up to 100 different atomic propositions. Formulas have the form: $\forall \pi, \pi'. (\wedge_{i=1}^{n_{in}}(in_{i,\pi} \leftrightarrow in_{i,\pi'})) \rightarrow \Box(\vee_{j=1}^{n_{out}}(out_{j,\pi} \leftrightarrow out_{j,\pi'}))$, where n_{in}, n_{out} represents the number of input and output atomic propositions, respectively. Results can be seen in Fig. 4. Note that RVHyper already fails to build monitor automata for $|n_{in} + n_{out}| > 10$.

6 Conclusion

We pursued the success story of rewrite-based monitors for trace properties by applying the technique to the runtime verification problem of Hyperproperties. We presented an algorithm that, given a $\forall^2$HyperLTL formula, incrementally constructs constraints that represent requirements on future traces, instead of storing traces during runtime. Our evaluation shows that our approach scales in parameters where existing automata-based approaches reach their limits.

Acknowledgments. We thank Bernd Finkbeiner for his valuable feedback on earlier versions of this paper.

References

1. Agrawal, S., Bonakdarpour, B.: Runtime verification of k-safety hyperproperties in HyperLTL. In: Proceedings of CSF, pp. 239–252. IEEE Computer Society (2016). https://doi.org/10.1109/CSF.2016.24
2. Bonakdarpour, B., Finkbeiner, B.: Runtime verification for HyperLTL. In: Falcone, Y., Sánchez, C. (eds.) RV 2016. LNCS, vol. 10012, pp. 41–45. Springer, Cham (2016). https://doi.org/10.1007/978-3-319-46982-9_4
3. Bonakdarpour, B., Finkbeiner, B.: The complexity of monitoring hyperproperties. In: Proceedings of CSF, pp. 162–174. IEEE Computer Society (2018). https://doi.org/10.1109/CSF.2018.00019
4. Bonakdarpour, B., Sánchez, C., Schneider, G.: Monitoring hyperproperties by combining static analysis and runtime verification. In: Margaria, T., Steffen, B. (eds.) ISoLA 2018. LNCS, vol. 11245, pp. 8–27. Springer, Cham (2018). https://doi.org/10.1007/978-3-030-03421-4_2
5. Brett, N., Siddique, U., Bonakdarpour, B.: Rewriting-based runtime verification for alternation-free HyperLTL. In: Legay, A., Margaria, T. (eds.) TACAS 2017. LNCS, vol. 10206, pp. 77–93. Springer, Heidelberg (2017). https://doi.org/10.1007/978-3-662-54580-5_5
6. Clarkson, M.R., Finkbeiner, B., Koleini, M., Micinski, K.K., Rabe, M.N., Sánchez, C.: Temporal logics for hyperproperties. In: Abadi, M., Kremer, S. (eds.) POST 2014. LNCS, vol. 8414, pp. 265–284. Springer, Heidelberg (2014). https://doi.org/10.1007/978-3-642-54792-8_15
7. Clarkson, M.R., Schneider, F.B.: Hyperproperties. J. Comput. Secur. **18**(6), 1157–1210 (2010). https://doi.org/10.3233/JCS-2009-0393
8. Clavel, M., et al.: The Maude 2.0 system. In: Nieuwenhuis, R. (ed.) RTA 2003. LNCS, vol. 2706, pp. 76–87. Springer, Heidelberg (2003). https://doi.org/10.1007/3-540-44881-0_7
9. Finkbeiner, B., Hahn, C.: Deciding hyperproperties. In: Proceedings of CONCUR. LIPIcs, vol. 59, pp. 13:1–13:14. Schloss Dagstuhl - Leibniz-Zentrum fuer Informatik (2016). https://doi.org/10.4230/LIPIcs.CONCUR.2016.13
10. Finkbeiner, B., Hahn, C., Lukert, P., Stenger, M., Tentrup, L.: Synthesizing reactive systems from hyperproperties. In: Chockler, H., Weissenbacher, G. (eds.) CAV 2018. LNCS, vol. 10981, pp. 289–306. Springer, Cham (2018). https://doi.org/10.1007/978-3-319-96145-3_16
11. Finkbeiner, B., Hahn, C., Stenger, M.: EAHyper: satisfiability, implication, and equivalence checking of hyperproperties. In: Majumdar, R., Kunčak, V. (eds.) CAV 2017. LNCS, vol. 10427, pp. 564–570. Springer, Cham (2017). https://doi.org/10.1007/978-3-319-63390-9_29
12. Finkbeiner, B., Hahn, C., Stenger, M., Tentrup, L.: Monitoring hyperproperties. In: Lahiri, S., Reger, G. (eds.) RV 2017. LNCS, vol. 10548, pp. 190–207. Springer, Cham (2017). https://doi.org/10.1007/978-3-319-67531-2_12
13. Finkbeiner, B., Hahn, C., Stenger, M., Tentrup, L.: RVHyper: a runtime verification tool for temporal hyperproperties. In: Beyer, D., Huisman, M. (eds.) TACAS 2018. LNCS, vol. 10806, pp. 194–200. Springer, Cham (2018). https://doi.org/10.1007/978-3-319-89963-3_11

14. Finkbeiner, B., Hahn, C., Torfah, H.: Model checking quantitative hyperproperties. In: Chockler, H., Weissenbacher, G. (eds.) CAV 2018. LNCS, vol. 10981, pp. 144–163. Springer, Cham (2018). https://doi.org/10.1007/978-3-319-96145-3_8
15. Finkbeiner, B., Rabe, M.N., Sánchez, C.: Algorithms for model checking HyperLTL and HyperCTL*. In: Kroening, D., Păsăreanu, C.S. (eds.) CAV 2015. LNCS, vol. 9206, pp. 30–48. Springer, Cham (2015). https://doi.org/10.1007/978-3-319-21690-4_3
16. Goguen, J.A., Meseguer, J.: Security policies and security models. In: Proceedings of S&P, pp. 11–20. IEEE Computer Society (1982). https://doi.org/10.1109/SP.1982.10014
17. Havelund, K., Rosu, G.: Monitoring programs using rewriting. In: Proceedings of ASE, pp. 135–143. IEEE Computer Society (2001). https://doi.org/10.1109/ASE.2001.989799
18. Manna, Z., Pnueli, A.: Temporal Verification of Reactive Systems - Safety. Springer, New York (1995). https://doi.org/10.1007/978-1-4612-4222-2
19. McLean, J.: Proving noninterference and functional correctness using traces. J. Comput. Secur. 1(1), 37–58 (1992). https://doi.org/10.3233/JCS-1992-1103
20. Pnueli, A.: The temporal logic of programs. In: Proceedings of FOCS, pp. 46–57. IEEE Computer Society (1977). https://doi.org/10.1109/SFCS.1977.32
21. Roscoe, A.W.: CSP and determinism in security modelling. In: Proceedings of S&P, pp. 114–127. IEEE Computer Society (1995). https://doi.org/10.1109/SECPRI.1995.398927
22. Somenzi, F.: Cudd: Cu decision diagram package-release 2.4.0. University of Colorado at Boulder (2009)
23. Soos, M., Nohl, K., Castelluccia, C.: Extending SAT solvers to cryptographic problems. In: Kullmann, O. (ed.) SAT 2009. LNCS, vol. 5584, pp. 244–257. Springer, Heidelberg (2009). https://doi.org/10.1007/978-3-642-02777-2_24
24. Zdancewic, S., Myers, A.C.: Observational determinism for concurrent program security. In: Proceedings of CSFW, p. 29. IEEE Computer Society (2003). https://doi.org/10.1109/CSFW.2003.1212703

Hybrid and Stochastic Systems

Tail Probabilities for Randomized Program Runtimes via Martingales for Higher Moments

Satoshi Kura[1,2(✉)], Natsuki Urabe[1,2], and Ichiro Hasuo[2,3]

[1] Department of Computer Science, University of Tokyo, Tokyo, Japan
kurasatoshi@is.s.u-tokyo.ac.jp
[2] National Institute of Informatics, Tokyo, Japan
[3] The Graduate University for Advanced Studies (SOKENDAI), Kanagawa, Japan

Abstract. Programs with randomization constructs is an active research topic, especially after the recent introduction of martingale-based analysis methods for their termination and runtimes. Unlike most of the existing works that focus on proving almost-sure termination or estimating the expected runtime, in this work we study the *tail probabilities* of runtimes—such as "the execution takes more than 100 steps with probability at most 1%." To this goal, we devise a theory of supermartingales that overapproximate *higher moments* of runtime. These higher moments, combined with a suitable concentration inequality, yield useful upper bounds of tail probabilities. Moreover, our vector-valued formulation enables automated template-based synthesis of those supermartingales. Our experiments suggest the method's practical use.

1 Introduction

The important roles of *randomization* in algorithms and software systems are nowadays well-recognized. In algorithms, randomization can bring remarkable speed gain at the expense of small probabilities of imprecision. In cryptography, many encryption algorithms are randomized in order to conceal the identity of plaintexts. In software systems, randomization is widely utilized for the purpose of fairness, security and privacy.

Embracing randomization in programming languages has therefore been an active research topic for a long time. Doing so does not only offer a solid infrastructure that programmers and system designers can rely on, but also opens up the possibility of *language-based, static* analysis of properties of randomized algorithms and systems.

The current paper's goal is to analyze imperative programs with randomization constructs—the latter come in two forms, namely probabilistic branching

T. Vojnar and L. Zhang (Eds.): TACAS 2019, Part II, LNCS 11428, pp. 135–153, 2019.
https://doi.org/10.1007/978-3-030-17465-1_8

and assignment from a designated, possibly continuous, distribution. We shall refer to such programs as *randomized programs*.[1]

Runtime and Termination Analysis of Randomized Programs. The *runtime* of a randomized program is often a problem of our interest; so is *almost-sure termination*, that is, whether the program terminates with probability 1. In the programming language community, these problems have been taken up by many researchers as a challenge of both practical importance and theoretical interest.

Most of the existing works on runtime and termination analysis follow either of the following two approaches.

- *Martingale-based methods*, initiated with a notion of *ranking supermartingale* in [4] and extended [1,6,7,11,13], have their origin in the theory of stochastic processes. They can also be seen as a probabilistic extension of *ranking functions*, a standard proof method for termination of (non-randomized) programs. Martingale-based methods have seen remarkable success in *automated synthesis* using templates and constraint solving (like LP or SDP).
- The *predicate-transformer* approach, pursued in [2,17,19], uses a more syntax-guided formalism of program logic and emphasizes reasoning by *invariants*.

The essential difference between the two approaches is not big: an invariant notion in the latter is easily seen to be an adaptation of a suitable notion of supermartingale. The work [33] presents a comprehensive account on the order-theoretic foundation behind these techniques.

These existing works are mostly focused on the following problems: deciding almost-sure termination, computing termination probabilities, and computing expected runtime. (Here "computing" includes giving upper/lower bounds.) See [33] for a comparison of some of the existing martingale-based methods.

Our Problem: Tail Probabilities for Runtimes. In this paper we focus on the problem of *tail probabilities* that is not studied much so far.[2] We present a method for *overapproximating* tail probabilities; here is the problem we solve.

Input: a randomized program Γ, and a *deadline* $d \in \mathbb{N}$
Output: an upper bound of the *tail probability* $\Pr(T_{\mathrm{run}} \geq d)$, where T_{run} is the runtime of Γ

Our target language is a imperative language that features randomization (probabilistic branching and random assignment). We also allow nondeterminism; this makes the program's runtime depend on the choice of a *scheduler* (i.e. how nondeterminism is resolved). In this paper we study the longest, worst-case runtime (therefore our scheduler is *demonic*). In the technical sections, we use the presentation of these programs as *probabilistic control graphs (pCFGs)*—this is as usual in the literature. See e.g. [1,33].

[1] With the rise of statistical machine learning, *probabilistic programs* attract a lot of attention. Randomized programs can be thought of as a fragment of probabilistic programs without *conditioning* (or *observation*) constructs. In other words, the Bayesian aspect of probabilistic programs is absent in randomized programs.

[2] An exception is [5]; see Sect. 7 for comparison with the current work.

An example of our target program is in Fig. 1. It is an imperative program with randomization: in Line 3, the value of z is sampled from the uniform distribution over the interval $[-2, 1]$. The symbol $*$ in the line 4 stands for a nondeterministic Boolean value; in our analysis, it is resolved so that the runtime becomes the longest.

```
1  x := 2;  y := 2;
2  while (x > 0 && y > 0) do
3    z := Unif (-2,1);
4    if * then
5      x := x + z
6    else
7      y := y + z
8    fi
9  od
```

Fig. 1. An example program

Given the program in Fig. 1 and a choice of a deadline (say $d = 400$), we can ask the question "what is the probability $\Pr(T_{\mathrm{run}} \geq d)$ for the runtime T_{run} of the program to exceed $d = 400$ steps?" As we show in Sect. 6, our method gives a guaranteed upper bound 0.0684. This means that, if we allow the time budget of $d = 400$ steps, the program terminates with the probability at least 93%.

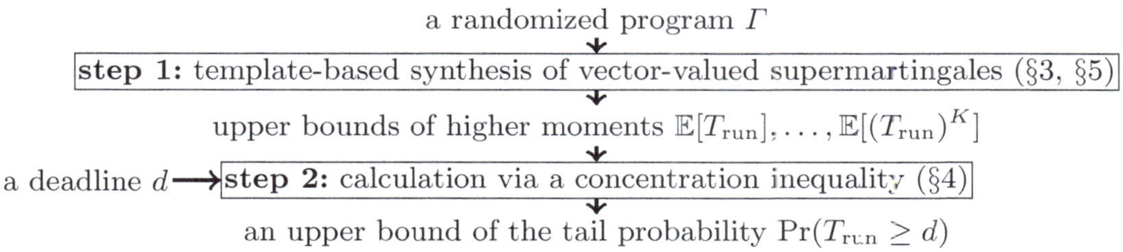

Fig. 2. Our workflow

Our Method: Concentration Inequalities, Higher Moments, and Vector-Valued Supermartingales. Towards the goal of computing tail probabilities, our approach is to use *concentration inequalities*, a technique from probability theory that is commonly used for overapproximating various tail probabilities. There are various concentration inequalities in the literature, and each of them is applicable in a different setting, such as a nonnegative random variable (Markov's inequality), known mean and variance (Chebyshev's inequality), a difference-bounded martingale (Azuma's inequality), and so on. Some of them were used for analyzing randomized programs [5] (see Sect. 7 for comparison).

In this paper, we use a specific concentration inequality that uses *higher moments* $\mathbb{E}[T_{\mathrm{run}}], \ldots, \mathbb{E}[(T_{\mathrm{run}})^K]$ of runtimes T_{run}, up to a choice of the maximum degree K. The concentration inequality is taken from [3]; it generalizes Markov's and Chebyshev's. We observe that a higher moment yields a tighter bound of the tail probability, as the deadline d grows bigger. Therefore it makes sense to strive for computing higher moments.

For computing higher moments of runtimes, we systematically extend the existing theory of ranking supermartingales, from the expected runtime (i.e. the first moment) to higher moments. The theory features a *vector-valued* supermartingale, which not only generalizes easily to degrees up to arbitrary $K \in \mathbb{N}$, but also allows automated synthesis much like usual supermartingales.

We also claim that the soundness of these vector-valued supermartingales is proved in a mathematically clean manner. Following our previous work [33], our arguments are based on the order-theoretic foundation of fixed points (namely the Knaster-Tarski, Cousot–Cousot and Kleene theorems), and we give upper bounds of higher moments by suitable least fixed points.

Overall, our workflow is as shown in Fig. 2. We note that the step 2 in Fig. 2 is computationally much cheaper than the step 1: in fact, the step 2 yields a symbolic expression for an upper bound in which d is a free variable. This makes it possible to draw graphs like the ones in Fig. 3. It is also easy to find a deadline d for which $\Pr(T_{\mathrm{run}} \geq d)$ is below a given threshold $p \in [0, 1]$.

We implemented a prototype that synthesizes vector-valued supermartingales using linear and polynomial templates. The resulting constraints are solved by LP and SDP solvers, respectively. Experiments show that our method can produce nontrivial upper bounds in reasonable computation time. We also experimentally confirm that higher moments are useful in producing tighter bounds.

Our Contributions. Summarizing, the contribution of this paper is as follows.

- We extend the existing theory of ranking supermartingales from expected runtimes (i.e. the first moment) to *higher moments*. The extension has a solid foundation of order-theoretic fixed points. Moreover, its clean presentation by vector-valued supermartingales makes automated synthesis as easy as before. Our target randomized programs are rich, embracing nondeterminism and continuous distributions.
- We study how these vector-valued supermartingales (and the resulting upper bounds of higher moments) can be used to yield upper bounds of *tail probabilities of runtimes*. We identify a concentration lemma that suits this purpose. We show that higher moments indeed yield tighter bounds.
- Overall, we present a comprehensive language-based framework for overapproximating tail probabilities of runtimes of randomized programs (Fig. 2). It has been implemented, and our experiments suggest its practical use.

Organization. We give preliminaries in Sect. 2. In Sect. 3, we review the order-theoretic characterization of ordinary ranking supermartingales and present an extension to higher moments of runtimes. In Sect. 4, we discuss how to obtain an upper bound of the tail probability of runtimes. In Sect. 5, we explain an automated synthesis algorithm for our ranking supermartingales. In Sect. 6, we give experimental results. In Sect. 7, we discuss related work. We conclude and give future work in Sect. 8. Some proofs and details are deferred to the appendices available in the extended version [22].

2 Preliminaries

We present some preliminary materials, including the definition of pCFGs (we use them as a model of randomized programs) and the definition of runtime.

Given topological spaces X and Y, let $\mathcal{B}(X)$ be the set of Borel sets on X and $\mathcal{B}(X, Y)$ be the set of Borel measurable functions $X \to Y$. We assume that the set $\mathbb{R}$ of reals, a finite set L and the set $[0, \infty]$ are equipped with the usual topology, the discrete topology, and the order topology, respectively. We use the induced Borel structures for these spaces. Given a measurable space X, let $\mathcal{D}(X)$ be the set of probability measures on X. For any $\mu \in \mathcal{D}(X)$, let $\mathrm{supp}(\mu)$ be the support of μ. We write $\mathbb{E}[X]$ for the expectation of a random variable X.

Our use of pCFGs follows recent works including [1].

Definition 2.1 (pCFG). A *probabilistic control flow graph (pCFG)* is a tuple $\Gamma = (L, V, l_{\mathrm{init}}, \boldsymbol{x}_{\mathrm{init}}, \mapsto, \mathrm{Up}, \mathrm{Pr}, G)$ that consists of the following.

- A finite set L of *locations*. It is a disjoint union of sets L_D, L_P, L_n and L_A of *deterministic*, *probabilistic*, *nondeterministic* and *assignment* locations.
- A finite set V of *program variables*.
- An *initial location* $l_{\mathrm{init}} \in L$.
- An *initial valuation* $\boldsymbol{x}_{\mathrm{init}} \in \mathbb{R}^V$
- A *transition relation* $\mapsto \subseteq L \times L$ which is total (i.e. $\forall l. \exists l'. l \mapsto l'$).
- An *update function* $\mathrm{Up} : L_A \to V \times \big(\mathcal{B}(\mathbb{R}^V, \mathbb{R}) \cup \mathcal{D}(\mathbb{R}) \cup \mathcal{B}(\mathbb{R}) \big)$ for assignment.
- A family $\mathrm{Pr} = (\mathrm{Pr}_l)_{l \in L_P}$ of probability distributions, where $\mathrm{Pr}_l \in \mathcal{D}(L)$, for probabilistic locations. We require that $l' \in \mathrm{supp}(\mathrm{Pr}_l)$ implies $l \mapsto l'$.
- A *guard function* $G : L_D \times L \to \mathcal{B}(\mathbb{R}^V)$ such that for each $l \in L_D$ and $\boldsymbol{x} \in \mathbb{R}^V$, there exists a unique location $l' \in L$ satisfying $l \mapsto l'$ and $\boldsymbol{x} \in G(l, l')$.

The update function can be decomposed into three functions $\mathrm{Up}_D : L_{AD} \to V \times \mathcal{B}(\mathbb{R}^V, \mathbb{R})$, $\mathrm{Up}_P : L_{AP} \to V \times \mathcal{D}(\mathbb{R})$ and $\mathrm{Up}_N : L_{AN} \to V \times \mathcal{B}(\mathbb{R})$, under a suitable decomposition $L_A = L_{AD} \cup L_{AP} \cup L_{AN}$ of assignment locations. The elements of L_{AD}, L_{AP} and L_{AN} represent *deterministic*, *probabilistic* and *nondeterministic* assignments, respectively. See e.g. [33].

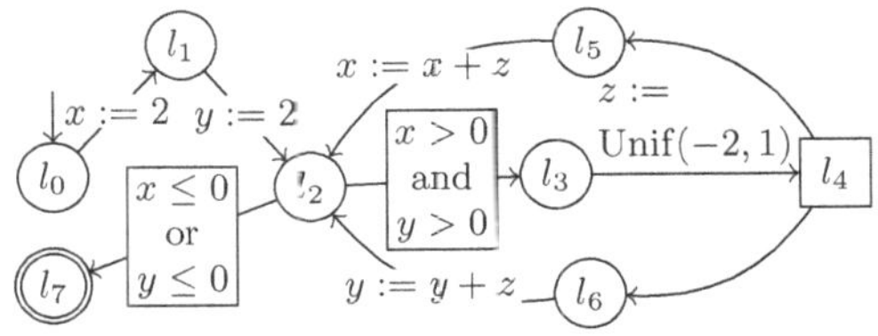

An example of a pCFG is shown on the right. It models the program in Fig. 1. The node l_4 is a nondeterministic location. $\mathrm{Unif}(-2, 1)$ is the uniform distribution on the interval $[-2, 1]$.

A *configuration* of a pCFG Γ is a pair $(l, \boldsymbol{x}) \in L \times \mathbb{R}^V$ of a location and a valuation. We regard the set $S = L \times \mathbb{R}^V$ of configurations is equipped with the product topology where L is equipped with the discrete topology. We say a configuration $(l', \boldsymbol{x}')$ is a *successor* of $(l, \boldsymbol{x})$, if $l \mapsto l'$ and the following hold.

- If $l \in L_D$, then $\boldsymbol{x}' = \boldsymbol{x}$ and $\boldsymbol{x} \in G(l, l')$.
- If $l \in L_N \cup L_P$, then $\boldsymbol{x}' = \boldsymbol{x}$.
- If $l \in L_A$, then $\boldsymbol{x}' = \boldsymbol{x}(x_j \leftarrow a)$, where $\boldsymbol{x}(x_j \leftarrow a)$ denotes the vector obtained by replacing the x_j-component of $\boldsymbol{x}$ by a. Here x_j is such that $\mathrm{Up}(l) = (x_j, u)$, and a is chosen as follows: (1) $a = u(\boldsymbol{x})$ if $u \in \mathcal{B}(\mathbb{R}^V, \mathbb{R})$; (2) $a \in \mathrm{supp}(u)$ if $u \in \mathcal{D}(\mathbb{R})$; and (3) $a \in u$ if $u \in \mathcal{B}(\mathbb{R})$.

An *invariant* of a pCFG Γ is a measurable set $I \in \mathcal{B}(S)$ such that $(l_{\mathrm{init}}, \boldsymbol{x}_{\mathrm{init}}) \in I$ and I is closed under taking successors (i.e. if $c \in I$ and c' is a successor of c then $c' \in I$). Use of invariants is a common technique in automated synthesis of supermartingales [1]: it restricts configuration spaces and thus makes the constraints on supermartingales weaker. It is also common to take an invariant as a measurable set [1]. A *run* of Γ is an infinite sequence of configurations $c_0 c_1 \dots$ such that c_0 is the initial configuration $(l_{\mathrm{init}}, \boldsymbol{x}_{\mathrm{init}})$ and c_{i+1} is a successor of c_i for each i. Let $\mathrm{Run}(\Gamma)$ be the set of runs of Γ.

A *scheduler* resolves nondeterminism: at a location in $L_N \cup L_{AN}$, it chooses a distribution of next configurations depending on the history of configurations visited so far. Given a pCFG Γ and a scheduler σ of Γ, a probability measure ν_σ^Γ on $\mathrm{Run}(\Gamma)$ is defined in the usual manner. See [22, Appendix B] for details.

Definition 2.2 (reaching time $T_C^\Gamma, T_{C,\sigma}^\Gamma$). Let Γ be a pCFG and $C \subseteq S$ be a set of configurations called a *destination.* The *reaching time* to C is a function $T_C^\Gamma : \mathrm{Run}(\Gamma) \to [0, \infty]$ defined by $(T_C^\Gamma)(c_0 c_1 \dots) = \mathrm{argmin}_{i \in \mathbb{N}}(c_i \in C)$. Fixing a scheduler σ makes T_C^Γ a random variable, since σ determines a probability measure ν_σ^Γ on $\mathrm{Run}(\Gamma)$. It is denoted by $T_{C,\sigma}^\Gamma$.

Runtimes of pCFGs are a special case of reaching times, namely to the set of terminating configurations.

The following higher moments are central to our framework. Recall that we are interested in demonic schedulers, i.e. those which make runtimes longer.

Definition 2.3 ($\mathbb{M}_{C,\sigma}^{\Gamma,k}$ and $\overline{\mathbb{M}}_C^{\Gamma,k}$). Assume the setting of Definition 2.2, and let $k \in \mathbb{N}$ and $c \in S$. We write $\mathbb{M}_{C,\sigma}^{\Gamma,k}(c)$ for the k-th moment of the reaching time of Γ from c to C under the scheduler σ, i.e. that is, $\mathbb{M}_{C,\sigma}^{\Gamma,k}(c) = \mathbb{E}[(T_{C,\sigma}^{\Gamma_c})^k] = \int (T_C^{\Gamma_c})^k \, \mathrm{d}\nu_\sigma^{\Gamma_c}$ where Γ_c is a pCFG obtained from Γ by changing the initial configuration to c. Their supremum under varying σ is denoted by $\overline{\mathbb{M}}_C^{\Gamma,k} := \sup_\sigma \mathbb{M}_{C,\sigma}^{\Gamma,k}$.

3 Ranking Supermartingale for Higher Moments

We introduce one of the main contributions in the paper, a notion of ranking supermartingale that overapproximates higher moments. It is motivated by the following observation: martingale-based reasoning about the second moment must concur with one about the first moment. We conduct a systematic theoretical extension that features an order-theoretic foundation and vector-valued supermartingales. The theory accommodates nondeterminism and continuous distributions, too. We omit some details and proofs; they are in [22, Appendix C].

The fully general theory for higher moments will be presented in Sect. 3.2; we present its restriction to the second moments in Sect. 3.1 for readability.

Prior to these, we review the existing theory of ranking supermartingales, through the lens of order-theoretic fixed points. In doing so we follow [33].

Definition 3.1 ("nexttime" operation $\overline{\mathbb{X}}$ (pre-expectation)). Given $\eta : S \to [0, \infty]$, let $\overline{\mathbb{X}}\eta : S \to [0, \infty]$ be the function defined as follows.

- If $l \in L_D$ and $\boldsymbol{x} \models G(l, l')$, then $(\overline{\mathbb{X}}\eta)(l, \boldsymbol{x}) = \eta(l', \boldsymbol{x})$.
- If $l \in L_P$, then $(\overline{\mathbb{X}}\eta)(l, \boldsymbol{x}) = \sum_{l \mapsto l'} \Pr_l(l')\eta(l', \boldsymbol{x})$.
- If $l \in L_N$, then $(\overline{\mathbb{X}}\eta)(l, \boldsymbol{x}) = \sup_{l \mapsto l'} \eta(l', \boldsymbol{x})$.
- If $l \in L_A$, $\mathrm{Up}(l) = (x_j, u)$ and $l \mapsto l'$, if $u \in \mathcal{B}(\mathbb{R}^V, \mathbb{R})$, then $(\overline{\mathbb{X}}\eta)(l, \boldsymbol{x}) = \eta(l', \boldsymbol{x}(x_j \leftarrow u(\boldsymbol{x})))$; if $u \in \mathcal{D}(\mathbb{R})$, then $(\overline{\mathbb{X}}\eta)(l, \boldsymbol{x}) = \int_{\mathbb{R}} \eta(l', \boldsymbol{x}(x_j \leftarrow y))\, du(y)$; and if $u \in \mathcal{B}(\mathbb{R})$, then $(\overline{\mathbb{X}}\eta)(l, \boldsymbol{x}) = \sup_{y \in u} \eta(l', \boldsymbol{x}(x_j \leftarrow y))$.

Intuitively, $\overline{\mathbb{X}}\eta$ is the expectation of η after one transition. Nondeterminism is resolved by the maximal choice.

We define $F_1 : (S \to [0, \infty]) \to (S \to [0, \infty])$ as follows.

$$(F_1(\eta))(c) = \begin{cases} 1 + (\overline{\mathbb{X}}\eta)(c) & c \in I \setminus C \\ 0 & \text{otherwise} \end{cases} \qquad \text{(Here “1+” accounts for time elapse)}$$

The function F_1 is an adaptation of the *Bellman operator*, a classic notion in the theory of Markov processes. A similar notion is used e.g. in [19]. The function space $(S \to [0, \infty])$ is a complete lattice structure, because $[0, \infty]$ is; moreover F_1 is easily seen to be monotone. It is not hard to see either that the expected reaching time $\overline{\mathbb{M}}_C^{\Gamma,1}$ to C coincides with the least fixed point μF_1.

The following theorem is fundamental in theoretical computer science.

Theorem 3.2 (Knaster–Tarski, [34]). *Let $(L, \leq)$ be a complete lattice and $f : L \to L$ be a monotone function. The least fixed point μf is the least prefixed point, i.e. $\mu f = \min\{l \in L \mid f(l) \leq l\}$.* □

The significance of the Knaster-Tarski theorem in verification lies in the induced proof rule: $f(l) \leq l \Rightarrow \mu f \leq l$. Instantiating to the expected reaching time $\overline{\mathbb{M}}_C^{\Gamma,1} = \mu F_1$, it means $F_1(\eta) \leq \eta \Rightarrow \overline{\mathbb{M}}_C^{\Gamma,1} \leq \eta$, i.e. an arbitrary prefixed point of F_1—which coincides with the notion of ranking supermartingale [4]—overapproximates the expected reaching time. This proves soundness of ranking supermartingales.

3.1 Ranking Supermartingales for the Second Moments

We extend ranking supermartingales to the second moments. It paves the way to a fully general theory (up to the K-th moments) in Sect. 3.2.

The key in the martingale-based reasoning of expected reaching times (i.e. first moments) was that they are characterized as the least fixed point of a function F_1. Here it is crucial that for an arbitrary random variable T, we have $\mathbb{E}[T + 1] = \mathbb{E}[T] + 1$ and therefore we can calculate $\mathbb{E}[T + 1]$ from $\mathbb{E}[T]$. However, this is not the case for second moments. As $\mathbb{E}[(T + 1)^2] = \mathbb{E}[T^2] + 2\mathbb{E}[T] + 1$, calculating the second moment requires not only $\mathbb{E}[T^2]$ but also $\mathbb{E}[T]$. This encourages us to define a vector-valued supermartingale.

Definition 3.3 (time-elapse function El_1). A function $\mathrm{El}_1 : [0, \infty]^2 \to [0, \infty]^2$ is defined by $\mathrm{El}_1(x_1, x_2) = (x_1 + 1, x_2 + 2x_1 + 1)$.

Then, an extension of F_1 for second moments can be defined as a combination of the time-elapse function El_1 and the pre-expectation $\overline{\mathbb{X}}$.

Definition 3.4 (F_2). Let I be an invariant and $C \subseteq I$ be a Borel set. We define $F_2 : (S \to [0,\infty]^2) \to (S \to [0,\infty]^2)$ by

$$(F_2(\eta))(c) = \begin{cases} (\overline{\mathbb{X}}(\mathrm{El}_1 \circ \eta))(c) & c \in I \setminus C \\ (0,0) & \text{otherwise.} \end{cases}$$

Here $\overline{\mathbb{X}}$ is applied componentwise: $(\overline{\mathbb{X}}(\eta_1,\eta_2))(c) = ((\overline{\mathbb{X}}\eta_1)(c), (\overline{\mathbb{X}}\eta_2)(c))$.

We can extend the complete lattice structure of $[0,\infty]$ to the function space $S \to [0,\infty]^2$ in a pointwise manner. It is a routine to prove that F_2 is monotone with respect to this complete lattice structure. Hence F_2 has the least fixed point. In fact, while $\overline{\mathbb{M}}_C^{\Gamma,1}$ was characterized as the least fixed point of F_1, a tuple $(\overline{\mathbb{M}}_C^{\Gamma,1}, \overline{\mathbb{M}}_C^{\Gamma,2})$ is *not* the least fixed point of F_2 (cf. Example 3.8 and Theorem 3.9). However, the least fixed point of F_2 *overapproximates* the tuple of moments.

Theorem 3.5. *For any configuration $c \in I$, $(\mu F_2)(c) \geq (\overline{\mathbb{M}}_C^{\Gamma,1}(c), \overline{\mathbb{M}}_C^{\Gamma,2}(c))$.* □

Let $T^{\Gamma}_{C,\sigma,n} = \min\{n, T^{\Gamma}_{C,\sigma}\}$. To prove the above theorem, we inductively prove

$$(F_2)^n(\bot)(c) \geq \left(\int T^{\Gamma_c}_{C,\sigma,n}\, \mathrm{d}\nu^{\Gamma_c}_{\sigma},\ \int (T^{\Gamma_c}_{C,\sigma,n})^2\, \mathrm{d}\nu^{\Gamma_c}_{\sigma}\right)$$

for each σ and n, and take the supremum. See [22, Appendix C] for more details.

Like ranking supermartingale for first moments, ranking supermartingale for second moments is defined as a prefixed point of F_2, i.e. a function η such that $\eta \geq F_2(\eta)$. However, we modify the definition for the sake of implementation.

Definition 3.6 (ranking supermartingale for second moments). A ranking supermartingale for second moments is a function $\eta : S \to \mathbb{R}^2$ such that: (i) $\eta(c) \geq (\overline{\mathbb{X}}(\mathrm{El}_1 \circ \eta))(c)$ for each $c \in I \setminus C$; and (ii) $\eta(c) \geq 0$ for each $c \in I$.

Here, the time-elapse function El_1 captures a positive decrease of the ranking supermartingale. Even though we only have inequality in Theorem 3.5, we can prove the following desired property of our supermartingale notion.

Theorem 3.7. *If $\eta : S \to \mathbb{R}^2$ is a supermartingale for second moments, then $(\overline{\mathbb{M}}_C^{\Gamma,1}(c), \overline{\mathbb{M}}_C^{\Gamma,2}(c)) \leq \eta(c)$ for each $c \in I$.* □

The following example and theorem show that we cannot replace $\geq$ with $=$ in Theorem 3.5 in general, but it is possible in the absence of nondeterminism.

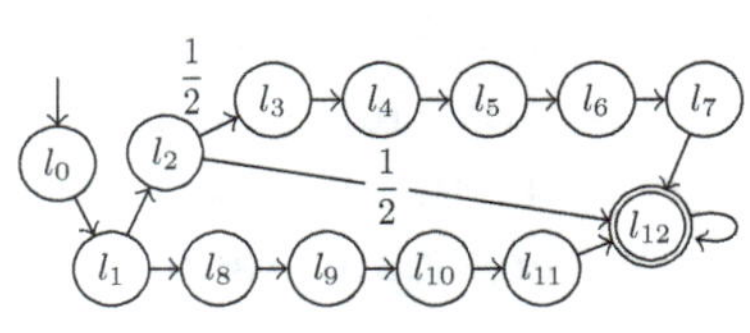

Example 3.8. The figure on the right shows a pCFG such that $l_2 \in L_P$ and all the other locations are in L_N, the initial location is l_0 and l_{12} is a terminating location. For the pCFG, the left-hand side of the inequality in Theorem 3.5 is $\mu F_2(l_0) = (6, 37.5)$. In contrast, if a scheduler σ takes a transition from l_1 to l_2 with probability p, $(\mathbb{M}^{\Gamma,1}_{C,\sigma}(l_0), \mathbb{M}^{\Gamma,2}_{C,\sigma}(l_0)) = (6 - \frac{1}{2}p, 36 - \frac{5}{2}p)$. Hence the right-hand side is $(\overline{\mathbb{M}}_C^{\Gamma,1}(l_0), \overline{\mathbb{M}}_C^{\Gamma,2}(l_0)) = (6, 36)$.

Theorem 3.9. *If* $L_N = L_{AN} = \emptyset$, $\forall c \in I.\,(\mu F_2)(c) = (\overline{\mathbb{M}}_C^{\Gamma,1}(c), \overline{\mathbb{M}}_C^{\Gamma,2}(c))$. □

3.2 Ranking Supermartingales for the Higher Moments

We extend the result in Sect. 3.1 to moments higher than second.

Firstly, the time-elapse function El_1 is generalized as follows.

Definition 3.10 (time-elapse function $\mathrm{El}_1^{K,k}$). For $K \in \mathbb{N}$ and $k \in \{1, \ldots, K\}$, a function $\mathrm{El}_1^{K,k} : [0,\infty]^K \to [0,\infty]$ is defined by $\mathrm{El}_1^{K,k}(x_1, \ldots, x_K) = 1 + \sum_{j=1}^{k} \binom{k}{j} x_j$. Here $\binom{k}{j}$ is the binomial coefficient.

Again, a monotone function F_K is defined as a combination of the time-elapse function $\mathrm{El}_1^{K,k}$ and the pre-expectation $\overline{\mathbb{X}}$.

Definition 3.11 (F_K). Let I be an invariant and $C \subseteq I$ be a Borel set. We define $F_K : (S \to [0,\infty]^K) \to (S \to [0,\infty]^K)$ by $F_K(\eta)(c) = (F_{K,1}(\eta)(c), \ldots, F_{K,K}(\eta)(c))$, where $F_{K,k} : (S \to [0,\infty]^K) \to (S \to [0,\infty])$ is given by

$$(F_{K,k}(\eta))(c) = \begin{cases} (\overline{\mathbb{X}}(\mathrm{El}_1^{K,k} \circ \eta))(c) & c \in I \setminus C \\ 0 & \text{otherwise.} \end{cases}$$

As in Definition 3.6, we define a supermartingale as a prefixed point of F_K.

Definition 3.12 (ranking supermartingale for K-th moments). We define $\eta_1, \ldots, \eta_K : S \to \mathbb{R}$ by $(\eta_1(c), \ldots, \eta_K(c)) = \eta(c)$. A *ranking supermartingale for K-th moments* is a function $\eta : S \to \mathbb{R}^K$ such that for each k, (i) $\eta_k(c) \geq (\overline{\mathbb{X}}(\mathrm{El}_1^{K,k} \circ \eta_k))(c)$ for each $c \in I \setminus C$; and (ii) $\eta_k(c) \geq 0$ for each $c \in I$.

For higher moments, we can prove an analogous result to Theorem 3.7.

Theorem 3.13. *If η is a supermartingale for K-th moments, then for each $c \in I$,* $(\overline{\mathbb{M}}_C^{\Gamma,1}(c), \ldots, \overline{\mathbb{M}}_C^{\Gamma,K}(c)) \leq \eta(c)$. □

4 From Moments to Tail Probabilities

We discuss how to obtain upper bounds of tail probabilities of runtimes from upper bounds of higher moments of runtimes. Combined with the result in Sect. 3, it induces a martingale-based method for overapproximating tail probabilities.

We use a concentration inequality. There are many choices of concentration inequalities (see e.g. [3]), and we use a variant of Markov's inequality. We prove that the concentration inequality is not only sound but also complete in a sense.

Formally, our goal is to calculate is an upper bound of $\Pr(T_{C,\sigma}^{\Gamma} \geq d)$ for a given deadline $d > 0$, under the assumption that we know upper bounds $u_1, \ldots, u_K$ of moments $\mathbb{E}[T_{C,\sigma}^{\Gamma}], \ldots, \mathbb{E}[(T_{C,\sigma}^{\Gamma})^K]$. In other words, we want to overapproximate $\sup_\mu \mu([d,\infty])$ where μ ranges over the set of probability measures on $[0,\infty]$ satisfying $\left(\int x \,\mathrm{d}\mu(x), \ldots, \int x^K \,\mathrm{d}\mu(x)\right) \leq (u_1, \ldots, u_K)$.

To answer this problem, we use a generalized form of Markov's inequality.

Proposition 4.1 (see e.g. [3, §2.1]). *Let X be a real-valued random variable and ϕ be a nondecreasing and nonnegative function. For any $d \in \mathbb{R}$ with $\phi(d) > 0$,*

$$\Pr(X \geq d) \leq \frac{\mathbb{E}[\phi(X)]}{\phi(d)}.$$

□

By letting $\phi(x) = x^k$ in Proposition 4.1, we obtain the following inequality. It gives an upper bound of the tail probability that is "tight."

Proposition 4.2. *Let X be a nonnegative random variable. Assume $\mathbb{E}[X^k] \leq u_k$ for each $k \in \{0, \ldots, K\}$. Then, for any $d > 0$,*

$$\Pr(X \geq d) \leq \min_{0 \leq k \leq K} \frac{u_k}{d^k}. \tag{1}$$

Moreover, this upper bound is tight: for any $d > 0$, there exists a probability measure such that the above equation holds.

Proof. The former part is immediate from Proposition 4.1. For the latter part, consider $\mu = p\delta_d + (1-p)\delta_0$ where δ_x is the Dirac measure at x and p is the value of the right-hand side of (1). □

By combining Theorem 3.13 with Proposition 4.2, we obtain the following corollary. We can use it for overapproximating tail probabilities.

Corollary 4.3. *Let $\eta : S \to \mathbb{R}^K$ be a ranking supermartingale for K-th moments. For each scheduler σ and a deadline $d > 0$,*

$$\Pr(T^{\Gamma}_{C,\sigma} \geq d) \leq \min_{0 \leq k \leq K} \frac{\eta_k(l_{\mathrm{init}}, \boldsymbol{x}_{\mathrm{init}})}{d^k}. \tag{2}$$

Here $\eta_0, \ldots, \eta_K$ are defined by $\eta_0(c) = 1$ and $\eta(c) = (\eta_1(c), \ldots, \eta_K(c))$. □

Note that if $K = 1$, Corollary 4.3 is essentially the same as [5, Thm 4]. Note also that for each K there exists $d > 0$ such that $\frac{\eta_K(l_{\mathrm{init}}, \boldsymbol{x}_{\mathrm{init}})}{d^K} = \min_{0 \leq k \leq K} \frac{\eta_k(l_{\mathrm{init}}, \boldsymbol{x}_{\mathrm{init}})}{d^k}$. Hence higher moments become useful in overapproximating tail probabilities as d gets large. Later in Sect. 6, we demonstrate this fact experimentally.

5 Template-Based Synthesis Algorithm

We discuss an automated synthesis algorithm that calculates an upper bound for the k-th moment of the runtime of a pCFG using a supermartingale in Definitions 3.6 or 3.12. It takes a pCFG Γ, an invariant I, a set $C \subseteq I$ of configurations, and a natural number K as input and outputs an upper bound of K-th moment.

Our algorithm is adapted from existing template-based algorithms for synthesizing a ranking supermartingale (for first moments) [4,6,7]. It fixes a linear or polynomial template with unknown coefficients for a supermartingale and using numerical methods like linear programming (LP) or semidefinite programming

(SDP), calculate a valuation of the unknown coefficients so that the axioms of ranking supermartingale for K-th moments are satisfied.

We hereby briefly explain the algorithms. See [22, Appendix D] for details.

Linear Template. Our linear template-based algorithm is adapted from [4,7]. We should assume that Γ, I and C are all "linear" in the sense that expressions appearing in Γ are all linear and I and C are represented by linear inequalities. To deal with assignments from a distribution like $x := \mathrm{Norm}(0, 1)$, we also assume that expected values of distributions appearing in Γ are known.

The algorithm first fixes a template for a supermartingale: for each location l, it fixes a K-tuple $\left(\sum_{j=1}^{|V|} a^l_{j,1} x_j + b^l_1, \ldots, \sum_j^{|V|} a^l_{j,K} x_j + b^l_K\right)$ of linear formulas. Here each $a^l_{j,i}$ and b^l_i are unknown variables called *parameters*. The algorithm next collects conditions on the parameters so that the tuples constitute a ranking supermartingale for K-th moments. It results in a conjunction of formulas of a form $\varphi_1 \geq 0 \land \cdots \land \varphi_m \geq 0 \Rightarrow \psi \geq 0$. Here $\varphi_1, \ldots, \varphi_m$ are linear formulas without parameters and ψ is a linear formula where parameters linearly appear in the coefficients. By Farkas' lemma (see e.g. [29, Cor 7.1h]) we can turn such formulas into linear inequalities over parameters by adding new variables. Its feasibility is efficiently solvable with an LP solver. We naturally wish to minimize an upper bound of the K-th moment, i.e. the last component of $\eta(l_{\mathrm{init}}, \boldsymbol{x}_{\mathrm{init}})$. We can minimize it by setting it to the objective function of the LP problem.

Polynomial Template. The polynomial template-based algorithm is based on [6]. This time, Γ, I and C can be "polynomial." To deal with assignments of distributions, we assume that the n-th moments of distributions in Γ are easily calculated for each $n \in \mathbb{N}$. It is similar to the linear template-based one.

It first fixes a polynomial template for a supermartingale, i.e. it assigns each location l a K-tuple of polynomial expressions with unknown coefficients. Likewise the linear template-based algorithm, the algorithm reduces the axioms of supermartingale for higher moments to a conjunction of formulas of a form $\varphi_1 \geq 0 \land \cdots \land \varphi_m \geq 0 \Rightarrow \psi \geq 0$. This time, each φ_i is a polynomial formula without parameters and ψ is a polynomial formula whose coefficients are *linear* formula over the parameters. In the polynomial case, a conjunction of such formula is reduced to an SDP problem using a theorem called Positivstellensatz (we used a variant called Schmüdgen's Positivstellensatz [28]). We solve the resulting problem using an SDP solver setting $\eta(l_{\mathrm{init}}, \boldsymbol{x}_{\mathrm{init}})$ as the objective function.

6 Experiments

We implemented two programs in OCaml to synthesize a supermartingale based on (a) a linear template and (b) a polynomial template. The programs translate a given randomized program to a pCFG and output an LP or SDP problem as described in Sect. 5. An invariant I and a terminal configuration C for the input program are specified manually. See e.g. [20] for automatic synthesis of an invariant. For linear templates, we have used GLPK (v4.65) [12] as an LP solver. For polynomial templates, we have used SOSTOOLS (v3.03) [31] (a sums of squares optimization tool that internally uses an SDP solver) on Matlab (R2018b). We used SDPT3 (v4.0) [30] as an SDP solver. The experiments were carried out on a Surface Pro 4 with an Intel Core i5-6300U (2.40 GHz) and 8 GB RAM. We tested our implementation for the following two programs and their variants, which were also used in the literature [7,19]. Their code is in [22, Appendix E].

Coupon collector's problem. A probabilistic model of collecting coupons enclosed in cereal boxes. There exist n types of coupons, and one repeatedly buy cereal boxes until all the types of coupons are collected. We consider two cases: (1-1) $n = 2$ and (1-2) $n = 4$. We tested the linear template program for them.

Random walk. We used three variants of 1-dimensional random walks: (2-1) integer-valued one, (2-2) real-valued one with assignments from continuous distributions, (2-3) with adversarial nondeterminism; and two variants of 2-dimensional random walks (2-4) and (2-5) with assignments from continuous distributions and adversarial nondeterminism. We tested both the linear and the polynomial template programs for these examples.

Experimental results. We measured execution times needed for Step 1 in Fig. 2. The results are in Table 1. Execution times are less than 0.2 s for linear template programs and several minutes for polynomial template programs. Upper bounds of tail probabilities obtained from Proposition 4.2 are in Fig. 3.

We can see that our method is applicable even with nondeterministic branching ((2-3), (2-4) and (2-5)) or assignments from continuous distributions ((2-2), (2-4) and (2-5)). We can use a linear template for bounding higher moments as long as there exists a supermartingale for higher moments representable by linear expressions ((1-1), (1-2) and (2-3)). In contrast, for (2-1), (2-2) and (2-4), only a polynomial template program found a supermartingale for second moments.

It is expectable that the polynomial template program gives a better bound than the linear one because a polynomial template is more expressive than a linear one. However, it did not hold for some test cases, probably because of numerical errors of the SDP solver. For example, (2-1) has a supermartingale for third moments that can be checked by a hand calculation, but the SDP solver returned "infeasible" in the polynomial template program. It appears that our program fails when large numbers are involved (e.g. the third moments of (2-1), (2-2) and (2-3)). We have also tested a variant of (2-1) where the initial position is multiplied by 10000. Then the SDP solver returned "infeasible" in the polynomial template program while the linear template program returns a nontrivial bound. Hence it seems that numerical errors are likely to occur to the polynomial template program when large numbers are involved.

Figure 3 shows that the bigger the deadline d is, the more useful higher moments become (cf. a remark just after Corollary 4.3). For example, in (1-2), an upper bound of $\Pr(T^{\Gamma}_{C,\sigma} \geq 100)$ calculated from the upper bound of the first moment is 0.680 while that of the fifth moment is 0.105.

To show the merit of our method compared with sampling-based methods, we calculated a tail probability bound for a variant of (2-2) (shown in Fig. 4 on

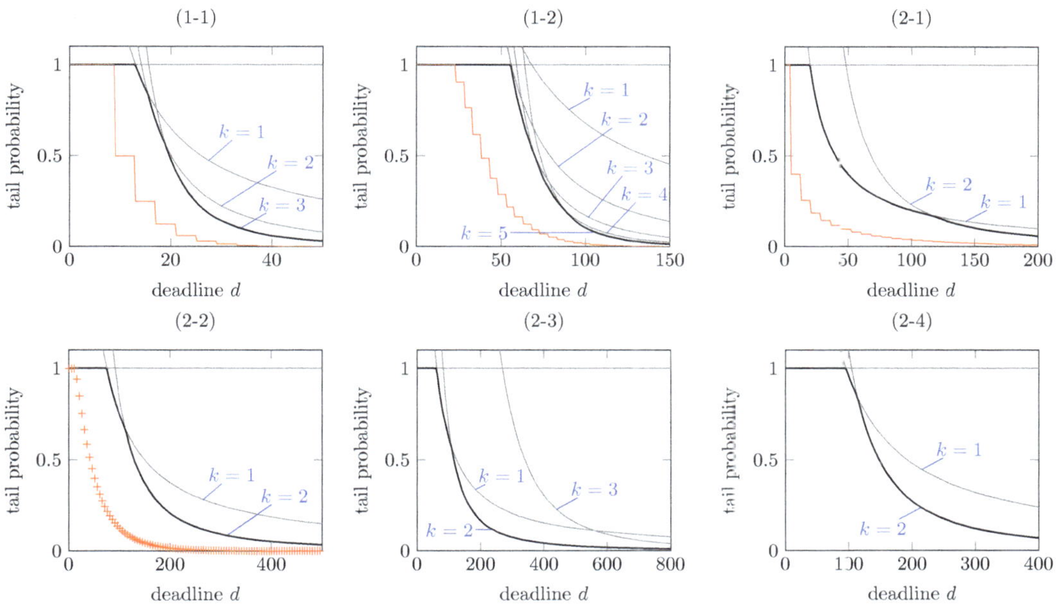

Fig. 3. Upper bounds of the tail probabilities (except (2-5)). Each gray line is the value of $\frac{u_k}{d^k}$ where u_k is the best upper bound in Table 1 of k-th moments and d is a deadline. Each black line is the minimum of gray lines, i.e. the upper bound by Proposition 4.2. The red lines in (1-1), (1-2) and (2-1) show the true tail probabilities calculated analytically. The red points in (2-2) show tail probabilities calculated by Monte Carlo sampling where the number of trials is 100000000. We did not calculate the true tail probabilities nor approximate them for (2-4) and (2-5) because these examples seem difficult to do so due to nondeterminism. (Color figure online)

Table 1. Upper bounds of the moments of runtimes. "-" indicates that the LP or SDP solver returned "infeasible". The "degree" column shows the degree of the polynomial template used in the experiments.

		(a) linear template		(b) polynominal template		
	moment	upper bound	time (s)	upper bound	time (s)	degree
(1-1)	1st	13	0.012			
	2nd	201	0.019			
	3rd	3829	0.023			
(1-2)	1st	68	0.024			
	2nd	3124	0.054			
	3rd	171932	0.089			
	4th	12049876	0.126			
	5th	1048131068	0.191			
(2-1)	1st	20	0.024	20.0	24.980	2
	2nd	-	0.013	2320.0	37.609	2
	3rd	-	0.017	-	30.932	3
(2-2)	1st	75	0.009	75.0	33.372	2
	2nd	-	0.014	8375.0	73.514	2
	3rd	-	0.021	-	170.416	3
(2-3)	1st	62	0.020	62.0	40.746	2
	2nd	28605.4	0.038	6710.0	97.156	2
	3rd	19567043.36	0.057	-	35.427	3
(2-4)	1st	96	0.020	95.95	157.748	2
	2nd	-	0.029	10944.0	361.957	2
(2-5)	1st	90	0.022	-	143.055	2
	2nd	-	0.042	-	327.202	2

```
x := 200000000;
while true do
  if prob(0.7) then
    z := Unif(0,1);
    x := x - z
  else
    z := Unif(0,1);
    x := x + z
  fi;
  refute (x < 0)
od
```

Fig. 4. A variant of (2-2).

p. 12) with a deadline $d = 10^{11}$. Because of its very long expected runtime, a sampling-based method would not work for it. In contrast, the linear template-based program gave an upper bound $\Pr(T^{\Gamma}_{C,\sigma} \geq 10^{11}) \leq 5000000025/10^{11} \approx 0.05$ in almost the same execution time as (2-2) (< 0.02 s).

7 Related Work

Martingale-Based Analysis of Randomized Programs. Martingale-based methods are widely studied for the termination analysis of randomized programs. One of the first is *ranking supermartingales*, introduced in [4] for proving almost sure termination. The theory of ranking supermartingales has since been extended actively: accommodating nondeterminism [1,6,7,11], syntax-oriented composition of supermartingales [11], proving properties beyond termination/reachability [13], and so on. Automated template-based synthesis of supermartingales by constraint solving has been pursued, too [1,4,6,7].

Other martingale-based methods that are fundamentally different from ranking supermartingales have been devised, too. They include: different notions of *repulsing supermartingales* for refuting termination (in [8,33]; also studied in control theory [32]); and *multiply-scaled submartingales* for underapproximating reachability probabilities [33,36]. See [33] for an overview.

In the literature on martingale-based methods, the one closest to this work is [5]. Among its contribution is the analysis of tail probabilities. It is done by either of the following combinations: (1) *difference-bounded* ranking supermartingales and the corresponding Azuma's concentration inequality; and (2) (not necessarily difference-bounded) ranking supermartingales and Markov's concentration inequality. When we compare these two methods with ours, the first method requires repeated martingale synthesis for different parameter values, which can pose a performance challenge. The second method corresponds to the restriction of our method to the first moment; recall that we showed the advantage of using higher moments, theoretically (Sect. 4) and experimentally (Sect. 6). See [22, Appendix F.1] for detailed discussions. Implementation is lacking in [5], too.

We use Markov's inequality to calculate an upper bound of $\Pr(T_{\mathrm{run}} \geq d)$ from a ranking supermartingale. In [7], Hoeffding's and Bernstein's inequalities are used for the same purpose. As the upper bounds obtained by these inequalities are exponentially decreasing with respect to d, they are asymptotically tighter than our bound obtained by Markov's inequality, assuming that we use the same ranking supermartingale. However, Hoeffding's and Bernstein's inequalities are applicable to limited classes of ranking supermartingales (so-called difference-bounded and incremental ones, respectively). There exists a randomized program whose tail probability for runtimes is decreasing only polynomially (not exponentially, see [22, Appendix G]); this witnesses that there are cases where the methods in [7] do not apply but ours can.

The work [1] is also close to ours in that their supermartingales are vector-valued. The difference is in the orders: in [1] they use the *lexicographic* order between vectors, and they aim to prove almost sure termination. In contrast, we use the *pointwise* order between vectors, for overapproximating higher moments.

The Predicate-Transformer Approach to Runtime Analysis. In the runtime/termination analysis of randomized programs, another principal line of work uses *predicate transformers* [2,17,19], following the precedent works on probabilistic predicate transformers such as [21,25]. In fact, from the mathematical point of view, the main construct for witnessing runtime/termination in those predicate transformer calculi (called *invariants*, see e.g. in [19]) is essentially the same thing as ranking supermartingales. Therefore the difference between the martingale-based and predicate-transformer approaches is mostly the matter of presentation—the predicate-transformer approach is more closely tied to program syntax and has a stronger deductive flavor. It also seems that there is less work on automated synthesis in the predicate-transformer approach.

In the predicate-transformer approach, the work [17] is the closest to ours, in that it studies *variance* of runtimes of randomized programs. The main differences are as follows: (1) computing tail probabilities is not pursued [17]; (2) their extension from expected runtimes to variance involves an additional variable τ, which poses a challenge in automated synthesis as well as in generalization to even higher moments; and (3) they do not pursue automated analysis. See Appendix F.2 of the extended version [22] for further details.

Higher Moments of Runtimes. Computing and using higher moments of runtimes of probabilistic systems—generalizing randomized programs—has been pursued before. In [9], computing moments of runtimes of *finite-state* Markov chains is reduced to a certain linear equation. In the study of randomized algorithms, the survey [10] collects a number of methods, among which are some tail probability bounds using higher moments. Unlike ours, none of these methods are language-based static ones. They do not allow automated analysis.

Other Potential Approaches to Tail Probabilities. We discuss potential approaches to estimating tail probabilities, other than the martingale-based one.

Sampling is widely employed for approximating behaviors of probabilistic systems; especially so in the field of probabilistic programming languages, since exact symbolic reasoning is hard in presence of conditioning. See e.g. [35]. We also used sampling to estimate tail probabilities in (2-2), Fig. 3. The main advantages of our current approach over sampling are threefold: (1) our upper bounds come with a mathematical guarantee, while the sampling bounds can always be erroneous; (2) it requires ingenuity to sample programs with nondeterminism; and (3) programs whose execution can take millions of years can still be analyzed by our method in a reasonable time, without executing them. The latter advantage is shared by static, language-based analysis methods in general; see e.g. [2].

Another potential method is probabilistic model checkers such as PRISM [23]. Their algorithms are usually only applicable to finite-state models, and thus not to randomized programs in general. Nevertheless, fixing a deadline d can make the reachable part $S_{\leq d}$ of the configuration space S finite, opening up the possibility of use of model checkers. It is an open question how to do so precisely, and the following challenges are foreseen: (1) if the program contains continuous distributions, the reachable part $S_{\leq d}$ becomes infinite; (2) even if $S_{\leq d}$ is finite, one has to repeat (supposedly expensive) runs of a model checker for each choice of d. In contrast, in our method, an upper bound for the tail probability $\Pr(T_{\text{run}} \geq d)$ is symbolically expressed as a function of d (Proposition 4.2). Therefore, estimating tail probabilities for varying d is computationally cheap.

8 Conclusions and Future Work

We provided a technique to obtain an upper bound of the tail probability of runtimes given a randomized algorithm and a deadline. We first extended the ordinary ranking supermartingale notion using the order-theoretic characterization so that it can calculate upper bounds of higher moments of runtimes for randomized programs. Then by using a suitable concentration inequality, we introduced a method to calculate an upper bound of tail probabilities from upper bounds of higher moments. Our method is not only sound but also complete in a sense. Our method was obtained by combining our supermartingale and the concentration inequality. We also implemented an automated synthesis algorithm and demonstrated the applicability of our framework.

Future Work. Example 3.8 shows that our supermartingale is not complete: it sometimes fails to give a tight bound for higher moments. Studying and improving the incompleteness is one possible direction of future work. For example, the following questions would be interesting: Can bounds given by our supermartingale be arbitrarily bad? Can we remedy the completeness by restricting the type of nondeterminism? Can we define a complete supermartingale?

Making our current method compositional is another direction of future research. Use of continuations, as in [18], can be a technical solution.

We are also interested in improving the implementation. The polynomial template program failed to give an upper bound for higher moments because of numerical errors (see Sect. 6). We wish to remedy this situation. There exist several studies for using numerical solvers for verification without affected by numerical errors [14–16, 26, 27]. We might make use of these works for improvements.

Acknowledgement. We thank the anonymous referees for useful comments. The authors are supported by JST ERATO HASUO Metamathematics for Systems Design Project (No. JPMJER1603), the JSPS-INRIA Bilateral Joint Research Project "CRECOGI," and JSPS KAKENHI Grant No. 15KT0012 & 15K11984. Natsuki Urabe is supported by JSPS KAKENHI Grant No. 16J08157.

References

1. Agrawal, S., Chatterjee, K., Novotný, P.: Lexicographic ranking supermartingales: an efficient approach to termination of probabilistic programs. PACMPL **2**(POPL), 34:1–34:32 (2018)
2. Batz, K., Kaminski, B.L., Katoen, J.-P., Matheja, C.: How long, O Bayesian network, will I sample thee? - A program analysis perspective on expected sampling times. In: Ahmed, A. (ed.) ESOP 2018. LNCS, vol. 10801, pp. 186–213. Springer, Cham (2018). https://doi.org/10.1007/978-3-319-89884-1_7
3. Boucheron, S., Lugosi, G., Massart, P.: Concentration Inequalities: A Nonasymptotic Theory of Independence. Oxford University Press, Oxford (2013)
4. Chakarov, A., Sankaranarayanan, S.: Probabilistic program analysis with martingales. In: Sharygina, N., Veith, H. (eds.) CAV 2013. LNCS, vol. 8044, pp. 511–526. Springer, Heidelberg (2013). https://doi.org/10.1007/978-3-642-39799-8_34
5. Chatterjee, K., Fu, H.: Termination of nondeterministic recursive probabilistic programs. CoRR, abs/1701.02944 (2017)
6. Chatterjee, K., Fu, H., Goharshady, A.K.: Termination analysis of probabilistic programs through Positivstellensatz's. In: Chaudhuri, S., Farzan, A. (eds.) CAV 2016. LNCS, vol. 9779, pp. 3–22. Springer, Cham (2016). https://doi.org/10.1007/978-3-319-41528-4_1
7. Chatterjee, K., Fu, H., Novotný, P., Hasheminezhad, R.: Algorithmic analysis of qualitative and quantitative termination problems for affine probabilistic programs. ACM Trans. Program. Lang. Syst. **40**(2), 7:1–7:45 (2018)
8. Chatterjee, K., Novotný, P., Zikelic, D.: Stochastic invariants for probabilistic termination. In: POPL, pp. 145–160. ACM (2017)
9. Dayar, T., Akar, N.: Computing moments of first passage times to a subset of states in markov chains. SIAM J. Matrix Anal. Appl. **27**(2), 396–412 (2005)
10. Doerr, B.: Probabilistic tools for the analysis of randomized optimization heuristics. CoRR, abs/1801.06733 (2018)
11. Ferrer Fioriti, L.M., Hermanns, H.: Probabilistic termination: soundness, completeness, and compositionality. In: POPL, pp. 489–501. ACM (2015)
12. The GNU linear programming kit. https://www.gnu.org/software/glpk/
13. Jagtap, P., Soudjani, S., Zamani, M.: Temporal logic verification of stochastic systems using barrier certificates. In: Lahiri and Wang [24], pp. 177–193
14. Jansson, C.: Termination and verification for ill-posed semidefinite programming problems. Optimization Online (2005)
15. Jansson, C.: VSDP: a MATLAB software package for verified semidefinite programming. In: NOLTA, pp. 327–330 (2006)
16. Jansson, C., Chaykin, D., Keil, C.: Rigorous error bounds for the optimal value in semidefinite programming. SIAM J. Numer. Anal. **46**(1), 180–200 (2007)
17. Kaminski, B.L., Katoen, J.-P., Matheja, C.: Inferring covariances for probabilistic programs. In: Agha, G., Van Houdt, B. (eds.) QEST 2016. LNCS, vol. 9826, pp. 191–206. Springer, Cham (2016). https://doi.org/10.1007/978-3-319-43425-4_14
18. Kaminski, B.L., Katoen, J.-P., Matheja, C., Olmedo, F.: Weakest precondition reasoning for expected run–times of probabilistic programs. In: Thiemann, P. (ed.) ESOP 2016. LNCS, vol. 9632, pp. 364–389. Springer, Heidelberg (2016). https://doi.org/10.1007/978-3-662-49498-1_15
19. Kaminski, B.L., Katoen, J.-P., Matheja, C., Olmedo, F.: Weakest precondition reasoning for expected runtimes of randomized algorithms. J. ACM **65**(5), 30:1–30:68 (2018)

20. Katoen, J.-P., McIver, A., Meinicke, L., Morgan, C.C.: Linear-invariant generation for probabilistic programs: automated support for proof-based methods. In: Cousot, R., Martel, M. (eds.) SAS 2010. LNCS, vol. 6337, pp. 390–406. Springer, Heidelberg (2010). https://doi.org/10.1007/978-3-642-15769-1_24
21. Kozen, D.: Semantics of probabilistic programs. J. Comput. Syst. Sci. **22**(3), 328–350 (1981)
22. Kura, S., Urabe, N., Hasuo, I.: Tail probabilities for randomized program runtimes via martingales for higher moments. CoRR, abs/1811.06779 (2018)
23. Kwiatkowska, M.Z., Norman, G., Parker, D.: PRISM 4.0: verification of probabilistic real-time systems. In: Gopalakrishnan, G., Qadeer, S. (eds.) CAV 2011. LNCS, vol. 6806, pp. 585–591. Springer, Heidelberg (2011). https://doi.org/10.1007/978-3-642-22110-1_47
24. Lahiri, S.K., Wang, C. (eds.): ATVA 2018. LNCS, vol. 11138. Springer, Cham (2018). https://doi.org/10.1007/978-3-030-01090-4
25. Morgan, C., McIver, A., Seidel, K.: Probabilistic predicate transformers. ACM Trans. Program. Lang. Syst. **18**(3), 325–353 (1996)
26. Roux, P., Iguernlala, M., Conchon, S.: A non-linear arithmetic procedure for control-command software verification. In: Beyer, D., Huisman, M. (eds.) TACAS 2018. LNCS, vol. 10806, pp. 132–151. Springer, Cham (2018). https://doi.org/10.1007/978-3-319-89963-3_8
27. Roux, P., Voronin, Y.-L., Sankaranarayanan, S.: Validating numerical semidefinite programming solvers for polynomial invariants. Form. Methods Syst. Des. **53**(2), 286–312 (2018)
28. Schmüdgen, K.: The k-moment problem for compact semi-algebraic sets. Math. Ann. **289**(1), 203–206 (1991)
29. Schrijver, A.: Theory of Linear and Integer Programming. Wiley, New York (1986)
30. SDPT3. http://www.math.nus.edu.sg/~mattohkc/SDPT3.html
31. SOSTOOLS. http://sysos.eng.ox.ac.uk/sostools/
32. Steinhardt, J., Tedrake, R.: Finite-time regional verification of stochastic non-linear systems. Int. J. Robot. Res. **31**(7), 901–923 (2012)
33. Takisaka, T., Oyabu, Y., Urabe, N., Hasuo, I.: Ranking and repulsing supermartingales for reachability in probabilistic programs. In: Lahiri and Wang [24], pp. 476–493
34. Tarski, A.: A lattice-theoretical fixpoint theorem and its applications. Pac. J. Math. **5**, 285–309 (1955)
35. Tolpin, D., van de Meent, J.-W., Yang, H., Wood, F.D.: Design and implementation of probabilistic programming language anglican. In: IFL, pp. 6:1–6:12. ACM (2016)
36. Urabe, N., Hara, M., Hasuo, I.: Categorical liveness checking by corecursive algebras. In: Proceedings of LICS 2017, pp. 1–12. IEEE Computer Society (2017)

Computing the Expected Execution Time of Probabilistic Workflow Nets

Philipp J. Meyer(✉), Javier Esparza, and Philip Offtermatt

Technical University of Munich, Munich, Germany
{meyerphi,esparza,offtermp}@in.tum.de

Abstract. Free-Choice Workflow Petri nets, also known as Workflow Graphs, are a popular model in Business Process Modeling.

In this paper we introduce Timed Probabilistic Workflow Nets (TPWNs), and give them a Markov Decision Process (MDP) semantics. Since the time needed to execute two parallel tasks is the maximum of the times, and not their sum, the expected time cannot be directly computed using the theory of MDPs with rewards. In our first contribution, we overcome this obstacle with the help of "earliest-first" schedulers, and give a single exponential-time algorithm for computing the expected time.

In our second contribution, we show that computing the expected time is #P-hard, and so polynomial algorithms are very unlikely to exist. Further, #P-hardness holds even for workflows with a very simple structure in which all transitions times are 1 or 0, and all probabilities are 1 or 0.5.

Our third and final contribution is an experimental investigation of the runtime of our algorithm on a set of industrial benchmarks. Despite the negative theoretical results, the results are very encouraging. In particular, the expected time of every workflow in a popular benchmark suite with 642 workflow nets can be computed in milliseconds. Data or code related to this paper is available at: [24].

1 Introduction

Workflow Petri Nets are a popular model for the representation and analysis of business processes [1,3,7]. They are used as back-end for different notations like BPMN (Business Process Modeling Notation), EPC (Event-driven Process Chain), and UML Activity Diagrams.

The project has received funding from the European Research Council (ERC) under the European Union's Horizon 2020 research and innovation programme under grant agreement No. 787367 (PaVeS). Further it is partially supported by the DFG Project No. 273811150 (Negotiations: A Model for Tractable Concurrency).

T. Vojnar and L. Zhang (Eds.): TACAS 2019, Part II, LNCS 11428, pp. 154–171, 2019.
https://doi.org/10.1007/978-3-030-17465-1_9

There is recent interest in extending these notations with quantitative information, like probabilities, costs, and time. The final goal is the development of tool support for computing performance metrics, like the average cost or the average runtime of a business process.

In a former paper we introduced Probabilistic Workflow Nets (PWN), a foundation for the extension of Petri nets with probabilities and rewards [11]. We presented a polynomial time algorithm for the computation of the expected cost of free-choice workflow nets, a subclass of PWN of particular interest for the workflow process community (see e.g. [1,10,13,14]). For example, 1386 of the 1958 nets in the most popular benchmark suite in the literature are free-choice Workflow Nets [12].

In this paper we introduce Timed PWNs (TPWNs), an extension of PWNs with time. Following [11], we define a semantics in terms of Markov Decision Processes (MDPs), where, loosely speaking, the nondeterminism of the MDP models absence of information about the order in which concurrent transitions are executed. For every scheduler, the semantics assigns to the TPWN an expected time to termination. Using results of [11], we prove that this expected time is actually independent of the scheduler, and so that the notion "expected time of a TPWN" is well defined.

We then proceed to study the problem of computing the expected time of a sound TPWN (loosely speaking, of a TPWN that terminates successfully with probability 1). The expected cost and the expected time have a different interplay with concurrency. The cost of executing two tasks in parallel is the sum of the costs (cost models e.g. salaries of power consumption), while the execution time of two parallel tasks is the maximum of their individual execution times. For this reason, standard reward-based algorithms for MDPs, which assume additivity of the reward along a path, cannot be applied.

Our solution to this problem uses the fact that the expected time of a TPWN is independent of the scheduler. We define an "earliest-first" scheduler which, loosely speaking, resolves the nondeterminism of the MDP by picking transitions with earliest possible firing time. Since at first sight the scheduler needs infinite memory, its corresponding Markov chain is infinite-state, and so of no help. However, we show how to construct another finite-state Markov chain with additive rewards, whose expected reward is equal to the expected time of the infinite-state chain. This finite-state Markov chain can be exponentially larger than the TPWN, and so our algorithm has exponential complexity. We prove that computing the expected time is #P-hard, even for free-choice TPWNs in which all transitions times are either 1 or 0, and all probabilities are 1 or $1/2$. So, in particular, the existence of a polynomial algorithm implies $\mathsf{P} = \mathsf{NP}$.

In the rest of the paper we show that, despite these negative results, our algorithm behaves well in practice. For all 642 sound free-choice nets of the benchmark suite of [12], computing the expected time never takes longer than a few milliseconds. Looking for a more complicated set of examples, we study a TPWN computed from a set of logs by process mining. We observe that the computation of the expected time is sensitive to the distribution of the execution time of a task. Still, our experiments show that even for complicated distributions leading to TPWNs with hundreds of transitions and times spanning two orders of magnitude the expected time can be computed in minutes.

All missing proofs can be found in the Appendix of the full version [19].

2 Preliminaries

We introduce some preliminary definitions. The full version [19] gives more details.

Workflow Nets. A *workflow net* is a tuple $\mathbf{N} = (P, T, F, i, o)$ where P and T are disjoint finite sets of *places* and *transitions*; $F \subseteq (P \times T) \cup (T \times P)$ is a set of *arcs*; $i, o \in P$ are distinguished *initial* and *final* places such that i has no incoming arcs, o has no outgoing arcs, and the graph $(P \cup T, F \cup \{(o, i)\})$ is strongly connected. For $x \in P \cup T$, we write ${}^\bullet x$ for the set $\{y \mid (y, x) \in F\}$ and $x^\bullet$ for $\{y \mid (x, y) \in F\}$. We call ${}^\bullet x$ (resp. $x^\bullet$) the *preset* (resp. *postset*) of x. We extend this notion to sets $X \subseteq P \cup T$ by ${}^\bullet X \stackrel{\text{def}}{=} \cup_{x \in X} {}^\bullet x$ resp. $X^\bullet \stackrel{\text{def}}{=} \cup_{x \in X} x^\bullet$. The notions of marking, enabled transitions, transition firing, firing sequence, and reachable marking are defined as usual. The *initial marking* (resp. *final marking*) of a workflow net, denoted by $\boldsymbol{i}$ (resp. $\boldsymbol{o}$), has one token on place i (resp. o), and no tokens elsewhere. A firing sequence σ is a *run* if $\boldsymbol{i} \xrightarrow{\sigma} \boldsymbol{o}$, i.e. if it leads to the final marking. $Run_{\mathbf{N}}$ denotes the set of all runs of $\mathbf{N}$.

Soundness and 1-safeness. Well designed workflows should be free of deadlocks and livelocks. This idea is captured by the notion of soundness [1,2]: A workflow net is *sound* if the final marking is reachable from any reachable marking.[1] Further, in this paper we restrict ourselves to 1-safe workflows: A marking M of a workflow net $\mathcal{W}$ is *1-safe* if $M(p) \leq 1$ for every place p, and $\mathcal{W}$ itself is *1-safe* if every reachable marking is 1-safe. We identify 1-safe markings M with the set $\{p \in P \mid M(p) = 1\}$.

Independence, concurrency, conflict [22]**.** Two transitions t_1, t_2 of a workflow net are *independent* if ${}^\bullet t_1 \cap {}^\bullet t_2 = \emptyset$, and *dependent* otherwise. Given a 1-safe marking M, two transitions are *concurrent at* M if M enables both of them, and they are independent, and *in conflict at* M if M enables both of them, and they are dependent. Finally, we recall the definition of Mazurkiewicz equivalence. Let $\mathbf{N} = (P, T, F, i, o)$ be a 1-safe workflow net. The relation $\equiv_1 \subseteq T^* \times T^*$ is defined as follows: $\sigma \equiv_1 \tau$ if there are independent transitions t_1, t_2 and sequences $\sigma', \sigma'' \in T^*$ such that $\sigma = \sigma' \, t_1 \, t_2 \sigma''$ and $\tau = \sigma' \, t_2 \, t_1 \sigma''$. Two sequences $\sigma, \tau \in T^*$ are *Mazurkiewicz equivalent* if $\sigma \equiv \tau$, where $\equiv$ is the reflexive and transitive closure of $\equiv_1$. Observe that $\sigma \in T^*$ is a firing sequence iff every sequence $\tau \equiv \sigma$ is a firing sequence.

Confusion-freeness, free-choice workflows. Let t be a transition of a workflow net, and let M be a 1-safe marking that enables t. The *conflict set of* t

[1] In [2], which examines many different notions of soundness, this is called *easy* soundness.

at M, denoted $C(t, M)$, is the set of transitions in conflict with t at M. A set U of transitions is a *conflict set* of M if there is a transition t such that $U = C(t, M)$. The conflict sets of M are given by $\mathcal{C}(M) \stackrel{\text{def}}{=} \cup_{t \in T} C(t, M)$. A 1-safe workflow net is *confusion-free* if for every reachable marking M and every transition t enabled at M, every transition u concurrent with t at M satisfies $C(u, M) = C(u, M \setminus {}^\bullet t) = C(u, (M \setminus {}^\bullet t) \cup t^\bullet)$. The following result follows easily from the definitions (see also [11]):

Lemma 1 [11]. *Let* $\mathbf{N}$ *be a 1-safe workflow net. If* $\mathbf{N}$ *is confusion-free then for every reachable marking* M *the conflict sets* $\mathcal{C}(M)$ *are a partition of the set of transitions enabled at* M*.*

A workflow net is *free-choice* if for every two places p_1, p_2, if $p_1^\bullet \cap p_2^\bullet \neq \emptyset$, then $p_1^\bullet = p_2^\bullet$. Any free-choice net is confusion-free, and the conflict set of a transition t enabled at a marking M is given by $C(t, M) = ({}^\bullet t)^\bullet$ (see e.g. [11]).

3 Timed Probabilistic Workflow Nets

In [11] we introduced a probabilistic semantics for confusion-free workflow nets. Intuitively, at every reachable marking a choice between two concurrent transitions is resolved nondeterministically by a scheduler, while a choice between two transitions in conflict is resolved probabilistically; the probability of choosing each transition is proportional to its *weight*. For example, in the net in Fig. 1a, at the marking $\{p_1, p_3\}$, the scheduler can choose between the conflict sets $\{t_2, t_3\}$ and $\{t_4\}$, and if $\{t_2, t_3\}$ is chosen, then t_2 is chosen with probability $1/5$ and t_3 with probability $4/5$. We extend Probabilistic Workflow Nets by assigning to each transition t a natural number $\tau(t)$ modeling the time it takes for the transition to fire, once it has been selected.[2]

Definition 1 (Timed Probabilistic Workflow Nets). *A* Timed Probabilistic Workflow Net *(TPWN) is a tuple* $\mathcal{W} = (\mathbf{N}, w, \tau)$ *where* $\mathbf{N} = (P, T, F, i, o)$ *is a 1-safe confusion-free workflow net,* $w \colon T \to \mathbb{Q}_{>0}$ *is a* weight function, *and* $\tau \colon T \to \mathbb{N}$ *is a* time function *that assigns to every transition a duration.*

Timed sequences. We assign to each transition sequence σ of $\mathcal{W}$ and each place p a *timestamp* $\mu(\sigma)_p$ through a *timestamp function* $\mu : T^* \to \mathbb{N}_\perp^P$. The set $\mathbb{N}_\perp$ is defined by $\mathbb{N}_\perp \stackrel{\text{def}}{=} \{\perp\} \cup \mathbb{N}$ with $\perp \leq x$ and $\perp + x = \perp$ for all $x \in \mathbb{N}_\perp$. Intuitively, if a place p is marked after σ, then $\mu(\sigma)_p$ records the "arrival time" of the token in p, and if p is unmarked, then $\mu(\sigma)_p = \perp$. When a transition occurs, it removes all tokens in its preset, and $\tau(t)$ time units later, puts tokens into its postset.

[2] The semantics of the model can be defined in the same way for both discrete and continuous time, but, since our results only concern discrete time, we only consider this case.

Formally, we define $\mu(\epsilon)_i \stackrel{\text{def}}{=} 0$, $\mu(\epsilon)_p \stackrel{\text{def}}{=} \bot$ for $p \neq i$, and $\mu(\sigma t) \stackrel{\text{def}}{=} \mathit{upd}(\mu(\sigma), t)$, where the update function $\mathit{upd} : \mathbb{N}_\bot^P \times T \to \mathbb{N}_\bot^P$ is given by:

$$\mathit{upd}(\boldsymbol{x}, t)_p \stackrel{\text{def}}{=} \begin{cases} \max_{q \in {}^\bullet t} \boldsymbol{x}_q + \tau(t) & \text{if } p \in t^\bullet \\ \bot & \text{if } p \in {}^\bullet t \setminus t^\bullet \\ \boldsymbol{x}_p & \text{if } p \notin {}^\bullet t \cup t^\bullet \end{cases}$$

We then define $\mathit{tm}(\sigma) \stackrel{\text{def}}{=} \max_{p \in P} \mu(\sigma)_p$ as the time needed to fire σ. Further $[\![\boldsymbol{x}]\!] \stackrel{\text{def}}{=} \{p \in P \mid \boldsymbol{x}_p \neq \bot\}$ is the marking represented by a timestamp $\boldsymbol{x} \in \mathbb{N}_\bot^P$.

Example 1. The net in Fig. 1a is a TPWN. Weights are shown in red next to transitions, and times are written in blue into the transitions. For the sequence $\sigma_1 = t_1 t_3 t_4 t_5$, we have $\mathit{tm}(\sigma_1) = 9$, and for $\sigma_2 = t_1 t_2 t_3 t_4 t_5$, we have $\mathit{tm}(\sigma_2) = 10$. Observe that the time taken by the sequences is *not* equal to the sum of the durations of the transitions.

Markov Decision Process semantics. A *Markov Decision Process* (MDP) is a tuple $\mathcal{M} = (Q, q_0, \mathit{Steps})$ where Q is a finite set of states, $q_0 \in Q$ is the initial state, and $\mathit{Steps}\colon Q \to 2^{\mathit{dist}(Q)}$ is the probability transition function. Paths of an MDP, schedulers, and the probability measure of paths compatible with a scheduler are defined as usual (see the Appendix of the full version [19]).

The semantics of a TPWN $\mathcal{W}$ is a Markov Decision Process $\mathit{MDP}_\mathcal{W}$. The states of $\mathit{MDP}_\mathcal{W}$ are either markings M or pairs (M, t), where t is a transition enabled at M. The intended meanings of M and (M, t) are "the current marking is M", and "the current marking is M, and t has been selected to fire next." Intuitively, t is chosen in two steps: first, a conflict set enabled at M is chosen nondeterministically, and then a transition of this set is chosen at random, with probability proportional to its weight.

Formally, let $\mathcal{W} = (\mathbf{N}, w, \tau)$ be a TPWN where $\mathbf{N} = (P, T, F, i, o)$, let M be a reachable marking of $\mathcal{W}$ enabling at least one transition, and let C be a conflict set of M. Let $w(C)$ be the sum of the weights of the transitions in C. The *probability distribution* $P_{M,C}$ *over* T is given by $P_{M,C}(t) = \frac{w(t)}{w(C)}$ if $t \in C$ and $P_{M,C}(t) = 0$ otherwise. Now, let $\mathcal{M}$ be the set of 1-safe markings of $\mathcal{W}$, and let $\mathcal{E}$ be the set of pairs (M, t) such that $M \in \mathcal{M}$ and M enables t. We define the Markov decision process $\mathit{MDP}_\mathcal{W} = (Q, q_0, \mathit{Steps})$, where $Q = \mathcal{M} \cup \mathcal{E}$, $q_0 = \mathbf{i}$, the initial marking of $\mathcal{W}$, and $\mathit{Steps}(M)$ is defined for markings of $\mathcal{M}$ and $\mathcal{E}$ as follows. For every $M \in \mathcal{M}$,

- if M enables no transitions, then $\mathit{Steps}(M)$ contains exactly one distribution, which assigns probability 1 to M, and 0 to all other states.
- if M enables at least one transition, then $\mathit{Steps}(M)$ contains a distribution λ for each conflict set C of M. The distribution is defined by: $\lambda(M, t) = P_{M,C}(t)$ for every $t \in C$, and $\lambda(s) = 0$ for every other state s.

For every $(M, t) \in \mathcal{E}$, $\mathit{Steps}(M, t)$ contains one single distribution that assigns probability 1 to the marking M' such that $M \xrightarrow{t} M'$, and probability 0 to every other state.

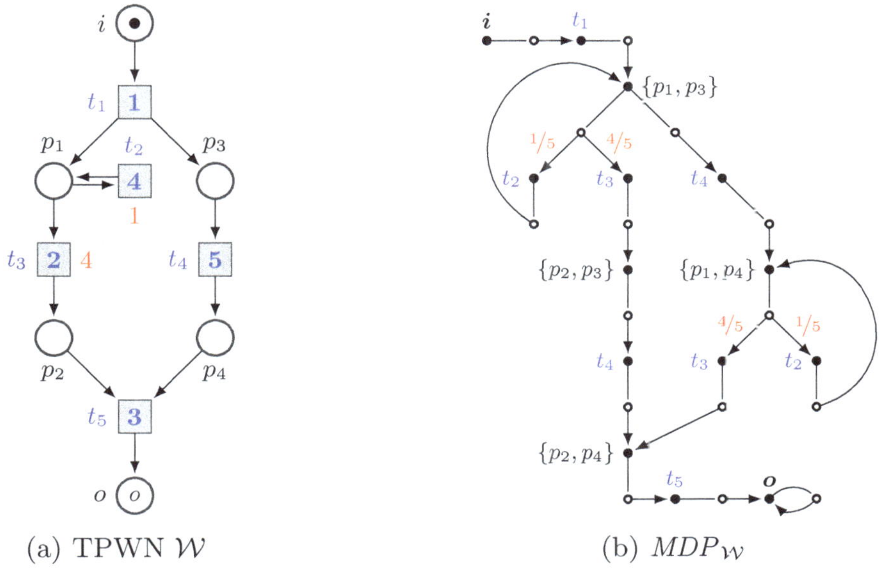

Fig. 1. A TPWN and its associated MDP. (Color figure online)

Example 2. Figure 1b shows a graphical representation of the MDP of the TPWN in Fig. 1a. Black nodes represent states, white nodes probability distributions. A black node q has a white successor for each probability distribution in $Steps(q)$. A white node λ has a black successor for each node q such that $\lambda(q) > 0$; the arrow leading to this black successor is labeled with $\lambda(q)$, unless $\lambda(q) = 1$, in which case there is no label. States (M, t) are abbreviated to t.

Schedulers. Given a TPWN $\mathcal{W}$, a scheduler of $MDP_{\mathcal{W}}$ is a function $\gamma : T^* \to 2^T$ assigning to each firing sequence $\boldsymbol{i} \xrightarrow{\sigma} M$ with $\mathcal{C}(M) \neq \emptyset$ a conflict set $\gamma(\sigma) \in \mathcal{C}(M)$. A firing sequence $\boldsymbol{i} \xrightarrow{\sigma} M$ is *compatible* with a scheduler γ if for all partitions $\sigma = \sigma_1 t \sigma_2$ for some transition t, we have $t \in \gamma(\sigma_1)$.

Example 3. In the TPWN of Fig. 1a, after firing t_1 two conflict sets become concurrently enabled: $\{t_2, t_3\}$ and $\{t_4\}$. A scheduler picks one of the two. If the scheduler picks $\{t_2, t_3\}$ then t_2 may occur, and in this case, since firing t_2 does not change the marking, the scheduler chooses again one of $\{t_2, t_3\}$ and $\{t_4\}$. So there are infinitely many possible schedulers, differing only in how many times they pick $\{t_2, t_3\}$ before picking t_4.

Definition 2 ((Expected) Time until a state is reached). *Let π be an infinite path of $MDP_{\mathcal{W}}$, and let M be a reachable marking of $\mathcal{W}$. Observe that M is a state of $MDP_{\mathcal{W}}$. The* time needed to reach M along π, *denoted $tm(M, \pi)$, is defined as follows: If π does not visit M, then $tm(M, \pi) \stackrel{def}{=} \infty$; otherwise, $tm(M, \pi) \stackrel{def}{=} tm(\Sigma(\pi'))$, where $\Sigma(\pi')$ is the transition sequence corresponding to the shortest prefix π' of π ending at M. Given a scheduler S, the expected time until reaching M is defined as*

$$ET^S_{\mathcal{W}}(M) \stackrel{def}{=} \sum_{\pi \in Paths^S} tm(M, \pi) \cdot Prob^S(\pi).$$

and the expected time $ET^S_{\mathcal{W}}$ *is defined as* $ET^S_{\mathcal{W}} \stackrel{def}{=} ET^S_{\mathcal{W}}(\boldsymbol{o})$*, i.e. the expected time until reaching the final marking.*

In [11] we proved a result for Probabilistic Workflow Nets (PWNs) with rewards, showing that the expected reward of a PWN is independent of the scheduler (intuitively, this is the case because in a confusion-free Petri net the scheduler only determines the logical order in which transitions occur, but not which transitions occur). Despite the fact that, contrary to rewards, the execution time of a firing sequence is not the sum of the execution times of its transitions, the proof carries over to the expected time with only minor modifications.

Theorem 1. *Let* $\mathcal{W}$ *be a TPWN.*

(1) There exists a value $ET_{\mathcal{W}}$ *such that for every scheduler* S *of* $\mathcal{W}$*, the expected time* $ET^S_{\mathcal{W}}$ *of* $\mathcal{W}$ *under* S *is equal to* $ET_{\mathcal{W}}$*.*
(2) $ET_{\mathcal{W}}$ *is finite iff* $\mathcal{W}$ *is sound.*

By this theorem, the expected time $ET_{\mathcal{W}}$ can be computed by choosing a suitable scheduler S, and computing $ET^S_{\mathcal{W}}$.

4 Computation of the Expected Time

We show how to compute the expected time of a TPWN. We fix an appropriate scheduler, show that it induces a finite-state Markov chain, define an appropriate reward function for the chain, and prove that the expected time is equal to the expected reward.

4.1 Earliest-First Scheduler

Consider a firing sequence $\boldsymbol{i} \xrightarrow{\sigma} M$. We define the *starting time* of a conflict set $C \in \mathcal{C}(M)$ as the earliest time at which the transitions of C become enabled. This occurs after *all* tokens of ${}^\bullet C$ arrive[3], and so the starting time of C is the maximum of $\mu(\sigma)_p$ for $p \in {}^\bullet C$ (recall that $\mu(\sigma)_p$ is the latest time at which a token arrives at p while firing σ).

Intuitively, the "earliest-first" scheduler always chooses the conflict set with the earliest starting time (if there are multiple such conflict sets, the scheduler chooses any one of them). Formally, recall that a scheduler is a mapping $\gamma \colon T^* \to 2^T$ such that for every firing sequence $\boldsymbol{i} \xrightarrow{\sigma} M$, the set $\gamma(\sigma)$ is a conflict set of M. We define the *earliest-first scheduler* γ by:

$$\gamma(\sigma) \stackrel{\text{def}}{=} \arg\min_{C \in \mathcal{C}(M)} \max_{p \in {}^\bullet C} \mu(\sigma)_p \qquad \text{where } M \text{ is given by } \boldsymbol{i} \xrightarrow{\sigma} M.$$

[3] This is proved in Lemma 7 in the Appendix of the full version [19].

Example 4. Figure 2a shows the Markov chain induced by the "earliest-first" scheduler defined above in the MDP of Fig. 1b. Initially we have a token at $\boldsymbol{i}$ with arrival time 0. After firing t_1, which takes time 1, we obtain tokens in p_1 and p_3 with arrival time 1. In particular, the conflict sets $\{t_2, t_3\}$ and $\{t_4\}$ become enabled at time 1. The scheduler can choose any of them, because they have the same starting time. Assume it chooses $\{t_2, t_3\}$. The Markov chain now branches into two transitions, corresponding to firing t_2 and t_3 with probabilities $1/5$ and $4/5$, respectively. Consider the branch in which t_2 fires. Since t_2 starts at time 1 and takes 4 time units, it removes the token from p_1 at time 1, and adds a new token to p_1 with arrival time 5; the token at p_3 is not affected, and it keeps its arrival time of 1. So we have $\mu(t_1t_2) = \{\substack{p_1\\5}, \substack{p_3\\1}\}$ (meaning $\mu(t_1t_2)_{p_1} = 5$, $\mu(t_1t_2)_{p_3} = 1$, and $\mu(t_1t_2)_p = \bot$ otherwise). Now the conflict sets $\{t_2, t_3\}$ and $\{t_4\}$ are enabled again, but with a difference: while $\{t_4\}$ has been enabled since time 1, the set $\{t_2, t_3\}$ is now enabled since time $\mu(t_1t_2)_{p_1} = 5$. The scheduler must now choose $\{t_4\}$, leading to the marking that puts tokens on p_1 and p_4 with arrival times $\mu(t_1t_2t_4)_{p_1} = 5$ and $\mu(t_1t_2t_4)_{p_4} = 6$. In the next steps the scheduler always chooses $\{t_2, t_3\}$ until t_5 becomes enabled. The final marking $\boldsymbol{o}$ can be reached after time 9, through $t_1t_3t_4t_5$ with probability $4/5$, or with times $10 + 4k$ for $k \in \mathbb{N}$, through $t_1t_2t_4t_2^kt_3t_5$ with probability $(1/5)^{k-1} \cdot 4/5$ (the times at which the final marking can be reached are written in blue inside the final states).

Theorem 2 below shows that the earliest-first scheduler only needs finite memory, which is not clear from the definition. The construction is similar to those of [6,15,16]. However, our proof crucially depends on TPWNs being confusion-free.

Theorem 2. *Let $H \stackrel{def}{=} \max_{t \in T} \tau(t)$ be the maximum duration of the transitions of T, and let $[H]_\bot \stackrel{def}{=} \{\bot, 0, 1, \ldots, H\} \subseteq \mathbb{N}_\bot$. There are functions $\nu\colon T^* \to [H]_\bot^P$ (compare with $\mu\colon T^* \to \mathbb{N}_\bot^P$), $f\colon [H]_\bot^P \times T \to [H]_\bot^P$ and $r\colon [H]_\bot^P \to \mathbb{N}$ such that for every $\sigma = t_1 \ldots t_n \in T^*$ compatible with γ and for every $t \in T$ enabled by σ:*

$$\gamma(\sigma) = \mathop{\arg\min}_{C \in \mathcal{C}([\![\nu(\sigma)]\!])} \max_{p \in {}^\bullet C} \nu(\sigma)_p \tag{1}$$

$$\nu(\sigma t) = f(\nu(\sigma), t) \tag{2}$$

$$tm(\sigma) = \max_{p \in P} \nu(\sigma)_p + \sum_{k=0}^{n-1} r(\nu(t_1 \ldots t_k)) \tag{3}$$

Observe that, unlike μ, the range of ν is finite. We call it the *finite abstraction* of μ. Equation 1 states that γ can be computed directly from the finite abstraction ν. Equation 2 shows that $\nu(\sigma t)$ can be computed from $\nu(\sigma)$ and t. So γ only needs to remember an element of $[H]_\bot^P$, which implies that it only requires finite memory. Finally, observe that the function r of Eq. 3 has a finite domain, and so it allows us to use ν to compute the time needed by σ.

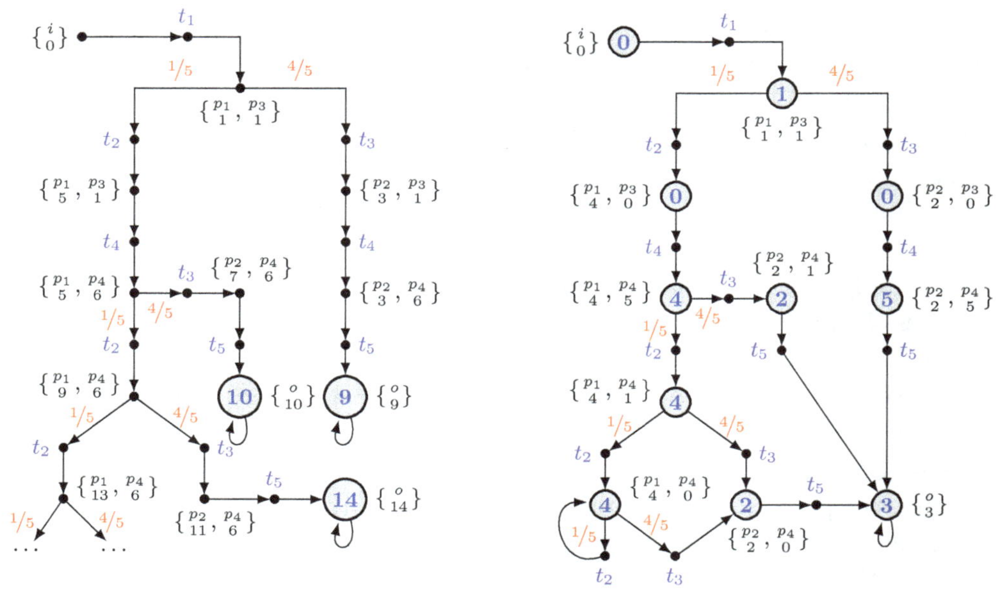

(a) Infinite MC for scheduler using $\mu(\sigma)$, with final states labeled by $tm(\sigma)$.

(b) Finite MC for scheduler using $\nu(\sigma)$, with states labeled by rewards $r(\nu(\sigma))$.

Fig. 2. Two Markov chains for the "earliest-first" scheduler. (Color figure online)

The formal definition of the functions ν, f, and r is given below, together with the definition of the auxiliary operator $\ominus\colon \mathbb{N}_\perp^P \times \mathbb{N} \to \mathbb{N}_\perp^P$:

$$(\boldsymbol{x} \ominus n)_p \stackrel{\text{def}}{=} \begin{cases} \max(\boldsymbol{x}_p - n, 0) & \text{if } \boldsymbol{x}_p \neq \perp \\ \perp & \text{if } \boldsymbol{x}_p = \perp \end{cases} \qquad f(\boldsymbol{x}, t) \stackrel{\text{def}}{=} upd(\boldsymbol{x}, t) \ominus \max_{p \in {}^\bullet t} \boldsymbol{x}_p$$

$$\nu(\epsilon) \stackrel{\text{def}}{=} \mu(\epsilon) \text{ and } \nu(\sigma t) \stackrel{\text{def}}{=} \mu(\sigma t) \ominus \max_{p \in {}^\bullet t} \mu(\sigma)_p \qquad r(\boldsymbol{x}) \stackrel{\text{def}}{=} \min_{C \in \mathcal{C}([\![\boldsymbol{x}]\!])} \max_{p \in {}^\bullet C} \boldsymbol{x}_p$$

Example 5. Figure 2b shows the finite-state Markov chain induced by the "earliest-first" scheduler computed using the abstraction ν. Consider the firing sequence $t_1 t_3$. We have $\mu(t_1 t_3) = \left\{ {p_2 \atop 3}, {p_3 \atop 1} \right\}$, i.e. the tokens in p_2 and p_3 arrive at times 3 and 1, respectively. Now we compute $\nu(t_1 t_3)$, which corresponds to the *local* arrival times of the tokens, i.e. the time elapsed *since the last transition starts to fire until the token arrives.* Transition t_3 starts to fire at time 1, and so the local arrival times of the tokens in p_2 and p_3 are 2 and 0, respectively, i.e. we have $\nu(t_1 t_3) = \left\{ {p_2 \atop 2}, {p_3 \atop 0} \right\}$. Using these local times we compute the local starting time of the conflict sets enabled at $\{p_2, p_3\}$. The scheduler always chooses the conflict set with earliest local starting time. In Fig. 2b the earliest local starting time of the state reached by firing σ, which is denoted $r(\nu(\sigma))$, is written in blue inside the state. The theorem above shows that this scheduler always chooses the same conflict sets as the one which uses the function μ, and that the time of a sequence can be obtained by adding the local starting times. This allows us to consider the earliest local starting time of a state as a *reward* associated to the state; then, the time taken by a sequence is equal to the sum of the rewards along the corresponding path of the chain. For example, we have $tm(t_1t_2t_4t_3t_5) = 0 + 1 + 0 + 4 + 2 + 3 = 10$.

Finally, let us see how $\nu(\sigma t)$ is computed from $\nu(\sigma)$ for $\sigma = t_1t_2t_4$ and $t = t_2$. We have $\nu(\sigma) = \left\{ {p_1 \atop 4}, {p_4 \atop 5} \right\}$, i.e. the local arrival times for the tokens in p_1 and p_4 are 4 and 5, respectively. Now $\{t_2, t_3\}$ is scheduled next, with local starting time $r(\nu(\sigma)) = \nu(\sigma)_{p_1} = 4$. If t_2 fires, then, since $\tau(t_2) = 4$, we first add 4 to the time of p_1, obtaining $\left\{ {p_1 \atop 8}, {p_4 \atop 5} \right\}$. Second, we subtract 4 from *all* times, to obtain the time elapsed since t_2 started to fire (for local times the origin of time changes every time a transition fires), yielding the final result $\nu(\sigma t_2) = \left\{ {p_1 \atop 4}, {p_4 \atop 1} \right\}$.

4.2 Computation in the Probabilistic Case

Given a TPWN and its corresponding MDP, in the previous section we have defined a finite-state earliest-first scheduler and a reward function of its induced Markov chain. The reward function has the following property: the execution time of a firing sequence compatible with the scheduler is equal to the sum of the rewards of the states visited along it. From the theory of Markov chains with rewards, it follows that the expected accumulated reward until reaching a certain state, provided that this state is reached with probability 1, can be computed by solving a linear equation system. We use this result to compute the expected time $ET_{\mathcal{W}}$.

Let $\mathcal{W}$ be a sound TPWN. For every firing sequence σ compatible with the earliest-first scheduler γ, the finite-state Markov chain induced by γ contains a state $\boldsymbol{x} = \nu(\sigma) \in [H]_{\perp}^{P}$. Let $C_{\boldsymbol{x}}$ be the conflict set scheduled by γ at $\boldsymbol{x}$. We define a system of linear equations with variables $X_{\boldsymbol{x}}$, one for each state $\boldsymbol{x}$:

$$\begin{aligned} X_{\boldsymbol{x}} &= r(\boldsymbol{x}) + \sum_{t \in C_{\boldsymbol{x}}} \frac{w(t)}{w(C_{\boldsymbol{x}})} \cdot X_{f(\boldsymbol{x},t)} && \text{if } [\![\boldsymbol{x}]\!] \neq \boldsymbol{o} \\ X_{\boldsymbol{x}} &= \max_{p \in P} \boldsymbol{x}_p && \text{if } [\![\boldsymbol{x}]\!] = \boldsymbol{o} \end{aligned} \tag{4}$$

The solution of the system is the expected reward of a path leading from $\boldsymbol{i}$ to $\boldsymbol{o}$. By the theory of Markov chains with rewards/costs ([4], Chap. 10.5), we have:

Lemma 2. *Let $\mathcal{W}$ be a sound TPWN. Then the system of linear equations (4) has a unique solution $\boldsymbol{X}$, and $ET_{\mathcal{W}} = \boldsymbol{X}_{\nu(\epsilon)}$.*

Theorem 3. *Let $\mathcal{W}$ be a TPWN. Then $ET_{\mathcal{W}}$ is either ∞ or a rational number and can be computed in single exponential time.*

Proof. We assume that the input has size n and all times and weights are given in binary notation. Testing whether $\mathcal{W}$ is sound can be done by exploration of the state space of reachable markings in time $\mathcal{O}(2^n)$. If $\mathcal{W}$ is unsound, we have $ET_{\mathcal{W}} = \infty$.

Now assume that $\mathcal{W}$ is sound. By Lemma 2, $ET_{\mathcal{W}}$ is the solution to the linear equation system (4), which is finite and has rational coefficients, so it is a rational number. The number of variables $|\boldsymbol{X}|$ of (4) is bounded by the size of $[H]_{\perp}^{P}$, and as $H = \max_{t \in T} \tau(t)$ we have $|\boldsymbol{X}| \leq (1+H)^{|P|} \leq (1+2^n)^n \leq 2^{n^2+n}$. The linear equation system can be solved in time $\mathcal{O}\left(n^2 \cdot |\boldsymbol{X}|^3\right)$ and therefore in time $\mathcal{O}(2^{p(n)})$ for some polynomial p.

5 Lower Bounds for the Expected Time

We analyze the complexity of computing the expected time of a TPWN. Botezano *et al.* show in [5] that deciding if the expected time exceeds a given bound is NP-hard. However, their reduction produces TPWNs with weights and times of arbitrary size. An open question is if the expected time can be computed in polynomial time when the times (and weights) must be taken from a finite set. We prove that this is not the case unless P = NP, even if all times are 0 or 1, all weights are 1, the workflow net is sound, acyclic and free-choice, and the size of each conflict set is at most 2 (resulting only in probabilities 1 or 1/2). Further, we show that even computing an ϵ-approximation is equally hard. These two results above are a consequence of the main theorem of this section: computing the expected time is #P-hard [23]. For example, counting the number of satisfying assignments for a boolean formula (#SAT) is a #P-complete problem. Therefore a polynomial-time algorithm for a #P-hard problem would imply P = NP.

The problem used for the reduction is defined on PERT networks [9], in the specialized form of *two-state stochastic PERT networks* [17], described below.

Definition 3. *A* two-state stochastic PERT network *is a tuple* $\mathbf{PN} = (G, s, t, \boldsymbol{p})$, *where* $G = (V, E)$ *is a directed acyclic graph with vertices* V, *representing events, and edges* E, *representing tasks, with a single source vertex* s *and sink vertex* t, *and where the vector* $\boldsymbol{p} \in \mathbb{Q}^E$ *assigns to each edge* $e \in E$ *a rational probability* $p_e \in [0,1]$. *We assume that all* p_e *are written in binary.*

Each edge $e \in E$ *of* $\mathbf{PN}$ *defines a random variable* X_e *with distribution* $\Pr(X_e = 1) = p_e$ *and* $\Pr(X_e = 0) = 1 - p_e$. *All* X_e *are assumed to be independent. The* project duration PD *of* $\mathbf{PN}$ *is the length of the longest path in the network*

$$PD(\mathbf{PN}) \stackrel{def}{=} \max_{\pi \in \Pi} \sum_{e \in \pi} X_e$$

where Π *is the set of paths from vertex* s *to vertex* t. *As this defines a random variable, the* expected project duration *of* $\mathbf{PN}$ *is then given by* $\mathbb{E}(PD(\mathbf{PN}))$.

Example 6. Figure 3a shows a small PERT network (without $\boldsymbol{p}$), where the project duration depends on the paths $\Pi = \{e_1e_3e_6, e_1e_4e_7, e_2e_5e_7\}$.

The following problem is #P-hard (from [17], using the results from [20]):

Given: A two-state stochastic PERT network $\mathbf{PN}$.
Compute: The expected project duration $\mathbb{E}(PD(\mathbf{PN}))$.

First reduction: 0/1 times, arbitrary weights. We reduce the problem above to computing the expected time of an acyclic TPWN with 0/1 times but arbitrary weights. Given a two-state stochastic PERT network **PN**, we construct a timed probabilistic workflow net $\mathcal{W}_{\mathbf{PN}}$ as follows:

- For each edge $e = (u, v) \in E$, add the "gadget net" shown in Fig. 3b. Assign $w(t_{e,0}) = 1 - p_e$, $w(t_{e,1}) = p_e$, $\tau(t_{e,0}) = 0$, and $\tau(t_{e,1}) = 1$.
- For each vertex $v \in V$, add a transition t_v with arcs from each $[e, v]$ such that $e = (u, v) \in E$ for some u and arcs to each $[v, e]$ such that $e = (v, w) \in E$ for some w. Assign $w(t_v) = 1$ and $\tau(t_v) = 0$.
- Add the place i with an arc to t_s and the place o with an arc from t_t.

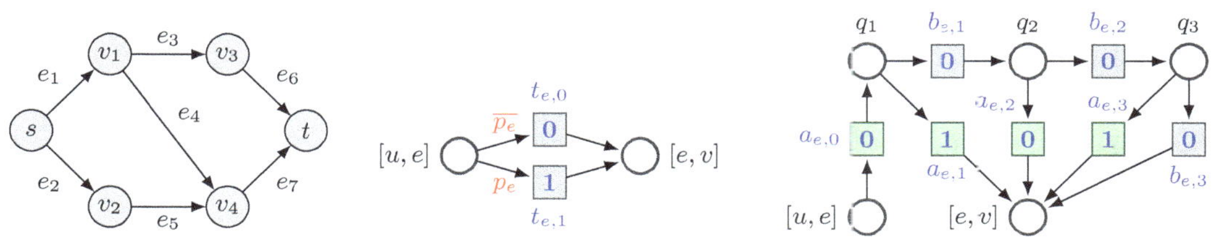

(a) PERT network **PN**. (b) Gadget for $e = (u, v)$ with rational weights $p_e, \overline{p_e}$. (c) Equivalent gadget for e with weights 1 for $p_e = 5/8 = (0.101)_2$.

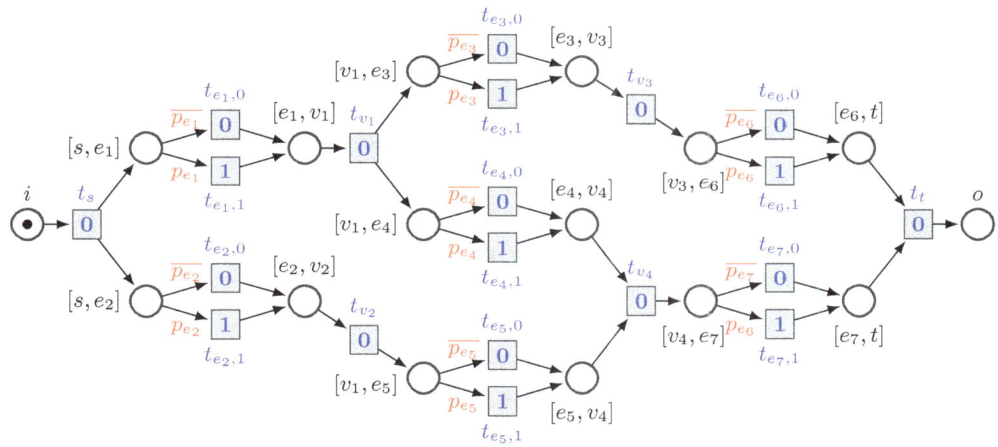

(d) Timed probabilistic workflow net $\mathcal{W}_{\mathbf{PN}}$.

Fig. 3. A PERT network and its corresponding timed probabilistic workflow net. The weight $\overline{p}$ is short for $1 - p$. Transitions without annotations have weight 1.

The result of applying this construction to the PERT network from Fig. 3a is shown in Fig. 3d. It is easy to see that this workflow net is sound, as from any reachable marking, we can fire enabled transitions corresponding to the edges and vertices of the PERT network in the topological order of the graph, eventually firing t_t and reaching $\boldsymbol{o}$. The net is also acyclic and free-choice.

Lemma 3. *Let* **PN** *be a two-state stochastic PERT network and let* $\mathcal{W}_{\mathbf{PN}}$ *be its corresponding TPWN by the construction above. Then* $ET_{\mathcal{W}_{\mathbf{PN}}} = \mathbb{E}(PD(\mathbf{PN}))$.

Second reduction: 0/1 times, 0/1 weights. The network constructed this way already uses times 0 and 1, however the weights still use arbitrary rational numbers. We now replace the gadget nets from Fig. 3b by equivalent nets where all transitions have weight 1. The idea is to use the binary encoding of the probabilities p_e, deciding if the time is 0 or 1 by a sequence of coin flips. We assume that $p_e = \sum_{i=0}^{k} 2^{-i} p_i$ for some $k \in \mathbb{N}$ and $p_i \in \{0, 1\}$ for $0 \leq i \leq k$. The replacement is shown in Fig. 3c for $p_e = 5/8 = (0.101)_2$.

Approximating the expected time is #P-hard. We show that computing an ϵ-approximation for $ET_{\mathcal{W}}$ is #P-hard [17,20].

Theorem 4. *The following problem is #P-hard:*

> **Given:** *A sound, acyclic and free-choice TPWN $\mathcal{W}$ where all transitions t satisfy $w(t) = 1$, $\tau(t) \in \{0, 1\}$ and $|({}^{\bullet}t)^{\bullet}| \leq 2$, and an $\epsilon > 0$.*
> **Compute:** *A rational r such that $r - \epsilon < ET_{\mathcal{W}} < r + \epsilon$.*

6 Experimental Evaluation

We have implemented our algorithm to compute the expected time of a TPWN as a package of the tool `ProM`[4]. It is available via the package manager of the latest nightly build under the package name `WorkflowNetAnalyzer`.

We evaluated the algorithm on two different benchmarks. All experiments in this section were run on the same machine equipped with an Intel Core i7-6700K CPU and 32 GB of RAM. We measure the actual runtime of the algorithm, split into construction of the Markov chain and solving the linear equation system, and exclude the time overhead due to starting `ProM` and loading the plugin.

6.1 IBM Benchmark

We evaluated the tool on a set of 1386 workflow nets extracted from a collection of five libraries of industrial business processes modeled in the IBM WebSphere Business Modeler [12]. All of the 1386 nets in the benchmark libraries are free-choice and therefore confusion-free. We selected the sound and 1-safe nets among them, which are 642 nets. Out of these, 409 are marked graphs, i.e. the size of any conflict set is 1. Out of the remaining 233 nets, 193 are acyclic and 40 cyclic.

As these nets do not come with probabilistic or time information, we annotated transitions with integer weights and times chosen uniformly from different intervals: (1) $w(t) = \tau(t) = 1$, (2) $w(t), \tau(t) \in [1, 10^3]$ and (3) $w(t), \tau(t) \in [1, 10^6]$. For each interval, we annotated the transitions of each net with random weights and times, and computed the expected time of all 642 nets.

For all intervals, we computed the expected time for any net in less than 50 ms. The analysis time did not differ much for different intervals. The solving time for the linear equation system is on average 5% of the total analysis time,

[4] http://www.promtools.org/.

and at most 68%. The results for the nets with the longest analysis times are given in Table 1. They show that even for nets with a huge state space, thanks to the earliest-first scheduler, only a small number of reachable markings is explored.

Table 1. Analysis times and size of the state space $|\boldsymbol{X}|$ for the 4 nets with the highest analysis times, given for each of the three intervals $[1], [10^3], [10^6]$ of possible times. Here, $|\mathcal{R}^N|$ denotes the number of reachable markings of the net.

Net	Net info & size				Analysis time (ms)			$\|\boldsymbol{X}\|$		
	cyclic	$\|P\|$	$\|T\|$	$\|\mathcal{R}^N\|$	[1]	$[10^3]$	$[10^6]$	[1]	$[10^3]$	$[10^6]$
m1.s30_s703	no	264	286	6117	40.3	44.6	43.8	304	347	347
m1.s30_s596	yes	214	230	623	21.6	24.4	23.6	208	232	234
b3.s371_s1986	no	235	101	$2 \cdot 10^{17}$	16.8	16.4	16.5	101	102	102
b2.s275_s2417	no	103	68	237626	14.2	17.8	15.9	355	460	431

6.2 Process Mining Case Study

As a second benchmark, we evaluated the algorithm on a model of a loan application process. We used the data from the BPI Challenge 2017 [8], an event log containing 31509 cases provided by a financial institute, and took as a model of the process the final net from the report of the winner of the academic category [21], a simple model with high fitness and precision w.r.t. the event log.

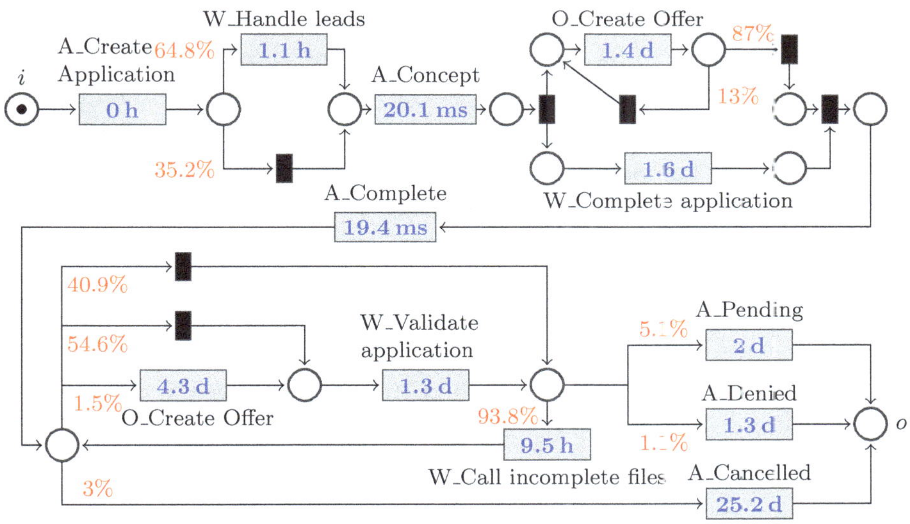

Fig. 4. Net from [21] of process for personal loan applications in a financial institute, annotated with mean waiting times and local trace weights. Black transitions are invisible transitions not appearing in the event log with time 0.

Table 2. Expected time, analysis time and state space size for the net in Fig. 4 for various distributions, where `memout` denotes reaching the memory limit.

Distribution	$\|T\|$	ET_W	$\|\boldsymbol{X}\|$	Analysis time		
				Total	Construction	Solving
Deterministic	19	24 d 1 h	33	40 ms	18 ms	22 ms
Histogram/12 h	141	24 d 18 h	4054	244 ms	232 ms	12 ms
Histogram/6 h	261	24 d 21 h	15522	2.1 s	1.8 s	0.3 s
Histogram/4 h	375	24 d 22 h	34063	10 s	6 s	4 s
Histogram/2 h	666	24 d 23 h	122785	346 s	52 s	294 s
Histogram/1 h	1117	—	422614	—	12.7 min	`memout`

Using the `ProM` plugin "Multi-perspective Process Explorer" [18] we annotated each transition with waiting times and each transition in a conflict set with a local percentage of traces choosing this transition when this conflict set is enabled. The net with mean times and weights as percentages is displayed in Fig. 4.

For a first analysis, we simply set the execution time of each transition deterministically to its mean waiting time. However, note that the two transitions "O_Create Offer" and "W_Complete application" are executed in parallel, and therefore the distribution of their execution times influences the total expected time. Therefore we also annotated these two transitions with a histogram of possible execution times from each case. Then we split them up into multiple transitions by grouping the times into buckets of a given interval size, where each bucket creates a transition with an execution time equal to the beginning of the interval, and a weight equal to the number of cases with a waiting time contained in the interval. The times for these transitions range from 6 ms to 31 days. As bucket sizes we chose $12, 6, 4, 2$ and 1 hour(s). The net always has 14 places and 15 reachable markings, but a varying number of transitions depending on the chosen bucket size. For the net with the mean as the deterministic time and for the nets with histograms for each bucket size, we then analyzed the expected execution time using our algorithm.

The results are given in Table 2. They show that using the complete distribution of times instead of only the mean can lead to much more precise results. When the linear equation system becomes very large, the solver time dominates the construction time of the system. This may be because we chose to use an exact solver for sparse linear equation systems. In the future, this could possibly be improved by using an approximative iterative solver.

7 Conclusion

We have shown that computing the expected time to termination of a probabilistic workflow net in which transition firings have deterministic durations is

#P-hard. This is the case even if the net is free-choice, and both probabilities and times can be written down with a constant number of bits. So, surprisingly, computing the expected time is much harder than computing the expected cost, for which there is a polynomial algorithm [11].

We have also presented an exponential algorithm for computing the expected time based on earliest-first schedulers. Its performance depends crucially on the maximal size of conflict sets that can be concurrently enabled. In the most popular suite of industrial benchmarks this number turns out to be small. So, very satisfactorily, the expected time of any of these benchmarks, some of which have hundreds of transitions, can still be computed in milliseconds.

Acknowledgements. We thank Hagen Völzer for input on the implementation and choice of benchmarks.

References

1. van der Aalst, W.M.P.: The application of Petri nets to workflow management. J. Circ. Syst. Comput. **8**(1), 21–66 (1998). https://doi.org/10.1142/S0218126698000043
2. van der Aalst, W.M.P., et al.: Soundness of workflow nets: classification, decidability, and analysis. Formal Asp. Comput. **23**(3), 333–363 (2011). https://doi.org/10.1007/s00165-010-0161-4
3. van der Aalst, W., van Hee, K.M.: Workflow Management: Models, Methods, and Systems. MIT Press, Cambridge (2004)
4. Baier, C., Katoen, J.P.: Principles of Model Checking. The MIT Press, Cambridge (2008)
5. Botezatu, M., Völzer, H., Thiele, L.: The complexity of deadline analysis for workflow graphs with multiple resources. In: La Rosa, M., Loos, P., Pastor, O. (eds.) BPM 2016. LNCS, vol. 9850, pp. 252–268. Springer, Cham (2016). https://doi.org/10.1007/978-3-319-45348-4_15
6. Carlier, J., Chrétienne, P.: Timed Petri net schedules. In: Rozenberg, G. (ed.) APN 1987. LNCS, vol. 340, pp. 62–84. Springer, Heidelberg (1988). https://doi.org/10.1007/3-540-50580-6_24
7. Desel, J., Erwin, T.: Modeling, simulation and analysis of business processes. In: van der Aalst, W., Desel, J., Oberweis, A. (eds.) Business Process Management. LNCS, vol. 1806, pp. 129–141. Springer, Heidelberg (2000). https://doi.org/10.1007/3-540-45594-9_9
8. van Dongen, B.F.: BPI Challenge 2017 (2017). https://doi.org/10.4121/uuid:5f3067df-f10b-45da-b98b-86ae4c7a310b
9. Elmaghraby, S.E.: Activity Networks: Project Planning and Control by Network Models. Wiley, Hoboken (1977)
10. Esparza, J., Hoffmann, P.: Reduction rules for colored workflow nets. In: Stevens, P., Wąsowski, A. (eds.) FASE 2016. LNCS, vol. 9633, pp. 342–358. Springer, Heidelberg (2016). https://doi.org/10.1007/978-3-662-49665-7_20
11. Esparza, J., Hoffmann, P., Saha, R.: Polynomial analysis algorithms for free choice probabilistic workflow nets. Perform. Eval. **117**, 104–129 (2017). https://doi.org/10.1016/j.peva.2017.09.006

12. Fahland, D., et al.: Instantaneous soundness checking of industrial business process models. In: Dayal, U., Eder, J., Koehler, J., Reijers, H.A. (eds.) BPM 2009. LNCS, vol. 5701, pp. 278–293. Springer, Heidelberg (2009). https://doi.org/10.1007/978-3-642-03848-8_19
13. Favre, C., Fahland, D., Völzer, H.: The relationship between workflow graphs and free-choice workflow nets. Inf. Syst. **47**, 197–219 (2015). https://doi.org/10.1016/j.is.2013.12.004
14. Favre, C., Völzer, H., Müller, P.: Diagnostic information for control-flow analysis of workflow graphs (a.k.a. free-choice workflow nets). In: Chechik, M., Raskin, J.-F. (eds.) TACAS 2016. LNCS, vol. 9636, pp. 463–479. Springer, Heidelberg (2016). https://doi.org/10.1007/978-3-662-49674-9_27
15. Gaubert, S., Mairesse, J.: Asymptotic analysis of heaps of pieces and application to timed Petri nets. In: Proceedings of the 8th International Workshop on Petri Nets and Performance Models, PNPM 1999, Zaragoza, Spain, 8–10 September 1999, pp. 158–169 (1999). https://doi.org/10.1109/PNPM.1999.796562
16. Gaubert, S., Mairesse, J.: Modeling and analysis of timed Petri nets using heaps of pieces. IEEE Trans. Autom. Control **44**(4), 683–697 (1999). https://doi.org/10.1109/9.754807
17. Hagstrom, J.N.: Computational complexity of PERT problems. Networks **18**(2), 139–147 (1988). https://doi.org/10.1002/net.3230180206
18. Mannhardt, F., de Leoni, M., Reijers, H.A.: The multi-perspective process explorer. In: Proceedings of the BPM Demo Session 2015 Co-located with the 13th International Conference on Business Process Management, BPM 2015, Innsbruck, Austria, 2 September 2015, pp. 130–134 (2015)
19. Meyer, P.J., Esparza, J., Offtermatt, P.: Computing the expected execution time of probabilistic workflow nets. arXiv:1811.06961 [cs.LO] (2018)
20. Provan, J.S., Ball, M.O.: The complexity of counting cuts and of computing the probability that a graph is connected. SIAM J. Comput. **12**(4), 777–788 (1983). https://doi.org/10.1137/0212053
21. Rodrigues, A., et al.: Stairway to value: mining a loan application process (2017). https://www.win.tue.nl/bpi/lib/exe/fetch.php?media=2017:bpi2017_winner_academic.pdf
22. Rozenberg, G., Thiagarajan, P.S.: Petri nets: basic notions, structure, behaviour. In: de Bakker, J.W., de Roever, W.-P., Rozenberg, G. (eds.) Current Trends in Concurrency. LNCS, vol. 224, pp. 585–668. Springer, Heidelberg (1986). https://doi.org/10.1007/BFb0027048
23. Valiant, L.G.: The complexity of computing the permanent. Theoret. Comput. Sci. **8**, 189–201 (1979). https://doi.org/10.1016/0304-3975(79)90044-6
24. Meyer, P.J., Esparza, J., Offtermatt, P.: Artifact and instructions to generate experimental results for TACAS 2019 paper: Computing the Expected Execution Time of Probabilistic Workflow Nets (artifact). Figshare (2019). https://doi.org/10.6084/m9.figshare.7831781.v1

Shepherding Hordes of Markov Chains

Milan Češka[1], Nils Jansen[2], Sebastian Junges[3(✉)], and Joost-Pieter Katoen[3]

[1] Brno University of Technology, Brno, Czech Republic
[2] Radboud University, Nijmegen, The Netherlands
[3] RWTH Aachen University, Aachen, Germany
sebastian.junges@cs.rwth-aachen.de

Abstract. This paper considers large families of Markov chains (MCs) that are defined over a set of parameters with finite discrete domains. Such families occur in software product lines, planning under partial observability, and sketching of probabilistic programs. Simple questions, like 'does at least one family member satisfy a property?', are NP-hard. We tackle two problems: distinguish family members that satisfy a given quantitative property from those that do not, and determine a family member that satisfies the property optimally, i.e., with the highest probability or reward. We show that combining two well-known techniques, MDP model checking and abstraction refinement, mitigates the computational complexity. Experiments on a broad set of benchmarks show that in many situations, our approach is able to handle families of millions of MCs, providing superior scalability compared to existing solutions.

1 Introduction

Randomisation is key to research fields such as dependability (uncertain system components), distributed computing (symmetry breaking), planning (unpredictable environments), and probabilistic programming. Families of alternative designs differing in the structure and system parameters are ubiquitous. Software dependability has to cope with configuration options, in distributed computing the available memory per process is highly relevant, in planning the observability of the environment is pivotal, and program synthesis is all about selecting correct program variants. The automated analysis of such families has to face a formidable challenge—in addition to the state-space explosion affecting each family member, the family size typically grows exponentially in the number of features, options, or observations. This affects the analysis of (quantitative) software product lines [18,28,43,45,46], strategy synthesis in planning under partial observability [12,14,29,36,41], and probabilistic program synthesis [9,13,27,40].

This paper considers families of Markov chains (MCs) to describe configurable probabilistic systems. We consider finite MC families with finite-state family members. Family members may have different transition probabilities and distinct topologies—thus different reachable state spaces. The latter aspect

This work has been supported by the DFG RTG 2236 "UnRAVeL" and the Czech Science Foundation grant No. Robust 17-12465S.

T. Vojnar and L. Zhang (Eds.): TACAS 2019, Part II, LNCS 11428, pp. 172–190, 2019.
https://doi.org/10.1007/978-3-030-17465-1_10

goes beyond the class of parametric MCs as considered in parameter synthesis [10,22,24,31] and model repair [6,16,42].

For an MC family $\mathfrak{D}$ and quantitative specification φ, with φ a reachability probability or expected reward objective, we consider the following synthesis problems: (a) does some member in $\mathfrak{D}$ satisfy a threshold on φ? (aka: *feasibility* synthesis), (b) which members of $\mathfrak{D}$ satisfy this threshold on φ and which ones do not? (aka: *threshold synthesis*), and (c) which family member(s) satisfy φ optimally, e.g., with highest probability? (aka: *optimal synthesis*).

The simplest synthesis problem, feasibility, is NP-complete and can naively be solved by analysing all individual family members—the so-called *one-by-one* approach. This approach has been used in [18] (and for qualitative systems in e.g. [19]), but is infeasible for large systems. An alternative is to model the family $\mathfrak{D}$ by a single Markov decision process (MDP)—the so-called *all-in-one* MDP [18]. The initial MDP state non-deterministically chooses a family member of $\mathfrak{D}$, and then evolves in the MC of that member. This approach has been implemented in tools such as ProFeat [18], and for purely qualitative systems in [20]. The MDP representation avoids the individual analysis of all family members, but its size is proportional to the family size. This approach therefore does not scale to large families. A symbolic BDD-based approach is only a partial solution as family members may induce different reachable state-sets.

This paper introduces an *abstraction-refinement* scheme over the MDP representation[1]. The abstraction *forgets* in which family member the MDP operates. The resulting *quotient* MDP has a single representative for every reachable state in a family member. It typically provides a very compact representation of the family $\mathfrak{D}$ and its analysis using off-the-shelf MDP model-checking algorithms yields a speed-up compared to the all-in-one approach. Verifying the quotient MDP yields under- and over-approximations of the min and max probability (or reward), respectively. These bounds are safe as all *consistent* schedulers, i.e., those that pick actions according to a single family member, are contained in all schedulers considered on the quotient MDP. (CEGAR-based MDP model checking for partial information schedulers, a slightly different notion than restricting schedulers to consistent ones, has been considered in [30]. In contrast to our setting, [30] considers history-dependent schedulers and in this general setting no guarantee can be given that bounds on suprema converge [29]).

Model-checking results of the quotient MDP do provide useful insights. This is evident if the resulting scheduler is consistent. If the verification reveals that the min probability exceeds r for a specification φ with a $\leq r$ threshold, then—even for inconsistent schedulers—it holds that all family members violate φ. If the model checking is inconclusive, i.e., the abstraction is too coarse, we iteratively refine the quotient MDP by splitting the family into sub-families. We do so in an efficient manner that avoids rebuilding the sub-families. Refinement employs a light-weight analysis of the model-checking results.

[1] Classical CEGAR for model checking of software product lines has been proposed in [21]. This uses feature transition systems, is purely qualitative and exploits existential state abstraction.

We implemented our abstraction-refinement approach using the Storm model checker [25]. Experiments with case studies from software product lines, planning, and distributed computing yield possible speed-ups of up to 3 orders of magnitude over the one-by-one and all-in-one approaches (both symbolic and explicit). Some benchmarks include families of millions of MCs where family members are thousands of states. The experiments reveal that—as opposed to parameter synthesis [10,24,31]—the threshold has a major influence on the synthesis times.

To summarise, this work presents: (a) MDP-based abstraction-refinement for various synthesis problems over large families of MCs, (b) a refinement strategy that mitigates the overhead of analysing sub-families, and (c) experiments showing substantial speed-ups for many benchmarks. Extra material can be found in [1,11].

2 Preliminaries

We present the basic foundations for this paper, for details, we refer to [4,5].

Probabilistic models. A *probability distribution* over a finite or countably infinite set X is a function $\mu\colon X \to [0,1]$ with $\sum_{x \in X} \mu(x) = \mu(X) = 1$. The set of all distributions on X is denoted $Distr(X)$. The support of a distribution μ is $\mathrm{supp}(\mu) = \{x \in X \mid \mu(x) > 0\}$. A distribution is *Dirac* if $|\mathrm{supp}(\mu)| = 1$.

Definition 1 (MC). *A* discrete-time Markov chain *(MC) D is a triple $(S, s_0, \mathbf{P})$, where S is a finite set of states, $s_0 \in S$ is an initial state, and $\mathbf{P}\colon S \to Distr(S)$ is a transition probability matrix.*

MCs have unique distributions over successor states at each state. Adding nondeterministic choices over distributions leads to Markov decision processes.

Definition 2 (MDP). *A* Markov decision process *(MDP) is a tuple $M = (S, s_0, Act, \mathcal{P})$ where S, s_0 as in Definition 1, Act is a finite set of actions, and $\mathcal{P}\colon S \times Act \nrightarrow Distr(S)$ is a partial transition probability function.*

The *available actions* in $s \in S$ are $Act(s) = \{a \in Act \mid \mathcal{P}(s,a) \neq \bot\}$. An MDP with $|Act(s)| = 1$ for all $s \in S$ is an MC. For MCs (and MDPs), a state-reward function is $rew\colon S \to \mathbb{R}_{\geq 0}$. The reward $rew(s)$ is earned upon leaving s.

A *path* of an MDP M is an (in)finite sequence $\pi = s_0 \xrightarrow{a_0} s_1 \xrightarrow{a_1} \cdots$, where $s_i \in S$, $a_i \in Act(s_i)$, and $\mathcal{P}(s_i, a_i)(s_{i+1}) \neq 0$ for all $i \in \mathbb{N}$. For finite π, $\mathrm{last}(\pi)$ denotes the last state of π. The set of (in)finite paths of M is Paths^M_{fin} (Paths^M). The notions of paths carry over to MCs (actions are omitted). Schedulers resolve all choices of actions in an MDP and yield MCs.

Definition 3 (Scheduler). *A* scheduler *for an MDP $M = (S, s_0, Act, \mathcal{P})$ is a function $\sigma\colon \mathsf{Paths}^M_{fin} \to Act$ such that $\sigma(\pi) \in Act(\mathrm{last}(\pi))$ for all $\pi \in \mathsf{Paths}^M_{fin}$. Scheduler σ is* memoryless *if $\mathrm{last}(\pi) = \mathrm{last}(\pi') \implies \sigma(\pi) = \sigma(\pi')$ for all $\pi, \pi' \in \mathsf{Paths}^M_{fin}$. The set of all schedulers of M is Σ^M.*

Definition 4 (Induced Markov Chain). *The MC* induced by MDP M and $\sigma \in \Sigma^M$ *is given by* $M_\sigma = (\mathsf{Paths}^M_{fin}, s_0, \mathbf{P}^\sigma)$ *where:*

$$\mathbf{P}^\sigma(\pi, \pi') = \begin{cases} \mathcal{P}(\text{last}(\pi), \sigma(\pi))(s') & \textit{if } \pi' = \pi \xrightarrow{\sigma(\pi)} s' \\ 0 & \textit{otherwise.} \end{cases}$$

Specifications. For a MC D, we consider unbounded reachability specifications of the form $\varphi = \mathbb{P}_{\sim\lambda}(\lozenge G)$ with $G \subseteq S$ a set of goal states, $\lambda \in [0,1] \subseteq \mathbb{R}$, and $\sim \in \{<, \leq, \geq, >\}$. The probability to satisfy the path formula $\phi = \lozenge G$ in D is denoted by $\texttt{Prob}(D, \phi)$. If φ holds for D, that is, $\texttt{Prob}(D, \phi) \sim \lambda$, we write $D \models \varphi$. Analogously, we define expected reward specifications of the form $\varphi = \mathbb{E}_{\sim\kappa}(\lozenge G)$ with $\kappa \in \mathbb{R}_{\geq 0}$. We refer to λ/κ as *thresholds*. While we only introduce reachability specifications, our approaches may be extended to richer logics like arbitrary PCTL [32], PCTL* [3], or ω-regular properties.

For an MDP M, a specification φ holds ($M \models \varphi$) if and only if it holds for the induced MCs of all schedulers. The maximum probability $\texttt{Prob}^{\max}(M, \phi)$ to satisfy a path formula ϕ for an MDP M is given by a maximising scheduler $\sigma^{\max} \in \Sigma^M$, that is, there is no scheduler $\sigma' \in \Sigma^M$ such that $\texttt{Prob}(M_{\sigma^{\max}}, \phi) < \texttt{Prob}(M_{\sigma'}, \phi)$. Analogously, we define the minimising probability $\texttt{Prob}^{\min}(M, \phi)$, and the maximising (minimising) expected reward $\texttt{ExpRew}^{\max}(M, \phi)$ ($\texttt{ExpRew}^{\min}(M, \phi)$).

The probability (expected reward) to satisfy path formula ϕ from state $s \in S$ in MC D is $\texttt{Prob}(D, \phi)(s)$ ($\texttt{ExpRew}(D, \phi)(s)$). The notation is analogous for maximising and minimising probability and expected reward measures in MDPs. Note that the expected reward $\texttt{ExpRew}(D, \phi)$ to satisfy path formula ϕ is only defined if $\texttt{Prob}(D, \phi) = 1$. Accordingly, the expected reward for MDP M under scheduler $\sigma \in \Sigma^M$ requires $\texttt{Prob}(M_\sigma, \phi) = 1$.

3 Families of MCs

We present our approaches on the basis of an explicit representation of a *family of MCs* using a parametric transition probability function. While arbitrary probabilistic programs allow for more modelling freedom and complex parameter structures, the explicit representation alleviates the presentation and allows to reason about practically interesting synthesis problems. In our implementation, we use a more flexible high-level modelling language, cf. Sect. 5.

Definition 5 (Family of MCs). *A* family of MCs *is defined as a tuple* $\mathfrak{D} = (S, s_0, K, \mathfrak{P})$ *where* S *is a finite set of states,* $s_0 \in S$ *is an initial state,* K *is a finite set of discrete parameters such that the domain of each parameter* $k \in K$ *is* $T_k \subseteq S$*, and* $\mathfrak{P}\colon S \to Distr(K)$ *is a family of transition probability matrices.*

The transition probability function of MCs maps states to distributions over successor states. For families of MCs, this function maps states to distributions over parameters. Instantiating each of these parameters with a value from its domain yields a "concrete" MC, called a *realisation*.

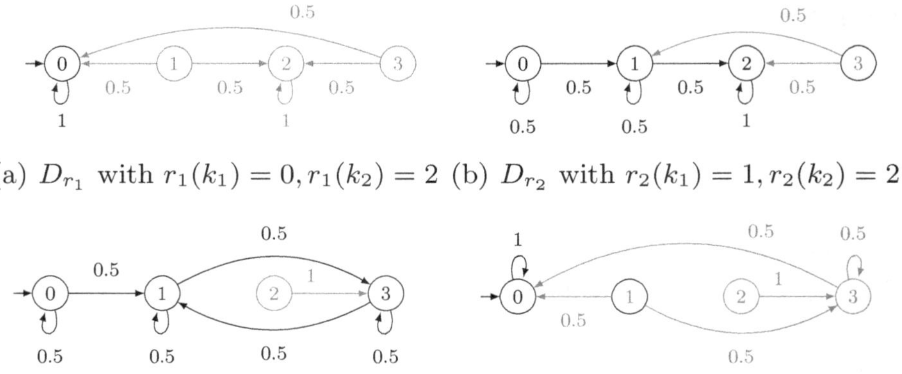

(a) D_{r_1} with $r_1(k_1) = 0, r_1(k_2) = 2$ (b) D_{r_2} with $r_2(k_1) = 1, r_2(k_2) = 2$

(c) D_{r_3} with $r_3(k_1) = 1, r_3(k_2) = 3$ (d) D_{r_4} with $r_4(k_1) = 0, r_4(k_2) = 3$

Fig. 1. The four different realisations of $\mathfrak{D}$.

Definition 6 (Realisation). *A* realisation *of a family $\mathfrak{D} = (S, s_0, K, \mathfrak{P})$ is a function $r\colon K \to S$ where $\forall k \in K\colon r(k) \in T_k$. A realisation r yields a MC $D_r = (S, s_0, \mathfrak{P}(r))$, where $\mathfrak{P}(r)$ is the transition probability matrix in which each $k \in K$ in $\mathfrak{P}$ is replaced by $r(k)$. Let $\mathcal{R}^{\mathfrak{D}}$ denote the* set of all realisations *for $\mathfrak{D}$.*

As a family $\mathfrak{D}$ of MCs is defined over finite parameter domains, the number of family members (i.e. realisations from $\mathcal{R}^{\mathfrak{D}}$) of $\mathfrak{D}$ is finite, viz. $|\mathfrak{D}| := |\mathcal{R}^{\mathfrak{D}}| = \prod_{k \in K} |T_k|$, but exponential in $|K|$. Subsets of $\mathcal{R}^{\mathfrak{D}}$ induce so-called *subfamilies* of $\mathfrak{D}$. While all these MCs share the same state space, their *reachable* states may differ, as demonstrated by the following example.

Example 1 (Family of MCs). Consider a family of MCs $\mathfrak{D} = (S, s_0, K, \mathfrak{P})$ where $S = \{0, 1, 2, 3\}$, $s_0 = 0$, and $K = \{k_0, k_1, k_2\}$ with domains $T_{k_0} = \{0\}, T_{k_1} = \{0, 1\}$, and $T_{k_2} = \{2, 3\}$. The parametric transition function $\mathfrak{P}$ is defined by:

$$\mathfrak{P}(0) = 0.5\colon k_0 + 0.5\colon k_1 \qquad \mathfrak{P}(1) = 0.5\colon k_1 + 0.5\colon k_2$$
$$\mathfrak{P}(2) = 1\colon k_2 \qquad \mathfrak{P}(3) = 0.5\colon k_1 + 0.5\colon k_2$$

Figure 1 shows the four MCs that result from the realisations $\{r_1, r_2, r_3, r_4\} = \mathcal{R}^{\mathfrak{D}}$ of $\mathfrak{D}$. States that are unreachable from the initial state are greyed out.

We state two synthesis problems for families of MCs. The first is to identify the set of MCs satisfying and violating a given specification, respectively. The second is to find a MC that maximises/minimises a given objective. We call these two problems *threshold synthesis* and *max/min synthesis*.

Problem 1 (Threshold synthesis). *Let $\mathfrak{D}$ be a family of MCs and φ a probabilistic reachability or expected reward specification. The* threshold synthesis problem *is to partition $\mathcal{R}^{\mathfrak{D}}$ into T and F such that $\forall r \in T\colon D_r \models \varphi$ and $\forall r \in F\colon D_r \not\models \varphi$.*

As a special case of the threshold synthesis problem, the *feasibility synthesis problem* is to find just one realisation $r \in \mathcal{R}^{\mathfrak{D}}$ such that $D_r \models \varphi$.

Problem 2 (Max synthesis). *Let $\mathfrak{D}$ a family of MCs and $\phi = \lozenge G$ for $G \subseteq S$. The* max synthesis problem *is to find a realisation $r^* \in \mathcal{R}^{\mathfrak{D}}$ such that* $\texttt{Prob}(D_{r^*}, \phi) = \max_{r \in \mathcal{R}^{\mathfrak{D}}} \{\texttt{Prob}(D_r, \phi)\}$. *The problem is defined analogously for an expected reward measure or minimising realisations.*

Example 2 (Synthesis problems). Recall the family of MCs $\mathfrak{D}$ from Example 1. For the specification $\varphi = \mathbb{P}_{\geq 0.1}(\lozenge\{1\})$, the solution to the threshold synthesis problem is $T = \{r_2, r_3\}$ and $F = \{r_1, r_4\}$, as the goal state 1 is not reachable for D_{r_1} and D_{r_4}. For $\phi = \lozenge\{1\}$, the solution to the max synthesis problem on $\mathfrak{D}$ is r_2 or r_3, as D_{r_2} and D_{r_3} have probability one to reach state 1.

Approach 1 (One-by-one [18]). *A straightforward solution to both synthesis problems is to enumerate all realisations $r \in \mathcal{R}^{\mathfrak{D}}$, model check the MCs D_r, and either compare all results with the given threshold or determine the maximum.*

We already saw that the number of realisations is exponential in $|K|$.

Theorem 1. *The feasibility synthesis problem is NP-complete.*

The theorem even holds for almost-sure reachability properties. The proof is a straightforward adaption of results for augmented interval Markov chains [17, Theorem 3], partial information games [15], or partially observable MDPs [14].

4 Guided Abstraction-Refinement Scheme

In the previous section, we introduced the notion of a family of MCs, two synthesis problems and the one-by-one approach. Yet, for a sufficiently high number of realisations such a straightforward analysis is not feasible. We propose a novel approach allowing us to more efficiently analyse families of MCs.

4.1 All-in-one MDP

We first consider a single MDP that subsumes all individual MCs of a family $\mathfrak{D}$, and is equipped with an appropriate action and state labelling to identify the underlying realisations from $\mathcal{R}^{\mathfrak{D}}$.

Definition 7 (All-in-one MDP [18,28,43]). *The* all-in-one MDP *of a family $\mathfrak{D} = (S, s_0, K, \mathfrak{P})$ of MCs is given as $M^{\mathfrak{D}} = (S^{\mathfrak{D}}, s_0^{\mathfrak{D}}, Act^{\mathfrak{D}}, \mathcal{P}^{\mathfrak{D}})$ where $S^{\mathfrak{D}} = S \times \mathcal{R}^{\mathfrak{D}} \cup \{s_0^{\mathfrak{D}}\}$, $Act^{\mathfrak{D}} = \{a^r \mid r \in \mathcal{R}^{\mathfrak{D}}\}$, and $\mathcal{P}^{\mathfrak{D}}$ is defined as follows:*

$$\mathcal{P}^{\mathfrak{D}}(s_0^{\mathfrak{D}}, a^r)((s_0, r)) = 1 \quad \textit{and} \quad \mathcal{P}^{\mathfrak{D}}((s, r), a^r)((s', r)) = \mathfrak{P}(r)(s)(s').$$

Example 3 (All-in-one MDP). Figure 2 shows the all-in-one MDP $M^{\mathfrak{D}}$ for the family $\mathfrak{D}$ of MCs from Example 1. Again, states that are not reachable from the initial state $s_0^{\mathfrak{D}}$ are marked grey. For the sake of readability, we only include the transitions and states that correspond to realisations r_1 and r_2.

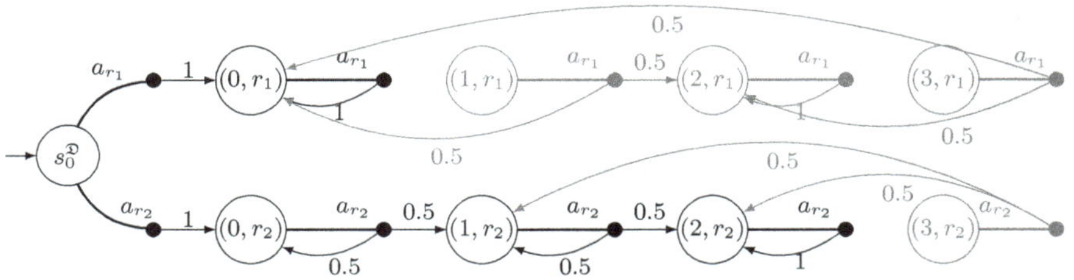

Fig. 2. Reachable fragment of the all-in-one MDP $M^{\mathfrak{D}}$ for realisations r_1 and r_2.

From the (fresh) initial state $s_0^{\mathfrak{D}}$ of the MDP, the choice of an action a_r corresponds to choosing the realisation r and entering the concrete MC D_r. This property of the all-in-one MDP is formalised as follows.

Corollary 1. *For the all-in-one MDP $M^{\mathfrak{D}}$ of family $\mathfrak{D}$ of MCs*[2]*:*

$$\{M^{\mathfrak{D}}_{\sigma^r} \mid \sigma^r \textit{ memoryless deterministic scheduler}\} = \{D_r \mid r \in \mathcal{R}^{\mathfrak{D}}\}.$$

Consequently, the feasibility synthesis problem for φ has the solution $r \in \mathcal{R}^{\mathfrak{D}}$ iff there exists a memoryless deterministic scheduler σ^r such that $M^{\mathfrak{D}}_{\sigma^r} \models \varphi$.

Approach 2 (All-in-one [18]). *Model checking the all-in-one MDP determines max or min probability (or expected reward) for all states, and thereby for all realisations, and thus provides a solution to both synthesis problems.*

As also the all-in-one MDP may be too large for realistic problems, we merely use it as formal starting point for our abstraction-refinement loop.

4.2 Abstraction

First, we define a predicate abstraction that at each state of the MDP *forgets* in which realisation we are, i.e., abstracts the second component of a state (s, r).

Definition 8 (Forgetting). *Let $M^{\mathfrak{D}} = (S^{\mathfrak{D}}, s_0^{\mathfrak{D}}, Act^{\mathfrak{D}}, \mathcal{P}^{\mathfrak{D}})$ be an all-in-one MDP.* Forgetting *is an equivalence relation $\sim_f \subseteq S^{\mathfrak{D}} \times S^{\mathfrak{D}}$ satisfying*

$$(s, r) \sim_f (s', r') \iff s = s' \textit{ and } s_0^{\mathfrak{D}} \sim_f (s_0^{\mathfrak{D}}, r)\ \forall r \in \mathcal{R}^{\mathfrak{D}}.$$

Let $[s]_\sim$ denote the equivalence class wrt. $\sim_f$ containing state $s \in S^{\mathfrak{D}}$.

Forgetting induces the quotient MDP $M^{\mathfrak{D}}_\sim = (S^{\mathfrak{D}}_\sim, [s_0^{\mathfrak{D}}]_\sim, Act^{\mathfrak{D}}, \mathcal{P}^{\mathfrak{D}}_\sim)$, *where* $\mathcal{P}^{\mathfrak{D}}_\sim([s]_\sim, a_r)([s']_\sim) = \mathfrak{P}(r)(s)(s')$.

At each state of the quotient MDP, the actions correspond to any realisation. It includes states that are unreachable in every realisation.

Remark 1 (Action space). According to Definition 8, for every state $[s]_\sim$ there are $|\mathfrak{D}|$ actions. Many of these actions lead to the same distributions over successor states. In particular, two different realisations r and r' lead to the same distribution in s if $r(k) = r'(k)$ for all $k \in K$ where $\mathfrak{P}(s)(k) \neq 0$. To avoid this spurious blow-up of actions, we *a-priori* merge all actions yielding the same distribution.

[2] The original initial state s_0 of the family of MCs needs to be the initial state of $M^{\mathfrak{D}}_{\sigma^r}$.

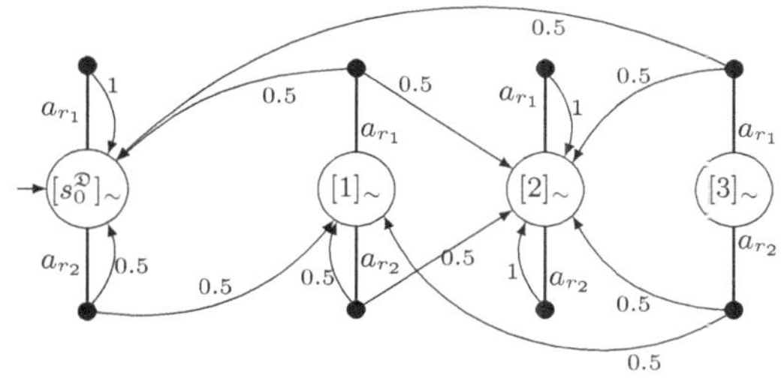

Fig. 3. The quotient MDP $M^{\mathfrak{D}}_{\sim}$ for realisations r_1 and r_2.

The quotient MDP under forgetting involves that the available actions allow to switch realisations and thereby create induced MCs different from any MC in $\mathfrak{D}$. We formalise the notion of a consistent realisation with respect to parameters.

Definition 9 (Consistent realisation). *For a family $\mathfrak{D}$ of MCs and $k \in K$,* k-realisation-consistency *is an equivalence relation $\approx_k \subseteq \mathcal{R}^{\mathfrak{D}} \times \mathcal{R}^{\mathfrak{D}}$ satisfying:*

$$r \approx_k r' \iff r(k) = r'(k).$$

Let $[r]_{\approx_k}$ denote the equivalence class w.r.t. $\approx_k$ containing $r \in \mathcal{R}^{\mathfrak{D}}$.

Definition 10 (Consistent scheduler). *For quotient MDP $M^{\mathfrak{D}}_{\sim}$ after forgetting and $k \in K$, a scheduler $\sigma \in \Sigma^{M^{\mathfrak{D}}_{\sim}}$ is* k-consistent *if for all $\pi, \pi' \in \mathsf{Paths}^{M^{\mathfrak{D}}_{\sim}}_{fin}$:*

$$\sigma(\pi) = a_r \wedge \sigma(\pi') = a_{r'} \Longrightarrow r \approx_k r' \ .$$

A scheduler is K-consistent *(short:* consistent*) if it is k-consistent for all $k \in K$.*

Lemma 1. *For the quotient MDP $M^{\mathfrak{D}}_{\sim}$ of family $\mathfrak{D}$ of MCs:*

$$\{(M^{\mathfrak{D}}_{\sim})_{\sigma^{r^*}} \mid \sigma^{r^*} \text{ consistent scheduler}\} = \{D_r \mid r \in \mathcal{R}^{\mathfrak{D}}\}.$$

Proof (Idea). For $\sigma^r \in \Sigma^{M^{\mathfrak{D}}}$, we construct $\sigma^{r^*} \in \Sigma^{M^{\mathfrak{D}}_{\sim}}$ such that $\sigma^{r^*}([s]_\sim) = a_r$ for all s. Clearly σ^{r^*} is consistent and $M^{\mathfrak{D}}_{\sigma^r} = (M^{\mathfrak{D}}_{\sim})_{\sigma^{r^*}}$ is obtained via a map between (s, r) and $[s]_\sim$. For $\sigma^{r^*} \in \Sigma^{M^{\mathfrak{D}}_{\sim}}$, we construct $\sigma^r \in \Sigma^{M^{\mathfrak{D}}}$ such that if $\sigma^{r^*}([s]_\sim) = a_r$ then $\sigma^r(s_0^{\mathfrak{D}}) = a_r$. For all other states, we define $\sigma^r((s, r')) = a^{r'}$ independently of σ^{r^*}. Then $M^{\mathfrak{D}}_{\sigma^r} = (M^{\mathfrak{D}}_{\sim})_{\sigma^{r^*}}$ is obtained as above.

The following theorem is a direct corollary: we need to consider exactly the consistent schedulers.

Theorem 2. *For all-in-one MDP $M^{\mathfrak{D}}$ and specification φ, there exists a memoryless deterministic scheduler $\sigma^r \in \Sigma^{M^{\mathfrak{D}}}$ such that $M^{\mathfrak{D}}_{\sigma^r} \models \varphi$ iff there exists a consistent deterministic scheduler $\sigma^{r^*} \in \Sigma^{M^{\mathfrak{D}}_{\sim}}$ such that $(M^{\mathfrak{D}}_{\sim})_{\sigma^{r^*}} \models \varphi$.*

Example 4. Recall the all-in-one MDP $M^{\mathfrak{D}}$ from Example 3. The quotient MDP $M^{\mathfrak{D}}_{\sim}$ is depicted in Fig. 3. Only the transitions according to realisations r_1 and r_2 are included. Transitions from previously unreachable states, marked grey in Example 3, are now available due to the abstraction. The scheduler $\sigma \in \Sigma^{M^{\mathfrak{D}}_{\sim}}$ with $\sigma([s_0^{\mathfrak{D}}]_{\sim}) = a_{r_2}$ and $\sigma([1]_{\sim}) = a_{r_1}$ is *not* k_1*-consistent* as different values are chosen for k_1 by r_1 and r_2. In the MC $M^{\mathfrak{D}}_{\sim\sigma}$ induced by σ and $M^{\mathfrak{D}}_{\sim}$, the probability to reach state $[2]_{\sim}$ is one, while under realisation r_1, state 2 is not reachable.

Approach 3 (Scheduler iteration). *Enumerating all consistent schedulers for $M^{\mathfrak{D}}_{\sim}$ and analysing the induced MC provides a solution to both synthesis problems.*

However, optimising over exponentially many consistent schedulers solves the NP-complete feasibility synthesis problem, rendering such an iterative approach unlikely to be efficient. Another natural approach is to employ solving techniques for NP-complete problems, like satisfiability modulo linear real arithmetic.

Approach 4 (SMT). *A dedicated SMT-encoding (in [11]) of the induced MCs of consistent schedulers from $M^{\mathfrak{D}}_{\sim}$ that solves the feasibility problem.*

4.3 Refinement Loop

Although iterating over consistent schedulers (Approach 3) is not feasible, model checking of $M^{\mathfrak{D}}_{\sim}$ still provides useful information for the analysis of the family $\mathfrak{D}$. Recall the feasibility synthesis problem for $\varphi = \mathbb{P}_{\leq\lambda}(\phi)$. If $\texttt{Prob}^{\max}(M^{\mathfrak{D}}_{\sim}, \phi) \leq \lambda$, then all realisations of $\mathfrak{D}$ satisfy φ. On the other hand, $\texttt{Prob}^{\min}(M^{\mathfrak{D}}_{\sim}, \phi) > \lambda$ implies that there is no realisation satisfying φ. If λ lies between the min and max probability, and the scheduler inducing the min probability is not consistent, we cannot conclude anything yet, i.e., the abstraction is too coarse. A natural countermeasure is to refine the abstraction represented by $M^{\mathfrak{D}}_{\sim}$, in particular, split the set of realisations leading to two synthesis sub-problems.

Definition 11 (Splitting). *Let $\mathfrak{D}$ be a family of MCs, and $\mathcal{R} \subseteq \mathcal{R}^{\mathfrak{D}}$ a set of realisations. For $k \in K$ and predicate A_k over S,* splitting *partitions $\mathcal{R}$ into*

$$\mathcal{R}_{\top} = \{r \in \mathcal{R} \mid A_k(r(k))\} \quad \textit{and} \quad \mathcal{R}_{\bot} = \{r \in \mathcal{R} \mid \neg A_k(r(k))\}.$$

Splitting the set of realisations, and considering the subfamilies separately, rather than splitting states in the quotient MDP, is crucial for the performance of the synthesis process as we avoid rebuilding the quotient MDP in each iteration. Instead, we only restrict the actions of the MDP to the particular subfamily.

Definition 12 (Restricting). *Let $M^{\mathfrak{D}}_{\sim} = (S^{\mathfrak{D}}_{\sim}, [s_0^{\mathfrak{D}}]_{\sim}, Act^{\mathfrak{D}}, \mathcal{P}^{\mathfrak{D}}_{\sim})$ be a quotient MDP and $\mathcal{R} \subseteq \mathcal{R}^{\mathfrak{D}}$ a set of realisations. The* restriction *of $M^{\mathfrak{D}}_{\sim}$ wrt. $\mathcal{R}$ is the MDP $M^{\mathfrak{D}}_{\sim}[\mathcal{R}] = (S^{\mathfrak{D}}_{\sim}, [s_0^{\mathfrak{D}}]_{\sim}, Act^{\mathfrak{D}}[\mathcal{R}], \mathcal{P}^{\mathfrak{D}}_{\sim})$ where $Act^{\mathfrak{D}}[\mathcal{R}] = \{a_r \mid r \in \mathcal{R}\}$.*[3]

[3] Naturally, $\mathcal{P}^{\mathfrak{D}}_{\sim}$ in $M^{\mathfrak{D}}_{\sim}[\mathcal{R}]$ is restricted to $Act^{\mathfrak{D}}[\mathcal{R}]$.

Algorithm 1. Threshold synthesis

Input: A family $\mathfrak{D}$ of MCs with the set $\mathcal{R}^{\mathfrak{D}}$ of realisations, and specification $\mathbb{P}_{\leq\lambda}(\phi)$
Output: A partition of $\mathcal{R}^{\mathfrak{D}}$ into subsets T and F according to Problem 1.

$F \leftarrow \emptyset,\ T \leftarrow \emptyset,\ U \leftarrow \{\mathcal{R}^{\mathfrak{D}}\}$
$M^{\mathfrak{D}}_{\sim} \leftarrow$ `buildQuotientMDP`$(\mathfrak{D}, \mathcal{R}^{\mathfrak{D}}, \sim_f)$ ▷ Applying Def. 7 and 8
while $U \neq \emptyset$ **do**
  select $\mathcal{R} \in U$ **and** $\mathcal{U} \leftarrow \mathcal{U} \setminus \{\mathcal{R}\}$
  $M^{\mathfrak{D}}_{\sim}[\mathcal{R}] \leftarrow$ `restrict`$(M^{\mathfrak{D}}_{\sim}, \mathcal{R})$ ▷ Applying Def. 12
  $(\max, \sigma_{\max}) \leftarrow$ `solveMaxMDP`$(M^{\mathfrak{D}}_{\sim}[\mathcal{R}], \phi)$
  $(\min, \sigma_{\min}) \leftarrow$ `solveMinMDP`$(M^{\mathfrak{D}}_{\sim}[\mathcal{R}], \phi)$
  if $\max < \lambda$ **then** $T \leftarrow T \cup \mathcal{R}$
  if $\min > \lambda$ **then** $F \leftarrow F \cup \mathcal{R}$
  if $\min \leq \lambda \leq \max$ **then**
    $U \leftarrow U \cup$ `split`$(\mathcal{R},$ `selPredicate`$(\max, \sigma_{\max}, \min, \sigma_{\min}))$ ▷ See Sect. 4.4
return T, F

The splitting operation is the core of the proposed abstraction-refinement. Due to space constraints, we do not consider feasibility separately.

Algorithm 1 illustrates the *threshold synthesis* process. Recall that the goal is to decompose the set $\mathcal{R}^{\mathfrak{D}}$ into realisations satisfying and violating a given specification, respectively. The algorithm uses a set U to store subfamilies of $\mathcal{R}^{\mathfrak{D}}$ that have not been yet classified as satisfying or violating. It starts building the quotient MDP with merged actions. That is, we never construct the all-in-one MDP, and we merge actions as discussed in Remark 1. For every $\mathcal{R} \in U$, the algorithm restricts the set of realisations to obtain the corresponding subfamily. For the restricted quotient MDP, the algorithm runs standard MDP model checking to compute the max and min probability and corresponding schedulers, respectively. Then, the algorithm either classifies $\mathcal{R}$ as satisfying/violating, or splits it based on a suitable predicate, and updates U accordingly. We describe the splitting strategy in the next subsection. The algorithm terminates if U is empty, i.e., all subfamilies have been classified. As only a finite number of subfamilies of realisations has to be evaluated, termination is guaranteed.

The refinement loop for max synthesis is very similar, cf. Algorithm 2. Recall that now the goal is to find the realisation r^* that maximises the satisfaction probability $\max^*$ of a path formula. The difference between the algorithms lies in the interpretation of the results of the underlying MDP model checking. If the max probability for $\mathcal{R}$ is below $\max^*$, $\mathcal{R}$ can be discarded. Otherwise, we check whether the corresponding scheduler $\sigma_{\max}$ is consistent. If consistent, the algorithm updates r^* and $\max^*$, and discards $\mathcal{R}$. If the scheduler is not consistent but $\min > \max^*$ holds, we can still update $\max^*$ and improve the pruning process, as it means that some realisation (we do not know which) in $\mathcal{R}$ induces a higher probability than $\max^*$. Regardless whether $\max^*$ has been updated, the algorithm has to split $\mathcal{R}$ based on some predicate, and analyse its subfamilies as they may include the maximising realisation.

Algorithm 2. Max synthesis

Input: A family $\mathfrak{D}$ of MCs with the set $\mathcal{R}^{\mathfrak{D}}$ of realisations, and a path formula ϕ
Output: A realisation $r^* \in \mathcal{R}^{\mathfrak{D}}$ according to Problem 2.

$\max^* \leftarrow -\infty$, $U \leftarrow \{\mathcal{R}^{\mathfrak{D}}\}$
$M^{\mathfrak{D}}_{\sim} \leftarrow \texttt{buildQuotientMDP}(\mathfrak{D}, \mathcal{R}^{\mathfrak{D}}, \sim_f)$ ▷ Applying Def. 7 and 8
while $U \neq \emptyset$ **do**
  select $\mathcal{R} \in U$ **and** $\mathcal{U} \leftarrow \mathcal{U} \setminus \{\mathcal{R}\}$
  $M^{\mathfrak{D}}_{\sim}[\mathcal{R}] \leftarrow \texttt{restrict}(M^{\mathfrak{D}}_{\sim}, \mathcal{R})$ ▷ Applying Def. 12
  $(\max, \sigma_{\max}) \leftarrow \texttt{solveMaxMDP}(M^{\mathfrak{D}}_{\sim}[\mathcal{R}], \phi)$
  $(\min, \sigma_{\min}) \leftarrow \texttt{solveMinMDP}(M^{\mathfrak{D}}_{\sim}[\mathcal{R}], \phi)$
  if $\max > \max^*$ **then**
    if $\texttt{isConsistent}(\sigma_{\max})$ **then** $r^* \leftarrow q_{\max}, \max^* \leftarrow \max$
    else
      if $\min > \max^*$ **then** $\max^* \leftarrow \min$
      $U \leftarrow U \cup \texttt{split}(\mathcal{R}, \texttt{selPredicate}(\max, \sigma_{\max}, \min, \sigma_{\min}))$ ▷ See Sect. 4.4
return r^*

4.4 Splitting Strategies

If verifying the quotient MDP $M^{\mathfrak{D}}_{\sim}[\mathcal{R}]$ cannot classify the (sub-)realisation $\mathcal{R}$ as satisfying or violating, we split $\mathcal{R}$, while we guide the splitting strategy by using the obtained verification results. The splitting operation chooses a suitable parameter $k \in K$ and predicate A_k that partition the realisations $\mathcal{R}$ into $\mathcal{R}_\top$ and $\mathcal{R}_\bot$ (see Definition 11). A good splitting strategy globally reduces the number of model-checking calls required to classify all $r \in \mathcal{R}$.

The two key aspects to locally determine a good k are: (1) the *variance*, that is, how the splitting may narrow the difference between $\max = \texttt{Prob}^{\max}(M^{\mathfrak{D}}_{\sim}[\mathcal{X}], \phi)$ and $\min = \texttt{Prob}^{\min}(M^{\mathfrak{D}}_{\sim}[\mathcal{X}], \phi)$ for both $\mathcal{X} = \mathcal{R}_\top$ or $\mathcal{X} = \mathcal{R}_\bot$, and (2) the *consistency*, that is, how the splitting may reduce the inconsistency of the schedulers $\sigma_{\max}$ and $\sigma_{\min}$. These aspects cannot be evaluated precisely without applying all the split operations and solving the new MDPs $M^{\mathfrak{D}}_{\sim}[\mathcal{R}_\bot]$ and $M^{\mathfrak{D}}_{\sim}[\mathcal{R}_\top]$. Therefore, we propose an efficient strategy that selects k and A_k based on a light-weighted analysis of the model-checking results for $M^{\mathfrak{D}}_{\sim}[\mathcal{R}]$. The strategy applies two *scores* $\texttt{variance}(k)$ and $\texttt{consistency}(k)$ that estimate the influence of k on the two key aspects. For any k, the scores are accumulated over all *important states* s (reachable via $\sigma_{\max}$ or $\sigma_{\min}$, respectively) where $\mathfrak{P}(s)(k) \neq 0$. A state s is important for $\mathcal{R}$ and some $\delta \in \mathbb{R}_{\geq 0}$ if

$$\frac{\texttt{Prob}^{\max}(M^{\mathfrak{D}}_{\sim}[\mathcal{R}], \phi)(s) - \texttt{Prob}^{\min}(M^{\mathfrak{D}}_{\sim}[\mathcal{R}], \phi)(s)}{\texttt{Prob}^{\max}(M^{\mathfrak{D}}_{\sim}[\mathcal{R}], \phi) - \texttt{Prob}^{\min}(M^{\mathfrak{D}}_{\sim}[\mathcal{R}], \phi)} \geq \delta$$

where $\texttt{Prob}^{\min}(.)(s)$ and $\texttt{Prob}^{\max}(.)(s)$ is the min and max probability in the MDP with initial state s. To reduce the overhead of computing the scores, we simplify the scheduler representation. In particular, for $\sigma_{\max}$ and every $k \in K$, we extract a map $C^k_{\max} : T_k \to \mathbb{N}$, where $C^k_{\max}(t)$ is the number of important states for which $\sigma_{\max}(s) = a_r$ with $r(k) = t$. The mapping $C^k_{\min}$ represents $\sigma_{\min}$.

We define $\texttt{variance}(k) = \sum_{t\in T_k} |C^k_{\max}(t) - C^k_{\min}(t)|$, leading to high scores if the two schedulers vary a lot. Further, we define $\texttt{consistency}(k) = \texttt{size}\left(C^k_{\max}\right)\cdot \texttt{max}\left(C^k_{\max}\right) + \texttt{size}\left(C^k_{\min}\right)\cdot \texttt{max}\left(C^k_{\min}\right)$, where $\texttt{size}\left(C\right) = |\{t \in T_k \mid C(t) > 0\}| - 1$ and $\texttt{max}\left(C\right) = \max_{t\in T_k}\{C(t)\}$, leading to high scores if the parameter has clear favourites for $\sigma_{\max}$ and $\sigma_{\min}$, but values from its full range are chosen.

As indicated, we consider different strategies for the two synthesis problems. For threshold synthesis, we favour the impact on the variance as we principally do not need consistent schedulers. For the max synthesis, we favour the impact on the consistency, as we need a consistent scheduler inducing the max probability.

Predicate A_k is based on reducing the variance: The strategy selects $T' \subset T_k$ with $|T'| = \frac{1}{2}\lceil |T_k| \rceil$, containing those t for which $C^k_{\max}(t) - C^k_{\min}(t)$ is the largest. The goal is to get a set of realisations that induce a large probability (the ones including T' for parameter k) and the complement inducing a small probability.

Approach 5 (MDP-based abstraction refinement). *The methods underlying Algorithms 1 and 2, together with the splitting strategies, provide solutions to the synthesis problems and are referred to as* MDP abstraction *methods.*

5 Experiments

We implemented the proposed synthesis methods as a Python prototype using Storm [25]. In particular, we use the Storm Python API for model-adaption, -building, and -checking as well as for scheduler extraction. For SMT solving, we use Z3 [39] via pySMT [26]. The tool-chain takes a PRISM [38] or JANI [8] model with open integer constants, together with a set of expressions with possible values for these constants. The model may include the parallel composition of several modules/automata. The open constants may occur in guards[4], probability definitions, and updates of the commands/edges. Via adequate annotations, we identify the parameter values that yield a particular action. The annotations are key to interpret the schedulers, and to restrict the quotient without rebuilding.

All experiments were executed on a Macbook MF839LL/A with 8 GB RAM memory limit and a 12 h time out. All algorithms can significantly benefit from coarse-grained parallelisation, which we therefore do not consider here.

5.1 Research Questions and Benchmarks

The goal of the experimental evaluation is to answer the research question: *How does the proposed MDP-based abstraction methods (Approaches 3–5) cope with the inherent complexity (i.e. the NP-hardness) of the synthesis problems (cf. Problems 1 and 2)?* To answer this question, we compare their performance with Approaches 1 and 2 [18], representing state-of-the-art solutions and the base-line algorithms. The experiments show that the performance of the

[4] Slight care by the user is necessary to avoid deadlocks.

Table 1. Benchmarks and timings for Approaches 1–3

Bench.	Range	$\|K\|$	$\|\mathcal{D}\|$	Member size Avg. $\|S\|$	Avg. $\|T\|$	Quotient size $\|S\|$	$\|A\|$	$\|T\|$	Run time 1-by-1	All-in-1	Sched. Enum.
Pole	[3.35, 3.82]	17	1327104	5689	16896	6793	7897	22416	130k*	MO	26k
Maze	[9.8, 9800]	20	1048576	134	211	203	277	409	28k*	TO	2.7k
Herman	[1.86, 2.44]	9	576	5287	6948	21313	102657	184096	55*	72	246
DPM	[68, 210]	9	32768	5572	18147	35154	66096	160146	2.9k*	MO	7.2k
BSN	[0, 0.988]	10	1024	116	196	382	457	762	31*	2	2

MDP abstraction significantly varies for different case studies. Thus, we consider benchmarks from various application domains to *identify the key characteristics of the synthesis problems affecting the performance of our approach.*

Benchmarks description. We consider the following case studies: *Maze* is a planning problem typically considered as POMDP, e.g. in [41]. The family describes all MCs induced by small-memory [14,35] observation-based deterministic strategies (with a fixed upper bound on the memory). We are interested in the expected time to the goal. In [35], parameter synthesis was used to find randomised strategies, using [22]. *Pole* considers balancing a pole in a noisy and unknown environment (motivated by [2,12]). At deploy time, the controller has a prior over a finite set of environment behaviours, and should optimise the expected behavior without depending on the actual (hidden) environment. The family describes schedulers that do not depend on the hidden information. We are interested in the expected time until failure. *Herman* is an asynchronous encoding of the distributed Herman protocol for self-stabilising rings [33,37]. The protocol is extended with a bit of memory for each station in the ring, and the choice to flip various unfair coins. Nodes in the ring are anonymous, they all behave equivalently (but may change their local memory based on local events). The family describes variations of memory-updates and coin-selection, but preserves anonymity. We are interested in the expected time until stabilisation. *DPM* considers a partial information scheduler for a disk power manager motivated by [7,27]. We are interested in the expected energy consumption. *BSN* (Body sensor network, [43]) describes a network of connected sensors that identify health-critical situations. We are interested in the reliability. The family contains various configurations of the used sensors. *BSN* is the largest software product line benchmark used in [18]. We drop some implications between features (parameters for us) as this is not yet supported by our modelling language. We thereby extended the family.

Table 1 shows the relevant statistics for each benchmark: the benchmark name, the (approximate) range of the min and max probability/reward for the given family, the number of non-singleton parameters $|K|$, and the number of family members $|\mathfrak{D}|$. Then, for the family members the average number of states and transitions of the MCs, and the states, actions ($= \sum_{s \in S} |Act(s)|$), and transitions of the quotient MDP. Finally, it lists in seconds the run time of the base-line

Table 2. Results for threshold synthesis via abstraction-refinement

Inst	λ	# Below	# Subf below	# Above	# Subf above	Singles	# Iter	Time	Build	Check	Anal.	Speedup
Pole	3.37	697	176	1326407	2186	920	4723	308	117	60	118	**421**
	3.73	1307077	7854	20027	3279	1294	22265	1.7k	576	317	396	**77**
	3.76	1322181	3140	4923	1025	1022	8329	584	187	114	197	**222**
	3.79	1326502	572	602	123	74	1389	58	23	10	23	**2.2k**
Maze	10	4	3	1048572	92	4	189	5	<1	3	<1	**26k**
	20	4247	2297	1044329	4637	3400	13867	114	21	43	29	**246**
	30	18188	9934	1030388	18004	14010	55875	608	80	127	270	**46**
	8000	1046285	846	2291	1125	969	3941	136	9	106	13	**1.0k**
Herman	1.9	6	6	570	368	320	747	333	303	11	18	**0.2**
	1.71	0	0	576	258	184	515	232	206	8	17	**0.3**
DPM	80	160	141	32608	1292	356	2865	1.0k	602	322	64	**3**
	70	6	6	32762	443	40	897	380	190	156	32	**8**
	60	0	0	32768	104	6	207	99	42	48	8	**29**
BSN	.965	544	81	480	81	25	321	2	<1	<1	<1	**1**
	.985	994	41	30	8	5	97	<1	<1	<1	<1	**3**

algorithms and the consistent scheduler enumeration[5]. The base-line algorithms employ the one-by-one and the all-in-one technique, using either a BDD or a sparse matrix representation. We report the best results. MOs indicate breaking the memory limit. Only the all-in-one approach required significant memory. As expected, the SMT-based implementation provides an inferior performance and thus we do not report its results.

5.2 Results and Discussion

To simplify the presentation, we focus primarily on the threshold synthesis problem as it allows a compact presentation of the key aspects. Below, we provide some remarks about the performance for the max and feasibility synthesis.

Results. Table 2 shows results for threshold synthesis. The first two columns indicate the benchmark and the various thresholds. For each threshold λ, the table lists the number of family members below (above) λ, each with the number of subfamilies that together contain these instances, and the number of singleton subfamilies that were considered. The last table part gives the number of iterations of the loop in Algorithm 1, and timing information (total, build/restrict times, model checking times, scheduler analysis times). The last column gives the speed-up over the best base-line (based on the estimates).

Key observations. The speed-ups drastically vary, which shows that the MDP abstraction often achieves a superior performance but may also lead to a performance degradation in some cases. We identify four key factors.

[5] Values with a * are estimated by sampling a large fraction of the family.

Iterations. As typical for CEGAR approaches, the key characteristic of the benchmark that affects the performance is the number N of iterations in the refinement loop. The abstract action introduces an overhead per iteration caused by performing two MDP verification calls and by the scheduler analysis. The run time for *BSN*, with a small $|\mathfrak{D}|$ is actually significantly affected by the initialisation of various data structures; thus only a small speedup is achieved.

Abstraction size. The size of the quotient, compared to the average size of the family members, is relevant too. The quotient includes at least all reachable states of all family members, and may be significantly larger if an inconsistent scheduler reaches states which are unreachable under any consistent scheduler. The existence of such states is a common artefact from encoding families in high-level languages. Table 1, however, indicates that we obtain a very compact representation for *Maze* and *Pole*.

Thresholds. The most important aspect is the threshold λ. If λ is closer to the optima, the abstraction requires a smaller number of iterations, which directly improves the performance. We emphasise that in various domains, thresholds that ask for close-to-optimal solutions are indeed of highest relevance as they typically represent the system designs developers are most interested in [44]. *Why do thresholds affect the number of iterations?* Consider a family with $T_k = \{0, 1\}$ for each k. Geometrically, the set $\mathcal{R}^{\mathfrak{D}}$ can be visualised as $|K|$-dimensional cube. The cube-vertices reflect family members. Assume for simplicity that one of these vertices is optimal with respect to the specification. Especially in benchmarks where parameters are equally important, the induced probability of a vertex roughly corresponds to the Manhattan distance to the optimal vertex. Thus, vertices above the threshold induce a diagonal hyperplane, which our splitting method approximates with orthogonal splits. Splitting diagonally is not possible, as it would induce optimising over observation-based schedulers. Consequently, we need more and more splits the more the diagonal goes through the middle of the cube. *Even when splitting optimally, there is a combinatorial blow-up in the required splits when the threshold is further from the optimal values.* Another effect is that thresholds far from optima are more affected by the over-approximation of the MDP model-checking results and thus yield more inconclusive answers.

Refinement strategy. So far, we reasoned about optimal splits. Due to the computational overhead, our strategy cannot ensure optimal splits. Instead, the strategy depends mostly on information encoded in the computed MDP strategies. *In models where the optimal parameter value heavily depends on the state, the obtained schedulers are highly inconsistent and carry only limited information for splitting.* Consequently, in such benchmarks we split sub-optimally. The sub-optimality has a major impact on the performance for *Herman* as all obtained strategies are highly inconsistent – they take a different coin for each node, which is good to speed up the stabilisation of the ring.

Summary. MDP abstraction is not a silver bullet. It has a lot of potential in threshold synthesis when the threshold is close to the optima. Consequently, *feasibility synthesis with unsatisfiable specifications is handled perfectly well by MDP abstraction*, while this is the worst-case for enumeration-based approaches. Likewise, *max synthesis* can be understood as threshold synthesis with a shifting threshold $\max^*$: If the $\max^*$ is quickly set close to max, MDP abstraction yields superior performance. Roughly, we can quickly approximate $\max^*$ when some of the parameter values are clearly beneficial for the specification.

6 Conclusion and Future Work

We contributed to the efficient analysis of families of Markov chains. In particular, we discussed and implemented existing approaches to solve practically interesting synthesis problems, and devised a novel abstraction refinement scheme that mitigates the computational complexity of the synthesis problems, as shown by the empirical evaluation. In the future, we will include refinement strategies based on counterexamples as in [23,34].

References

1. Repository with benchmarks. https://github.com/moves-rwth/shepherd
2. Arming, S., Bartocci, E., Chatterjee, K., Katoen, J.-P., Sokolova, A.: Parameter-independent strategies for pMDPs via POMDPs. In: McIver, A., Horvath, A. (eds.) QEST 2018. LNCS, vol. 11024, pp. 53–70. Springer, Cham (2018). https://doi.org/10.1007/978-3-319-99154-2_4
3. Aziz, A., Singhal, V., Balarin, F., Brayton, R.K., Sangiovanni-Vincentelli, A.L.: It usually works: the temporal logic of stochastic systems. In: Wolper, P. (ed.) CAV 1995. LNCS, vol. 939, pp. 155–165. Springer, Heidelberg (1995). https://doi.org/10.1007/3-540-60045-0_48
4. Baier, C., de Alfaro, L., Forejt, V., Kwiatkowska, M.: Model checking probabilistic systems. In: Clarke, E., Henzinger, T., Veith, H., Bloem, R. (eds.) Handbook of Model Checking, pp. 963–999. Springer, Cham (2018). https://doi.org/10.1007/978-3-319-10575-8_28
5. Baier, C., Katoen, J.: Principles of Model Checking. MIT Press, Cambridge (2008)
6. Bartocci, E., Grosu, R., Katsaros, P., Ramakrishnan, C.R., Smolka, S.A.: Model repair for probabilistic systems. In: Abdulla, P.A., Leino, K.R.M. (eds.) TACAS 2011. LNCS, vol. 6605, pp. 326–340. Springer, Heidelberg (2011). https://doi.org/10.1007/978-3-642-19835-9_30
7. Benini, L., Bogliolo, A., Paleologo, G., Micheli, G.D.: Policy optimization for dynamic power management. IEEE Trans. Comput.-Aided Des. Integr. Circ. Syst. **8**(3), 299–316 (2000)
8. Budde, C.E., Dehnert, C., Hahn, E.M., Hartmanns, A., Junges, S., Turrini, A.: JANI: quantitative model and tool interaction. In: Legay, A., Margaria, T. (eds.) TACAS 2017. LNCS, vol. 10206, pp. 151–168. Springer, Heidelberg (2017). https://doi.org/10.1007/978-3-662-54580-5_9
9. Calinescu, R., Češka, M., Gerasimou, S., Kwiatkowska, M., Paoletti, N.: Efficient synthesis of robust models for stochastic systems. J. Syst. Softw. **143**, 140–158 (2018)

10. Češka, M., Dannenberg, F., Paoletti, N., Kwiatkowska, M., Brim, L.: Precise parameter synthesis for stochastic biochemical systems. Acta Informatica **54**(6), 589–623 (2017)
11. Češka, M., Jansen, N., Junges, S., Katoen, J.P.: Shepherding hordes of Markov chains. CoRR abs/1902.xxxxx (2019)
12. Chades, I., Carwardine, J., Martin, T.G., Nicol, S., Sabbadin, R., Buffet, O.: MOMDPs: a solution for modelling adaptive management problems. In: AAAI. AAAI Press (2012)
13. Chasins, S., Phothilimthana, P.M.: Data-driven synthesis of full probabilistic programs. In: Majumdar, R., Kunčak, V. (eds.) CAV 2017. LNCS, vol. 10426, pp. 279–304. Springer, Cham (2017). https://doi.org/10.1007/978-3-319-63387-9_14
14. Chatterjee, K., Chmelik, M., Davies, J.: A symbolic SAT-based algorithm for almost-sure reachability with small strategies in POMDPs. In: AAAI, pp. 3225–3232. AAAI Press (2016)
15. Chatterjee, K., Kößler, A., Schmid, U.: Automated analysis of real-time scheduling using graph games. In: HSCC, pp. 163–172. ACM (2013)
16. Chen, T., Hahn, E.M., Han, T., Kwiatkowska, M.Z., Qu, H., Zhang, L.: Model repair for Markov decision processes. In: TASE, pp. 85–92. IEEE (2013)
17. Chonev, V.: Reachability in augmented interval Markov chains. CoRR abs/1701.02996 (2017)
18. Chrszon, P., Dubslaff, C., Klüppelholz, S., Baier, C.: ProFeat: feature-oriented engineering for family-based probabilistic model checking. Formal Asp. Comput. **30**(1), 45–75 (2018)
19. Classen, A., Cordy, M., Heymans, P., Legay, A., Schobbens, P.: Model checking software product lines with SNIP. STTT **14**(5), 589–612 (2012)
20. Classen, A., Cordy, M., Heymans, P., Legay, A., Schobbens, P.: Formal semantics, modular specification, and symbolic verification of product-line behaviour. Sci. Comput. Program. **80**, 416–439 (2014)
21. Cordy, M., Heymans, P., Legay, A., Schobbens, P.Y., Dawagne, B., Leucker, M.: Counterexample guided abstraction refinement of product-line behavioural models. In: SIGSOFT FSE, pp. 190–201. ACM (2014)
22. Cubuktepe, M., Jansen, N., Junges, S., Katoen, J.-P., Topcu, U.: Synthesis in pMDPs: a tale of 1001 parameters. In: Lahiri, S.K., Wang, C. (eds.) ATVA 2018. LNCS, vol. 11138, pp. 160–176. Springer, Cham (2018). https://doi.org/10.1007/978-3-030-01090-4_10
23. Dehnert, C., Jansen, N., Wimmer, R., Ábrahám, E., Katoen, J.-P.: Fast debugging of PRISM models. In: Cassez, F., Raskin, J.-F. (eds.) ATVA 2014. LNCS, vol. 8837, pp. 146–162. Springer, Cham (2014). https://doi.org/10.1007/978-3-319-11936-6_11
24. Dehnert, C., et al.: PROPhESY: a PRObabilistic ParamEter SYnthesis tool. In: Kroening, D., Păsăreanu, C.S. (eds.) CAV 2015. LNCS, vol. 9206, pp. 214–231. Springer, Cham (2015). https://doi.org/10.1007/978-3-319-21690-4_13
25. Dehnert, C., Junges, S., Katoen, J.-P., Volk, M.: A storm is coming: a modern probabilistic model checker. In: Majumdar, R., Kunčak, V. (eds.) CAV 2017. LNCS, vol. 10427, pp. 592–600. Springer, Cham (2017). https://doi.org/10.1007/978-3-319-63390-9_31
26. Gario, M., Micheli, A.: PySMT: a solver-agnostic library for fast prototyping of SMT-based algorithms. In: SMT Workshop 2015 (2015)
27. Gerasimou, S., Calinescu, R., Tamburrelli, G.: Synthesis of probabilistic models for quality-of-service software engineering. Autom. Softw. Eng. **25**(4), 785–831 (2018)

28. Ghezzi, C., Sharifloo, A.M.: Model-based verification of quantitative non-functional properties for software product lines. Inf. Softw. Technol. **55**(3), 508–524 (2013)
29. Giro, S., D'Argenio, P.R., Fioriti, L.M.F.: Distributed probabilistic input/output automata: expressiveness, (un)decidability and algorithms. Theor. Comput. Sci. **538**, 84–102 (2014)
30. Giro, S., Rabe, M.N.: Verification of partial-information probabilistic systems using counterexample-guided refinements. In: Chakraborty, S., Mukund, M. (eds.) ATVA 2012. LNCS, vol. 7561, pp. 333–348. Springer, Heidelberg (2012). https://doi.org/10.1007/978-3-642-33386-6_26
31. Hahn, E.M., Hermanns, H., Zhang, L.: Probabilistic reachability for parametric Markov models. Softw. Tools Technol. Transfer **13**(1), 3–19 (2011)
32. Hansson, H., Jonsson, B.: A logic for reasoning about time and reliability. Formal Aspects Comput. **6**(5), 512–535 (1994)
33. Herman, T.: Probabilistic self-stabilization. Inf. Process. Lett. **35**(2), 63–67 (1990)
34. Jansen, N., et al.: Symbolic counterexample generation for large discrete-time Markov chains. Sci. Comput. Program. **91**, 90–114 (2014)
35. Junges, S., et al.: Finite-state controllers of POMDPs using parameter synthesis. In: UAI, pp. 519–529. AUAI Press (2018)
36. Kochenderfer, M.J.: Decision Making Under Uncertainty: Theory and Application, 1st edn. The MIT Press, Cambridge (2015)
37. Kwiatkowska, M., Norman, G., Parker, D.: Probabilistic verification of Herman's self-stabilisation algorithm. Formal Aspects Comput. **24**(4), 661–670 (2012)
38. Kwiatkowska, M., Norman, G., Parker, D.: PRISM 4.0: verification of probabilistic real-time systems. In: Gopalakrishnan, G., Qadeer, S. (eds.) CAV 2011. LNCS, vol. 6806, pp. 585–591. Springer, Heidelberg (2011). https://doi.org/10.1007/978-3-642-22110-1_47
39. de Moura, L., Bjørner, N.: Z3: an efficient SMT solver. In: Ramakrishnan, C.R., Rehof, J. (eds.) TACAS 2008. LNCS, vol. 4963, pp. 337–340. Springer, Heidelberg (2008). https://doi.org/10.1007/978-3-540-78800-3_24
40. Nori, A.V., Ozair, S., Rajamani, S.K., Vijaykeerthy, D.: Efficient synthesis of probabilistic programs. In: PLDI, pp. 208–217. ACM (2015)
41. Norman, G., Parker, D., Zou, X.: Verification and control of partially observable probabilistic systems. Real-Time Syst. **53**(3), 354–402 (2017)
42. Pathak, S., Ábrahám, E., Jansen, N., Tacchella, A., Katoen, J.-P.: A greedy approach for the efficient repair of stochastic models. In: Havelund, K., Holzmann, G., Joshi, R. (eds.) NFM 2015. LNCS, vol. 9058, pp. 295–309. Springer, Cham (2015). https://doi.org/10.1007/978-3-319-17524-9_21
43. Rodrigues, G.N., et al.: Modeling and verification for probabilistic properties in software product lines. In: HASE, pp. 173–180. IEEE (2015)
44. Skaf, J., Boyd, S.: Techniques for exploring the suboptimal set. Optim. Eng. **11**(2), 319–337 (2010)
45. Vandin, A., ter Beek, M.H., Legay, A., Lluch-Lafuente, A.: QFLan: a tool for the quantitative analysis of highly reconfigurable systems. In: Havelund, K., Peleska, J., Roscoe, B., de Vink, E. (eds.) FM 2018. LNCS, vol. 10951, pp. 329–337. Springer, Cham (2018). https://doi.org/10.1007/978-3-319-95582-7_19
46. Varshosaz, M., Khosravi, R.: Discrete time Markov chain families: modeling and verification of probabilistic software product lines. In: SPLC Workshops, pp. 34–41. ACM (2013)

Optimal Time-Bounded Reachability Analysis for Concurrent Systems

Yuliya Butkova(✉) and Gereon Fox

Saarland University, Saarbrücken, Germany
{butkova,fox}@depend.uni-saarland.de

Abstract. Efficient optimal scheduling for concurrent systems on a finite horizon is a challenging task up to date: Not only does time have a continuous domain, but in addition there are exponentially many possible decisions to choose from at every time point.

In this paper we present a solution to the problem of optimal time-bounded reachability for Markov automata, one of the most general formalisms for modelling concurrent systems. Our algorithm is based on the discretisation of the time horizon. In contrast to most existing algorithms for similar problems, the discretisation step is not fixed. We attempt to discretise only in those time points when the optimal scheduler *in fact* changes its decision. Our empirical evaluation demonstrates that the algorithm improves on existing solutions up to several orders of magnitude.

1 Introduction

Modern technologies grow and complexify rapidly, making it hard to ensure their dependability and reliability. Formal approaches to describing these systems include (generalised) stochastic Petri nets [Mol82, MCB84, MBC+98, Bal07], stochastic activity networks [MMS85], dynamic fault trees [BCS10] and others. The semantics of these modelling languages is often defined in terms of *continuous time Markov chains* (CTMCs). CTMCs can model the behaviour of seemingly independent processes evolving in memoryless continuous time (according to exponential distributions).

Modelling a system as a CTMC, however, strips it of any notion of *choice*, e.g., which of a number of requests to process first, or how to optimally balance the load over multiple servers of a cluster. Making sure that the system is safe for all possible choices of this kind is an important issue when assessing its reliability. *Non-determinism* allows the modeller to capture these choices. Modelling systems with non-determinism is possible in formalisms such as *interactive Markov chains* [Her02], or *Markov automata* (MA) [EHKZ13]. The latter are one

This work is supported by the ERC Advanced Investigators Grant 695614 (POWVER) and by the German Research Foundation (DFG) Grant 389792660, as part of CRC 248 (see https://perspicuous-computing.science).

T. Vojnar and L. Zhang (Eds.): TACAS 2019, Part II, LNCS 11428, pp. 191–208, 2019.
https://doi.org/10.1007/978-3-030-17465-1_11

of the most general models for concurrent systems available and can serve as a semantics for generalised stochastic Petri nets and dynamic fault trees.

A similar formalism, *continuous time Markov decision processes* (CTMDPs) [Ber00,Put94], has seen wide-spread use in control theory and operations research. In fact, MA and CTMDPs are closely related: They both can model exponential Markovian transitions and non-determinism. However, MA are *compositional*, while CTMDPs are not: In general it is not possible to model a system as a CTMDP by modelling each of its sub-components as smaller CTMDP and then combining them. This is why modelling large systems with many communicating sub-components as a CTMDP is cumbersome and error-prone. In fact, most modern model checkers, such as `Storm` [DJKV17], `Modest` [HH14] and `PRISM` [KNP11], do not offer any support for CTMDPs.

In the analysis of MA and CTMDPs, one of the most challenging problems is the approximation of *optimal time-bounded reachability probability*, i. e. the maximal (or minimal) probability of a system to reach a set of goal states (e. g. unsafe states) within a given time bound. Due to the presence of non-determinism this value depends on which decisions are taken at which time points. Since the optimal strategy is time dependent there are continuously many different strategies. Classically, one deals with continuity by discretising the values, as is the case in most algorithms for CTMDPs and MA [Neu10,FRSZ16,HH15,BS11]: The time horizon is discretised into finitely many intervals, and the value within each interval is approximated by e. g. polynomial or exponential functions.

Discretisation is closely related to the scheduler that is optimal for a specific MA. As an example, consider Fig. 1: The plot shows the probabilities of reaching a goal state for a certain time bound, by choosing options 1 and 2. If less than 0.9 seconds remain, option 1 has a higher probability of reaching the goal set, while option 2 is preferable as long as more than 0.9 seconds are left. In this example it is enough to discretise the time horizon with roughly 2 intervals: $[0, 0.9]$ and $(0.9, 1.5]$. The algorithms known to date however use from 200 to $2 \cdot 10^6$ intervals, which is far too many. The solution that we present in this paper discretises the time horizon in only *three* intervals for this example.

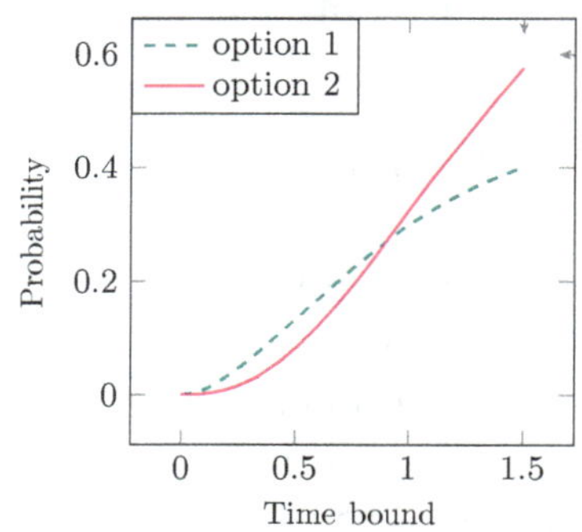

Fig. 1. Reachability probability for different decisions

Our contribution consists in an algorithm that computes time bounded reachability probabilities for Markov automata. The algorithm discretises the time horizon by intervals of variable length, making them smaller near those time points where the optimal scheduler switches from one decision to another. We give a characterisation of these time points, as well as tight sufficient conditions for no such time point to exist within an interval. We present an empirical evaluation of the performance of the algorithm and compare it to other algorithms available for Markov automata. The algorithm does perform well in the comparison, improving in some cases by several orders of magnitude, but does not strictly outperform available solutions.

2 Preliminaries

Given a finite set S, a *probability distribution* over S is a function $\mu : S \to [0,1]$, s. t. $\sum_{s \in S} \mu(s) = 1$. We denote the set of all probability distributions over S by $\mathrm{Dist}(S)$. The sets of rational, real and natural numbers are denoted with $\mathbb{Q}$, $\mathbb{R}$ and $\mathbb{N}$ resp., $X_{\trianglerighteq 0} = \{x \in X \mid x \trianglerighteq 0\}$, for $X \in \{\mathbb{Q}, \mathbb{R}\}, \trianglerighteq \in \{>, \geqslant\}$, $\mathbb{N}_{\geqslant 0} = \mathbb{N} \cup \{0\}$.

Definition 1. *A* Markov automaton (MA)[1] *is a tuple* $\mathcal{M} = (S, Act, \mathbf{P}, \mathrm{Q}, G)$ *where S is a finite set of states partitioned into* probabilistic *(PS) and* Markovian *(MS), $G \subseteq S$ is a set of* goal states, *Act is a finite set of actions,* $\mathbf{P} : PS \times Act \to \mathrm{Dist}(S)$ *is the probabilistic transition matrix,* $\mathrm{Q} : MS \times S \to \mathbb{Q}$ *is the Markovian transition matrix, s. t.* $\mathrm{Q}(s, s') \geqslant 0$ *for* $s \neq s'$, $\mathrm{Q}(s, s) = -\sum_{s' \neq s} \mathrm{Q}(s, s')$.

Figure 2 shows an example MA. Grey and white colours denote Markovian and probabilistic states correspondingly. Transitions labelled as α or β are actions of state s_1. Dashed transitions associated with an action represent the distribution assigned to the action. Purely solid transitions are Markovian.

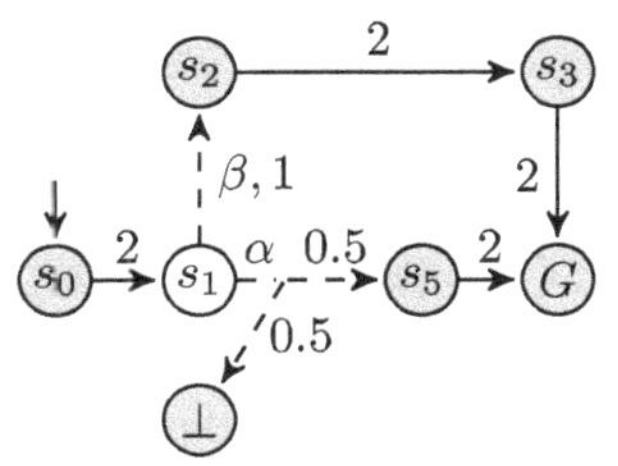

Fig. 2. An example MA.

Notation and further definitions: For a Markovian state $s \in MS$ and $s' \neq s$, we call $\mathrm{Q}(s, s')$ the *transition rate* from s to s'. The *exit rate* of a Markovian state s is $\mathrm{E}(s) := \sum_{s' \neq s} \mathrm{Q}(s, s')$. $\mathbf{E}_{\max}$ denotes the maximal exit rate among all the Markovian states of $\mathcal{M}$. For a probabilistic state $s \in PS$, $\mathrm{Act}(s) = \{\alpha \in \mathrm{Act} \mid \exists \mu \in \mathrm{Dist}(S) : \mathbf{P}(s, \alpha) = \mu\}$ denotes the set of actions that are *enabled* in s. $\mathbb{P}[s, \alpha, \cdot] \in \mathrm{Dist}(S)$ is defined by $\mathbb{P}[s, \alpha, s'] := \mu(s')$, where $\mathbf{P}(s', \alpha) = \mu$. We impose the usual *non-zenoness* [GHH+14] restriction on MA. This disallows e. g., probabilistic states with no outgoing transitions, or with only self-loop transitions.

A *(timed) path* in $\mathcal{M}$ is a finite or infinite sequence $\rho = s_0 \xrightarrow{\alpha_0, t_0} s_1 \xrightarrow{\alpha_1, t_1} \cdots \xrightarrow{\alpha_k, t_k} s_{k+1} \xrightarrow{\alpha_{k+1}, t_{k+1}} \cdots$, where $\alpha_i \in \mathrm{Act}(s_i)$ for $s_i \in PS$, and $\alpha_i = \perp$ for $s_i \in MS$. For a finite path $\rho = s_0 \xrightarrow{\alpha_0, t_0} s_1 \xrightarrow{\alpha_1, t_1} \cdots \xrightarrow{\alpha_{k-1}, t_{k-1}} s_k$ we define $\rho{\downarrow} = s_k$. The set of all finite (infinite) paths of $\mathcal{M}$ is denoted by $Paths^*$ ($Paths$).

Time passes continuously in Markovian states. The system leaves the state after the amount of time that is governed by an exponential distribution, i. e. the probability of leaving $s \in MS$ within $t \geq 0$ time units is given by $1 - \mathrm{e}^{-\mathrm{E}(s) \cdot t}$, after which the next state s' is chosen with probability $\mathrm{Q}(s, s')/\mathrm{E}(s)$.

Probabilistic transitions happen instantaneously. Whenever the system is in a probabilistic state s and an action $\alpha \in \mathrm{Act}(s)$ is chosen, the successor s' is

[1] Strictly speaking, this is the definition of a *closed* Markov automaton in which no state has two actions with the same label. This is however not a restriction since the analysis of *general* Markov automata is always performed only after the composition under the urgency assumption is performed. Additional renaming of the actions does not affect the properties considered in this work.

selected according to the distribution $\mathbb{P}[s, \alpha, \cdot]$ and the system moves from s to s' right away. Thus, the residence time in probabilistic states is always 0.

2.1 Time-Bounded Reachability

In this work we are interested in the probability to reach a certain set of states of a Markov automaton within a given time bound. However, due to the presence of multiple actions in probabilistic states the behaviour of a Markov automaton is not a stochastic process and thus no probability measure can be defined. This issue is resolved by introducing the notion of a scheduler.

A *general scheduler (or strategy)* $\pi : \mathit{Paths}^* \rightarrow \mathrm{Dist}(\mathrm{Act})$ is a measurable function, s. t. $\forall \rho \in \mathit{Paths}^*$ if $\rho\downarrow \in \mathit{PS}$ then $\pi(\rho) \in \mathrm{Dist}(\mathrm{Act}(\rho\downarrow))$. General schedulers provide a distribution over enabled actions of a probabilistic state given that the path ρ has been observed from the beginning of the system evolution. We call *stationary* such a general scheduler π that can be represented as $\pi : \mathit{PS} \rightarrow \mathrm{Act}$, i. e. it is non-randomised and depends only on the current state. The set of all general (stationary) schedulers is denoted by $\Pi_{\mathtt{gen}}$ ($\Pi_{\mathtt{stat}}$ resp.).

Given a general scheduler π, the behaviour of a Markov automaton is a fully defined stochastic process. For the definition of the probability measure $\mathrm{Pr}^{\pi}_{\mathcal{M}}$ on Markov automata we refer to [Hat17].

Let $s \in S$, $T \in \mathbb{Q}_{\geqslant 0}$ be a time bound and $\pi \in \Pi_{\mathtt{gen}}$ be a general scheduler. The *(time-bounded) reachability probability* (or *value*) for a scheduler π and state s in $\mathcal{M}$ is defined as follows:

$$\mathrm{val}^{\mathcal{M},\pi}_{s}(T) := \mathrm{Pr}^{\pi}_{\mathcal{M}}\left[\Diamond^{\leqslant T}_{s} G\right],$$

where $\Diamond^{\leqslant T}_{s} G = \{s \xrightarrow{\alpha_0, t_0} s_1 \xrightarrow{\alpha_1, t_1} s_2 \ldots \mid \exists i : s_i \in G \wedge \sum_{j=0}^{i-1} t_j \leq T\}$ is the set of paths starting from s and reaching G before T.

For opt $\in \{\sup, \inf\}$, the *optimal (time-bounded) reachability probability* (or *value*) of state s in $\mathcal{M}$ is defined as follows:

$$\mathrm{val}^{\mathcal{M}}_{s}(T) := \mathrm{opt}_{\pi \in \Pi_{\mathtt{gen}}} \mathrm{val}^{\mathcal{M},\pi}_{s}(T)$$

We denote by $\mathrm{val}^{\mathcal{M},\pi}(T)$ ($\mathrm{val}^{\mathcal{M}}(T)$) the vector of values $\mathrm{val}^{\mathcal{M},\pi}_{s}(T)$ ($\mathrm{val}^{\mathcal{M}}_{s}(T)$) for all $s \in S$. A general scheduler that achieves optimum for $\mathrm{val}^{\mathcal{M}}(T)$ is called *optimal*, and the one that achieves value $\boldsymbol{v}$, s. t. $||\boldsymbol{v} - \mathrm{val}^{\mathcal{M}}(T)||_{\infty} < \varepsilon$, is *$\varepsilon$-optimal.*

Optimal Schedulers. For the time-bounded reachability problem it is known [RS13] that there exists an optimal scheduler π of the form $\pi : \mathit{PS} \times \mathbb{R}_{\geqslant 0} \rightarrow \mathrm{Act}$. This scheduler does not need to know the full history of the system, but only the current probabilistic state it is in and the total time left until time bound. It is deterministic, i. e. *not randomised*, and additionally, this scheduler is *piecewise constant*, meaning that there exists a finite partition $\mathcal{I}(\pi)$ of the time interval $[0, T]$ into intervals $I_0 = [t_0, t_1], I_1 = (t_1, t_2], \cdots, I_{k-1} = (t_{k-1}, t_k]$, such that

$t_0 = 0, t_k = T$ and the value of the scheduler remains constant throughout each interval of the partition, i. e. $\forall I \in \mathcal{I}(\pi), \forall t_1, t_2 \in I, \forall s \in PS : \pi(s, t_1) = \pi(s, t_2)$. The value of π on an interval $I \in \mathcal{I}(\pi)$ and $s \in PS$ is denoted by $\pi(s, I)$, i. e. $\pi(s, I) = \pi(s, t)$ for any $t \in I$.

As an example, consider the MA in Fig. 2 and time bound $T = 1$. Here the optimal scheduler for state s_1 chooses the reliable but slow action β if there is enough time, i. e. if at least 0.62 time is left. Otherwise the optimal scheduler switches to a more risky, but faster path via action α.

In the literature this subclass of schedulers is sometimes referred to as *total-time positional deterministic, piecewise constant schedulers*. From now on we call a scheduler from this subclass simply a *scheduler (or strategy)* and denote the set of such schedulers with Π. An important notion of schedulers is the *switching point*, the point of time separating two intervals of constant decisions:

Definition 2. *For a scheduler π and $s \in PS$ we call $\tau \in \mathbb{R}_{\geqslant 0}$ a* switching point, *iff $\exists I_1, I_2 \in \mathcal{I}(\pi)$, s. t. $\tau = \sup I_1$ and $\tau = \inf I_2$ and $\exists s \in PS : \pi(s, I_1) \neq \pi(s, I_2)$.*

Whether the switching points can be computed exactly or not is an open problem. In fact, the theorem of Lindemann-Weierstrass suggests that switching points are non-algebraic numbers, what hints at a negative answer.

3 Related Work

In this section we briefly review the algorithms designed to approximate time bounded reachability probabilities. We only discuss the algorithms that guarantee to compute ε-close approximation of the reachability value.

The majority of the algorithms [Neu10, BS11, FRSZ16, SSM18, BHHK15] are available for continuous time Markov decision processes (CTMDPs) [Ber00]. Two of those, [Neu10] and [BHHK15], are also applicable to MA. We compare to them in our empirical evaluation in Sect. 5. All the algorithms utilise such known techniques as discretisation, uniformisation, or a combination thereof. The drawback of most of the algorithms is that they do not adapt to a specific instance of a problem. Namely, given a model $\mathcal{M}$ to analyse, they perform as many computations as is needed for $\widehat{\mathcal{M}}$, which is the worst-case model in a subclass of models that share certain parameters with $\mathcal{M}$, such as $\mathbf{E}_{\max}$, for example. Experimental evaluation performed in [BHHK15] shows that such approaches are not promising, because most of the time the algorithms perform too many unnecessary computations. This is not the case for [BS11] and [BHHK15]. The latter performs the analysis via uniformisation and schedulers that cannot observe time. The former, designed for CTMDPs, performs discretisation of the time horizon with intervals of variable length, however is not applicable to MA. Just like in [BS11], our approach is to adapt the discretisation of the time horizon to a specific instance of the problem.

4 Our Solution

In this section we present a novel approach to approximating optimal time-bounded reachability and the optimal scheduler for an arbitrary Markov automaton. Throughout the section we work with an MA $\mathcal{M} = (S, \mathrm{Act}, \mathbf{P}, \mathrm{Q}, G)$, time bound $T \in \mathbb{Q}_{\geqslant 0}$ and precision $\varepsilon \in \mathbb{Q}_{>0}$. To simplify the presentation we concentrate on supremum reachability probability.

Given a scheduler, computation (or approximation) of the reachability probability is relatively easy:

Lemma 1. *For a scheduler* $\pi \in \Pi$ *and a state* $s \in S$*, the function* $\mathrm{val}_s^{\mathcal{M},\pi} : [0, T] \to [0, 1]$ *is the solution to the following system of equations:*

$$\begin{aligned} f_s(t) &= 1 && \textit{if } s \in G \\ -\frac{\mathrm{d}f_s(t)}{\mathrm{d}t} &= \sum_{s' \in S} \mathrm{Q}(s, s') \cdot f_{s'}(t) && \textit{else if } s \in MS \\ f_s(t) &= \sum_{s' \in S} \mathbb{P}[s, \pi(s,t), s'] \cdot f_{s'}(t) && \textit{else if } s \in PS \end{aligned} \tag{1}$$

$$f_s(0) = \begin{cases} 1 & \textit{if } s \in G \\ \sum_{s' \in S} \mathbb{P}[s, \pi(s,0), s'] \cdot f_{s'}(0) & \textit{else if } s \in PS \\ 0 & \textit{otherwise} \end{cases} \tag{2}$$

Let $0 = \tau_0 < \tau_1 < \ldots < \tau_{k-1} < \tau_k = T$, where τ_i are the switching points of π for $i = 1..k-1$. The solution of the system of Equations (1)–(2) can be obtained separately on each of the intervals $(\tau_{i-1}, \tau_i], \forall i = 1..k$, where the value of the scheduler remains constant for all states. Given the solution $\mathrm{val}_s^{\mathcal{M},\pi}(t)$ on interval $(\tau_{i-1}, \tau_i]$, we derive the solution for $(\tau_i, \tau_{i+1}]$ by using the values $\mathrm{val}_s^{\mathcal{M},\pi}(\tau_i)$ as boundary conditions. Later in Sect. 4.1 we will show that the approximation of the solution for each interval $(\tau_{i-1}, \tau_i]$ can be achieved via a combination of known techniques, such as *uniformisation* (for the Markovian states) and *untimed reachability analysis* (for probabilistic states).

Thus, given an optimal scheduler, Lemma 1 can be used to compute or approximate the optimal reachability value. Finding an optimal scheduler is therefore *the* challenge for optimal time-bounded reachability analysis. Our solution is based on approximating the optimal reachability value up to an arbitrary $\varepsilon > 0$ by discretising the time horizon with intervals of variable length. On each interval the value of our ε-optimal scheduler remains constant. The discretisation we use attempts to reflect the partition $\mathcal{I}(\pi)$ of a minimal[2] optimal scheduler π, i. e. it mimics intervals on which π has constant value.

Our solution is presented in Algorithm 1. It computes an ε-optimal scheduler $\pi_{\mathtt{opt}}$ and approximates the system of Equations (1)–(2) for $\pi_{\mathtt{opt}}$. The algorithm iterates over intervals of constant decisions of an ε-optimal strategy. At each

[2] In the size of $\mathcal{I}(\pi)$.

iteration it computes: (i) a stationary scheduler π that is close to be optimal on the current interval (line 7), (ii) length δ of the interval, on which π introduces acceptable error (line 8) and (iii) the reachability values for time $t+\delta$ (line 9). The following sections discuss the steps of the algorithm in more detail.

Theorem 1. *Algorithm 1 approximates the value of an arbitrary Markov automaton for time bound $T \in \mathbb{Q}_{\geqslant 0}$ up to a given $\varepsilon \in \mathbb{Q}_{>0}$.*

Algorithm 1. `SwitchStep`

Input: MA $\mathcal{M} = (S, \mathrm{Act}, \mathbf{P}, \mathrm{Q}, G)$, time bound $T \in \mathbb{Q}_{\geqslant 0}$, precision $\varepsilon \in \mathbb{Q}_{>0}$
Output: $\boldsymbol{u}(T) \in [0,1]^{|S|}$, s. t. $||\boldsymbol{u}(T) - \mathrm{val}^{\mathcal{M}}(T)||_\infty < \varepsilon$, ε-optimal scheduler $\pi_{\mathtt{opt}}$
Parameters: $w \in (0,1)$, and $\varepsilon_i < \varepsilon$, by default $w = 0.1, \varepsilon_i = w \cdot \varepsilon$

1: $\delta_{\min} = (1-w) \cdot 2 \cdot (\varepsilon - \varepsilon_i)/{\mathbf{E}_{\max}}^2/T$
2: $\varepsilon_\Psi = \varepsilon_\mathrm{r} = w\varepsilon\delta_{\min}/T$
3: $t = 0$, $\varepsilon^t_{\mathrm{acc}} = \varepsilon_i$
4: $\forall s \in MS : \boldsymbol{u}_s(t) = (s \in G)?1:0$ and $\forall s \in PS : \boldsymbol{u}_s(t) = \mathcal{R}^*_{\varepsilon_i}(s, G)$
5: $\forall s \in PS : \pi_{\mathtt{opt}}(s, 0) = \arg\max \mathcal{R}^*_{\varepsilon_i}(s, G)$
6: **while** $t < T$ **do**
7: $\pi = \textsc{FindStrategy}(\boldsymbol{u}(t))$
8: $\delta, \varepsilon_\delta = \textsc{FindStep}(\mathcal{M}, T-t, \delta_{\min}, \boldsymbol{u}(t), \varepsilon_\Psi, \varepsilon_\mathrm{r}, \pi)$
9: compute $\boldsymbol{u}(t+\delta)$ according to (5) for ε_Ψ and ε_r
10: $t = t+\delta$, $\varepsilon^t_{\mathrm{acc}} = \varepsilon^{t-\delta}_{\mathrm{acc}} + \varepsilon_\delta$
11: $\forall s \in PS, \tau \in (0, \delta] : \pi_{\mathtt{opt}}(s, t+\tau) = \pi(s)$
12: **return** $\boldsymbol{u}_s(T), \pi_{\mathtt{opt}}$

4.1 Computing the Reachability Value

In this section we discuss steps 4 and 9, that require computation of the reachability probability according to the system of Equations (1)–(2). Our approach is based on the approximation of the solution. The presence of two types of states, probabilistic and Markovian, demands separate treatment of those. Informally, we will combine two techniques: time-bounded reachability analysis on continuous time Markov chains[3] for Markovian states and time-unbounded reachability analysis on discrete time Markov chains[4] for probabilistic states. Parameters w and ε_i of Algorithm 1 control the error allowed by the approximation. Here ε_i bounds the error for the very first instance of time-unbounded reachability in line 4. While w defines the fraction of the error that can be used by the approximations in subsequent iterations (ε_Ψ and ε_r).

We start with time-unbounded reachability analysis for probabilistic states. Let $\pi \in \Pi_{\mathtt{stat}}, s, s' \in S$. We define

[3] Markov automata without probabilistic states.

[4] Markov automata without Markovian states and such that $\forall s \in PS : |\mathrm{Act}(s)| = 1$.

$$\mathcal{R}(s,\pi,s') = \begin{cases} 1 & \text{if } s = s' \\ \sum\limits_{p\in S} \mathbb{P}[s,\pi(s),p]\cdot\mathcal{R}(p,\pi,s') & \text{else if } s\in PS \\ 0 & \text{otherwise} \end{cases} \tag{3}$$

This value denotes the probability to reach state s' starting from state s by performing any number of probabilistic transitions and no Markovian transitions. This system of linear equations can be either solved exactly, e.g. via Gaussian elimination, or approximated (numerical methods). If $\mathcal{R}(s,\pi,s')$ is under-approximated we denote it by $\mathcal{R}_\epsilon(s,\pi,s')$, where ϵ is the approximation error. For $A\subseteq S$ we define $\mathcal{R}(s,\pi,A) = \sum_{s'\in A}\mathcal{R}(s,\pi,s')$, $\mathcal{R}_\epsilon(s,\pi,A) = \sum_{s'\in A}\mathcal{R}_\epsilon(s,\pi,s')$.

For time bound $0, s\in PS$ the value $\mathrm{val}_s^{\mathcal{M}}(0)$ is the optimal probability to reach any goal state via only probabilistic transitions. We denote it by $\mathcal{R}^*(s,G) = \max_{\pi\in\Pi_{\mathtt{stat}}}\mathcal{R}(s,\pi,G)$ (step 4). It is a well-known problem on *discrete time Markov decision processes* [Put94] and can be computed or approximated by policy iteration, linear programming [Put94] or interval value iteration [HM14, QK18, BKL+17]. If the value is approximated up to ϵ, we denote it by $\mathcal{R}^*_\epsilon(s,G)$.

The reachability analysis on Markovian states is solved with the well-known *uniformisation* approach [Jen53]. Informally, Markovian states will be implicitly *uniformised*: The exit rate for each Markovian state will be equal $\mathbf{E}_{\max}$ (by adding a self-loop transition), but this will not affect the reachability value.

We will first define the discrete probability to reach the target vector within k Markovian transitions. Let $\boldsymbol{x}\in[0,1]^{|S|}$ be a vector of values for each state. For $k\in\mathbb{N}_{\geqslant 0}, \pi\in\Pi_{\mathtt{stat}}$ we define $\mathbf{D}^k_{\boldsymbol{x}}(s,\pi) = 1$ if $s\in G$ and otherwise:

$$\mathbf{D}^k_{\boldsymbol{x}}(s,\pi) = \begin{cases} \boldsymbol{x}_s & \text{if } k=0 \\ \sum\limits_{s'\neq s}\frac{\mathrm{Q}(s,s')}{\mathbf{E}_{\max}}\cdot\mathbf{D}^{k-1}_{\boldsymbol{x}}(s',\pi) + (1-\frac{\mathrm{E}(s)}{\mathbf{E}_{\max}})\cdot\mathbf{D}^{k-1}_{\boldsymbol{x}}(s,\pi) & \text{if } k>0, s\in MS \\ \sum\limits_{s'\in MS\cup G}\mathcal{R}(s,\pi,s')\cdot\mathbf{D}^k_{\boldsymbol{x}}(s',\pi) & \text{if } k>0, s\in PS \end{cases} \tag{4}$$

The value $\mathbf{D}^k_{\boldsymbol{x}}(s,\pi)$ is the weighted sum over all states s' of the value $\boldsymbol{x}_{s'}$ and the probability to reach s' starting from s within k Markovian transitions. Therefore the counter k decreases only when a Markovian state performs a transition and is not affected by probabilistic transitions. If values $\mathcal{R}(s,\pi,s')$ are approximated up to precision ϵ, i.e. $\mathcal{R}_\epsilon(s,\pi,s')$ is used for probabilistic states instead of $\mathcal{R}(s,\pi,s')$ in (4), we use the notation $\mathbf{D}^k_{\boldsymbol{x},\epsilon}(s,\pi)$.

We denote with Ψ_λ the probability mass function of the Poisson distribution with parameter λ. For a $\tau\in\mathbb{R}_{\geqslant 0}$ and $\varepsilon_\Psi\in(0,1]$, $N(\tau,\varepsilon_\Psi)$ is some natural number satisfying $\sum_{i=0}^{N(\tau,\varepsilon_\Psi)}\Psi_{\mathbf{E}_{\max}\cdot\tau}(i)\geqslant 1-\varepsilon_\Psi$, e.g. $N(\tau,\varepsilon_\Psi) = \lceil\mathbf{E}_{\max}\cdot\tau\cdot e^2 - ln(\varepsilon_\Psi)\rceil$ [BHHK15], where e is the Euler's number.

We are now in position to describe a way to compute $\boldsymbol{u}(t+\delta)$ at line 9 of Algorithm 1. Let $\boldsymbol{u}(t)\in[0,1]^{|S|}$ be a vector of values computed by the previous iteration of Algorithm 1 for time t. Let $\widetilde{\mathrm{val}}^{\mathcal{M},\pi}(t+\delta)$ be the solution of the system of Equation (1) for time point $t+\delta$, a stationary scheduler $\pi : PS \to \text{Act}$ and where $\boldsymbol{u}(t)$ is used instead of $\text{val}^{\mathcal{M},\pi}(t)$ as the boundary condition[5]. The following Lemma shows that $\widetilde{\text{val}}^{\mathcal{M},\pi}(t+\delta)$ can be efficiently approximated up to $\varepsilon_\Psi + \varepsilon_r$:

Lemma 2. *Let $\varepsilon_\Psi \in (0,1], \varepsilon_r \in [0,1], \varepsilon_N = \varepsilon_r / N((T-t), \varepsilon_\Psi)$ and $\delta \in [0, T-t]$. Then $\forall s \in S : \boldsymbol{u}_s(t+\delta) \leqslant \widetilde{\text{val}}_s^{\mathcal{M},\pi}(t+\delta) \leqslant \boldsymbol{u}_s(t+\delta) + \varepsilon_\Psi + \varepsilon_r$, where:*

$$\boldsymbol{u}_s(t+\delta) = \begin{cases} 1 & \text{if } s \in G \\ \sum_{i=0}^{N(\delta,\varepsilon_\Psi)} \Psi_{\mathbf{E}_{max}\cdot\delta}(i) \cdot \mathbf{D}^i_{\boldsymbol{u}(t),\varepsilon_N}(s,\pi) & \text{else if } s \in MS \\ \sum_{s' MS \cup G} \mathcal{R}_{\varepsilon_N}(s,\pi,s') \cdot \boldsymbol{u}_{s'}(t+\delta) & \text{else if } s \in PS \end{cases} \tag{5}$$

4.2 Choosing a Strategy

The strategy for the next interval is computed in Step 7 and implicitly in Step 4. The latter has been discussed in Sect. 4.1. We proceed to Step 7.

Here we search for a strategy that remains constant for all time points within interval $(t, t+\delta]$, for some $\delta > 0$, and introduces only an acceptable error. Analogously to results for *continuous time Markov decision processes* [Mil68], we prove that derivatives of function $\boldsymbol{u}(\tau)$ at time $\tau = t$ help finding the strategy π that remains optimal for interval $(t, t+\delta]$, for some $\delta > 0$. This is rooted in the Taylor expansion of function $\boldsymbol{u}(t+\delta)$ via the values of $\boldsymbol{u}(t)$. We define sets

$$\mathcal{F}_0 = \{\pi \in \Pi_{\texttt{stat}} \mid \forall s \in PS : \pi = \arg\max\nolimits_{\pi' \in \Pi_{\texttt{stat}}} \boldsymbol{d}^{(0)}_{\pi'}(s)\}$$
$$\mathcal{F}_i = \{\pi \in \mathcal{F}_{i-1} \mid \forall s \in PS : \pi = \arg\max\nolimits_{\pi' \in \mathcal{F}_{i-1}} (-1)^{i-1} \boldsymbol{d}^{(i)}_{\pi'}(s)\}, i \geqslant 1,$$

where for $\pi \in \Pi_{\texttt{stat}}$, $s \in G : \boldsymbol{d}^{(0)}_\pi(s) = 1$, for $s \in MS \setminus G : \boldsymbol{d}^{(0)}_\tau(s) = \boldsymbol{u}_s(t)$, for $s \in PS \setminus G$: $\boldsymbol{d}^{(0)}_\pi(s) = \sum_{s' \in MS \cup G} \mathcal{R}(s,\pi,s') \cdot \boldsymbol{u}_{s'}(t)$ and for $i \geqslant 1$:

$$\boldsymbol{d}^{(i)}_\pi(s) = \begin{cases} 0 & \text{if } s \in G \\ \sum_{s' \in S} \mathrm{Q}(s,s') \cdot \boldsymbol{d}^{(i-1)}(s') & \text{if } s \in MS \setminus G \\ \sum_{s' \in MS} \mathcal{R}(s,\pi,s') \cdot \boldsymbol{d}^{(i)}(s') & \text{if } s \in PS \setminus G \end{cases} \qquad \boldsymbol{d}^{(i)} = \boldsymbol{d}^{(i)}_\pi \text{ for any } \pi \in \mathcal{F}_i,$$

The value $\boldsymbol{d}^{(i)}_\pi(s)$ is the ith derivative of $\boldsymbol{u}_s(t)$ at time t for a scheduler π.

Lemma 3. *If $\pi \in \mathcal{F}_{|S|+1}$ then $\exists \delta > 0$ such that π is optimal on $(t, t+\delta]$.*

Thus in order to compute a stationary strategy that is optimal on time-interval $(t, t+\delta]$, for some $\delta > 0$, one needs to compute at most $|S|+1$ derivatives

[5] $\widetilde{\text{val}}^{\mathcal{M},\pi}(t+\delta)$ may differ from $\text{val}^{\mathcal{M},\pi}(t+\delta)$ since its boundary condition $\boldsymbol{u}(t)$ is an approximation of the boundary condition $\text{val}^{\mathcal{M},\pi}(t)$, used by $\text{val}^{\mathcal{M},\pi}(t+\delta)$.

of $\boldsymbol{u}(\tau)$ at time t. Procedure FINDSTRATEGY does exactly that. It computes sets $\mathcal{F}_i$ until for some $j \in 0..(|S|+1)$ there is only 1 strategy left, i.e. $|\mathcal{F}_j| = 1$. Otherwise it outputs any strategy in $\mathcal{F}_{|S|+1}$. Similarly to Sect. 4.1, the scheduler that maximises the values $\mathcal{R}(s, \pi, s')$ can be approximated. This question and other optimisations are discussed in detail in Sect. 4.4.

4.3 Finding Switching Points

Given that a strategy π is computed by FINDSTRATEGY, we need to know for how long this strategy can be followed before the action has to change for at least one of the states. We consider the behaviour of the system in the time interval $[t, T]$. Recall the function $\widetilde{\text{val}}^{\pi}(t+\delta), \delta \in [0, T-t]$, defined in Sect. 4.1 (Lemma 2) as the solution of the system of Equation (1) with the boundary condition $\boldsymbol{u}(t)$, for a stationary scheduler π. For a probabilistic state s the following holds:

$$\widetilde{\text{val}}_s^{\pi}(t+\delta) = \sum_{s' \in MS \cup G} \mathcal{R}(s, \pi, s') \cdot \widetilde{\text{val}}_{s'}^{\pi}(t+\delta) \tag{6}$$

Let $s \in PS, \pi \in \Pi_{\mathtt{stat}}, \alpha \in \text{Act}(s)$. Consider the following function:

$$\widetilde{\text{val}}_s^{\pi, s \to \alpha}(t+\delta) = \sum_{s' \in MS \cup G} \underbrace{\sum_{s'' \in S} \mathbb{P}[s, \alpha, s''] \cdot \mathcal{R}(s'', \pi, s')}_{\mathcal{R}_{s \to \alpha}(s, \pi, s')} \cdot \widetilde{\text{val}}_{s'}^{\pi}(t+\delta)$$

This function denotes the reachability value for time bound $t+\delta$ and a scheduler that is different from π. Namely, this is such a scheduler, that all states follow strategy π, except for state s, that selects action α for the very first transition, and afterwards selects action $\pi(s)$. Between two switching points the strategy π is optimal and therefore the value of $\widetilde{\text{val}}_s^{\pi, s \to \alpha}(t+\delta)$ is not greater than $\widetilde{\text{val}}_s^{\pi}(t+\delta)$ for all $s \in PS, \alpha \in \text{Act}(s)$. If for some $\delta \in [0, T-t], s \in PS, \alpha \in \text{Act}(s)$ it holds that $\widetilde{\text{val}}_s^{\pi, s \to \alpha}(t+\delta) > \widetilde{\text{val}}_s^{\pi}(t+\delta)$, then action α is better for s then $\pi(s)$, and therefore $\pi(s)$ is not optimal for s at $t+\delta$. We show that the next switching point after time point t is such a value $t+\delta, \delta \in (0, T-t]$, that

$$\begin{aligned} &\forall s \in PS, \forall \alpha \in \text{Act}(s), \forall \tau \in [0, \delta) : \widetilde{\text{val}}_s^{\pi}(t+\tau) \geqslant \widetilde{\text{val}}_s^{\pi, s \to \alpha}(t+\tau) \\ &\text{and } \exists s \in PS, \alpha \in \text{Act}(s) : \widetilde{\text{val}}_s^{\pi}(t+\delta) < \widetilde{\text{val}}_s^{\pi, s \to \alpha}(t+\delta) \end{aligned} \tag{7}$$

Procedure FINDSTEP approximates switching points iteratively. It splits the time interval $[0, T]$ into subintervals $[t_1, t_2], \ldots, [t_{n-1}, t_n]$ and at each iteration k checks whether (7) holds for some $\delta \in [t_k, t_{k+1}]$. The latter is performed by procedure CHECKINTERVAL. If $\forall \delta \in [t_k, t_{k+1}]$ (7) does not hold, FINDSTEP repeats by increasing k. Otherwise, it outputs the largest $\delta \in [t_k, t_{k+1}]$ for which (7) does not hold (line 11). This is done by binary search up to distance $\delta_{\min}$. Later in this section we will show that establishing that (7) does not hold for all $\delta \in [t_k, t_{k+1}]$ can be efficiently performed by considering only 2 time points of the interval $[t_k, t_{k+1}]$ and a subset of state-action pairs.

Algorithm 2. FINDSTEP

Input: MA $\mathcal{M} = (S, \text{Act}, \mathbf{P}, \text{Q}, G)$, time left $t \in \mathbb{Q}_{\geqslant 0}$, minimal step size $\delta_{\min}$, vector $\boldsymbol{u} \in [0,1]^{|S|}$, $\varepsilon_\Psi \in (0,1]$, $\varepsilon_{\text{r}} \in [0,1]$, $\pi \in \Pi_{\texttt{stat}}$
Output: step $\delta \in [\delta_{\min}, t]$ and upper bound on accumulated error $\varepsilon_\delta \geqslant 0$

if $(t \leqslant \delta_{\min})$ **then return** $t, (\mathbf{E}_{\max} \cdot t)^2/2$
$k = 1, t_1 = \delta_{\min}$
do
  $t_{k+1} = \min\{t, T_\Psi(k+1, \varepsilon_\Psi), (\lfloor t_k \cdot \mathbf{E}_{\max} \rfloor + 1)/\mathbf{E}_{\max}\}$
  set $A = \mathcal{T}_{\max}(k+1)$ or $A = PS \times \text{Act}$ ▷ see discussion in the end of Sect. 4.3
  toswitch = CHECKINTERVAL$(\mathcal{M}, [t_k, t_{k+1}], A, \varepsilon_\Psi, \varepsilon_{\text{r}})$
  $k = k + 1$
while (not *toswitch*) and $t_k < t$)
$k = k - 1$
if (*toswitch* = *true*) **then**
  find the largest $\delta \in [t_k, t_{k+1}]$, s.t. CHECKINTERVAL$(\mathcal{M}, [t_k, \delta], A, \varepsilon_\Psi, \varepsilon_{\text{r}})$ =false
  if $(\delta > \delta_{\min})$ **then** $\epsilon = 0$ **else** $\epsilon = (\mathbf{E}_{\max}\delta_{\min})^2/2$
  return δ, ϵ
else **return** $t, 0$

Selectingt_k. This step is a heuristic. The correctness of our algorithm does not depend on the choices of t_k, but its runtime is supposed to benefit from it: Obviously, the runtime of FINDSTRATEGY is best given an oracle that produces time points t_k which are exactly the switching points of the optimal strategy. Any other heuristic is just a guess.

At every iteration k we choose such a time point t_k that the MA is very likely to perform at most k Markovian transitions within time t_k. "Very likely" here means with probability $1 - \varepsilon_\Psi$. For $k \in \mathbb{N}$ we define $T_\Psi(k, \varepsilon_\Psi)$ as follows: $T_\Psi(1, \varepsilon_\Psi) = \delta_{\min}$, and for $k > 1$: $T_\Psi(k, \varepsilon_\Psi)$ satisfies $\sum_{i=0}^{k} \Psi_{\mathbf{E}_{\max} \cdot T_\Psi(k,\varepsilon_\Psi)}(i) \geqslant 1 - \varepsilon_\Psi$.

Searching for switching points within $[t_k, t_{k+1}]$. In order to check whether $\widetilde{\text{val}}^\pi(t + \delta) \geqslant \widetilde{\text{val}}^{\pi, s\to\alpha}(t+\delta)$ for *all* $\delta \in [t_k, t_{k+1}]$ we only have to check whether the maximum of function $\text{diff}(s, \alpha, t+\delta) = \widetilde{\text{val}}_s^{\pi, s\to\alpha}(t+\delta) - \widetilde{\text{val}}_s^\pi(t+\delta)$ is at most 0 on this interval for all $s \in PS, \alpha \in \text{Act}(s)$. In order to achieve this we work on the approximation of $\text{diff}(s, \alpha, t+\delta)$ derived from Lemma 2, thus establishing a sufficient condition for the scheduler to remain optimal:

$$\begin{aligned} \widetilde{\text{val}}_s^{\pi, s\to\alpha}(t+\delta) &= \sum_{s' \in MS \cup G} \mathcal{R}_{s\to\alpha}(s, \pi, s') \cdot \widetilde{\text{val}}_{s'}^\pi(t+\delta) \\ &\leqslant \sum_{s' \in MS \setminus G} \mathcal{R}_{s\to\alpha, \varepsilon_{\text{N}}}(s, \pi, s') \sum_{i=0}^{k} \Psi_{\mathbf{E}_{\max}\cdot\delta}(i) \cdot \mathbf{D}^i_{\boldsymbol{u}(t), \varepsilon_{\text{N}}}(s', \pi) \\ &\quad + \mathcal{R}_{s\to\alpha, \varepsilon_{\text{N}}}(s, \pi, G) + \varepsilon_\Psi + \varepsilon_{\text{r}} \end{aligned} \tag{8}$$

Here $\mathcal{R}_{s\to\alpha,\varepsilon_{\mathrm{N}}}(s,\pi,s')$ ($\mathcal{R}_{s\to\alpha,\varepsilon_{\mathrm{N}}}(s,\pi,G)$) denotes an under-approximation of the value $\mathcal{R}_{s\to\alpha}(s,\pi,s')$ ($\mathcal{R}_{s\to\alpha}(s,\pi,G)$ resp.) up to ε_{N}, defined in Lemma 2. And analogously for $\widetilde{\mathrm{val}}^{\pi}(t+\delta)$. Simple rewriting leads to the following:

$$\widetilde{\mathrm{val}}_s^{\pi,s\to\alpha}(t+\delta)-\widetilde{\mathrm{val}}_s^{\pi}(t+\delta)\leqslant\sum_{i=0}^{k}\Psi_{\mathbf{E}_{\max}\cdot\delta}(i)\cdot B^i_{\pi,\varepsilon_{\mathrm{N}}}(s,\alpha)+C_{\pi,\varepsilon_{\mathrm{N}}}(s,\alpha),\quad(9)$$

where $B^i_{\pi,\varepsilon_{\mathrm{N}}}(s,\alpha)=\sum_{s'\in MS\setminus G}\left(\mathcal{R}_{s\to\alpha,\varepsilon_{\mathrm{N}}}(s,\pi,s')-\mathcal{R}_{\varepsilon_{\mathrm{N}}}(s,\pi,s')\right)\cdot\mathbf{D}^i_{\boldsymbol{u}(t),\varepsilon_{\mathrm{N}}}(s',\pi)$ and $C_{\pi,\varepsilon_{\mathrm{N}}}(s,\alpha)=\mathcal{R}_{s\to\alpha,\varepsilon_{\mathrm{N}}}(s,\pi,G)-\mathcal{R}_{\varepsilon_{\mathrm{N}}}(s,\pi,G)+\varepsilon_{\Psi}+\varepsilon_{\mathrm{r}}$. In order to find the supremum of the right-hand side of (9) over all $\delta\in[a,b]$ we search for extremum of each $y_i(\delta)=\Psi_{\mathbf{E}_{\max}(t+\delta)}(i)\cdot B^i_{\pi,\varepsilon_{\mathrm{N}}}(s,\alpha), i=0..k$, separately as a function of δ. Simple derivative analysis shows that the extremum of these functions is achieved at $\delta=i/\mathbf{E}_{\max}$. Truncation of the time interval by $(\lfloor t_k\cdot\mathbf{E}_{\max}\rfloor+1)/\mathbf{E}_{\max}$ (step 4, Algorithm 2) ensures that for all $i=0..k$ the extremum of $y_i(\delta)$ is attained at either $\delta=t_k$ or $\delta=t_{k+1}$.

Lemma 4. *Let $[t_k,t_{k+1}]$ be the interval considered by* CheckInterval *at iteration k. $\forall\delta\in[t_k,t_{k+1}], s\in PS, \alpha\in Act$:*

$$\mathrm{diff}(s,\alpha,t+\delta)\leqslant\sum_{i=0}^{k}\Psi_{\mathbf{E}_{max}\delta(s,\alpha,i)}(i)\cdot B^i_{\pi,\varepsilon_N}(s,\alpha)+C_{\pi,\varepsilon_N}(s,\alpha),\qquad(10)$$

where

$$\delta(s,\alpha,i)=\begin{cases}t_k & \text{if } B^i_{\pi,\varepsilon_N}(s,\alpha)\geqslant 0 \text{ and } i/\mathbf{E}_{max}\leqslant t_k\\ & \text{or } B^i_{\pi,\varepsilon_N}(s,\alpha)\leqslant 0 \text{ and } i/\mathbf{E}_{max}>t_k\\ t_{k+1} & \text{otherwise}\end{cases}$$

CheckInterval returns false iff for all $s\in PS,\alpha\in\mathrm{Act}$ the right-hand side of (10) is less or equal to 0. Since Lemma 4 over-approximates $\mathrm{diff}(s,\alpha,t+\delta)$ false positives are inevitable. Namely, it is possible that procedure CheckInterval suggests that there exists a switching point within $[t_k,t_{k+1}]$, while in reality there is none. This however does not affect correctness of the algorithm and only its running time.

Finding Maximal Transitions. Here we show that there exists a subset of states, such that, if the optimal strategy for these states does not change on an interval, then the optimal strategy for *all* states does not change on this interval.

In the following we call a pair $(s,\alpha)\in PS\times\mathrm{Act}$ a *transition*. For transitions $(s,\alpha),(s',\alpha')\in PS\times\mathrm{Act}$ we write $(s,\alpha)\preceq_k(s',\alpha')$ iff $C_{\pi,\varepsilon_{\mathrm{N}}}(s,\alpha)\leqslant C_{\pi,\varepsilon_{\mathrm{N}}}(s',\alpha')$ and $\forall i=0..k: B^i_{\pi,\varepsilon_{\mathrm{N}}}(s,\alpha)\leqslant B^i_{\pi,\varepsilon_{\mathrm{N}}}(s',\alpha')$. We say that a transition (s,α) is *maximal* if there exists no other transition (s',α') that satisfies the following: $(s,\alpha)\preceq_k(s',\alpha')$ and at least one of the following conditions hold: $C_{\pi,\varepsilon_{\mathrm{N}}}(s,\alpha)<C_{\pi,\varepsilon_{\mathrm{N}}}(s',\alpha')$ or $\exists i=0..k: B^i_{\pi,\varepsilon_{\mathrm{N}}}(s,\alpha)<B^i_{\pi,\varepsilon_{\mathrm{N}}}(s',\alpha')$. The set of all maximal transitions is denoted with $\mathcal{T}_{\max}(k)$.

We prove that if inequality (10) holds for all transitions from $\mathcal{T}_{\max}(k)$, then it holds for all transitions. Thus only transitions from $\mathcal{T}_{\max}(k)$ have to be checked by procedure CHECKINTERVAL. In our implementation we only compute $\mathcal{T}_{\max}(k)$ before the call to CHECKINTERVAL at line 11 of Algorithm 2. and use the set $A = PS \times \text{Act}$ within the while-loop.

4.4 Optimisation for Large Models

Here we discuss a number of implementation improvements developers should consider when applying our algorithm to large case studies:

Switching points. It may happen that the optimal strategy switches very often on a time interval, while the effect of these frequent switches is negligible. The difference may be so small that the ε-optimal strategy actually stays stationary on this interval. In addition, floating-point computations may lead to imprecise results: Values that are 0 in theory might be represented by non-zero float-point numbers, making it seem as if the optimal strategy changed its decision, when in fact it did not. To counteract these issues we can modify CHECKINTERVAL such that it outputs false even if the right-hand side of (10) is positive, as long as it is sufficiently small. The following lemma proves that the error introduced by not switching the decision is acceptable:

Lemma 5. *Let* $\delta = t_{k+1} - t_k$, $\varepsilon' = \varepsilon - \varepsilon_i, \epsilon \in (0, \varepsilon' \cdot \delta/T)$ *and* $N(\delta, \epsilon) = (\mathbf{E}_{max}\delta)^2/2.0/\epsilon$. *If* $\forall s \in PS, \alpha \in Act, \tau \in [t_k, t_{k+1}]$ *the right-hand side of (10) is not greater than* $(\varepsilon'\delta/T - \epsilon)/N(\delta, \epsilon)$, *then* π *is* $\varepsilon'\delta/T$*-optimal in* $[t_k, t_{k+1}]$.

Optimal strategy. In some cases computation of the optimal strategy in the way it was described in Sect. 4.2 is computationally expensive, or is not possible at all. For example, if some values $|\boldsymbol{d}_\pi^{(i)}(s)|$ are larger than the maximal floating point number that a computer can store, or if the computation of $|S|+1$ derivatives is already too prohibitive for models of large state space, or if the values $\mathcal{R}(s, \pi, s')$ can only be approximated and not computed precisely. With the help of Lemma 5 and minor modifications to Algorithm 1, the correctness and convergence of Algorithm 1 can be preserved even when the strategy computed by FINDSTRATEGY is not guaranteed to be optimal.

5 Empirical Evaluation

We implemented our algorithm as a part of `IMCA` [GHKN12]. Experiments were conducted as single-thread processes on an Intel Core i7-4790 with 32 GB of RAM. We compare the algorithm presented in this paper with [Neu10] and [BHHK15]. Both are available in `IMCA`. We use the following abbreviations to refer to the algorithms: `FixStep` for [Neu10], `Unif`$^+$ for [BHHK15] and `SwitchStep` for Algorithm 1. The value of the parameter w in Algorithm 1 is set to 0.1, $\varepsilon_i = 0$. We keep the default values of all other algorithms.

Table 1. The discretisation step used in some of the experiments shown in Fig. 3.

	δ_F	$\min \delta_S$	avg δ_S	$\max \delta_S$	T	precision
dpm-5-2	$3.7 \cdot 10^{-6}$	$3.65 \cdot 10^{-5}$	0.27	3.97	15	0.001
qs-2-3	$1.04 \cdot 10^{-6}$	$1.04 \cdot 10^{-6}$	0.017	7.56	15	0.001
ps-2-6	$3.54 \cdot 10^{-6}$	0.0003	6	17.4	18	0.001

The evaluation is performed on a set of published benchmarks:

dpm-j-k: A model of a *dynamic power management system* [QWP99], representing the internals of a Fujitsu disk drive. The model contains a queue, service requester, service provider and a power manager. The requester generates tasks of j types differing in energy requirements, that are stored in the queue of size k. The power manager selects the processing mode for the service provider. A state is a goal state if the queue of at least one task type is full.

qs-j-k and **ps-j-k:** Models of a *queuing system* [HH12] and a *polling system* [GHH+13] where incoming requests of j types are buffered in two queues of size k each, until they are processed by the server. We consider the state with both queues being full to form the goal state set.

The memory required by all three algorithms is polynomial in the size of the model. For the evaluation we therefore concentrate on runtime only. We set the time limit for the experiments to 15 minutes. Timeouts are marked by x in the plots. Runtimes are given in seconds. All the plots use the log-log axis.

Results

SwitchStep vs FixStep. Figure 3 compares runtimes of SwitchStep and FixStep. For these experiments precision is set to 10^{-3} and the state space size ranges from 10^2 to 10^5.

This plot represents the general trend observed in many experiments: The algorithm FixStep does not scale well with the size of the problem (state space, precision, time bound). For larger benchmarks it usually required more than 15 minutes. This is likely due to the fact that the discretisation step used by FixStep is very small, which means that the algorithm performs many iterations. In fact Table 1 reports on the size of the discretisation steps for both FixStep and SwitchStep on a few benchmarks. Here the column δ_F shows the length of the discretisation step of FixStep. As we mentioned in Sect. 3, this step is fixed for the selected values of time bound and precision. Columns $\min \delta_S$, avgδ_S and $\max \delta_S$ show minimal, average

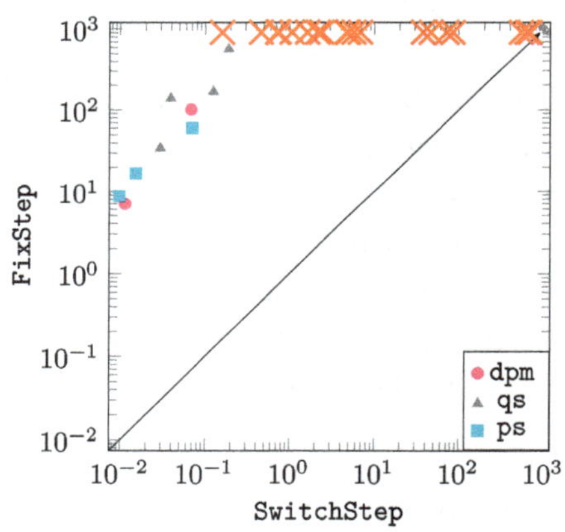

Fig. 3. Running time comparison of FixStep and SwitchStep.

and maximal steps used by `SwitchStep` respectively. The average step used by `SwitchStep` is several orders of magnitude larger than that of `FixStep`. Therefore `SwitchStep` performs much less iterations. Even though each iteration takes longer, overall significant decrease in the amount of iterations leads to much smaller total runtime.

`SwitchStep` **vs** `Unif`$^+$. In order to compare `SwitchStep` with `Unif`$^+$ we have to restrict ourselves to a subclass of Markov automata in which probabilistic and Markovian states alternate, and probabilistic states have only 1 successor for each action. This is due to the fact that `Unif`$^+$ is available in `IMCA` only for this subclass of models.

Table 2. Parameters of the experiments shown in Fig. 4.

	$\lvert S\rvert$	$\lvert Act\rvert$	$\mathbf{E}_{\max}$	T
dpm-[4..7]-2	2061 - 158,208	4 - 7	4.6 - 9.1	15
dpm-3-[2..20]	412 - 115,108	3	3.3	100
qs-1-[2..7]	124 - 3,614	4 - 14	11.3 - 35.3	6
qs-[1..4]-2	124 - 16,924	4 - 8	11.3	6
ps-[1..8]-2	47 - 156,315	3 - 8	3.6 - 257.6	18
ps-2-[1-7]	65 - 743,969	2 - 4	4.8 - 5.6	18

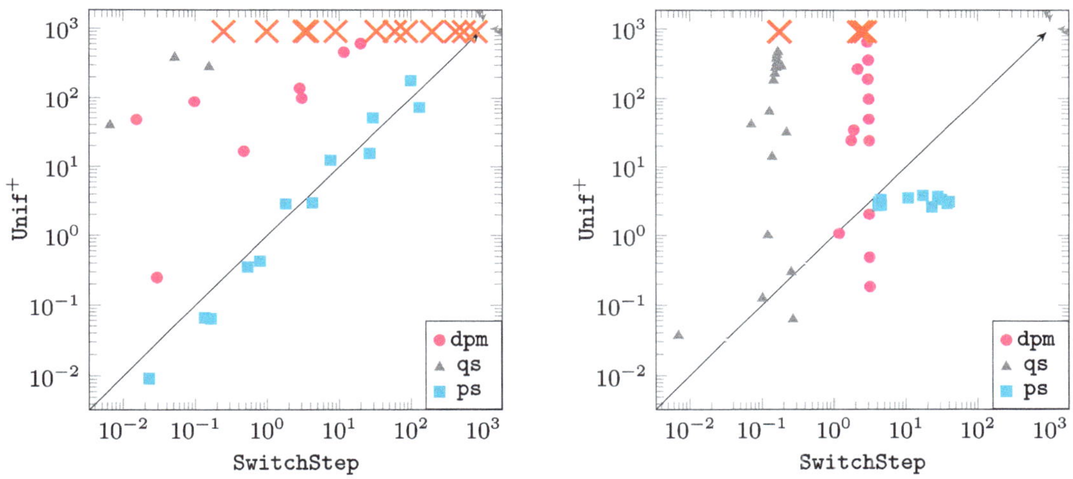

Fig. 4. Running times of algorithms `SwitchStep` and `Unif`$^+$.

Figure 4 shows the comparison of running times of `SwitchStep` and `Unif`$^+$. For the plot on the left we varied those model parameters that affect state space size, number of non-deterministic actions and maximal exit rate. In the plot on the right the model parameters are fixed, but precision and time bounds used for the experiments are differing. Table 2 shows the parameters of the models used in these experiments. We observe that there are cases in which `SwitchStep` performs remarkably better than `Unif`$^+$, and cases of the opposite. Consider the experiments in Fig. 4, right. They show that `Unif`$^+$ may be highly sensitive to variations of time bounds and precision, while `SwitchStep` is more robust in this respect. This is due to the fact that the scheduler computed by `Unif`$^+$ does not have means to observe time precisely and can only guess it. This may be good enough, which is the case on the `ps` benchmark. However if it is not, then better precision will require many more computations. Additionally `Unif`$^+$ does not use discretisation. This means that the increase of the time bound from T_1 to T_2 may significantly increase the overall running time, even if no new switching points appear on the interval $[T_1, T_2]$. `SwitchStep` does not suffer from these issues due to the fact that it considers schedulers that observe the time precisely and uses the discretisation. Large time intervals that introduce no switching points will likely be handled within one iteration.

In general, `SwitchStep` performs at its best when there are not too many switching points, which is what is observed in most published case studies.

Conclusions: We conclude that `SwitchStep` does not replace all existing algorithms for time bounded reachability. However it does improve the state of the art in many cases and thus occupies its own niche among available solutions.

References

[Bal07] Balbo, G.: Introduction to generalized stochastic Petri nets. In: Bernardo, M., Hillston, J. (eds.) SFM 2007. LNCS, vol. 4486, pp. 83–131. Springer, Heidelberg (2007). https://doi.org/10.1007/978-3-540-72522-0_3

[BCS10] Boudali, H., Crouzen, P., Stoelinga, M.: A rigorous, compositional, and extensible framework for dynamic fault tree analysis. IEEE Trans. Dependable Sec. Comput. **7**(2), 128–143 (2010). https://doi.org/10.1109/TDSC.2009.45

[Ber00] Bertsekas, D.P.: Dynamic Programming and Optimal Control, 2nd edn. Athena Scientific, Belmont (2000)

[BHHK15] Butkova, Y., Hatefi, H., Hermanns, H., Krčál, J.: Optimal continuous time Markov decisions. In: Finkbeiner, B., Pu, G., Zhang, L. (eds.) ATVA 2015. LNCS, vol. 9364, pp. 166–182. Springer, Cham (2015). https://doi.org/10.1007/978-3-319-24953-7_12

[BKL+17] Baier, C., Klein, J., Leuschner, L., Parker, D., Wunderlich, S.: Ensuring the reliability of your model checker: interval iteration for Markov decision processes. In: Majumdar, R., Kunčak, V. (eds.) CAV 2017. LNCS, vol. 10426, pp. 160–180. Springer, Cham (2017). https://doi.org/10.1007/978-3-319-63387-9_8

[BS11] Buchholz, P., Schulz, I.: Numerical analysis of continuous time Markov decision processes over finite horizons. Comput. OR **38**(3), 651–659 (2011). https://doi.org/10.1016/j.cor.2010.08.011

[DJKV17] Dehnert, C., Junges, S., Katoen, J., Volk, M.: A storm is coming: a modern probabilistic model checker. In: Majumdar, R., Kunčak, V. (eds.) CAV 2017. LNCS, vol. 10427, pp. 592–600. Springer, Cham (2017). https://doi.org/10.1007/978-3-319-63390-9_31

[EHKZ13] Eisentraut, C., Hermanns, H., Katoen, J., Zhang, L.: A semantics for every GSPN. In: Colom, J.-M., Desel, J. (eds.) PETRI NETS 2013. LNCS, vol. 7927, pp. 90–109. Springer, Heidelberg (2013). https://doi.org/10.1007/978-3-642-38697-8_6

[FRSZ16] Fearnley, J., Rabe, M.N., Schewe, S., Zhang, L.: Efficient approximation of optimal control for continuous-time Markov games. Inf. Comput. **247**, 106–129 (2016). https://doi.org/10.1016/j.ic.2015.12.002

[GHH+13] Guck, D., Hatefi, H., Hermanns, H., Katoen, J., Timmer, M.: Modelling, reduction and analysis of Markov automata. In: Joshi, K., Siegle, M., Stoelinga, M., D'Argenio, P.R. (eds.) QEST 2013. LNCS, vol. 8054, pp. 55–71. Springer, Heidelberg (2013). https://doi.org/10.1007/978-3-642-40196-1_5

[GHH+14] Guck, D., Hatefi, H., Hermanns, H., Katoen, J., Timmer, M.: Analysis of timed and long-run objectives for Markov automata. Log. Methods Comput. Sci. **10**(3) (2014). https://doi.org/10.2168/LMCS-10(3:17)2014

[GHKN12] Guck, D., Han, T., Katoen, J.-P., Neuhäußer, M.R.: Quantitative timed analysis of interactive Markov chains. In: Goodloe, A.E., Person, S. (eds.) NFM 2012. LNCS, vol. 7226, pp. 8–23. Springer, Heidelberg (2012). https://doi.org/10.1007/978-3-642-28891-3_4

[Hat17] Hatefi-Ardakani, H.: Finite horizon analysis of Markov automata. Ph.D. thesis, Saarland University, Germany (2017). http://scidok.sulb.uni-saarland.de/volltexte/2017/6743/

[Her02] Hermanns, H.: Interactive Markov Chains: The Quest for Quantified Quality. LNCS, vol. 2428. Springer, Heidelberg (2002). https://doi.org/10.1007/3-540-45804-2

[HH12] Hatefi, H., Hermanns, H.: Model checking algorithms for Markov automata. ECEASST **53** (2012). http://journal.ub.tu-berlin.de/eceasst/article/view/783

[HH14] Hartmanns, A., Hermanns, H.: The modest toolset: an integrated environment for quantitative modelling and verification. In: Ábrahám, E., Havelund, K. (eds.) TACAS 2014. LNCS, vol. 8413, pp. 593–598. Springer, Heidelberg (2014). https://doi.org/10.1007/978-3-642-54862-8_51

[HH15] Hatefi, H., Hermanns, H.: Improving time bounded reachability computations in interactive Markov chains. Sci. Comput. Program. **112**, 58–74 (2015). https://doi.org/10.1016/j.scico.2015.05.003

[HM14] Haddad, S., Monmege, B.: Reachability in MDPs: refining convergence of value iteration. In: Ouaknine, J., Potapov, I., Worrell, J. (eds.) RP 2014. LNCS, vol. 8762, pp. 125–137. Springer, Cham (2014). https://doi.org/10.1007/978-3-319-11439-2_10

[Jen53] Jensen, A.: Markoff chains as an aid in the study of markoff processes. Scand. Actuarial J. **1953**(sup1), 87–91 (1953). https://doi.org/10.1080/03461238.1953.10419459

[KNP11] Kwiatkowska, M.Z., Norman, G., Parker, D.: PRISM 4.0: verification of probabilistic real-time systems. In: Gopalakrishnan, G., Qadeer, S. (eds.) CAV 2011. LNCS, vol. 6806, pp. 585–591. Springer, Heidelberg (2011). https://doi.org/10.1007/978-3-642-22110-1_47

[MBC+98] Marsan, M.A., Balbo, G., Conte, G., Donatelli, S., Franceschinis, G.: Modelling with generalized stochastic Petri nets. SIGMETRICS Perform. Eval. Rev. **26**(2), 2 (1998). https://doi.org/10.1145/288197.581193

[MCB84] Marsan, M.A., Conte, G., Balbo, G.: A class of generalized stochastic Petri nets for the performance evaluation of multiprocessor systems. ACM Trans. Comput. Syst. **2**(2), 93–122 (1984). https://doi.org/10.1145/190.191

[Mil68] Miller, B.: Finite state continuous time Markov decision processes with a finite planning horizon. SIAM J. Control **6**(2), 266–280 (1968). https://doi.org/10.1137/0306020

[MMS85] Meyer, J.F., Movaghar, A., Sanders, W.H.: Stochastic activity networks: structure, behavior, and application. In: International Workshop on Timed Petri Nets, Torino, pp. 106–115. IEEE Computer Society (1985)

[Mol82] Molloy, M.K.: Performance analysis using stochastic Petri nets. IEEE Trans. Comput. **C–31**(9), 913–917 (1982)

[Neu10] Neuhäußer, M.R.: Model checking nondeterministic and randomly timed systems. Ph.D. thesis, RWTH Aachen University (2010). http://darwin.bth.rwth-aachen.de/opus3/volltexte/2010/3136/

[Put94] Puterman, M.L.: Markov Decision Processes: Discrete Stochastic Dynamic Programming, 1st edn. Wiley, Hoboken (1994)

[QK18] Quatmann, T., Katoen, J.-P.: Sound value iteration. In: Chockler, H., Weissenbacher, G. (eds.) CAV 2018. LNCS, vol. 10981, pp. 643–661. Springer, Cham (2018). https://doi.org/10.1007/978-3-319-96145-3_37

[QWP99] Qiu, Q. Wu, Q., Pedram, M.: Stochastic modeling of a power-managed system: construction and optimization. In: ISLPED, 1999, pp. 194–199. ACM (1999). https://doi.org/10.1145/313817.313923

[RS13] Rabe, M.N., Schewe, S.: Optimal time-abstract schedulers for CTMDPs and continuous-time Markov games. Theor. Comput. Sci. **467**, 53–67 (2013). https://doi.org/10.1016/j.tcs.2012.10.001

[SSM18] Salamati, M., Soudjani, S., Majumdar, R.: Approximate time bounded reachability for CTMCs and CTMDPs: a Lyapunov approach. In: McIver, A., Horvath, A. (eds.) QEST 2018. LNCS, vol. 11024, pp. 389–406. Springer, Cham (2018). https://doi.org/10.1007/978-3-319-99154-2_24

Synthesis

Minimal-Time Synthesis for Parametric Timed Automata

Étienne André[1,2,3], Vincent Bloemen[4(✉)], Laure Petrucci[1], and Jaco van de Pol[4,5]

[1] LIPN, CNRS UMR 7030, Université Paris 13, Villetaneuse, France
[2] JFLI, CNRS, Tokyo, Japan
[3] National Institute of Informatics, Tokyo, Japan
[4] University of Twente, Enschede, The Netherlands
v.bloemen@utwente.nl
[5] University of Aarhus, Aarhus, Denmark

Abstract. Parametric timed automata (PTA) extend timed automata by allowing parameters in clock constraints. Such a formalism is for instance useful when reasoning about unknown delays in a timed system. Using existing techniques, a user can synthesize the parameter constraints that allow the system to reach a specified goal location, regardless of how much time has passed for the internal clocks.

We focus on synthesizing parameters such that not only the goal location is reached, but we also address the following questions: *what is the minimal time to reach the goal location?* and *for which parameter values can we achieve this?* We analyse the problem and present a semi-algorithm to solve it. We also discuss and provide solutions for minimizing a specific parameter value to still reach the goal.

We empirically study the performance of these algorithms on a benchmark set for PTAs and show that *minimal-time reachability synthesis* is more efficient to compute than the standard synthesis algorithm for reachability. Data or code related to this paper is available at: [26].

1 Introduction

Timed Automata (TA) [2] extend finite automata with *clocks*, for instance to model real-time systems. Timed automata allow for reasoning about temporal properties of the designed system. In addition to reachability problems, it is possible to compute for TAs the minimal or maximal time required to reach a specific goal location. Such a result is valuable in practice, as it can describe the response time of a system or it may indicate when a component failure occurs.

This work is partially supported by the ANR national research program PACS (ANR-14-CE28-0002) and PHC Van Gogh project PAMPAS.
É. André—Partially supported by ERATO HASUO Metamathematics for Systems Design Project (No. JPMJER1603), JST.
V. Bloemen—Supported by the 3TU.BSR project.

T. Vojnar and L. Zhang (Eds.): TACAS 2019, Part II, LNCS 11428, pp. 211–228, 2019.
https://doi.org/10.1007/978-3-030-17465-1_12

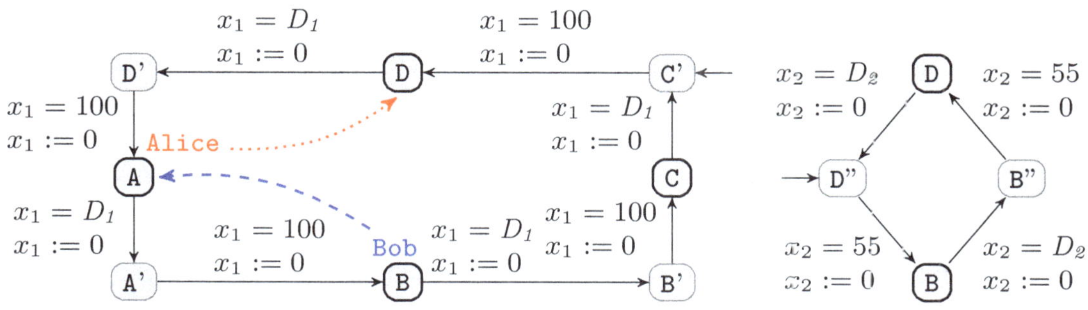

(a) Train 1 (b) Train 2

Fig. 1. Train delay scheduling problem: `Alice` (depicted in dotted red), located at `A`, wants to go to station `D`. `Bob` (depicted in dashed blue), located at `B`, wants to go to `A`. By setting the train delays D_1 and D_2 for train 1 and 2, make sure that both `Alice` and `Bob` reach their target station in minimum total time. (Color figure online)

It may not always be possible to describe a real-time system with a TA. There are often uncertainties in the timing constraints, for instance how long it takes between sending and receiving a message. Optimising specific timing delays to improve the overall throughput of the system may also be considered, as shown in Example 1. Such uncertainties can however be modelled using a *parametric timed automaton (PTA)* [3]. A PTA adds parameters, or unknown constants, to the TA formalism. By examining the reachability of a goal location, the parameters get constrained and we can observe which parameter valuations preserve the reachability of the goal location.

This process, also called *parameter synthesis*, is definitely useful for analysing reachability properties of a system. However, this technique does disregard timing aspects to some extent. Given the parameter constraints, it is no longer possible to give clear boundaries on the time to reach the goal, as this may depend on the parameter valuations. We focus on the parameter synthesis problem while reaching the goal location in minimal time, as demonstrated in Example 1.

Example 1. Consider the example in Fig. 1, which depicts a train network consisting of two trains. Both trains share locations `B` and `D` (the station platforms) while locations $\mathtt{A}', \mathtt{B}', \mathtt{C}', \mathtt{D}', \mathtt{B}''$, and $\mathtt{D}''$ represent a train travelling (tracks). The travel time for train 1 between any two stations is 100, and 55 for train 2. Train 1 stops at stations `A`, `B`, `C`, and `D`, for time D_1 (and train 2 stops for D_2 time units at `B` and `D`). Here, the train delays D_1 and D_2 are parameters and x_1 and x_2 are clocks. Both clocks start at 0 and reset after every transition. We assume that the trains use different tracks and changing trains at the platform of a station can be done in negligible time.

`Alice` is starting her journey from `A` and would like to go to `D`. `Bob` is located at `B` and wants to go to `A`. Train 1 and/or 2 can be used to travel, if both the train and the person are at the same location. Initially, both `Alice` and `Bob` wait for a train, since the initial positions of train 1 and 2 are respectively `C'` and `D"`.

We would like to set the train delays D_1 and D_2 in such a way that the total time for `Alice` and `Bob` to reach their target location, i. e. the PTA location for which `Alice` is at station `D` and `Bob` is at station `A`, is minimal. The optimal solution is $D_1 = 25 \wedge D_2 = 15$, which leads to a total time of 405 units[1]. Note that this is neither optimal for `Alice` (the fastest would be $D_1 = 0 \wedge D_2 = 5$), nor optimal for `Bob` ($D_1 = 10 \wedge D_2 = 0$).

Note that in other instances, the time to reach a goal location may be an interval, describing the lower- and upper-bound on the time. This can be achieved in the example by changing the travel time from train 1 to be between 95 and 105, by guarding the outgoing transitions from locations $\mathtt{A}'$, $\mathtt{B}'$, $\mathtt{C}'$ and $\mathtt{D}'$ with $95 \leq x_1 \leq 105$ (instead of $x_1 = 100$). We focus on the lower-bound *global time*, meaning that we look at the minimal *total* time passed in the system, which may differ from the clock values as the clocks can be reset.
In this paper, we address the following problems:

- *minimal-time reachability*: synthesizing *a single* parameter valuation for which the goal location can be reached in minimal (lower-bound) time,
- *minimal-time reachability synthesis*: synthesizing all parameter valuations such that the time to reach the goal location is minimized, and
- *parameter minimization synthesis*: synthesizing all parameter valuations such that a particular parameter is minimized and the goal location can still be reached (this problem can also address the *minimal-time reachability synthesis problem* by adding a parameter to equal with the final clock value).

For all stated problems we provide algorithms to solve them and empirically compare them with a set of benchmark experiments for PTAs, obtained from [5]. Interestingly, compared to standard reachability and synthesis, minimal-time reachability and synthesis is in general computed faster as fewer states have to be considered in the exploration. We also look at the computability and intractability of the problems for PTAs and L/U-PTAs (PTAs for which each parameter only appears as a lower- or upper-bound).

Related work. The earliest work on minimal-time reachability for timed automata was by Courcoubetis and Yannakis [17], who first addressed the problem of computing lower and upper bounds. Several algorithms have been developed since to improve performance [22,24,25], by e. g. using parallelism. Related problems have been studied, such as minimal-time reachability for weighted timed automata [4], minimal-cost reachability in priced timed automata [12], and job scheduling for timed automata [1].

Concerning parametric timed automata, to the best of our knowledge, the minimal-time reachability problem was not tackled in the past. The reachability-emptiness problem ("the emptiness of the parameter valuation set for which a

[1] `Alice` waits for train 1 to reach `A` at time 225, then she hops on and exits the train on time 350 at `B`. There she can immediately take train 2 and reach `D` at time 405. `Bob` waits for train 2 to reach `B` at time 55 and takes this train. At time 125 he reaches `D` and can immediately hop on train 1. Bob reaches `A` at time 225.

given set of locations is reachable") is undecidable [3], with various settings considered, notably a single clock compared to parameters [21] or a single rational-valued or integer-valued parameter [14,21] (see [6] for a survey). Only severely limiting the number of clocks (e. g. [3,11,14,16]), and often restricting to integer-valued parameters, can bring some decidability. Emptiness for the subclass of L/U-PTAs is also decidable [13]. Minimizing a parameter can however be considered done in the setting of upper-bound PTAs (PTAs in which the clocks are only restricted from above): the exact synthesis of integer valuations for which a location is reachable can be done [15], and therefore the minimum valuation of a parameter can be obtained.

2 Preliminaries

We assume a set $\mathbb{X} = \{x_1, \dots, x_{|\mathbb{X}|}\}$ of *clocks*, i. e. real-valued variables that evolve at the same rate. A clock valuation is $\nu_{\mathbb{X}} : \mathbb{X} \rightarrow \mathbb{R}_{\geq 0}$. We write $\mathbf{0}$ for the clock valuation assigning 0 to all clocks. Given $d \in \mathbb{R}_{\geq 0}$, $\nu_{\mathbb{X}} + d$ is the valuation s.t. $(\nu_{\mathbb{X}} + d)(x) = \nu_{\mathbb{X}}(x) + d$, for all $x \in \mathbb{X}$. Given $R \subseteq \mathbb{X}$, we define the *reset* of a valuation $\nu_{\mathbb{X}}$, denoted by $[\nu_{\mathbb{X}}]_R$, as follows: $[\nu_{\mathbb{X}}]_R(x) = 0$ if $x \in R$, and $[\nu_{\mathbb{X}}]_R(x) = \nu_{\mathbb{X}}(x)$ otherwise.

We assume a set $\mathbb{P} = \{p_1, \dots, p_{|\mathbb{P}|}\}$ of *parameters*. A parameter *valuation* $\nu_{\mathbb{P}}$ is $\nu_{\mathbb{P}} : \mathbb{P} \rightarrow \mathbb{Q}_+$. We denote $\bowtie \in \{<, \leq, =, \geq, >\}$, $\triangleleft \in \{<, \leq\}$, and $\triangleright \in \{>, \geq\}$. A guard g is a constraint over $\mathbb{X} \cup \mathbb{P}$ defined by a conjunction of inequalities of the form $x \bowtie d$ or $x \bowtie p$, with $x \in \mathbb{X}$, $d \in \mathbb{N}$ and $p \in \mathbb{P}$. Given a guard g, we write $\nu_{\mathbb{X}} \models \nu_{\mathbb{P}}(g)$ if the expression obtained by replacing each clock $x \in C$ appearing in g by $\nu_{\mathbb{X}}(x)$ and each parameter $p \in \mathbb{P}$ appearing in g by $\nu_{\mathbb{P}}(p)$ evaluates to true.

2.1 Parametric Timed Automata

Definition 1 (PTA). *A PTA $\mathcal{A}$ is a tuple $\mathcal{A} = (\Sigma, L, \ell_0, \mathbb{X}, \mathbb{P}, \mathcal{I}, E)$, where: (i) Σ is a finite set of actions, (ii) L is a finite set of locations, (iii) $\ell_0 \in L$ is the initial location, (iv) $\mathbb{X}$ is a finite set of clocks, (v) $\mathbb{P}$ is a finite set of parameters, (vi) $\mathcal{I}$ is the invariant, assigning to every $\ell \in L$ a guard $\mathcal{I}(\ell)$, (vii) E is a finite set of edges $e = (\ell, g, a, R, \ell')$ where $\ell, \ell' \in L$ are the source and target locations, $a \in \Sigma$, $R \subseteq \mathbb{X}$ is a set of clocks to be reset, and g is a guard.*

Given a parameter valuation $\nu_{\mathbb{P}}$ and PTA $\mathcal{A}$, we denote by $\nu_{\mathbb{P}}(\mathcal{A})$ the non-parametric structure where all occurrences of a parameter $p \in \mathbb{P}$ have been replaced by $\nu_{\mathbb{P}}(p)$. Any structure $\nu_{\mathbb{P}}(\mathcal{A})$ is also a *timed automaton*. By assuming a rescaling of the constants (multiplying all constants in $\nu_{\mathbb{P}}(\mathcal{A})$ by their least common denominator), we obtain an equivalent (integer-valued) TA.

Definition 2 (L/U-PTA). *An* L/U-PTA *is a PTA where the set of parameters is partitioned into lower-bound parameters and upper-bound parameters, i. e. parameters that appear only in guards and invariants in inequalities of the form $p \triangleleft x$, or of the form $p \triangleright x$, respectively.*

Definition 3 (Semantics of a PTA). *Given a PTA $\mathcal{A} = (\Sigma, L, \ell_0, \mathbb{X}, \mathbb{P}, \mathcal{I}, E)$, and a parameter valuation $\nu_\mathbb{P}$, the semantics of $\nu_\mathbb{P}(\mathcal{A})$ is given by the timed transition system (TTS) $(S, s_0, \rightarrow)$, with:*

- $S = \{(\ell, \nu_\mathbb{X}) \in L \times \mathbb{R}_{\geq 0}^{|\mathbb{X}|} \mid \nu_\mathbb{X} \models \nu_\mathbb{P}(\mathcal{I}(\ell))\}$, $s_0 = (\ell_0, \mathbf{0})$,
- $\rightarrow$ *consists of the discrete and (continuous) delay transition relations: (i) discrete transitions:* $(\ell, \nu_\mathbb{X}) \overset{e}{\mapsto} (\ell', \nu'_\mathbb{X})$, *if* $(\ell, \nu_\mathbb{X}), (\ell', \nu'_\mathbb{X}) \in S$, *and there exists* $e = (\ell, g, a, R, \ell') \in E$, *such that* $\nu'_\mathbb{X} = [\nu_\mathbb{X}]_R$, *and* $\nu_\mathbb{X} \models \nu_\mathbb{P}(g)$, *(ii) delay transitions:* $(\ell, \nu_\mathbb{X}) \overset{d}{\mapsto} (\ell, \nu_\mathbb{X} + d)$, *with* $d \in \mathbb{R}_{\geq 0}$, *if* $\forall d' \in [0, d], (\ell, \nu_\mathbb{X} + d') \in S$.

Moreover we write $(\ell, \nu_\mathbb{X}) \overset{(d,e)}{\longrightarrow} (\ell', \nu'_\mathbb{X})$ for a combination of a delay and discrete transition if $\exists \nu''_\mathbb{X} : (\ell, \nu_\mathbb{X}) \overset{d}{\mapsto} (\ell, \nu''_\mathbb{X}) \overset{e}{\mapsto} (\ell', \nu'_\mathbb{X})$.

Given a TA $\nu_\mathbb{P}(\mathcal{A})$ with concrete semantics $(S, s_0, \rightarrow)$, we refer to the states of S as the *concrete states* of $\nu_\mathbb{P}(\mathcal{A})$. A *run* ρ of $\nu_\mathbb{P}(\mathcal{A})$ is a possibly infinite alternating sequence of concrete states of $\nu_\mathbb{P}(\mathcal{A})$, and pairs of edges and delays, starting from the initial state s_0 of the form $s_0, (d_0, e_0), s_1, \cdots$, with $i = 0, 1, \ldots$, and $d_i \in \mathbb{R}_{\geq 0}$, $e_i \in E$, and $(s_i, e_i, s_{i+1}) \in \rightarrow$. The set of all finite runs over $\nu_\mathbb{P}(\mathcal{A})$ is denoted by $Runs(\nu_\mathbb{P}(\mathcal{A}))$. The *duration* of a finite run $\rho = s_0, (d_0, e_0), s_1, \cdots, s_i$, is given by $duration(\rho) = \sum_{0 \leq j \leq i-1} d_j$.

Given a state $s = (\ell, \nu_\mathbb{X})$, we say that s is reachable in $\nu_\mathbb{P}(\mathcal{A})$ if s is the last state of a run of $\nu_\mathbb{P}(\mathcal{A})$. By extension, we say that ℓ is reachable; and by extension again, given a set T of locations, we say that T is reachable if there exists $\ell \in T$ such that ℓ is reachable in $\nu_\mathbb{P}(\mathcal{A})$. The set of all finite runs of $\nu_\mathbb{P}(\mathcal{A})$ that reach T is denoted by $Reach(\nu_\mathbb{P}(\mathcal{A}), T)$.

Minimal reachability. As the minimal time may not be an integer, but also the smallest value larger than an integer[2], we define a minimum as either a pair in $\mathbb{Q}_+ \times \{=, >\}$ or ∞. The comparison operators function as follows: $(c, =) < \infty$, $(c, >) < \infty$, and $(c_1, \succ_1) < (c_2, \succ_2)$ iff either $c_1 < c_2$ or $c_1 = c_2$, $\succ_1$ is $=$ and $\succ_2$ is $>$[3].

Given a set of locations T, the minimal time reachability of T in $\nu_\mathbb{P}(\mathcal{A})$, denoted by $MinTimeReach(\nu_\mathbb{P}(\mathcal{A}), T) = \min\{duration(\rho) \mid \rho \in Reach(\nu_\mathbb{P}(\mathcal{A}), T)\}$, is the minimal duration over all runs of $\nu_\mathbb{P}(\mathcal{A})$ reaching T.

By extension, given a PTA, we denote by $MinTimePTA(\mathcal{A}, T)$ the minimal time reachability of T over all valuations, i.e. $MinTimePTA(\mathcal{A}, T) = \min_{\nu_\mathbb{P}} MinTimeReach(\nu_\mathbb{P}(\mathcal{A}), T)$. As we will be interested in synthesizing the valuations leading to the minimal time, let us define $MinTimeSynth(\mathcal{A}, T) = \{\nu_\mathbb{P} \mid MinTimeReach(\nu_\mathbb{P}(\mathcal{A}), T) = MinTimePTA(\mathcal{A}, T)\}$.

We will also be interested in minimizing the valuation of a given parameter p_i (without any notion of time) reaching a given location, and we therefore

[2] Consider a TA with a transition guarded by $x > 1$ from ℓ_0 to ℓ_1, then the minimal duration of runs reaching ℓ_1 is not 1 but slightly more.

[3] When we compute the minimum over a set, we actually calculate its infimum and combine the value with either $=$ or $>$ to indicate if the value is present in the set.

define $MinParamReach(\mathcal{A}, p_i, T) = \min_{\nu_{\mathbb{P}}}\{\nu_{\mathbb{P}}(p_i) \mid Reach(\nu_{\mathbb{P}}(\mathcal{A}), T) \neq \emptyset\}$. Similarly, we will be interested in synthesizing *all* valuations leading to the minimal valuation of p_i reaching T, so let us define $MinParamSynth(\mathcal{A}, p_i, T) = \{\nu_{\mathbb{P}} \mid Reach(\nu_{\mathbb{P}}(\mathcal{A}), T) \neq \emptyset \wedge \nu_{\mathbb{P}}(p_i) = MinParamReach(\mathcal{A}, p_i, T)\}$.

2.2 Computation Problems

Minimal-time reachability problem:
INPUT: A PTA $\mathcal{A}$, a subset $T \subseteq L$ of its locations.
PROBLEM: Compute $MinTimePTA(\mathcal{A}, T)$.

Minimal-time reachability synthesis problem:
INPUT: A PTA $\mathcal{A}$, a subset $T \subseteq L$ of its locations.
PROBLEM: Compute $MinTimeSynth(\mathcal{A}, T)$.

Before addressing these problems, we will address the slightly different problem of minimal-parameter reachability, i. e. the minimization of a parameter reaching a given location (independently of time). We will see in Lemma 1 that this problem can also give an answer to the minimal-time reachability (synthesis) problem.

Minimal-parameter reachability problem:
INPUT: A PTA $\mathcal{A}$, a parameter p, a subset $T \subseteq L$ of the locations of $\mathcal{A}$.
PROBLEM: Compute $MinParamReach(\mathcal{A}, T, p)$.

Minimal-parameter reachability synthesis problem:
INPUT: A PTA $\mathcal{A}$, a parameter p, a subset $T \subseteq L$ of the locations of $\mathcal{A}$.
PROBLEM: Synthesize $MinParamSynth(\mathcal{A}, T, p)$.

2.3 Symbolic Semantics

Let us now recall the symbolic semantics of PTAs (see e. g. [8, 19]), that we will use to solve these problems.

Constraints. We first define operations on constraints. A linear term over $\mathbb{X} \cup \mathbb{P}$ is of the form $\sum_{1 \leq i \leq |\mathbb{X}|} \alpha_i x_i + \sum_{1 \leq j \leq |\mathbb{P}|} \beta_j p_j + d$, with $x_i \in \mathbb{X}$, $p_j \in \mathbb{P}$, and $\alpha_i, \beta_j, d \in \mathbb{Z}$. A *constraint* C (i. e. a convex polyhedron) over $\mathbb{X} \cup \mathbb{P}$ is a conjunction of inequalities of the form $lt \bowtie 0$, where lt is a linear term. $\perp$ denotes the false parameter constraint, i. e. the constraint over $\mathbb{P}$ containing no valuation.

Given a parameter valuation $\nu_{\mathbb{P}}$, $\nu_{\mathbb{P}}(C)$ denotes the constraint over $\mathbb{X}$ obtained by replacing each parameter p in C with $\nu_{\mathbb{P}}(p)$. Likewise, given a clock valuation $\nu_{\mathbb{X}}$, $\nu_{\mathbb{X}}(\nu_{\mathbb{P}}(C))$ denotes the expression obtained by replacing each clock x in $\nu_{\mathbb{P}}(C)$ with $\nu_{\mathbb{X}}(x)$. We say that $\nu_{\mathbb{P}}$ *satisfies* C, denoted by $\nu_{\mathbb{P}} \models C$, if the set of clock valuations satisfying $\nu_{\mathbb{P}}(C)$ is non-empty. Given a parameter valuation $\nu_{\mathbb{P}}$ and a clock valuation $\nu_{\mathbb{X}}$, we denote by $\nu_{\mathbb{X}}|\nu_{\mathbb{P}}$ the valuation over $\mathbb{X} \cup \mathbb{P}$ such that for all clocks x, $\nu_{\mathbb{X}}|\nu_{\mathbb{P}}(x) = \nu_{\mathbb{X}}(x)$ and for all parameters p, $\nu_{\mathbb{X}}|\nu_{\mathbb{P}}(p) = \nu_{\mathbb{P}}(p)$. We use the notation $\nu_{\mathbb{X}}|\nu_{\mathbb{P}} \models C$ to indicate that $\nu_{\mathbb{X}}(\nu_{\mathbb{P}}(C))$ evaluates to true. We say that C is *satisfiable* if $\exists \nu_{\mathbb{X}}, \nu_{\mathbb{P}}$ s.t.$\nu_{\mathbb{X}}|\nu_{\mathbb{P}} \models C$.

We define the *time elapsing* of C, denoted by $C^{\nearrow}$, as the constraint over $\mathbb{X}$ and $\mathbb{P}$ obtained from C by delaying all clocks by an arbitrary amount of time. That is, $\nu'_{\mathbb{X}}|\nu_{\mathbb{P}} \models C^{\nearrow}$ iff $\exists \nu_{\mathbb{X}} : \mathbb{X} \rightarrow \mathbb{R}_+, \exists d \in \mathbb{R}_+$ s.t. $\nu'_{\mathbb{X}}|\nu_{\mathbb{P}} \models C \wedge \nu'_{\mathbb{X}} = \nu_{\mathbb{X}} + d$. Given $R \subseteq \mathbb{X}$, we define the *reset* of C, denoted by $[C]_R$, as the constraint obtained from C by resetting the clocks in R, and keeping the other clocks unchanged. Given a subset $\mathbb{P}' \subseteq \mathbb{P}$ of parameters, we denote by $C{\downarrow_{\mathbb{P}'}}$ the projection of C onto $\mathbb{P}'$, i. e. obtained by eliminating the clock variables and the parameters in $\mathbb{P} \setminus \mathbb{P}'$ (e. g. using Fourier-Motzkin). Therefore, $C{\downarrow_{\mathbb{P}}}$ denotes the elimination of the clock variables only, i. e. the projection onto $\mathbb{P}$. Given p, we denote by $\mathsf{GetMin}(C,p)$ the minimum of p in a form $(c, \succ)$. Technically, GetMin can be implemented using polyhedral operations as follows: $C{\downarrow_{\{p\}}}$ is computed, and then the infimum is extracted; then the operator in $\{=, >\}$ is inferred depending whether $C{\downarrow_{\{p\}}}$ is bounded from below using a closed or an open constraint. We extend GetMin to accommodate clocks, thus $\mathsf{GetMin}(C,x)$ returns the minimal clock value that x can take, while conforming to C.

A symbolic state is a pair (ℓ, C) where $\ell \in L$ is a location, and C its associated constraint, called *parametric zone*.

Definition 4 (Symbolic semantics). *Given a PTA* $\mathcal{A} = (\Sigma, L, \ell_0, \mathbb{X}, \mathbb{P}, \mathcal{I}, E)$, *the symbolic semantics of* $\mathcal{A}$ *is defined by the labelled transition system called the* parametric zone graph $\mathcal{PZG} = (E, \mathbf{S}, \mathbf{s}_0, \Rightarrow)$, *with*

- $\mathbf{S} = \{(\ell, C) \mid C \subseteq \mathcal{I}(\ell)\}$, $\mathbf{s}_0 = \big(\ell_0, (\bigwedge_{1 \leq i \leq |\mathbb{X}|} x_i = 0)^{\nearrow} \wedge \mathcal{I}(\ell_0)\big)$, *and*
- $\big((\ell, C), e, (\ell', C')\big) \in \Rightarrow$ *if* $e = (\ell, g, a, R, \ell') \in E$ *and* $C' = \big([(C \wedge g)]_R \wedge \mathcal{I}(\ell')\big)^{\nearrow} \wedge \mathcal{I}(\ell')$ *with* C' *satisfiable.*

That is, in the parametric zone graph, nodes are symbolic states, and arcs are labeled by *edges* of the original PTA. Given $\mathbf{s} = (\ell, C)$, if $\big((\ell, C), e, (\ell', C')\big) \in \Rightarrow$, we write $\mathsf{Succ}(\mathbf{s}, e) = (\ell', C')$. By extension, we write $\mathsf{Succ}(\mathbf{s})$ for $\cup_{e \in E} \mathsf{Succ}(\mathbf{s}, e)$. Well-known results (see [19]) connect the concrete and the symbolic semantics.

3 Computability and Intractability

3.1 Minimal-Time Reachability

The following result is a consequence of a monotonicity property of L/U-PTAs [19]. We can safely replace parameters with some constants in order to compute the solution to the minimal-time reachability problem, which reduces to the minimal-time reachability in a TA, which is PSPACE-complete [17]. All proofs are given in [7].

Proposition 1 (minimal-time reachability for L/U-PTAs). *The minimal-time reachability problem for L/U-PTAs is PSPACE-complete.*

Computing the minimal time for which a location is reached (Proposition 1) does not mean that we are able to compute exactly all valuations for which this location is reachable in minimal time. In fact, we show that it is not possible in a formalism for which the emptiness of the intersection is decidable—which notably rules out its representation as a finite union of polyhedra. The proof idea is that representing it in such a formalism would contradict the undecidability of the emptiness problem for (normal) PTAs.

Proposition 2 (intractability of minimal-time reachability synthesis for L/U-PTAs). *The solution to the minimal-time reachability synthesis problem for L/U-PTAs cannot be represented in a formalism for which the emptiness of the intersection is decidable.*

3.2 Minimal-Parameter Reachability

For the full class of PTAs, we will see that these problems are clearly out of reach: if it was possible to compute the solution to the minimal-parameter reachability or minimal-parameter reachability synthesis, then it would be possible to answer the reachability emptiness problem—which is undecidable in most settings [6].

We first show that an algorithm for the minimal-parameter synthesis problem can be used to solve the minimal-time synthesis problem, i. e. the minimal-parameter synthesis problem is at least as hard as the minimal-time synthesis problem.

Lemma 1 (minimal-time from minimal-parameter synthesis). *An algorithm that solves the minimal-parameter synthesis problem can be used to solve the minimal-time synthesis problem by extending the PTA.*

Proof. Assume we are given an arbitrary PTA $\mathcal{A}$, a set of target locations T, and a global clock x_{global} that never resets. We construct the PTA $\mathcal{A}'$ from $\mathcal{A}$ by adding a new parameter p_{global}, and for every edge (ℓ, g, a, R, ℓ') in $\mathcal{A}'$ such that $\ell' \in T$, we replace g by $g \wedge x_{global} = p_{global}$. Note that when a target location from T is reached, we have that $x_{global} = p_{global}$, hence by minimizing p_{global} we also minimize x_{global}. Thus, by solving $\mathit{MinParamSynth}(\mathcal{A}', T, p_{global})$, we effectively solve $\mathit{MinTimeSynth}(\mathcal{A}, T)$.

The following result states that synthesis of the minimal-value of the parameter is intractable for PTAs.

Proposition 3 (intractability of minimal-parameter reachability for PTAs). *The solution to the minimal-parameter reachability for PTAs cannot be computed in general.*

Proof (sketch). By showing that testing equality of "$p = 0$" against the solution of the minimal-parameter reachability problem for the PTA in Fig. 2 and ℓ'_f is equivalent to solving reachability emptiness of ℓ_f in $\mathcal{A}$—which is undecidable [3]. Therefore, the solution cannot be computed in general.

The intractability of minimal-parameter reachability synthesis for PTAs will be implied by the upcoming Proposition 4 in a more restricted setting.

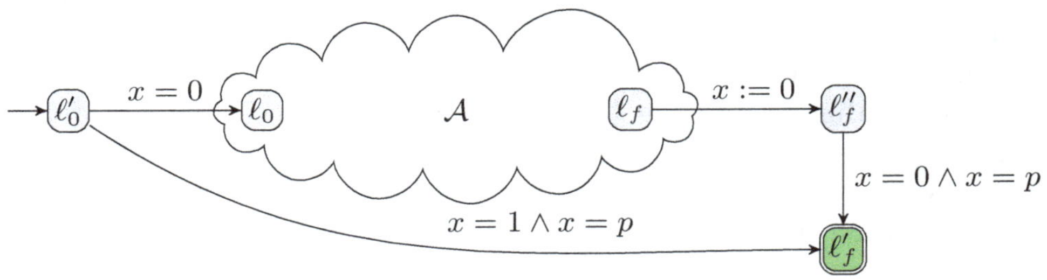

Fig. 2. Intractability of minimal-parameter reachability for PTAs

Intractability of the synthesis for L/U-PTAs. The following result states that synthesis is intractable for L/U-PTAs. In particular, this rules out the possibility to represent the result using a finite union of polyhedra.

Proposition 4 (intractability of minimal-parameter reachability synthesis for L/U-PTAs). *The solution to the minimal-parameter reachability synthesis for L/U-PTAs cannot always be represented in a formalism for which the emptiness of the intersection is decidable and for which the minimization of a variable is computable.*

Proof. From Lemma 1 and Proposition 2. □

The minimal-parameter reachability problem remains open for L/U-PTAs (see Sect. 7). Despite these negative results, we will define procedures that address not only the class of L/U-PTAs, but in fact the class of full PTAs. Of course, these procedures are not guaranteed to terminate.

4 Minimal Parameter Reachability Synthesis

We give $\mathsf{MinParamSynth}(\mathcal{A}, T, p)$ in Algorithm 1. It maintains a set $\mathbf{W}$ of waiting symbolic states, a set $\mathbf{P}$ of passed states, a current optimum *Opt* and the associated optimal valuations K. While $\mathbf{W}$ is not empty, a state is picked in line 6. If it is a target state (i. e. $\ell \in T$) then the projection of its constraint onto p is computed, and the minimum is inferred (line 10). If that projection improves the known optimum, then the associated parameter valuations K are completely replaced by the one obtained from the current state (i. e. the projection of C onto $\mathbb{P}$). Otherwise, if $C\downarrow_{\{p\}}$ is equal to the known optimum (line 14), then we add (using disjunction) the associated valuations. Finally, if the current state is not a target state and has not been visited before, then we compute its successors and add them to $\mathbf{W}$ in lines 17 and 18.

Note that if $\mathbf{W}$ is implemented as a FIFO list with "pick" the first element, then this algorithm is a classical BFS procedure.

Also note that if we replace lines 10–15 with the statement $K \leftarrow K \vee C\downarrow_{\mathbb{P}}$ (i. e. adding the parameter valuations to K every time the algorithm reaches a target location), we obtain the standard synthesis algorithm $\mathsf{EFSynth}$ from e. g. [20], that synthesizes all parameter valuations for which a set of locations is reachable.

Algorithm 1: MinParamSynth($\mathcal{A}, T, p$)

```
input   : A PTA A with symbolic initial state s0 = (ℓ0, C0), a set of target locations T,
          a parameter p.
output  : Constraint K over the parameters.
W ← {s0}                                                    // waiting set
P ← ∅                                                       // passed set
Opt ← ∞                                                     // current optimum
K ← ⊥                                                       // current optimum valuations
while W ≠ ∅ do
    Pick s = (ℓ, C) from W
    W ← W \ {s}
    P ← P ∪ {s}
    if ℓ ∈ T then                                           // s is a target state
        s_opt ← GetMin(C, p)                                // compute local optimum
        if s_opt < Opt then                                 // the optimum is strictly better
            Opt ← s_opt                                     // we found a new best optimum: replace it
            K ← C↓ℙ                                         // completely replace the found valuations
        else if s_opt = Opt then                            // the optimum is equal to the one known
            K ← K ∨ C↓ℙ                                     // add the found valuations
    else                                                    // otherwise explore successors
        for each s' ∈ Succ(s) do
            if s' ∉ W ∧ s' ∉ P then W ← W ∪ {s'}
return K
```

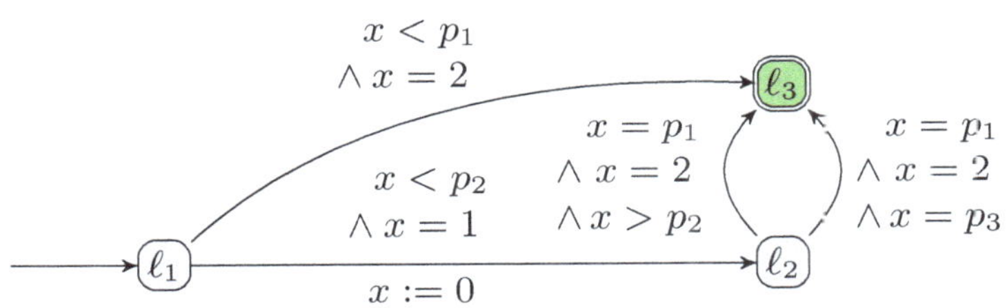

Fig. 3. PTA exemplifying Algorithm 1.

Example 2. Consider the PTA $\mathcal{A}$ in Fig. 3, and run MinParamSynth($\mathcal{A}, \{\ell_3\}, p_1$). The initial state is $\mathbf{s}_1 = (\ell_1, x \geq 0)$ (we omit the trivial constraints $p_i \geq 0$). Its successors $\mathbf{s}_2 = (\ell_3, x \geq 2 \wedge p_1 > 2)$ and $\mathbf{s}_3 = (\ell_2, x \geq 0 \wedge p_2 > 1)$ are added to $\mathbf{W}$. Pick $\mathbf{s}_2$ from $\mathbf{W}$: it is a target, and therefore GetMin(C_2, p_1) is computed, which gives $(2, >)$. Since $(2, >) < \infty$, we found a new minimum, and K becomes $C_2{\downarrow_{\mathbb{P}}}$, i. e. $p_1 > 2$. Pick $\mathbf{s}_3$ from $\mathbf{W}$: it is not a target, therefore we compute its successors $\mathbf{s}_4 = (\ell_3, x \geq 2 \wedge p_1 = 2 \wedge 1 < p_2 < 2)$ and $\mathbf{s}_5 = (\ell_3, x \geq 2 \wedge p_1 = p_3 = 2 \wedge p_2 > 1)$. Pick $\mathbf{s}_4$: it is a target, with GetMin(C_4, p_1) $= (2, =)$. As $(2, =) < (2, >)$, we found a new minimum, and K is replaced with $C_4{\downarrow_{\mathbb{P}}}$, i. e. $p_1 = 2 \wedge 1 < p_2 < 2$. Pick $\mathbf{s}_5$: it is a target, with GetMin(C_4, p_1) $= (2, =)$. As $(2, =) = (2, =)$, we found an equally good minimum, and K is improved with $C_5{\downarrow_{\mathbb{P}}}$, giving a new K equal to $(p_1 = 2 \wedge 1 < p_2 < 2) \vee (p_1 = p_3 = 2 \wedge p_2 > 1)$. As $\mathbf{W} = \emptyset$, K is returned.

Algorithm 1 is a semi-algorithm; if it terminates with result K, then K is a solution for the MinParamSynth problem. Correctness follows from the fact that the algorithm explores the entire parametric zone graph, except for successors of target states (from [19,20] we have that successors of a symbolic state can only restrict the parameter constraint, hence we cannot improve). Furthermore, the minimum is tracked and updated whenever a target state is reached.

We show that synthesis can effectively be achieved for PTAs with a single clock, a decidable subclass.

Proposition 5 (synthesis for one-clock PTAs). *The solution to the minimal-parameter reachability synthesis can be computed for 1-clock PTAs using a finite union of polyhedra.*

5 Minimal Time Reachability Synthesis

For minimal-time reachability and synthesis, we assume that the PTA contains a global clock x_{global} that is never reset. Otherwise, we extend the PTA by simply adding a 'dummy' clock x_{global} without any associated guards, invariants or resets.

Algorithm 2: $\mathsf{MinTimeSynth}(\mathcal{A}, T, x_{global})$

input : A PTA $\mathcal{A}$ with symbolic initial state $\mathbf{s}_0 = (\ell_0, C_0)$, a set of target locations T, a global clock that never resets x_{global}.
output : Minimal time T_{opt} constraint K over the parameters.

$\mathbf{Q} \leftarrow \{(0, \mathbf{s}_0)\}$ // priority queue ordered by time
$\mathbf{P} \leftarrow \emptyset$ // passed set
$K \leftarrow \bot$ // current optimum parameter valuations
$T_{opt} \leftarrow \infty$ // current optimum time
while $\mathbf{Q} \neq \emptyset$ **do**
    $(t, \mathbf{s} = (\ell, C)) = \mathbf{Q}.\mathsf{Pop}()$ // take head of the queue and remove it
    $\mathbf{P} \leftarrow \mathbf{P} \cup \{\mathbf{s}\}$
    if $t > T_{opt}$ **then break**
    else if $\ell \in T$ **then** // when s is a target state and $t \leq T_{opt}$
        $K \leftarrow K \vee (C \wedge x_{global} = t)\downarrow_{\mathbb{P}}$ // valuations for which $t = T_{opt}$
    else // otherwise explore successors
        for each $\mathbf{s}' \in \mathsf{Succ}(\mathbf{s})$ **do**
            if $\mathbf{s}' \in \mathbf{Q} \vee \mathbf{s}' \in \mathbf{P}$ **then continue** // ignore seen states
            $t' \leftarrow \mathsf{GetMin}(\mathbf{s}'.C, x_{global})$ // get minimal time of $\mathbf{s}'.C$
            if $t' \leq T_{opt}$ **then** // only add states not exceeding T_{opt}
                if $\mathbf{s}'.\ell \in T \wedge t' < T_{opt}$ **then**
                    $T_{opt} \leftarrow t'$ // new lower time to target
                $\mathbf{Q}.\mathsf{Push}((t', \mathbf{s}'))$ // add to the priority queue
return (T_{opt}, K)

We give $\mathsf{MinTimeSynth}(\mathcal{A}, T, x_{global})$ in Algorithm 2. We maintain a *priority queue* $\mathbf{Q}$ of waiting symbolic states and order these by their minimal time (for the initial state this is 0). We further maintain a set $\mathbf{P}$ of passed states, a current time optimum T_{opt} (initially ∞), and the associated optimal valuations K. We first explain the synthesis algorithm and then the reachability variant.

Minimal-time reachability synthesis. While $\mathbf{Q}$ is not empty, the state with the lowest associated minimal time t is popped from the head of the queue (line 6). If this time t is larger than T_{opt} (line 8), then this also holds for all remaining states in $\mathbf{Q}$. Also all successor states from $\mathbf{s}$ (or successors of any state from $\mathbf{Q}$) cannot have a better minimal time, thus we can end the algorithm.

Otherwise, if $\mathbf{s}$ is a target state, we assume that $t \not< T_{opt}$ and thus $t = T_{opt}$ (we guarantee this property when pushing states to the queue). Before adding the parameter valuations to K in line 10, we intersect the constraint with $x_{global} = t$ in case the clock value depends on parameters, e. g. if C is $x_{global} = p$.[4]

If $\mathbf{s}$ is not a target state, then we consider its successors in lines 12–18. We ignore states that have been visited before (line 13), and compute the minimal time of $\mathbf{s}'$ in line 14. We compare t' with T_{opt} in line 15. All successor states for which t' exceeds T_{opt} are ignored, as they cannot improve the result.

If $\mathbf{s}'$ is a target state and $t' < T_{opt}$, then we update T_{opt}. Finally, the successor state is pushed to the priority queue in line 18. Note that we preserve the property that $t \not< T_{opt}$ for the states in $\mathbf{Q}$.

Minimal-time reachability. When we are interested in just a single parameter valuation, we may end the algorithm early. The algorithm can be terminated as soon as it reaches line 10. We can assert at this point that T_{opt} will not decrease any further, since all remaining unexplored states have a minimal time that is larger than or equal to T_{opt}.

Algorithm 2 is a semi-algorithm; if it terminates with result (T_{opt}, K), then K is a solution for the MinTimeSynth problem. Correctness follows from the fact that the algorithm explores exactly all symbolic states in the parametric zone graph that can be reached in at most T_{opt} time, except for successors of target states. Note (again) that successors of a symbolic state can only restrict the parameter constraint. Furthermore, T_{opt} is checked and updated for every encountered successor to ensure that the first time a target state is popped from the priority queue $\mathbf{Q}$, it is reached in T_{opt} time (after which T_{opt} never changes).

6 Experiments

We implemented all our algorithms in the IMITATOR tool [9] and compared their performance with the standard (non-minimization) EFSynth parameter synthesis algorithm from [20]. For the experiments, we are interested in analysing the performance (in the form of computation time) of each algorithm, and comparing that with the performance of standard synthesis.

Benchmark models. We collected PTA models and properties from the IMITATOR benchmarks library [5] which contains numerous benchmark models from

[4] In case t is of the form $(c, >)$ with $c \in \mathbb{Q}_+$, then the intersection of C with the linear term $x_{global} = t$ would result in $\bot$, as the exact value t is not part of the constraint. In the implementation, we intersect C with $x_{global} = t + \varepsilon$, for a small $\varepsilon > 0$.

scientific and industrial domains. We selected all models with reachability properties and extended these to include: (1) a new clock variable that represents the global time x_{global}, i.e. a clock that does not reset, and (2) a new parameter p_{global} along with the linear term $x_{global} = p_{global}$ for every transition that targets a goal location, to ensure that when minimizing p_{global} we effectively minimize x_{global}. In total we have 68 models, and for every experiment we used the extended model that includes both the global time clock x_{global} and the corresponding parameter p_{global}.

Subsumption. For each algorithm that we consider, it is possible to reduce the search space with the following two reduction techniques:

- *State inclusion* [18]: Given two symbolic states $\mathbf{s}_1 = (\ell_1, C_1)$ and $\mathbf{s}_2 = (\ell_2, C_2)$ with $\ell_1 = \ell_2$, we say that $\mathbf{s}_1$ is included in $\mathbf{s}_2$ if all parameter valuations for $\mathbf{s}_1$ are also contained in $\mathbf{s}_2$, e.g. C_1 is $p > 5$ and C_2 is $p > 2$. We may then conclude that $\mathbf{s}_1$ is redundant and can be ignored. This check can be performed in the successor computation (Succ) to remove included states, without altering correctness for minimal-time (or parameter) synthesis.
- *State merging* [10]: Two states $\mathbf{s}_1 = (\ell_1, C_1)$ and $\mathbf{s}_2 = (\ell_2, C_2)$ can be merged if $\ell_1 = \ell_2$ and $C_1 \cup C_2$ is a convex polyhedron. The resulting state $(\ell_1, C_1 \cup C_2)$ replaces $\mathbf{s}_1$ and $\mathbf{s}_2$ and is an over-approximation of both states. However, reachable locations, minimality, and executable actions are preserved.

State inclusion is a relatively inexpensive computational task and preliminary results showed that it caused the algorithm to perform equally fast or faster than without the check. Checking for merging is however a computationally expensive procedure and thus should not be performed for every newly found state. For all BFS-based algorithms (standard synthesis and minimal-parameter synthesis) we merge every BFS layer. For the minimal-time synthesis algorithm, we empirically studied various merging heuristics and found that merging every ten iterations of the algorithm yielded the best results. We assume that both the inclusion and merging state-space reductions are used in all experiments (all computation times include the overhead the reductions), unless otherwise mentioned.

Run configurations. For the experiments we used the following configurations:

- MTReach: Minimal-time reachability,
- MTSynth: Minimal-time synthesis,
- MTSynth-noRed: Minimal time synthesis, without reductions,
- MPReach: Minimal-parameter reachability (of p_{global}), and
- MPSynth: Minimal-parameter synthesis (of p_{global}), and
- EFSynth: Classical reachability synthesis.

Experimental setup. We performed all our experiments on an Intel® Core™ i7-4710MQ processor with 2.50 GHz and 7.4GiB memory, using a single thread. The six run configurations were executed on each benchmark model, with a timeout of 3600 s. All our models, results, and information on how to reproduce the results are available on https://github.com/utwente-fmt/OptTime-TACAS19.

Results. The results of our experiments are displayed in Fig. 4.

MTSynth vs EFSynth. We observe that for most of the models MTSynth clearly outperforms EFSynth. This is to be expected since all states that take more than the minimal time can be ignored. Note that the experiments that appear on a vertical line between $0.1s < x < 1s$ are a scaled-up variant of the same model, indicating that this scaling does not affect minimal-time synthesis. Finally, the model plotted at $(1346, 52)$ does not heavily modify the clocks. As a consequence, MTSynth has to explore most of the state space while continuously having to extract the time constraints, making it inefficient.

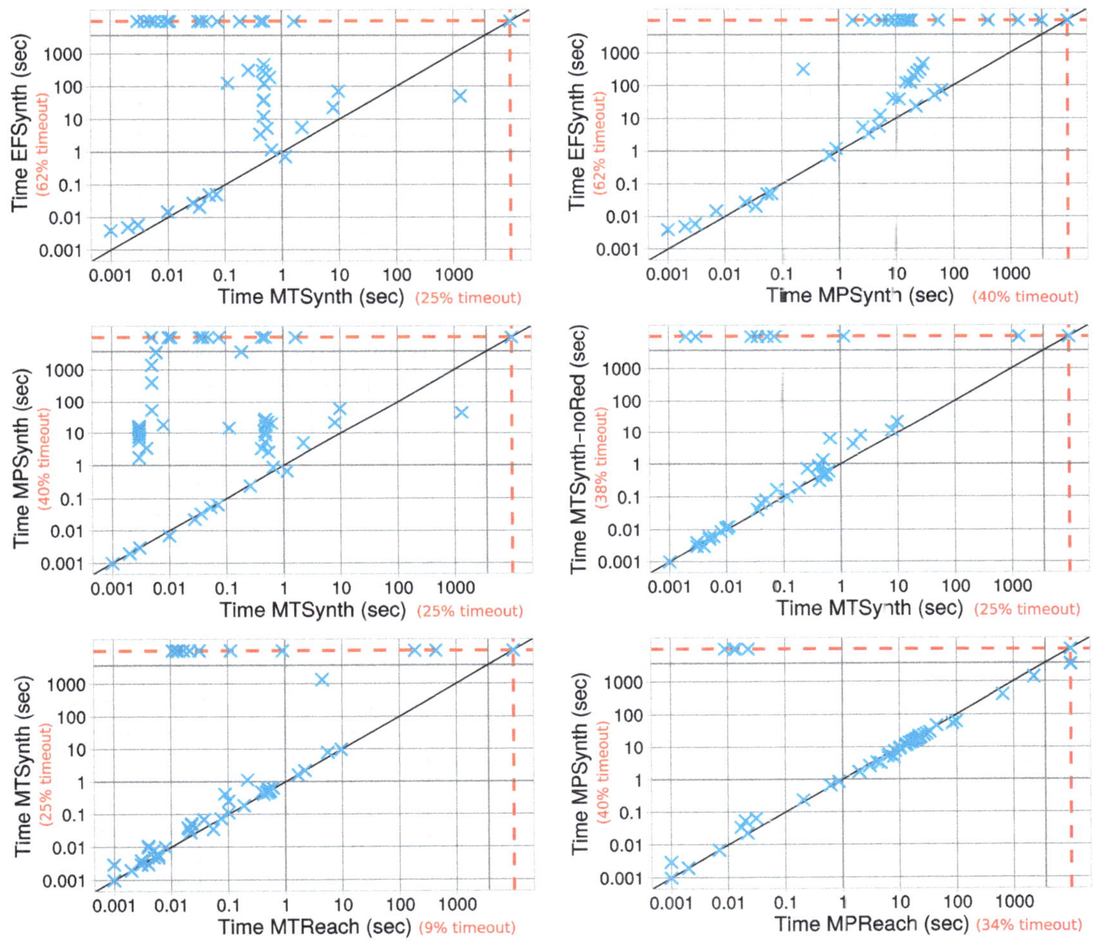

Fig. 4. Scatterplot comparisons of different algorithm configurations. The marks on the red dashed line did not finish computing within the allowed time (3600 s). (Color figure online)

MPSynth vs EFSynth. We can see that MPSynth performs more similar to EFSynth than MTSynth, which is to be expected as the algorithms differ less. Still, MPSynth significantly outperforms EFSynth. This is also because fewer states have to be explored to guarantee optimality (once a parameter exceeds the minimal value, all its successors can be ignored).

MTSynth vs MPSynth. Here, we find that MTSynth outperforms MPSynth, similar to the comparison with EFSynth. The results also show a second scalable model around $(0.003, 10)$ and we see that MPSynth is able to solve the 'bad performing model' for MTSynth as quickly as EFSynth. Still, we can conclude that the minimal-time synthesis problem is in general more efficiently solved with the MTSynth algorithm.

MTSynth vs MTSynth-noRed. Here we can see the advantage of using the inclusion and merging reductions to reduce the search space. For most models there is a non-existent to slight improvement, but for others it makes a large difference. While there is some computational overhead in performing these reductions, this overhead is not significant enough to outweigh their benefits.

MTReach vs MTSynth. With MTReach we expect faster execution times as the algorithm terminates once a parameter valuation is found. The experiments show that this is indeed the case (mostly visible from the timeout line). However, we also observe that for quite a few models the difference is not as significant, implying that synthesis results can often be quickly obtained once a single minimal-time valuation is found.

MPReach vs MPSynth. Here we also expect MPReach to be faster than its synthesis variant. While it does quickly solve six instances for which MPSynth timed out, other than that there is no real performance gain. We also argue here that synthesis is obtained quickly when a minimal parameter bound is found. Of course we are effectively computing a minimal global time, so results may change when a different parameter is minimized.

7 Conclusion

We have designed and implemented several algorithms to solve the minimal-time parameter synthesis and related problems for PTAs. From our experiments we observed in general that minimal-time reachability synthesis is in fact faster to compute compared to standard synthesis. We further show that synthesis while minimizing a parameter is also more efficient, and that existing search space reductions apply well to our algorithms.

Aside from the performance improvement, we deem minimal-time reachability synthesis to be useful in practice. It allows for evaluating which parameter valuations guarantee that the goal is reached in minimal time. We consider it particularly valuable when reasoning about real-time systems.

On the theoretical side, we did not address the minimal-parameter reachability problem for L/U-PTAs (we only showed intractability of the synthesis). While finding the minimal valuation of a given lower-bound parameter is trivial (the answer is 0 iff the target location is reachable), finding the minimum of an upper-bound parameter boils down to reachability-synthesis for U-PTAs, a problem that remains open in general (it is only solvable for integer-valued parameters [15]), as well as to shrinking timed automata [23], but with 0-coefficients in the shrinking vector—not allowed in [23].

A direction for future work is to improve performance by exploiting parallelism. Parallel random search could significantly speed up the computation process, as demonstrated for timed automata [24,25]. Another interesting research direction is to look at maximizing the time to reach the target, or to minimize the *upper-bound* time to reach the target (e. g. for minimizing the worst-case response-time in real-time systems); a preliminary study suggests that the latter problem is significantly more complex than the minimal-time synthesis problem. One may also study other quantitative criteria, e. g. minimizing cost parameters.

References

1. Abdeddaïm, Y., Asarin, E., Maler, O.: Scheduling with timed automata. Theoret. Comput. Sci. **354**(2), 272–300 (2006). https://doi.org/10.1016/j.tcs.2005.11.018
2. Alur, R., Dill, D.L.: A theory of timed automata. Theoret. Comput. Sci. **126**(2), 183–235 (1994)
3. Alur, R., Henzinger, T.A., Vardi, M.Y.: Parametric real-time reasoning. In: STOC, pp. 592–601. ACM, New York (1993)
4. Alur, R., La Torre, S., Pappas, G.J.: Optimal paths in weighted timed automata. Theoret. Comput. Sci. **318**(3), 297–322 (2004). https://doi.org/10.1016/j.tcs.2003.10.038
5. André, É.: A benchmark library for parametric timed model checking. In: Artho, C., Ölveczky, P.C. (eds.) FTSCS 2018. CCIS, vol. 1008, pp. 75–83. Springer, Cham (2019). https://doi.org/10.1007/978-3-030-12988-0_5
6. André, É.: What's decidable about parametric timed automata? Int. J. Softw. Tools Technol. Transfer (2018). https://doi.org/10.1007/s10009-017-0467-0
7. André, É., Bloemen, V., Van de Pol, J., Petrucci, L.: Minimal-time synthesis for parametric timed automata (long version) (2019). https://arxiv.org/abs/1902.03013
8. André, É., Chatain, Th., Encrenaz, E., Fribourg, L.: An inverse method for parametric timed automata. IJFCS **20**(5), 819–836 (2009). https://doi.org/10.1142/S0129054109006905
9. André, É., Fribourg, L., Kühne, U., Soulat, R.: IMITATOR 2.5: a tool for analyzing robustness in scheduling problems. In: Giannakopoulou, D., Méry, D. (eds.) FM 2012. LNCS, vol. 7436, pp. 33–36. Springer, Heidelberg (2012). https://doi.org/10.1007/978-3-642-32759-9_6
10. André, É., Fribourg, L., Soulat, R.: Merge and conquer: state merging in parametric timed automata. In: Van Hung, D., Ogawa, M. (eds.) ATVA 2013. LNCS, vol. 8172, pp. 381–396. Springer, Cham (2013). https://doi.org/10.1007/978-3-319-02444-8_27
11. André, É., Markey, N.: Language preservation problems in parametric timed automata. In: Sankaranarayanan, S., Vicario, E. (eds.) FORMATS 2015. LNCS, vol. 9268, pp. 27–43. Springer, Cham (2015). https://doi.org/10.1007/978-3-319-22975-1_3
12. Behrmann, G., Fehnker, A., Hune, T., Larsen, K., Pettersson, P., Romijn, J.: Efficient guiding towards cost-optimality in UPPAAL. In: Margaria, T., Yi, W. (eds.) TACAS 2001. LNCS, vol. 2031, pp. 174–188. Springer, Heidelberg (2001). https://doi.org/10.1007/3-540-45319-9_13

13. Behrmann, G., Larsen, K.G., Rasmussen, J.I.: Optimal scheduling using priced timed automata. SIGMETRICS Perform. Eval. Rev. **32**(4), 34–40 (2005). https://doi.org/10.1145/1059816.1059823
14. Beneš, N., Bezděk, P., Larsen, K.G., Srba, J.: Language emptiness of continuous-time parametric timed automata. In: Halldórsson, M.M., Iwama, K., Kobayashi, N., Speckmann, B. (eds.) ICALP 2015. LNCS, vol. 9135, pp. 69–81. Springer, Heidelberg (2015). https://doi.org/10.1007/978-3-662-47666-6_6
15. Bozzelli, L., La Torre, S.: Decision problems for lower/upper bound parametric timed automata. Formal Methods Syst. Des. **35**(2), 121–151 (2009). https://doi.org/10.1007/s10703-009-0074-0
16. Bundala, D., Ouaknine, J.: Advances in parametric real-time reasoning. In: Csuhaj-Varjú, E., Dietzfelbinger, M., Ésik, Z. (eds.) MFCS 2014. LNCS, vol. 8634, pp. 123–134. Springer, Heidelberg (2014). https://doi.org/10.1007/978-3-662-44522-8_11
17. Courcoubetis, C., Yannakakis, M.: Minimum and maximum delay problems in real-time systems. Formal Methods Syst. Des. **1**(4), 385–415 (1992). https://doi.org/10.1007/BF00709157
18. Daws, C., Tripakis, S.: Model checking of real-time reachability properties using abstractions. In: Steffen, B. (ed.) TACAS 1998. LNCS, vol. 1384, pp. 313–329. Springer, Heidelberg (1998). https://doi.org/10.1007/BFb0054180
19. Hune, T., Romijn, J., Stoelinga, M., Vaandrager, F.W.: Linear parametric model checking of timed automata. JLAP **52–53**, 183–220 (2002). https://doi.org/10.1016/S1567-8326(02)00037-1
20. Jovanović, A., Lime, D., Roux, O.H.: Integer parameter synthesis for timed automata. IEEE Trans. Softw. Eng. **41**(5), 445–461 (2015)
21. Miller, J.S.: Decidability and complexity results for timed automata and semi-linear hybrid automata. In: Lynch, N., Krogh, B.H. (eds.) HSCC 2000. LNCS, vol. 1790, pp. 296–310. Springer, Heidelberg (2000). https://doi.org/10.1007/3-540-46430-1_26
22. Niebert, P., Tripakis, S., Yovine, S.: Minimum-time reachability for timed automata. In: IEEE Mediteranean Control Conference (2000)
23. Sankur, O., Bouyer, P., Markey, N.: Shrinking timed automata. Inf. Comput. **234**, 107–132 (2014). https://doi.org/10.1016/j.ic.2014.01.002
24. Zhang, Z., Nielsen, B., Larsen, K.G.: Distributed algorithms for time optimal reachability analysis. In: Fränzle, M., Markey, N. (eds.) FORMATS 2016. LNCS, vol. 9884, pp. 157–173. Springer, Cham (2016). https://doi.org/10.1007/978-3-319-44878-7_10
25. Zhang, Z., Nielsen, B., Larsen, K.G.: Time optimal reachability analysis using swarm verification. In: SAC, pp. 1634–1640. ACM (2016). https://doi.org/10.1145/2851613.2851828
26. André, É., Bloemen, V., Petrucci, L., van de Pol, J.: Artifact for TACAS 2019 paper: Minimal-Time Synthesis for Parametric Timed Automata (artifact). Figshare (2019). https://doi.org/10.6084/m9.figshare.7813427.v1

Environmentally-Friendly GR(1) Synthesis

Rupak Majumdar[1], Nir Piterman[2], and Anne-Kathrin Schmuck[1(✉)]

[1] MPI-SWS, Kaiserslautern, Germany
akschmuck@mpi-sws.org
[2] University of Leicester, Leicester, UK

Abstract. Many problems in reactive synthesis are stated using two formulas—an *environment assumption* and a *system guarantee*—and ask for an implementation that satisfies the guarantee in environments that satisfy their assumption. Reactive synthesis tools often produce strategies that formally satisfy such specifications by actively preventing an environment assumption from holding. While formally correct, such strategies do not capture the intention of the designer. We introduce an additional requirement in reactive synthesis, *non-conflictingness*, which asks that a system strategy should always allow the environment to fulfill its liveness requirements. We give an algorithm for solving GR(1) synthesis that produces non-conflicting strategies. Our algorithm is given by a 4-nested fixed point in the μ-calculus, in contrast to the usual 3-nested fixed point for GR(1). Our algorithm ensures that, in every environment that satisfies its assumptions on its own, traces of the resulting implementation satisfy both the assumptions and the guarantees. In addition, the asymptotic complexity of our algorithm is the same as that of the usual GR(1) solution. We have implemented our algorithm and show how its performance compares to the usual GR(1) synthesis algorithm.

1 Introduction

Reactive synthesis from temporal logic specifications provides a methodology to automatically construct a system implementation from a declarative specification of correctness. Typically, reactive synthesis starts with a set of requirements on the system and a set of assumptions about the environment. The objective of the synthesis tool is to construct an implementation that ensures all guarantees are met in every environment that satisfies all the assumptions; formally, the synthesis objective is an implication $A \Rightarrow G$. In many synthesis problems, the system can actively influence whether an environment satisfies its assumptions. In such cases, an implementation that prevents the environment from satisfying its assumptions is considered correct for the specification: since the antecedent of the implication $A \Rightarrow G$ does not hold, the property is satisfied.

N. Piterman—Supported by project "d-SynMA" that is funded by the European Research Council (ERC) under the European Union's Horizon 2020 research and innovation programme (grant agreement No. 772459).

T. Vojnar and L. Zhang (Eds.): TACAS 2019, Part II, LNCS 11428, pp. 229–246, 2019.
https://doi.org/10.1007/978-3-030-17465-1_13

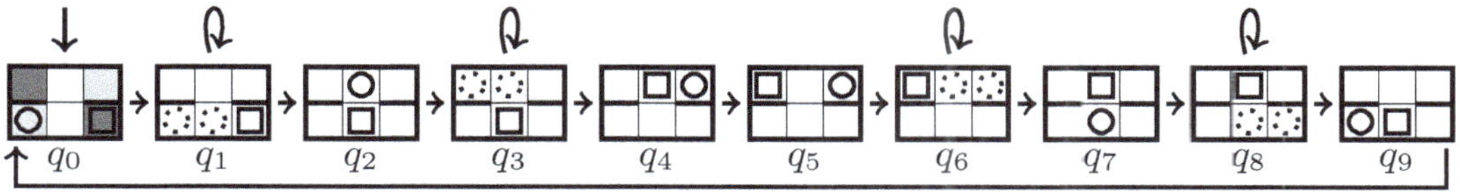

Fig. 1. Pictorial representation of a *desired* strategy for a robot (square) moving in a maze in presence of a moving obstacle (circle). Obstacle and robot start in the lower left and right corner, can move at most one step at a time (to non-occupied cells) and cells that they should visit infinitely often are indicated in light and dark gray (see q_0), respectively. Nodes with self-loops ($q_{\{1,3,6,8\}}$) can be repeated finitely often with the obstacle located at one of the dotted positions.

Such implementations satisfy the letter of the specification but not its intent. Moreover, assumption-violating implementations are not a theoretical curiosity but are regularly produced by synthesis tools such as `slugs` [14]. In recent years, a lot of research has thus focused on how to model environment assumptions [2, 4, 5, 11, 18], so that assumption-violating implementations are ruled out. Existing research either removes the "zero sum" assumption on the game by introducing different levels of co-operation [5], by introducing equilibrium notions inspired by non-zero sum games [7, 16, 20], or by introducing richer quantitative objectives on top of the temporal specifications [1, 3].

Contribution. In this paper, we take an alternative approach. We consider the setting of GR(1) specifications, where assumptions and guarantees are both conjunctions of safety and Büchi properties [6]. GR(1) has emerged as an expressive specification formalism [17, 24, 28] and, unlike full linear temporal logic, synthesis for GR(1) can be implemented in time quadratic in the state/transition space. In our approach, the environment is assumed to satisfy its assumptions provided the system does not prevent this. Conversely, the system is required to pick a strategy that ensures the guarantees whenever the assumptions are satisfied, but additionally ensures *non-conflictingness*: along each finite prefix of a play according to the strategy, there exists the persistent possibility for the environment to play such that its liveness assumptions will be met.

Our main contribution is to show a μ-calculus characterization of winning states (and winning strategies) that rules out system strategies that are winning by preventing the environment from fulfilling its assumptions. Specifically, we provide a 4-nested fixed point that characterizes winning states and strategies that are *non-conflicting* and ensure all guarantees are met if all the assumptions are satisfied. Thus, if the environment promises to satisfy its assumption if allowed, the resulting strategy ensures both the assumption and the guarantee.

Our algorithm does not introduce new notions of winning, or new logics or winning conditions. Moreover, since μ-calculus formulas with d alternations can be computed in $O(n^{\lceil d/2 \rceil})$ time [8, 26], the $O(n^2)$ asymptotic complexity for the new symbolic algorithm is the same as the standard GR(1) algorithm.

Motivating Example. Consider a small two-dimensional maze with 3×2 cells as depicted in Fig. 1, state q_0. A robot (square) and an obstacle (circle) are

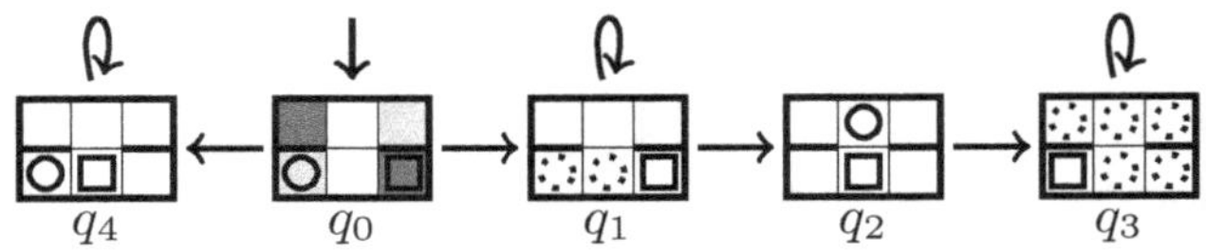

Fig. 2. Pictorial representation of the *GR(1) winning strategy* synthesized by **slugs** for the robot (square) in the game described in Fig. 1.

located in this maze and can move at most one step at a time to non-occupied cells. There is a wall between the lower and upper left cell and the lower and upper right cell. The interaction between the robot and the object is as follows: first the environment chooses where to move the obstacle to, and, after observing the new location of the obstacle, the robot chooses where to move.

Our objective is to synthesize a strategy for the robot s.t. it visits both the upper left and the lower right corner of the maze (indicated in dark gray in Fig. 1, state q_0) infinitely often. Due to the walls in the maze the robot needs to cross the two white middle cells infinitely often to fulfill this task. If we assume an arbitrary, adversarial behavior of the environment (e.g., placing the obstacle in one white cell and never moving it again) this desired robot behavior cannot be enforced. We therefore assume that the obstacle is actually another robot that is required to visit the lower left and the upper right corner of the maze (indicated in light gray in Fig. 1, state q_0) infinitely often. While we do not know the precise strategy of the other robot (i.e., the obstacle), its liveness assumption is enough to infer that the obstacle will always eventually free the white cells. Under this assumption the considered synthesis problem has a solution.

Let us first discuss one intuitive strategy for the robot in this scenario, as depicted in Fig. 1. We start in q_0 with the obstacle (circle) located in the lower left corner and the robot (square) located in the lower right corner. Recall that the obstacle will eventually move towards the upper right corner. The robot can therefore wait until it does so, indicated by q_1. Here, the dotted circles denote possible locations of the obstacle during the (finitely many) repetitions of q_1 by following its self loop. Whenever the obstacle moves to the upper part of the maze, the robot moves into the middle part (q_2). Now it waits until the obstacle reaches its goal in the upper right, which is ensured to happen after a finite number of visits to q_3. When the obstacle reaches the upper right, the robot moves up as well (q_4). Now the robot can freely move to its goal in the upper left (q_5). This process symmetrically repeats for moving back to the respective goals in the lower part of the maze (q_6 to q_9 and then back to q_0). With this strategy, the interaction between environment and system goes on for infinitely many cycles and the robot fulfills its specification.

The outlined synthesis problem can be formalized as a two player game with GR(1) winning condition. When solving this synthesis problem using the tool **slugs** [14], we obtain the strategy depicted in Fig. 2 (not the desired one in Fig. 1). The initial state, denoted by q_0 is the same as in Fig. 1 and if the environment moves the obstacle into the middle passage (q_1) the robot reacts as before; it waits until the object eventually proceeds to the upper part of the maze (q_2). However, after this happens the robot takes the chance to simply move to the lower left cell of the maze and stays there forever (q_3). By this, the robot prevents the environment from fulfilling its objective. Similarly, if the obstacle does not immediately start moving in q_0, the robot takes the chance to place itself in the middle passage and stays there forever (q_4). This obviously prevents the environment from fulfilling its liveness properties.

In contrast, when using our new algorithm to solve the given synthesis problem, we obtain the strategy given in Fig. 1, which satisfies the guarantees while allowing the environment assumptions to be satisfied.

Related Work. Our algorithm is inspired by supervisory controller synthesis for non-terminating processes [23,27], resulting in a fixed-point algorithm over a Rabin-Büchi automaton. This algorithm has been simplified for two interacting Büchi automata in [22] without proof. We adapt this algorithm to GR(1) games and provide a new, self-contained proof in the framework of two-player games, which is distinct from the supervisory controller synthesis setting (see [13,25] for a recent comparison of both frameworks).

The problem of correctly handling assumptions in synthesis has recently gained attention in the reactive synthesis community [4]. As our work does not assume precise knowledge about the environment strategy (or the ability to impose the latter), it is distinct from cooperative approaches such as assume-guarantee [9] or rational synthesis [16]. It is closest related to obliging games [10], cooperative reactive synthesis [5], and assume-admissible synthesis [7]. Obliging games [10] incorporate a similar notion of non-conflictingness as our work, but do not condition winning of the system on the environment fulfilling the assumptions. This makes obliging games harder to win. Cooperative reactive synthesis [5] tries to find a winning strategy enforcing $A \cap G$. If this specification is not realizable, it is relaxed and the obtained system strategy enforces the guarantees if the environment cooperates "in the right way". Instead, our work always assumes the same form of cooperation; coinciding with just one cooperation lever in [5]. Assume-admissible synthesis [7] for two players results in two individual synthesis problems. Given that both have a solution, only implementing the system strategy ensures that the game will be won if the environment plays *admissible*. This is comparable to the view taken in this paper, however, assuming that the environment plays *admissible* is stronger then our assumption on an environment attaining its liveness properties if not prevented from doing so. Moreover, we only need so solve one synthesis problem, instead of two. However, it should be noted that [5,7,10] handle ω-regular assumptions and guarantees. We focus on the practically important GR(1) fragment and our method better leverages the computational benefits for this fragment.

All proofs of our results and additional examples can be found in the extended version [21]. We further acknowledge that the same problem was independently solved in the context of reactive robot mission plans [12] which was brought to our attention only shortly before the final submission of this paper.

2 Two Player Games and the Synthesis Problem

2.1 Two Player Games

Formal Languages. Let Σ be a finite alphabet. We write Σ^*, Σ^+, and Σ^ω for the sets of finite words, non-empty finite words, and infinite words over Σ. We write $w \leq v$ (resp., $w < v$) if w is a prefix of v (resp., a strict prefix of v). The set of all prefixes of a word $w \in \Sigma^\omega$ is denoted $\text{pfx}(w) \subseteq \Sigma^*$. For $L \subseteq \Sigma^*$, we have $L \subseteq \text{pfx}(L)$. For $\mathcal{L} \subseteq \Sigma^\omega$ we denote by $\overline{\mathcal{L}}$ its complement $\Sigma^\omega \setminus \mathcal{L}$.

Game Graphs and Strategies. A *two player game graph* $H = (Q^0, Q^1, \delta^0, \delta^1, q_0)$ consists of two finite disjoint state sets Q^0 and Q^1, two transition functions $\delta^0 : Q^0 \to 2^{Q^1}$ and $\delta^1 : Q^1 \to 2^{Q^0}$, and an initial state $q_0 \in Q^0$. We write $Q = Q^0 \cup Q^1$. Given a game graph H, a *strategy* for player 0 is a function $f^0 : (Q^0Q^1)^*Q^0 \to Q^1$; it is *memoryless* if $f^0(\nu q^0) = f^1(q^0)$ for all $\nu \in (Q^0Q^1)^*$ and all $q^0 \in Q^0$. A *strategy* $f^1 : (Q^0Q^1)^+ \to Q^0$ for player 1 is defined analogously. The infinite sequence $\pi \in (Q^0Q^1)^\omega$ is called a play over H if $\pi(0) = q_0$ and for all $k \in \mathbb{N}$ holds that $\pi(2k+1) \in \delta^0(\pi(2k))$ and $\pi(2k+2) \in \delta^1(\pi(2k+1))$; π is compliant with f^0 and/or f^1 if additionally holds that $f^0(\pi|_{[0,2k]}) = \pi(2k+1)$ and/or $f^1(\pi|_{[0,2k+1]}) = \pi(2k+2)$. We denote by $\mathcal{L}(H, f^0)$, $\mathcal{L}(H, f^1)$ and $\mathcal{L}(H, f^0, f^1)$ the set of plays over H compliant with f^0, f^1, and both f^0 and f^1, respectively.

Winning Conditions. We consider winning conditions defined over sets of states of a given game graph H. Given $F \subseteq Q$, we say a play π satisfies the *Büchi condition* F if $\text{Inf}(\pi) \cap F \neq \emptyset$, where $\text{Inf}(\pi) = \{q \in Q \mid \pi(k) = q \text{ for infinitely many } k \in \mathbb{N}\}$. Given a set $\mathcal{F} = \{F_1, \ldots, F_m\}$, where each $F_i \subseteq Q$, we say a play π satisfies the *generalized Büchi condition* $\mathcal{F}$ if $\text{Inf}(\pi) \cap F_i \neq \emptyset$ for each $i \in [1; m]$. We additionally consider generalized reactivity winning conditions with rank 1 (GR(1) winning conditions in short). Given two generalized Büchi conditions $\mathcal{F}^0 = \{F_1^0, \ldots, F_m^0\}$ and $\mathcal{F}^1 = \{F_1^1, \ldots, F_n^1\}$, a play π satisfies the GR(1) condition if either $\text{Inf}(\pi) \cap F_i^0 = \emptyset$ for some $i \in [1; m]$ or $\text{Inf}(\pi) \cap F_j^1 \neq \emptyset$ for each $j \in [1; m]$. That is, whenever the play satisfies $\mathcal{F}^0$, it also satisfies $\mathcal{F}^1$. We use the tuples (H, F), $(H, \mathcal{F})$ and $(H, \mathcal{F}^0, \mathcal{F}^1)$ to denote a Büchi, generalized Büchi and GR(1) game over H, respectively, and collect all winning plays in these games in the sets $\mathcal{L}(H, F)$, $\mathcal{L}(H, \mathcal{F})$ and $\mathcal{L}(H, \mathcal{F}^0, \mathcal{F}^1)$. A strategy f^l is *winning* for player l in a Büchi, generalized Büchi, or GR(1) game, if $\mathcal{L}(H, f^l)$ is contained in the respective set of winning plays.

Set Transformers on Games. Given a game graph H, we define the existential, universal, and player 0-, and player 1-controllable pre-operators. Let $P \subseteq Q$.

$$\mathsf{Pre}^{\exists}(P) = \{q^0 \in Q^0 | \delta^0(q^0) \cap P \neq \emptyset\} \cup \{q^1 \in Q^1 | \delta^1(q^1) \cap P \neq \emptyset\}, \text{ and} \tag{1}$$

$$\mathsf{Pre}^{\forall}(P) = \{q^0 \in Q^0 | \delta^0(q^0) \subseteq P\} \cup \{q^1 \in Q^1 | \delta^1(q^1) \subseteq P\}, \tag{2}$$

$$\mathsf{Pre}^{0}(P) = \{q^0 \in Q^0 | \delta^0(q^0) \cap P \neq \emptyset\} \cup \{q^1 \in Q^1 | \delta^1(q^1) \subseteq P\}, \text{ and} \tag{3}$$

$$\mathsf{Pre}^1(P) = \{q^0 \in Q^0 | \delta^0(q^0) \subseteq P\} \cup \{q^1 \in Q^1 | \delta^1(q^1) \cap P \neq \emptyset\}. \tag{4}$$

Observe that $Q \setminus \mathsf{Pre}^{\exists}(P) = \mathsf{Pre}^{\forall}(Q \setminus P)$ and $Q \setminus \mathsf{Pre}^1(P) = \mathsf{Pre}^0(Q \setminus P)$.

We combine the operators in (1)–(4) to define a *conditional predecessor* $\mathsf{CondPre}$ and its dual $\overline{\mathsf{CondPre}}$ for sets $P, P' \subseteq Q$ by

$$\mathsf{CondPre}(P, P') := \mathsf{Pre}^{\exists}(P) \cap \mathsf{Pre}^1(P \cup P'), \text{ and} \tag{5}$$

$$\overline{\mathsf{CondPre}}(P, P') := \mathsf{Pre}^{\forall}(P) \cup \mathsf{Pre}^0(P \cap P'). \tag{6}$$

We see that $Q \setminus \mathsf{CondPre}(P, P') = \overline{\mathsf{CondPre}}(Q \setminus P, Q \setminus P')$.

μ-Calculus. We use the μ-calculus as a convenient logical notation used to define a symbolic algorithm (i.e., an algorithm that manipulates sets of states rather then individual states) for computing a set of states with a particular property over a given game graph H. The formulas of the μ-calculus, interpreted over a two-player game graph H, are given by the grammar

$$\varphi ::= p \mid X \mid \varphi \cup \varphi \mid \varphi_1 \cap \varphi_2 \mid pre(\varphi) \mid \mu X.\varphi \mid \nu X.\varphi$$

where p ranges over subsets of Q, X ranges over a set of formal variables, $pre \in \{\mathsf{Pre}^{\exists}, \mathsf{Pre}^{\forall}, \mathsf{Pre}^0, \mathsf{Pre}^1, \mathsf{CondPre}, \overline{\mathsf{CondPre}}\}$ ranges over set transformers, and μ and ν denote, respectively, the least and greatest fixpoint of the functional defined as $X \mapsto \varphi(X)$. Since the operations $\cup$, $\cap$, and the set transformers pre are all monotonic, the fixpoints are guaranteed to exist. A μ-calculus formula evaluates to a set of states over H, and the set can be computed by induction over the structure of the formula, where the fixpoints are evaluated by iteration. We omit the (standard) semantics of formulas [19].

2.2 The Considered Synthesis Problem

The GR(1) synthesis problem asks to synthesize a winning strategy for the system player (player 1) for a given GR(1) game $(H, \mathcal{F}_{\mathcal{A}}, \mathcal{F}_{\mathcal{G}})$ or determine that no such strategy exists. This can be equivalently represented in terms of ω-languages, by asking for a system strategy f^1 over H s.t.

$$\emptyset \neq \mathcal{L}(H, f^1) \subseteq \overline{\mathcal{L}(H, \mathcal{F}_{\mathcal{A}})} \cup \mathcal{L}(H, \mathcal{F}_{\mathcal{G}}).$$

That is, the system wins on plays $\pi \in \mathcal{L}(H, f^1)$ if either $\pi \notin \mathcal{L}(H, \mathcal{F}_{\mathcal{A}})$ or $\pi \in \mathcal{L}(H, \mathcal{F}_{\mathcal{A}}) \cap \mathcal{L}(H, \mathcal{F}_{\mathcal{G}})$. The only mechanism to ensure that *sufficiently* many computations will result from f^1 is the usage of the environment input, which enforces a minimal branching structure. However, the system could still win this game by *falsifying the assumptions*; i.e., by generating plays $\pi \notin \mathcal{L}(H, \mathcal{F}_{\mathcal{A}})$ that prevent the environment from fulfilling its liveness properties.

We suggest an alternative view to the usage of the assumptions on the environment $\mathcal{F}_{\mathcal{A}}$ in a GR(1) game. The condition $\mathcal{F}_{\mathcal{A}}$ can be interpreted abstractly as modeling an underlying mechanism that ensures that the environment player

(player 0) generates only inputs (possibly in response to observed outputs) that conform with the given assumption. In this context, we would like to ensure that the system (player 1) allows the environment, as much as possible, to fulfill its liveness and only *restricts* the environment behavior if needed to enforce the guarantees. We achieve this by forcing the system player to ensure that the environment is always able to play such that it fulfills its liveness, i.e.

$$\mathrm{pfx}(\mathcal{L}(H, f^1)) = \mathrm{pfx}(\mathcal{L}(H, f^1) \cap \mathcal{L}(H, \mathcal{F}_\mathcal{A}))\,.$$

As the $\supseteq$-inclusion trivially holds, the constraint is given by the $\subseteq$-inclusion. Intuitively, the latter holds if every finite play α compliant with f^1 over H can be extended (by a suitable environment strategy) to an infinite play π compliant with f^1 that fulfills the environment liveness assumptions. It is easy to see that not every solution to the GR(1) game $(H, \mathcal{F}_\mathcal{A}, \mathcal{F}_\mathcal{G})$ (in the classical sense) supplies this additional requirement. We therefore propose to synthesize a system strategy f^1 with the above properties, as summarized in the following problem statement.

Problem 1. Given a GR(1) game $(H, \mathcal{F}_\mathcal{A}, \mathcal{F}_\mathcal{G})$ synthesize a system strategy f^1

$$\text{s.t.}\quad \emptyset \neq \mathcal{L}(H, f^1) \subseteq \overline{\mathcal{L}(H, \mathcal{F}_\mathcal{A})} \cup \mathcal{L}(H, \mathcal{F}_\mathcal{G}), \tag{7a}$$

$$\text{and}\quad \mathrm{pfx}(\mathcal{L}(H, f^1)) = \mathrm{pfx}(\mathcal{L}(H, f^1) \cap \mathcal{L}(H, \mathcal{F}_\mathcal{A})) \tag{7b}$$

both hold, or verify that no such system strategy exists. □

Problem 1 asks for a strategy f^1 s.t. every play π compliant with f^1 over H fulfills the system guarantees, i.e., $\pi \in \mathcal{L}(H, \mathcal{F}_\mathcal{G})$, if the environment fulfills its liveness properties, i.e., if $\pi \in \mathcal{L}(H, \mathcal{F}_\mathcal{A})$ (from (7a)), while the latter always remains possible (by a suitably playing environment) due to (7b). Inspired by algorithms solving the supervisory controller synthesis problem for non-terminating processes [23,27], we propose a solution to Problem 1 in terms of a vectorized 4-nested fixed-point in the remaining part of this paper. We show that Problem 1 can be solved by a finite-memory strategy, if a solution exists.

We note that (7b) is not a linear time but a branching time property and can therefore not be "compiled away" into a different GR(1) or even ω-regular objective. Satisfaction of (7b) requires checking whether the set $F_\mathcal{A}$ remains reachable from any reachable state in the game graph realizing $\mathcal{L}(H, f^1)$[1].

3 Algorithmic Solution for Singleton Winning Conditions

We first consider the GR(1) game $(H, \mathcal{F}_\mathcal{A}, \mathcal{F}_\mathcal{G})$ with singleton winning conditions $\mathcal{F}_\mathcal{A} = \{F_\mathcal{A}\}$ and $\mathcal{F}_\mathcal{G} = \{F_\mathcal{G}\}$, i.e., $n = m = 1$. It is well known that a system winning strategy f^1 for this game can be synthesized by solving a three color parity game over H. This can be expressed by the μ-calculus formula (see [15])

$$\varphi_3 := \nu Z\ .\ \mu Y\ .\ \nu X\ .\ (F_\mathcal{G} \cap \mathsf{Pre}^1(Z)) \cup \mathsf{Pre}^1(Y) \cup (Q \setminus F_\mathcal{A} \cap \mathsf{Pre}^1(X)). \tag{8}$$

[1] It can indeed be expressed by the CTL* formula $\mathsf{AGEF}F_\mathcal{A}$ (see [13], Sect. 3.3.2).

It follows that $q_0 \in [\![\varphi_3]\!]$ if and only if the synthesis problem has a solution and the winning strategy f^1 is obtained from a ranking argument over the sets computed during the evaluation of (8).

To obtain a system strategy f^1 solving Problem 1 instead, we propose to extend (8) to a 4-nested fixed-point expressed by the μ-calculus formula

$$\varphi_4 = \nu Z \, . \, \mu Y \, . \, \nu X \, . \, \mu W \, . \\ (F_{\mathcal{G}} \cap \mathsf{Pre}^1(Z)) \;\cup\; \mathsf{Pre}^1(Y) \;\cup\; ((Q \setminus F_{\mathcal{A}}) \cap \mathsf{CondPre}(W, X \setminus F_{\mathcal{A}})) \, . \tag{9}$$

Compared to (8) this adds an inner-most largest fixed-point and substitutes the last controllable pre-operator by the conditional one. Intuitively, this distinguishes between states from which player 1 can force visiting $F_{\mathcal{G}}$ and states from which player 1 can force avoiding $F_{\mathcal{A}}$. This is in contrast to (8) and allows to exclude strategies that allow player 1 to win by falsifying the assumptions.

The remainder of this section shows that $q_0 \in [\![\varphi_4]\!]$ if and only if Problem 1 has a solution and the winning strategy f^1 fulfilling (7a) and (7b) can be obtained from a ranking argument over the sets computed during the evaluation of (9).

Soundness

We prove soundness of (9) by showing that every state $q \in [\![\varphi_4]\!]$ is winning for the system player. In view of Problem 1 this requires to show that there exists a system strategy f^1 s.t. all plays starting in a state $q \in [\![\varphi_4]\!]$ and evolving in accordance to f^1 result in an infinite play that fulfills (7a) and (7b).

We start by defining f^1 from a ranking argument over the iterations of (9). Consider the last iteration of the fixed-point in (9) over Z. As (9) terminates after this iteration we have $Z = Z^\infty = [\![\varphi_4]\!]$. Assume that the fixed point over Y is reached after k iterations. If Y^i is the set obtained after the i-th iteration, we have that $Z^\infty = \bigcup_{i=0}^{k} Y^i$ with $Y^i \subseteq Y^{i+1}$, $Y^0 = \emptyset$ and $Y^k = Z^\infty$. Furthermore, let $X^i = Y^i$ denote the fixed-point of the iteration over X resulting in Y^i and denote by W^i_j the set obtained in the jth iteration over W performed while using the value X^i for X and Y^{i-1} for Y. Then it holds that $Y^i = X^i = \bigcup_{j=0}^{l_i} W^i_j$ with $W^i_j \subseteq W^i_{j+1}$, $W^i_0 = \emptyset$ and $W^i_{l_i} = Y^i$ for all $i \in [0; k]$.

Using these sets, we define a ranking for every state $q \in Z^\infty$ s.t.

$$\mathsf{rank}(q) = (i, j) \text{ iff } q \in \left(Y^i \setminus Y^{i-1}\right) \cap \left(W^i_j \setminus W^i_{j-1}\right) \text{ for } i, j > 0. \tag{10}$$

We order ranks lexicographically. It further holds that (see [21])

$$q \in D \quad \Leftrightarrow \quad \mathsf{rank}(q) = (1,1) \qquad \Leftrightarrow \quad q \in F_{\mathcal{G}} \cap Z^\infty \tag{11a}$$

$$q \in E^i \quad \Leftrightarrow \quad \mathsf{rank}(q) = (i,1) \wedge i > 1 \qquad \Leftrightarrow \quad q \in (F_{\mathcal{A}} \setminus F_{\mathcal{G}}) \cap Z^\infty \tag{11b}$$

$$q \in R^i_j \quad \Leftrightarrow \quad \mathsf{rank}(q) = (i,j) \wedge j > 1 \qquad \Leftrightarrow \quad q \in (Z^\infty \setminus (F_{\mathcal{A}} \cup F_{\mathcal{G}})), \tag{11c}$$

where D, E^i and R^i_j denote the sets *added* to the winning state set by the first, second and third term of (9), respectively, in the corresponding iteration.

Figure 3 (left) shows a schematic representation of this construction for an example with $k = 3$, $l_1 = 4$, $l_2 = 2$ and $l_3 = 3$. The set $D = F_{\mathcal{G}} \cap Z^\infty$ is

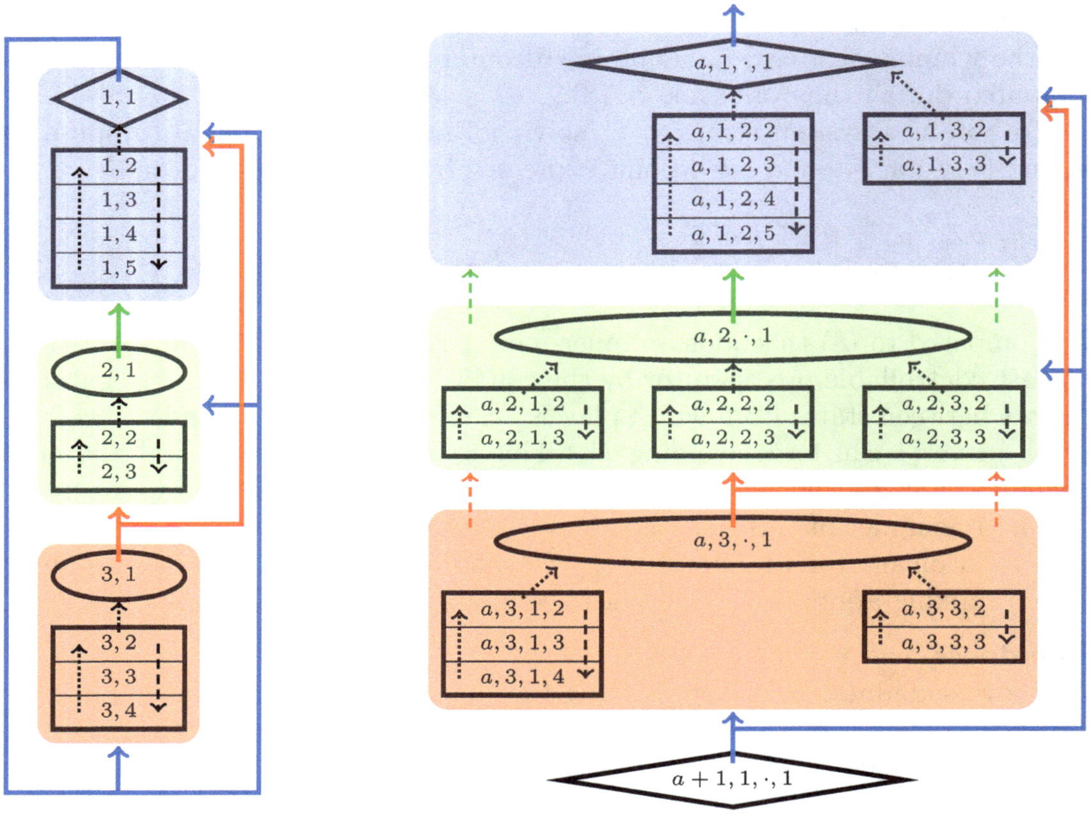

Fig. 3. Schematic representation of the ranking defined in (10) (left) and in (16) (right). Diamond, ellipses and rectangles represent the sets D, E^i and R^i_j, while blue, green and red indicate the sets Y^1, $Y^2 \setminus Y^1$ and $Y^3 \setminus Y^2$ (annotated by $^a/^{ab}$ for the right figure). Labels (i, j) and (a, i, b, j) indicate that all states q associated with this set fulfill $\mathsf{rank}(q) = (i, j)$ and $^{ab}\mathsf{rank}(q) = (i, j)$, respectively. Solid, colored arcs indicate system-enforceable moves, dotted arcs indicate existence of environment or system transitions and dashed arcs indicate possible existence of environment transitions. (Color figure online)

represented by the diamond at the top where the label $(1, 1)$ denotes the associated rank (see (11a)). The ellipses represent the sets $E^i \subseteq (F_{\mathcal{A}} \setminus F_{\mathcal{G}}) \cap Z^\infty$, where the corresponding $i > 1$ is indicated by the associated rank $(i, 1)$. Due to the use of the controllable pre-operator in the first and second term of (9), it is ensured that progress out of D and E^i can be enforced by the system, indicated by the solid arrows. This is in contrast to all states in $R^i_j \subseteq Z^\infty \setminus F_{\mathcal{A}} \setminus F_{\mathcal{G}}$, which are represented by the rectangular shapes in Fig. 3 (left). These states allow the environment to increase the ranking (dashed lines) as long as $Z^\infty \setminus F_{\mathcal{A}} \setminus F_{\mathcal{G}}$ is not left and there exists a possible move to decrease the j-rank (dotted lines). While this does not strictly enforce progress, we see that whenever the environment plays such that states in $F_{\mathcal{A}}$ (i.e., the ellipses) are visited infinitely often (i.e., the environment fulfills its assumptions), the system can enforce progress w.r.t. the defined ranking and states in $F_{\mathcal{G}}$ (i.e., the diamond shape) is eventually visited. The system is restricted to take the existing solid or dotted transitions in

Fig. 3 (left). With this, it is easy to see that the constructed strategy is winning if the environment fulfills its assumptions, i.e., (7a) holds. However, to ensure that (7b) also holds, we need an additional requirement. This is necessary as the used construction also allows plays to cycle through the blue region of Fig. 3 (left) only, and by this not surely visiting states in $F_{\mathcal{A}}$ infinitely often. However, if $\mathcal{L}(H, F_{\mathcal{G}}) \subseteq \mathcal{L}(H, F_{\mathcal{A}})$ we see that (7b) holds as well. It should be noted that the latter is a sufficient condition which can be easily checked symbolically on the problem instance but not a necessary one.

Based on the ranking in (10) we define a memory-less system strategy $f^1 : Q^1 \cap Z^\infty \to Q^0 \subseteq \delta^1$ s.t. the rank is always decreased, i.e.,

$$q' = f^1(q) \Rightarrow \begin{cases} \mathsf{rank}(q') < \mathsf{rank}(q), & \mathsf{rank}(q) > (1,1) \\ q' \in Z^\infty, & \text{otherwise} \end{cases} \tag{12}$$

The next theorem shows that this strategy indeed solves Problem 1.

Theorem 1. *Let $(H, \mathcal{F}_{\mathcal{A}}, \mathcal{F}_{\mathcal{G}})$ be a GR(1) game with singleton winning conditions $\mathcal{F}_{\mathcal{A}} = \{F_{\mathcal{A}}\}$ and $\mathcal{F}_{\mathcal{G}} = \{F_{\mathcal{G}}\}$. Suppose f^1 is the system strategy in* (12) *based on the ranking in* (10)*. Then it holds for all $q \in [\![\varphi_4]\!]$ that*[2]

$$\mathcal{L}_q(H, f^1) \subseteq \overline{\mathcal{L}_q(H, \mathcal{F}_{\mathcal{A}})} \cup \mathcal{L}_q(H, \mathcal{F}_{\mathcal{G}}), \tag{13a}$$

$$\mathcal{L}_q(H, f^1) \cap \mathcal{L}_q(H, \mathcal{F}_{\mathcal{G}}) \neq \emptyset, \text{ and} \tag{13b}$$

$$\mathcal{L}_q(H, \mathcal{F}_{\mathcal{G}}) \subseteq \mathcal{L}_q(H, \mathcal{F}_{\mathcal{A}}) \Rightarrow \mathrm{pfx}(\mathcal{L}_q(H, f^1)) = \mathrm{pfx}(\mathcal{L}_q(H, f^1) \cap \mathcal{L}_q(H, \mathcal{F}_{\mathcal{A}})). \tag{13c}$$

Completeness

We show completeness of (9) by establishing that every state $q \in Q \setminus [\![\varphi_4]\!] = [\![\overline{\varphi_4}]\!]$ is losing for the system player. In view of Problem 1 this requires to show that for all $q \in [\![\overline{\varphi_4}]\!]$ and all system strategies f^1 either (7a) or (7b) does not hold. This is formalized in [21] by first negating the fixed-point in (9) and deriving the induced ranking of this negated fixed-point. Using this ranking, we first show that the environment can (i) render the negated winning set $\overline{Z}^\infty$ invariant and (ii) can always enforce the play to visit $F_{\mathcal{G}}$ only finitely often, resulting in a violation of the guarantees. Using these observations we finally show that whenever (7a) holds for an arbitrary system strategy f^1 starting in $[\![\overline{\varphi_4}]\!]$, then (7b) cannot hold. With this, completeness, as formalized in the following theorem, directly follows.

Theorem 2. *Let $(H, \mathcal{F}_{\mathcal{A}}, \mathcal{F}_{\mathcal{G}})$ be a GR(1) game with singleton winning conditions $\mathcal{F}_{\mathcal{A}} = \{F_{\mathcal{A}}\}$ and $\mathcal{F}_{\mathcal{G}} = \{F_{\mathcal{G}}\}$. Then it holds for all $q \in [\![\overline{\varphi_4}]\!]$ and all system strategies f^1 over H that either*

$$\emptyset \neq \mathcal{L}_q(H, f^1) \subseteq \overline{\mathcal{L}_q(H, \mathcal{F}_{\mathcal{A}})} \cup \mathcal{L}_q(H, \mathcal{F}_{\mathcal{G}}), \text{ or} \tag{14a}$$

$$\mathrm{pfx}(\mathcal{L}_q(H, f^1)) = \mathrm{pfx}(\mathcal{L}_q(H, f^1) \cap \mathcal{L}_q(H, \mathcal{F}_{\mathcal{A}})) \text{ does not hold.} \tag{14b}$$

[2] Given a state $q \in Q = Q^0 \cup Q^1$ we use the subscript q to denote that the respective set of plays is defined by using q as the initial state of H.

A Solution for Problem 1
We note that the additional assumption in Theorem 1 is required only to ensure that the resulting strategy fulfills (7b). Suppose that this assumption holds for the initial state q_0 of H. That is, consider a GR(1) game $(H, \mathcal{F}_\mathcal{A}, \mathcal{F}_\mathcal{G})$ with singleton winning conditions $\mathcal{F}_\mathcal{A} = \{F_\mathcal{A}\}$ and $\mathcal{F}_\mathcal{G} = \{F_\mathcal{G}\}$ s.t. $\mathcal{L}(H, F_\mathcal{G}) \subseteq \mathcal{L}(H, F_\mathcal{A})$. Then it follows from Theorem 2 that Problem 1 has a solution iff $q_0 \in [\![\varphi_4]\!]$. Furthermore, if $q_0 \in [\![\varphi_4]\!]$, based on the intermediate values maintained for the computation of φ_4 in (10) and the ranking defined in (12), we can construct f^1 that wins the GR(1) condition in (7a) and is non-conflicting, as in (7b).

We can check symbolically whether $\mathcal{L}(H, F_\mathcal{G}) \subseteq \mathcal{L}(H, F_\mathcal{A})$. For this we construct a game graph H' from H by removing all states in $F_\mathcal{A}$, and then check whether $\mathcal{L}(H', F_\mathcal{G})$ is empty. The latter is decidable in logarithmic space and polynomial time. If this check fails, then $\mathcal{L}(H, F_\mathcal{G}) \not\subseteq \mathcal{L}(H, F_\mathcal{A})$. Furthermore, we can replace $\mathcal{L}(H, \mathcal{F}_\mathcal{G})$ in (7a) by $\mathcal{L}(H, \mathcal{F}_\mathcal{G}) \cap \mathcal{L}(H, \mathcal{F}_\mathcal{A})$ without affecting the restriction (7a) imposes on the choice of f^1. Given singleton winning conditions $F_\mathcal{G}$ and $F_\mathcal{A}$, we see that $\mathcal{L}(H, F_\mathcal{G}) \cap \mathcal{L}(H, F_\mathcal{A}) = \mathcal{L}(H, \{F_\mathcal{G}, F_\mathcal{A}\})$ and it trivially holds that $\mathcal{L}(H, \{F_\mathcal{G}, F_\mathcal{A}\}) \subseteq \mathcal{L}(H, F_\mathcal{A})$. That is, we fulfill the conditional by replacing the system guarantee $\mathcal{L}(H, \mathcal{F}_\mathcal{G})$ by $\mathcal{L}(H, \{F_\mathcal{G}, F_\mathcal{A}\})$. However, this results in a GR(1) synthesis problem with $m = 1$ and $n = 2$, which we discuss next.

4 Algorithmic Solution for GR(1) Winning Conditions

We now consider a general GR(1) game $(H, \mathcal{F}_\mathcal{A}, \mathcal{F}_\mathcal{G})$ with $\mathcal{F}_\mathcal{A} = \{{}^1F_\mathcal{A}, \ldots, {}^mF_\mathcal{A}\}$ and $\mathcal{F}_\mathcal{G} = \{{}^1F_\mathcal{G}, \ldots, {}^nF_\mathcal{G}\}$ s.t. $n, m > 1$. The known fixed-point for solving GR(1) games in [6] rewrites the three nested fixed-point in (8) in a vectorized version, which induces an order on the guarantee sets in $\mathcal{F}_\mathcal{G}$ and adds a disjunction over all assumption sets in $\mathcal{F}_\mathcal{A}$ to every line of this vectorized fixed-point. Adapting the same idea to the 4-nested fixed-point algorithm (9) results in

$$\varphi_4 = \nu \begin{bmatrix} {}^1Z \\ {}^2Z \\ \vdots \\ {}^nZ \end{bmatrix} . \begin{bmatrix} \mu\ {}^1Y \ . \ \left(\bigvee_{b=1}^m \ \nu\ {}^{1b}X \ . \ \mu\ {}^{1b}W\ {}^{1b}\Omega\right) \\ \mu\ {}^2Y \ . \ \left(\bigvee_{b=1}^m \ \nu\ {}^{2b}X \ . \ \mu\ {}^{2b}W\ {}^{2b}\Omega\right) \\ \vdots \\ \mu\ {}^nY \ . \ \left(\bigvee_{b=1}^m \ \nu\ {}^{nb}X \ . \ \mu\ {}^{nb}W\ {}^{nb}\Omega\right) \end{bmatrix}, \tag{15}$$

where, ${}^{ab}\Omega = ({}^aF_\mathcal{G} \cap \mathsf{Pre}^1({}^{a^+}Z)) \cup \mathsf{Pre}^1({}^aY) \cup (Q \setminus {}^bF_\mathcal{A} \cap \mathsf{CondPre}(W, X \setminus {}^bF_\mathcal{A}))$ and a^+ denotes $(a \mod n) + 1$.

The remainder of this section shows how soundness and completeness carries over from the 4-nested fixed-point algorithm (9) to its vectorized version in (15).

Soundness and Completeness
We refer to intermediate sets obtained during the computation of the fixpoints by similar notations as in Sect. 3. For example, the set ${}^aY^i$ is the i-th approximation of the fixpoint computing ${}^aY$ and ${}^{ab}W^i_j$ is the j-th approximation of ${}^{ab}W$ while computing the i-th approximation of ${}^aY$, i.e., computing ${}^aY^i$ and using ${}^aY^{i-1}$.

Similar to the above, we define a mode-based rank for every state $q \in {}^aZ^\infty$; we track the currently chased guarantee $a \in [1;n]$ (similar to [6]) and the currently avoided assumption set $b \in [1,m]$ as an additional internal mode. In analogy to (10) we define

$$ {}^{ab}\mathsf{rank}(q) = (i,j) \text{ iff } q \in \left({}^aY^i \setminus {}^aY^{i-1}\right) \cap \left({}^{ab}W^i_j \setminus {}^{ab}W^i_{j-1}\right) \text{ for } i,j > 0. \quad (16) $$

Again, we order ranks lexicographically, and, in analogy to (11a), (11b) and (11c), we have

$$ \begin{aligned} q \in {}^aD &\Leftrightarrow {}^a\mathsf{rank}(q) = (1,1) && \Rightarrow q \in {}^aF_{\mathcal{G}}, && (17a)\\ q \in {}^aE^i &\Leftrightarrow {}^a\mathsf{rank}(q) = (i,1) \wedge i > 1, && && (17b)\\ q \in {}^{ab}R^i_j &\Leftrightarrow {}^{ab}\mathsf{rank}(q) = (i,j) \wedge j > 1 && \Rightarrow q \notin {}^bF_{\mathcal{A}}. && (17c) \end{aligned} $$

The sets ${}^aY^i$, ${}^{ab}W^i_j$, ${}^aD$, ${}^aE^i$ and ${}^{ab}R^i_j$ are interpreted in direct analogy to Sect. 3, where a and b annotate the used line and conjunct in (15).

Figure 3 (right) shows a schematic representation of the ranking for an example with ${}^ak = 3$, ${}^{a1}l_1 = 0$, ${}^{a2}l_1 = 4$, ${}^{a3}l_1 = 2$, ${}^al_2 = 2$, ${}^{a1}l_3 = 3$, ${}^{a2}l_3 = 0$, and ${}^{a3}l_3 = 2$. Again, the set ${}^aD \subseteq {}^aF_{\mathcal{G}}$ is represented by the diamond at the top of the figure. Similarly, all ellipses represent sets ${}^aE^i$ added in the i-th iteration over line a of (15). Again, progress out of ellipses can be enforced by the system, indicated by the solid arrows leaving those shapes. However, this might not preserve the current b mode. It might be the environment choosing which assumption to avoid next. Further, the environment might choose to change the b mode along with decreasing the i-rank, as indicated by the colored dashed lines[3]. Finally, the interpretation of the sets represented by rectangular shapes in Fig. 3 (right), corresponding to (17c), is in direct analogy to the case with singleton winning conditions. It should be noticed that this is the only place where we preserve the current b-mode when constructing a strategy.

Using this intuition we define a system strategy that uses enforceable and existing transitions to decrease the rank if possible and preserves the current a mode until the diamond shape is reached. The b mode is only preserved within rectangular sets. This is formalized by a strategy

$$ f^1 : \textstyle\bigcup_{a\in[1;n]} \left((Q^1 \cap {}^aZ^\infty) \times a \times [1;m]\right) \rightarrow Q^0 \times [1;n] \times [1;m] \quad (18a) $$

s.t. $(q', \cdot, \cdot) = f^1(q, \cdot, \cdot)$ implies $q' \in \delta^1(q)$ and $(q', a', b') = f^1(q, a, b)$ implies

$$ \begin{cases} q' \in {}^{a^+}Z^\infty \wedge a' = a^+, & {}^{ab}\mathsf{rank}(q) = (1,1)\\ {}^{a'b'}\mathsf{rank}(q') \leq (i-1,\cdot) \wedge a' = a, & {}^{ab}\mathsf{rank}(q) = (i,1), i > 1\\ {}^{a'b'}\mathsf{rank}(q') \leq (i,j-1) \wedge a' = a \wedge b' = b, & {}^{ab}\mathsf{rank}(q) = (i,j), j > 1 \end{cases} . \quad (18b) $$

[3] The strategy extraction in (18a) and (18b) prevents the system from choosing a different b mode. The strategy choice could be optimized w.r.t. fast progress towards ${}^aF_{\mathcal{G}}$ in such cases.

We say that a play π over H is compliant with f^1 if there exist mode traces $\alpha \in [1;n]^\omega$ and $\beta \in [1;m]^\omega$ s.t. for all $k \in \mathbb{N}$ holds $(\pi(2k+2), \alpha(2k+2), \beta(2k+2)) = f^1(\pi(2k+1), \alpha(2k+1), \beta(2k+1))$, and (i) $\alpha(2k+1) = \alpha(2k)^+$ if ${}^{ab}\mathsf{rank}(\pi(2k+1)) = (1,1)$, (ii) $\alpha(2k+1) = \alpha(2k)$ if ${}^{ab}\mathsf{rank}(\pi(2k+1)) = (i,1), i > 1$, and (iii) $\alpha(2k+1) = \alpha(2k)$ and $\beta(2k+1) = \beta(2k)$ if ${}^{ab}\mathsf{rank}(\pi(2k+1)) = (i,j), j > 1$.

With this it is easy to see that the intuition behind Theorem 1 directly carries over to every line of (15). Additionally, using $\mathsf{Pre}^1({}^{a^+}Z)$ in ${}^aD$ allows to cycle through all the lines of (15), which ensures that every set ${}^aF_\mathcal{G} \in \mathcal{F}_\mathcal{G}$ is tried to be attained by the constructed system strategy in a pre-defined order. See [21] for a formalization of this intuition and a detailed proof.

To prove completeness, it is also shown in [21] that the negation of (15) can be over-approximated by negating every line separately. Therefore, the reasoning for every line of the negated fixed-point carries over from Sect. 3, resulting in the analogous completeness result. With this we obtain soundness and completeness in direct analogy to Theorems 1–2, formalized in Theorem 3.

Theorem 3. *Let $(H, \mathcal{F}_\mathcal{A}, \mathcal{F}_\mathcal{G})$ be a GR(1) game with $\mathcal{F}_\mathcal{A} = \{{}^1F_\mathcal{A}, \ldots, {}^mF_\mathcal{A}\}$ and $\mathcal{F}_\mathcal{G} = \{{}^1F_\mathcal{G}, \ldots, {}^nF_\mathcal{G}\}$. Suppose f^1 is the system strategy in (18a) and (18b) based on the ranking in (16). Then it holds for all $q \in [\![\varphi_4^v]\!]$ that (13a), (13b) and (13c) hold. Furthermore, it holds for all $q \notin [\![\varphi_4^v]\!]$ and all system strategies f^1 over H that either (14a) or (14b) does not hold.*

A Solution for Problem 1

Given that $\mathcal{L}(H, \mathcal{F}_\mathcal{G}) \subseteq \mathcal{L}(H, \mathcal{F}_\mathcal{A})$ it follows from Theorem 3 that Problem 1 has a solution iff $q_0 \in [\![\varphi_4^v]\!]$. Furthermore, if $q_0 \in [\![\varphi_4^v]\!]$ we can construct f^1 that wins the GR(1) condition in (7a) and is non-conflicting, as in (7b).

Using a similar construction as in Sect. 3, we can symbolically check whether $\mathcal{L}(H, \mathcal{F}_\mathcal{G}) \subseteq \mathcal{L}(H, \mathcal{F}_\mathcal{A})$. For this, we construct a new game graph H_b for every ${}^bF_\mathcal{A}$, $b \in [1;m]$ by removing the latter set from the state set of H and checking whether $\mathcal{L}(H_b, \mathcal{F}_\mathcal{G})$ is empty. If some of these m checks fail, we have $\mathcal{L}(H, \mathcal{F}_\mathcal{G}) \not\subseteq \mathcal{L}(H, \mathcal{F}_\mathcal{A})$. Now observe that by checking every ${}^bF_\mathcal{A}$ separately, we know which goals are not necessarily passed by infinite runs which visit all ${}^aF_\mathcal{G}$ infinitely often and can collect them in the set $\mathcal{F}_\mathcal{A}^{\text{failed}}$. Using the same reasoning as in Sect. 3, we can simply add the set $\mathcal{F}_\mathcal{A}^{\text{failed}}$ to the system guarantee set to obtain an equivalent synthesis problem which is solvable by the given algorithm, if it is realizable. More precisely, consider the new system guarantee set $\mathcal{F}'_\mathcal{G} = \mathcal{F}_\mathcal{G} \cup \mathcal{F}_\mathcal{A}^{\text{failed}}$ and observe that $\mathcal{L}(H, \mathcal{F}'_\mathcal{G}) \subseteq \mathcal{L}(H, \mathcal{F}_\mathcal{A})$ by definition, and therefore substituting $\mathcal{L}(H, \mathcal{F}_\mathcal{G})$ by $\mathcal{L}(H, \mathcal{F}'_\mathcal{G})$ in (7a) does not change the satisfaction of the given inclusion.

5 Complexity Analysis

We show that the search for a more elaborate strategy does not affect the worst case complexity. In Sect. 6 we show that this is also the case in practice. We state this complexity formally below.

Theorem 4. *Let* $(H, \mathcal{F}_\mathcal{A}, \mathcal{F}_\mathcal{G})$ *be a GR(1) game. We can check whether there is a winning non-conflicting strategy* f^1 *by a symbolic algorithm that performs* $O(|Q|^2|\mathcal{F}_\mathcal{G}||\mathcal{F}_\mathcal{A}|)$ *next step computations and by an enumerative algorithm that works in time* $O(m|Q|^2|\mathcal{F}_\mathcal{G}||\mathcal{F}_\mathcal{A}|)$*, where* m *is the number of transitions of the game.*

Proof. Each line of the fixed-point is iterated $O(|Q|^2)$ times [8]. As there are $|\mathcal{F}_\mathcal{G}||\mathcal{F}_\mathcal{A}|$ lines the upper bound follows. As we have to compute $|\mathcal{F}_\mathcal{G}||\mathcal{F}_\mathcal{A}|$ different ranks for each state, it follows that the complexity is $O(m|Q|^2|\mathcal{F}_\mathcal{G}||\mathcal{F}_\mathcal{A}|)$. □

We note that *enumeratively* our approach is theoretically worse than the classical approach to GR(1). This follows from the straight forward reduction to the rank computation in the rank lifting algorithm and the relative complexity of the new rank when compared to the general GR(1) rank. We conjecture that more complex approaches, e.g., through a reduction to a parity game and the usage of other enumerative algorithms, could eliminate this gap.

6 Experiments

We have implemented the 4-nested fixed-point algorithm in (15) and the corresponding strategy extraction in (18a) and (18b). It is available as an extension to the GR(1) synthesis tool `slugs` [14]. In this section we show how this algorithm (called 4FP) performs in comparison to the usual 3-nested fixed-point algorithm for GR(1) synthesis (called 3FP) available in `slugs`. All experiments were run on a computer with an Intel i5 processor running an x86 Linux at 2 GHz with 8 GB of memory.

We first run both algorithms on a benchmark set obtained from the maze example in the introduction by changing the number of rows and columns of the maze. We first increased the number of lines in the maze and added a goal state for both the obstacle and the robot per line. This results in a maze where in the first and last column, system and environment goals alternate and all adjacent cells are separated by a horizontal wall. Hence, both players need to cross the one-cell wide white space in the middle infinitely often to visit all their goal states infinitely often. The computation times and the number of states in the resulting strategy are shown in Table 1, upper part, column 3–6. Interestingly, we see that the 3FP always returns a strategy that blocks the environment. In contrast, the non-conflicting strategies computed by the 4FP are relatively larger (in state size) and computed about 10 times slower compared to the 3FP (compare column 3–4 and 5–6). When increasing the number of columns instead (lower part of Table 1), the number of goals is unaffected. We made the maze wider and left only a one-cell wide passage in the middle of the maze to allow crossings between its upper and lower row. Still, the 3FP only returns strategies that falsify the assumption, which have fewer states and are computed much faster than the environment respecting strategy returned by the 4FP. Unfortunately, the speed of computing a strategy or its size is immaterial if the winning strategy so computed wins only by falsifying assumptions.

To rule out the discrepancy between the two algorithms w.r.t. the size of strategies, we slightly modified the above maze benchmark s.t. the environment assumptions are not falsifiable anymore. We increased the capabilities of the obstacle by allowing it to move at most 2 steps in each round and to "jump over" the robot. Under these assumptions we repeated the above experiments. The computation times and the number of states in the resulting strategy are shown in Table 1, column 9–12. We see, that in this case the size of the strategies computed by the two algorithms are more similar. The larger number for the 4FP is due to the fact that we have to track both the a and the b mode, possibly resulting in multiple copies of the same a-mode state. We see that the state difference decreases with the number of goals (upper part of Table 1, column 9–12) and increases with the number of (non-goal) states (lower part of Table 1, column 9–12). In both cases, the 3FP still computes faster, but the difference decreases with the number of goals.

In addition to the 3FP and the 4FP we have also tested a sound but incomplete heuristic, which avoids the disjunction over all b's in every line of (15) by only investigating $a = b$. The state count and computation times for this heuristic are shown in Table 1, column 7–8 for the original maze benchmark, and in column 13–14 for the modified one. We see that in both cases the heuristic only returns a winning strategy if the maze is not wider then 3 cells. This is due to the fact that in all other cases the robot cannot prevent the obstacle from attaining a particular assumption state until the robot has moved from one goal to the next. The 4FP handles this problem by changing between avoided assumptions in between visits to different goals. Intuitively, the computation times and state counts for the heuristic should be smaller then for the 4FP, as the exploration of the disjunction over b's is avoided, which is true for many scenarios of the considered benchmark. It should however be noted that this is not always the case (compare e.g. line 3, column 6 and 8). This stems from the fact that restricting the synthesis to avoiding one particular assumption might require more iterations over W and Y within the fixed-point computation.

Table 1. Experimental results for the maze benchmark. The size of the maze is given in columns/lines, the number of goals is given per player. The states are counted for the returned winning strategies. Strategies preventing the environment from fulfilling its goals are indicated by a *. Recorded computation times are rounded wall-clock times.

		falsifiable assumptions						non-falsifiable assumptions					
		3FP		4FP		Heuristic		3FP		4FP		Heuristic	
size	goals	states	time	states	time	states	time	states	time	states	time	states	time
3/2	2	10*	< 1s	46	< 1s	12	< 1s	35	< 1s	50	< 1s	40	< 1s
3/10	10	34*	< 1s	1401	8s	1307	3s	1119	1s	1513	13s	1533	5s
3/20	20	64*	21s	5799	201s	5732	337s	3926	37s	6000	163s	6378	105s
25/2	2	94*	< 1s	2144	4s	n.r.	6s	744	< 1s	2318	4s	n.r.	5s
63/2	2	397*	< 1s	14259	32s	n.r.	101s	4938	2s	15465	54s	n.r.	66s

7 Discussion

We believe the requirement that a winning strategy be *non-conflicting* is a simple way to disallow strategies that win by actively preventing the environment from satisfying its assumptions, without significantly changing the theoretical formulation of reactive synthesis (e.g., by adding different winning conditions or new notions of equilibria). It is not a trace property, but our main results show that adding this requirement retains the algorithmic niceties of GR(1) synthesis: in particular, symbolic algorithms have the same asymptotic complexity.

However, non-conflictingness makes the implicit assumption of a "maximally flexible" environment: it is possible that because of unmodeled aspects of the environment strategy, it is not possible for the environment to satisfy its specifications in the precise way allowed by a non-conflicting strategy. In the maze example discussed in Sect. 1, the environment needs to move the obstacle to precisely the goal cell which is currently rendered reachable by the system. If the underlying dynamics of the obstacle require it to go back to the lower left from state q_3 before proceeding to the upper right (e.g., due to a required battery recharge), the synthesized robot strategy prevents the obstacle from doing so.

Finally, if there is no non-conflicting winning strategy, one could look for a "minimally violating" strategy. We leave this for future work. Additionally, we leave for future work the consideration of non-conflictingness for general LTL specifications or (efficient) fragments thereof.

References

1. Almagor, S., Kupferman, O., Ringert, J., Velner, Y.: Quantitative assume guarantee synthesis. In: Majumdar, R., Kunčak, V. (eds.) CAV 2017. LNCS, vol. 10427, pp. 353–374. Springer, Cham (2017). https://doi.org/10.1007/978-3-319-63390-9_19
2. Bloem, R., et al.: Synthesizing robust systems. Acta Informatika **51**(3–4), 193–220 (2014)
3. Bloem, R., Chatterjee, K., Henzinger, T., Jobstmann, B.: Better quality in synthesis through quantitative objectives. In: Bouajjani, A., Maler, O. (eds.) CAV 2009. LNCS, vol. 5643, pp. 140–156. Springer, Heidelberg (2009). https://doi.org/10.1007/978-3-642-02658-4_14
4. Bloem, R., Ehlers, R., Jacobs, S., Könighofer, R.: How to handle assumptions in synthesis. In: SYNT 2014, Vienna, Austria, pp. 34–50 (2014)
5. Bloem, R., Ehlers, R., Könighofer, R.: Cooperative reactive synthesis. In: Finkbeiner, B., Pu, G., Zhang, L. (eds.) ATVA 2015. LNCS, vol. 9364, pp. 394–410. Springer, Cham (2015). https://doi.org/10.1007/978-3-319-24953-7_29
6. Bloem, R., Jobstmann, B., Piterman, N., Pnueli, A., Sahar, Y.: Synthesis of reactive(1) designs. J. Comput. Syst. Sci. **78**(3), 911–938 (2012)
7. Brenguier, R., Raskin, J.-F., Sankur, O.: Assume-admissible synthesis. Acta Informatica **54**(1), 41–83 (2017)
8. Browne, A., Clarke, E., Jha, S., Long, D., Marrero, W.: An improved algorithm for the evaluation of fixpoint expressions. Theoret. Comput. Sci. **178**(1–2), 237–255 (1997)

9. Chatterjee, K., Henzinger, T.A.: Assume-guarantee synthesis. In: Grumberg, O., Huth, M. (eds.) TACAS 2007. LNCS, vol. 4424, pp. 261–275. Springer, Heidelberg (2007). https://doi.org/10.1007/978-3-540-71209-1_21
10. Chatterjee, K., Horn, F., Löding, C.: Obliging games. In: Gastin, P., Laroussinie, F. (eds.) CONCUR 2010. LNCS, vol. 6269, pp. 284–296. Springer, Heidelberg (2010). https://doi.org/10.1007/978-3-642-15375-4_20
11. D'Ippolito, N., Braberman, V., Piterman, N., Uchitel, S.: Synthesis of live behavior models. In: 18th International Symposium on Foundations of Software Engineering, pp. 77–86. ACM (2010)
12. Ehlers, R., Könighofer, R., Bloem, R.: Synthesizing cooperative reactive mission plans. In: IROS, pp. 3478–3485 (2015)
13. Ehlers, R., Lafortune, S., Tripakis, S., Vardi, M.Y.: Supervisory control and reactive synthesis: a comparative introduction. Discrete Event Dyn. Syst. **27**(2), 209–260 (2017)
14. Ehlers, R., Raman, V.: Slugs: extensible GR(1) synthesis. In: Chaudhuri, S., Farzan, A. (eds.) CAV 2016. LNCS, vol. 9780, pp. 333–339. Springer, Cham (2016). https://doi.org/10.1007/978-3-319-41540-6_18
15. Emerson, E., Jutla, C.: Tree automata, mu-calculus and determinacy. In: FOCS 1991, pp. 368–377, October 1991
16. Fisman, D., Kupferman, O., Lustig, Y.: Rational synthesis. In: Esparza, J., Majumdar, R. (eds.) TACAS 2010. LNCS, vol. 6015, pp. 190–204. Springer, Heidelberg (2010). https://doi.org/10.1007/978-3-642-12002-2_16
17. Johnson, B., Havlak, F., Kress-Gazit, H., Campbell, M.: Experimental evaluation and formal analysis of high-level tasks with dynamic obstacle anticipation on a full-sized autonomous vehicle. J. Field Robot. **34**, 897–911 (2017)
18. Klein, U., Pnueli, A.: Revisiting synthesis of GR(1) specifications. In: Barner, S., Harris, I., Kroening, D., Raz, O. (eds.) HVC 2010. LNCS, vol. 6504, pp. 161–181. Springer, Heidelberg (2011). https://doi.org/10.1007/978-3-642-19583-9_16
19. Kozen, D.: Results on the propositional μ-calculus. Theoret. Comput. Sci. **27**(3), 333–354 (1983)
20. Kupferman, O., Perelli, G., Vardi, M.: Synthesis with rational environments. Ann. Math. Artif. Intell. **78**(1), 3–20 (2016)
21. Majumdar, R., Piterman, N., Schmuck, A.-K.: Environmentally-friendly GR(1) synthesis (extended version). arXiv preprint (2019)
22. Moor, T.: Supervisory control on non-terminating processes: an interpretation of liveness properties. Technical report, Lehrstuhl für Regelungstechnik, Friedrich-Alexander Universität Erlangen-Nürnberg (2017)
23. Ramadge, P.J.: Some tractable supervisory control problems for discrete-event systems modeled by Büchi automata. IEEE Trans. Autom. Control **34**, 10–19 (1989)
24. Rogersten, R., Xu, H., Ozay, N., Topcu, U., Murray, R.M.: Control software synthesis and validation for a vehicular electric power distribution testbed. J. Aerosp. Inf. Syst. **11**(10), 665–678 (2014)
25. Schmuck, A.-K., Moor, T., Majumdar, R.: On the relation between reactive synthesis and supervisory control of non-terminating processes. In: WODES 2018 (2018)
26. Seidl, H.: Fast and simple nested fixpoints. Inf. Process. Lett. **59**(6), 303–308 (1996)
27. Thistle, J.G., Wonham, W.M.: Supervision of infinite behavior of discrete event systems. SIAM J. Control Optim. **32**, 1098–1113 (1994)
28. Xu, H., Topcu, U., Murray, R.M.: Specification and synthesis of reactive protocols for aircraft electric power distribution. IEEE Trans. Control Netw. Syst. **2**(2), 193–203 (2015)

StocHy: Automated Verification and Synthesis of Stochastic Processes

Nathalie Cauchi(✉) and Alessandro Abate

Department of Computer Science,
University of Oxford, Oxford, UK
nathalie.cauchi@cs.ox.ac.uk

Abstract. StocHy is a software tool for the quantitative analysis of discrete-time *stochastic hybrid systems* (SHS). StocHy accepts a high-level description of stochastic models and constructs an equivalent SHS model. The tool allows to (i) simulate the SHS evolution over a given time horizon; and to automatically construct formal abstractions of the SHS. Abstractions are then employed for (ii) formal verification or (iii) control (policy, strategy) synthesis. StocHy allows for modular modelling, and has separate simulation, verification and synthesis engines, which are implemented as independent libraries. This allows for libraries to be easily used and for extensions to be easily built. The tool is implemented in C++ and employs manipulations based on vector calculus, the use of sparse matrices, the symbolic construction of probabilistic kernels, and multi-threading. Experiments show StocHy's markedly improved performance when compared to existing abstraction-based approaches: in particular, StocHy beats state-of-the-art tools in terms of precision (abstraction error) and computational effort, and finally attains scalability to large-sized models (12 continuous dimensions). StocHy is available at www.gitlab.com/natchi92/StocHy. Data or code related to this paper is available at: [31].

1 Introduction

Stochastic hybrid systems (SHS) are a rich mathematical modelling framework capable of describing systems with complex dynamics, where uncertainty and hybrid (that is, both continuous and discrete) components are relevant. Whilst earlier instances of SHS have a long history, SHS proper have been thoroughly investigated only from the mid 2000s, and have been most recently applied to the study of complex systems, both engineered and natural. Amongst engineering case studies, SHS have been used for modelling and analysis of micro grids [29], smart buildings [23], avionics [7], automation of medical devices [3]. A benchmark for SHS is also described in [10]. However, a wider adoption of SHS in real-world applications is stymied by a few factors: (i) the complexity associated with modelling SHS; (ii) the generality of their mathematical framework, which requires an arsenal of advanced and diverse techniques to analyse them; and (iii) the undecidability of verification/synthesis problems over SHS and the curse of dimensionality associated with their approximations.

T. Vojnar and L. Zhang (Eds.): TACAS 2019, Part II, LNCS 11428, pp. 247–264, 2019.
https://doi.org/10.1007/978-3-030-17465-1_14

This paper introduces a new software tool - StocHy - which is aimed at simplifying both the modelling of SHS and their analysis, and which targets the wider adoption of SHS, also by non-expert users. With focus on the three limiting factors above, StocHy allows to describe SHS by parsing or extending well-known and -used state-space models and generates a standard SHS model automatically and formats it to be analysed. StocHy can (i) perform verification tasks, e.g., compute the probability of staying within a certain region of the state space from a given set of initial conditions; (ii) automatically synthesise policies (strategies) maximising this probability, and (iii) simulate the SHS evolution over time. StocHy is implemented in C++ and modular making it both extendible and portable.

Related work. There exist only a few tools that can handle (classes of) SHS. Of much inspiration for this contribution, FAUST^2 [28] generates abstractions for uncountable-state discrete-time stochastic processes, natively supporting SHS models with a single discrete mode and finite actions, and performs verification of reachability-like properties and corresponding synthesis of policies. FAUST^2 is naïvely implemented in MATLAB and lacks in scalability to large models. The MODEST TOOLSET [18] allows to model and to analyse classes of continuous-time SHS, particularly probabilistic hybrid automata (PHA) that combine probabilistic discrete transitions with deterministic evolution of the continuous variables. The tool for stochastic and dynamically coloured petri nets (SDCPN) [13] supports compositional modelling of PHA and focuses on simulation via Monte Carlo techniques. The existing tools highlight the need for a new software that allows for (i) straightforward and general SHS modelling construction and (ii) scalable automated analysis.

Contributions. The StocHy tool newly enables

- *formal verification* of SHS via either of two abstraction techniques:
  - for discrete-time, continuous-space models with additive disturbances, and possibly with multiple discrete modes, we employ formal abstractions as general Markov chains or Markov decision processes [28]; StocHy improves techniques in the FAUST^2 tool by simplifying the input model description, by employing sparse matrices to manipulate the transition probabilities and by reducing the computational time needed to generate the abstractions.
  - for models with a finite number of actions, we employ interval Markov decision processes and the model checking framework in [22]; StocHy provides a novel abstraction algorithm allowing for efficient computation of the abstract model, by means of an adaptive and sequential refining of the underlying abstraction. We show that we are able to generate significantly smaller abstraction errors and to verify models with up to 12 continuous variables.
- *control* (strategy, policy) *synthesis* via formal abstractions, employing:
  - stochastic dynamic programming; StocHy exploits the use of symbolic kernels.

- robust synthesis using interval Markov decision processes; StocHy automates the synthesis algorithm with the abstraction procedure and the temporal property of interest, and exploits the use of sparse matrices;

- *simulation* of complex stochastic processes, such as SHS, by means of Monte Carlo techniques; StocHy automatically generates statistics from the simulations in the form of histograms, visualising the evolution of both the continuous random variables and the discrete modes.

This contribution is structured as follows: Sect. 2 crisply presents the theoretical underpinnings (modelling and analysis) for the tool. We provide an overview of the implementation of StocHy in Sect. 3. We highlight features and use of StocHy by a set of experimental evaluations in Sect. 4: we provide four different case studies that highlight the applicability, ease of use, and scalability of StocHy. Details on executing all the case studies are detailed in this paper and within a Wiki page that accompanies the StocHy distribution.

2 Theory: Models, Abstractions, Simulations

2.1 Models - Discrete-Time Stochastic Hybrid Systems

StocHy supports the modelling of the following general class of SHS [1,4].

Definition 1. *A* SHS *[4] is a discrete-time model defined as the tuple*

$$\mathcal{H} = (\mathcal{Q}, n, \mathcal{U}, T_x, T_q), \quad \textit{where} \tag{1}$$

- $\mathcal{Q} = \{q_1, q_2, \ldots, q_m\}$, $m \in \mathbb{N}$, *represents a finite set of modes (locations);*
- $n \in \mathbb{N}$ *is the dimension of the continuous space* $\mathbb{R}^n$ *of each mode; the hybrid state space is then given by* $\mathcal{D} = \cup_{q \in \mathcal{Q}}\{q\} \times \mathbb{R}^n$*;*
- $\mathcal{U}$ *is a continuous set of actions, e.g.* $\mathbb{R}^v$*;*
- $T_q : \mathcal{Q} \times \mathcal{D} \times \mathcal{U} \to [0,1]$ *is a discrete stochastic kernel on* Q *given* $\mathcal{D} \times \mathcal{U}$*, which assigns to each* $s = (q,x) \in \mathcal{D}$ *and* $u \in \mathcal{U}$*, a probability distribution over* $\mathcal{Q} : T_q(\cdot|s,u)$*;*
- $T_x : \mathcal{B}(\mathbb{R}^n) \times \mathcal{D} \times \mathcal{U} \to [0,1]$ *is a Borel-measurable stochastic kernel on* $\mathbb{R}^n$ *given* $\mathcal{D} \times \mathcal{U}$*, which assigns to each* $s \in \mathcal{D}$ *and* $u \in \mathcal{U}$ *a probability measure on the Borel space* $(\mathbb{R}^n, \mathcal{B}(\mathbb{R}^n)) : T_x(\cdot|s,u)$*.*

In this model the discrete component takes values in a finite set $\mathcal{Q}$ of modes (a.k.a. locations), each endowed with a continuous domain (the Euclidean space $\mathbb{R}^n$). As such, a point s over the hybrid state space $\mathcal{D}$ is pair (q,x), where $q \in \mathcal{Q}$ and $x \in \mathbb{R}^n$. The semantics of transitions at any point over a discrete time domain, are as follows: given a point $s \in \mathcal{D}$, the discrete state is chosen from T_q, and depending on the selected mode $q \in \mathcal{Q}$ the continuous state is updated according to the probabilistic law T_x. Non-determinism in the form of actions can affect both discrete and continuous transitions.

Remark 1. A rigorous characterisation of SHS can be found in [1], which introduces a general class of models with probabilistic resets and a hybrid actions space. Whilst we can deal with general SHS models, in the case studies of this paper we focus on special instances, as described next. □

Remark 2 (Special instance). In Case Study 2 (see Sect. 4.2) we look at models where actions are associated to a deterministic selection of locations, namely $T_q : \mathcal{U} \rightarrow \mathcal{Q}$ and $\mathcal{U}$ is a finite set of actions. □

Remark 3 (Special instance). In Case Study 4 (Sect. 4.4) we consider non-linear dynamical models with bilinear terms, which are characterised for any $q \in \mathcal{Q}$ by $x_{k+1} = A_q x_k + B_q u_k + x_k \sum_{i=1}^{v} N_{q,i} u_{i,k} + G_q w_k$, where $k \in \mathbb{N}$ represents the discrete time index, A_q, B_q, G_q are appropriately sized matrices, $N_{q,i}$ represents the bilinear influence of the i−th input component u_i, and $w_k = w \sim \mathcal{N}(\cdot; 0, 1)$ and $\mathcal{N}(\cdot; \eta, \nu)$ denotes a Gaussian density function with mean η and covariance matrix ν^2. This expresses the continuous kernel $T_x : \mathcal{B}(\mathbb{R}^n) \times \mathcal{D} \times \mathcal{U} \rightarrow [0, 1]$ as

$$\mathcal{N}(\cdot; A_q x + B_q u + x \sum_{i=1}^{v} N_{q,i} u_i + F_q, G_q). \tag{2}$$

In Case Study 1-2-3 (Sects. 4.1–4.3), we look at the special instance from [22], where the dynamics are autonomous (no actions) and linear: here T_x is

$$\mathcal{N}(\cdot; A_q x + F_q, G_q), \tag{3}$$

where in Case Studies 1, 3 $\mathcal{Q}$ is a single element. □

Definition 2. *A Markov decision process (*MDP*) [5] is a discrete-time model defined as the tuple*

$$\mathcal{H} = (\mathcal{Q}, \mathcal{U}, T_q), \quad \textit{where} \tag{4}$$

- $\mathcal{Q} = \{q_1, q_2, \ldots, q_m\}$, $m \in \mathbb{N}$, *represents a finite set of modes;*
- $\mathcal{U}$ *is a finite set of actions;*
- $T_q : \mathcal{Q} \times \mathcal{Q} \times \mathcal{U} \rightarrow [0, 1]$ *is a discrete stochastic kernel that assigns, to each* $q \in \mathcal{Q}$ *and* $u \in \mathcal{U}$, *a probability distribution over* $\mathcal{Q} : T_q(\cdot|q, u)$.

Whenever the set of actions is trivial or a policy is synthesised and used (cf. discussion in Sect. 2.2) the MDP reduces to a Markov chain (MC), and a kernel $T_q : \mathcal{Q} \times \mathcal{Q} \rightarrow [0, 1]$ assigns to each $q \in \mathcal{Q}$ a distribution over $\mathcal{Q}$ as $T_q(\cdot|q)$.

Definition 3. *An interval Markov decision process (*IMDP*) [26] extends the syntax of an* MDP *by allowing for uncertain* T_q, *and is defined as the tuple*

$$\mathcal{H} = (\mathcal{Q}, \mathcal{U}, \check{P}, \hat{P}), \quad \textit{where} \tag{5}$$

- $\mathcal{Q}$ *and* $\mathcal{U}$ *are as in Definition 2;*
- $\check{P}$ *and* $\hat{P} : \mathcal{Q} \times \mathcal{U} \times \mathcal{Q} \rightarrow [0, 1]$ *is a function that assigns to each* $q \in \mathcal{Q}$ *a lower (upper) bound probability distribution over* $\mathcal{Q} : \check{P}(\cdot|q, u)$ $(\hat{P}(\cdot|q, u)$ *respectively).*

For all $q, q' \in \mathcal{Q}$ *and* $u \in \mathcal{U}$, *it holds that* $\check{P}(q'|q,u) \leq \hat{P}(q'|q,u)$ *and,*

$$\sum_{q' \in \mathcal{Q}} \check{P}(q'|q,u) \leq 1 \leq \sum_{q' \in \mathcal{Q}} \hat{P}(q'|q,u).$$

Note that when $\check{P}(\cdot|q,u) = \hat{P}(\cdot|q,u)$, *the* IMDP *reduces to the* MDP *with* $\check{P}(\cdot|q,u) = \hat{P}(\cdot|q,u) = T_q(\cdot|q,u)$.

2.2 Formal Verification and Strategy Synthesis via Abstractions

Formal verification and strategy synthesis over SHS are in general not decidable [4,30], and can be tackled via quantitative finite abstractions. These are precise approximations that come in two main different flavours: abstractions into MDP [4,28] and into IMDP [22]. Once the finite abstractions are obtained, and with focus on specifications expressed in (non-nested) PCTL or fragments of LTL [5], formal verification or strategy synthesis can be performed via probabilistic model checking tools, such as PRISM [21], STORM [12], ISCASMC [17]. We overview next the two alternative abstractions, as implemented in StocHy.

Abstractions into Markov decision processes. Following [27], MDP are generated by either (i) uniformly gridding the state space and computing an abstraction error, which depends on the continuity of the underlying continuous dynamics and on the chosen grid; or (ii) generating the grid adaptively and sequentially, by splitting the cells with the largest local abstraction error until a desired global abstraction error is achieved. The two approaches display an intuitive trade-off, where the first in general requires more memory but less time, whereas the second generates smaller abstractions. Either way, the probability to transit from each cell in the grid into any other cell characterises the MDP matrix T_q. Further details can be found in [28]. StocHy newly provides a C++ implementation and employs sparse matrix representation and manipulation, in order to attain faster generation of the abstraction and use in formal verification or strategy synthesis.

Verification via MDP (when the action set is trivial) is performed to check the abstraction against non-nested, bounded-until specifications in PCTL [5] or *co-safe linear temporal logic* (CSLTL) [20].

Strategy synthesis via MDP is defined as follows. Consider, the class of deterministic and memoryless Markov strategies $\pi = (\mu_0, \mu_1, \dots)$ where $\mu_k : \mathcal{Q} \to \mathcal{U}$. We compute the strategy $\pi^\star$ that maximises the probability of satisfying a formula, with algorithms discussed in [28].

Abstraction into Interval Markov decision processes (IMDP) is based on a procedure in [11] performed using a uniform grid and with a finite set of actions $\mathcal{U}$ (see Remark 2). StocHy newly provides the option to generate a grid using adaptive/sequential refinements (similar to the case in the paragraph above) [27], which is performed as follows: (i) define a required minimal maximum abstraction error ε_{max}; (ii) generate a coarse abstraction using the Algorithm in [11] and compute the local error ε_q that is associated to each abstract state q; (iii) split all cells where $\varepsilon_q > \varepsilon_{max}$ along the main axis of each dimension, and update the probability bounds (and errors); and (iv) repeat this process until $\forall q,\ \varepsilon_q < \varepsilon_{max}$.

Verification via IMDP is run over properties in CSLTL or bounded-LTL (BLTL) form using the IMDP model checking algorithm in [22].

Synthesis via IMDP [11] is carried out by extending the notions of strategies of MDP to depend on memory, that is on prefixes of paths.

2.3 Analysis via Monte Carlo Simulations

Monte Carlo techniques generate numerical sampled trajectories representing the evaluation of a stochastic process over a predetermined time horizon. Given a sufficient number of trajectories, one can approximate the statistical properties of the solution process with a required confidence level. This approach has been adopted for simulation of different types of SHS. [19] applies sequential Monte Carlo simulation to SHS to reason about rare-event probabilities. [13] performs Monte Carlo simulations of classes of SHS described as Petri nets. [8] proposes a methodology for efficient Monte Carlo simulations of continuous-time SHS. In this work, we analyse a SHS model using Monte Carlo simulations following the approach in [4]. Additionally, we generate histogram plots at each time step, providing further insight on the evolution of the solution process.

3 Overview of StocHy

Installation. StocHy is set up using the provided GET_DEP file found within the distribution package, which will automatically install all the required dependencies. The executable RUN.SH builds and runs StocHy. This basic installation setup has been successfully tested on machines running Ubuntu 18.04.1 LTS GNU and Linux operating systems.

Input interface. The user interacts with StocHy via the MAIN file and must specify (i) a high-level description of the model dynamics and (ii) the task to be performed. The description of model dynamics can take the form of a list of the transition probabilities between the discrete modes, and of the state-space models for the continuous variables in each mode; alternatively, a description can be obtained by specifying a path to a MATLAB file containing the model description in state-space form together with the transition probability matrix. Tasks can be of three kinds (each admitting specific parameters): simulation, verification, or synthesis. The general structure of the input interface is illustrated via an example in Listing 1.1: here the user is interested in simulating a SHS with two discrete modes $\mathcal{Q} = \{q_0, q_1\}$ and two continuous variables evolve according to (3). The model is autonomous and has no control actions. The relationship between the discrete modes is defined by a fixed transition probability (line 1). The evolution of the continuous dynamics are defined in lines 2–14. The initial condition for both the discrete modes and

```
1  arma::mat Tq = { {0.4, 0.6},{0.7,0.3}};      // Transition probabilities
2  // Evolution of the continuous variables for each discrete mode
3  // First model
4  arma::mat Aq0 = {{0.5, 0.4},{0.2,0.6}};
5  arma::mat Fq0 = { {0},{0}};
6  arma::mat Gq0 = {{0.4,0},{0.3, 0.3}};
7  ssmodels_t modelq0(Aq0, Fq0, Gq0);
8  // Second model
9  arma::mat Aq1 = {{0.6, 0.3},{0.1,0.7}};
10 arma::mat Fq1 = { {0},{0}};
11 arma::mat Gq1 = {{0.2,0},{0.1, 0}};
12 ssmodels_t modelq1(Aq1,Fq1, Gq1);
13 std::vector<ssmodels_t> models =
14 {modelq1,modelq2};
15 // Initial state q_0
16 arma::mat q_init = arma::zeros<arma::mat>(1,1);
17 // Initial continuous variables
18 arma::mat x1_init = arma::ones<arma:mat>(2,1);
19 exdata_t data(x1_init,q_init);
20 // Build shs
21 shs_t<arma::mat,int> mySHS(Tq,models,data);
22 // Time horizon
23 int K = 32;
24 // Task definition  (1 = simulator, 2 = faust^2, 3 = imdp)
25 int lb = 1;
26 taskSpec_t mySpec(lb,K);
27 // Combine
28 inputSpec_t<arma::mat,int> myInput(mySHS,mySpec);
29 // Perform task
30 performTask(myInput);
```

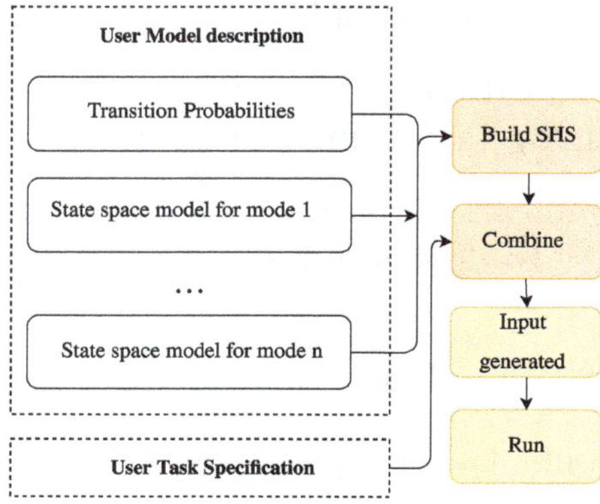

Listing 1.1: Description of MAIN file for simulating a SHS consisting of two discrete modes and two continuous variables evolving according to (2).

the continuous variables are set in lines 16–21 (this is needed for simulation tasks). The equivalent SHS model is then set up by instantiating an object of type `shs_t<arma::mat,int>` (line 23). Next, the task is defined in line 27 (simulation with a time horizon $K = 32$, as specified in line 25 and using the simulator library, as set in line 26). We combine the model and task specification together in line 29. Finally, StocHy carries out the simulation using the function `performTask` (line 31).

Modularity. StocHy comprises independent libraries for different tasks, namely (i) FAUST^2, (ii) IMDP, and (iii) simulator. Each of the libraries is separate and depends only on the model structure that has been entered. This allows for seamless extensions of individual sub-modules with new or existing tools and methods. The function `performTask` acts as multiplexer for calling any of the libraries depending on the input model and task specification.

Data structures. StocHy makes use of multiple techniques to minimise computational overhead. It employs vector algebra for efficient handling of linear operations, and whenever possible it stores and manipulates matrices as sparse structures. It uses the linear algebra library Armadillo [24,25], which applies multi-threading and a sophisticated expression evaluator that has been shown to speed up matrix manipulations in C++ when compared to other libraries. FAUST^2 based abstractions define the underlying kernel functions symbolically using the library GiNaC [6], for easy evaluation of the stochastic kernels.

Output interface. We provide outputs as text files for all three libraries, which are stored within the RESULTS folder. We also provide additional PYTHON scripts for generating plots as needed. For abstractions based on FAUST^2, the user has the additional option to export the generated MDP or MC to PRISM format, to interface with the popular model checker [21] (StocHy prompts the user this option following the completion of the verification or synthesis task). As a future extension, we plan to export the generated abstraction models to the model checker STORM [12] and to the modelling format JANI [9].

4 StocHy: Experimental Evaluation

We apply StocHy on four different case studies highlighting different models and tasks to be performed. All the experiments are run on a standard laptop, with an Intel Core i7-8550U CPU at 1.80 GHz × 8 and with 8 GB of RAM.

4.1 Case Study 1 - Formal Verification

We consider the SHS model first presented in [2]. The model takes the form of (1), and has one discrete mode and two continuous variables representing the level of CO_2 (x_1) and the ambient temperature (x_2), respectively. The continuous variables evolve according to

$$\begin{aligned} x_{1,k+1} &= x_{1,k} + \frac{\Delta}{V}(-\rho_m x_{1,k} + \varrho_c(C_{out} - x_{1,k})) + \sigma_1 w_k, \\ x_{2,k+1} &= x_{2,k} + \frac{\Delta}{C_z}(\rho_m C_{pa}(T_{set} - x_{2,k}) + \frac{\varrho_c}{R}(T_{out} - x_{2,k})) + \sigma_2 w_k, \end{aligned} \tag{6}$$

where Δ the sampling time $[min]$, V is the volume of the zone $[m^3]$, ρ_m is the mass air flow pumped inside the room $[m^3/min]$, ϱ_c is the natural drift air flow $[m^3/min]$, C_{out} is the outside CO_2 level $[ppm/min]$, T_{set} is the desired temperature $[^oC]$, T_{out} is the outside temperature $[\,^\circ C/min]$, C_z is the zone capacitance $[Jm^3/\,^\circ C]$, C_{pa} is the specific heat capacity of air $[J/\,^\circ C]$, R is the resistance to heat transfer $[\,^\circ C/J]$, and $\sigma_{(\cdot)}$ is a variance term associated to the noise $w_k \sim \mathcal{N}(0,1)$.

We are interested in verifying whether the continuous variables remain within the safe set $X_{safe} = [405, 540] \times [18, 24]$ over 45 min ($K = 3$). This property can be encoded as a BLTL property, $\varphi_1 := \Box^{\leq K} X_{safe}$, where $\Box$ is the "*always*" temporal operator considered over a finite horizon. The semantics of BLTL is defined over finite traces, denoted by $\zeta = \{\zeta_j\}_{j=0}^K$. A trace ζ satisfies φ_1 if $\forall j \leq K, \zeta_j \in X_{safe}$, and we quantify the probability that traces generated by the SHS satisfy φ_1.

Case study 1: Listings explaining task specification for (a) FAUST^2 and (b) IMDP

```
1  // Dynamics definition
2  shs_t<arma::mat,int>
       myShs('../CS1.mat');
3  // Specification for FAUST^2
4  // safe set
5  arma::mat safe =
       {{405,540},{18,24}};
6  // max error
7  double eps = 1;
8  // grid type
9  // (1 = uniform, 2 = adaptive)
10 int gridType = 1;
11 // time horizon
12 int K = 3;
13 // task and property type
14 // (1 = verify safety , 2 =
       verify reach-avoid,
15 // 3 = safety synthesis, 4 =
       reach-avoid synthesis)
16 int p = 1;
17 // library (1 = simulator, 2 =
       faust^2, 3 = imdp)
18 int lb = 2;
19 // task specification
20 taskSpec_t
       mySpec(lb,K,p,safe,eps,gridType);
```

Listing 1.2: (a) FAUST^2

```
1  // Dynamics definition
2  shs_t<arma::mat,int>
       myShs('../CS1.mat');
3  // Specification for IMDP
4  // safe set
5  arma::mat safe
       {{405,540},{18,24}};
6  // grid size for each dimension
7  arma::mat grid =
       {{0.0845,0.0845}};
9  // relative tolerance
10 arma::mat reft = {{1,1}};
11 // time horizon
12 int K = 3;
13 // task and property type
14 // (1 = verify safety , 2 =
       verify reach-avoid,
15 // 3 = safety synthesis, 4 =
       reach-avoid synthesis)
16 int p = 1;
17 // library (1 = simulator, 2 =
       faust^2, 3 = imdp)
18 int lb = 3;
19 // task specification
20 taskSpec_t
       mySpec(lb,K,p,safe,grid,reft);
```

Listing 1.3: (b) IMDP

When tackled with the method based on FAUST^2 that hinges on the computation of Lipschitz constants, this verification task is numerically tricky, in view of difference in dimensionality of the range of x_1 and x_2 within the safe set X_{safe} and the variance associated with each dimension $G_{q_0} = \left[\begin{smallmatrix}\sigma_1 & 0\\ 0 & \sigma_2\end{smallmatrix}\right] = \left[\begin{smallmatrix}40.096 & 0\\ 0 & 0.511\end{smallmatrix}\right]$. In order to mitigate this, StocHy automatically rescales the state space so all the dynamics evolve in a comparable range.

Implementation. StocHy provides two verification methods, one based on FAUST^2 and the second based on IMDP. We parse the model from file CS1.MAT (see line 2 of Listings 1.2(a) and 1.3(b), corresponding to the two methods). CS1.MAT sets parameter values to (6) and uses a $\Delta = 15$ $[min]$. As anticipated, we employ both techniques over the same model description:

- for FAUST^2 we specify the safe set (X_{safe}), the maximum allowable error, the grid type (whether uniform or adaptive grid), the time horizon, together with the type of property of interest (safety or reach-avoid). This is carried out in lines 5–21 in Listing 1.2(a).

Table 1. *Case study 1:* Comparison of verification results for φ_1 when using FAUST^2 vs IMDP.

Tool Method	Impl. Platform	$\lvert\mathcal{Q}\rvert$ [states]	Time [s]	Error ε_{max}
FAUST^2	MATLAB	576	186.746	1
FAUST^2	C++	576	51.420	1
IMDP	C++	576	87.430	0.236
FAUST^2	MATLAB	1089	629.037	1
FAUST^2	C++	1089	78.140	1
IMDP	C++	1089	387.940	0.174
FAUST^2	MATLAB	2304	2633.155	1
FAUST^2	C++	2304	165.811	1
IMDP	C++	2304	1552.950	0.121
FAUST^2	MATLAB	3481	7523.771	1
FAUST^2	C++	3481	946.294	1
IMDP	C++	3481	3623.090	0.098
FAUST^2	MATLAB	4225	10022.850	0.900
FAUST^2	C++	4225	3313.990	0.900
IMDP	C++	4225	4854.580	0.089

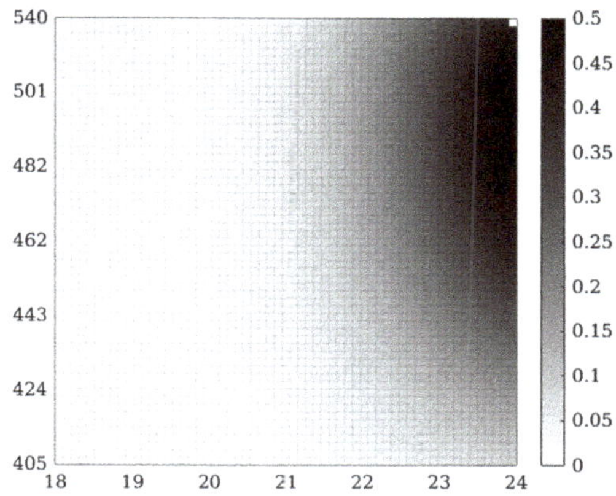

Fig. 1. *Case study 1:* Lower bound probability of satisfying φ_1 generated using IMDP with 3481 states.

- for the IMDP method, we define the safe set (X_{safe}), the grid size, the relative tolerance, the time horizon and the property type. This can be done by defining the task specification using lines 5–21 in Listing 1.3(b).

Finally, to run either of the methods on the defined input model, we combine the model and the task specification using `inputSpec_t<arma::mat,int> myInput(myShs,mySpec)`, then run the command `performTask(myInput)`. The verification results for both methods are stored in the RESULTS directory:

- for FAUST^2, StocHy generates four text files within the RESULTS folder: REPRESENTATIVE_POINTS.TXT contains the partitioned state space; TRANSITION_MATRIX.TXT consists of the transition probabilities of the generated abstract MC; PROBLEM_SOLUTION.TXT contains the sat probability for each state of the MC; and E.TXT stores the global maximum abstraction error.
- for IMDP, StocHy generates three text files in the same folder: STEPSMIN.TXT stores $\check{P}$ of the abstract IMDP; STEPSMAX.TXT stores $\hat{P}$; and SOLUTION.TXT contains the sat probability and the errors ε_q for each abstract state q.

Outcomes. We perform the verification task using both FAUST^2 and IMDP, over different sizes of the abstraction grid. We employ uniform gridding for both methods. We further compare the outcomes of StocHy against those of the FAUST^2 tool, which is implemented in MATLAB [28]. Note that the IMDP consists of $|\mathcal{Q}|+1$ states, where the additional state is the sink state $q_u = \mathcal{D}\backslash X_{safe}$. The results are shown in Table 1. We saturate (conservative) errors output that are greater than 1 to this value. We show the probability of satisfying the formula obtained from IMDP for a grid size of 3481 states in Fig. 1 – similar probabilities are obtained for the remaining grid sizes. As evident from Table 1, the new IMDP method outperforms the approach using FAUST^2 in terms of the

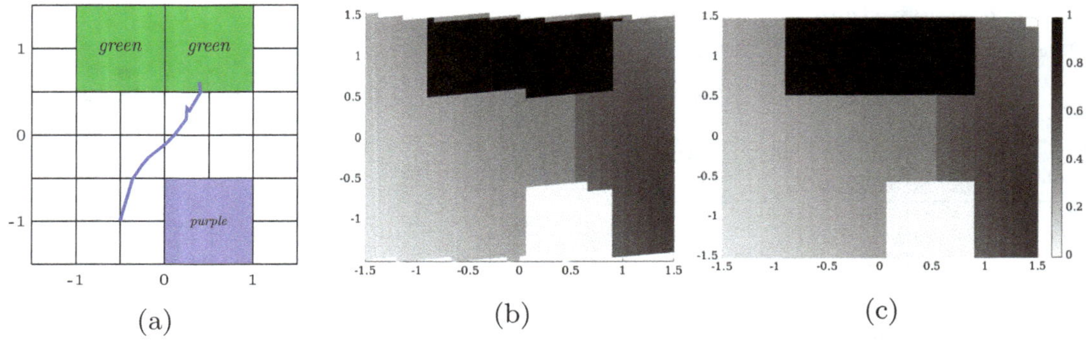

Fig. 2. *Case study 2:* (a) Gridded domain together with a superimposed simulation of trajectory initialised at $(-0.5, -1)$ within q_0, under the synthesised optimal switching strategy π^*. Lower probabilities of satisfying φ_2 for mode q_0 (b) and for mode q_1 (c), as computed by StocHy.

maximum error associated to the abstraction (FAUST^2 generates an abstraction error < 1 only with 4225 states). Comparing the FAUST^2 within StocHy and the original FAUST^2 implementation (running in MATLAB), StocHy offers computational speed-up for the same grid size. This is due to the faster computation of the transition probabilities, through StocHy's use of matrix manipulations. FAUST^2 within StocHy also simplifies the input of the dynamical model description: in the original FAUST^2 implementation, the user is asked to manually input the stochastic kernel in the form of symbolic equations in a MATLAB script. This is not required when using StocHy, automatically generates the underlying symbolic kernels from the input state-space model descriptions.

4.2 Case Study 2 - Strategy Synthesis

We consider a stochastic process with two modes $\mathcal{Q} = \{q_0, q_1\}$, which continuously evolves according to (3) with

$$A_{q_0} = \begin{bmatrix} 0.43 & 0.52 \\ 0.65 & 0.12 \end{bmatrix}, G_{q_0} = \begin{bmatrix} 1 & 0.1 \\ 0 & 0.1 \end{bmatrix}, A_{q_0} = \begin{bmatrix} 0.65 & 0.12 \\ 0.52 & 0.43 \end{bmatrix}, G_{q_1} = \begin{bmatrix} 0.2 & 0 \\ 0 & 0.2 \end{bmatrix}, F_{q_i} = \begin{bmatrix} 0 \\ 0 \end{bmatrix},$$

and $i \in \{0, 1\}$. Consider the continuous domain shown in Fig. 2a over both discrete locations. We plan to synthesise the optimal switching strategy $\pi^\star$ that maximises the probability of reaching the *green* region, whilst avoiding the *purple* one, over an unbounded time horizon, given any initial condition within the domain. This can be expressed with the LTL formula, $\varphi_2 := (\neg purple)\ \mathsf{U}\ green$, where U is the "*until*" temporal operator, and the atomic propositions $\{purple, green\}$ denote regions within the set $X = [-1.5, 1.5]^2$ (see Fig. 2a).

Implementation. We define the model dynamics following lines 3–14 in Listing 1.1, while we use Listing 1.3 to specify the synthesis task and together with its associated parameters. The LTL property φ_2 is over an unbounded time horizon, which leads to employing the IMDP method for synthesis (recall that the FAUST^2 implementation can only handle time-bounded properties, and its abstraction error monotonically increases with the time horizon of the formula). In order to encode the task we set the variable `safe` to correspond to X the grid size to 0.12 and the relative tolerance to 0.06 along both dimensions (cf. lines 5–10 in Listing 1.3). We set the time horizon `K = -1` to represent an unbounded time horizon, let `p = 4` to trigger the synthesis engine over the given specification and make `lb = 3` to use IMDP method (cf. lines 12–19 in Listing 1.3). This task specification partitions the set X into the underlying IMDP via uniform gridding. Alternatively, the user has the option to make use of the adaptive-sequential algorithm by defining a new variable `eps_max` which characterise the maximum allowable abstraction error and then specify the task using `taskSpec_t mySpec(lb,K,p,boundary,eps_max,grid,rtol);`. Next, we define two files (PHI1.TXT and PHI2.TXT) containing the coordinates within the gridded domain (see Fig. 2a) associated with the atomic propositions *purple* and *green*, respectively. This allows for automatic labelling of the state-space over which synthesis is to be performed. Running the main file, StocHy generates a SOLUTION.TXT file within the RESULTS folder. This contains the synthesised $\pi^\star$ policy, the lower bound for the probabilities of satisfying φ_2, and the local errors ε_q for any region q.

Outcomes. The case study generates an abstraction with a total of 2410 states, a maximum probability of 1, a maximum abstraction error of 0.21, and it requires a total time of 1639.3 [s]. In this case, we witness a slightly larger abstraction error via the IMDP method then in the previous case study. This is due the non-diagonal covariance matrix G_{q_0} which introduces a rotation in X within mode q_0. When labelling the states associated with the regions *purple* and *green*, an additional error is introduced due to the over- and under-approximation of states associated with each of the two regions. We further show the simulation of a trajectory under $\pi^\star$ with a starting point of $(-0.5, -1)$ in q_0, within Fig. 2a.

4.3 Case Study 3 - Scaling in Continuous Dimension of Model

We now focus on the continuous dynamics by considering a stochastic process with $\mathcal{Q} = \{q_0\}$ (single mode) and dynamics evolving according to (3), characterised by $A_{q_0} = 0.8\mathbf{I}_d$, $F_{q_0} = \mathbf{0}_d$ and $G_{q_0} = 0.2\mathbf{I}_d$, where d corresponds to the number of continuous variables. We are interested in checking the LTL specification $\varphi_3 := \Box X_{safe}$, where $X_{safe} = [-1, 1]^d$, as the continuous dimension d of the model varies. Here "$\Box$" is the "*always*" temporal operator and a trace ζ satisfies φ_3 if $\forall k \geq 0$, $\zeta_k \in X_{safe}$. In view of the focus on scalability for this Case Study 3, we disregard discussing the computed probabilities, which we instead covered in Sect. 4.1.

Implementation. Similar to Case Study 2, we follow lines 3–14 in Listing 1.1 to define the model dynamics, while we use Listing 1.3 to specify the verification task using the IMDP method. For this example, we employ a uniform grid having a grid size of 1 and relative tolerance of 1 for each dimension (cf. lines 5–10 in

Table 2. *Case study 3:* Verification results of the IMDP-based approach over φ_3, for varying dimension d of the stochastic process.

Dimensions [d]	2	3	4	5	6	7	8	9	10	11	12
$\|\mathcal{Q}\|$ [states]	4	14	30	62	126	254	510	1022	2046	4094	8190
Time taken [s]	0.004	0.06	0.21	0.90	4.16	19.08	79.63	319.25	1601.31	5705.47	21134.23
Error (ε_{max})	4.15e-5	3.34e-5	2.28e-5	9.70e-5	8.81e-6	1.10e-6	2.95e-6	4.50e-7	1.06e-7	4.90e-8	4.89e-8

Listing 1.3). We set `K = -1` to represent an unbounded time horizon, `p = 1` to perform verification over a safety property and `lb = 3` to use the IMDP method (cf. lines 12–19 in Listing 1.3). In Table 2 we list the number of states required for each dimension, the total computational time, and the maximum error associated with each abstraction.

Outcomes. From Table 2 we can deduce that by employing the IMDP method within StocHy, the generated abstract models have manageable state spaces, thanks to the tight error bounds that is obtained. Notice that since the number of cells per dimension is increased with the dimension d of the model, the associated abstraction error ε_{max} is decreased. The small error is also due to the underlying contractive dynamics of the process. This is a key fact leading to scalability over the continuous dimension d of the model: StocHy displays a significant improvement in scalability over the state of the art [28] and allows abstracting stochastic models with relevant dimensionality. Furthermore, StocHy is capable to handle specifications over infinite horizons (such as the considered *until* formula).

4.4 Case Study 4 - Simulations

For this last case study, we refer to the CO_2 model described in Case Study 1 (Sect. 4.1). We extend the CO_2 model to capture (i) the effect of occupants leaving or entering the zone within a time step (ii) the opening or closing of the windows in the zone [2]. ρ_m is now a control input and is an exogenous signal. This can be described as a SHS comprising two-dimensional dynamics, over discrete modes in the set $\{q_0 = (E, C), q_1 = (F, C), q_2 = (F, O), q_3 = (E, O)\}$ describing possible configurations of the room (empty (E) or full (F), and with windows open (O) or closed (C)). A MC representing the discrete modes and their dynamics is in Fig. 3a. The continuous variables evolve according to Eq. (6), which now captures the effect of switching between discrete modes, as

$$x_{1,k+1} = x_{1,k} + \frac{\Delta}{V}(-\rho_m x_{1,k} + \varrho_{o,c}(C_{out} - x_{1,k})) + \mathbf{1}_F C_{occ,k} + \sigma_1 w_k, \tag{7}$$

$$x_{2,k+1} = x_{2,k} + \frac{\Delta}{C_z}(\rho_m C_{pa}(T_{set} - x_{2,k}) + \frac{\varrho_{o,c}}{R}(T_{out} - x_{2,k})) + \mathbf{1}_F T_{occ,k} + \sigma_2 w_k,$$

where the additional terms are: $\varrho_{(\cdot)}$ is the natural drift air flow that changes depending whether the window is open (ϱ_o) or closed (ϱ_c) $[m^3/min]$; C_{occ} is the generated CO_2 level when the zone is occupied (it is multiplied by the indicator

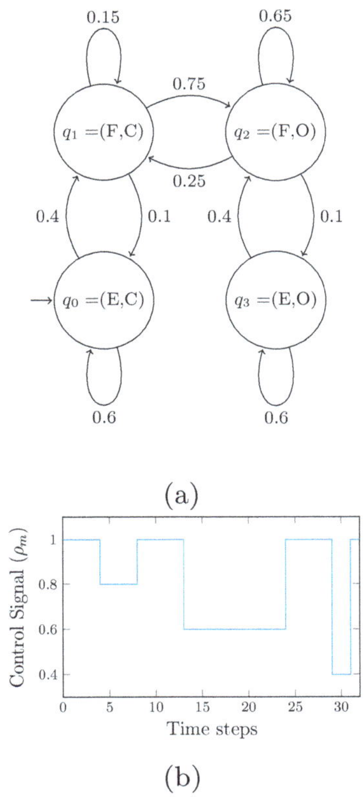

Fig. 3. *Case study 4:* (a) MC for the discrete modes of the CO_2 model and (b) input control signal.

```
1  // Number of simulations
2  int monte = 5000;
3  // Initial continuous variables
4  arma::mat x_init =
       arma::zeros<arma::mat>(2,monte);
5  // Initialise random generators
6  std::random_device rand_dev;
7  std::mt19937 generator(rand_dev());
8  // Define distributions
9  std::normal_distribution<double>
       d1{450,25};
10 std::normal_distribution<double> d2{17,2};
11 for(size_t i = 0; i < monte; ++i)
12 {
13  x_init(0,i) = d1(generator);
14  x_init(1,i) = d2(generator);
15 }
16 // Initial discrete mode q_0 = (E,C)
17 arma::mat q_init =
       arma::zeros<arma::mat>(1,monte);
18 // Definition of control signal
19 // Read from .txt/.mat file or define here
20 arma::mat u =readInputSignal("../u.txt");
21 //Combining
22 exdata_t data(x_init,u,q_init);
```

Listing 1.4: *Case study 4:* Definition of intial conditions for simulation

function $\mathbf{1}_F$) $[ppm/min]$; T_{occ} is the generated heat due to occupants $[\,^{\circ}C/min]$, which couples the dynamics in (7) as $T_{occ,k} = v x_{1,k} + \hbar$.

Implementation. The provided file CS4.MAT sets the values of the parameters in (7) and contains the transition probability matrix representing the relationships between discrete modes. We select a sampling time $\Delta = 15$ $[min]$ and simulate the evolution of this dynamical model over a fixed time horizon $K = 8$ h (i.e. 32 steps) with an initial CO_2 level $x_1 \sim \mathcal{N}(450, 25)$ $[ppm]$ and a temperature level of $x_2 \sim \mathcal{N}(17, 2)$ $[\,^{\circ}C]$. We define the initial conditions using Listing 1.4. Line 2 defines the number of Monte Carlo simulations using by the variable `monte` and sets this to 5000. We instantiate the initial values of the continuous variables using the term `x_init`, while we set the initial discrete mode using the variable `q_init`. This is done using lines 4–17 which defines independent normal distribution for each of the continuous variable from which we sample 5000 points for each of the continuous variables and defines the initial discrete mode to $q_0 = (E, C)$. We define the control signal ρ_m in line 20, by parsing the `u.txt` which contains discrete values of ρ_m for each time step (see Fig. 3b). Once the model is defined, we follow Listing 1.1 to perform the simulation. The simulation

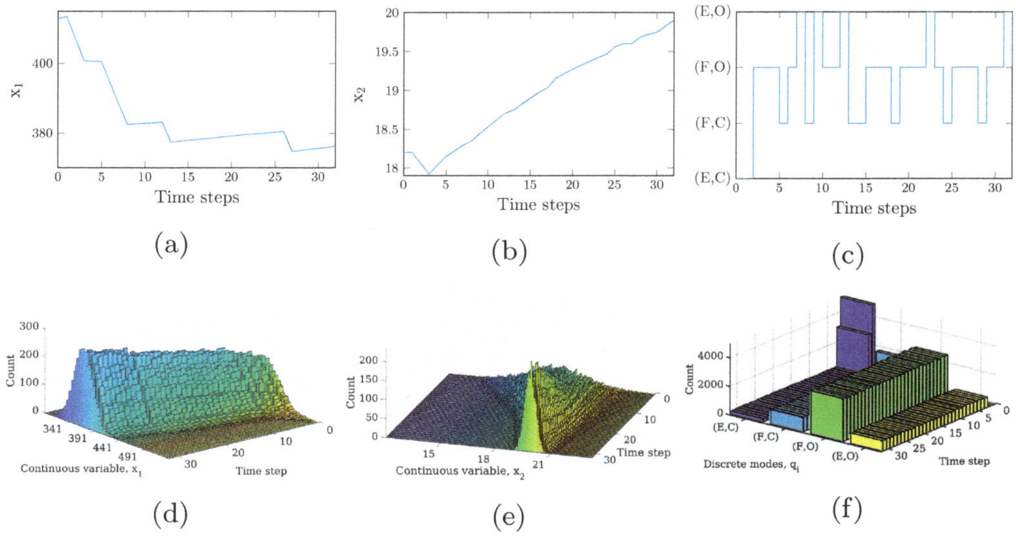

Fig. 4. *Case study 4:* Simulation single traces for continuous variables (a) x_1, (b) x_2 and discrete modes (c) q. Histogram plots with respect to time step for (d) x_1, (e) x_2 and discrete modes (f) q.

engine also generates a PYTHON script, `simPlots.py`, which gives the option to visualise the simulation outcomes offline.

Outcomes. The generated simulation plots are shown in Fig. 4, which depicts: (i) a sample trace for each continuous variable (the evolution of x_1 is shown in Fig. 4a, x_2 in Fig. 4b) and for the discrete modes (see Fig. 4c); and (ii) histograms depicting the range of values the continuous variables can be in during each time step and the associated count (see Fig. 4c for x_1 and Fig. 4e for x_2); and a histogram showing the likelihood of being in a discrete mode within each time step (see Fig. 4f). The total time taken to generate the simulations is 48.6 [s].

5 Conclusions and Extensions

We have presented StocHy, a new software tool for the quantitative analysis of stochastic hybrid systems. There is a plethora of enticing extensions that we are planning to explore. In the short term, we intend to: (i) interface with other model checking tools such as STORM [12] and the MODEST TOOLSET [16]; (ii) embed algorithms for policy refinement, so we can generate policies for models having numerous continuous input variables [15]; (iii) benchmarking the tool against a set of SHS models [10]. In the longer term, we plan to extend StocHy such that (i) it can employ a graphical user-interface; (ii) it can allow analysis of continuous-time SHS; and (iii) it can make use of data structures such as multi-terminal binary decision diagrams [14] to reduce the memory requirements during the construction of the abstract MDP or IMDP.

Acknowledgements. The author's would also like to thank Kurt Degiorgio, Sadegh Soudjani, Sofie Haesaert, Luca Laurenti, Morteza Lahijanian, Gareth Molyneux and Viraj Brian Wijesuriya. This work is in part funded by the Alan Turing Institute, London, and by Malta's ENDEAVOUR Scholarships Scheme.

References

1. Abate, A., Prandini, M., Lygeros, J., Sastry, S.: Probabilistic reachability and safety for controlled discrete time stochastic hybrid systems. Automatica **44**(11), 2724–2734 (2008)
2. Abate, A.: Formal verification of complex systems: model-based and data-driven methods. In: Proceedings of the 15th ACM-IEEE International Conference on Formal Methods and Models for System Design, MEMOCODE 2017, Vienna, Austria, 29 September–02 October 2017, pp. 91–93 (2017)
3. Abate, A., et al.: ARCH-COMP18 category report: stochastic modelling. EPiC Ser. Comput. **54**, 71–103 (2018)
4. Abate, A., Katoen, J.P., Lygeros, J., Prandini, M.: Approximate model checking of stochastic hybrid systems. Eur. J. Control **16**(6), 624–641 (2010)
5. Baier, C., Katoen, J.P.: Principles of Model Checking. MIT Press, Cambridge (2008)
6. Bauer, C., Frink, A., Kreckel, R.: Introduction to the GiNaC framework for symbolic computation within the C++ programming language. J. Symbolic Comput. **33**(1), 1–12 (2002)
7. Blom, H., Lygeros, J. (eds.): Stochastic Hybrid Systems: Theory and Safety Critical Applications. LNCIS, vol. 337. Springer, Heidelberg (2006). https://doi.org/10.1007/11587392
8. Bouissou, M., Elmqvist, H., Otter, M., Benveniste, A.: Efficient Monte Carlo simulation of stochastic hybrid systems. In: Proceedings of the 10th International Modelica Conference, Lund, Sweden, 10–12 March 2014, no. 96, pp. 715–725. Linköping University Electronic Press (2014)
9. Budde, C.E., Dehnert, C., Hahn, E.M., Hartmanns, A., Junges, S., Turrini, A.: JANI: quantitative model and tool interaction. In: Legay, A., Margaria, T. (eds.) TACAS 2017. LNCS, vol. 10206, pp. 151–168. Springer, Heidelberg (2017). https://doi.org/10.1007/978-3-662-54580-5_9
10. Cauchi, N., Abate, A.: Benchmarks for cyber-physical systems: a modular model library for building automation systems. IFAC-PapersOnLine **51**(16), 49–54 (2018). 6th IFAC Conference on Analysis and Design of Hybrid Systems ADHS 2018
11. Cauchi, N., Laurenti, L., Lahijanian, M., Abate, A., Kwiatkowska, M., Cardelli, L.: Efficiency through uncertainty: scalable formal synthesis for stochastic hybrid systems. In: 22nd ACM International Conference on Hybrid Systems: Computation and Control (HSCC) (2019). arXiv:1901.01576
12. Dehnert, C., Junges, S., Katoen, J.-P., Volk, M.: A storm is coming: a modern probabilistic model checker. In: Majumdar, R., Kunčak, V. (eds.) CAV 2017. LNCS, vol. 10427, pp. 592–600. Springer, Cham (2017). https://doi.org/10.1007/978-3-319-63390-9_31
13. Everdij, M.H., Blom, H.A.: Hybrid Petri Nets with diffusion that have into-mappings with generalised stochastic hybrid processes. In: Blom, H.A.P., Lygeros, J. (eds.) Stochastic Hybrid Systems. LNCIS, vol. 337, pp. 31–63. Springer, Heidelberg (2006). https://doi.org/10.1007/11587392_2
14. Fujita, M., McGeer, P.C., Yang, J.Y.: Multi-terminal binary decision diagrams: an efficient data structure for matrix representation. Formal Methods Syst. Des. **10**(2–3), 149–169 (1997)
15. Haesaert, S., Cauchi, N., Abate, A.: Certified policy synthesis for general Markov decision processes: an application in building automation systems. Perform. Eval. **117**, 75–103 (2017)

16. Hahn, E.M., Hartmanns, A., Hermanns, H., Katoen, J.P.: A compositional modelling and analysis framework for stochastic hybrid systems. Formal Methods Syst. Des. **43**(2), 191–232 (2013)
17. Hahn, E.M., Li, Y., Schewe, S., Turrini, A., Zhang, L.: iscasMc: a web-based probabilistic model checker. In: Jones, C., Pihlajasaari, P., Sun, J. (eds.) FM 2014. LNCS, vol. 8442, pp. 312–317. Springer, Cham (2014). https://doi.org/10.1007/978-3-319-06410-9_22
18. Hartmanns, A., Hermanns, H.: The modest toolset: an integrated environment for quantitative modelling and verification. In: Ábrahám, E., Havelund, K. (eds.) TACAS 2014. LNCS, vol. 8413, pp. 593–598. Springer, Heidelberg (2014). https://doi.org/10.1007/978-3-642-54862-8_51
19. Krystul, J., Blom, H.A.: Sequential Monte Carlo simulation of rare event probability in stochastic hybrid systems. IFAC Proc. Volumes **38**(1), 176–181 (2005)
20. Kupferman, O., Vardi, M.Y.: Model checking of safety properties. Formal Methods Syst. Des. **19**(3), 291–314 (2001)
21. Kwiatkowska, M., Norman, G., Parker, D.: PRISM 4.0: verification of probabilistic real-time systems. In: Gopalakrishnan, G., Qadeer, S. (eds.) CAV 2011. LNCS, vol. 6806, pp. 585–591. Springer, Heidelberg (2011). https://doi.org/10.1007/978-3-642-22110-1_47
22. Lahijanian, M., Andersson, S.B., Belta, C.: Formal verification and synthesis for discrete-time stochastic systems. IEEE Trans. Autom. Control **60**(8), 2031–2045 (2015)
23. Larsen, K.G., Mikučionis, M., Muñiz, M., Srba, J., Taankvist, J.H.: Online and compositional learning of controllers with application to floor heating. In: Chechik, M., Raskin, J.-F. (eds.) TACAS 2016. LNCS, vol. 9636, pp. 244–259. Springer, Heidelberg (2016). https://doi.org/10.1007/978-3-662-49674-9_14
24. Sanderson, C., Curtin, R.: Armadillo: a template-based C++ library for linear algebra. J. Open Source Softw. **1**, 26–32 (2016)
25. Sanderson, C., Curtin, R.: A user-friendly hybrid sparse matrix class in C++. In: Davenport, J.H., Kauers, M., Labahn, G., Urban, J. (eds.) ICMS 2018. LNCS, vol. 10931, pp. 422–430. Springer, Cham (2018). https://doi.org/10.1007/978-3-319-96418-8_50
26. Škulj, D.: Discrete time Markov chains with interval probabilities. Int. J. Approx. Reason. **50**(8), 1314–1329 (2009)
27. Soudjani, S.E.Z.: Formal abstractions for automated verification and synthesis of stochastic systems. Ph.D. thesis, TU Delft (2014)
28. Soudjani, S.E.Z., Gevaerts, C., Abate, A.: FAUST^2: formal abstractions of uncountable-STate STochastic processes. In: Baier, C., Tinelli, C. (eds.) TACAS 2015. LNCS, vol. 9035, pp. 272–286. Springer, Heidelberg (2015). https://doi.org/10.1007/978-3-662-46681-0_23
29. Střelec, M., Macek, K., Abate, A.: Modeling and simulation of a microgrid as a stochastic hybrid system. In: 2012 3rd IEEE PES Innovative Smart Grid Technologies Europe (ISGT Europe), pp. 1–9, October 2012
30. Summers, S., Lygeros, J.: Verification of discrete time stochastic hybrid systems: a stochastic reach-avoid decision problem. Automatica **46**(12), 1951–1961 (2010)
31. Cauchi, N., Abate, A.: Artifact and instructions to generate experimental results for TACAS 2019 paper: StocHy: automated verification and synthesis of stochastic processes (artifact). Figshare (2019). https://doi.org/10.6084/m9.figshare.7819487.v1

Synthesis of Symbolic Controllers: A Parallelized and Sparsity-Aware Approach

Mahmoud Khaled[1(✉)], Eric S. Kim[2], Murat Arcak[2], and Majid Zamani[3,4]

[1] Department of Electrical and Computer Engineering, Technical University of Munich, Munich, Germany
khaled.mahmoud@tum.de

[2] Department of Electrical Engineering and Computer Sciences, University of California Berkeley, Berkeley, CA, USA
{eskim,arcak}@berkeley.edu

[3] Department of Computer Science, University of Colorado Boulder, Boulder, USA
majid.zamani@colorado.edu

[4] Department of Computer Science, Ludwig Maximilian University of Munich, Munich, Germany

Abstract. The correctness of control software in many safety-critical applications such as autonomous vehicles is very crucial. One approach to achieve this goal is through "symbolic control", where complex physical systems are approximated by finite-state abstractions. Then, using those abstractions, provably-correct digital controllers are algorithmically synthesized for concrete systems, satisfying some complex high-level requirements. Unfortunately, the complexity of constructing such abstractions and synthesizing their controllers grows exponentially in the number of state variables in the system. This limits its applicability to simple physical systems.

This paper presents a unified approach that utilizes sparsity of the interconnection structure in dynamical systems for both construction of finite abstractions and synthesis of symbolic controllers. In addition, parallel algorithms are proposed to target high-performance computing (HPC) platforms and Cloud-computing services. The results show remarkable reductions in computation times. In particular, we demonstrate the effectiveness of the proposed approach on a 7-dimensional model of a BMW 320i car by designing a controller to keep the car in the travel lane unless it is blocked.

1 Introduction

Recently, the world has witnessed many emerging safety-critical applications such as smart buildings, autonomous vehicles and smart grids. These applications are examples of cyber-physical systems (CPS). In CPS, embedded control

This work was supported in part by the H2020 ERC Starting Grant AutoCPS and the U.S. National Science Foundation grant CNS-1446145.

T. Vojnar and L. Zhang (Eds.): TACAS 2019, Part II, LNCS 11428, pp. 265–281, 2019.
https://doi.org/10.1007/978-3-030-17465-1_15

software plays a significant role by monitoring and controlling several physical variables, such as pressure or velocity, through multiple sensors and actuators, and communicates with other systems or with supporting computing servers. A novel approach to design provably correct embedded control software in an automated fashion, is via formal method techniques [10,11], and in particular *symbolic control.*

Symbolic control provides algorithmically provably-correct controllers based on the dynamics of physical systems and some given high-level requirements. In symbolic control, physical systems are approximated by finite abstractions and then discrete (a.k.a. symbolic) controllers are automatically synthesized for those abstractions, using automata-theoretic techniques [5]. Finally, those controllers will be refined to hybrid ones applicable to the original physical systems. Unlike traditional design-then-test workflows, merging design phases with formal verification ensures that controllers are certified-by-construction. Current implementations of symbolic control, unfortunately, take a monolithic view of systems, where the entire system is modeled, abstracted, and a controller is synthesized from the overall state sets. This view interacts poorly with the symbolic approach, whose complexity grows exponentially in the number of state variables in the model. Consequently, the technique is limited to small dynamical systems.

1.1 Related Work

Recently, two promising techniques were proposed for mitigating the computational complexity of symbolic controller synthesis. The first technique [2] utilizes sparsity of internal interconnection of dynamical systems to efficiently construct their finite abstractions. It is only presented for constructing abstractions while controller synthesis is still performed monolithically without taking into account the sparse structure. The second technique [4] provides parallel algorithms targeting high performance (HPC) computing platforms, but suffers from state-explosion problem when the number of parallel processing elements (PE) is fixed. We briefly discuss each of those techniques and propose an approach that efficiently utilizes both of them.

Many abstraction techniques implemented in existing tools, including `SCOTS` [9], traverse the state space in a brute force way and suffer from an exponential runtime with respect to the number of state variables. The authors of [2] note that a majority of continuous-space systems exhibit a coordinate structure, where the governing equation for each state variable is defined independently. When the equations depend only on a few continuous variables, then they are said to be sparse. They proposed a modification to the traditional brute-force procedure to take advantage of such sparsity only in constructing abstractions. Unfortunately, the authors do not leverage sparsity to improve synthesis of symbolic controllers, which is, practically, more computationally complex. In this paper, we propose a parallel implementation of their technique to utilize HPC platforms. We also show how sparsity can be utilized, using a parallel implementation, during the controller synthesis phase as well.

The framework `pFaces` [4] is introduced as an acceleration ecosystem for implementations of symbolic control techniques. Parallel implementations of the abstraction and synthesis algorithms are introduced as computation kernels in `pFaces`, which are were originally done serially in `SCOTS` [9]. The proposed algorithms treat the problem as a data-parallel task and they scale remarkably well as the number of PEs increases. `pFaces` allows controlling the complexity of symbolic controller synthesis by adding more PEs. The results introduced in [4] outperform all exiting tools for abstraction construction and controller synthesis. However, for a fixed number of PEs, the algorithms still suffer from the state-explosion problem.

In this paper, we propose parallel algorithms that utilize the sparsity of the interconnection in the construction of abstraction and controller synthesis. In particular, the main contributions of this paper are twofold:

(1) We introduce a parallel algorithm for constructing abstractions with a distributed data container. The algorithm utilizes sparsity and can run on HPC platforms. We implement it in the framework of `pFaces` and it shows remarkable reduction in computation time compared to the results in [2].
(2) We introduce a parallel algorithm that integrates sparsity of dynamical systems into the controller synthesis phase. Specifically, a sparsity-aware preprocessing step concentrates computational resources in a small relevant subset of the state-input space. This algorithm returns the same result as the monolithic procedure, while exhibiting lower runtimes. To the best of our knowledge, the proposed algorithm is the first to merge parallelism with sparsity in the context of symbolic controller synthesis.

2 Preliminaries

Given two sets A and B, we denote by $|A|$ the cardinality of A, by 2^A the set of all subsets of A, by $A \times B$ the Cartesian product of A and B, and by $A \setminus B$ the Pontryagin difference between the sets A and B. Set $\mathbb{R}^n$ represents the n-dimensional Euclidean space of real numbers. This symbol is annotated with subscripts to restrict it in the obvious way, e.g., $\mathbb{R}^n_+$ denotes the positive (component-wise) n-dimensional vectors. We denote by $\pi_A : A \times B \to A$ the natural projection map on A and define it, for a set $C \subseteq A \times B$, as follows: $\pi_A(C) = \{a \in A \mid \exists_{b \in B}\ (a, b) \in C\}$. Given a map $R : A \to B$ and a set $\mathcal{A} \subseteq A$, we define $R(\mathcal{A}) := \bigcup_{a \in \mathcal{A}} \{R(a)\}$. Similarly, given a set-valued map $Z : A \to 2^B$ and a set $\mathcal{A} \subseteq A$, we define $Z(\mathcal{A}) := \bigcup_{a \in \mathcal{A}} Z(a)$.

We consider general discrete-time nonlinear dynamical systems given in the form of the update equation:

$$\Sigma : x^+ = f(x, u), \tag{1}$$

where $x \in X \subseteq \mathbb{R}^n$ is a state vector and $u \in U \subseteq \mathbb{R}^m$ is an input vector. The system is assumed to start from some initial state $x(0) = x_0 \in X$ and the map f is used to update the state of the system every τ seconds. Let set $\bar{X}$ be a finite partition on X constructed by a set of hyper-rectangles of identical widths

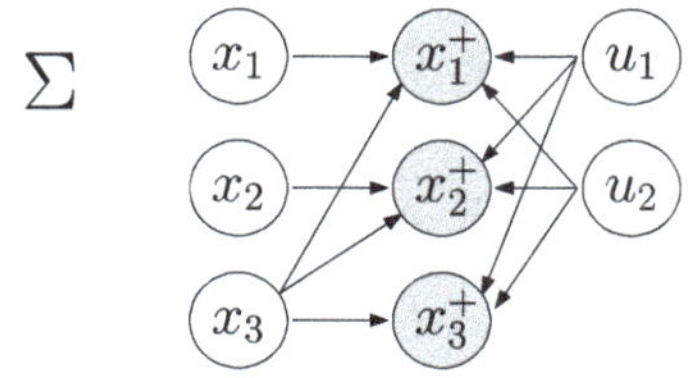

Fig. 1. The sparsity graph of the vehicle example as introduced in [2].

$\eta \in \mathbb{R}^n_+$ and let set $\bar{U}$ be a finite subset of U. A finite abstraction of (1) is a finite-state system $\bar{\Sigma} = (\bar{X}, \bar{U}, T)$, where $T \subseteq \bar{X} \times \bar{U} \times \bar{X}$ is a transition relation crafted so that there exists a feedback-refinement relation (FRR) $\mathcal{R} \subseteq X \times \bar{X}$ from Σ to $\bar{\Sigma}$. Interested readers are referred to [8] for details about FRRs and their usefulness on synthesizing controllers for concrete systems using their finite abstractions.

For a system Σ, an update-dependency graph is a directed graph of verticies representing input variables $\{u_1, u_2, \cdots, u_m\}$, state variables $\{x_1, x_2, \cdots, x_n\}$, and updated state variables $\{x_1^+, x_2^+, \cdots, x_n^+\}$, and edges that connect input (resp. states) variables to the affected updated state variables based on map f. For example, Fig. 1 depicts the update-dependency graph of the vehicle case-study presented in [2] with the update equation:

$$\begin{bmatrix} x_1^+ \\ x_2^+ \\ x_3^+ \end{bmatrix} = \begin{bmatrix} f_1(x_1, x_3, u_1, u_2) \\ f_2(x_2, x_3, u_1, u_2) \\ f_3(x_3, u_1, u_2) \end{bmatrix},$$

for some nonlinear functions f_1, f_2, and f_3. The state variable x_3 affects all updated state variables x_1^+, x_2^+, and x_3^+. Hence, the graph has edges connecting x_3 to x_1^+, x_2^+, and x_3^+, respectively. As update-dependency graphs become denser, sparsity of their corresponding abstract systems is reduced. The same graph applies to the abstract system $\bar{\Sigma}$.

We sometimes refer to $\bar{X}$, $\bar{U}$, and T as monolithic state set, monolithic input set and monolithic transition relation, respectively. A generic projection map

$$P_i^f : A \to \pi^i(A)$$

is used to extract elements of the corresponding subsets affecting the updated state $\bar{x}_i^+$. Note that $A \subseteq \bar{X} := \bar{X}_1 \times \bar{X}_2 \times \cdots \times \bar{X}_n$ when we are interested in extracting subsets of the state set and $A \subseteq \bar{U} := \bar{U}_1 \times \bar{U}_2 \times \cdots \times \bar{U}_m$ when we are interested in extracting subsets of the input set. When extracting subsets of the state set, π^i is the projection map $\pi_{\bar{X}_{k_1} \times \bar{X}_{k_2} \times \cdots \times \bar{X}_{k_K}}$, where $k_j \in \{1, 2, \cdots, n\}$, $j \in \{1, 2, \cdots, K\}$, and $\bar{X}_{k_1} \times \bar{X}_{k_2} \times \cdots \times \bar{X}_{k_K}$ is a subset of states affecting the updated state variable $\bar{x}_i^+$. Similarly, when extracting subsets of the input set, π^i is the projection map $\pi_{\bar{U}_{p_1} \times \bar{U}_{p_2} \times \cdots \times \bar{U}_{p_P}}$, where $p_i \in \{1, 2, \cdots, m\}$, $i \in \{1, 2, \cdots, P\}$, $\bar{U}_{p_1} \times \bar{U}_{p_2} \times \cdots \times \bar{U}_{p_P}$ is a subset of inputs affecting the updated state variable $\bar{x}_i^+$.

For example, assume that the monolithic state (resp. input) set of the system $\bar{\Sigma}$ in Fig. 1 is given by $\bar{X} := \bar{X}_1 \times \bar{X}_2 \times \bar{X}_3$ (resp. $\bar{U} := \bar{U}_1 \times \bar{U}_2$) such that for any $\bar{x} := (\bar{x}_1, \bar{x}_2, \bar{x}_3) \in \bar{X}$ and $\bar{u} := (\bar{u}_1, \bar{u}_2) \in \bar{U}$, one has $\bar{x}_1 \in \bar{X}_1$, $\bar{x}_2 \in \bar{X}_2$, $\bar{x}_3 \in \bar{X}_3$, $\bar{u}_1 \in \bar{U}_1$, and $\bar{u}_2 \in \bar{U}_2$. Now, based on the dependency graph, $P_1^f(\bar{x}) := \pi_{\bar{X}_1 \times \bar{X}_3}(\bar{x}) = (\bar{x}_1, \bar{x}_3)$ and $P_1^f(\bar{u}) := \pi_{\bar{U}_1 \times \bar{U}_2}(\bar{u}) = (\bar{u}_1, \bar{u}_2)$. We can also apply the map to subsets of $\bar{X}$ and $\bar{U}$, e.g., $P_1^f(\bar{X}) = \bar{X}_1 \times \bar{X}_3$, and $P_1^f(\bar{U}) = \bar{U}_1 \times \bar{U}_2$.

For a transition element $t = (\bar{x}, \bar{u}, \bar{x}') \in T$, we define $P_i^f(t) := (P_i^f(\bar{x}), P_i^f(\bar{u}), \pi_{\bar{X}_i}(\bar{x}'))$, for any component $i \in \{1, 2, \cdots, n\}$. Note that for t, the successor state $\bar{x}'$ is treated differently as it is related directly to the updated state variable $\bar{x}_i^+$. We can apply the map to subsets of T, e.g., for the given update-dependency graph in Fig. 1, one has $P_1^f(T) = \bar{X}_1 \times \bar{X}_3 \times \bar{U}_1 \times \bar{U}_2 \times \bar{X}_1$.

On the other hand, a generic recovery map

$$D_i^f : P_i^f(A) \to 2^A,$$

is used to recover elements (resp. subsets) from the projected subsets back to their original monolithic sets. Similarly, $A \subseteq \bar{X} := \bar{X}_1 \times \bar{X}_2 \times \cdots \times \bar{X}_n$ when we are interested in subsets of the state set and $A \subseteq \bar{U} := \bar{U}_1 \times \bar{U}_2 \times \cdots \times \bar{U}_m$ when we are interested in subsets of the input set.

For the same example in Fig. 1, let $\bar{x} := (\bar{x}_1, \bar{x}_2, \bar{x}_3) \in \bar{X}$ be a state. Now, define $\bar{x}_p := P_1^f(\bar{x}) = (\bar{x}_1, \bar{x}_3)$. We then have $D_1^f(\bar{x}_p) := \{(\bar{x}_1, \bar{x}_2^*, \bar{x}_3) \mid \bar{x}_2^* \in \bar{X}_2\}$. Similarly, for a transition element $t := ((\bar{x}_1, \bar{x}_2, \bar{x}_3), (\bar{u}_1, \bar{u}_2), (\bar{x}_1', \bar{x}_2', \bar{x}_3')) \in T$ and its projection $t_p := P_1^f(t) = ((\bar{x}_1, \bar{x}_3), (\bar{u}_1, \bar{u}_2), (\bar{x}_1'))$, the recovered transitions is the set $D_1^f(t_p) = \{((\bar{x}_1, \bar{x}_2^*, \bar{x}_3), (\bar{u}_1, \bar{u}_2), (\bar{x}_1', \bar{x}_2'^*, \bar{x}_3'^*)) \mid \bar{x}_2^* \in \bar{X}_2, \bar{x}_2'^* \in \bar{X}_2$, and $\bar{x}_3'^* \in \bar{X}_3\}$.

Given a subset $\widetilde{X} \subseteq \bar{X}$, let $[\widetilde{X}] := D_1^f \circ P_1^f(\widetilde{X})$. Note that $[\widetilde{X}]$ is not necessarily equal to $\widetilde{X}$. However, we have that $\widetilde{X} \subseteq [\widetilde{X}]$. Here, $[\widetilde{X}]$ over-approximates $\widetilde{X}$.

For an update map f in (1), a function $\Omega^f : \bar{X} \times \bar{U} \to X \times X$ characterizes hyper-rectangles that over-approximate the reachable sets starting from a set $\bar{x} \in \bar{X}$ when the input $\bar{u}$ is applied. For example, if a growth bound map ($\beta : \mathbb{R}^n \times U \to \mathbb{R}^n$) is used, Ω^f can be defined as follows:

$$\Omega^f(\bar{x}, \bar{u}) = (x_{lb}, x_{ub}) := (-r + f(\bar{x}_c, \bar{u}), r + f(\bar{x}_c, \bar{u})),$$

where $r = \beta(\eta/2, u)$, and $\bar{x}_c \in \bar{x}$ denotes the centroid of $\bar{x}$. Here, β is the growth bound introduced in [8, Section VIII]. An over-approximation of the reachable sets can then be obtained by the map $O^f : \bar{X} \times \bar{U} \to 2^{\bar{X}}$ defined by:

$$O^f(\bar{x}, \bar{u}) := Q \circ \Omega^f(\bar{x}, \bar{u}),$$

where Q is a quantization map defined by:

$$Q(x_{lb}, x_{ub}) = \{\bar{x}' \in \bar{X} \mid \bar{x}' \cap [\![x_{lb}, x_{ub}]\!] \neq \emptyset\}, \tag{2}$$

where $[\![x_{lb}, x_{ub}]\!] = [x_{lb,1}, x_{ub,1}] \times [x_{lb,2}, x_{ub,2}] \times \cdots \times [x_{lb,n}, x_{ub,n}]$.

We also assume that O^f can be decomposed component-wise (i.e., for each dimension $i \in \{1, 2, \cdots, n\}$) such that for any $(\bar{x}, \bar{u}) \in \bar{X} \times \bar{U}$, $O^f(\bar{x}, \bar{u}) = \bigcap_{i=1}^n D_i^f(O_i^f(P_i^f(\bar{x}), P_i^f(\bar{u})))$, where $O_i^f : P_i^f(\bar{X}) \times P_i^f(\bar{U}) \to 2^{P_i^f(\bar{X})}$ is an over-approximation function restricted to component $i \in \{1, 2, \cdots, n\}$ of f. The same assumption applies to the underlying characterization function Ω^f.

Algorithm 1: Serial algorithm for constructing abstractions (SA).

Input: $\bar{X}, \bar{U}, O^f$
Output: A transition relation $T \subseteq \bar{X} \times \bar{U} \times \bar{X}$.
$T \leftarrow \emptyset$; ▷ `Initialize the set of transitions`
for all $\bar{x} \in \bar{X}$ **do**
  for all $\bar{u} \in \bar{U}$ **do**
    for all $\bar{x}' \in O^f(\bar{x}, \bar{u})$ **do**
      $T \leftarrow T \cup \{(\bar{x}, \bar{u}, \bar{x}')\}$; ▷ `Add a new transition`
    end
  end
end

Algorithm 2: Serial sparsity-aware algorithm for constructing abstractions (Sparse-SA) as introduced in [2].

Input: $\bar{X}, \bar{U}, O^f$
Output: A transition relation $T \subseteq \bar{X} \times \bar{U} \times \bar{X}$.
1 $T \leftarrow \bar{X} \times \bar{U} \times \bar{X}$; ▷ `Initialize the set of transitions`
2 **for all** $i \in \{1, 2, \cdots, n\}$ **do**
3   $T_i \leftarrow SA(P_i^f(\bar{X}), P_i^f(\bar{U}), O_i^f)$; ▷ `Transitions of sub-spaces`
4   $T \leftarrow T \cap D_i^f(T_i)$; ▷ `Add transitions of sub-spaces`
5 **end**

3 Sparsity-Aware Distributed Constructions of Abstractions

Traditionally, constructing $\bar{\Sigma}$ is achieved monolithically and sequentially. This includes current state-of-the-art tools, e.g. `SCOTS` [9], `PESSOA` [6], `CoSyMa` [7], and `SENSE` [3]. More precisely, such tools have implementations that serially traverse each element $(\bar{x}, \bar{u}) \in \bar{X} \times \bar{U}$ to compute a set of transitions $\{(\bar{x}, \bar{u}, \bar{x}') \mid \bar{x}' \in O^f(\bar{x}, \bar{u})\}$. Algorithm 1 presents the traditional serial algorithm (denoted by SA) for constructing $\bar{\Sigma}$.

The drawback of this exhaustive search was mitigated by the technique introduced in [2] which utilizes the sparsity of $\bar{\Sigma}$. The authors suggest constructing T by applying Algorithm 1 to subsets of each component. Algorithm 2 presents a sparsity-aware serial algorithm (denoted by Sparse-SA) for constructing $\bar{\Sigma}$, as introduced in [2]. If we assume a bounded number of elements in subsets of each component (i.e., $|P_i^f(\bar{X})|$ and $|P_i^f(\bar{U})|$ from line 3 in Algorithm 2), we would expect a near-linear complexity of the algorithm. This is not clearly the case in [2, Figure 3] as the authors decided to use Binary Decision Diagrams (BDD) to represent transition relation T.

Clearly, representing T as a single storage entity is a drawback in Algorithm 2. All component-wise transition sets T_i will eventually need to push their results into T. This hinders any attempt to parallelize it unless a lock-free data structure is used, which affects the performance dramatically.

Algorithm 3: Proposed sparsity-aware parallel algorithm for constructing discrete abstractions.

Input: $\bar{X}, \bar{U}, \Omega^f$

Output: A list of characteristic sets: $K := \bigcup_{p=1}^{P} \bigcup_{i=1}^{n} K_{loc,i}^{p}$.

1 **for all** $i \in \{1, 2, \cdots, n\}$ **do**
2   **for all** $p \in \{1, 2, \cdots, P\}$ **do**
3         $K_{loc,i}^{p} \leftarrow \emptyset$; ▷ `Initialize local containers`
4   **end**
5 **end**
6 **for all** $i \in \{1, 2, \cdots, n\}$ **in parallel do**
7   **for all** $(\bar{x}, \bar{u}) \in P_i^f(\bar{X}) \times P_i^f(\bar{U})$ **in parallel with index** j **do**
8         $p = I(i, j)$; ▷ `Identify target PE`
9         $(x_{lb}, x_{ub}) \leftarrow \Omega^f(\bar{x}, \bar{u})$; ▷ `Calculate characteristics`
10         $K_{loc,i}^{p} \leftarrow K_{loc,i}^{p} \cup \{(\bar{x}, \bar{u}, (x_{lb}, x_{ub}))\}$; ▷ `Store characteristics`
11   **end**
12 **end**

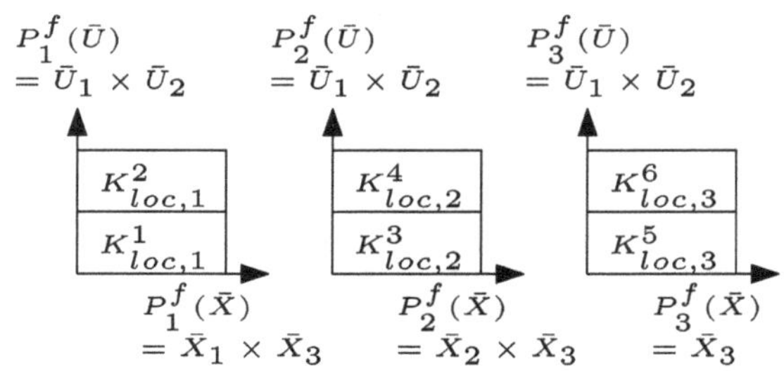

Fig. 2. An example task distributions for the parallel sparsity-aware abstraction.

On the other hand, Algorithm 2 in [4] introduces a technique for constructing $\bar{\Sigma}$ by using a distributed data container to maintain the transition set T without constructing it explicitly. In [4], using a continuous over-approximation Ω^f is favored as opposed to the discrete over-approximation O^f since it requires less memory in practice. The actual computation of transitions (i.e., using O^f to compute discrete successor states) is delayed to the synthesis phase and done on the fly. The parallel algorithm scales remarkably with respect to the number of PEs, denoted by P, since the task is parallelizable with no data dependency. However, it still handles the problem monolithically which means, for a fixed P, it will not probably scale as the system dimension n grows.

We then introduce Algorithm 3 which utilizes sparsity to construct $\bar{\Sigma}$ in parallel, and is a combination of Algorithm 2 in [4] and Algorithm 2. Function $I : \mathbb{N}_+ \setminus \{\infty\} \times \mathbb{N}_+ \setminus \{\infty\} \rightarrow \{1, 2, \cdots, P\}$ maps a parallel job (i.e., lines 9 and 10 inside the inner **parallel for-all statement**), for a component i and a tuple $(\bar{x}, \bar{u})$ with index j, to a PE with an index $p = I(i, j)$. $K_{loc,i}^{p}$ stores the characterizations of abstraction of ith component and is located in PE of index p. Collectively, $K_{loc,1}^{1}, \ldots, K_{loc,i}^{p}, \ldots, K_{loc,n}^{P}$ constitute a distributed container that stores the abstraction of the system.

Figure 2 depicts an example of the job and task distributions for the example presented in Fig. 1. Here, we use $P = 6$ with a mapping I that distributes one

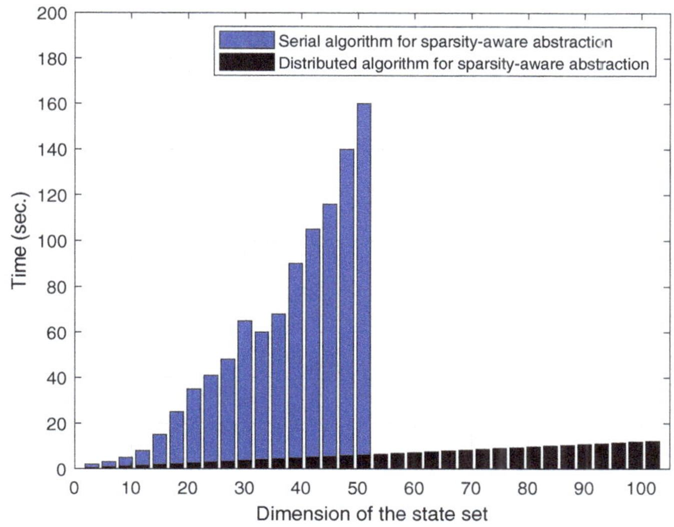

Fig. 3. Comparison between the serial and parallel algorithms for constructing abstractions of a traffic network model by varying the dimensions.

partition element of one subset $P_i^f(\bar{X}) \times P_i^f(\bar{U})$ to one PE. We also assume that the used PEs have equal computation power. Consequently, we try to divide each subset $P_i^f(\bar{X}) \times P_i^f(\bar{U})$ into two equal partition elements such that we have, in total, 6 similar computation spaces. Inside each partition element, we indicate which distributed storage container $K_{loc,i}^p$ is used.

To assess the distributed algorithm in comparison with the serial one presented in [2], we implement it in `pFaces`. We use the same traffic model presented in [2, Subsection VI-B] and the same parameters. For this example, the authors of [2] construct T_i, for each component $i \in \{1, 2, \cdots, n\}$. They combine them incrementally in a BDD that represents T. A monolithic construction of T from T_i is required in [2] since symbolic controllers synthesis is done monolithically. On the other hand, using $K_{loc,i}^p$ in our technique plays a major role in reducing the complexity of constructing higher dimensional abstractions. In Sect. 4, we utilize $K_{loc,i}^p$ directly to synthesize symbolic controllers with no need to explicitly construct T.

Figure 3 depicts a comparison between the results reported in [2, Figure 3] and the ones obtained from our implementation in `pFaces`. We use an Intel Core i5 CPU, which comes equipped with an internal GPU yielding around 24 PEs being utilized by `pFaces`. The implementation stores the distributed containers $K_{loc,i}^p$ as raw-data inside the memories of their corresponding PEs. As expected, the distributed algorithm scales linearly and we are able to go beyond 100 dimensions in a few seconds, whereas Figure 3 in [2] shows only abstractions up to a 51-dimensional traffic model because constructing the monolithic T begins to incur an exponential cost for higher dimensions.

Remark 1. Both Algorithms 2 and 3 utilize sparsity of Σ to reduce the space complexity of abstractions from $|\bar{X} \times \bar{U}|$ to $\sum_{i=1}^{n} |P_i^f(\bar{X}) \times P_i^f(\bar{U})|$. However, Algorithm 2 iterates over the space serially. Algorithm 3, on the other hand, handles the computation over the space in parallel using P PEs.

4 Sparsity-Aware Distributed Synthesis of Symbolic Controllers

Given an abstract system $\bar{\Sigma} = (\bar{X}, \bar{U}, T)$, we define the controllable predecessor map $CPre^T : 2^{\bar{X}\times\bar{U}} \to 2^{\bar{X}\times\bar{U}}$ for $Z \subseteq \bar{X} \times \bar{U}$ by:

$$CPre^T(Z) = \{(\bar{x}, \bar{u}) \in \bar{X} \times \bar{U} \mid \emptyset \neq T(\bar{x}, \bar{u}) \subseteq \pi_{\bar{X}}(Z)\}, \tag{3}$$

where $T(\bar{x}, \bar{u})$ is an interpretation of the transitions set T as a map $T : \bar{X} \times \bar{U} \to 2^{\bar{X}}$ that evaluates a set of successor states from a state-input pair. Similarly, we introduce a component-wise controllable predecessor map $CPre^{T_i} : 2^{P_i^f(\bar{X})\times P_i^f(\bar{U})} \to 2^{P_i^f(\bar{X})\times P_i^f(\bar{U})}$, for any component $i \in \{1, 2, \cdots, n\}$ and any $\widetilde{Z} := P_i^f(Z) := \pi_{P_i^f(\bar{X})\times P_i^f(\bar{U})}(Z)$, as follows:

$$CPre^{T_i}(\widetilde{Z}) = \{(\bar{x}, \bar{u}) \in P_i^f(\bar{X}) \times P_i^f(\bar{U}) \mid \emptyset \neq T_i(\bar{x}, \bar{u}) \subseteq \pi_{\bar{X}_i}(\widetilde{Z})\}. \tag{4}$$

Proposition 1. *The following inclusion holds for any $i \in \{1, 2, \cdots, n\}$ and any $Z \subseteq \bar{X} \times \bar{U}$:*

$$P_i^f(CPre^T(Z)) \subseteq CPre^{T_i}(P_i^f(Z)).$$

Proof. Consider an element $z_p \in P_i^f(CPre^T(Z))$. This implies that there exists $z \in \bar{X} \times \bar{U}$ such that $z \in CPre^T(Z)$ and $z_p = P_i^f(z)$. Consequently, $T_i(z_p) \neq \emptyset$ since $T(z) \neq \emptyset$. Also, since $z \in CPre^T(Z)$, then $T(z) \subseteq \pi_{\bar{X}}(Z)$. Now, recall how T_i is constructed as a component-wise set of transitions in line 2 in Algorithm 2. Then, we conclude that $T_i(z_p) \subseteq \pi_{\bar{X}_i}(P_i^f(Z))$. By this, we already satisfy the requirements in (4) such that $z_p = (\bar{x}, \bar{u}) \in CPre^{T_i}(Z)$.

Here, we consider reachability and invariance specifications given by the LTL formulae $\Diamond\psi$ and $\Box\psi$, respectively, where ψ is a propositional formula over a set of atomic propositions AP. We first construct an initial winning set $Z_\psi = \{(\bar{x}, \bar{u}) \in \bar{X} \times \bar{U} \mid L(\bar{x}, \bar{u}) \models \psi)\}$, where $L : \bar{X} \times \bar{U} \to 2^{AP}$ is some labeling function. During the rest of this section, we focus on reachability specifications for the sake of space and a similar discussion can be pursued for invariance specifications.

Traditionally, to synthesize symbolic controllers for the reachability specifications $\Diamond\psi$, a monotone function:

$$\underline{G}(Z) := CPre^T(Z) \cup Z_\psi \tag{5}$$

is employed to iteratively compute $Z_\infty = \mu Z.\underline{G}(Z)$ starting with $Z_0 = \emptyset$. Here, a notation from μ-calculus is used with μ as the minimal fixed point operator and $Z \subseteq \bar{X} \times \bar{U}$ is the operated variable representing the set of winning pairs $(\bar{x}, \bar{u}) \in \bar{X} \times \bar{U}$. Set $Z_\infty \subseteq \bar{X} \times \bar{U}$ represents the set of final winning pairs, after a finite number of iterations. Interested readers can find more details in [5] and the references therein. The transition map T is used in this fixed-point

Algorithm 4: Traditional serial algorithm to synthesize $\underline{C}$ enforcing the specification $\Diamond\psi$.

Input: Initial winning domain $Z_\psi \subset \bar{X} \times \bar{U}$ and T

Output: A controller $\underline{C} : \bar{X}_w \rightarrow 2^{\bar{U}}$.

$Z_\infty \leftarrow \emptyset$; ▷ Initialize a running win-pairs set
$\bar{X}_w \leftarrow \emptyset$; ▷ Initialize a running win-states set
do
  $Z_0 \leftarrow Z_\infty$; ▷ Current win-pairs gets latest win-pairs
  $Z_\infty \leftarrow CPre^T(Z_0) \cup Z_\psi$; ▷ Update the running win-pairs set
  $D \leftarrow Z_\infty \setminus Z_0$; ▷ Separate the new win-pairs
  foreach $\bar{x} \in \pi_{\bar{X}}(D)$ *with* $\bar{x} \notin \bar{X}_w$ **do**
    $\bar{X}_w \leftarrow \bar{X}_w \cup \{\bar{x}\}$; ▷ Add new win-states
    $\underline{C}(\bar{x}) := \{\bar{u} \in \bar{U} | (\bar{x}, \bar{u}) \in D\}$; ▷ Add new control actions
  end
while $Z_\infty \neq Z_0$;

computation and, hence, the technique suffers directly from the state-explosion problem. Algorithm 4 depicts a traditional serial algorithm of symbolic controller synthesis for reachability specifications. The synthesized controller is a map $\underline{C} : \bar{X}_w \rightarrow 2^{\bar{U}}$, where $\bar{X}_w \subseteq \bar{X}$ represents a winning (a.k.a. controllable) set of states. Map $\underline{C}$ is defined as: $\underline{C}(\bar{x}) = \{\bar{u} \in \bar{U} \mid (\bar{x}, \bar{u}) \in \mu^{j(\bar{x})} Z.\underline{G}(Z)\}$, where $j(\bar{x}) = \inf\{i \in \mathbb{N} \mid \bar{x} \in \pi_{\bar{X}}(\mu^i Z.\underline{G}(Z))\}$, and $\mu^i Z.\underline{G}(Z)$ represents the set of state-input pairs by the end of the ith iteration of the minimal fixed point computation.

A parallel implementation that mitigates the complexity of the fixed-point computation is introduced in [4, Algorithm 4]. Briefly, for a set $Z \subseteq \bar{X} \times \bar{U}$, each iteration of $\mu Z.\underline{G}(Z)$ is computed via parallel traversal in the complete space $\bar{X} \times \bar{U}$. Each PE is assigned a disjoint set of state-input pairs from $\bar{X} \times \bar{U}$ and it declares whether, or not, each pair belongs to the next winning pairs (i.e., $\underline{G}(Z)$). Although the algorithm scales well w.r.t P, it still suffers from the state-explosion problem for a fixed P. We present a modified algorithm that utilizes sparsity to reduce the parallel search space at each iteration.

First, we introduce the component-wise monotone function:

$$\underline{G}_i(Z) := CPre^{T_i}(P_i^f(Z)) \cup P_i^f(Z_\psi), \tag{6}$$

for any $i \in \{1, 2, \cdots, n\}$ and any $Z \in \bar{X} \times \bar{U}$. Now, an iteration in the sparsity-aware fixed-point can be summarized by the following three steps:

(1) Compute the component-wise sets $\underline{G}_i(Z)$. Note that $\underline{G}_i(Z)$ lives in the set $P_i^f(\bar{X}) \times P_i^f(\bar{U})$.
(2) Recover a monolithic set $\underline{G}_i(Z)$, for each $i \in \{1, 2, \cdots, n\}$, using the map D_i^f and intersect these sets. Formally, we denote this intersection by:

$$[\underline{G}(Z)] := \bigcap_{i=1}^{n} (D_i^f(\underline{G}_i(Z))). \tag{7}$$

Note that $[\underline{G}(Z)]$ is an over-approximation of the monolithic set $\underline{G}(Z)$, which we prove in Theorem 1.

(3) Now, based on the next theorem, there is no need for a parallel search in $\bar{X} \times \bar{U}$ and the search can be done in $[\underline{G}(Z)]$. More accurately, the search for new elements in the next winning set can be done in $[\underline{G}(Z)] \setminus Z$.

Theorem 1. *Consider an abstract system* $\bar{\Sigma} = (\bar{X}, \bar{U}, T)$. *For any set* $Z \in \bar{X} \times \bar{U}$, $\underline{G}(Z) \subseteq [\underline{G}(Z)]$.

Proof. Consider any element $z \in \underline{G}(Z)$. This implies that $z \in Z$, $z \in Z_\psi$ or $z \in CPre^T(Z)$. We show that $z \in [\underline{G}(Z)]$ for any of these cases.

Case 1 $[z \in Z]$: By the definition of map P_i^f, we know that $P_i^f(z) \in P_i^f(Z)$. By the monotonicity of map $\underline{G}_i$, $P_i^f(Z) \subseteq \underline{G}_i(Z)$. This implies that $P_i^f(z) \in \underline{G}_i(Z)$. Also, by the definition of map D_i^f, we know that $z \in D_i^f(\underline{G}_i(Z))$. The above argument holds for any component $i \in \{1, 2, \cdots, n\}$ which implies that $z \in \bigcap_{i=1}^n (D_i^f(\underline{G}_i(Z))) = [\underline{G}(Z)]$.

Case 2 $[z \in Z_\psi]$: The same argument used for the previous case can be used for this one as well.

Case 3 $[z \in CPre^T(Z)]$: We apply the map P_i^f to both sides of the inclusion. We then have $P_i^f(z) \in P_i^f(CPre^T(Z))$. Using Proposition 1, we know that $P_i^f(CPre^T(Z)) \subseteq CPre^{T_i}(Z)$. This implies that $P_i^f(z) \in CPre^{T_i}(P_i^f(Z))$. From (6) we obtain that $P_i^f(z) \in \underline{G}_i(Z)$, and consequently, $z \in D_i^f(\underline{G}_i(Z))$. The above argument holds for any component $i \in \{1, 2, \cdots, n\}$. This, consequently, implies that $z \in \bigcap_{i=1}^n (D_i^f(\underline{G}_i(Z))) = [\underline{G}(Z)]$, which completes the proof.

Remark 2. An initial computation of the controllable predecessor is done component-wise in step (1) which utilizes the sparsity of $\bar{\Sigma}$ and can be easily implemented in parallel. Only in step (3) a monolithic search is required. However, unlike the implementation in [4, Algorithm 4], the search is performed only for a subset of $\bar{X} \times \bar{U}$, which is $[\underline{G}(Z)] \setminus Z$.

Note that dynamical systems pose some locality property (i.e., starting from nearby states, successor states are also nearby) and an initial winning set will grow incrementally with each fixed-point iteration. This makes the set $[\underline{G}(Z)] \setminus Z$ relatively small w.r.t $|\bar{X} \times \bar{U}|$. We clarify this and the result in Theorem 1 with a small example.

4.1 An Illustrative Example

For the sake of illustrating the proposed sparsity-aware synthesis technique, we provide a simple two-dimensional example. Consider a robot described by the following difference equation:

$$\begin{bmatrix} x_1^+ \\ x_2^+ \end{bmatrix} = \begin{bmatrix} x_1 + \tau u_1 \\ x_2 + \tau u_2 \end{bmatrix},$$

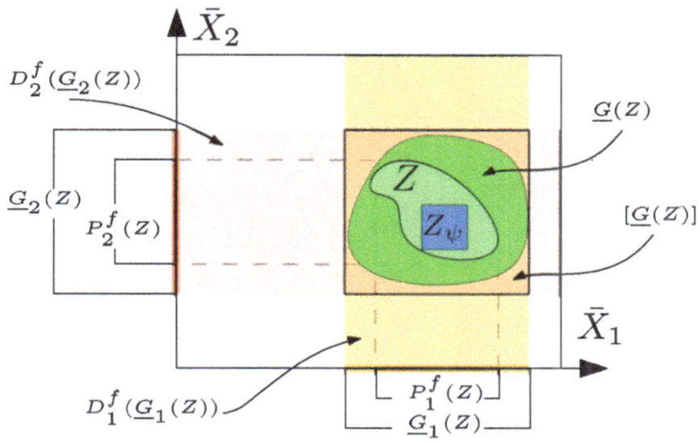

Fig. 4. A visualization of one arbitrary fixed-point iteration of the sparsity-aware synthesis technique for a two-dimensional robot system.

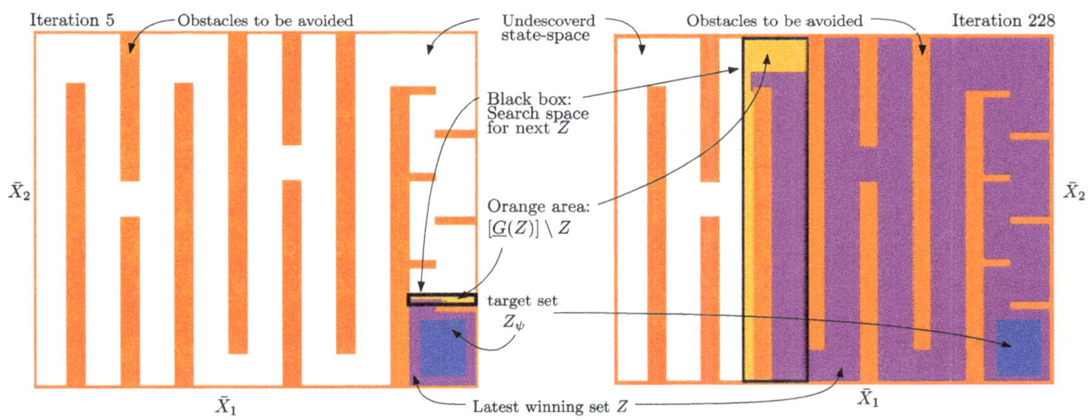

Fig. 5. The evolution of the fixed-point sets for the robot example by the end of fixed-point iterations 5 (left side) and 228 (right side). A video of all iterations can be found in: http://goo.gl/aegznf.

where $(x_1, x_2) \in \bar{X} := \bar{X}_1 \times \bar{X}_2$ is a state vector and $(u_1, u_2) \in \bar{U} := \bar{U}_1 \times \bar{U}_2$ is an input vector. Figure 4 shows a visualization of the sets related to this sparsity-aware technique for symbolic controller synthesis for one fixed-point iteration. Set Z_ψ is the initial winning-set (a.k.a. target-set for reachability specifications) constructed from a given specification (e.g., a region in $\bar{X}$ to be reached by the robot) and Z is the winning-set of the current fixed-point iteration. For simplicity, all sets are projected on $\bar{X}$ and the readers can think of $\bar{U}$ as an additional dimension perpendicular to the surface of this paper.

As depicted in Fig. 4, the next winning-set $\underline{G}(Z)$ is over-approximated by $[\underline{G}(Z)]$, as a result of Theorem 1. Algorithm 4 in [4] searches for $\underline{G}(Z)$ in $(\bar{X}_1 \times \bar{X}_2) \times (\bar{U}_1 \times \bar{U}_2)$. This work suggests searching for $\underline{G}(Z)$ in $[\underline{G}(Z)] \setminus Z$ instead.

4.2 A Sparsity-Aware Parallel Algorithm for Symbolic Controller Synthesis

We propose Algorithm 5 to parallelize sparsity-aware controller synthesis. The main difference between this and Algorithm 4 in [4] are lines 9–12. They

Algorithm 5: Proposed parallel sparsity-aware algorithm to synthesize $\underline{C}$ enforcing specification $\Diamond\psi$.

Input: Initial winning domain $Z_\psi \subset \bar{X} \times \bar{U}$ and T
Output: A controller $\underline{C} : \bar{X}_w \to 2^{\bar{U}}$.
1 $Z_\infty \leftarrow \emptyset$; ▷ `Initialize a shared win-pairs set`
2 $\bar{X}_w \leftarrow \emptyset$; ▷ `Initialize a shared win-states set`
3 **do**
4   $Z_0 \leftarrow Z_\infty$; ▷ `Current win-pairs set gets latest win-pairs`
5   **for all** $p \in \{1, 2, \cdots, P\}$ **do**
6     $Z^p_{loc} \leftarrow \emptyset$; ▷ `Initialize a local win-pairs set`
7     $\bar{X}^p_{w,loc} \leftarrow \emptyset$; ▷ `Initialize a local win-states set`
8   **end**
9   $[\underline{G}] \leftarrow \bar{X} \times \bar{U}$; ▷ `Initialize` $[\underline{G}(Z)]$
10   **for all** $i \in \{1, 2, \cdots, n\}$ **do**
11     $[\underline{G}] \leftarrow [\underline{G}] \cap D^f_i(\underline{G}_i(Z_\infty))$; ▷ `Over-approximate`
12   **end**
13   **for all** $(\bar{x}, \bar{u}) \in [\underline{G}] \setminus Z_\infty$ **in parallel with index** j **do**
14     $p = I(i)$; ▷ `Identify a PE`
15     $Posts \leftarrow Q \circ K^p_{loc}(\bar{x}, \bar{u})$; ▷ `Compute successor states`
16   **if** $Posts \subseteq Z_0 \cup Z_\psi$ **then**
17       $Z^p_{loc} \leftarrow Z^p_{loc} \cup \{(\bar{x}, \bar{u})\}$; ▷ `Record a winning pair`
18       $\bar{X}^p_{w,loc} \leftarrow \bar{X}^p_{w,loc} \cup \{\bar{x}\}$; ▷ `Record a winning state`
19   **if** $\bar{x} \notin \pi_{\bar{X}}(Z_0)$ **then**
20         $\underline{C}(\bar{x}) \leftarrow \underline{C}(\bar{x}) \cup \{\bar{u}\}$; ▷ `Record a control action`
21   **end**
22   **end**
23   **end**
24   **for all** $p \in \{1, 2, \cdots, P\}$ **do**
25     $Z_\infty \leftarrow Z_\infty \cup Z^p_{loc}$; ▷ `Update the shared win-pairs set`
26     $\bar{X}_w \leftarrow \bar{X}_w \cup \bar{X}^p_{w,loc}$; ▷ `Update the shared win-states set`
27   **end**
28 **while** $Z_\infty \neq Z_0$;

correspond to computing $[\underline{G}(Z)]$ at each iteration of the fixed-point computation. Line 13 is modified to do the parallel search inside $[\underline{G}(Z)] \setminus Z$ instead of $\bar{X} \times \bar{U}$ in the original algorithm. The rest of the algorithm is well documented in [4].

The algorithm is implemented in `pFaces` as updated versions of the kernels `GBFP` and `GBFP`$_\mathtt{m}$ in [4]. We synthesize a reachability controller for the robot example presented earlier. Figure 5 shows an arena with obstacles depicted as red boxes. It depicts the result at the fixed point iterations 5 and 228. The blue box indicates the target set (i.e., Z_ψ). The region colored with purple indicates the current winning states. The orange region indicates $[\underline{G}(Z)] \setminus Z$. The black box is the next search region which is a rectangular over approximation of the $[\underline{G}(Z)] \setminus Z$. We over-approximate $[\underline{G}(Z)] \setminus Z$ with such rectangle as it is straightforward for PEs in `pFaces` to work with rectangular parallel jobs. The synthesis problem is solved in 322 fixed-point iterations. Unlike the parallel algorithm in

[4] which searches for the next winning region inside $\bar{X} \times \bar{U}$ at each iteration, the implementation of the proposed algorithm reduces the parallel search by an average of 87% when searching inside the black boxes in each iteration.

Fig. 6. An autonomous vehicle trying to avoid a sudden obstacle on the highway.

5 Case Study: Autonomous Vehicle

We consider a vehicle described by the following 7-dimensional discrete-time single track (ST) model [1]:

$$
\begin{aligned}
x_1^+ &= x_1 + \tau x_4 \cos(x_5 + x_7),\\
x_2^+ &= x_2 + \tau x_4 \sin(x_5 + x_7),\\
x_3^+ &= x_3 + \tau u_1,\\
x_4^+ &= x_4 + \tau u_2,\\
x_5^+ &= x_5 + \tau x_6,\\
x_6^+ &= x_6 + \tfrac{\tau \mu m}{I_z(l_r + l_f)}(l_f C_{S,f}(g l_r - u_2 h_{cg}) x_3 + (l_r C_{S,r}(g l_f - u_2 h_{cg}) - l_f C_{S,f}(g l_r\\
&\quad - u_2 h_{cg})) x_7 - (l_f l_f C_{S,f}(g l_r - u_2 h_{cg}) + l_r^2 C_{S,r}(g l_f + u_2 h_{cg})) \tfrac{x_6}{x_4}),\\
x_7^+ &= x_7 + \tfrac{\tau \mu}{x4*(lf+lr)}(C_{S,f}(g l_r - u_2 h_{cg}) x_3 - (C_{S,r}(g l_f + u_2 h_{cg}) + C_{S,f}(g l_r\\
&\quad - u_2 h_{cg})) x_7 + (C_{s,r}(g l_f + u_2 h_{cg}) l_r - C_{S,f}(g l_r - u_2 h_c g) l_f) \tfrac{x_6}{x_4}) - x_6,
\end{aligned}
$$

where x_1 and x_2 are the position coordinates, x_3 is the steering angle, x_4 is the heading velocity, x_5 is the yaw angle, x_6 is the yaw rate, and x_7 is the slip angle. Variables u_1 and u_2 are inputs and they control the steering angle and heading velocity, respectively. Input and state variables are all members of $\mathbb{R}$. The model takes into account tire slip making it a good candidate for studies that consider planning of evasive maneuvers that are very close to the physical limits. We consider an update period $\tau = 0.1$ s and the following parameters for a BMW 320i car: $m = 1093$ [kg] as the total mass of the vehicle, $\mu = 1.048$ as the friction coefficient, $l_f = 1.156$ [m] as the distance from the front axle to center of gravity (CoG), $l_r = 1.422$ [m] as the distance from the rear axle to CoG, $h_{cg} = 0.574$ [m] as the height of CoG, $I_z = 1791.0$ [kg m^2] as the moment of inertia for entire mass around z axis, $C_{S,f} = 20.89$ [1/rad] as the front cornering stiffness coefficient, and $C_{S,r} = 19.89$ [1/rad] as the rear cornering stiffness coefficient.

To construct an abstract system $\bar{\Sigma}$, we consider a bounded version of the state set $X := [0, 84] \times [0, 6] \times [-0.18, 0.8] \times [12, 21] \times [-0.5, 0.5] \times [-0.8, 0.8] \times [-0.1, 0.1]$, a state quantization vector $\eta_X = (1.0, 1.0, 0.01, 3.0, 0.05, 0.1, 0.02)$, a input set $U := [-0.4, 0.4] \times [-4, 4]$, and an input quantization vector $\eta_U = (0.1, 0.5)$.

Table 1. Used HW configurations for testing the proposed technique.

Identifier	Description	PEs	Frequency
HW_1	Local machine: Intel Xeon E5-1620	8	3.6 GHz
HW_2	AWS instance `p3.16xlarge`: Intel(R) Xeon(R) E5-2686	64	2.3 GHz
HW_3	AWS instance `c5.18xlarge`: Intel Xeon Platinum 8000	72	3.6 GHz

Table 2. Results obtained after running the experiments $\texttt{EX}_1$ and $\texttt{EX}_2$.

$\texttt{EX}_1$ (Memory = 22.1 G.B.) $\lvert\bar{X} \times \bar{U}\rvert = 23.8 \times 10^9$				$\texttt{EX}_2$ (Memory = 49.2 G.B.) $\lvert\bar{X} \times \bar{U}\rvert = 52.9 \times 10^9$			
HW	Time pFaces/$\texttt{GBFP}_\texttt{m}$	Time This work	Speedup	HW	Time pFaces/$\texttt{GBFP}_\texttt{m}$	Time This work	Speedup
HW_2	2.1 h	0.5 h	4.2x	HW_1	≥24 h	8.7 h	≥2.7x
HW_3	1.9 h	0.4 h	4.7x	HW_2	8.1 h	3.2 h	2.5x

We are interested in an autonomous operation of the vehicle on a highway. Consider a situation on two-lane highway when an accident happens suddenly on the same lane on which our vehicle is traveling. The vehicle's controller should find a safe maneuver to avoid the crash with the next-appearing obstacle. Figure 6 depicts such a situation. We over-approximate the obstacle with the hyper-box $[28, 50] \times [0, 3] \times [-0.18, 0.8] \times [12, 21] \times [-0.5, 0.5] \times [-0.8, 0.8] \times [-0.1, 0.1]$.

We run the implementation on different HW configurations. We use a local machine and instances from Amazon Web Services (AWS) cloud computing services. Table 1 summarizes those configurations. We also run two different experiments. For the first one (denoted by $\texttt{EX}_1$), the goal is to only avoid the crash with the obstacle. We use a smaller version of the original state set $X := [0, 50] \times [0, 6] \times [-0.18, 0.8] \times [11, 19] \times [-0.5, 0.5] \times [-0.8, 0.8] \times [-0.1, 0.1]$. The second one (denoted by $\texttt{EX}_2$) targets the full-sized highway window (84 m), and the goal is to avoid colliding with the obstacle and get back to the right lane. Table 2 reports the obtained results. The reported times are for constructing finite abstractions of the vehicle and synthesizing symbolic controllers. Note that our results outperform easily the initial kernels in `pFaces` which itself outperforms serial implementations with speedups up to 30000x as reported in [4]. The speedup in $\texttt{EX}_1$ is higher as the obstacle consumes a relatively bigger volume in the state space. This makes $[\underline{G}(Z)] \setminus Z$ smaller and, hence, faster for our implementation.

6 Conclusion and Future Work

A unified approach that utilizes sparsity of the interconnection structure in dynamical systems is introduced for the construction of finite abstractions and synthesis of their symbolic controllers. In addition, parallel algorithms are designed to target HPC platforms and they are implemented within the framework of `pFaces`. The results show remarkable reductions in computation times.

We showed the effectiveness of the results on a 7-dimensional model of a BMW 320i car by designing a controller to keep the car in the travel lane unless it is blocked.

The technique still suffers from the memory inefficiency as inherited from `pFaces`. More specifically, the data used during the computation of abstraction and the synthesis of symbolic controllers is not encoded. Using raw data requires larger amounts of memory. Future work will focus on designing distributed data-structures that achieve a balance between memory size and access time.

References

1. Althof, M.: Commonroad: vehicle models (version 2018a). Technical report, Technical University of Munich, Garching, Germany, October 2018. https://commonroad.in.tum.de
2. Gruber, F., Kim, E.S., Arcak, M.: Sparsity-aware finite abstraction. In: Proceedings of 56th IEEE Annual Conference on Decision and Control (CDC), pp. 2366–2371. IEEE, USA, December 2017. https://doi.org/10.1109/CDC.2017.8263995
3. Khaled, M., Rungger, M., Zamani, M.: SENSE: abstraction-based synthesis of networked control systems. In: Electronic Proceedings in Theoretical Computer Science (EPTCS), vol. 272, pp. 65–78. Open Publishing Association (OPA), Waterloo, June 2018. https://doi.org/10.4204/EPTCS.272.6, http://www.hcs.ei.tum.de/software/sense
4. Khaled, M., Zamani, M.: pFaces: an acceleration ecosystem for symbolic control. In: Proceedings of the 22nd ACM International Conference on Hybrid Systems: Computation and Control, HSCC 2019. ACM, New York (2019). https://doi.org/10.1145/3302504.3311798
5. Maler, O., Pnueli, A., Sifakis, J.: On the synthesis of discrete controllers for timed systems. In: Mayr, E.W., Puech, C. (eds.) STACS 1995. LNCS, vol. 900, pp. 229–242. Springer, Heidelberg (1995). https://doi.org/10.1007/3-540-59042-0_76
6. Mazo, M., Davitian, A., Tabuada, P.: PESSOA: a tool for embedded controller synthesis. In: Touili, T., Cook, B., Jackson, P. (eds.) CAV 2010. LNCS, vol. 6174, pp. 566–569. Springer, Heidelberg (2010). https://doi.org/10.1007/978-3-642-14295-6_49
7. Mouelhi, S., Girard, A., Gössler, G.: CoSyMA: a tool for controller synthesis using multi-scale abstractions. In: Proceedings of 16th International Conference on Hybrid Systems: Computation and Control, HSCC 2013, pp. 83–88. ACM, New York (2013). https://doi.org/10.1145/2461328.2461343
8. Reissig, G., Weber, A., Rungger, M.: Feedback refinement relations for the synthesis of symbolic controllers. IEEE Trans. Autom. Control **62**(4), 1781–1796 (2017). https://doi.org/10.1109/TAC.2016.2593947
9. Rungger, M., Zamani, M.: SCOTS: a tool for the synthesis of symbolic controllers. In: Proceedings of the 19th International Conference on Hybrid Systems: Computation and Control, HSCC 2016, pp. 99–104. ACM, New York (2016). https://doi.org/10.1145/2883817.2883834
10. Tabuada, P.: Verification and Control of Hybrid Systems: A Symbolic Approach. Springer, Heidelberg (2009). https://doi.org/10.1007/978-1-4419-0224-5
11. Zamani, M., Pola, G., Mazo Jr., M., Tabuada, P.: Symbolic models for nonlinear control systems without stability assumptions. IEEE Trans. Autom. Control **57**(7), 1804–1809 (2012). https://doi.org/10.1109/TAC.2011.2176409

Symbolic Verification

$\mathrm{i}_{\mathrm{Rank}}$: A Variable Order Metric for DEDS Subject to Linear Invariants

Elvio Gilberto Amparore[1], Gianfranco Ciardo[2], Susanna Donatelli[1(✉)], and Andrew Miner[2]

[1] Dipartimento di Informatica, Università di Torino, Torino, Italy
{amparore,donatelli}@di.unito.it
[2] Iowa State University, Ames, IA, USA
{ciardo,asminer}@iastate.edu

Abstract. Finding good variable orders for decision diagrams is essential for their effective use. We consider Multiway Decision Diagrams (MDDs) encoding a set of fixed-size vectors satisfying a set of linear invariants. Two critical applications of this problem are encoding the state space of a discrete-event discrete state system (DEDS) and encoding all solutions to a set of integer constraints. After studying the relations between the MDD structure and the constraints imposed by the linear invariants, we define $\mathrm{i}_{\mathrm{Rank}}$, a new variable order metric that exploits the knowledge embedded in these invariants. We evaluate $\mathrm{i}_{\mathrm{Rank}}$ against other previously proposed metrics on a benchmark of 40 different DEDS and show that it is a better predictor of the MDD size and it is better at driving heuristics for the generation of good variable orders.

Keywords: Decision diagrams · Variable order metrics and computation

1 Introduction

Decision diagrams (DDs) are a popular data structure to encode large sets of structured data, for example vectors whose elements take values over finite domains, but it is well-known [10] that the size of the DD strongly depends on how the structure of the data (its "variables") is mapped to the structure of the DD (its "levels"). The problem of determining the association of variable(s) to levels is the "variable ordering problem" and it is known that finding an optimal order is an NP-complete problem [9] for any DD class, including binary DDs (BDDs [10]) and multiway DDs (MDDs [19]). This has given rise to a variety of metrics (to compare the effectiveness of two orders without actually building the corresponding DDs) and of heuristics (to compute sub-optimal orders, often by attempting to optimize a given metric). DDs play a central role in many system verification tools [4,11,14,20,22], where they typically support state space exploration. Tools often make use of general-purpose DD libraries [8,18,26,27]. Libraries typically support dynamic reordering to improve the current order at

T. Vojnar and L. Zhang (Eds.): TACAS 2019, Part II, LNCS 11428, pp. 285–302, 2019.
https://doi.org/10.1007/978-3-030-17465-1_16

run-time, while the definition of an initial order (static ordering) is typically up to the verification tool, which can rely on domain knowledge. The two problems are synergistic: reordering works better if the initial order is at least fairly good.

Our research seeks to find good variable order metrics and good variable order heuristics for MDDs encoding sets of fixed-size vectors, when these vectors satisfy some linear invariants. We want to answer whether it is possible to *leverage invariant information to define effective metrics and heuristics for variable order.* Two applications where this is important are *encoding the state space of a discrete-event discrete state system* and *encoding all solutions to a set of integer constraints.* In this paper, we concentrate on the first problem, but also address a special case of the second. Specifically, we study the relationship between MDDs and linear invariants with integer coefficients, and define two new metrics, PF and $\mathrm{i}_{\mathrm{Rank}}$, and associated heuristic and meta-heuristic. PF and $\mathrm{i}_{\mathrm{Rank}}$ exploit the constraint imposed by the invariants. Our evaluation shows that $\mathrm{i}_{\mathrm{Rank}}$ is superior to any other metric we consider, in all experiments we performed.

We do not discuss the state-of-the art on heuristics, see [7] for a full survey, but only metrics and on how metric optimization can guide a meta-heuristic. After the necessary background in Sect. 2, Sects. 3 and 4 define the metrics PF and $\mathrm{i}_{\mathrm{Rank}}$, based on a number of observation and propositions on the relation between MDD and invariants. Section 5 experimentally evaluates the two metrics against several other metrics on 40 different models, considering thousands of variable orders. Section 6 summarizes our results and discusses future work.

2 Background

Let $\mathbb{B} = \{\bot, \top\}$, $\mathbb{N}$ and $\mathbb{Z}$ denote the set of booleans, natural numbers, and integers, respectively. All other sets are denoted by calligraphic letters, e.g., $\mathcal{A}$.

2.1 Discrete-Event Discrete-State System and Their State Space

A *discrete-event discrete-state system* can be generally described by providing:

(1) The set of *potential* states $\mathcal{S}_{pot}$, defining the type of system states. We assume $\mathcal{S}_{pot} = \mathbb{N}^{\mathcal{V}}$; i.e., a state $\mathbf{m}$ is a valuation of a finite set $\mathcal{V}$ of natural variables.
(2) The state $\mathbf{m}_{init} \in \mathcal{S}_{pot}$, describing the *initial* state of the system.
(3) The relation $\mathcal{R} \subseteq \mathcal{S}_{pot} \times \mathcal{S}_{pot}$, describing the state-to-state transitions; if $(\mathbf{m}, \mathbf{m}') \in \mathcal{R}$, the system can move from $\mathbf{m}$ to $\mathbf{m}'$ in one step. We assume that $\mathcal{R}$ is defined by a finite set of *events* $\mathcal{E}$ and a function *Effect* $: \mathcal{E} \times \mathcal{S}_{pot} \to (\mathcal{S}_{pot} \cup \{\circ\})$, specifying the unique state $\mathbf{m}'$ reached if event e occurs in state $\mathbf{m}$, none if $\mathit{Effect}(e, \mathbf{m}) = \circ$ (e is *disabled* in $\mathbf{m}$). We write $\mathbf{m} \xrightarrow{e} \mathbf{m}'$ iff $\mathit{Effect}(e, \mathbf{m}) = \mathbf{m}' \neq \circ$.

The *reachable* states are $\mathcal{S}_{rch} = \{\mathbf{m} : \exists e_1, \ldots, e_n \in \mathcal{E}, \mathbf{m}_{init} \xrightarrow{e_1} \cdots \xrightarrow{e_n} \mathbf{m}\}$ and, for such a system, an *invariant* is a boolean function $f : \mathcal{S}_{pot} \to \mathbb{B}$ with the property that it evaluates to $\top$ in all reachable states: $\mathbf{m} \in \mathcal{S}_{rch} \Rightarrow f(\mathbf{m})$, while it may be either $\top$ or $\bot$ in the unreachable states $\mathcal{S}_{pot} \setminus \mathcal{S}_{rch}$.

We specify DEDSs as Petri nets, because of their widespread use and the large body of literature on Petri net invariants. In Petri net terminology, the evaluation of variables describes the number of *tokens* in the set $\mathcal{P}$ of *places* (thus the state, or *marking*, is a vector in $\mathbb{N}^{\mathcal{P}}$), the events $\mathcal{E}$ correspond to the *transitions* $\mathcal{T}$, while two $\mathbb{N}^{\mathcal{P}\times\mathcal{T}}$ matrices $\mathbf{C}^-$ and $\mathbf{C}^+$ define the system evolution. *Effect*$(t,\mathbf{m}) = \mathbf{m}+\mathbf{C}^+[\mathcal{P},t]-\mathbf{C}^-[\mathcal{P},t]$ (transition firing) iff $\mathbf{m} \geq \mathbf{C}^-[\mathcal{P},t]$, otherwise *Effect*$(t,\mathbf{m}) = \circ$, i.e., t is disabled in $\mathbf{m}$, where $\geq$ is interpreted componentwise. The *incidence* matrix $\mathbf{C} = \mathbf{C}^+ - \mathbf{C}^-$ is the net change to the marking caused by firing transition t is $\mathbf{C}[\mathcal{P},t]$. Figure 1 shows two Petri nets used as running example. Places are shown as circles, transitions as bars, and $\mathbf{C}^-$ ($\mathbf{C}^+$) as incoming (outgoing) arcs for transitions with the corresponding value in $\mathbf{C}^-$ ($\mathbf{C}^+$) shown on the arc (omitted if 1). The incidence matrix and initial marking are next to the nets.

A *p-flow* is a vector $\boldsymbol{\pi} \in \mathbb{Z}^{\mathcal{P}} \setminus \{\mathbf{0}\}$ such that $\boldsymbol{\pi}^T \cdot \mathbf{C} = \mathbf{0}$, and its *support* is $Supp(\boldsymbol{\pi}) = \{v \in \mathcal{P} : \boldsymbol{\pi}[v] \neq 0\}$. A p-flow $\boldsymbol{\pi}$ implies a *linear invariant* of the form $\forall \mathbf{m} \in \mathcal{S}_{rch} : \boldsymbol{\pi}^T \cdot \mathbf{m} = \boldsymbol{\pi}^T \cdot \mathbf{m}_{init}$, where $\boldsymbol{\pi}^T \cdot \mathbf{m}_{init} = Tc(\boldsymbol{\pi})$ is obviously a constant value, the *token count* of the invariant, which depends only on $\mathbf{m}_{init}$. If clear from the context, $\boldsymbol{\pi}$ may refer to either a p-flow or the implied invariant.

P-flows with no negative entries are called *p-semiflows*. Let $\mathcal{F}$ be the set of p-flows, $\mathcal{F}^+$ the set of p-semiflows, and $\mathcal{F}^- = \mathcal{F} \setminus \mathcal{F}^+$ the p-flows that are not p-semiflows. Since multiplying a p-flow by a non-zero integer results in a p-flow, these sets are either empty or infinite. Figure 1 shows the *minimal* p-flows (defined later) as column vectors, with the token count below the vector.

A p-semiflow $\boldsymbol{\pi}$ describes a *conservative invariant*, which implies a *bound* $\mathbf{m}[v] \leq Tc(\boldsymbol{\pi})/\boldsymbol{\pi}[v]$ on the number of tokens in each place v of the support of $\boldsymbol{\pi}$ for any reachable marking $\mathbf{m}$. Column "bnd" in Fig. 1 reports these bounds. The two p-semiflows in Fig. 1(A) express the following invariants:

$$f_1 : \quad \forall \mathbf{m} \in \mathcal{S}_{rch},\ \mathbf{m}[P_0] + \mathbf{m}[P_1 b] + \mathbf{m}[P_2 b] + \mathbf{m}[P_3 b] = 2$$
$$f_2 : \quad \forall \mathbf{m} \in \mathcal{S}_{rch},\ \mathbf{m}[P_0] + \mathbf{m}[P_1 a] + \mathbf{m}[P_2 a] + \mathbf{m}[P_3 a] = 2.$$

These in turn imply that the number of tokens in each place is bounded by 2. We assume that each place v is bounded by some $n_v \in \mathbb{N}$, and redefine $\mathcal{S}_{pot}$ as $\times_{v\in\mathcal{P}}[0,1,\ldots,n_v]$. This ensures that $\mathcal{S}_{rch}$ is finite and therefore can be encoded in a (large enough but finite) MDD. This is the case if the Petri net is covered by conservative invariants, i.e., each place is in the support of some p-semiflow.

Work on Petri net invariants has mainly targeted $\mathcal{F}^+$ rather than $\mathcal{F}$, possibly because it is easier to compute properties, like the bounds of places, with $\mathcal{F}^+$. On the other hand, $\mathcal{F}$ can be characterized by a basis (whose size equals to the dimension of the null space of $\mathbf{C}$, thus cannot exceed the smaller of $|\mathcal{P}|$ and $|\mathcal{T}|$), while $\mathcal{F}^+$ can only be characterized by a *minimal generator*, the smallest set of vectors that can generate its elements through non-negative integer linear combinations of its elements. It has been shown [15] that this set is finite, is unique (thus we can denote it as $\mathcal{F}^+_{min}$), and consists of all *minimal* p-semiflows

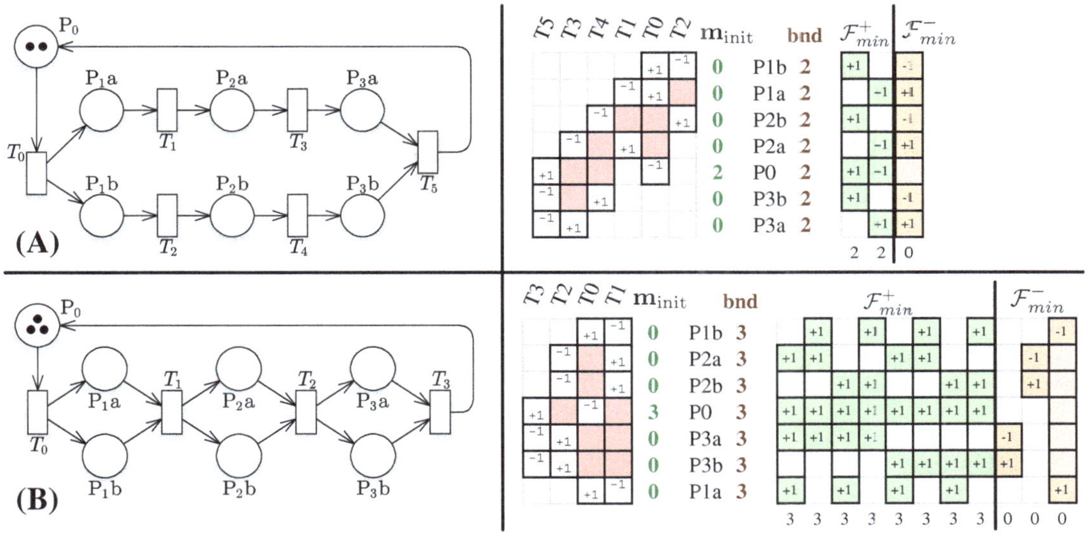

Fig. 1. Two Petri nets, their incidence matrices, and their p-flows.

(where a p-semiflow is minimal if the g.c.d. of its coefficients is 1 and its support does not strictly contain the support of another p-semiflow). However, $\mathcal{F}^+_{min}$ may have size exponential in $|\mathcal{P}|$. A classic example of this is a Petri net sequence of fork and join models with $n+1$ transitions and $2n+1$ places whose $\mathcal{F}^+_{min}$ has size 2^n. Figure 1(B) shows the case $n = 3$. The reader can find in [15] full details and a thorough analysis of the cost of computing $\mathcal{F}^+_{min}$.

In addition to $\mathcal{S}_{rch}$, we can define $\mathcal{S}_{sat} = \{\mathbf{m} \in \mathbb{N}^{\mathcal{P}} : \forall \boldsymbol{\pi} \in \mathcal{F}, \mathbf{m} \cdot \boldsymbol{\pi} = Tc(\boldsymbol{\pi})\}$. Obviously $\mathcal{S}_{rch} \subseteq \mathcal{S}_{sat}$. We let $\mathcal{S}$ refer to either when the distinction is not relevant. Note that $\mathcal{S}_{sat}$ is a superset of the *linearized reachability set* [21] $\{\mathbf{m} \in \mathbb{N}^{\mathcal{P}} : \exists\, \mathbf{y} \in \mathbb{N}^{\mathcal{T}}, \mathbf{m} = \mathbf{m}_{init} + \mathbf{C} \cdot \mathbf{y}^T\}$, used in Petri net theory to devise a semi-decidable procedure for safety properties.

2.2 Multiway Decision Diagrams

Definition 1 (MDD). Given a *global domain* $\mathcal{X} = \times_{k=1}^{L} \mathcal{X}_k$, where each *local domain* $\mathcal{X}_k$ is of the form $\{0, 1, \ldots, n_k\}$ for some $n_k \in \mathbb{N}$, an (ordered, quasi-reduced) MDD over $\mathcal{X}$ is a directed acyclic graph with exactly two terminal nodes, $\top$ and $\bot$, at *level* 0 (we write $\top.lvl = \bot.lvl = 0$), with each non-terminal node p at some level $p.lvl = k \in \{1, \ldots, L\}$ having one outgoing edge for each $i \in \mathcal{X}_k$, pointing to a node $p[i]$ at level $k-1$ or to $\bot$, and with no *duplicates* (there cannot be nodes p and q at level k with $p[i] = q[i]$ for all $i \in \mathcal{X}_k$) or *redundant* nodes (node p at level k is redundant if $p[0] = p[i]$ for all $i \in \mathcal{X}_k$) pointing to $\bot$. The function $f_p : \mathcal{X} \rightarrow \mathbb{B}$ encoded by an MDD node p is recursively defined as $f_p(i_1, \ldots, i_L) = f_{p[i_k]}(i_1, \ldots, i_L)$ if $p.lvl = k > 0$, and $f_p(i_1, \ldots, i_L) = p$ if $p.lvl = 0$. Interpreting f_p as an indicator function, p also encodes the set $\mathcal{S}_p \subseteq \mathcal{X}$, defined as $\mathcal{S}_p = \{(i_1, \ldots, i_L) : f_p(i_1, \ldots, i_L)\}$. This is the set of variable assignments compatible with the paths from p to $\top$. $\square$

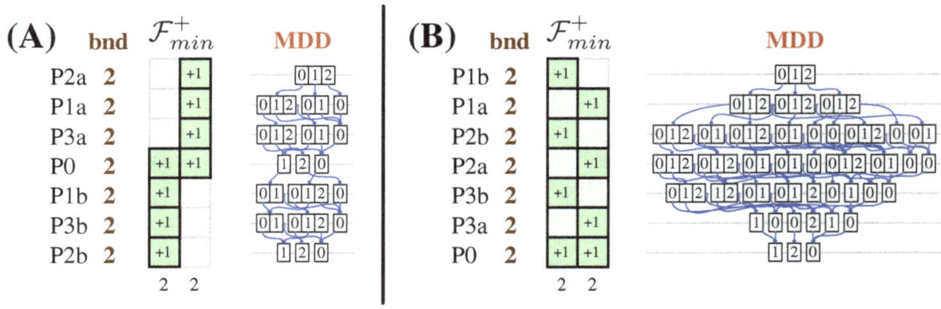

Fig. 2. P-semiflows and MDD for two variable orders for the net in Fig. 1(A).

MDDs are a *canonical* representation of subsets of $\mathcal{X}$: given MDD nodes p and q at the same level, $\mathcal{S}_p = \mathcal{S}_q$ iff $p = q$. We observe that quasi-reduced MDDs differ from the more common *fully-reduced* MDDs, which allow edges to skip levels by eliminating all redundant nodes, not just those encoding $\bot$. As it will be clear, though, the quasi-reduced MDD encoding the state space of a Petri net covered by invariants *cannot contain redundant nodes*, thus coincides with the fully-reduced MDD for such models. When drawing MDDs, edges point down and we omit node $\bot$, edges pointing to it, and the corresponding cells in the originating node, so that, if node p at level k with $\mathcal{X}_k = \{0, \ldots, 4\}$ is drawn as $\boxed{2|3}$, it means that $p[0] = p[1] = p[4] = \bot$. We also omit node $\top$ and edges pointing to it, but not the corresponding cell in the originating node.

MDDs have been successfully employed to generate and store the reachable state space of DEDSs, in particular Petri nets, using fixpoint *symbolic* iterations. The MDD representation of a state space $\mathcal{S}_{rch}$ is computed as the least fixpoint of the equation $\mathcal{Z} = \mathcal{Z} \cup \{\mathbf{m}_{init}\} \cup \{\mathbf{m}' : \mathbf{m} \in \mathcal{Z} \wedge \exists e \in \mathcal{E}, \mathbf{m} \xrightarrow{e} \mathbf{m}'\}$, while the generation of $\mathcal{S}_{sat}$ simply needs to consider one flow (and associated invariant) at a time, thus can be achieved by performing exactly $|\mathcal{F}| - 1$ intersections of the sets of assignments satisfying each individual constraint.

Since we focus on the size of the MDD encoding $\mathcal{S}$, we only consider MDDs with a single root node r, so that $\mathcal{S}_r = \mathcal{S}$. Letting $\mathcal{N}_k$ be the set of MDD nodes al level k, we characterize the MDD size in terms of its nonterminal nodes $\mathcal{N}$, i.e., $|\mathcal{N}| = \sum_{k=1}^{L} |\mathcal{N}_k|$ (although, unlike for BDDs [10] where nodes have exactly two outgoing edges, the number of MDD edges $\sum_{k=1}^{L} |\{(p, i) : p \in \mathcal{N}_k, p[i] \neq \bot\}|$ could also be a meaningful measure of size). The first step to generate $\mathcal{S}$ is to map the places $\mathcal{P}$ of the Petri net to the L levels of the MDD. We limit ourselves to mapping each place to a different level, i.e., requiring a *variable order* $\lambda : \mathcal{P} \to \{1, \ldots, L\}$, where $L = |\mathcal{P}|$. It is known that the choice of λ can exponentially affect the size of MDD and finding an optimal mapping is NP-complete [9]. We stress that we consider only the *final* size of the MDD. In reality, the fixpoint iterations to compute $\mathcal{S}_{rch}$ or the intersections to compute $\mathcal{S}_{sat}$ can lead to an intermediate size of the MDD (*peak* size) that is normally much larger than the final size. However, our work to reduce the final MDD size is largely orthogonal to other strategies (like *saturation* [13] for $\mathcal{S}_{rch}$ construction) aimed at reducing the peak size, thus both can be employed to improve efficiency.

The MDDs in Fig. 2 encode $\mathcal{S}_{rch}$ for the Petri net of Fig. 1(A), for two different variable orders. More precisely Fig. 2 shows, left to right, and for each order, the variable order (with level L at the top), the place bounds, the p-semiflows $\mathcal{F}^{+}_{min}$ (with the token count at the bottom), and the corresponding MDDs. The variable order in (B) is poor, resulting in an MDD with 40 nodes, while that in (A) requires only 19 nodes.

2.3 Metrics for Variable Orders

A metric M is a *perfect* predictor of MDD size if $M(\lambda_1) \leq M(\lambda_2)$ implies $|\mathcal{N}(\lambda_1)| \leq |\mathcal{N}(\lambda_2)|$ for any variable orders λ_1 and λ_2, where $\mathcal{N}(\lambda)$ is the number of nodes in the MDD for $\mathcal{S}$ when using variable order λ; no efficiently-computable perfect predictor is known. Metrics have been defined based on the *span of events* in the incidence matrix $\mathbf{C}$, on the *bandwidth* of $\mathbf{C}$, on the *center of gravity* of events, and on p-semiflows. Metrics that consider the span of each event t (distance between the top and bottom nonzero in $\mathbf{C}^{-}[\mathcal{P}, t]$ or $\mathbf{C}^{+}[\mathcal{P}, t]$ for the given variable order) are the Normalized sum of Event Span (NES), the Weighted NES (WES), Sum of Span (SOS) [24], Sum of Tops (SOT) [11] and Sum of Unique and Productive Spans (SOUPS) [25]. Classic bandwidth reduction techniques from linear algebra were applied to variable order computation for the first time in [23]. The corresponding metrics are Bandwidth (BW), Profile (PROF), or Wavefront (WF), computed on a squared matrix derived from the incidence matrix $\mathbf{C}$. Point-transition spans (PTS) is the metric used as a convergence criterion by the widely used heuristic FORCE [3], an algorithm for multi-dimensional clustering of graphs that has been adapted to variable order generation. A center of gravity for the variables is defined and the orders are measured in terms of *hyperdistance* of the variable from the center of gravity. PTS^P [6] is a variation of PTS to consider also the effect of p-semiflows in the PTS variable clustering. Finally, the p-semiflow span (PSF) is the metric optimized by the heuristic defined in [5], which works by ordering the variables according to p-semiflows. PSF is a measure of the proximity of places that belong to the same p-semiflow.

An overview of these metrics can be found in [6], which also studies their coefficient of correlation to determine the predictive power of each metric over a large set of models and of orders. All models in the study are Petri nets, mostly conservative. We now provide some details for SOUPS and PSF which, together with PTS^P, have been reported as valuable predictors [6].

SOUPS modifies the *sum of transition spans* (SOS) metric [24] by considering only once the maximal common portion of multiple transition spans having the same effect on the marking and avoids counting the bottom portion of a transition span if it checks but does not change the marking of the corresponding places. SOUPS performs particularly well in conjunction with saturation [13], as it tends to result in even smaller peak MDDs. SOS and SOUPS, just like WES and NES [24] or SOT [11], are easily computed from the matrices $\mathbf{C}^{-}$ and $\mathbf{C}^{+}$.

PSF is computed analogously to SOS, but considering p-semiflow spans instead of transition spans:

$$\text{PSF}(\lambda) = \sum_{\pi \in \mathcal{F}^+_{min}} \Big(\max\{\lambda(v) : \pi[v] \neq 0\} - \min\{\lambda(v) : \pi[v] \neq 0\} + 1\Big).$$

In our figures, the column for p-flow π has a dark cell with $\pi[v]$ in it for each place v in $Supp(\pi)$, a light empty cell for each place not in the support but bracketed by places in the support, and a white empty cell for the remaining places not in the support. With this notation, PSF is just the count of the number of non-white squares in the matrix of $\mathcal{F}^+_{min}$.

There has been a proposal [16] to use of p-semiflows to *eliminate* some state variables (decision diagram levels) through a greedy heuristic, but later work [12] observed that this leads to a loss of *locality* in the MDD representation of the transition relation, and suggested instead to use p-semiflows to *merge* variables, proving that this always reduces the MDD size. The same paper [12] also proposed to modify the sum-of-transition-tops (SOT) metric so that it considers also a set of linearly independent p-semiflows, but provided no hints about the relative weight given to transitions vs. p-semiflows when computing the metric.

3 MDD and Invariants: The PF Metric

We now begin investigating the relationship between p-flows and the shape of the MDD encoding $\mathcal{S}_{rch}$ and $\mathcal{S}_{sat}$, and introduce the new metric PF.

P-flows and information remembered at level k. The invariant corresponding to a p-flow π imposes a constraint on the reachable markings, since it implies a constant weighted sum of the tokens in the places belonging to $Supp(\pi)$. Thus, the MDD must "remember" (using distinct nodes at level k) the possible partial weighted sums corresponding to places in the invariant support that are above level k, as long as the invariant is *active*, i.e., its support contains places mapped to levels k or below, and this is true even if the place mapped to level k is not in the support. Thus, intuitively, places in the support should be mapped to levels close to each other. This can be easily seen seen in Fig. 2(B), where the places in the support of the two p-semiflows in $\mathcal{F}^+_{min}$ are not in consecutive levels, resulting in more nodes: the level for P_2b has 9 nodes, since the MDD must remember the partial sum of tokens of the places in the two branches of the Petri net of Fig. 1(A), and each of them can range from 0 to 2. In the order of Fig. 2(A), all places in the top branch are instead above the level of place P_0, which is in turn above all places in the bottom branch. Thus, level P_0 has only three possible values to remember: whether in the top (and thus in the bottom) branch there are 0, 1, or 2 tokens (and therefore P_0 has 2, 1, or 0 tokens, respectively). This dependence is captured by the metric PSF of Sect. 2.3. The PSF value for order (B) is 13, while it is 8 for order (A), consistent with the intuition that a smaller value of PSF results in a smaller MDD.

P-flows and singletons. The token count of an invariant π determines a *single* possible value for the number of tokens in the level "completing" π (the lowest level corresponding to a place in $Supp(\pi)$), which can then only contain *singletons* (nodes with a single outgoing edge). This is the case for level P_0 in the

MDD of Fig. 2(A) and P_0 in the MDD of Fig. 2(B). Interestingly, level P_3a in the MDD of Fig. 2(B) also contains only singletons. This is due to an invariant generated by a p-flow in $\mathcal{F}^-$:

$$\boldsymbol{\pi}_3 : \quad \mathbf{m}[P_1a] + \mathbf{m}[P_2a] + \mathbf{m}[P_3a] - \mathbf{m}[P_1b] - \mathbf{m}[P_2b] - \mathbf{m}[P_3b] = 0,$$

As p-flows in $\mathcal{F}^-$ have similar implications on the MDD structure as those in $\mathcal{F}^+$, we define a new metric PF, by extending PSF to consider also non-positive p-flows. Give a set of p-flows $\mathcal{F}_{min}$, we can then define:

$$\mathrm{PF}(\lambda) = \textstyle\sum_{\boldsymbol{\pi} \in \mathcal{F}_{min}} \Big(\max\{\lambda(p) : \boldsymbol{\pi}(p) \neq 0\} - \min\{\lambda(p) : \boldsymbol{\pi}(p) \neq 0\} + 1\Big),$$

But what is an appropriate choice for $\mathcal{F}_{min}$? To have a consistent definition of the metric we need $\mathcal{F}_{min}$ to be uniquely and appropriately defined. While p-semiflows are characterized by a unique generator set $\mathcal{F}^+_{min}$, p-flows can be characterized by a *basis*, but the choice of basis is not unique and can lead to meaningless value of PF (for example if we choose a basis where each p-flow has the same span over the places, so that any variable order results in the same value for the PF metric).

Continuing the analogy with PSF, we define $\mathcal{F}_{min}$ as the set of minimal p-flows, i.e., the g.c.d. of their entries is 1 and their support does not strictly include the support of any other p-flow; in addition, to avoid considering both a p-flow and its negative, we assume an arbitrary place order (unrelated to the MDD variable order) and require the first nonzero entry to be positive. We now prove that this set $\mathcal{F}_{min}$ is unique and that it can generate a multiple of any p-flow. In the figures, the set $\mathcal{F}_{min}$ is shown partitioned into $\mathcal{F}^+_{min}$ and $\mathcal{F}^-_{min} = \mathcal{F}_{min} \backslash \mathcal{F}^+_{min}$.

Theorem 1. Set $\mathcal{F}_{min}$ is unique, and it spans all p-flow directions, i.e., given $\boldsymbol{\pi} \in \mathcal{F}$, for some $a \in \mathbb{Z}$, $a\boldsymbol{\pi}$ equals a linear combination of elements in $\mathcal{F}_{min}$.

Proof. To prove uniqueness, it suffices to show that there can be at most one minimal p-flow with a given support. Assume by contradiction that there are two distinct minimal p-flows $\boldsymbol{\pi}_1$ and $\boldsymbol{\pi}_2$ with $Supp(\boldsymbol{\pi}_1) = Supp(\boldsymbol{\pi}_2) = \mathcal{Q}$, and let $a_1 > 0$ and $a_2 > 0$ be the coefficients in $\boldsymbol{\pi}_1$ and $\boldsymbol{\pi}_2$ corresponding to the first place $v \in \mathcal{Q}$, respectively. Then, define $\boldsymbol{\pi} = a_2\boldsymbol{\pi}_1 - a_1\boldsymbol{\pi}_2$, so that $\boldsymbol{\pi}[v] = 0$.
If $\boldsymbol{\pi} \neq \mathbf{0}$, then $\boldsymbol{\pi} \in \mathcal{F}$ but $Supp(\boldsymbol{\pi}) \subseteq \mathcal{Q} \backslash \{v\}$, thus $\boldsymbol{\pi}_1$ and $\boldsymbol{\pi}_2$ cannot be minimal p-flows since their support strictly contains the support of $\boldsymbol{\pi}$, a contradiction.
If $\boldsymbol{\pi} = \mathbf{0}$, then $a_2\boldsymbol{\pi}_1 = a_1\boldsymbol{\pi}_2$, which implies $a_2 = a_1$, since the g.c.d. of both $\boldsymbol{\pi}_1$ and $\boldsymbol{\pi}_2$ is 1. But then, $\boldsymbol{\pi}_1 = \boldsymbol{\pi}_2$, again a contradiction.
To prove that $\mathcal{F}_{min}$ spans all p-flow directions, consider $\boldsymbol{\pi}'_1 \in \mathcal{F}$. There must exist $\boldsymbol{\pi}_1 \in \mathcal{F}_{min}$ with $Supp(\boldsymbol{\pi}_1) \subseteq Supp(\boldsymbol{\pi}'_1)$; pick $v \in Supp(\boldsymbol{\pi}_1)$ and let $a_1 = \boldsymbol{\pi}_1[v]$ and $b_1 = \boldsymbol{\pi}'_1[v]$, so that $a_1\boldsymbol{\pi}'_1 = b_1\boldsymbol{\pi}_1 + \boldsymbol{\pi}'_2$, with $Supp(\boldsymbol{\pi}'_2) \subseteq Supp(\boldsymbol{\pi}'_1) \setminus \{v\}$. Either $Supp(\boldsymbol{\pi}'_2) = \emptyset$, or it is a p-flow, in which case we can repeat the process to obtain $a_2\boldsymbol{\pi}'_2 = b_2\boldsymbol{\pi}_2 + \boldsymbol{\pi}'_3$, and so on. Eventually, we must reach the case $Supp(\boldsymbol{\pi}'_{n+1}) = \emptyset$, i.e., $\boldsymbol{\pi}'_{n+1} = \mathbf{0}$, at which point we can write $a_1 \cdots a_n\boldsymbol{\pi}'_1 = b_1a_2 \cdots a_n\boldsymbol{\pi}_1 + b_2a_3 \cdots a_n\boldsymbol{\pi}_2 + \cdots + b_n\boldsymbol{\pi}_n$, where $\boldsymbol{\pi}_1, \ldots, \boldsymbol{\pi}_n \in \mathcal{F}_{min}$, i.e., we can express a multiple of $\boldsymbol{\pi}'_1$ as a linear combination of elements of $\mathcal{F}_{min}$. □

We observe that the size of $\mathcal{F}_{min}$, like that of $\mathcal{F}^+_{min}$, is at most exponential in $|\mathcal{P}|$, since the proof of Theorem 1 shows that the elements of $\mathcal{F}_{min}$ must have uncomparable supports.

4 MDD and Invariants: The i_{Rank} Metric

As we shall see in Sect. 5, both PSF and PF exhibit significant correlation with the MDD size. However, there are cases where they do not perform well, especially when $\mathcal{F}_{min}$ is large. Consider for example the Petri net of Fig. 1(B), and the three MDDs corresponding to different variable orders in Fig. 3. This Petri net has many minimal p-flows, $|\mathcal{F}^+_{min}| = 8$ and $|\mathcal{F}_{min}| = 11$. The three p-flows in $\mathcal{F}^-_{min}$ relate the places inside each fork-and-join subnet ($P_ia = P_ib$, for $i = 1, 2, 3$), while the eight p-semiflows in $\mathcal{F}^+_{min}$ relate the tokens in the three fork-and-join subnets with those in place P_0. The order in Fig. 3(B) produces the smallest MDD size (37 nodes against the 49 nodes of order (A) and 69 of (C)), but it is the one with the worst (highest) value of PSF. On the other side also PF fails to chose the order with the smallest MDD: the smallest value for PF is 55 for order (A), which is only the second best for MDD size. One reason is that, when $\mathcal{F}_{min}$ contains many related, dependent constraints affecting a given MDD level, counting all of them may confuse the metric. On the other hand, we have seen that considering instead a basis depends strongly on the choice of vectors included in the basis, with a meaningless metric in the worst case.

We then propose i_{Rank}, a new variable order metric which, like PSF and PF, is based on linear invariants but, unlike PSF and PF, *is unaffected by redundant minimal p-flows* and *is independent of the choice of the specific p-flows* being considered, as long as they constitute a generator set. i_{Rank} focuses on the number $\rho(k)$ of *linearly independent partial p-flows* that are still active at level k. The definition of i_{Rank} requires a deeper understanding of the relationships among the MDD structure and the p-flows, as illustrated next.

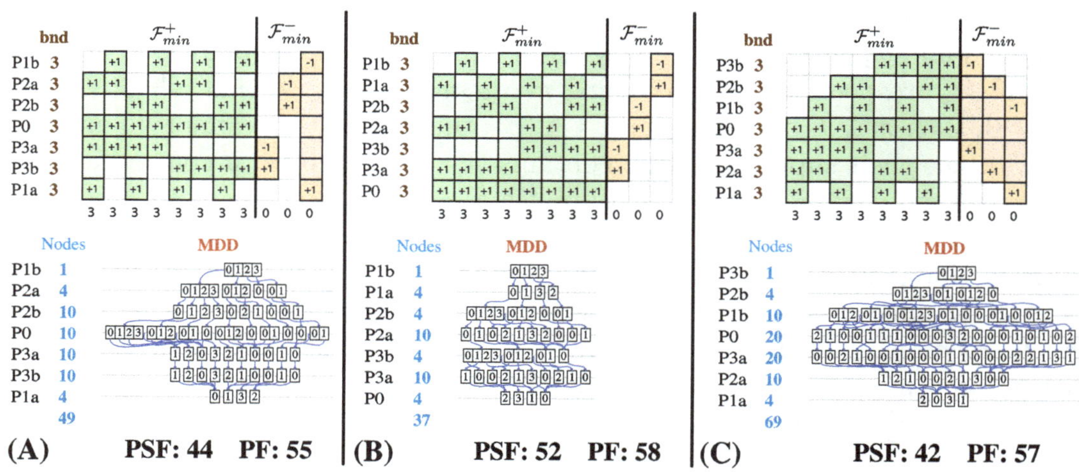

Fig. 3. Three variable orders for the Petri net of Fig. 1(B), and the resulting MDDs.

Given an MDD with root node r and two MDD nodes $p, q \neq \bot$ with $p.lvl = k$ and $q.lvl = h$, let $\mathcal{A}_p$ (for above) be the set of paths from r to p, $\mathcal{B}_p$ (for below) the set of paths from p to $\top$, and $\mathcal{C}_{p,q}$ the set of paths from p to q:

$$\mathcal{A}_p = \{(i_L, \ldots, i_{k+1}) : r[i_L] \cdots [i_{k+1}] = p\}$$
$$\mathcal{B}_p = \{(i_k, \ldots, i_1) : p[i_k] \cdots [i_1] = \top\}$$
$$\mathcal{C}_{p,q} = \{(i_k, \ldots, i_{h+1}) : p[i_k] \cdots [i_{h+1}] = q\},$$

thus $\mathcal{A}_r = \mathcal{B}_\top = \{()\}$, $\mathcal{A}_\top = \mathcal{B}_r = \mathcal{S}_r$, $\mathcal{A}_p = \mathcal{C}_{r,p}$, $\mathcal{B}_p = \mathcal{C}_{p,\top}$, $\mathcal{C}_{p,q} = \emptyset$ if $q.lvl \geq p.lvl$. When using an MDD to store $\mathcal{S}$ with a given variable order λ, the sets of paths defined by $\mathcal{A}_p$, $\mathcal{B}_p$, and $\mathcal{C}_{p,q}$ also denote sets of submarkings, by interpreting i_k as the number of tokens in place $v = \lambda^{-1}(k)$, and so on.

Theorem 2 [28]**.** The nodes at level k can be used to define a partition of $\mathcal{S}_r$: $\bigcup_{p \in \mathcal{N}_k} \mathcal{A}_p \times \mathcal{B}_p = \mathcal{S}_r$, and $\forall p, q \in \mathcal{N}_k, p \neq q \Rightarrow \mathcal{A}_p \times \mathcal{B}_p \cap \mathcal{A}_q \times \mathcal{B}_q = \emptyset$.

We can relate MDD nodes and the p-flows by proving that all submarkings described by $\mathcal{C}_{p,q}$, therefore by $\mathcal{A}_p$, have the same partial sum for any given p-flow. Given nodes p and q with $p.lvl = k > q.lvl = h$, $\sigma = (i_k, \ldots, i_{h+1}) \in \mathcal{C}_{p,q}$, and a p-flow $\boldsymbol{\pi} \in \mathcal{F}$, we let the partial sum of submarking σ for invariant $\boldsymbol{\pi}$ be:

$$Sum(p, q, \sigma, \boldsymbol{\pi}) = \textstyle\sum_{p.lvl \geq j > q.lvl} i_j \cdot \boldsymbol{\pi}[\lambda^{-1}(j)].$$

In particular, for any $\sigma \in \mathcal{C}_{r,\top} = \mathcal{S}_{rch}$, we have $Sum(r, \top, \sigma, \boldsymbol{\pi}) = Tc(\boldsymbol{\pi})$.

We can now introduce two fundamental properties enjoyed by an MDD encoding a state space subject to a set of p-flows $\mathcal{F}$, which will pave the way to the definition of our new metric called $\mathrm{i}_{\mathrm{Rank}}$.

Theorem 3. Assume a set of states $\mathcal{S}$ subject to the set of p-flows $\mathcal{F}$ is encoded by an MDD rooted at r. Then, all paths between a given pair of nodes have the same partial sum for any given invariant: $\forall \sigma, \sigma' \in \mathcal{C}_{p,q}, \forall \boldsymbol{\pi} \in \mathcal{F}, Sum(p, q, \sigma, \boldsymbol{\pi}) = Sum(p, q, \sigma', \boldsymbol{\pi})$. We can therefore write $Sum(p, q, \boldsymbol{\pi})$.

Proof. Consider two nodes p and q, with $p.lvl = k > q.lvl = h$, two paths σ and σ' from p to q, and any $\sigma_a \in \mathcal{A}_p$ and $\sigma_b \in \mathcal{B}_q$, so that both $(\sigma_a, \sigma, \sigma_b)$ and $(\sigma_a, \sigma', \sigma_b)$ describe markings in $\mathcal{S}$. Then, for any p-flow $\boldsymbol{\pi} \in \mathcal{F}$, we have that $Sum(r, \top, (\sigma_a, \sigma, \sigma_b), \boldsymbol{\pi}) = Sum(r, \top, (\sigma_a, \sigma', \sigma_b), \boldsymbol{\pi}) = Tc(\boldsymbol{\pi})$. However, $Sum(r, \top, (\sigma_a, \sigma, \sigma_b), \boldsymbol{\pi}) = Sum(r, p, \sigma_a, \boldsymbol{\pi}) + Sum(p, q, \sigma, \boldsymbol{\pi}) + Sum(q, \top, \sigma_b, \boldsymbol{\pi}) = Sum(r, \top, (\sigma_a, \sigma', \sigma_b), \boldsymbol{\pi}) = Sum(r, p, \sigma_a, \boldsymbol{\pi}) + Sum(p, q, \sigma', \boldsymbol{\pi}) + Sum(q, \top, \sigma_b, \boldsymbol{\pi})$, thus we must have $Sum(p, q, \sigma, \boldsymbol{\pi}) = Sum(p, q, \sigma', \boldsymbol{\pi})$. □

An even stronger property holds if the MDD encodes $\mathcal{S}_{sat}$: then, every node in the MDD is completely identified by a unique pattern of partial p-flow sums.

Theorem 4. Let $\mathcal{S}_{sat}$ be encoded by an MDD rooted at r. Then, the nodes at level k have different partial sums:

$$\forall p, p' \in \mathcal{N}_k,\ p \neq p' \ \Rightarrow\ \exists \boldsymbol{\pi} \in \mathcal{F},\ Sum(r, p, \boldsymbol{\pi}) \neq Sum(r, p', \boldsymbol{\pi}).$$

Proof. Remember that $\mathcal{S}_{sat} = \{\mathbf{m} \in \mathbb{N}^{\mathcal{P}} : \forall \boldsymbol{\pi} \in \mathcal{F}, \mathbf{m} \cdot \boldsymbol{\pi} = Tc(\boldsymbol{\pi})\}$. Assume that distinct nodes $p, p' \in \mathcal{N}_k$ satisfy $\forall \boldsymbol{\pi} \in \mathcal{F} : Sum(r,p,\boldsymbol{\pi}) = Sum(r,p',\boldsymbol{\pi})$. Since the MDD is canonical, p and p' must encode different sets, thus there must be a σ in $\mathcal{B}_p \setminus \mathcal{B}_{p'}$ or in $\mathcal{B}_{p'} \setminus \mathcal{B}_p$ (w.l.o.g. assume the former case). Then, considering any $\sigma_a \in \mathcal{A}_p$ and $\sigma'_a \in \mathcal{A}_{p'}$, we have $(\sigma_a, \sigma) \in \mathcal{S}_{sat}$ and $(\sigma'_a, \sigma) \notin \mathcal{S}_{sat}$. But $(\sigma_a, \sigma) \in \mathcal{S}_{sat}$ implies $\forall \boldsymbol{\pi} \in \mathcal{F}, Sum(r, \top, (\sigma_a, \sigma), \boldsymbol{\pi}) = Tc(\boldsymbol{\pi})$ and, since $Sum(r, \top, (\sigma_a, \sigma), \boldsymbol{\pi}) = Sum(r, p, \sigma_a, \boldsymbol{\pi}) + Sum(p, \top, \sigma, \boldsymbol{\pi}) = Sum(r, p', \sigma'_a, \boldsymbol{\pi}) + Sum(p, \top, \sigma, \boldsymbol{\pi}) = Sum(r, \top, (\sigma'_a, \sigma), \boldsymbol{\pi})$, and this holds for any $\boldsymbol{\pi}$ in $\mathcal{F}$, we should also have $(\sigma'_a, \sigma) \in \mathcal{S}_{sat}$, a contradiction. □

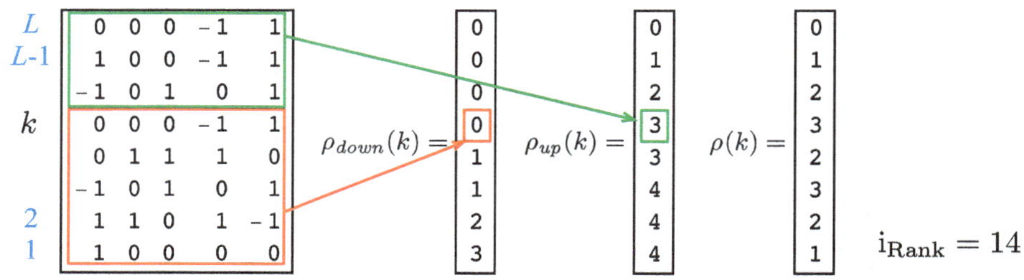

Fig. 4. Computations of the rank weights from a matrix $\mathbf{F}$ with $\text{rank}(\mathbf{F}) = 4$.

Theorem 4 implies that every node in the MDD encoding $\mathcal{S}_{sat}$ is completely identified by a unique pattern of partial p-flow sums. However, not every p-flow is relevant at a given level k of the MDD, and, more importantly, the portions from level L to level k of different p-flows may encode the same information, i.e., may be *linearly dependent*, yet these redundant portions contribute to the computation of the PF metric. iRank, then, attempts to estimate the number of *possible* combinations of partial path sums that may actually be found in the nodes at level k of the MDD, taking into account these linear dependencies.

To this end, we consider the $|\mathcal{P}| \times |\mathcal{F}_{min}|$ matrix $\mathbf{F}$ (rows ordered according to λ, columns in any order) describing the p-flows in $\mathcal{F}_{min}$, and define the number $\rho_{up}(k)$ of linearly independent partial p-flows up to level k:

$$\rho_{up}(k) = \text{rank}\big(\mathbf{F}[L : k+1, \cdot]\big),$$

where $\mathbf{F}[L : k+1, \cdot]$ is the submatrix of $\mathbf{F}$ with rows L through $k+1$ (level k is excluded because we are counting the partial sums *reaching* level k). $\rho_{up}(k)$ counts both p-flows active at level k and those that are not, as the lowest place in their support is mapped to a level above k (p-flow already "closed" at level k). The number $\rho_{down}(k)$ of linearly independent closed p-flows at level k is obtained by subtracting the rank of submatrix $\mathbf{F}[k : 1, \cdot]$ from the rank of the entire matrix $\mathbf{F}$:

$$\rho_{down}(k) = \text{rank}(\mathbf{F}) - \text{rank}\big(\mathbf{F}[k : 1, \cdot]\big).$$

Then, the value we are seeking is the difference of these two quantities:

$$\rho(k) = \rho_{up}(k) - \rho_{down}(k).$$

Figure 4 depicts the definition of $\rho_{up}(k)$ and $\rho_{down}(k)$. The rectangles in the invariant matrix $\mathbf{F}$ represents the portions used to compute the ranks for level k. The values of $\rho_{up}(k)$, $\rho_{down}(k)$, and $\rho(k)$, for all levels k, are listed on the right.

The value of the $\mathrm{i}_{\mathrm{Rank}}$ metric is then the sum of all the $\rho(k)$ values:

$$\mathrm{i}_{\mathrm{Rank}} = \textstyle\sum_{1 \le k \le L} \rho(k),$$

which can be thought of as an estimate of the number of independent factors affecting the number of MDD nodes at the various levels. Thus, we should expect that a linear increase in $\mathrm{i}_{\mathrm{Rank}}$ implies an exponential increase in the MDD size. The main advantage of $\mathrm{i}_{\mathrm{Rank}}$ is that it does not suffer in the presence of an excessive number of p-flows (as do PF and PSF). Indeed, since the metric is computed on the rank of $\mathbf{F}$ and on the rank of sets of rows of $\mathbf{F}$, and since these ranks do not change while adding linear combinations of p-flows (larger $\mathbf{F}$) or by removing p-flows (smaller $\mathbf{F}$) as long as we remove only linear dependent vectors, we have a metric that is rather robust. Additionally, it is also fairly inexpensive to compute, $O(\min\{\mathcal{P}, \mathcal{T}\}^3)$.

5 Experimental Assessment of the Metrics

We now experimentally assess the efficacy of PF and $\mathrm{i}_{\mathrm{Rank}}$: since the relationship between p-flows and MDD nodes is stronger for $\mathcal{S}_{sat}$ than for $\mathcal{S}_{rch}$ (Theorem 4), we expect higher correlation when the MDD encodes the former. We also seek to determine whether these metrics can be used to drive iterative heuristics or meta-heuristics that compute variable orders. All experiments are on different sets of orders for 40 models taken from the Petri Net Repository [2]. The experiments have been conducted using the GreatSPN tool [1,4], which uses the Meddly library [8]. All MDDs generated had fewer than one million nodes. We follow the evaluation procedure of [6] and compute the Spearman coefficient of correlation (CC), whose interpretation is: $[1, 0.8]$ means very strong correlation, $[0.6, 0.8]$ strong correlation, $[0.4, 0.6]$ moderate correlation, and so on decreasing. Negative values indicate anti-correlation.

Figure 5 compares the correlation of $\mathrm{i}_{\mathrm{Rank}}$ and PF to that of the metrics of Sect. 2.3. Although all experiments have been performed, for sake of space only 6 metrics are considered in the tables. We have chosen to include PSF, PF and $\mathrm{i}_{\mathrm{Rank}}$ (for obvious reasons), plus the best among the $\mathbf{C}$ span metrics (SOUPS), and two versions of PTS (PTS and PTS^P, without and with p-flow) since PTS is the metrics implicitly optimized by the widely used FORCE heuristic. No bandwidth metric is reported since they all exhibit at best a moderate correlation. Each row represents a metric, columns report the CC of the metrics with the MDD encoding $\mathcal{S}_{sat}$ (columns [A] and [B]) and $\mathcal{S}_{rch}$ (columns [C] and [D]) for two different sets of orders. The CC of a single model for a single metric is computed from the bivariate series relating, for each variable order λ, the MDD size built using λ with the value of the metric for that λ. ICC is the CC computed over the set of orders λ in $\mathcal{V}_{\mathrm{IMPR}}$ and BCC is computed over $\mathcal{V}_{\mathrm{BEST}}$. The sets $\mathcal{V}_{\mathrm{IMPR}}$ and $\mathcal{V}_{\mathrm{BEST}}$ are built from 1,000 initial random orders by generating sequences of

	[A] ICC (S_{sat})		[B] BCC (S_{sat})		[C] ICC (S_{rch})		[D] BCC (S_{rch})	
Metric	Distribution	Mean	Distribution	Mean	Distribution	Mean	Distribution	Mean
iRank		0.963		0.914		0.921		0.744
PSF		0.845		0.685		0.798		0.538
SOUPS		0.775		0.530		0.767		0.489
PTS_P		0.759		0.437		0.753		0.408
PF		0.721		0.668		0.666		0.516
PTS		0.668		0.379		0.673		0.363
	−1 0 1		−1 0 1		−1 0 1		−1 0 1	

Fig. 5. Two correlation coefficients for different metrics for $\mathcal{S}_{sat}$ and $\mathcal{S}_{rch}$

increasingly better orders (in terms of MDD final size) until a convergence criterion is satisfied; $\mathcal{V}_{\text{IMPR}}$ retains all orders while $\mathcal{V}_{\text{BEST}}$ retains only the last orders in each sequence (thus exactly 1,000 orders). This construction is explained in [6], where it was observed that $\mathcal{V}_{\text{BEST}}$ tends to contain mostly good orders, and $\mathcal{V}_{\text{IMPR}}$ a mixture of good and bad orders. The above sets have been built for each of the 40 models. For each combination, we report the mean CC (over all models) and the CC distribution for the 40 models; the x axis is partitioned into 20 bins, so the y axis indicates the number of models whose CC falls into each bin. All plots have the same scale on the y axis. and the height of the bar at 0 is fixed at 36 for all rows.

The results of Fig. 5 indicate that i_{Rank} has the highest correlation for both ICC and BCC and for both $\mathcal{S}_{rch}$ and $\mathcal{S}_{sat}$. i_{Rank} is better than the second best by 12% (ICC on $\mathcal{S}_{sat}$) and up to 28% (BCC on $\mathcal{S}_{rch}$). The comparison with PTS (the metric used as a convergence criteria by the widely used FORCE heuristic) is even more striking. It is also evident that in none of the four cases PF performs better than PSF, supporting our observation that considering more p-flows is not always (or even usually) a good idea. Figure 5 also indicates that all metrics have better CC when the MDD encodes $\mathcal{S}_{sat}$ (column [A] vs. [C], and column [B] vs. [D]). This is not surprising for i_{Rank}, given Theorem 4, but it also holds for all other metrics. This could be due to the fact that, since $\mathcal{S}_{rch} \subseteq \mathcal{S}_{sat}$, the MDD for $\mathcal{S}_{rch}$ encodes additional constraints not captured by any of the metrics.

Comparing columns [A] and [B] (and columns [C] and [D]) of Fig. 5, we observe that ICC is higher than BCC for all metrics, meaning that they have better correlation when the set of considered orders is $\mathcal{V}_{\text{IMPR}}$ (mix of good and bad orders) rather than $\mathcal{V}_{\text{BEST}}$ (mostly good orders). This is related to the use of the Spearman CC, which quantifies how well the i-th largest value of the metric correlates with the i-th largest value of the MDD size: certainly with $\mathcal{V}_{\text{BEST}}$ we tend to have more MDDs of similar size, making it more difficult to discriminate.

The experiments reported in Fig. 6 serve to evaluate whether the metrics can be used as an objective function inside a simulated annealing procedure (columns [A] and [C]) or as a meta-heuristic to select one among the orders produced during the simulated annealing (columns [B] and [D]). Given an initial variable order and a metric m the procedure searches an "optimal" order through

Metric	[A] Ann. Distrib. (S_{sat})	Mean	[B] Metaheuristic (S_{sat})	Mean	[C] Ann. Distrib. (S_{rch})	Mean	[D] Metaheuristic (S_{rch})	Mean
iRank		0.819		0.885		0.665		0.806
PSF		0.748		0.806		0.607		0.719
PF		0.717		0.785		0.574		0.703
SOUPS		0.690		0.759		0.590		0.731
PTS_P		0.684		0.762		0.584		0.716
PTS		0.641		0.726		0.554		0.684
	0 0.2 0.4 0.6 0.8 1		0 0.2 0.4 0.6 0.8 1		0 0.2 0.4 0.6 0.8 1		0 0.2 0.4 0.6 0.8 1	

Fig. 6. Evaluation of metrics on simulated annealing produced orders

Metric	RND+Force Score (S_{sat})	Mean	RND+Force Score (S_{rch})	Mean
iRank		0.898		0.853
PSF		0.873		0.829
PF		0.870		0.822
SOUPS		0.860		0.842
PTS_P		0.829		0.813
PTS		0.812		0.794
Baseline		0.834		0.721
	0 0.2 0.4 0.6 0.8 1		0 0.2 0.4 0.6 0.8 1	

Fig. 7. Evaluation of metrics on FORCE-produced orders.

a simulated annealing procedure [17], aimed at minimizing the value of m. We employ a standard simulated annealing procedure, described in [6]. Unlike the construction of the set of orders used for the computation of ICC and BCC in Fig. 5, no MDD is built during the construction of the candidate variable order. For each metric, the simulated annealing procedure is run 1,000 times, from different initial orders, and Fig. 6 reports, in columns [A] and [C], the mean and distribution of the "score" of the MDDs built using the 1,000 orders produced by the 1,000 runs of the simulated annealing for each metric m, for the 40 models. The score is the distance from the size of the smallest MDD built, normalized on the distance between the smallest and the largest MDD size built (see [6], Eq. 5), obviously computed separately for each model. A value of 1 for order λ for a given model indicates that the smallest MDD seen for that model was built using λ. A value of 0 indicates the worst order. Column [A] refers to the MDDs storing $\mathcal{S}_{sat}$, while column [C] refers to $\mathcal{S}_{rch}$. Again, i_{Rank} performs better than any other metrics in both cases.

Columns [B] and [D] instead report the results of using each metric m as a meta-heuristic: for each model a single order is chosen (the order with the best value for metric m), and the 40 resulting scores are plotted. This corresponds to using metrics in practice to select a given order for a model. Again, i_{Rank} shows the best performance, indicating that it can select good candidate orders.

Figure 7 shows the evaluation of a meta-heuristic also defined in [6], based on FORCE. Each metric m is used to drive the selection of the "best" variable order among a set of variable orders produced using FORCE from an initial set of 1,000 random orders. This is done for each of the 40 models. The last row is the baseline (40×1,000 points, all computed using FORCE), while all other histograms are built out of 40 MDD sizes, one per model. A mean value greater than the baseline mean indicates that the metric selects the best orders among the ones computed by FORCE. A mean below the baseline indicates otherwise. Again, when we employ $\mathrm{i}_{\mathrm{Rank}}$ to select the order to use, we get a better score than with any other metric for both $\mathcal{S}_{sat}$ (left column) and $\mathcal{S}_{rch}$ (right column).

6 Conclusion and Future Work

We considered the problem of defining and evaluating variable orders for MDDs encoding either the reachable states of a DEDS ($\mathcal{S}_{rch}$) or the states satisfying a set of linear invariants ($\mathcal{S}_{sat}$). We studied the relation between the MDD size and structure and the linear invariants, and proposed two new metrics: PF, a trivial extension to PSF; and $\mathrm{i}_{\mathrm{Rank}}$. Through a set of experiments, metrics have been evaluated both as predictors of the MDD size and as drivers for two heuristics (and associated meta-heuristics). The experiments follow the procedure proposed in [6], as defining a good and fair procedure to compare metrics and MDD sizes for a set of models is a nontrivial task. The results show that $\mathrm{i}_{\mathrm{Rank}}$ is better than any other metrics we found in the literature.

The definition of $\mathrm{i}_{\mathrm{Rank}}$, and PF, assumes that linear invariants are available. For DEDSs specified as Petri nets, the linear invariants are derived from the p-flows, the left annullers of the incidence matrix, an integer matrix describing how an event modifies a state. Clearly, whenever a DEDS can be specified through a similar matrix, the application of our method is straightforward, as in the case of various formalisms used in system modeling and verification. For other formalisms, this may be less immediate, but our method only assumes a set of linear invariants on the state space, regardless of how they are computed.

In our experiments, we considered only *conservative* Petri nets, where each place appears in at least one invariant. This allowed us to compare with previously defined metrics that exploit linear invariants generated from p-semiflows. If no invariants are available, or if most places are not part of any invariant, PF and $\mathrm{i}_{\mathrm{Rank}}$ could perform very poorly. If a net is not conservative, a subset of places may "lose" tokens, "gain tokens", or both. The last two cases cause $\mathcal{S}_{rch}$ to be infinite, but the first case can still be managed by our approach, thanks to p-flows. As an example, consider the net obtained from the net in Fig. 1(B) by removing the arc from transition T_3 back to P_0 Such a net does not have any p-semiflow, but all the places between each pair of fork-and-join belong to a p-flow, allowing us to apply our method. A further extension could consider invariants where the weighted sum of tokens in a subset of places is less than or equal a constant (instead of just equal).

Several directions for additional exploration remain. First, $\mathrm{i}_{\mathrm{Rank}}$ does not consider the initial state of the DEDS, but the number of nodes at a given level depends on the token count of the p-flows, and this may be especially important when the p-flows have significantly different token counts. Then, the efficient computation of $\mathrm{i}_{\mathrm{Rank}}$ is obviously important, as heuristics using it could probably evaluate it many times. The computation could be expensive since it involves matrix rank computations.

Finally, we are interested in extending i_{Rank} to more general constraints, which can still provide hints on good variable orders; for example, a constraint "if $A = 3$ then $B = C$" imposes no limitations on C along paths where $A \neq 3$, (assuming A is above B and B is above C in the MDD), but, requires to remember the value of B until reaching C along paths where $A = 3$.

References

1. The GreatSPN tool homepage. http://www.di.unito.it/~greatspn/index.html
2. MCC: The Model Checking Competition. https://mcc.lip6.fr
3. Aloul, F.A., Markov, I.L., Sakallah, K.A.: FORCE: a fast and easy-to-implement variable-ordering heuristic. In: Proceedings of GLSVLSI, pp. 116–119. ACM, New York (2003)
4. Amparore, E.G., Balbo, G., Beccuti, M., Donatelli, S., Franceschinis, G.: 30 years of GreatSPN. In: Fiondella, L., Puliafito, A. (eds.) Principles of Performance and Reliability Modeling and Evaluation. SSRE, pp. 227–254. Springer, Cham (2016). https://doi.org/10.1007/978-3-319-30599-8_9
5. Amparore, E.G., Beccuti, M., Donatelli, S.: Gradient-based variable ordering of decision diagrams for systems with structural units. In: D'Souza, D., Narayan Kumar, K. (eds.) ATVA 2017. LNCS, vol. 10482, pp. 184–200. Springer, Cham (2017). https://doi.org/10.1007/978-3-319-68167-2_13
6. Amparore, E.G., Ciardo, G., Donatelli, S.: Variable order metrics for decision diagrams in system verification (2018, submitted for publication). http://www.di.unito.it/~amparore/metrics_STTT.pdf
7. Amparore, E.G., Donatelli, S., Beccuti, M., Garbi, G., Miner, A.: Decision diagrams for Petri nets: which variable ordering? In: Transactions on Petri Nets and Other Models of Concurrency XI. Springer, Heidelberg (2019, to appear)
8. Babar, J., Miner, A.: Meddly: multi-terminal and edge-valued decision diagram library. In: International Conference on Quantitative Evaluation of Systems, pp. 195–196. IEEE Computer Society, Los Alamitos (2010)
9. Bollig, B., Wegener, I.: Improving the variable ordering of OBDDs is NP-complete. IEEE Trans. Comput. **45**(9), 993–1002 (1996)
10. Bryant, R.E.: Graph-based algorithms for Boolean function manipulation. IEEE Trans. Comput. **35**(8), 677–691 (1986)
11. Ciardo, G., Jones, R.L., Miner, A.S., Siminiceanu, R.: Logical and stochastic modeling with SMART. Perf. Eval. **63**, 578–608 (2006)
12. Ciardo, G., Lüttgen, G., Yu, A.J.: Improving static variable orders via invariants. In: Kleijn, J., Yakovlev, A. (eds.) ICATPN 2007. LNCS, vol. 4546, pp. 83–103. Springer, Heidelberg (2007). https://doi.org/10.1007/978-3-540-73094-1_8
13. Ciardo, G., Zhao, Y., Jin, X.: Ten years of saturation: a Petri net perspective. In: Jensen, K., Donatelli, S., Kleijn, J. (eds.) Transactions on Petri Nets and Other Models of Concurrency V. LNCS, vol. 6900, pp. 51–95. Springer, Heidelberg (2012). https://doi.org/10.1007/978-3-642-29072-5_3
14. Cimatti, A., Clarke, E.M., Giunchiglia, F., Roveri, M.: NuSMV: a new symbolic model verifier. In: Halbwachs, N., Peled, D. (eds.) CAV 1999. LNCS, vol. 1633, pp. 495–499. Springer, Heidelberg (1999). https://doi.org/10.1007/3-540-48683-6_44
15. Colom, J.M., Silva, M.: Convex geometry and semiflows in P/T nets. A comparative study of algorithms for computation of minimal p-semiflows. In: Rozenberg, G. (ed.) ICATPN 1989. LNCS, vol. 483, pp. 79–112. Springer, Heidelberg (1991). https://doi.org/10.1007/3-540-53863-1_22

16. Davies, I., Knottenbelt, W., Kritzinger, P.S.: Symbolic methods for the state space exploration of GSPN models. In: Field, T., Harrison, P.G., Bradley, J., Harder, U. (eds.) TOOLS 2002. LNCS, vol. 2324, pp. 188–199. Springer, Heidelberg (2002). https://doi.org/10.1007/3-540-46029-2_12
17. Du, K.L., Swamy, M.N.S.: Search and Optimization by Metaheuristics. Springer, Basel (2016). https://doi.org/10.1007/978-3-319-41192-7
18. Lind-Nielsen, J.: BuDDy Manual, July 2003. http://buddy.sourceforge.net/manual/main.html
19. Kam, T., Villa, T., Brayton, R.K., Sangiovanni-Vincentelli, A.: Multi-valued decision diagrams: theory and applications. Multiple-Valued Logic **4**(1), 9–62 (1992)
20. Kwiatkowska, M., Norman, G., Parker, D.: PRISM: probabilistic model checking for performance and reliability analysis. Perform. Eval. **36**(4), 40–45 (2009)
21. Martinez, J., Silva, M.: A simple and fast algorithm to obtain all invariants of a generalized Petri net. In: Girault, C., Reisig, W. (eds.) Application and Theory of Petri Nets. INFORMATIK, vol. 52, pp. 301–310. Springer, Heidelberg (1982). https://doi.org/10.1007/978-3-642-68353-4_47
22. McMillan, K.L.: Symbolic Model Checking. Kluwer Academic Publishers, Norwell (1993)
23. Meijer, J., van de Pol, J.: Bandwidth and wavefront reduction for static variable ordering in symbolic reachability analysis. In: Rayadurgam, S., Tkachuk, O. (eds.) NFM 2016. LNCS, vol. 9690, pp. 255–271. Springer, Cham (2016). https://doi.org/10.1007/978-3-319-40648-0_20
24. Siminiceanu, R.I., Ciardo, G.: New metrics for static variable ordering in decision diagrams. In: Hermanns, H., Palsberg, J. (eds.) TACAS 2006. LNCS, vol. 3920, pp. 90–104. Springer, Heidelberg (2006). https://doi.org/10.1007/11691372_6
25. Smith, B., Ciardo, G.: SOUPS: a variable ordering metric for the saturation algorithm. In: Proceedings of the International Conference on Application of Concurrency to System Design (ACSD). IEEE Computer Society Press (2018)
26. Somenzi, F.: Efficient manipulation of decision diagrams. STTT **3**(2), 171–181 (2001)
27. Thierry-Mieg, Y.: Symbolic model-checking using ITS-tools. In: Baier, C., Tinelli, C. (eds.) TACAS 2015. LNCS, vol. 9035, pp. 231–237. Springer, Heidelberg (2015). https://doi.org/10.1007/978-3-662-46681-0_20
28. Wan, M., Ciardo, G., Miner, A.S.: Approximate steady-state analysis of large Markov models based on the structure of their decision diagram encoding. Perf. Eval. **68**, 463–486 (2011)

Binary Decision Diagrams with Edge-Specified Reductions

Junaid Babar(✉), Chuan Jiang, Gianfranco Ciardo, and Andrew Miner

Department of Computer Science, Iowa State University, Ames, IA 50011, USA
{junaid,cjiang,ciardo,asminer}@iastate.edu

Abstract. Various versions of binary decision diagrams (BDDs) have been proposed in the past, differing in the reduction rule needed to give meaning to edges skipping levels. The most widely adopted, fully-reduced BDDs and zero-suppressed BDDs, excel at encoding different types of boolean functions (if the function contains subfunctions independent of one or more underlying variables, or it tends to have value zero when one of its arguments is nonzero, respectively). Recently, new classes of BDDs have been proposed that, at the cost of some additional complexity and larger memory requirements per node, exploit both cases. We introduce a new type of BDD that we believe is conceptually simpler, has small memory requirements in terms of node size, tends to result in fewer nodes, and can easily be further extended with additional reduction rules. We present a formal definition, prove canonicity, and provide experimental results to support our efficiency claims.

1 Introduction

Decision diagrams (DDs) have been widely adopted for a variety of applications. This is due to their often compact, graph-based representations of functions over boolean variables, along with operations to manipulate those boolean functions based on the sizes of the graph representations, rather than the size of the domain of the function. Most DD types are canonical for boolean functions: for a fixed ordering of the function variables, each function has a unique (modulo graph isomorphism) DD representation, or encoding.

Compactness, and canonicity, is achieved through careful rules for eliminating nodes. All canonical DDs eliminate nodes that duplicate information: if nodes p and q encode the same function, one of them is discarded. Additional compactness comes from a reduction rule (or rules) that specifies both how to interpret "long" edges that skip over function variables, and how to eliminate nodes and replace them with long edges. Two popular forms of decision diagrams, Binary Decision Diagrams (BDDs) [1] and Zero-suppressed binary Decision Diagrams (ZDDs) [8], use different reduction rules. Some applications are more suitable for BDDs while others are more suitable for ZDDs, depending on which of the two reductions can be applied to a greater number of nodes. Unfortunately, it is not always easy to know, *a priori*, which reduction rule is best for a particular application. Worse, there are applications where *both* rules are useful.

T. Vojnar and L. Zhang (Eds.): TACAS 2019, Part II, LNCS 11428, pp. 303–318, 2019.
https://doi.org/10.1007/978-3-030-17465-1_17

Recently, Tagged BDDs (TBDDs) [10] and Chain-reduced BDDs (CBDDs) or ZDDs (CZDDs) [2] have been introduced to combine the reduction rules of BDDs and ZDDs. We introduce a new type of BDD, called *Edge Specified Reduction* BDDs (ESRBDDs), that we believe is conceptually simpler and has smaller node storage requirements than TBDDs, CBDDs, and CZDDs, while still exploiting the BDD and ZDD reduction rules. Additionally, ESRBDDs are flexible in that additional reduction rules may be added with low cost. Finally, unlike TBDDs, CBDDs, and CZDDs, ESRBDDs treat the BDD and ZDD reduction rules equally: there is no need to prioritize one rule over another.

The paper is organized as follows. Section 2 recalls definitions for BDDs and ZDDs and describes related work. Section 3 formally defines ESRBDDs, gives their reduction algorithm, proves that they are a canonical form, and compares them with related DDs. Section 4 gives detailed experimental results to show how the various DDs compare in practice. Section 5 provides conclusions.

2 Related Decision Diagrams

We focus on various types of DDs that have been proposed to efficiently encode boolean functions of boolean variables, and briefly recall DDs relevant to our work. For consistency in notation, all DD types we present encode functions of the form $f : \mathbb{B}^L \to \mathbb{B}$ and have L levels, with level L at the top.

The first and most widely-known type is the *reduced-ordered binary decision diagrams* (BDDs) [1]. A BDD is a directed acyclic graph where the two terminal nodes $\mathbf{0}$ and $\mathbf{1}$ are at level 0, we write $lvl(\mathbf{0}) = lvl(\mathbf{1}) = 0$, while each nonterminal node p belongs to a level $lvl(p) \in \{1, ..., L\}$ and has two outgoing edges, $p[0]$ and $p[1]$, pointing to nodes at lower levels (this is the "ordered" property). The "reduced" property instead forbids both *duplicate* nodes (p and q are duplicates if $lvl(p) = lvl(q)$, $p[0] = q[0]$, and $p[1] = q[1]$), and *redundant* nodes (p is redundant if $p[0] = p[1]$). The function F_p encoded by BDD node p is defined as

$$F_p(x_{1:L}) = \begin{cases} F_{p[x_{lvl(p)}]}(x_{1:L}) & lvl(p) > 0 \\ p & lvl(p) = 0, \end{cases}$$

where $(x_{1:L})$ is a shorthand for the boolean tuple $(x_1, ..., x_L)$.

Another widely-used type is the *zero-suppressed binary decision diagrams* (ZDDs) [8], which differ from BDDs only in that they forbid *high-zero* nodes (node p is high-zero if $p[1] = \mathbf{0}$) instead of redundant nodes. The function encoded by ZDD node p is defined with respect to a level $n \geq m = lvl(p)$, as

$$F_p^n(x_{1:n}) = \begin{cases} \mathbf{0} & n > m \land \exists i, m < i \leq n, x_i = 1 \\ F_p^m(x_{1:m}) & n > m \land \forall i, m < i \leq n, x_i = 0 \\ F_{p[x_m]}^{m-1}(x_{1:m-1}) & n = m > 0 \\ p & n = m = 0. \end{cases}$$

Both BDDs and ZDDs are *canonical*: any function $f : \mathbb{B}^L \to \mathbb{B}$ has a unique node p encoding it, an essential property guaranteeing *time* efficiency. Just as important is their *memory* efficiency, i.e., the number of nodes required to encode a given function. In this respect, BDDs and ZDDs are particularly suited to different situations. BDDs require fewer nodes if there are many "don't cares", i.e., it often happens that $F_p(x_{1:L}) = F_p(y_{1:L})$ when $x_{1:L}$ and $y_{1:L}$ differ in one position, as this corresponds to redundant nodes, not stored in BDDs. ZDDs require fewer nodes if the function tends to have value 0 when many arguments have value 1 as this corresponds to high-zero nodes, not stored in ZDDs.

Quasi-reduced BDDs (QBDDs) [5] are also canonical: they are just like BDDs (or ZDDs) except they only forbid duplicate nodes. QBDD edges connect nodes on adjacent levels. Since edges are not allowed to *skip* levels, nodes do not need to store level information, and redundant and high-zero nodes cannot be eliminated. A useful variation is to eliminate only redundant (or high-zero) nodes whose children are **0**, and thus allow long edges directly to **0**. In either case, QBDDs require at least as many nodes as BDDs and ZDDs to encode a given function, so they provide an upper bound on both the BDD and the ZDD sizes.

Various decision diagrams have been proposed to combine the characteristics of BDDs and ZDDs and exploit the reduction potential of both. *Tagged binary decision diagrams* (TBDDs) [10] associate a level tag to each edge. BDD reductions are implied along the edge from the level of the node to the level of the tag, and ZDD reductions are implied from the level of the tag to the level of the node pointed to by the edge. Alternatively, TBDDs can apply reductions in the reverse order along an edge: ZDD reductions first and BDD reductions second. Either reduction order can be used in TBDDs, but a TBDD can only use one of them, i.e., they cannot both be used in the same TBDD.

Chain-reduced BDDs (CBDDs) and *chain-reduced ZDDs* (CZDDs) [2] augment BDDs and ZDDs by using nodes to encode chains of high-zero nodes and redundant nodes, respectively. Each node specifies two levels, the first level indicating where the chain starts (similar to the level of an ordinary BDD or ZDD node), and the second, additional, level indicating where the chain ends.

Finally, *ordered Kronecker functional decision diagrams* [3] allow multiple decomposition types (Shannon, positive Davio, and negative Davio), enabling both BDD and ZDD reductions. However, each level has a fixed decomposition type, thus this approach is less flexible, potentially less efficient, and hindered by the need to know which decomposition will perform best for each level.

3 ESRBDDs

Definition 1. An L-level *(ordered) edge-specified reduction* binary decision diagram (ESRBDD) is a directed acyclic graph where the two *terminal* nodes **0** and **1** are at level 0, $lvl(\mathbf{0}) = lvl(\mathbf{1}) = 0$, while each *nonterminal* node p belongs to a level $lvl(p) \in \{1, ..., L\}$ and has two outgoing edges, $p[0]$ and $p[1]$, pointing to nodes at lower levels. An edge is a pair $e = \langle e.rule, e.node \rangle$, where $e.rule$ is a *reduction rule* in $\{\mathtt{S}, \mathtt{L_0}, \mathtt{H_0}, \mathtt{X}\}$ and $e.node$ is the node to which edge e points. For $i \in \{0, 1\}$, if $lvl(p[i].node) = lvl(p) - 1$, we say that $p[i]$ is a *short* edge and require that $p[i].rule = \mathtt{S}$. If instead $lvl(p[i].node) < lvl(p) - 1$, the only other possibility, we say that $p[i]$ is a *long* edge, since it "skips over" one or more levels, and require that $p[i].rule \in \{\mathtt{H_0}, \mathtt{L_0}, \mathtt{X}\}$.

The reduction rule on an edge specifies its meaning when skipping levels, thus it is just S for short edges while, for long edges, the rules $\mathtt{H_0}$, $\mathtt{L_0}$, and X correspond to the "zero-suppressed" rule of [8], the "one-suppressed" rule (a new rule analogous to the zero-suppressed, as we shall see), and the "fully-reduced" rule of [1], respectively. To make this more precise, we recursively define the boolean function $F^n_{\langle\kappa,p\rangle} : \mathbb{B}^n \rightarrow \mathbb{B}$ encoded by an ESRBDD edge $\langle\kappa,p\rangle$ with respect to a level $n \in \{0, ..., L\}$, subject to $lvl(p) \leq n$, as

$$F^n_{\langle\kappa,p\rangle}(x_{1:n}) = \begin{cases} \text{if } lvl(p) = n = 0 & p \\ \text{if } lvl(p) = n > 0 & (x_n)\ ?\ F^{n-1}_{p[1]}(x_{1:n-1}) \ :\ F^{n-1}_{p[0]}(x_{1:n-1}) \\ \text{if } lvl(p) < n, \kappa = \mathtt{X}, & (x_n)\ ?\ F^{n-1}_{\langle\kappa,p\rangle}(x_{1:n-1}) \ :\ F^{n-1}_{\langle\kappa,p\rangle}(x_{1:n-1}) \\ \text{if } lvl(p) < n, \kappa = \mathtt{H_0}, & (x_n)\ ?\ \mathbf{0} \ :\ F^{n-1}_{\langle\kappa,p\rangle}(x_{1:n-1}) \\ \text{if } lvl(p) < n, \kappa = \mathtt{L_0}, & (x_n)\ ?\ F^{n-1}_{\langle\kappa,p\rangle}(x_{1:n-1}) \ :\ \mathbf{0}, \end{cases}$$

where the if-then-else operator $(x_n)?f_1{:}f_0$ is a shorthand for $(\neg x_n \wedge f_0) \vee (x_n \wedge f_1)$.

We defined an ESRBDD as a directed acyclic graph, so it can potentially have multiple *roots* (nodes with no incoming edges). However, since our focus is on the size of the DD encoding a given function, we assume from now on that our ESRBDDs have a single root node $p^\star$, pointed to by a *dangling edge* with rule $\kappa^\star$. We denote the set of all nodes reachable from $p^\star$ (and therefore all nodes in the ESRBDD) as $Nodes(p^\star)$. The dangling edge $\langle\kappa^\star,p^\star\rangle$ encodes the function $F^L_{\langle\kappa^\star,p^\star\rangle}$, which is independent of $\kappa^\star$ only if $lvl(p^\star) = L$, in which case we require $\kappa^\star = \mathtt{S}$, while we require $\kappa^\star \in \{\mathtt{L_0}, \mathtt{H_0}, \mathtt{X}\}$ if $lvl(p^\star) < L$. Finally, we will informally say "ESRBDD $\langle\kappa^\star,p^\star\rangle$" to refer to the entire graph below (and including) dangling edge $\langle\kappa^\star,p^\star\rangle$.

Before introducing reduced ESRBDDs and showing they are canonical, we need some terminology. We say that an ESRBDD nonterminal node q:

- *duplicates* node p if $lvl(p) = lvl(q)$, $p[0] = q[0]$, and $p[1] = q[1]$,
- is *redundant* if $q[0] = q[1] = \langle\kappa,p\rangle$, with $\kappa \in \{\mathtt{S}, \mathtt{X}\}$,
- is *high-zero* if $q[0].rule \in \{\mathtt{S}, \mathtt{H_0}\}$, $q[1].rule \in \{\mathtt{S}, \mathtt{X}\}$, and $q[1].node = \mathbf{0}$,
- is *low-zero* if $q[0].rule \in \{\mathtt{S}, \mathtt{X}\}$, $q[0].node = \mathbf{0}$, and $q[1].rule \in \{\mathtt{S}, \mathtt{L_0}\}$.

Note that BDDs [1] can be viewed as ESRBDDs where the edge labels are restricted to $\{\mathtt{S}, \mathtt{X}\}$, and a reduced BDD corresponds to an ESRBDD with no duplicate nodes and no redundant nodes. Similarly, ZDDs [8] can be viewed as ESRBDDs where edge labels are restricted to $\{\mathtt{S}, \mathtt{H_0}\}$, and a reduced ZDD corresponds to an ESRBDD with no duplicate nodes and no high-zero nodes. Also, we note that there is no corresponding definition in the existing literature for the version of ESRBDDs where the edge labels are restricted to $\{\mathtt{S}, \mathtt{L_0}\}$.

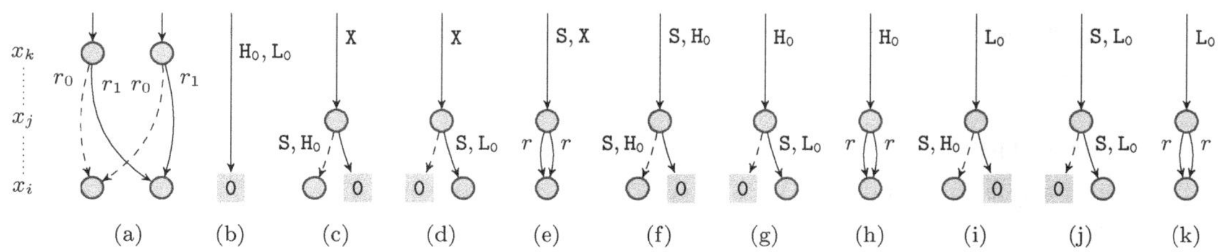

Fig. 1. Patterns not allowed in RESRBDDs

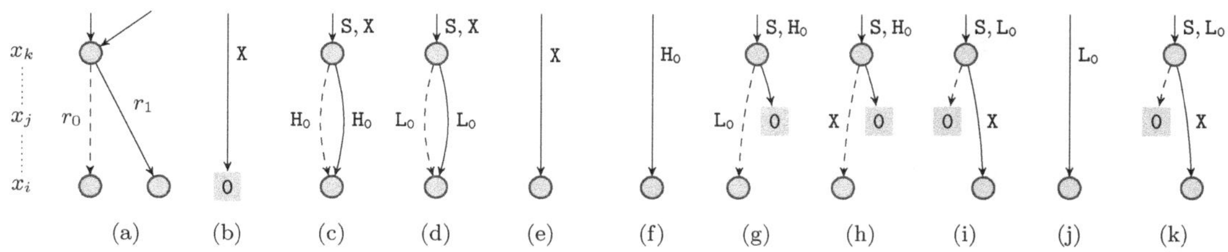

Fig. 2. Replacement rules for patterns in Fig. 1

Definition 2. An ESRBDD is *reduced* if the following restrictions hold:

R1. There are no duplicate nodes.
R2. There are no redundant nodes.
R3. There are no high-zero nodes.
R4. There are no low-zero nodes.
R5. For any edge $e = \langle \kappa, \mathbf{0} \rangle$, $\kappa \in \{\mathtt{S}, \mathtt{X}\}$.

The last restriction disallows edges $\langle \mathtt{H_0}, \mathbf{0} \rangle$ and $\langle \mathtt{L_0}, \mathbf{0} \rangle$ in the reduced ESRBDD. This is because $F^n_{\langle \mathtt{H_0}, \mathbf{0} \rangle} \equiv F^n_{\langle \mathtt{L_0}, \mathbf{0} \rangle} \equiv F^n_{\langle \mathtt{X}, \mathbf{0} \rangle} \equiv \mathbf{0}$, and since we want to enforce canonicity in the reduced ESRBDD, we have *arbitrarily* chosen $\langle \mathtt{X}, \mathbf{0} \rangle$ as the unique representation for such long edges.

3.1 Reducing an ESRBDD

An ESRBDD can be converted into a reduced ESRBDD using Algorithm 1. The algorithm first replaces any edges $\langle \mathtt{H_0}, \mathbf{0} \rangle$ or $\langle \mathtt{L_0}, \mathbf{0} \rangle$ with $\langle \mathtt{X}, \mathbf{0} \rangle$, to satisfy restriction R5. Then, it repeatedly chooses a high-zero, low-zero, redundant, or duplicate node q and eliminates it. If node q duplicates node p, then it redirects all incoming edges from q to p (line 7). Otherwise, q is a high-zero, low-zero, or redundant node, and lines 9–14 find a node d' with $lvl(d') < lvl(q) = n - 1$, and a rule $\kappa' \in \{\mathtt{X}, \mathtt{H_0}, \mathtt{L_0}\}$ such that $F^n_{\langle \mathtt{S}, q \rangle}(x_{1:n}) = F^n_{\langle \kappa', d' \rangle}(x_{1:n})$. Note that a short edge to node q becomes a long edge to node d' because $lvl(d') < lvl(q)$. For the special case of $d' = \mathbf{0}$, *any* edge to q is equivalent to edge $\langle \mathtt{X}, \mathbf{0} \rangle$, so the algorithm replaces those edges (line 16).

When $d' \neq \mathbf{0}$, we have $F^n_{\langle \mathtt{S}, q \rangle}(x_{1:n}) = F^n_{\langle \kappa', d' \rangle}(x_{1:n})$ for $n = lvl(q) + 1$, and these edges are replaced in line 18. It follows that $F^n_{\langle \kappa', q \rangle}(x_{1:n}) = F^n_{\langle \kappa', d' \rangle}(x_{1:n})$ for $n > lvl(q)+1$; these replacements are made in line 19. For rules $\kappa \in \{\mathtt{X}, \mathtt{H_0}, \mathtt{L_0}\}$

Algorithm 1. Reduce an ESRBDD

```
1: procedure Reduce(ESRBDD ⟨κ*,p*⟩)
2:     V ← Nodes(p*);
3:     ∀κ ∈ {H0, L0}, replace all ⟨κ,0⟩ edges with ⟨X,0⟩;
4:     while V contains a high-zero, low-zero, redundant, or duplicate node do
5:         Choose a high-zero, low-zero, redundant, or duplicate node q ∈ V;
6:         if q duplicates p then
7:             ∀κ ∈ {S, X, H0, L0}, replace all ⟨κ,q⟩ edges with ⟨κ,p⟩;
8:         else
9:             if q is a redundant node then
10:                κ' ← X;    d' ← q[1].node;
11:            else if q is a high-zero node then
12:                κ' ← H0;   d' ← q[0].node;
13:            else if q is a low-zero node then
14:                κ' ← L0;   d' ← q[1].node;
15:            if d' = 0 then
16:                ∀κ ∈ {S, X, H0, L0}, replace all ⟨κ,q⟩ edges with ⟨X,0⟩;
17:            else
18:                Replace all ⟨S,q⟩ edges with ⟨κ',d'⟩;
19:                Replace all ⟨κ',q⟩ edges with ⟨κ',d'⟩;
20:                for all rules κ ∈ {X, H0, L0} \ {κ'}, such that an edge ⟨κ,q⟩ exists do
21:                    Create node q' at level lvl(q) + 1 and add q' to V;
22:                    if κ = X then
23:                        q'[0] ← ⟨κ',d'⟩;   q'[1] ← ⟨κ',d'⟩;
24:                    else if κ = H0 then
25:                        q'[0] ← ⟨κ',d'⟩;   q'[1] ← ⟨X,0⟩;
26:                    else if κ = L0 then
27:                        q'[0] ← ⟨X,0⟩;   q'[1] ← ⟨κ',d'⟩;
28:                    Replace all ⟨κ,q⟩ edges with ⟨κ,q'⟩ or ⟨S,q'⟩;
29:        Remove q from V;
```

with $\kappa \neq \kappa'$, we cannot replace $\langle\kappa,q\rangle$ with a single long edge to node d', because the edge needs different reduction rules: the κ rule is needed above level $lvl(q)$, and the κ' rule is needed from level $lvl(q)$ down. So lines 21–27 of the algorithm create a new node q' at level $lvl(q)+1$, of the appropriate shape such that $F^n_{\langle\kappa,q\rangle}(x_{1:n}) = F^n_{\langle \mathtt{S},q'\rangle}(x_{1:n})$ for $n = lvl(q')+1$. It then follows that $F^n_{\langle\kappa,q\rangle}(x_{1:n}) = F^n_{\langle\kappa,q'\rangle}(x_{1:n})$ for $n > lvl(q')+1$. These replacements are made in line 28, where the replacement $\langle\kappa,q'\rangle$ is used for long edges, and $\langle \mathtt{S},q'\rangle$ is used for short edges.

In the above discussion, any edge that is replaced by the algorithm encodes the same function as its replacement, giving us the following lemma.

Lemma 1. In Algorithm 1, each edge replacement preserves the function encoded by the ESRBDD $\langle\kappa^\star,p^\star\rangle$.

It remains to show that the algorithm always terminates.

Lemma 2. Algorithm 1 terminates in $\mathcal{O}(|Nodes(p^\star)|)$ steps.

Proof: The proof is based on the observation that, at every iteration of the algorithm, a node q is chosen to be processed (line 5), at most two nodes are created at level $lvl(q)+1$ (line 21), and node q is removed (line 29). These new nodes (q' on line 21), by construction, satisfy one of the following patterns:

- $q'[0] = q'[1] = \langle\kappa',d'\rangle$, where $d' \neq \mathbf{0}$, and $\kappa' \in \{\mathtt{H_0}, \mathtt{L_0}\}$,
- $q'[0] = \langle\mathtt{X},\mathbf{0}\rangle$, and $q'[1] = \langle\kappa',d'\rangle$, where $d' \neq \mathbf{0}$, and $\kappa' \in \{\mathtt{X}, \mathtt{H_0}\}$,
- $q'[0] = \langle\kappa',d'\rangle$, and $q'[1] = \langle\mathtt{X},\mathbf{0}\rangle$, where $d' \neq \mathbf{0}$, and $\kappa' \in \{\mathtt{X}, \mathtt{L_0}\}$.

These nodes are neither redundant, high-zero, nor low-zero, but they could be duplicates. Since the elimination of duplicate nodes (line 7) does not create new nodes, the two nodes created at $lvl(q)+1$ result in at most two additional iterations of the algorithm. Therefore, for every node in the original ESRBDD, the algorithm iterates at most three times. □

Theorem 1. Algorithm 1 converts ESRBDD $\langle\kappa^\star,p^\star\rangle$ to an equivalent reduced ESRBDD in $\mathcal{O}(|Nodes(p^\star)|)$ steps.

Proof: Lemma 2 establishes that Algorithm 1 terminates in $\mathcal{O}(|Nodes(p^\star)|)$ steps. Based on the condition of the while loop, when the loop terminates, we know that the ESRBDD contains no high-zero, low-zero, redundant, or duplicate nodes. From line 3 and the fact that the algorithm never adds an edge of the form $\langle\mathtt{H_0},\mathbf{0}\rangle$ or $\langle\mathtt{L_0},\mathbf{0}\rangle$, we conclude that when Algorithm 1 terminates, any edge to terminal node $\mathbf{0}$ must have edge rule $\mathtt{S}$ or $\mathtt{X}$. Therefore, when the Algorithm terminates, the ESRBDD is reduced. Lemma 1 establishes that Algorithm 1 produces an equivalent (in terms of encoded function) ESRBDD. □

While we have established that Algorithm 1 always terminates and produces a reduced ESRBDD, we have not yet established that the Algorithm produces the *same* reduced ESRBDD, regardless of the order in which nodes are chosen in line 5. This is guaranteed by the canonicity property, discussed next. Additionally, we note here that, unlike most other decision diagrams (including BDDs, ZDDs, CBDDs, CZDDs, and TDDs), a reduced ESRBDD is not necessarily a minimum size ESRBDD encoding of a function, even for a fixed variable order, as elimination of some node q during the reduction could trigger the creation of two new nodes. An example of this is shown in Fig. 3, where redundant node q is eliminated. Edges $\langle\mathtt{S},q\rangle$ and $\langle\mathtt{X},q\rangle$ can be simply redirected as $\langle\mathtt{X},p\rangle$, but the $\langle\mathtt{H_0},q\rangle$ and $\langle\mathtt{L_0},q\rangle$ edges require the creation of two new nodes $q_{\mathtt{H_0}}$ and $q_{\mathtt{L_0}}$.

While the "chaotic" non-deterministic reduction procedure in Algorithm 1 is handy in proving termination under the most general conditions, in practice we utilize a deterministic depth-first version of this algorithm that reduces a node only after having reduced its children.

3.2 Canonicity of Reduced ESRBDDs

We are now ready to discuss the *canonicity* of reduced ESRBDDs, i.e., to show that a function has a unique encoding as a reduced ESRBDD. In the following, we say that functions $F^n_{\langle\kappa,p\rangle}$ and $F^n_{\langle\kappa',p'\rangle}$ are *equivalent*, written $F^n_{\langle\kappa,p\rangle} \equiv F^n_{\langle\kappa',p'\rangle}$, if $F^n_{\langle\kappa,p\rangle}(x_{1:n}) = F^n_{\langle\kappa',p'\rangle}(x_{1:n})$ for all possible inputs $(x_{1:n}) \in \mathbb{B}^n$.

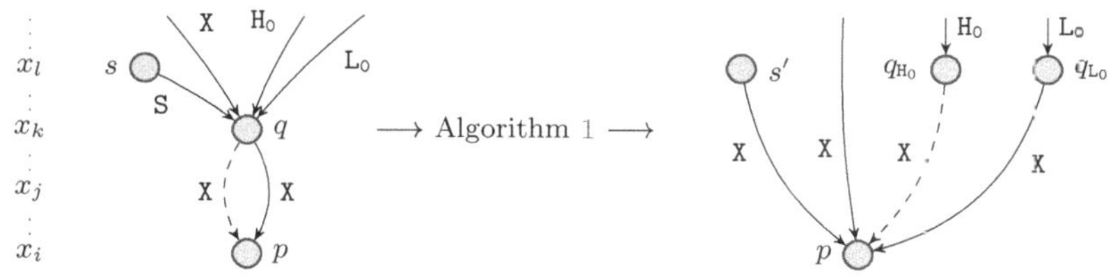

Fig. 3. A worst-case example where elimination of node q creates two nodes.

Theorem 2. In a reduced ESRBDD, for any $n \in \mathbb{N}$, for any two edges $e = \langle \kappa, p \rangle$, $e' = \langle \kappa', p' \rangle$ with $lvl(p) \le n$, $lvl(p') \le n$, if $F_e^n \equiv F_{e'}^n$ then (1) $p = p'$, and (2) if $lvl(p) < n$ then $\kappa = \kappa'$.

Proof: The proof is by induction on n. For the base case, we use $n = 0$ and from the definition of F we have $F_e^0 \equiv F_{e'}^0 \ \rightarrow \ p = p'$.

Now, suppose the theorem holds for $n = m$, where $m \ge 0$, we will prove it holds for $n = m + 1$. Regardless of $\langle \kappa, p \rangle$, we have

$$F^n_{\langle \kappa, p \rangle}(x_{1:n}) = (x_n)?f_1(x_{1:n-1}):f_0(x_{1:n-1})$$

for some functions f_0 and f_1. Similarly, we have

$$F^n_{\langle \kappa', p' \rangle}(x_{1:n}) = (x_n)?f'_1(x_{1:n-1}):f'_0(x_{1:n-1}).$$

It follows that $F^n_{\langle \kappa, p \rangle} \equiv F^n_{\langle \kappa', p' \rangle}$ if and only if $f_0 \equiv f'_0$ and $f_1 \equiv f'_1$.
First, suppose $lvl(p) = n$ and $lvl(p') = n$. From the definition of F, it follows that $F^{n-1}_{p[0]} \equiv F^{n-1}_{p'[0]}$ and $F^{n-1}_{p[1]} \equiv F^{n-1}_{p'[1]}$. By inductive hypothesis, $p[0].node = p'[0].node$ and $p[1].node = p'[1].node$. If $lvl(p[0].node) < n-1$, then by inductive hypothesis, $p[0] = p'[0]$; otherwise, $lvl(p[0].node) = n-1$ and we must have $p[0].rule = \texttt{S}$ and $p'[0].rule = \texttt{S}$, thus $p[0] = p'[0]$. By a similar argument, it follows that $p[1] = p'[1]$. We therefore have either that $p = p'$ and the theorem holds, or that p duplicates p', which is impossible because of restriction R1.
Next, suppose $lvl(p) < n$ and $lvl(p') < n$. If $\kappa = \kappa'$, then in all cases for F we conclude that $F^{n-1}_{\langle \kappa, p \rangle} \equiv F^{n-1}_{\langle \kappa', p' \rangle}$ and by inductive hypothesis we have that $p = p'$, so the theorem holds. We now show that $\kappa \ne \kappa'$ is impossible, by contradiction. Consider the possible cases for $\kappa \ne \kappa'$:

1. $\kappa = \texttt{X}$: If $\kappa' = \texttt{L}_0$ or $\kappa' = \texttt{H}_0$, from the definition of F we conclude that $F^{n-1}_{\langle \kappa, p \rangle} \equiv F^{n-1}_{\langle \kappa', p' \rangle}$ and that $F^{n-1}_{\langle \kappa, p \rangle} \equiv \mathbf{0}$.
2. $\kappa = \texttt{L}_0$: If $\kappa' = \texttt{H}_0$, from the definition of F we conclude that $F^{n-1}_{\langle \kappa, p \rangle} \equiv \mathbf{0}$ and $F^{n-1}_{\langle \kappa', p' \rangle} \equiv \mathbf{0}$.
3. The remaining cases are symmetric.

In all cases, we conclude that $F^{n-1}_{\langle \kappa, p \rangle} \equiv \mathbf{0}$ and $F^{n-1}_{\langle \kappa', p' \rangle} \equiv \mathbf{0}$. By the inductive hypothesis, we have that $p = \mathbf{0}$ and $p' = \mathbf{0}$. According to R5, if $p = \mathbf{0}$ then κ cannot be $\texttt{L}_0$ or $\texttt{H}_0$. But this implies $\kappa = \texttt{X}$ and $\kappa' = \texttt{X}$, contradicting our assumption that $\kappa \ne \kappa'$.

Finally, suppose $lvl(p) = n$ and $lvl(p') < n$ (the case $lvl(p) < n$ and $lvl(p') = n$ is symmetric). We show that this is impossible, by contradiction. Consider the possible cases for κ':

1. $\kappa' = \texttt{X}$: From the definition of F, we must have $F^{n-1}_{p[0]} \equiv F^{n-1}_{\langle\kappa',p'\rangle}$ and $F^{n-1}_{p[1]} \equiv F^{n-1}_{\langle\kappa',p'\rangle}$. By the inductive hypothesis, we conclude that $p[0].node = p'$ and $p[1].node = p'$. If $lvl(p') = n-1$, then we have $p[0] = p[1] = \langle\texttt{S},p'\rangle$; otherwise, we have $lvl(p') < n-1$ and by inductive hypothesis, $p[0] = p[1] = \langle\kappa',p'\rangle = \langle\texttt{X},p'\rangle$. Either way, node p is redundant, and from R2 we have a contradiction.
2. $\kappa' = \texttt{H}_0$: From the definition of F, we must have $F^{n-1}_{p[0]} \equiv F^{n-1}_{\langle\kappa',p'\rangle}$ and $F^{n-1}_{p[1]} \equiv \mathbf{0}$. By the inductive hypothesis, we conclude that $p[0].node = p'$ and $p[1].node = \mathbf{0}$. If $lvl(p') = n-1$, then we have $p[0] = \langle\texttt{S},p'\rangle$; otherwise, we have $lvl(p') < n-1$ and by inductive hypothesis, $p[0] = \langle\kappa',p'\rangle = \langle\texttt{H}_0,p'\rangle$. Either way, node p is high-zero, and from R3 we have a contradiction.
3. $\kappa' = \texttt{L}_0$: From the definition of F, we must have $F^{n-1}_{p[0]} \equiv \mathbf{0}$ and $F^{n-1}_{p[1]} \equiv F^{n-1}_{\langle\kappa',p'\rangle}$. By the inductive hypothesis, we conclude that $p[0].node = \mathbf{0}$ and $p[1].node = p'$. If $lvl(p') = n-1$, then we have $p[1] = \langle\texttt{S},p'\rangle$; otherwise, we have $lvl(p') < n-1$ and by inductive hypothesis, $p[1] = \langle\kappa',p'\rangle = \langle\texttt{L}_0,p'\rangle$. Either way, node p is low-zero, and from R4 we have a contradiction. □

The canonicity result establishes that, regardless of how a ESRBDD is constructed for a given function, the resulting reduced ESRBDD is guaranteed to be unique (assuming a given variable order). Thus, we can determine in constant time whether two functions encoded as reduced ESRBDDs are equivalent (as is already the case for reduced ordered BDDs and ZDDs). From now on, unless otherwise specified, we assume that all ESRBDDs are reduced.

3.3 Comparing ESRBDDs to Other Types of Decision Diagrams

For the remainder of the paper, we consider the relative size of the different types of DD based on the interpretation of long edges, namely, BDDs, ZDDs, CBDDs, CZDDs, TBDDs, and ESRBDDs. We also consider ESRBDDs without the $\texttt{L}_0$ edge label, denoted ESRBDD$-\texttt{L}_0$. These are summarized in Table 1, some entries (comparisons between BDDs, ZDDs, CBDDs, and CZDDs) are known from prior work [2,6], some entries are discussed below, and some entries are unknown. Entry $[T_1, T_2]$ describes the worst-case increase in the number of nodes, as a multiplicative factor, More formally, it is the bound for "number of nodes required to encode f using T_2" divided by "number of nodes required to encode f using T_1" for all functions f over L boolean variables. Note that the node counts always include both terminal nodes. A factor of 1 indicates that type T_1 cannot require fewer nodes than type T_2.

First, we discuss how an arbitrary BDD can be converted into a TBDD or ESRBDD, and fill in the BDD row in Table 1. To build a TBDD from a BDD, every edge to a non-terminal node p in the BDD is annotated with the level tag $lvl(p)$. By definition, any such annotated edge in a TBDD implies BDD

Table 1. Worst-case relative increase when converting one DD type into another.

	BDD	ZDD	CBDD	CZDD	TBDD	ESR−L_0	ESR
BDD →	—	$L/2$ [6]	1 [2]	2 [2]	1	1	1
ZDD →	$L/2$ [6]	—	3 [2]	1 [2]	1	1	1
CBDD →	?	?	—	2 [2]	?	2	2
CZDD →	?	?	3 [2]	—	?	2	2
TBDD →	?	?	?	?	—	3	3
ESRBDD−L_0 →	$L/2$	$L/2$	3	2	1	—	3/2
ESRBDD →	$2L/3$	$2L/3$	$L/2$	$L/2$	$L/2$	$L/2$	—

reductions for the skipped levels. A TBDD thus constructed is no larger than the BDD, and may be further reduced (since it could contain high-zero nodes) by applying the TBDD reduction described in [10]. Similarly, we can annotate long edges in the BDD with X (Fig. 4(a)), and short edges with S, to obtain an unreduced ESRBDD. We then apply Algorithm 1. We now show that this will not increase the ESRBDD size, and thus the resulting ESRBDD cannot be larger than the original BDD.

Lemma 3. Suppose we have an unreduced ESRBDD where, for every node q, there exists a rule $\kappa \in \{\mathtt{X}, \mathtt{H_0}, \mathtt{L_0}\}$ such that every edge to q is either $\langle \mathtt{S}, q\rangle$ or $\langle \kappa, q\rangle$. Then reducing the ESRBDD will not increase the number of nodes.

Proof: Apply Algorithm 1 and in line 5, always choose a node at the lowest level. Then, when a node q is chosen, all incoming edges to q will be labeled either with S or with κ. The $\langle \mathtt{S}, q\rangle$ edges will not cause any node to be created. The $\langle \kappa, q\rangle$ edges will cause at most one node to be created. But then node q is removed. Thus, the overall number of nodes cannot increase. □

It is also easy to convert a ZDD into a TBDD or ESRBDD. To obtain a TBDD, annotate every edge from non-terminal node p with the level tag $lvl(p)$, so that ZDD reductions are used for all the edges; then reduce the TBDD. To obtain an ESRBDD, annotate long edges in the ZDD with $\mathtt{H_0}$, see Fig. 4(b), and short edges with S, and apply Algorithm 1.

The conversion from a chained DD to an unreduced ESRBDD is illustrated in Fig. 4(c) and (d). For each chain node $x_k : x_i$ with $x_k > x_i$, create a "top node" with variable x_k, and a "bottom node" with variable x_i, that is only pointed to by its corresponding top node. In a CBDD, the top node will be a high-zero node, and all top nodes and non-chained nodes will have incoming edges labeled with X or S. In a CZDD, the top node will be a redundant node, and all top nodes and non-chained nodes will have incoming edges labeled with $\mathtt{H_0}$ or S. At worst, the unreduced ESRBDD has twice the nodes of the original CBDD or CZDD and, from Lemma 3, reducing this ESRBDD does not increase its size.

In a TBDD, each edge can be characterized as short, purely X, purely $\mathtt{H_0}$, or partly X and partly $\mathtt{H_0}$. To convert into an ESRBDD, the short edges are labeled with S, the purely X edges are labeled with X, the purely $\mathtt{H_0}$ edges are labeled

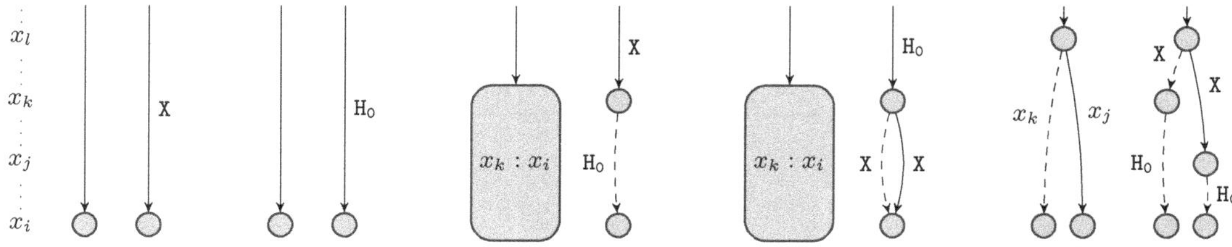

Fig. 4. Converting to ESRBDDs.

with $\mathtt{H_0}$. Edges that are partly X and partly $\mathtt{H_0}$ require the addition of a node at the level where the reduction rule changes, as shown in Fig. 4(e). The worst case occurs when *every* edge requires such a node. Then, since every TBDD node has two outgoing edges, the resulting unreduced ESRBDD will have triple the number of nodes. Since all of the introduced nodes have incoming X edges, and all other nodes have incoming S or $\mathtt{H_0}$ edges, from Lemma 3 this ESRBDD will not increase in size when it is reduced. We note here that, if there are some purely X edges in the TBDD, then Lemma 3 no longer applies; however, the number of nodes that would be added during reduction is no more than the number of nodes saved by not having to introduce a node on the purely X edges.

We now consider converting from ESRBDDs into the other DD types. In the case where $\mathtt{L_0}$ edges are not allowed (row ESRBDD$-\mathtt{L_0}$ in Table 1), the worst case BDD is from ESRBDD $\langle \mathtt{H_0}, \mathbf{1}\rangle$ and the worst case ZDD is from ESRBDD $\langle \mathtt{X}, \mathbf{1}\rangle$. In both cases, the ESRBDD has 2 nodes, while the resulting BDD/ZDD has $L+2$ nodes, giving ratios of $L/2 + o(L)$, similar to the discussion in [6, p. 250]. The example ZDD in [2], which produces a CBDD with three times as many nodes, can be converted into an ESRBDD of the same size. Similarly, the example BDD in [2], which produces a CZDD with twice as many nodes, can be converted into an ESRBDD of the same size. Any ESRBDD without $\mathtt{L_0}$ edges can be converted into a TBDD by labeling X edges with a level tag such that the X rule is always applied, and labelling $\mathtt{H_0}$ edges with a level tag such that the $\mathtt{H_0}$ rule is always applied. Therefore, the TBDD cannot be larger than the ESRBDD. An ESRBDD$-\mathtt{L_0}$ can be converted into an ESRBDD by running Algorithm 1 to eliminate any low-zero nodes. For each low-zero node that is eliminated, we could have an incoming X and $\mathtt{H_0}$ edge, causing the creation of two nodes. Suppose we eliminate n low-zero nodes that cause creation of two nodes. Then, because each low-zero node must have 2 incoming edges, we must have $2n$ incoming edges to these nodes. Above, we must have at least $2n-1$ nodes to produce these edges. We could then "stack" such a pattern m times. This gives an ESRBDD with $m(n+2n-1)+2 = m(3n-1)+2$ nodes, and a reduced ESRBDD with $m(2n+2n-1)+2 = m(4n-1)+2$ nodes. The upper bound of this ratio is $3/2$, which occurs when $n=1$ and m goes to infinity.

For the case of ESRBDDs with all types of edges (row ESRBDD in Table 1), the $\mathtt{L_0}$ edge allows us to build different worst cases. Consider an ESRBDD $\langle \mathtt{S}, p\rangle$ where $lvl(p) = L$, $p[0] = \langle \mathtt{H_0}, \mathbf{1}\rangle$, and $p[1] = \langle \mathtt{L_0}, \mathbf{1}\rangle$. This ESRBDD has 3 nodes.

Table 2. Numbers of nodes for dictionary benchmarks.

Word List		QBDD	BDD	CBDD	ZDD	CZDD	TBDD	ESR
Binary	Compact	1,120,437	1,120,250	971,387	657,969	657,969	657,902	**484,765**
	Full	1,285,501	1,285,285	1,153,438	851,555	851,554	851,479	**520,576**
One-hot	Compact	9,739,638	9,739,638	656,649	**311,227**	**311,227**	**311,227**	**311,227**
	Full	22,775,492	22,775,492	656,712	**311,227**	**311,227**	**311,227**	**311,227**

Password List		QBDD	BDD	CBDD	ZDD	CZDD	TBDD	ESR
Binary	Compact	5,705,516	5,704,777	4,542,925	2,960,478	2,960,435	2,960,209	**2,399,272**
	Full	5,649,626	5,648,670	4,960,446	3,532,847	3,532,816	3,532,467	**2,410,589**
One-hot	Compact	72,858,088	72,858,088	3,055,784	**1,486,430**	**1,486,430**	**1,486,430**	**1,486,430**
	Full	101,737,047	101,737,047	3,056,067	**1,486,430**	**1,486,430**	**1,486,430**	**1,486,430**

Because BDDs cannot exploit $\mathtt{H}_0$ or $\mathtt{L}_0$ edges, this will produce a BDD with $2(L-1)+3 = 2L+1$ nodes, giving a worst-case ratio of $2L/3$. The ZDD worst-case is similar, using instead $p[0] = \langle \mathtt{X}, \mathbf{1} \rangle$. Finally, for DD types that can exploit both X and $\mathtt{H}_0$ edges, the ESRBDD $\langle \mathtt{L}_0, \mathbf{1} \rangle$ corresponds to the worst case: the CBDD, CZDD, TBDD, and ESRBDD$-\mathtt{L}_0$ will all require $L+2$ nodes.

4 Experimental Results

We compare the performance of QBDDs (with long edges to **0**), BDDs, ZDDs, CBDDs, CZDDs, TBDDs, and ESRBDDs on three sets of benchmarks. The first two benchmarks are similar to those used in [2], and are representative of general textual information and digital logic functions, respectively. The third benchmark is typical in state space analysis of concurrent systems.

4.1 Dictionaries

A dictionary can be encoded as an indicator function over the set of strings of a given length from either the `compact` alphabet consisting of the distinct symbols found in the dictionary plus `NULL`, or the `full` alphabet of all 128 ASCII characters (to ensure that all encoded strings have the same length, shorter ones are padded with the ASCII symbol `NULL`). We use the encoding schemes described in [2]: *one-hot* and *binary*. Therefore, each dictionary generates four benchmarks, one for each choice of encoding and alphabet.

We compare the different DD types on two dictionaries. The first one is the English words in file `/usr/share/dict/words` under MacOS, containing 235,886 words with lengths ranging from 1 to 24. Its compact alphabet contains lower and upper case letters plus hyphen and `NULL` (54 in total). The second one is a set of passwords from SecLists [7] (non-ASCII characters are replaced with `NULL`), containing 999,999 passwords with lengths ranging from 1 to 39. Its compact alphabet consists of 91 symbols including `NULL`.

Table 3. Numbers of nodes for combinational circuit benchmarks.

Circuit	QBDD	BDD	CBDD	ZDD	CZDD	TBDD	ESR
C432	2,675	1,506	1,506	2,658	2,189	**1,494**	1,498
C499	29,483	28,769	28,769	29,316	28,749	28,610	**28,428**
C880	15,048	6,496	6,496	15,044	9,640	6,496	**6,491**
C1355	85,694	75,498	75,498	85,439	77,976	75,243	**74,757**
C1908	18,456	16,210	16,174	17,859	16,047	15,687	**15,685**
C2670	74,940	15,662	15,658	74,468	21,012	**15,539**	15,601
C3540	152,523	51,878	51,778	150,539	64,563	**50,871**	51,146
C5315	26,011	3,793	3,784	25,785	4,749	**3,716**	3,742

Table 2 reports the number of nodes required to store each dictionary, according to different encodings and alphabets (the best result on each row is in boldface). Except for QBDDs and BDDs, the one-hot encoding results in fewer nodes, demonstrating the effectiveness of the zero-suppressed idea when encoding large, sparse data. Among the DD types we consider, ESRBDDs have the fewest nodes, regardless of encoding and alphabet. For binary encodings, ESRBDDs use 19%–39% fewer nodes than TBDDs, the second best choice. With one-hot encodings, ZDDs, CZDDs, TBDDs, and ESRBDDs tie for best because (a) there are no redundant nodes and (b) any low-zero nodes that are eliminated do not cause an overall decrease in the number nodes in the ESRBDDs. Indeed, redundant nodes are rare even with binary encodings, as they arise when two words w_1 and w_2 not only have bit patterns that differ in a position, but they also share all their possible continuations, i.e., w_1w' is a word if and only if w_2w' is also a word, for all w'. In the English word list, "Hlidhskjalf" and its alternate spelling "Hlithskjalf" is one such rare instance (note that no w' can continue either of them to form an additional word).

4.2 Combinational Circuits

BDDs are commonly used to synthesize and verify digital circuits. We select a set of combinational circuits from the LGSynth'91 benchmarks [11] and, for each circuit, we build a DD encoding all its output logic functions. For each circuit, the variable order is determined using Sifting [9] while building the BDD.

Table 3 reports the number of nodes needed to encode all outputs of each circuit. In contrast to the dictionaries, these benchmarks place importance on the ability to eliminate redundant nodes. Thus, QBDDs and ZDDs have the worst performance. TBDDs and ESRBDDs are always the two best representations, and the difference between them is less than 0.7%.

4.3 Safe Petri Nets

Decision diagrams are frequently used in symbolic model checking to represent sets of states. We have selected a set of 37 *safe* Petri nets from the 2018 Model Checking Contest https://mcc.lip6.fr/2018/. A Petri net is safe if each one of its places can contain at most one token—each place can, therefore, be mapped

Table 4. Final scores for the safe Petri net benchmarks.

QBDD	BDD	CBDD	ZDD	CZDD	TBDD	ESR
3.108	2.971	2.038	1.215	1.167	1.160	**1.001**

Table 5. Number of nodes for a subset of the safe Petri net benchmarks.

Model	QBDD	BDD	CBDD	ZDD	CZDD	TBDD	ESR
DiscoveryGPU-PT-14a	80,865	75,682	75,571	43,016	43,016	**39,689**	40,953
BusinessProcesses-PT-04	282,787	282,787	130,825	67,228	67,228	67,228	**66,983**
Referendum-PT-0020	343,676	343,676	339,552	194,607	194,607	194,607	**184,789**
NeoElection-PT-3	414,962	414,962	34,860	15,519	15,519	15,519	**15,507**
SimpleLoadBal-PT-10	503,777	503,777	376,896	191,460	191,460	191,460	**182,403**
LamportFastMutEx-PT-4	507,897	507,897	252,361	122,487	122,487	122,487	**119,111**
AutoFlight-PT-06a	520,755	520,755	356,729	207,409	207,409	207,409	**178,855**
RwMutex-PT-r0020w0010	553,073	553,073	502,831	358,580	358,580	358,580	**195,377**
DES-PT-01b	709,303	709,303	442,610	246,647	246,647	246,647	**217,325**
Dekker-PT-015	1,191,942	1,191,942	844,466	504,726	504,726	504,726	**403,801**
Railroad-PT-010	2,109,610	2,109,610	1,096,122	554,541	554,541	554,541	**516,121**
NQueens-PT-08	3,698,534	3,698,534	2,295,689	1,443,628	1,443,628	1,443,628	**1,069,242**
ResAllocation-PT-R020C002	5,532,167	5,532,167	4,554,792	2,826,856	2,826,856	2,826,856	**2,167,111**

directly to a boolean variable. Most of these models have scaling parameters that affect their size and complexity, yielding $N = 103$ model instances.

Providing detailed results for all the model instances would require excessive space, so to summarize over all model instances, Table 4 shows a score for each DD type i. The score is the geometric mean [4]:

$$score(i) = \sqrt[N]{\prod_{n=1}^{N} \frac{T_i(n)}{T_{min}(n)}}$$

where N is the total number of model instances, $T_i(n)$ is the number of nodes needed to represent the state space of instance n using DD type i, and $T_{min}(n)$ is the smallest number of nodes needed to represent the state space of instance n by any of the DD types we consider. ESRBDDs have by far the smallest overall score, barely larger than 1, indicating that they are either the smallest or slightly larger than the smallest for each model instance.

Table 5 shows $T_i(n)$ for model instances n that required more than 250,000 nodes in the QBDD representation. For parameterized models that had multiple model instances satisfying this criterion, we present data for only the largest such model instance. We have also included the results for *DiscoveryGPU*—the only model where ESRBDDs were not the best (they were a close second).

4.4 Memory Considerations: The Size of Nodes

So far, we have compared DD types based on how many nodes they require. However, the actual memory consumption also depends on the size of the respective nodes. All of these DDs store two child pointers. In addition, BDDs and ZDDs

Table 6. Overhead of node sizes (bits per node) as compared to QBDD nodes.

Level bits	BDD	ZDD	CBDD	CZDD	TBDD	ESR−L_0	ESR
16	+16	+16	+32	+32	+48	+18	+20
20	+20	+20	+40	+40	+60	+22	+24
32	+32	+32	+64	+64	+96	+34	+36

store a level, CBDDs and CZDDs store two levels, TBDDs store three levels, while ESRBDDs store a level and two edge rules. Since all short edges must be labeled by S, it is only necessary to label the long edges, and this requires $\log_2 n$ bits per edge if there are n non-S reduction rules. Without L_0 edges, a single bit distinguishes H_0 from X; otherwise, two bits are required for rules $\{H_0, L_0, X\}$. QBDD nodes are therefore the smallest (typically requiring 64 or 128 bits, when 32–bit or 64–bit pointers are used, respectively) and Table 6 indicates the *additional* cost required for each node type, when the level integers are stored using 16 bits (as suggested by [2]), 20 bits (as suggested by [10]), and 32 bits.

ESRBDDs are clearly more memory efficient than CBDDs, CZDDs and TBDDs. There are a few instances in our experiments where TBDDs use marginally fewer nodes than ESRBDDs (less than 3.2% fewer nodes in every such instance), but not enough to overcome their per-node memory overhead.

5 Conclusions

We have shown that ESRBDDs are a simple, yet efficient, generalization of previous attempts at combining reduction rules. Unlike previous efforts, they are not biased towards any particular reduction rule and therefore eliminate the need for the user to prioritize the reduction rules. They also provide a framework for further generalizations through additional reduction rules—for example, "high-one" and "low-one", the duals of "low-zero" and "high-zero" respectively.

ESRBDDs allow users to select a subset of reduction rules that suit their needs, and make it possible to integrate domain-specific reduction rules (a common phenomenon) with a subset of existing ones. ESRBDD nodes are also more compact than all previous such efforts, and new reduction rules can be added at a small cost—$\log_2 n$ bits per edge, where n is the number of reduction rules. Our future efforts will be directed towards adapting BDD manipulation operations (such as *Apply*) to work with the reduction rules in ESRBDDs, and towards including complement edges and other reduction rules, such as "high-one", "low-one", or "identity" reductions, while maintaining canonicity.

Acknowledgments. This work was supported in part by National Science Foundation grant ACI-1642397.

References

1. Bryant, R.E.: Graph-based algorithms for Boolean function manipulation. IEEE Trans. Comp. **35**(8), 677–691 (1986)
2. Bryant, R.E.: Chain reduction for binary and zero-suppressed decision diagrams. In: Beyer, D., Huisman, M. (eds.) TACAS 2018. LNCS, vol. 10805, pp. 81–98. Springer, Cham (2018). https://doi.org/10.1007/978-3-319-89960-2_5
3. Drechsler, R., Becker, B.: Ordered Kronecker functional decision diagrams – a data structure for representation and manipulation of Boolean functions. Trans. Comput. Aided Des. Integr. Circ. Syst. **17**(10), 965–973 (2006)
4. Fleming, P.J., Wallace, J.J.: How not to lie with statistics: the correct way to summarize benchmark results. Commun. ACM **29**(3), 218–221 (1986)
5. Kimura, S., Clarke, E.M.: A parallel algorithm for constructing binary decision diagrams. In: Proceedings of International Conference on Computer Design (ICCD), pp. 220–223. IEEE Computer Society Press, September 1990
6. Knuth, D.E.: The Art of Computer Programming, Volume 4A: Combinatorial Algorithms, Part I. Addison-Wesley, Boston (2011)
7. Miessler, D., Haddix, J.: SecLists. https://github.com/danielmiessler/SecLists
8. Minato, S.-I.: Zero-suppressed BDDs and their applications. Softw. Tools Technol. Transf. **3**, 156–170 (2001)
9. Rudell, R.: Dynamic variable ordering for ordered binary decision diagrams. In: International Conference on CAD, pp. 139–144, November 1993
10. van Dijk, T., Wille, R., Meolic, R.: Tagged BDDs: combining reduction rules from different decision diagram types. In: Proceedings of the 17th Conference on Formal Methods in Computer-Aided Design, FMCAD 2017, Austin, TX, pp. 108–115. FMCAD Inc. (2017)
11. Yang, S.: Logic synthesis and optimization benchmarks user guide: version 3.0. Microelectronics Center of North Carolina (MCNC) (1991)

Effective Entailment Checking for Separation Logic with Inductive Definitions

Jens Katelaan[1(✉)], Christoph Matheja[2], and Florian Zuleger[1]

[1] TU Wien, Vienna, Austria
jkatelaan@forsyte.at
[2] RWTH Aachen University, Aachen, Germany

Abstract. Symbolic-Heap Separation logic is a popular formalism for automated reasoning about heap-manipulating programs, which allows the user to give customized data structure definitions.

In this paper, we give a new decidability proof for the separation logic fragment of Iosif, Rogalewicz and Simacek. We circumvent the reduction to MSO from their proof and provide a direct model-theoretic construction with elementary complexity. We implemented our approach in the Harrsh analyzer and evaluate its effectiveness. In particular, we show that Harrsh can decide the entailment problem for data structure definitions for which no previous decision procedures have been implemented.

1 Introduction

Separation logic (SL) [12,18] is a popular formalism for Hoare-style verification of imperative, heap-manipulating programs. In particular, the *symbolic heap* separation logic fragment has received a lot of attention: Symbolic heaps serve as the basis of various automated verification tools, such as Infer [6], Sleek [7], Songbird [19], GRASSHopper [17], VCDryad [16], VeriFast [13], SLS [20], and Spen [9]. Many of the aforementioned tools rely on *systems of inductive predicate definitions* (SID) that serve as specifications of dynamic data structures, e.g., linked lists and trees.

At the heart of every Hoare-style verification procedure based on separation logic lies the *entailment problem*: Given two SL formulas, say φ and ψ, is every model of φ also a model of ψ? While the entailment problem is undecidable in general [2], there are various approaches to decide entailments between symbolic heaps ranging from complete methods for fixed SIDs [3], over decision procedures for restricted classes of SIDs [10,11], to incomplete approaches, such as fold/unfold reasoning [7] or cyclic proofs [5].

Among the largest decidable fragments of symbolic heaps with inductive definitions is the fragment of *symbolic heaps with bounded tree-width* (SL_{btw}) [10]. This fragment supports a rich class of data structures in SID specifications, such as doubly-linked lists and binary trees with linked leaves. SL_{btw} introduces

T. Vojnar and L. Zhang (Eds.): TACAS 2019, Part II, LNCS 11428, pp. 319–336, 2019.
https://doi.org/10.1007/978-3-030-17465-1_18

$$
\begin{array}{rcl}
\mathtt{tree}(x_1, x_2) & \Leftarrow & x_1 \mapsto (\mathbf{null}, \mathbf{null}, x_2) \\
\mathtt{tree}(x_1, x_2) & \Leftarrow & \exists \ell, r \colon x_1 \mapsto (\ell, r, x_2) * \mathtt{tree}(\ell, x_1) * \mathtt{tree}(r, x_1) \\
\hline
\mathtt{rtree}(x_1, x_2, x_3) & \Leftarrow & \exists r \colon x_1 \mapsto (x_3, r, x_2) * \mathtt{parent}(x_3, x_1) * \mathtt{tree}(r, x_1) \\
\mathtt{parent}(x_1, x_2) & \Leftarrow & x_1 \mapsto (\mathbf{null}, \mathbf{null}, x_2) \\
\mathtt{rtree}(x_1, x_2, x_3) & \Leftarrow & \exists \ell, r \colon x_1 \mapsto (\ell, r, x_2) * \mathtt{rtree}(\ell, x_1, x_3) * \mathtt{tree}(r, x_1) \\
\hline
\mathtt{ltree}(x_1, x_2, x_3) & \Leftarrow & \exists p \colon x_1 \mapsto (\mathbf{null}, \mathbf{null}, p) * \mathtt{lltree}(p, x_1, x_2, x_3) \\
\mathtt{lltree}(x_1, x_2, x_3, x_4) & \Leftarrow & \exists r \colon x_1 \mapsto (x_2, r, x_3) * \mathtt{tree}(r, x_1) * \mathtt{lroot}(x_3, x_1, x_4) \\
\mathtt{lltree}(x_1, x_2, x_3, x_4) & \Leftarrow & \exists r, p \colon x_1 \mapsto (x_2, r, p) * \mathtt{lltree}(p, x_1, x_3, x_4) * \mathtt{tree}(r, x_1) \\
\mathtt{lroot}(x_1, x_2, x_3) & \Leftarrow & \exists r \colon x_1 \mapsto (x_2, r, x_3) * \mathtt{tree}(r, x_1)
\end{array}
$$

Fig. 1. An SID Φ with three predicates for binary trees with parent pointers.

three syntactic conditions on SIDs—progress, connectivity, and establishment—that enable a reduction from the entailment problem for $\mathrm{SL}_{\mathrm{btw}}$ to the (decidable) satisfiability problem for monadic second-order logic (MSO) over graphs of bounded tree width. This gives rise to a decision procedure of non-elementary complexity—at least without an in-depth analysis of the quantifier alternations involved in the reduction. The reduction to MSO is also technically involved and has—to the best of our knowledge—never been implemented. The authors remark in the follow-up paper [11] that "the method from [10] causes a blowup of several exponentials in the size of the input problem and is unlikely to produce an effective decision procedure."

Contributions. We give a new proof for the decidability of the entailment problem for the $\mathrm{SL}_{\mathrm{btw}}$ fragment. In contrast to [10], we circumvent the reduction to MSO and give a direct model-theoretic construction with elementary complexity. This yields an easy-to-implement decision procedure for entailments in the full $\mathrm{SL}_{\mathrm{btw}}$ fragment. We implemented our approach in the Harrsh analyzer and report on promising results for challenging examples (Sect. 6). In particular, we show that Harrsh can decide the entailment problem for data structure definitions for which no previous decision procedures have been implemented.

A challenging example. To highlight the challenges faced when developing and implementing decision procedures for entailments in $\mathrm{SL}_{\mathrm{btw}}$, consider the SID Φ consisting of the rules in Fig. 1.[1] There are three predicates, namely `tree`, `rtree`, and `ltree`, that specify binary trees with parent pointers (treep for short). The predicate `tree` takes two parameters representing the root of the tree and its parent. Predicates `rtree` and `ltree` both have the leftmost leaf of the tree as an additional parameter. Such a parameter may, for example, be required to specify tree segments for an automated program analysis. Although both `rtree` and `ltree` describe treeps, they take radically different approaches: Predicate `rtree` defines a treep starting at the root, i.e., it specifies the root of the treep

[1] The syntax and semantics of SIDs are defined formally in Sect. 3.

and then states that both subtrees are treeps (the parameter representing the leftmost leaf is additionally passed to the left subtree). In contrast, predicate `ltree` specifies treeps starting at the leftmost leaf and moving up to the root. Consequently, the models of these predicates are derived in completely different ways, which is a challenge for commonly applied approaches, such as fold/unfold (cf. [7]) or inductive reasoning (cf. [5,19,20]). In fact, the entailment $\mathtt{ltree}(x_1, x_2, x_3) \models \mathtt{rtree}(x_2, x_3, x_1)$ holds, whereas the entailment $\mathtt{rtree}(x_2, x_3, x_1) \models \mathtt{ltree}(x_1, x_2, x_3)$ is violated: Intuitively, `rtree` admits models in which all shortest paths from the root to the leftmost leaf have length one. In contrast, for `ltree`, the minimal length of all shortest paths is two. Thus, the heap illustrated in Fig. 2 is a model of `rtree`, but not of `ltree`. In fact, if we rule out this model, `rtree` and `ltree` entail each other. That is, the entailment below and its converse are both valid:

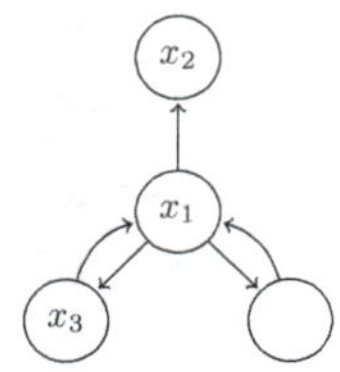

Fig. 2. treep

$$\mathtt{ltree}(x_1, x_2, x_3) \models \exists \ell, r \colon x_2 \mapsto (l, r, x_3) * \mathtt{rtree}(l, x_2, x_1) * \mathtt{tree}(r, x_2) \qquad (\clubsuit)$$

HARRSH solved the entailment (♣) from above in less than a second. The only other tool capable of successfully solving (♣) is SLIDE [11], which is based on tree automata. However, the approach in [11] is not complete for $\mathrm{SL}_{\mathrm{btw}}$.

Overview of our approach. We first present an algebra à la Courcelle [8] to systematically construct models of separation logic formulas (Sect. 2). This algebra enables us to conveniently formalize the semantics of separation logic (Sect. 3). To decide entailments, we then develop an abstraction mechanism for models with the following properties (Sect. 4):

1. The abstraction is *compositional*, i.e., we can perform our algebraic operations on abstractions instead of models (Theorem 2).
2. The abstraction is *finite*, i.e., each model of a predicate is abstracted to one of finitely many abstractions (Lemma 3).
3. The abstraction *refines* the predicate satisfaction relation, i.e., models with the same abstraction entail the same predicates among those relevant for the entailment (Lemma 2).
4. The abstraction is *effective*, i.e., for a given abstraction, one can determine which predicates are entailed (Theorem 3).

How do we obtain a decision procedure from these properties for an entailment, say $\mathsf{pred}_1(\mathbf{x_1}) \models_{\Phi} \mathsf{pred}_2(\mathbf{x_2})$? We iteratively compute all abstractions corresponding to models of $\mathsf{pred}_1(\mathbf{x_1})$. Due to compositionality (1), this can be achieved by applying the same operations used to construct models on previously computed abstractions until a fixed point is reached. Finiteness of the abstraction (2) ensures termination. We then exploit that the abstraction is well-defined (3) and effective (4) to decide the entailment: $\mathsf{pred}_1(\mathbf{x_1}) \models_{\Phi} \mathsf{pred}_2(\mathbf{x_2})$ holds iff all computed abstractions of models of $\mathsf{pred}_1(\mathbf{x_1})$ yield that they are also models of $\mathsf{pred}_2(\mathbf{x_2})$ (Sect. 5).

Due to space constraints, all proofs are in the supplementary material [1].

Notation. The set of all (non-empty) finite sequences over a set S is S^* (S^+). Bold letters denote sequences, e.g., $\mathbf{x} = \langle x_1, \ldots, x_k \rangle$. $\mathbf{x}[i]$ refers to the i-th element of $\mathbf{x}$. We often treat sequences as sets, i.e. we write $y \in \mathbf{x}$ if y occurs in $\mathbf{x}$, $\mathbf{x} \cup \mathbf{z}$ for the set of all elements in $\mathbf{x}$ or $\mathbf{z}$, etc. $f = \{x_1 \mapsto y_1, \ldots, x_n \mapsto y_n\}$ is the function given by $f(x_i) = y_i$ for $i \in [1, n]$, $n \geq 0$. Moreover, functions $f\colon X \to Y$ are lifted to functions on sequences $f\colon X^* \to Y^*$ by pointwise application.

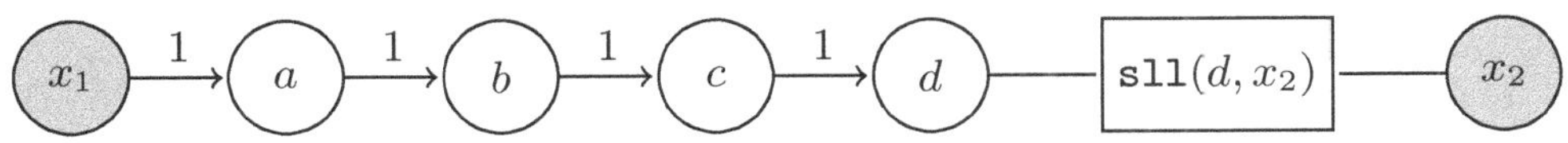

Fig. 3. A heap graph modeling a list segment of length at least 5 from x_1 to x_2.

2 Heap Graphs

Separation logic is typically interpreted in terms of stack-heap pairs consisting of a stack, i.e., an evaluation of variables, and a heap, i.e., a finite mapping from memory locations to values. In our setting, however, it is more convenient to abstract from locations and consider labeled graphs.

Formally, let **Var** be a set of variables containing a special variable **null** $\in$ **Var**. Moreover, let **Preds** be a set of *predicate identifiers*; each predicate $\mathsf{pred} \in$ **Preds** is equipped with an arity $\mathrm{ar}(\mathsf{pred}) \in \mathbb{N}$. $\mathsf{pred}(\mathbf{x})$ is a *predicate call* if the length of sequence $\mathbf{x} \in \mathbf{Var}^*$ is $\mathrm{ar}(\mathsf{pred})$.

Definition 1 (Heap Graph). *A* heap graph $\mathcal{M} = \langle \mathsf{Ptr}, \mathsf{FV}, \mathsf{calls} \rangle$ *is a graph whose nodes are a finite set of variables in* **Var**. *The edges of* $\mathcal{M}$ *are given by a partial points-to function* $\mathsf{Ptr}\colon \mathbf{Var} \setminus \{\mathbf{null}\} \rightharpoonup_{\mathit{finite}} \mathbf{Var}^+$ *mapping variables to finite tuples of variables. Moreover,* $\mathsf{FV} \subseteq \mathbf{Var}$ *is a finite set of* free variables *and* calls *is a finite set of* predicate calls. *A heap graph is* concrete *if* $\mathsf{calls} = \emptyset$. *We collect all variables in* Ptr, FV, *and* calls *in* $\mathsf{vars}(\mathcal{M})$. *Finally, we write* $\mathsf{Ptr}_{\mathcal{M}}$, $\mathsf{FV}_{\mathcal{M}}$, *and* $\mathsf{calls}_{\mathcal{M}}$ *to refer to the individual components of heap graph* $\mathcal{M}$. △

Example 1. Figure 3 depicts a heap graph modeling a singly-linked list of length at least five with head x_1 and tail x_2 (assuming the predicate call $\mathtt{sll}(d, x_2)$ stands for non-empty lists segments from d to x_2; see the left part of Fig. 5). In our graphical notation, every node corresponds to the variable it is labeled with. Gray nodes correspond to the free variables in FV. For each variable, say x, the pointers $\mathsf{Ptr}(x) = \langle y_1, \ldots, y_k \rangle$ are represented by directed edges—labeled with the position $1, 2, \ldots, k$—from the node labeled with x to nodes labeled with $y_1, \ldots, y_k$, respectively. We usually omit the edge labels if each node has at most one outgoing edge. Finally, a predicate call is drawn as a box labeled with the predicate call and connected to the nodes representing the variables occurring in the call's parameters. Formally, the heap graph in Fig. 3 is given by $\mathcal{M} = \langle \mathsf{Ptr}, \mathsf{FV}, \mathsf{calls} \rangle$ with points-to mapping $\mathsf{Ptr} = \{x_1 \mapsto a, a \mapsto b, b \mapsto c, c \mapsto d\}$, free variables $\mathsf{FV} = \{x_1, x_2\}$ and predicate calls $\mathsf{calls} = \{\mathtt{sll}(d, x_2)\}$. △

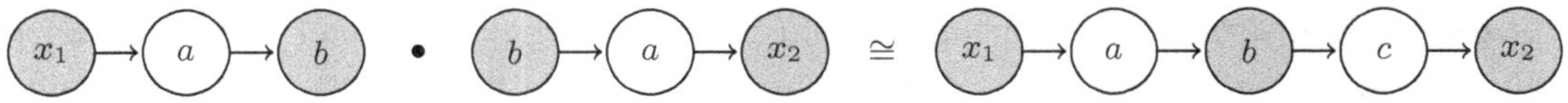

Fig. 4. Illustration of composition of two heap graphs.

Heap graphs are an abstraction of the classical stack-heap model. To reason about separation logic with heap graphs (and their abstractions), we need a few operations for their systematic construction: Let $f\colon \mathbf{Var} \to \mathbf{Var}$ be a partial function and $f(\mathcal{M})$ its application to every variable in every component of $\mathcal{M}$.

Isomorphic heap graphs. We call a variable $x \in \mathbf{Var}$ an *auxiliary variable* of heap graph $\mathcal{M}$ if x is not a free variable of $\mathcal{M}$. Throughout this article, we do not distinguish between isomorphic heap graphs, i.e., heap graphs that are identical up to renaming of auxiliary variables. Formally, two heap graphs $\mathcal{M}_1$ and $\mathcal{M}_2$ are *isomorphic*, written $\mathcal{M}_1 \cong \mathcal{M}_2$, if there exists a bijective function $f\colon \mathsf{vars}(\mathcal{M}_1) \to \mathsf{vars}(\mathcal{M}_2)$ such that (1) $\mathsf{FV}_{\mathcal{M}_1} = \mathsf{FV}_{\mathcal{M}_2}$, (2) $f(x) = x$ for all $x \in \mathsf{FV}_{\mathcal{M}_1}$, and (3) $f(\mathcal{M}_1) = \mathcal{M}_2$.

Renaming heap graphs. Our first operation enables renaming of free variables. Formally, let $\mathcal{M}$ be a heap graph and $\mathbf{x} \in \mathsf{FV}^*_{\mathcal{M}}$, $\mathbf{y} \in \mathbf{Var}^*$ be repetition free sequences of variables of the same length. Then the *renaming* of $\mathbf{x}$ to $\mathbf{y}$ in $\mathcal{M}$ is given by $\mathsf{rename}_{\mathbf{x},\mathbf{y}}(\mathcal{M}) = f(\mathcal{M})$, where

$$f\colon \mathbf{Var} \to \mathbf{Var}, \quad z \mapsto \begin{cases} \mathbf{y}[i] & \text{if } \mathbf{x}[i] = z \\ z & \text{otherwise.} \end{cases}$$

Composition. Our next operation allows composing heap graphs by "gluing" them together at their common free variables. Formally, let $\mathcal{M}_1, \mathcal{M}_2$ be heap graphs such that (1) $\mathsf{vars}(\mathcal{M}_1) \cap \mathsf{vars}(\mathcal{M}_2) \subseteq \mathsf{FV}_{\mathcal{M}_1} \cap \mathsf{FV}_{\mathcal{M}_2}$ and (2) $\mathsf{Ptr}_{\mathcal{M}_1}$ and $\mathsf{Ptr}_{\mathcal{M}_1}$ are domain disjoint, i.e., $\mathrm{dom}(\mathsf{Ptr}_{\mathcal{M}_1}) \cap \mathrm{dom}(\mathsf{Ptr}_{\mathcal{M}_2}) = \emptyset$. Then the componentwise union $\mathcal{M}_1 \cup \mathcal{M}_2$ of $\mathcal{M}_1$ and $\mathcal{M}_2$ is $\langle \mathsf{Ptr}_{\mathcal{M}_1} \cup \mathsf{Ptr}_{\mathcal{M}_2}, \mathsf{FV}_{\mathcal{M}_1} \cup \mathsf{FV}_{\mathcal{M}_2}, \mathsf{calls}_{\mathcal{M}_1} \cup \mathsf{calls}_{\mathcal{M}_2} \rangle$. Otherwise, $\mathcal{M}_1 \cup \mathcal{M}_2$ is undefined. We then define the composition $\mathcal{M}_1 \bullet \mathcal{M}_2$ of heap graphs $\mathcal{M}_1, \mathcal{M}_2$ as

$$\mathcal{M}_1 \bullet \mathcal{M}_2 = \begin{cases} \mathcal{M}_1 \cup \mathcal{M} & \text{where } \mathcal{M} \cong \mathcal{M}_2 \text{ and } \mathcal{M}_1 \cup \mathcal{M} \text{ is defined} \\ \text{undefined} & \text{otherwise.} \end{cases}$$

Example 2. Figure 4 depicts the composition of two heap graphs representing lists of length two. Since both heap graphs share a variable $a \notin \mathsf{FV}$, we first compute an isomorphic heap graph in which variable a is substituted by c in the second graph. Both heap graphs are then merged at their common free variable b. This results in a heap graph modeling a list of length four. △

Forgetting free variables. To construct larger heap graphs from smaller ones, we often need additional free variables to glue the right nodes together, e.g., the variable b in Example 2. Consequently, we need a mechanism for subsequent removal of these variables from the set of free variables. To this end, for every heap graph $\mathcal{M}$ and sequence of free variables $\mathbf{x} \in \mathsf{FV}^*_{\mathcal{M}}$, we define the operation $\mathsf{forget}_{\mathbf{x}}(\mathcal{M}) = \langle \mathsf{Ptr}_{\mathcal{M}}, \mathsf{FV}_{\mathcal{M}} \setminus \mathbf{x}, \mathsf{calls}_{\mathcal{M}} \rangle$.

Single allocations. The simplest non-empty heap graph is a single variable, say x with pointers to a sequence $\mathbf{y}$ of finitely many other variables. We write $x \rightarrowtail \mathbf{y}$ to denote this *single-allocation heap graph* $\langle \{x \mapsto \mathbf{y}\}, \{x\} \cup \mathbf{y}, \emptyset \rangle$.

Theorem 1 ([8]). *Every non-empty heap graph of tree width at most k can be constructed from heap graphs $x \rightarrowtail \mathbf{y}$, renaming, composition, and forgetting using at most $k+1$ free variables.*

3 Symbolic Heap Separation Logic

We consider the symbolic heap fragment of separation logic with user-defined inductive predicate definitions. We omit pure formulas to simplify the presentation. Notice, however, that our implementation supports reasoning about symbolic heaps with pure formulas.

Syntax. The syntax of our simplified symbolic heap fragment is then given by the following context-free grammar:

$$\varphi ::= \mathbf{emp} \mid x \mapsto \mathbf{y} \mid \mathsf{pred}(\mathbf{y}) \mid \exists x \colon \varphi \mid \varphi * \varphi,$$

where $x \in \mathbf{Var} \setminus \{\mathbf{null}\}$ is a variable, $\mathbf{y} \in \mathbf{Var}^+$ is a sequence of variables, and $\mathsf{pred}(\mathbf{y})$ is a predicate call. Here, $\mathbf{emp}$ is the *empty heap*, $x \mapsto \mathbf{y}$ asserts that x *points-to* the locations captured by $\mathbf{y}$, $\exists x \colon \varphi$ is *existential quantification*, and $*$ is the *separating conjunction*. Because $*$ is commutative and associative and because existential quantifiers can always be moved to the front, we will always consider symbolic heaps to be of form $\exists \mathbf{y} \colon (x_1 \rightarrow \mathbf{y}_1) * \cdots * (x_m \mapsto \mathbf{y}_m) * \mathsf{pred}_1(\mathbf{z}_1) * \cdots * \mathsf{pred}_n(\mathbf{z}_n)$.

Inductive definitions. Before we assign formal semantics to symbolic heaps, we clarify how custom predicates are specified. To this end, a *system of inductive definitions* (SID) is a finite set Φ of rules of the form $\mathsf{pred} \Leftarrow \varphi$, where $\mathsf{pred} \in \mathbf{Preds}$ is a predicate symbol and φ is a symbolic heap. We assume that all symbolic heaps of rules with head pred have the same sequence of free variables $(x_1, \ldots, x_{\mathsf{ar}(\mathsf{pred})})$[2] and collect these variables in the set $\mathsf{fv}(\mathsf{pred})$. Moreover, we collect all predicates that occur in SID Φ in the set $\mathbf{Preds}(\Phi)$ and all rules of SID Φ in the set $\mathbf{Rules}(\Phi)$. Examples of SIDs are found in Figs. 1 and 5.

[2] A variable is in the set $\mathsf{fv}(\varphi)$ of free variables of φ if it is not bound by a quantifier.

Semantics. We define the semantics of symbolic heaps φ for a given SID Φ in terms of a force relation $\models_\Phi$, which determines whether a heap graph $\mathcal{M}$ satisfies φ. To this end, let $\varphi[\mathbf{x}/\mathbf{y}]$ denote the symbolic heap φ in which every free occurrence of variable $\mathbf{x}[i]$ is substituted by variable $\mathbf{y}[i]$, where $1 \leq i \leq |\mathbf{x}| = |\mathbf{y}|$. Then the relation $\models_\Phi$ is defined inductively on the syntax of symbolic heaps:

$$\begin{aligned}
\mathcal{M} \models_\Phi \mathbf{emp} &\text{ iff ex. } \mathbf{x} \in \mathbf{Var}^* \text{ s.t. } \mathcal{M} = \langle \emptyset, \mathbf{x}, \emptyset \rangle \\
\mathcal{M} \models_\Phi x \mapsto \mathbf{y} &\text{ iff ex. } \mathbf{z} \supseteq \{x\} \cup \mathbf{y} \text{ s.t. } \mathcal{M} = \langle \{x \mapsto \mathbf{y}\}, \mathbf{z}, \emptyset \rangle \\
\mathcal{M} \models_\Phi \mathsf{pred}(\mathbf{y}) &\text{ iff ex. } \mathbf{z} \supseteq \mathbf{y} \text{ s.t. } \mathcal{M} \cong \langle \emptyset, \mathbf{z}, \{\mathsf{pred}(\mathbf{y})\} \rangle \\
&\quad \text{or ex. } (\mathsf{pred} \Leftarrow \psi) \in \mathbf{Rules}(\Phi) \text{ s.t. } \mathcal{M} \models_\Phi \psi[\mathsf{fv}(\mathsf{pred})/\mathbf{y}] \\
\mathcal{M} \models_\Phi \exists x \colon \varphi &\text{ iff ex. } y \in \mathbf{Var} \text{ s.t. } \langle \mathsf{Ptr}_\mathcal{M}, \mathsf{FV}_\mathcal{M} \cup \{y\}, \mathsf{calls}_\mathcal{M} \rangle \models_\Phi \varphi[x/y] \\
\mathcal{M} \models_\Phi \varphi_1 * \varphi_2 &\text{ iff ex. } \mathcal{M}_1, \mathcal{M}_2 \text{ s.t. } \mathcal{M} \cong \mathcal{M}_1 \bullet \mathcal{M}_2 \\
&\quad \text{and } \mathcal{M}_1 \models_\Phi \varphi_1 \text{ and } \mathcal{M}_2 \models_\Phi \varphi_2
\end{aligned}$$

The above semantics coincides with the standard least fixed-point semantics of symbolic heaps (cf. [4]) for stack-heap pairs if we restrict ourselves to concrete heap graphs. Moreover, there is a strong relationship between our SL semantics and the operations on heap graphs defined in Sect. 2.

Lemma 1. *Let* $\varphi = \exists \mathbf{y} \colon (x_1 \mapsto \mathbf{y}_1) * \cdots * (x_m \mapsto \mathbf{y}_m) * \mathsf{pred}_1(\mathbf{z}_1) * \cdots * \mathsf{pred}_n(\mathbf{z}_n)$ *be a symbolic heap.* $\mathcal{M} \models_\Phi \varphi$ *iff there exist* $\mathcal{M}_1, \ldots, \mathcal{M}_{m+n}$ *such that (1)* $\mathcal{M}_i \models_\Phi x \mapsto \mathbf{y}_i$ *for* $1 \leq i \leq m$, *(2)* $\mathcal{M}_{m+j} \models_\Phi \mathsf{pred}_j(\mathsf{fv}(\mathsf{pred}_j))$ *for* $1 \leq j \leq n$, *and (3)* $\mathcal{M} = \mathsf{forget}_\mathbf{y}(\mathcal{M}_1 \bullet \cdots \bullet \mathcal{M}_m \bullet \mathsf{rename}_{\mathsf{fv}(\mathsf{pred}_1),\mathbf{z}_1}(\mathcal{M}_{m+1}) \bullet \cdots \bullet \mathsf{rename}_{\mathsf{fv}(\mathsf{pred}_n),\mathbf{z}_n}(\mathcal{M}_{m+n}))$.

Symbolic heaps with bounded tree-width. Our goal is to develop a decision procedure for symbolic heaps with inductive definitions in the bounded tree-width fragment developed by Iosif et al. [10]. This fragment imposes three conditions on SIDs, which we assume for all SIDs Φ considered in the following:

1. *Progress:* Every rule *allocates* exactly one variable x, i.e. every rule contains exactly one points-to assertion $x \mapsto \mathbf{y}$.
2. *Connectivity:* Every predicate call $\mathsf{pred}(\mathbf{z})$ of a rule has a parameter $\mathbf{z}[i]$ that is referenced by the rule's allocated variable, i.e., $\mathbf{z}[i] \in \mathbf{y}$. Moreover, the i-th free variable of predicate pred must be allocated in all rules $\mathsf{pred} \Leftarrow \varphi$ of Φ.
3. *Establishment:* All existentially quantified variables are eventually allocated.

Assumptions. We make two further assumptions for all SIDs throughout this paper: (1) *Predicates are called with pairwise different parameters.* (2) *Unfolding predicates (iteratively substituting predicate calls* $\mathsf{pred}(\mathbf{y})$ *with the right-hand sides* $\varphi[\mathsf{fv}(\mathsf{pred})/\mathbf{y}]$ *of rules* $\mathsf{pred} \Leftarrow \varphi$*) always yields satisfiable symbolic heaps.* SIDs can be transformed automatically to satisfy (1) and (2) before applying our decision procedure (cf. [1,14]). The SIDs in Figs. 1 and 5 satisfy all assumptions.

4 Profiles: An Abstraction for Concrete Heap Graphs

Entailment problem. We present our approach for entailments $\mathsf{pred}_1(\mathbf{x}) \models_\Phi \mathsf{pred}_2(\mathbf{y})$ between predicate calls $\mathsf{pred}_1(\mathbf{x})$, and $\mathsf{pred}_2(\mathbf{y})$ of an SID Φ. We discuss the treatment of more general entailments at the end of Sect. 5. Formally, the entailment $\mathsf{pred}_1(\mathbf{x}) \models_\Phi \mathsf{pred}_2(\mathbf{y})$ holds iff for all concrete heap graphs $\mathcal{M}$, we have $\mathcal{M} \models_\Phi \mathsf{pred}_1(\mathbf{x})$ implies $\mathcal{M} \models_\Phi \mathsf{pred}_2(\mathbf{y})$.

Model reconstruction. Recall from Lemma 1 that $\mathcal{M} \models_\Phi \mathsf{pred}_1(\mathbf{x})$ can be interpreted as being able to construct $\mathcal{M}$ as a model of $\mathsf{pred}_1(\mathbf{x})$ using the rules of SID Φ and our operations on heap graphs introduced in Sect. 2. To prove the entailment $\mathsf{pred}_1(\mathbf{x}) \models_\Phi \mathsf{pred}_2(\mathbf{y})$, we then have to "reconstruct" any such $\mathcal{M}$ as a model of $\mathsf{pred}_2(\mathbf{y})$. Since infinitely many model reconstructions might be required—after all there might be infinitely many $\mathcal{M}$ with $\mathcal{M} \models_\Phi \mathsf{pred}_1(\mathbf{x})$—we now develop an abstraction of heap graphs such that finitely many abstract model reconstructions suffice to cover all models of $\mathsf{pred}_1(\mathbf{x})$.

Running example. To sharpen our intuition, we present the technical details of our abstraction together with a running example: Fig. 5 shows an SID Φ_{lists} specifying predicates for various singly-linked list segments. The predicate $\mathtt{sll}(x_1, x_2)$ specifies non-empty singly-linked list segments with head x_1 and tail x_2. Similarly, the predicates $\mathsf{odd}(x_1, x_2)$ and $\mathsf{even}(x_1, x_2)$ restrict such list segments to odd and even length, respectively. In the remainder of this and the next section, we will use our abstraction to show that the entailment $\mathtt{sll}(x_1, x_2) \models_{\Phi_{\text{lists}}} \mathsf{odd}(x_1, x_2)$ does *not* hold.

$$\begin{aligned} \mathtt{sll}(x_1,x_2) &\Leftarrow x_1 \mapsto x_2 \\ \mathtt{sll}(x_1,x_2) &\Leftarrow \exists y\colon x_1 \mapsto y * \mathtt{sll}(y,x_2) \end{aligned} \qquad \begin{aligned} \mathsf{odd}(x_1,x_2) &\Leftarrow x_1 \mapsto x_2 \\ \mathsf{odd}(x_1,x_2) &\Leftarrow \exists y\colon x_1 \mapsto y * \mathsf{even}(y,x_2) \\ \mathsf{even}(x_1,x_2) &\Leftarrow \exists y\colon x_1 \mapsto y * \mathsf{odd}(y,x_2) \end{aligned}$$

Fig. 5. SIDs Φ_{sll} (left) and $\Phi_{\text{o/e}}$ (right) specifying singly-linked list segments with head x_1 and tail x_2. Moreover, we define $\Phi_{\text{lists}} = \Phi_{\text{sll}} \cup \Phi_{\text{o/e}}$.

4.1 Context Profiles as an Abstract Domain

Contexts. Our proposed abstraction is based on *contexts*. Intuitively, every context describes an extension of a concrete heap graph by predicate calls such that the resulting graph satisfies a fixed predicate call. Thus, contexts reveal what is missing in a concrete heap graph to reconstruct models of predicate calls.

Definition 2 (Context). *A triple $\mathcal{C} = \langle \mathsf{V}, \mathsf{pred}(\mathbf{x}), \mathsf{calls}\rangle$ is a* context *of a concrete heap graph $\mathcal{M}$ w.r.t. SID Φ if (1) $\mathsf{V} = \mathsf{FV}_{\mathcal{M}}$, (2) $\langle \mathsf{Ptr}_{\mathcal{M}}, \mathbf{x}, \mathsf{calls}\rangle \models_\Phi \mathsf{pred}(\mathbf{x})$, and (3) neither $\mathbf{x}$ nor calls contain auxiliary variables of $\mathcal{M}$. Moreover, we define the set of* free variables *of context $\mathcal{C}$ as $\mathsf{fv}(\mathcal{C}) := \mathsf{V}$. We call variables in $\mathbf{x}$ or calls, but not in $\mathsf{fv}(\mathcal{C})$, the* auxiliary variables *of $\mathcal{C}$.* △

Example 3. Figure 6 shows contexts for two concrete heap graphs $\mathcal{M}_{\text{odd}}$ and $\mathcal{M}_{\text{even}}$ of odd and even length (without dashes), respectively. The extension by calls from the contexts is illustrated by dashed lines. Intuitively, context $\mathcal{C}_1$ states that no extension of $\mathcal{M}_{\text{odd}}$ is needed to obtain a model of predicate $\mathsf{odd}(x_1, x_2)$. Context $\mathcal{C}_2$ states that—in order to obtain an odd list segment from x_1 to a, where a is an additional free variable—we have to add an even list segment from x_2 to a. Similarly, we obtain an even list segment from x_1 to some fresh variable a by adding an odd list segment from x_2 to a. The interpretation of contexts $\mathcal{C}_4$, $\mathcal{C}_5$, and $\mathcal{C}_6$ of $\mathcal{M}_{\text{even}}$ is analogous. △

Contexts decompositions. A context of heap graph $\mathcal{M}$ stores the free variables of $\mathcal{M}$. These variables are important, because additional free variables might allow to split a heap graph into several smaller ones. For example, the additional free variable b in Fig. 4 (read from right to left) allows to decompose a list into two lists. Since our goal is to develop a compositional abstraction, we have to take contexts of decompositions of heap graphs into account. In general, these decompositions are relevant for entailment when considering more complicated SIDs, e.g., doubly-linked binary trees or trees with linked leaves. We thus have to compute decompositions $\mathcal{M}_1 \bullet \ldots \bullet \mathcal{M}_k$, $k \geq 1$, of a concrete heap graph $\mathcal{M}$ and then consider a context for each component.

Definition 3 (Context decomposition). *A* context decomposition *of a concrete heap graph $\mathcal{M}$ w.r.t. SID Φ is a set $\mathcal{E} = \{\mathcal{C}_1, \ldots, \mathcal{C}_k\}$ such that $\mathcal{M} = \mathcal{M}_1 \bullet \ldots \bullet \mathcal{M}_k$, $k \geq 1$, is a decomposition of $\mathcal{M}$ and $\mathcal{C}_1, \ldots, \mathcal{C}_k$ are contexts of the concrete heap graphs $\mathcal{M}_1, \ldots, \mathcal{M}_k$ w.r.t. Φ, respectively. Moreover, we define the set of* free variables *of context decomposition $\mathcal{E}$ as* $\mathsf{fv}(\mathcal{E}) := \bigcup_{\mathcal{C} \in \mathcal{E}} \mathsf{fv}(\mathcal{C})$. △

$\mathcal{C}_1 = \langle \{x_1, x_2\}, \mathsf{odd}(x_1, x_2), \emptyset \rangle$

$\mathcal{C}_2 = \langle \{x_1, x_2\}, \mathsf{odd}(x_1, a), \{\mathsf{even}(x_2, a)\} \rangle$

$\mathcal{C}_3 = \langle \{x_1, x_2\}, \mathsf{even}(x_1, a), \{\mathsf{odd}(x_2, a)\} \rangle$

$\mathcal{C}_4 = \langle \{x_1, x_2\}, \mathsf{even}(x_1, x_2), \emptyset \rangle$

$\mathcal{C}_5 = \langle \{x_1, x_2\}, \mathsf{even}(x_1, a), \{\mathsf{even}(x_2, a)\} \rangle$

$\mathcal{C}_6 = \langle \{x_1, x_2\}, \mathsf{odd}(x_1, a), \{\mathsf{odd}(x_2, a)\} \rangle$

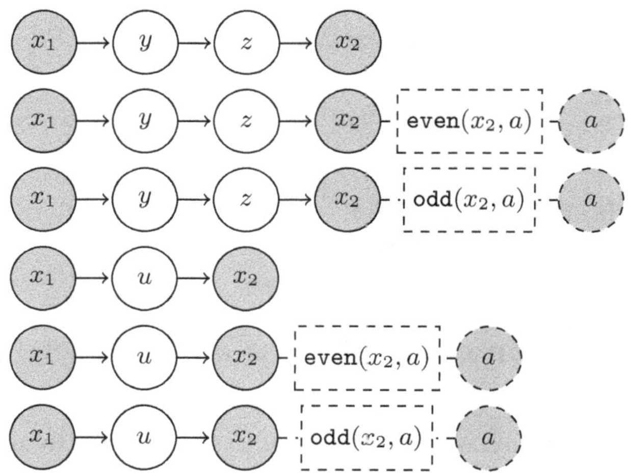

Fig. 6. Contexts of concrete heap graphs $\mathcal{M}_{\text{odd}}$ (first graph) and $\mathcal{M}_{\text{even}}$ (fourth graph). The extensions by a context are drawn in dashed lines.

Example 4. The concrete heap graph $\mathcal{M}_{\text{odd}}$ in Fig. 6 cannot be decomposed into smaller graphs due to a lack of free variables. Hence, context decompositions of $\mathcal{M}_{\text{odd}}$ are singletons consisting of $\mathcal{C}_1$, $\mathcal{C}_2$, and $\mathcal{C}_3$ in Fig. 6, respectively. △

Profiles. As the above example shows, concrete heap graphs may have multiple context decompositions. We thus abstract a concrete heap graph $\mathcal{M}$ by the set of all context decompositions of $\mathcal{M}$:

Definition 4 (Profiles). *The* profile $\mathsf{profile}_{\Phi}(\mathcal{M})$ *of a concrete heap graph* $\mathcal{M}$ *w.r.t. SID* Φ *is the set of all context decompositions of* $\mathcal{M}$ *w.r.t.* Φ*. Moreover, since all* $\mathcal{E} \in \mathcal{P}$ *have the same free variables, we define the free variables of* $\mathcal{P}$ *as* $\mathsf{fv}(\mathcal{P}) := \mathsf{fv}(\mathcal{E})$ *for some* $\mathcal{E} \in \mathcal{P}$*.* △

Refinement property. We propose profiles as a suitable abstraction for deciding entailments. We will argue that they comply with the four essential correctness properties discussed in Sect. 1: refinement, finiteness, compositionality, and effectiveness. Refinement means that two concrete heap graphs with the same profiles entail the same SID predicates. Hence, for each profile and predicate pred, it suffices to find a single model of pred with that profile. Formally,

Lemma 2. *Let* $\mathcal{M}, \mathcal{M}'$ *be concrete heap graphs with* $\mathsf{profile}_{\Phi}(\mathcal{M}) = \mathsf{profile}_{\Phi}(\mathcal{M}')$*. Then, for all* $\mathsf{pred} \in \mathbf{Preds}(\Phi)$*, we have* $\mathcal{M} \models_{\Phi} \mathsf{pred}(\mathbf{x})$ *iff* $\mathcal{M}' \models_{\Phi} \mathsf{pred}(\mathbf{x})$*.*

Finiteness. In general, the set of profiles of concrete heap graphs is infinite due to different names for additional free variables, e.g., variable a in Fig. 6. To obtain a finite set of profiles, we thus (a) limit the total number of free variables, (b) consider profiles up to renaming of additional free variables, and (c) exploit the *connectivity condition.* Notice that condition (a) is not a restriction, because the number of free variables for every SID and thus every entailment query is bounded. For condition (b), we have to lift the notion of isomorphism from heap graphs to profiles. Formally, contexts $\mathcal{C}_1 = \langle \mathbf{z}_1, \mathsf{pred}_1(\mathbf{x}_1), \mathsf{calls}_1 \rangle$ and $\mathcal{C}_2 = \langle \mathbf{z}_2, \mathsf{pred}_2(\mathbf{x}_2), \mathsf{calls}_2 \rangle$ are isomorphic iff $\mathbf{z}_1 = \mathbf{z}_2$, $\mathsf{pred}_1 = \mathsf{pred}_2$ and there exists a bijective function $f \colon \mathbf{Var} \to \mathbf{Var}$ such that (1) for all $z \in \mathbf{z}_1$, $f(z) = z$, (2) $f(\mathbf{x}_1) = \mathbf{x}_2$, and (3) $\mathsf{calls}_2 = \{\mathsf{pred}(f(\mathbf{y})) \mid \mathsf{pred}(\mathbf{y}) \in \mathsf{calls}_1\}$. Moreover, two context decompositions $\mathcal{E}_1$, $\mathcal{E}_2$ are isomorphic iff for all $i \in \{1, 2\}$ and contexts $\mathcal{C} \in \mathcal{E}_i$ there is a context $\mathcal{C}' \in \mathcal{E}_{3-i}$ that is isomorphic to $\mathcal{C}$. Analogously, two profiles $\mathcal{P}_1$, $\mathcal{P}_2$ are isomorphic iff for all $i \in \{1, 2\}$ and context decompositions $\mathcal{E} \in \mathcal{P}_i$ there exists a context decomposition $\mathcal{E}' \in \mathcal{P}_{3-i}$ that is isomorphic to $\mathcal{E}_i$.

Throughout this paper, we do not distinguish between isomorphic contexts, context decompositions, or profiles.

Lemma 3. *For every SID* Φ *and variable sequence* $\mathbf{x} \in \mathbf{Var}^*$*, the set of profiles* $\mathbf{Profiles}^{\mathbf{x}}(\Phi) = \{\mathsf{profile}_{\Phi}(\mathcal{M}) \mid \mathcal{M}$ *concrete heap graph,* $\mathsf{fv}(\mathsf{profile}_{\Phi}(\mathcal{M})) \subseteq \mathbf{x}\}$ *is finite up to profile isomorphism.*

Example 5. Recall from Fig. 5 the SID $\Phi_{\mathsf{o/e}}$. Moreover, recall from Fig. 6 the concrete heap graphs $\mathcal{M}_{\mathrm{odd}}$ and $\mathcal{M}_{\mathrm{even}}$ and their contexts $\mathcal{C}_1$, $\mathcal{C}_2$, $\mathcal{C}_3$ and $\mathcal{C}_4$, $\mathcal{C}_5$, $\mathcal{C}_6$, respectively. Then the profiles of $\mathcal{M}_{\mathrm{odd}}$ and $\mathcal{M}_{\mathrm{even}}$ w.r.t. $\Phi_{\mathsf{o/e}}$ are (up to isomorphism) $\mathsf{profile}_{\Phi_{\mathsf{o/e}}}(\mathcal{M}_{\mathrm{odd}}) = \{\{\mathcal{C}_1\}, \{\mathcal{C}_2\}, \{\mathcal{C}_2\}\}$ and $\mathsf{profile}_{\Phi_{\mathsf{o/e}}}(\mathcal{M}_{\mathrm{even}}) = \{\{\mathcal{C}_4\}, \{\mathcal{C}_5\}, \{\mathcal{C}_6\}\}$. In fact, the profile of every singly-linked list segment from x_1

to x_2 of odd (even) length is isomorphic to $\mathsf{profile}_{\Phi_{o/e}}(\mathcal{M}_{\text{odd}})$ ($\mathsf{profile}_{\Phi_{o/e}}(\mathcal{M}_{\text{even}})$). Hence, the profile of every model of the singly-linked list predicate $\texttt{sll}(x_1, x_2)$ is either $\mathsf{profile}_{\Phi_{o/e}}(\mathcal{M}_{\text{odd}})$ or $\mathsf{profile}_{\Phi_{o/e}}(\mathcal{M}_{\text{even}})$. △

4.2 Computation of Profiles

Due to Lemmas 2 and 3, we can decide an entailment $\mathsf{pred}_1(\mathbf{x}) \models_\Phi \mathsf{pred}_2(\mathbf{x})$, once the profiles of all models of $\mathsf{pred}_1(\mathbf{x})$ with respect to the rules relevant for $\mathsf{pred}_2(\mathbf{x})$ are known. The key insight underlying our entailment checker is that profiles can be computed automatically in a compositional manner. To this end, recall from Theorem 1 that every concrete heap graph can be constructed from single-allocation heap graphs $x \rightarrowtail \mathbf{y}$ by means of renaming, forgetting, and composition. We exploit this by (1) devising an algorithm to compute $\mathsf{profile}_\Phi(x \rightarrowtail \mathbf{y})$ and (2) lifting the operations $\mathsf{rename}_{\mathbf{x},\mathbf{y}}$, $\mathsf{forget}_{\mathbf{x}}$, and $\bullet$ for renaming, forgetting, and composition of heap graphs to operations $\overline{\mathsf{rename}}_{\mathbf{x},\mathbf{y}}$, $\overline{\mathsf{forget}}_{\mathbf{x}}$, and $\overline{\bullet}$ on profiles.

Profiles of single allocations. Since single allocations $x \rightarrowtail \mathbf{y}$ cannot be further decomposed, every context decomposition of $x \rightarrowtail \mathbf{y}$ w.r.t. an SID Φ is a singleton. Due to the progress condition, every rule of Φ contains exactly one points-to assertion. For each SID rule $\mathsf{pred} \Leftarrow \exists \mathbf{z}\colon x' \mapsto \mathbf{y}' * \mathsf{pred}_1(\mathbf{y}_1) * \cdots * \mathsf{pred}_k(\mathbf{y}_k)$, the corresponding context $\langle \{x'\} \cup \mathbf{y}', \mathsf{pred}(\mathbf{x}), \{\mathsf{pred}_1(\mathbf{y}_1), \ldots, \mathsf{pred}_k(\mathbf{y}_k)\}\rangle$ must be in the profile of $x \rightarrowtail \mathbf{y}$ iff $x \rightarrowtail \mathbf{y}$ is a model of $\exists \mathbf{z}\colon x' \mapsto \mathbf{y}'$. Hence:

Lemma 4. *Profiles of single allocations, i.e.,* $\mathsf{profile}_\Phi(x \rightarrowtail \mathbf{y})$*, are computable.*

Rename for profiles. We lift the operation $\mathsf{rename}_{\mathbf{x},\mathbf{y}}$, which renames each variable in $\mathbf{x}$ to the corresponding variable in $\mathbf{y}$ according to their position, from heap graphs to contexts, context decompositions, and profiles by componentwise application. That is, for a context $\mathcal{C} = \langle \mathbf{z}, \mathsf{pred}(\mathbf{u}), \mathsf{calls}\rangle$, a context decomposition $\mathcal{E}$, and a profile $\mathcal{P}$, we define:

$$\begin{aligned}
\mathsf{rename}_{\mathbf{x},\mathbf{y}}(\mathcal{C}) &:= \langle \mathsf{rename}_{\mathbf{x},\mathbf{y}}(\mathbf{z}), \mathsf{pred}(\mathsf{rename}_{\mathbf{x},\mathbf{y}}(\mathbf{u})), \\
&\qquad \{\mathsf{pred}'(\mathsf{rename}_{\mathbf{x},\mathbf{y}}(\mathbf{v}) \mid \mathsf{pred}'(\mathbf{v}) \in \mathsf{calls}\}\rangle \\
\mathsf{rename}_{\mathbf{x},\mathbf{y}}(\mathcal{E}) &:= \{\mathsf{rename}_{\mathbf{x},\mathbf{y}}(\mathcal{C}) \mid \mathcal{C} \in \mathcal{E}\} \\
\overline{\mathsf{rename}}_{\mathbf{x},\mathbf{y}}(\mathcal{P}) &:= \{\mathsf{rename}_{\mathbf{x},\mathbf{y}}(\mathcal{E}) \mid \mathcal{E} \in \mathcal{P}\}
\end{aligned}$$

Forget for profiles. Next, we lift the operation $\mathsf{forget}_{\mathbf{x}}$, which removes variables in $\mathbf{x}$ from the set of free variables, to contexts, context decompositions, and profiles. For a profile, forgetting a free variable means that some of its constituting context decompositions do not have to be considered anymore, because the composition of their underlying models is no longer defined. Hence, these decompositions are removed. Formally, for a context $\mathcal{C} = \langle \mathbf{z}, \mathsf{pred}(\mathbf{u}), \mathsf{calls}\rangle$, a context decomposition $\mathcal{E}$, and a profile $\mathcal{P}$, we define:

$$\mathsf{forget}_{\mathbf{x}}(\mathcal{C}) := \langle \mathbf{z} \setminus \mathbf{x}, \mathsf{pred}(\mathbf{u}), \mathsf{calls}\rangle \qquad \mathsf{forget}_{\mathbf{x}}(\mathcal{E}) := \{\mathsf{forget}_{\mathbf{x}}(\mathcal{C}) \mid \mathcal{C} \in \mathcal{E}\}$$
$$\overline{\mathsf{forget}}_{\mathbf{x}}(\mathcal{P}) := \{\mathsf{forget}_{\mathbf{x}}(\mathcal{E}) \mid \mathcal{E} \in \mathcal{P} \text{ and } \mathbf{x} \cap \mathsf{usedvs}(\mathcal{E}) = \emptyset\}$$
$$\mathsf{usedvs}(\mathcal{E}) := \bigcup_{\mathcal{C} \in \mathcal{E}} \mathsf{usedvs}(\mathcal{C}) \qquad \mathsf{usedvs}(\mathcal{C}) := \mathbf{u} \cup \bigcup_{\mathsf{prec}'(\mathbf{y}) \in \mathsf{calls}} \mathbf{y}$$

Composition for profiles. It remains to lift heap graph composition to profiles. This is formalized as substituting predicate calls of contexts by other contexts:

Definition 5 (Context substitution). *Let* $\mathcal{C}_1 = \langle \mathbf{x}_1, \mathsf{pred}_1(\mathbf{z}_1), \mathsf{calls}_1\rangle$ *and* $\mathcal{C}_2 = \langle \mathbf{x}_2, \mathsf{pred}_2(\mathbf{z}_2), \mathsf{calls}_2\rangle$ *be contexts such that (1)* $\mathsf{pred}_1(\mathbf{z}_1) \in \mathsf{calls}_2$ *and (2) no auxiliary variable of* $\mathcal{C}_2$ *is a free variable of* $\mathcal{C}_1$ *and vice versa. Then the* substitution *of* $\mathsf{pred}_1(\mathbf{z})$ *in* $\mathcal{C}_2$ *by* $\mathcal{C}_1$ *is given by*

$$\mathcal{C}_2\,[\mathcal{C}_1] := \langle\, \mathbf{x_1} \cup \mathbf{x_2},\ \mathsf{pred}_2(\mathbf{z_2}),\ (\mathsf{calls}_2 \setminus \{\mathsf{pred}_1(\mathbf{z}_1)\}) \cup \mathsf{calls}_1\rangle. \qquad \triangle$$

To compose profiles, we attempt to substitute the underlying contexts with each other in all possible ways. Formally, a context decomposition $\mathcal{E}_1$ *derives* a context decomposition $\mathcal{E}_2$, written $\mathcal{E}_1 \rhd \mathcal{E}_2$, iff there exist contexts $\mathcal{C}_1, \mathcal{C}_2 \in \mathcal{E}_1$ such that $\mathcal{E}_2 = (\mathcal{E}_1 \setminus \{\mathcal{C}_1, \mathcal{C}_2\}) \cup \{\mathcal{C}_2\,[\mathcal{C}_1]\}$.[3] We denote by $\rhd^*$ the reflexive-transitive closure of the derivation relation $\rhd$. The composition of two profiles then consists of all context decompositions derivable from some decompositions of both profiles:

Definition 6 (Composition of profiles). *Let* $\mathcal{P}_1$ *and* $\mathcal{P}_2$ *be profiles w.r.t.* Φ. *Then the* composition $\mathcal{P}_1 \mathbin{\bar{\bullet}} \mathcal{P}_2$ *of* $\mathcal{P}_1$ *and* $\mathcal{P}_2$ *is defined as*

$$\mathcal{P}_1 \mathbin{\bar{\bullet}} \mathcal{P}_2 := \{\mathcal{E} \mid \exists \mathcal{E}_1 \in \mathcal{P}_1, \mathcal{E}_2 \in \mathcal{P}_2 \colon \mathcal{E}_1 \cup \mathcal{E}_2 \rhd^* \mathcal{E}\}. \qquad \triangle$$

Compositionality. Our lifted heap graph operations satisfy the compositionality property mentioned in Sect. 1. That is,

Theorem 2. *For all concrete heap graphs* $\mathcal{M}$, $\mathcal{M}'$ *and every SID* Φ, *we have*

$$\begin{aligned}
\overline{\mathsf{rename}}_{\mathbf{x},\mathbf{y}}(\mathsf{profile}_{\Phi}(\mathcal{M})) &= \mathsf{profile}_{\Phi}(\mathsf{rename}_{\mathbf{x},\mathbf{y}}(\mathcal{M}))\\
\overline{\mathsf{forget}}_{\mathbf{x}}(\mathsf{profile}_{\Phi}(\mathcal{M})) &= \mathsf{profile}_{\Phi}(\mathsf{forget}_{\mathbf{x}}(\mathcal{M}))\\
\mathsf{profile}_{\Phi}(\mathcal{M}) \mathbin{\bar{\bullet}} \mathsf{profile}_{\Phi}(\mathcal{M}') &= \mathsf{profile}_{\Phi}(\mathcal{M} \bullet \mathcal{M}')
\end{aligned}$$

provided that $\mathsf{rename}_{\mathbf{x},\mathbf{y}}(\mathcal{M})$, $\mathsf{forget}_{\mathbf{x}}(\mathcal{M})$, *and* $\mathcal{M} \bullet \mathcal{M}'$ *are defined, respectively.*

Example 6. Recall from Fig. 6 the heap graphs $\mathcal{M}_{\text{odd}}$ and $\mathcal{M}_{\text{even}}$ whose profiles w.r.t. $\Phi_{\text{o/e}}$ capture all singly-linked lists. We can construct a concrete heap graph $\mathcal{M}$ representing a list of length five from x_1 to x_2 by computing

$$\mathcal{M} := \mathsf{rename}_{v,x_2}\left(\mathsf{forget}_{x_2}\left(\mathcal{M}_{\text{odd}} \bullet \mathsf{rename}_{(x_1,x_2),(x_2,v)}(\mathcal{M}_{\text{even}})\right)\right).$$

[3] Recall that all definitions are to be read up to isomorphism, i.e., auxiliary variables of $\mathcal{C}_1$, $\mathcal{C}_2$, and $\mathcal{E}_2$ may be renamed prior to the substitution.

Then, by Theorem 2, the corresponding profile $\mathsf{profile}_{\Phi_{\mathsf{o/e}}}(M)$ is given by:

$$\overline{\mathsf{rename}}_{v,x_2}\Big(\overline{\mathsf{forget}}_{x_2}\Big(\mathsf{profile}_{\Phi_{\mathsf{o/e}}}(\mathcal{M}_{\mathrm{odd}})\mathbin{\overline{\bullet}}\overline{\mathsf{rename}}_{(x_1,x_2),(x_2,v)}(\mathsf{profile}_{\Phi_{\mathsf{o/e}}}(\mathcal{M}_{\mathrm{even}})\Big)\Big)$$

This profile, in turn, coincides with the profile of $\mathcal{M}_{\mathrm{odd}}$, i.e., we have

$$\mathsf{profile}_{\Phi_{\mathsf{o/e}}}(\mathcal{M}) \;=\; \mathsf{profile}_{\Phi_{\mathsf{o/e}}}(\mathcal{M}_{\mathrm{odd}}).$$

In particular, notice that without the forget statement, we would obtain a heap graph $\mathcal{M}'$ with an additional free variable. The additional free variable would also influence the profile of $\mathcal{M}'$, because there exist more decompositions of $\mathcal{M}'$ into heap graphs $\mathcal{M}_1 \bullet \mathcal{M}_2$. Consequently, there are also more context decompositions of $\mathcal{M}'$ and thus $\mathcal{M}'$ has a larger profile. △

5 An Effective Decision Procedure for Entailment

Profile analysis. We now exploit our abstract domain to develop a decision procedure for entailments of the form $\mathsf{pred}_1(\mathbf{a}) \models_{\Phi} \mathsf{pred}_2(\mathbf{b})$. Let us first consider the case in which the parameters $\mathbf{a}$ and $\mathbf{b}$ coincide with the free variables in the rules of the SID, i.e., $\mathbf{a} = \mathsf{fv}(\mathsf{pred}_1) =: \mathbf{x_1}$ and $\mathbf{b} = \mathsf{fv}(\mathsf{pred}_2) =: \mathbf{x_2}$. Our key observation is then that analyzing profiles of the entailment's left-hand side suffices to discharge it: The entailment $\mathsf{pred}_1(\mathbf{x_1}) \models_{\Phi} \mathsf{pred}_2(\mathbf{x_2})$ holds iff the profile of every model $\mathcal{M}$ of $\mathsf{pred}_1(\mathbf{x_1})$ contains a context decomposition stating that a model of $\mathsf{pred}_2(\mathbf{x_2})$ can be reconstructed from $\mathcal{M}$. Formally,

Theorem 3. *The entailment* $\mathsf{pred}_1(\mathbf{x_1}) \models_{\Phi} \mathsf{pred}_2(\mathbf{x_2})$ *holds iff for all concrete heap graphs* $\mathcal{M}$ *with* $\mathcal{M} \models \mathsf{pred}_1(\mathbf{x_1})$, $\{\langle \mathsf{FV}_{\mathcal{M}}, \mathsf{pred}_2(\mathbf{x_2}), \emptyset\rangle\} \in \mathsf{profile}_{\Phi}(\mathcal{M})$.

Example 7. Recall the profiles $\mathsf{profile}_{\Phi_{\mathsf{o/e}}}(\mathcal{M}_{\mathrm{even}})$ and $\mathsf{profile}_{\Phi_{\mathsf{o/e}}}(\mathcal{M}_{\mathrm{odd}})$ from Example 5 computed for models of $\mathtt{sll}(x_1, x_2)$ w.r.t. SID $\Phi_{\mathsf{o/e}}$ (Fig. 5). We now use these profiles to disprove the entailment $\mathtt{sll}(x_1, x_2) \models_{\Phi_{\mathrm{lists}}} \mathsf{odd}(x_1, x_2)$: First, observe that all predicates relevant for constructing models of $\mathsf{odd}(x_1, x_2)$ belong to $\Phi_{\mathsf{o/e}} \subseteq \Phi_{\mathrm{lists}}$. Second, the $\mathsf{profile}_{\Phi_{\mathsf{o/e}}}(\mathcal{M}_{\mathrm{even}})$ does not contain a context decomposition $\{\langle\{x_1, x_2\}, \mathsf{odd}(x_1, x_2), \emptyset\rangle\}$. Hence, by Theorem 3, the entailment does not hold as we cannot reconstruct $\mathcal{M}_{\mathrm{even}}$ as a model of predicate $\mathsf{odd}(x_1, x_2)$. △

Computing profiles. By Theorem 3, to decide whether $\mathsf{pred}_1(\mathbf{x_1}) \models_{\Phi} \mathsf{pred}_2(\mathbf{x_2})$ holds, it suffices to compute the finite (by Lemma 3) set of all profiles of models of $\mathsf{pred}_1(\mathbf{x_1})$. This is performed by the procedure $\mathsf{abstractSID}(\Phi)$ shown in Algorithm 1. To understand how the algorithm works, recall how predicates can be unrolled to compute a model: We select an SID rule and replace all of its predicate calls with previously computed models. By Lemma 1, this amounts to performing heap graph operations. That is, we first rename the free variables of previously computed models to match the parameters of predicate calls. After

Algorithm 1: The algorithm $\mathsf{abstractSID}(\Phi)$ computes a function f that maps each predicate $\mathsf{pred} \in \mathbf{Preds}(\Phi)$ to the set of profiles $\{\mathsf{profile}_\Phi(\mathcal{M}) \mid \mathcal{M} \models_\Phi \mathsf{pred}(\mathsf{fv}(\mathsf{pred}))\}$.

1 $f_{curr} := \lambda \mathsf{pred}\ .\ \emptyset$;
2 **repeat**
3   $f_{prev} := f_{curr}$;
4   **for** $\mathsf{pred} \in \mathbf{Preds}(\Phi)$ **do**
5   **for** $(\mathsf{pred} \Leftarrow \exists \mathbf{y} \colon x \mapsto \mathbf{z_0} * \mathsf{pred}_1(\mathbf{z_1}) * \cdots * \mathsf{pred}_k(\mathbf{z_k})) \in \mathbf{Rules}(\Phi)$ **do**
6       $\mathcal{P}_0 := \mathsf{profile}_\Phi(x \rightarrowtail \mathbf{z_0})$;
7   **for** $\mathcal{F}_1 \in f_{prev}(\mathsf{pred}_1), \ldots, \mathcal{F}_k \in f_{prev}(\mathsf{pred}_k)$ **do**
8   **for** $i \in \{1, \ldots, k\}$ **do**
9           $\mathcal{P}_i := \overline{\mathsf{rename}}_{\mathsf{fv}(\mathsf{pred}_i), \mathbf{z_i}}(\mathcal{F}_i)$;
10         $\mathcal{P} := \overline{\mathsf{forget}}_{\mathbf{y}}(\mathcal{P}_0 \mathbin{\bar{\bullet}} \mathcal{P}_1 \mathbin{\bar{\bullet}} \cdots \mathbin{\bar{\bullet}} \mathcal{P}_k)$;
11         $f_{curr}(\mathsf{pred}) := f_{curr}(\mathsf{pred}) \cup \{\mathcal{P}\}$;
12 **until** $f_{curr} = f_{prev}$;
13 **return** f_{curr}

that, the resulting models and the single allocation (due to the progress condition) of the rule are composed into a single heap graph. Finally, we apply a forget operation to remove free variables that have been existentially quantified.

Algorithm 1 behaves analogously. However, instead of applying operations on heap graphs, it applies our *abstract* operations on profiles (cf. Theorem 2): We select an SID rule $\mathsf{pred} \Leftarrow \varphi$ in line 5. By Lemma 4, we can compute the profile of the single allocation in φ. (l. 6). We then select previously computed profiles for the predicate rules and rename their free variables to match the parameters of the predicate calls in φ (l. 7–9). Finally, the selected profiles are composed and added to the computed profiles of predicate pred (l. 10, 11). The algorithm then proceeds by computing profiles until a fixed point is reached (l. 12).

Correctness. Algorithm 1 is guaranteed to terminate due to the finiteness of our abstract domain (Lemma 3). Moreover, it computes the desired set of profiles:

Theorem 4. $\mathsf{abstractSID}(\Phi)(\mathsf{pred}) = \{\mathsf{profile}_\Phi(\mathcal{M}) \mid \mathcal{M} \models_\Phi \mathsf{pred}(\mathsf{fv}(\mathsf{pred}))$ *and* $\mathsf{FV}_\mathcal{M} \subseteq \mathsf{fv}(\mathsf{pred})\}$.

To check entailments $\mathsf{pred}_1(\mathbf{a}) \models_\Phi \mathsf{pred}_2(\mathbf{b})$, where $\mathbf{a}$ and $\mathbf{b}$ do not coincide with the free variables of pred_1 and pred_2 in the rules of Φ, it suffices to apply an additional rename operation. Hence, by combining Theorems 3 and 4, we obtain a constructive decidability proof for entailments between predicate calls. Moreover, a close inspection of the size of the set of profiles and the runtime of Algorithm 1 reveals that our decision procedure runs in time doubly exponential in the size of a given SID. A detailed analysis is found in [1, Sect. 7.4].

Corollary 1. *It is decidable in doubly exponential time whether the entailment* $\mathsf{pred}_1(\mathbf{a}) \models_{\Phi} \mathsf{pred}_2(\mathbf{b})$ *holds.*

Generalizations. Several of our assumptions about SIDs and entailments have been made purely to simplify the presentation. In fact, Corollary 1 can be generalized to (1) decide entailments $\varphi \models_{\Phi} \psi$ for symbolic heaps φ, ψ (instead of predicate calls) and (2) SIDs with pure formulas. Both extensions are supported by our implementation. Further details are found in [1].

6 Experiments

We implemented our decision procedure for entailment in the separation logic prover HARRSH [1,15], which is written in Scala. HARRSH supports the full $\mathrm{SL}_{\mathrm{btw}}$ fragment, including pure formulas, parameter repetitions, and entailments between symbolic heaps (as opposed to single predicate calls). Table 1 summarizes the results of our evaluation for a selection of entailments and SIDs. Our full collection of 101 benchmarks and all experimental results are available online [1].

Methodology. We compared HARRSH against SONGBIRD [19], the winner of the SID entailment category of this year's separation logic competition, SL-COMP'18; and against SLIDE [11], the tool that is most closely related to our approach but that is complete only for a subclass of $\mathrm{SL}_{\mathrm{btw}}$. Experiments were conducted using the popular benchmarking harness JMH on an Intel® Core™ i7-7500U CPU running at 2.70 GHz with a memory limit of 4 GB. We report the average run times obtained by running JMH on each benchmark for 100 s.

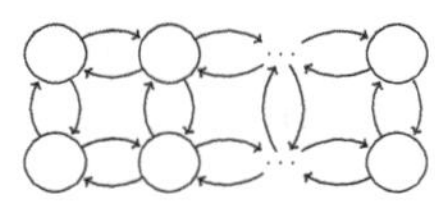

Fig. 7. dlgrid

Benchmarks. Besides the running example (with `sll`, `even` and `odd` as in Fig. 5) and the entailments for doubly-linked trees discussed in the introduction (with `ltree`, `rtree` as defined in Fig. 1), we show results on standard data-structure specifications from the SL literature: Several variants of trees with linked leaves (`tll` [10], `atll`, $\mathtt{tll}^{lin}$) and doubly-linked lists (`dllht` [18] defining lists from head to tail, `dllth` from tail to head). Beyond lists and trees, we checked an entailment between *doubly-linked 2-grid segments* (see Fig. 7) defined forwards `dlgridr` and backwards `dlgridl`.[4]

Size of the abstraction. Beside the run times, we report the size of the abstraction computed by HARRSH. More specifically, we report (1) the total number of profiles in the fixed point of $\mathsf{abstractSID}$ (#P), (2) the total number of context decompositions across all profiles (#D), and (3) the total number of contexts across all decompositions of all profiles (#C). This shows that even though the abstract domain $\mathbf{Profiles}^{\mathsf{x}}(\Phi)$ is very large in general, HARRSH typically only needs to explore a small portion of it to decide an entailment.

[4] Formal definitions of all SIDs are found in the supplementary material [1].

Table 1. The performance of Harrsh (HRS), Songbird (SB) and Slide (SLD) on a variety of SIDs; and the size of the abstraction computed by Harrsh. The timeout (TO) was 180,000 ms. Termination before the timeout but without result is denoted (U). Wrong results/crashes are marked (X).

Benchmark		Time (ms)			Profiles		
Query	Status	HRS	SB	SLD	#P	#D	#C
$\mathtt{sll}(x_1, x_2) \models \mathtt{odd}(x_1, x_2)$	false	4	11	43	2	6	6
$\mathtt{even}(x_1, x_2) \models \mathtt{sll}(x_1, x_2)$	true	2	26	43	2	4	4
$\mathtt{rtree}(x_1, x_2, x_3) \models \mathtt{ltree}(x_1, x_2, x_3)$	false	16	(U)	53	3	14	21
Entailment (♣) (Sect. 1), left to right	true	393	TO	53	7	70	116
Entailment (♣) (Sect. 1), right to left	true	532	1274	54	9	57	87
$\mathtt{atll}(x_1, x_2, x_3) \models \mathtt{tll}(x_1, x_2, x_3)$	true	9	8519	TO	2	2	2
$\mathtt{tll}(x_1, x_2, x_3) \models \mathtt{atll}(x_1, x_2, x_3)$	false	2	119	TO	2	1	1
$\mathtt{tll}^{lin}(x_1, x_2, x_3) \models \mathtt{tll}(x_1, x_2, x_3)$	true	2	34	(X)	3	3	4
$\mathtt{dllht}(x_1, x_2, x_3, x_4) \models \mathtt{dllth}(x_3, x_4, x_1, x_2)$	true	16	37	50	3	27	45
$\mathtt{dllth}(x_1, x_2, x_3, x_4) \models \mathtt{dllht}(x_3, x_4, x_1, x_2)$	true	16	37	50	3	27	45
$\mathtt{dlgridr}(x_1, \dots, x_8) \models \mathtt{dlgridl}(x_1, \dots, x_8)$	true	172	TO	(X)	5	87	208

Results. Table 1 reveals that our decision procedure—being the first implemented decision procedure that is complete for the entire SL fragment SL_{btw}—is not only of theoretical interest, but can also solve challenging entailment problems efficiently in practice. While Slide was faster on some benchmarks that fall into the fragment defined in [11], as well as on some SIDs outside of that fragment, Harrsh was able to solve several benchmarks on which Slide failed. Two benchmarks led to errors: One wrong result and one program crash (the first and the second entries marked by (X) in Table 1, respectively). We are unsure whether the timeouts encountered on the TLL benchmarks are caused by a bug in Slide, as Slide is quite efficient on other TLL variants (see [11, Table 1]). Furthermore, note that Harrsh significantly outperformed Songbird, providing further evidence of the effectiveness of our profile-based abstraction.

7 Conclusion

We presented an alternative proof for decidability of entailment in separation logic with bounded tree width [10]. In contrast to the original proof, we give a direct model theoretic construction. We implemented the resulting decision procedure in the tool Harrsh and obtained promising experimental results. For future work, we plan to extend our approach to the bi-abduction problem.

References

1. Supplementary material. The webpage below provides access to proofs, our tool, its source code, and our benchmarks. https://github.com/katelaan/harrsh
2. Antonopoulos, T., Gorogiannis, N., Haase, C., Kanovich, M.I., Ouaknine, J.: Foundations for decision problems in separation logic with general inductive predicates. In: Muscholl, A. (ed.) FoSSaCS 2014. LNCS, vol. 8412, pp. 411–425. Springer, Heidelberg (2014). https://doi.org/10.1007/978-3-642-54830-7_27
3. Berdine, J., Calcagno, C., O'Hearn, P.W.: A decidable fragment of separation logic. In: Lodaya, K., Mahajan, M. (eds.) FSTTCS 2004. LNCS, vol. 3328, pp. 97–109. Springer, Heidelberg (2004). https://doi.org/10.1007/978-3-540-30538-5_9
4. Brotherston, J.: Formalised inductive reasoning in the logic of bunched implications. In: Nielson, H.R., Filé, G. (eds.) SAS 2007. LNCS, vol. 4634, pp. 87–103. Springer, Heidelberg (2007). https://doi.org/10.1007/978-3-540-74061-2_6
5. Brotherston, J., Distefano, D., Petersen, R.L.: Automated cyclic entailment proofs in separation logic. In: Bjørner, N., Sofronie-Stokkermans, V. (eds.) CADE 2011. LNCS (LNAI), vol. 6803, pp. 131–146. Springer, Heidelberg (2011). https://doi.org/10.1007/978-3-642-22438-6_12
6. Calcagno, C., Distefano, D.: Infer: an automatic program verifier for memory safety of C programs. In: Bobaru, M., Havelund, K., Holzmann, G.J., Joshi, R. (eds.) NFM 2011. LNCS, vol. 6617, pp. 459–465. Springer, Heidelberg (2011). https://doi.org/10.1007/978-3-642-20398-5_33
7. Chin, W., David, C., Nguyen, H.H., Qin, S.: Automated verification of shape, size and bag properties via user-defined predicates in separation logic. Sci. Comput. Program. **77**(9), 1006–1036 (2012)
8. Courcelle, B., Engelfriet, J.: Graph Structure and Monadic Second-Order Logic - A Language-Theoretic Approach, Encyclopedia of Mathematics and Its Applications, vol. 138. Cambridge University Press, Cambridge (2012)
9. Enea, C., Lengál, O., Sighireanu, M., Vojnar, T.: SPEN: a solver for separation logic. In: Barrett, C., Davies, M., Kahsai, T. (eds.) NFM 2017. LNCS, vol. 10227, pp. 302–309. Springer, Cham (2017). https://doi.org/10.1007/978-3-319-57288-8_22
10. Iosif, R., Rogalewicz, A., Simácek, J.: The tree width of separation logic with recursive definitions. In: Bonacina, M.P. (ed.) CADE 2013. LNCS (LNAI), vol. 7898, pp. 21–38. Springer, Heidelberg (2013). https://doi.org/10.1007/978-3-642-38574-2_2
11. Iosif, R., Rogalewicz, A., Vojnar, T.: Deciding entailments in inductive separation logic with tree automata. In: Cassez, F., Raskin, J.-F. (eds.) ATVA 2014. LNCS, vol. 8837, pp. 201–218. Springer, Cham (2014). https://doi.org/10.1007/978-3-319-11936-6_15
12. Ishtiaq, S.S., O'Hearn, P.W.: BI as an assertion language for mutable data structures. In: Conference Record of POPL 2001: The 28th ACM SIGPLAN-SIGACT Symposium on Principles of Programming Languages, London, UK, 17–19 January 2001, pp. 14–26 (2001)
13. Jacobs, B., Smans, J., Philippaerts, P., Vogels, F., Penninckx, W., Piessens, F.: VeriFast: a powerful, sound, predictable, fast verifier for C and Java. In: Bobaru, M., Havelund, K., Holzmann, G.J., Joshi, R. (eds.) NFM 2011. LNCS, vol. 6617, pp. 41–55. Springer, Heidelberg (2011). https://doi.org/10.1007/978-3-642-20398-5_4

14. Jansen, C., Katelaan, J., Matheja, C., Noll, T., Zuleger, F.: Unified reasoning about robustness properties of symbolic-heap separation logic. In: Yang, H. (ed.) ESOP 2017. LNCS, vol. 10201, pp. 611–638. Springer, Heidelberg (2017). https://doi.org/10.1007/978-3-662-54434-1_23
15. Katelaan, J., Matheja, C., Noll, T., Zuleger, F.: Harrsh: a tool for unified reasoning about symbolic-heap separation logic. In: Proceedings of the 13th International Workshop on the Implementation of Logics (IWIL) (2018)
16. Pek, E., Qiu, X., Madhusudan, P.: Natural proofs for data structure manipulation in C using separation logic. In: ACM SIGPLAN Conference on Programming Language Design and Implementation, PLDI 2014, Edinburgh, United Kingdom, 09–11 June 2014, pp. 440–451 (2014)
17. Piskac, R., Wies, T., Zufferey, D.: GRASShopper - complete heap verification with mixed specifications. In: Ábrahám, E., Havelund, K. (eds.) TACAS 2014. LNCS, vol. 8413, pp. 124–139. Springer, Heidelberg (2014). https://doi.org/10.1007/978-3-642-54862-8_9
18. Reynolds, J.C.: Separation logic: a logic for shared mutable data structures. In: Proceedings 17th IEEE Symposium on Logic in Computer Science (LICS 2002), Copenhagen, Denmark, 22–25 July 2002, pp. 55–74 (2002)
19. Ta, Q., Le, T.C., Khoo, S., Chin, W.: Automated mutual explicit induction proof in separation logic. In: Fitzgerald, J., Heitmeyer, C., Gnesi, S., Philippou, A. (eds.) FM 2016. LNCS, vol. 9995, pp. 659–676. Springer, Cham (2016). https://doi.org/10.1007/978-3-319-48989-6_40
20. Ta, Q., Le, T.C., Khoo, S., Chin, W.: Automated lemma synthesis in symbolic-heap separation logic. PACMPL **2**(POPL), 9:1–9:29 (2018)

Safety and Fault-Tolerant Systems

Digital Bifurcation Analysis of TCP Dynamics

Nikola Beneš, Luboš Brim, Samuel Pastva(✉), and David Šafránek

Faculty of Informatics, Masaryk University, Brno, Czech Republic
{xbenes3,brim,xpastva,safranek}@fi.muni.cz

Abstract. Digital bifurcation analysis is a new algorithmic method for exploring how the behaviour of a parameter-dependent computer system varies with a change in its parameters and, in particular, for identification of bifurcation points where such variation becomes dramatic. We have developed the method in an analogy with the traditional bifurcation theory and have it successfully applied to models taken from systems biology. In this case study paper, we demonstrate the appropriateness and usefulness of the digital bifurcation analysis as a push-button alternative to the classical approaches as traditionally used for analysing the stability of TCP/IP protocols. We consider two typical examples (congestion control and buffer sizes throughput influence) and show that the method provides the same results as obtained with classical non-automatic analytical and numerical methods.

1 Introduction

The objective of the bifurcation theory is to study qualitative changes to the properties of a parameter-dependent system as parameters are varied. The method is typically applied to continuous-time or discrete-time dynamical systems. Even a tiny change in parameters may cause a dynamical system to exhibit entirely different qualitative features. Such dramatic changes in the topology of the phase space of a dynamical system are known as *bifurcations*, and the values of the parameters for which a bifurcation occurs are called *bifurcation points*. For a complete global understanding of a complex dynamical system, it is essential to know the bifurcation points, as well as the parameter ranges in which there is no fundamental change. A simple example of a real-life bifurcation is the phase transition of water to ice at the temperature of 0 °C. At this critical temperature, a tiny change in the temperature results in a "sudden" systematic change in the substance. The two materials are governed by a different set of parameters and qualitative properties. For example, we can talk about cracking ice but not water.

Non-linear dynamical systems appearing in physics, biology or economy are not the only source of bifurcation phenomena. Even computer systems can

This work has been partially supported by the Czech Science Foundation grant No. 18-00178S.

T. Vojnar and L. Zhang (Eds.): TACAS 2019, Part II, LNCS 11428, pp. 339–356, 2019.
https://doi.org/10.1007/978-3-030-17465-1_19

suddenly alter the quality of their behaviour. A simple example might be a significant performance degradation of a computation caused by system swapping. Studying bifurcations in computer systems can provide an additional formal analysis ingredient leading to a better understanding of critical systems properties, like stability or robustness.

Inspired by the bifurcation theory for dynamical systems, we have developed an approach that allows analysing how the dynamics (runs, state transitions) of a discrete computer system changes when its parameters are changed [6,11]. We call the method *digital bifurcation analysis*. In the approach, the qualitative changes in the behaviour are represented as changes in the truth-value of temporal formulae defining specific behaviour (portrait) pattern of the system. The method for computing results of the bifurcation analysis (typically presented as *bifurcation diagrams*) uses our novel symbolic parallel parameter synthesis algorithm [3] which itself builds on the model-checking technology. As the approach employs a hybrid temporal logic for which the algorithm is computationally demanding we have also developed specialised algorithms dedicated to some specific formulae/patterns and thus working more efficiently.

Example of such patterns are attractors, which we see as a particular class of patterns representing the states of the system in which the system's execution persists in the long-time horizon, i.e., the so-called invariant subsets of the state-space towards which the system's runs are attracted. In computer systems, the most typical attractors can be observed in the form of terminal strongly connected components (tSCCs) [38]. We have developed an efficient parallel algorithm for detecting tSCCs in parametrised graphs in [1], and we use this algorithm in our two case studies. We have already successfully applied the digital bifurcation analysis to several models from systems biology [4,5].

In this case-study paper, we report on the application of digital bifurcation analysis to the Transmission Control Protocol (TCP) which currently facilitates most of the internet communication. One of the severe problems in practical applications of TCP is congestion, appearing when the required resources overrun the capacity of internet communication. Over the past years, many internet congestion control mechanisms have been developed to ensure the reliable and efficient exchange of information across the internet, such as Active Queue Management (AQM). Bifurcation analysis of TCP under various congestion control mechanisms have been studied by several authors [16,25,30,32,40,41]. All have used a continuous-time model (e.g., the fluid model) and applied traditional mathematical methods of bifurcation analysis, including simulations, to detect parameter values when the system passes through a critical point, the system loses its stability, and a so-called Hopf bifurcation occurs [22].

Our approach to bifurcation analysis does not require to remodel the given discrete system in terms of a continuous-time dynamical system. Digital bifurcation analysis works directly on discrete models represented as state transition systems. Furthermore, the method is, unlike mathematical methods, fully automatic and does not need mathematical skills to be utilised. Another advantage is that the method is scalable to state spaces with tens of variables and tens of possibly dependent parameters, overcoming thus significantly the limits of traditional mathematical methods. Last but not least the method is advantageous in performing global bifurcation analysis, which is harder to compute than the local analysis where bifurcation points are expected to be approximately known in advance.

It is important to stress that the purpose of this case-study paper is not to propose any new congestion control mechanisms or protocols. We aim to provide a demonstration of the appropriateness and usefulness of the digital bifurcation analysis as a push-button technique that makes a promising alternative to the classical approaches when analysing stability and robustness of TCP protocol specifications and implementations. To that end, we consider two different case studies targeting TCP. In both of them, we analyse how the structure and quality of attractors change when the parameters change. The first one deals with TCP that uses the Random Early Detection (RED) method [14] as an active queue management mechanism to control congestion. Although the RED mechanism alone is easy to understand, its interaction with TCP connections is rather complicated and is not well understood. In [33] the authors used a deterministic non-linear dynamical model of the TCP-RED protocol (together with detailed simulations) to demonstrate that the model exhibits a transition between a stable fixed point and an oscillatory or chaotic behaviour as parameters are varied. In our case study, we were able to achieve the same results fully automatically using our method. In the second example, we consider TCP itself combined with essential performance-oriented extensions. We analyse how the sizes of the send and receive socket buffers influence the throughput; in particular, we identify the combinations of sizes (bifurcation points) for which we observe a dramatic drop. The results we have achieved are in accordance with [28].

It is worth noting that bifurcation analysis provides a conceptually very different view of the protocol functionality than what is usually addressed by formal verification methods. The goal of verification is to prove the correctness of a system specification for all initial states and in the case of parametrised verification also regardless of the number of its components, or the parametrised domain of variables. On the other hand, the goal of bifurcation analysis of parametrised systems is to identify parameter values for which the system suddenly changes its behaviour regardless of its correctness.

Several examples of the TCP protocol verification are in [8,13,18,23,35–37]. As regards parametric verification, the Bounded Retransmission Protocol (BRP) for manually derived constraints has been checked by parametric model-checking in [19], the Stop-and-Wait Protocol (SWP) has been targeted in [15] for all possible values of the maximum sequence number and the maximum number of retransmissions parameters. We are not aware of any formal verification method that would address the bifurcations of the protocol behaviour.

Finally, we discuss the approaches related to bifurcation analysis. To the best of our knowledge, the only related approach to bifurcation analysis that also employs methods of formal verification has been presented in [20,21]. The authors address the identification of bifurcation points in non-trivial dynamics of a numerical cardiac-cell model represented using a hybrid automaton. The method is based on guided-search-based bounded-time reachability analysis used to estimate ranges of parameter values displaying two complementary patterns of systems behaviour. These ranges are computed for bounded-time reachability and over-approximated up to a particular δ-precision due to the underlying δ-decision algorithm.

2 Attractor Analysis Workflow

We first describe the standard scenario for digital bifurcation analysis focused on attractor analysis. The input is a parametrised system and a certain classification of stability-based attractor properties that we are interested in. The system is in the model design phase formalised as a discrete finite-state model and subsequently via the state-space generation procedure turned into a parametrised graph. How the initial model is obtained and what language the model is written in is domain-specific and is explained later when describing the case studies. The classification of the attractor properties specifies what shapes and forms of attractors we want to consider distinct enough to express a dramatic change in the system's behaviour. In the simplest case, which we call the *counting version* of our problem, we may be merely interested in the number of attractors and consider two parametrisations of a system non-equivalent if this number changes. More interesting cases may classify the attractors according to various stability-related properties, such as oscillations. The core parametric analysis algorithm then computes the parametric tSCC map. The resulting map is post-processed, producing e.g. the visualisation of bifurcation diagram, plots, tables, etc. The workflow of our method for the digital bifurcation analysis of attractors is summarised in Fig. 1.

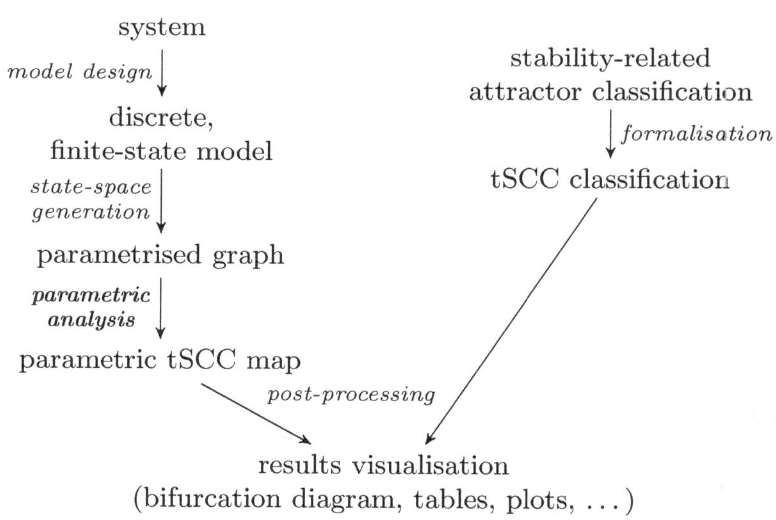

Fig. 1. Attractor analysis method workflow.

In general, our digital bifurcation analysis algorithm presupposes that the state space of the model has the form of a parametrised Kripke structure. In this case study, we are interested in attractor properties that are independent of the atomic proposition valuation. We, therefore, consider a simpler formalism here, namely that of parametrised graphs which are directed graphs with self-loops allowed and edges labelled by parameters taken from a given parameter set.

Definition 1. *A* graph *is a pair* (V, E) *where* V *is a finite set of* vertices *and* $E \subseteq V \times V$ *is a set of* edges. *A* parametrised graph *is a triple* $G = (V, E, \mathbb{P})$ *where* $\mathbb{P}$ *is a set of* parametrisations *and* $E : V \times V \to 2^{\mathbb{P}}$ *such that for each* $p \in \mathbb{P}$, $G_p = (V, E_p = \{(u, v) \mid p \in E(u, v)\})$ *is a graph. We call* G_p *the* projection of G on p.

To be able to investigate the properties of the attractors in the system, we need to use a notion that is analogous to an attractor in a parametrised graph. In dynamical systems theory, an attractor [27] is the smallest set of states (points in the phase space) invariant under the system dynamics. Parametrised graphs can be regarded as discrete abstractions of a dynamical system in which the dynamics are represented using paths in the graph. The respective abstraction of the notion of an attractor thus coincides with the notion of a terminal strongly connected component (tSCC) of a graph.

Definition 2. *Let* $G = (V, E)$ *be a graph. We say that a vertex* $t \in V$ is reachable *from a vertex* $s \in V$ *if* $(s, t) \in E^*$ *where* E^* *denotes the reflexive and transitive closure of* E. *A set of vertices* $C \subseteq V$ *is* strongly connected, *if* v *is reachable from* u *for any two vertices* u, $v \in C$. *A* strongly connected component *(SCC) is a* maximal *strongly connected set* $C \subseteq V$, *i.e. such that no* C' *with* $C \subsetneq C' \subseteq V$ *is strongly connected. A strongly connected component* C *is called* terminal *(tSCC) if* $(C \times (V \setminus C)) \cap E = \emptyset$, *i.e. there are no edges leaving* C.

We are now ready to state the algorithmic problem whose solution forms the basis of our method.

Terminal SCCs Enumeration Problem. Let $G = (V, E, \mathbb{P})$ be a parametrised graph. The goal is to enumerate, for every parametrisation $p \in \mathbb{P}$, all tSCCs in the graph G_p, the projection of G on p.

In this general version of our problem, the output is going to be a mapping that assigns to each $p \in \mathbb{P}$ the set of all tSCCs of G_p. We call this the *parametric tSCC map*. This map may be then further processed and visualised. We are mainly interested in the *bifurcation diagram* of the model. This diagram is a plot which partitions the parameter space into regions where the behaviour of the system is qualitatively invariant. In the case of a single parameter, this type of one-dimensional diagram is typically augmented by a second dimension which presents the location of the tSCCs with respect to a chosen system variable.

To be able to distinguish between quantitatively different behaviour of the system, we need to formalise the classification of stability-based attractor properties in terms of tSCCs. We thus get a classification function that separates tSCCs into classes. Two parametrisations of a system are then said to be qualitatively different if their respective graphs differ in the count of tSCCs belonging to each class. In the case of the counting version, we thus consider one class of tSCCs only. Here, parametrisations of a system are considered to be qualitatively different if their graphs contain a different number of tSCCs. In the more detailed cases, we can classify tSCCs according to size (small vs large), density (sparse vs dense), graph-specific properties (bipartite vs non-bipartite) etc.

For an example of how these classifications relate to the classical bifurcation analysis, we may see bipartite tSCCs as representing oscillatory patterns in attractors. The change from a small non-bipartite tSCC to a bipartite tSCC can be thus seen as an analogy of the Hopf bifurcation. In our two case studies, we distinguish between sinks (single-state tSCCs), bipartite (oscillatory) tSCC, and other tSCCs, which are further differentiated between small and large, based on a chosen domain-specific threshold.

The rest of this section gives a brief overview of the parallel algorithm for solving the tSCCs enumeration problem that we have developed in [1].

2.1 Core Algorithm

First, note that a simple *sequential* solution to the problem is to use any reasonable SCC decomposition algorithm (e.g. Tarjan's [39]) and enumerate the tSCCs in the residual graph. However, all known optimal sequential SCC decomposition algorithms use the depth-first search algorithm, which is suspected to be non-parallelisable [34]. There are known parallel SCC decomposition algorithms; for a survey, we refer to [2]. Our approach is based on the observation that we do not have to compute all of the SCCs to enumerate the terminal ones.

Furthermore, instead of scanning through all parametrisations and solving the problem for every one of them separately our approach deals with sets of parametrisations directly. This makes our algorithm suitable for use in connection with various kinds of symbolic set representations. The reason for using a parallel algorithm is the necessity to deal with the high computational demands of the method as discussed in [1].

The main idea of the Terminal Component Detection (TCD) algorithm lies in repeated reachability, which is known to be easily parallelisable. To explain the method, we start with a non-parametrised version of the algorithm. The following explication is illustrated in Fig. 2. Let us assume a given (non-parametrised) graph $G = (V, E)$. We choose an arbitrary vertex $v \in V$ (denoted by the double circle in the illustration) and compute all vertices reachable from v; let us call the resulting set of vertices F. We further compute the set of all vertices backwards-reachable from v inside F; we call the resulting set B. Finally, we compute all vertices backwards-reachable from any vertex of F; let us call this set B'.

Clearly, B is an SCC of the graph, and moreover, it is a terminal SCC iff $F \setminus B$ is empty. Furthermore, $B' \setminus F$ contains no tSCCs: all vertices in $B' \setminus F$ have a path to a vertex in F. We recursively run the algorithm in $F \setminus B$ and $V \setminus B'$ if non-empty. Observe that no tSCC may intersect both of these sets and these two subproblems can be thus dealt with independently (i.e. in parallel). Note that

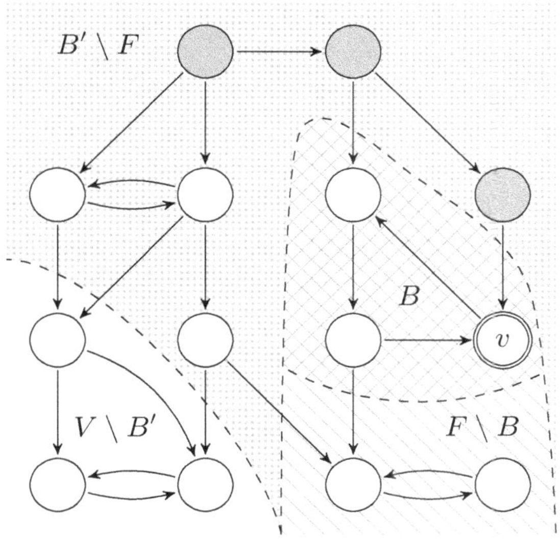

Fig. 2. Illustration of the non-parametrised version of our algorithm.

every time the algorithm is (recursively) started, its input is an induced subgraph of the original graph that satisfies the precondition that all its tSCCs are tSCCs of the original graph. These observations together imply the correctness of the algorithm.

The asymptotic complexity of the algorithm in its non-parametric version is of the order $\mathcal{O}(|V| \cdot (|V| + |E|))$ as in the worst case, every iteration may eliminate a single vertex of the graph. The actual performance of the algorithm strongly depends on the choice of the initial vertex v. If we consistently choose v that lies close to (or directly in) a tSCC of the graph, the complexity gets linear. Of course, such choice cannot be made in advance. The paper [1] discusses the impact of several heuristics that try to approximate this choice.

The algorithm can also be made more efficient using a *trimming* subprocedure in the manner of [26], i.e. removing all vertices without incoming edges. In Fig. 2, the removed vertices are marked in grey; furthermore, the $V \setminus B'$ part of the graph contains one vertex that would be removed in the next recursive run.

To extend the basic idea to parametrised graphs, we use a notion of parametrised sets of vertices. Formally, a parametrised set of vertices $\widehat{A}$ is a function $\widehat{A} : V \to 2^{\mathbb{P}}$. To deal with parametrised sets, we use a generalisation of the standard set operations. All the operations are performed element-wise, e.g. the union of parametrised sets $\widehat{A} \cup \widehat{B}$ is defined as the parametrised set $\widehat{C}$ such that $\widehat{C}(v) = \widehat{A}(v) \cup \widehat{B}(v)$ for all v. The parametrised set of all vertices and all parametrisations is given by $\widehat{V}$ such that $\widehat{V}(v) = \mathbb{P}$ for all $v \in V$.

The notions of the forward and backward reachable sets can be easily extended to the parametrised setting. They can be computed by a fixed-point algorithm which iterates the parametrised successor (or predecessor) operator. Given a parametrised set of vertices $\widehat{X}$, the successor operator computes the parametrised set $\widehat{Y}$ such that $\widehat{Y}(v) = \widehat{X}(v) \cup \bigcup_{u \in V}(\widehat{X}(u) \cap E(u,v))$ and similarly for the predecessor operator.

The parametrised algorithm then proceeds as described in the previous, extended with the parametrised sets. One further key difference is that instead of choosing one starting vertex, we need to choose a set of starting vertices with disjoint parametrisation sets that together cover all parametrisations that are present in the currently explored parametrised subgraph. The reason for this, as well as a discussion on heuristics that allow choosing such sets efficiently, can be again found in [1].

In the worst case, when parametrisations are represented explicitly, the asymptotic complexity of the algorithm is of the order $\mathcal{O}(|\mathbb{P}| \cdot |V| \cdot (|V| + |E|))$. The actual performance of the algorithm depends on various choices and heuristics. It can also be strongly influenced by the usage of a symbolic encoding of the parametrised sets. In this paper, the sets of parametrisations are represented symbolically using an interval encoding, similar to the one used in [10]. Other options for a symbolic representation of parameters include SMT formulae [3].

3 Case Studies

In this section, we present two case studies focusing on discovering bifurcations in the behaviour of the TCP protocol. Each of them addresses a different essential aspect of the protocol, namely congestion control and packet flow stability. We demonstrate how the digital bifurcation analysis can aid in the design, analysis and control of these discrete reactive systems.

In the first case study, we consider a relatively common setting in the standard bifurcation theory: A discrete map governing the behaviour of the RED congestion control mechanism. This mechanism prevents congestion on network nodes such as routers and is subject to changes in its behaviour due to different internal and external parameters. We show how different parameters influence the stability of the mechanism and how a hypothetical system administrator or an automated controller can use this information to avoid faulty behaviour.

The second case study presents an entirely discrete model of the basic TCP focusing on the stability of packet flow. We study the influence of the sender and receiver buffer sizes on the behaviour of the protocol and its ability to transfer packets in a timely manner. We assume the role of a hypothetical protocol designer and consider a set of extensions and modifications to the protocol proposed by various networking experts. We observe that such extensions and their interplay can introduce bifurcations leading to serious degradation of the protocol performance.

The case studies are implemented with the help of the tool Pithya [7] which provides the necessary parametrised graph analysis algorithms. The source code of this implementation is available at https://github.com/sybila/tcp-bifurcation. All experiments were performed on a typical 4-core 3 GHz desktop computer with 16 GB of RAM.

3.1 Instabilities in TCP-RED

This case study addresses the congestion control in TCP. The congestion control mechanism prevents the protocol from overloading the network with too many packets. The problem has two important aspects. The first aspect is the congestion control on the sender side that has to ensure maximal throughput for a single flow of packets. The second aspect is the congestion control on other network nodes, such as routers, where several connections meet.

One of the common approaches to implementing the congestion control on routers is the Random Early Drop (RED) method proposed in [14]. This technique explicitly drops packets as the router queue starts to fill up. Consequently, senders are indirectly notified (by observing the packet loss) that the link is approaching a congested state before the situation becomes critical.

Model Description. To study the RED mechanism, we use a discrete time model proposed in [33]. In Fig. 3, we present the model equations and a basic description of all model variables and constants. Detailed aspects of the model design are given in the original paper.

$$p_t(\overline{q}_t) = \begin{cases} 0 & \overline{q}_t \in [0, q_l] \\ \frac{\overline{q}_t - q_l}{q_u - q_l} p_{max} & \overline{q}_t \in (q_l, q_u) \\ 1 & \overline{q}_t \in [q_u, B] \end{cases} \quad (1) \qquad q_t(p_t) = \begin{cases} B & p_t \in [0, p_l] \\ \frac{n \cdot k}{\sqrt{p_t}} - \frac{c \cdot d}{m} & p_t \in (p_l, p_u) \\ 0 & p_t \in [p_u, 1] \end{cases} \quad (2)$$

$$\overline{q}_{t+1}(\overline{q}_t) = (1 - w) \cdot \overline{q}_t + w \cdot q_t(p_t(\overline{q}_t)) \quad (3)$$

maximum buffer size $B = 3750$
lower queue threshold $q_l = 250$
upper queue threshold $q_u = 750$
packet size $m = 4\text{kb}$
maximum drop rate $p_{max} = 0.1$
number of TCP connections $n = 250$
propagation delay $d = 0.1\text{s}$
link capacity $c = 75\text{Mb/s}$

drop rate $p_t \in [0, 1]$
queue size $q_t \in [0, B]$
average queue size $\overline{q}_t \in [0, B]$
lower drop threshold $p_l = \left(\frac{n \cdot m \cdot k}{dc + Bm}\right)^2$
upper drop threshold $p_u = \left(\frac{n \cdot m \cdot k}{dc}\right)^2$
rate constant $k = \sqrt{3/2}$
averaging weight $w = 0.15$

Fig. 3. A discrete time model of the RED congestion control behaviour. The individual constants are stated with basic explanations and default values. The parameters are selected from the given set of constants and their bounds are specified later with the corresponding experiments.

The model assumes n connections flowing through a single RED-capable router. All connections share basic properties, namely the packet size and the propagation delay. In such a case, the situation can be simplified by considering only a single combined flow, as the router cannot differentiate between the individual flows anyway. The router then maintains the current drop rate p_t (Eq. 1) and the queue size q_t (Eq. 2) based on the current exponentially weighted average queue size $\overline{q}_t$ (Eq. 3).

A typical scenario is that a network administrator takes control over parameters such as the averaging weight w or the queue thresholds q_l and q_u. Furthermore, it is also important to consider the influence of the connection count n and the propagation delay d, as these numbers will change depending on the current network load.

Parametrised Graph. To analyse the model, we require a finite parametrised graph $G = (V, E, \mathbb{P})$. Here, $\mathbb{P}$ is the parameter space given by the chosen model parameters (we specify the chosen parameters for each experiment later). In Eq. 3, we write $\overline{q}_{t+1}(\overline{q}, \lambda)$ for $\lambda \in \mathbb{P}$ to specify the parametrised version of the model.

We assume $s + 1$ thresholds $t_0 < t_1 < \ldots < t_s$ such that $t_0 = 0$ and $t_s = B$. These thresholds partition the state space of the variable $\overline{q}$ into s intervals $[t_0, t_1], \ldots, [t_{s-1}, t_s]$, denoted as $I_1, \ldots, I_s$. These intervals then represent vertices of our parametrised graph $V = \{I_i \mid i \in [1, s]\}$.

Next, we construct the parametrised edges between our intervals so that they over-approximate the behaviour of the original discrete map. Let us consider two intervals I_i and I_j and the edge from I_i to I_j. Clearly, the set of parametrisations $E(I_i, I_j)$ has to include all parametrisations λ such that for some $\overline{q}_t \in I_i$ it holds that $\overline{q}_{t+1}(\overline{q}_t, \lambda) \in I_j$. We compute these sets using interval arithmetic, ensuring that all such parametrisations are included.

Finally, since our graph over-approximates the original discrete map, each tSCC over-approximates some attractor(s) of the original system. Furthermore, the precision of this over-approximation can be refined by introducing additional thresholds or substituting interval arithmetic for a more sophisticated approximation method, e.g., Taylor models [24].

Analysis Results. The analysis procedure consists of two scenarios:

Scenario 1: Consider a system designer who studies the effects of parameters to assess correct settings ensuring the stable behaviour of the protocol. In Fig. 4(a) and (b), the locations and types of attractors are shown for parameters w and n, respectively. It can be seen that increasing the parameter w has a destabilising effect – the small (stable) tSCC (component size $\leq 0.01 \cdot B$) turns into a bipartite tSCC (representing oscillation) and finally into a large non-bipartite tSCC. On the other hand, the effect of the connection count n is complementary: a higher number of connections stabilise the behaviour (Fig. 4b). Additionally, the protocol behaves as expected in the stable region – w does not influence the location of the steady state whereas a higher number of connections require higher queue sizes to accommodate the increased data flow. Using this

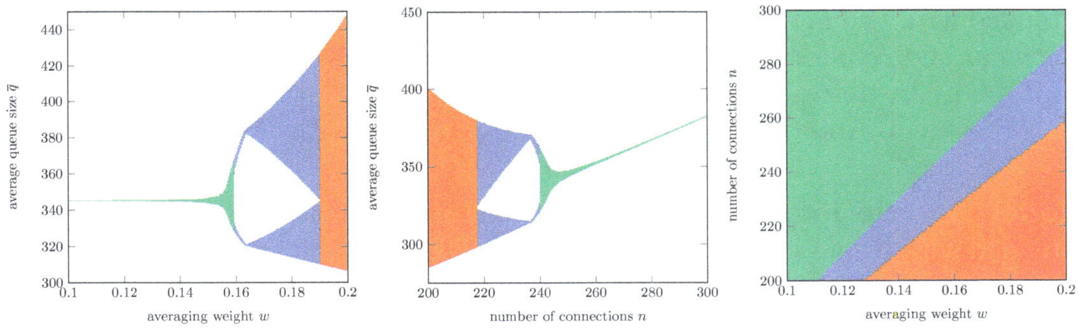

(a) (b) (c)

Fig. 4. Bifurcation diagrams showing the location and character of the tSCC depending on model parameters in the RED model. The green region indicates a small component ($\leq 0.01 \cdot B$), the blue region shows oscillatory behaviour (bipartite graph), and the red region corresponds to a large non-bipartite tSCC. (a) $w \in [0.1, 0.2]$ and $n = 250$; (b) $n \in [200, 300]$ and $w = 0.15$; (c) $w \in [0.1, 0.2]$ and $n \in [200, 300]$. (Color figure online)

kind of analysis, a general overview of the systems behaviour w.r.t. the given parameters can be directly obtained in a matter of minutes.

Scenario 2: Assume an administrator (or an automated controller) is supposed to adjust the parameter w to preserve the correct functionality of the system subject to a varying number of connections n. In Fig. 4c, it is shown how the character of the attractor changes with the controllable parameter w and the external condition n. This allows the administrator to select optimal values for the given situation. Note that while this specific type of diagram does not show the concrete location of components, it is still contained in the method results and can be used to support the decision further. While this type of analysis is certainly more computationally challenging, it can still be performed in under one hour.

3.2 Packet Flow Stability

The TCP specification as defined in RFC 793 [31] provides a fundamental description of the TCP protocol such as the packet format or the state machine for event processing. However, many implementation and performance aspects were not addressed in the original specification. Therefore in the subsequent years, several extensions and improvements of the protocol functionality have been introduced [9, 12, 29].

Nowadays, many well-tested, production ready implementations of TCP exist. However, as demonstrated in [28], non-standard network configurations and combinations of various modifications can cause problems even in well-established implementations. Furthermore, new implementations are still being developed where such fundamental problems can easily re-appear [17].

In this case study, we assume the role of a hypothetical protocol engineer. We introduce a basic parametrised model of TCP according to RFC 793 [31] extended with two performance-oriented modifications, namely *delayed acknowledgement* and *Nagle's algorithm*. We observe that these modifications, while useful in many instances, can introduce unexpected bifurcations in the behaviour of the protocol. Additionally, we compare our results with [28].

Model Description. We consider a model of TCP based on RFC 793 [31] extended with Nagle's algorithm according to RFC 896 [29] and delayed acknowledgement according to RFC 813 [12] and RFC 1122 [9]. We assume a single sender which sends an uni-directional infinite stream of data to a single receiver connected by a reliable link with unlimited capacity. As parameters, we assume a fixed maximal buffer size S for the sender and R for the receiver. Finally, the size of each packet is limited by the Maximum Segment Size (MSS) set by the network administrator.

Since we are not interested in the exact values of the transmitted data bytes, we can model the state of the protocol using the number of bytes in each protocol phase. This abstraction leads to the following five state variables:

- `W` – the number of bytes in the send buffer waiting to be sent;
- `D` – the list of data packet sizes in transit;
- `U` – the number of bytes in the receive buffer waiting to be acknowledged;
- `A` – the list of acknowledgement packets in transit;
- `ACK` – the out-of-order acknowledgement flag.

Furthermore, we use **`outstanding`** to denote the number of unacknowledged bytes (`U` plus the sum of all elements in `D` and `A`). Since the protocol is not limited by the link capacity, we assume the available **`window`** is always equal to $min(S, R)$ minus **`outstanding`** bytes. Notice that all the bytes considered by the model variables must be stored in the send buffer (the sender must keep the data until acknowledgement arrives), whereas only the bytes waiting to be acknowledged are stored in the receive buffer.

The dynamics of the model is governed by a set of discrete asynchronous events. Each event can be only executed when its preconditions are met. As our parametrised graph, we consider the graph of the protocol states reachable from the initial configuration where all channels are empty, and all variables are zero. The model consists of the following discrete events:

Copy data from the application: Before sending, the data needs to be copied from the application to the kernel memory where the networking layer operates. This occurs in 1024-byte chunks such that at least for every four chunks, the copying is interrupted to send available data right away [28] if possible:

$$\mathtt{W} = \mathtt{W} + k \cdot 1024;\ \text{where } k \in [1..4] \text{ is maximal}$$
$$\text{such that } (k \cdot 1024 + \mathtt{W} + \mathtt{outstanding} \leq S)$$

Send full packet: When MSS unsent bytes are available in the send buffer and the **`window`** capacity is sufficient, a full packet can be constructed and sent:

$$\mathtt{W} = \mathtt{W} - \text{MSS};\ \mathtt{D} = \mathit{append}(\mathtt{D}, \text{MSS});\ \text{when } (\mathtt{window} \geq \text{MSS} \wedge \mathtt{W} \geq \text{MSS})$$

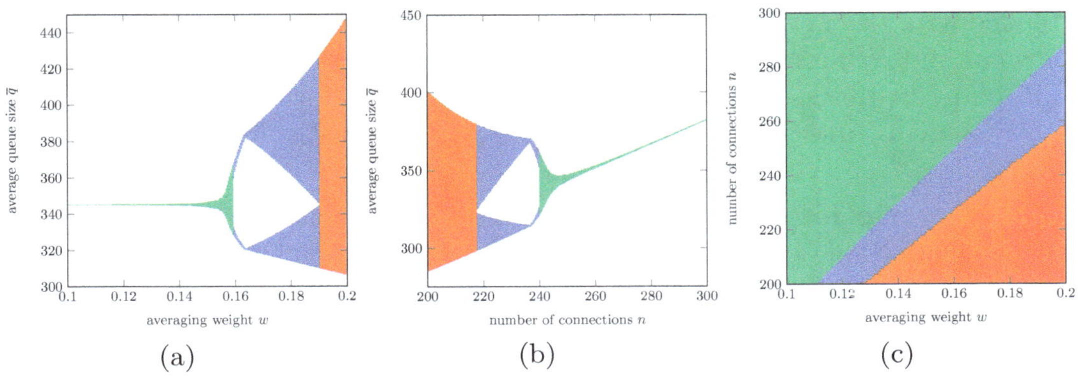

Fig. 4. Bifurcation diagrams showing the location and character of the tSCC depending on model parameters in the RED model. The green region indicates a small component ($\leq 0.01 \cdot B$), the blue region shows oscillatory behaviour (bipartite graph), and the red region corresponds to a large non-bipartite tSCC. (a) $w \in [0.1, 0.2]$ and $n = 250$; (b) $n \in [200, 300]$ and $w = 0.15$; (c) $w \in [0.1, 0.2]$ and $n \in [200, 300]$. (Color figure online)

kind of analysis, a general overview of the systems behaviour w.r.t. the given parameters can be directly obtained in a matter of minutes.

Scenario 2: Assume an administrator (or an automated controller) is supposed to adjust the parameter w to preserve the correct functionality of the system subject to a varying number of connections n. In Fig. 4c, it is shown how the character of the attractor changes with the controllable parameter w and the external condition n. This allows the administrator to select optimal values for the given situation. Note that while this specific type of diagram does not show the concrete location of components, it is still contained in the method results and can be used to support the decision further. While this type of analysis is certainly more computationally challenging, it can still be performed in under one hour.

3.2 Packet Flow Stability

The TCP specification as defined in RFC 793 [31] provides a fundamental description of the TCP protocol such as the packet format or the state machine for event processing. However, many implementation and performance aspects were not addressed in the original specification. Therefore in the subsequent years, several extensions and improvements of the protocol functionality have been introduced [9,12,29].

Nowadays, many well-tested, production ready implementations of TCP exist. However, as demonstrated in [28], non-standard network configurations and combinations of various modifications can cause problems even in well-established implementations. Furthermore, new implementations are still being developed where such fundamental problems can easily re-appear [17].

In this case study, we assume the role of a hypothetical protocol engineer. We introduce a basic parametrised model of TCP according to RFC 793 [31] extended with two performance-oriented modifications, namely *delayed acknowledgement* and *Nagle's algorithm*. We observe that these modifications, while useful in many instances, can introduce unexpected bifurcations in the behaviour of the protocol. Additionally, we compare our results with [28].

Model Description. We consider a model of TCP based on RFC 793 [31] extended with Nagle's algorithm according to RFC 896 [29] and delayed acknowledgement according to RFC 813 [12] and RFC 1122 [9]. We assume a single sender which sends an uni-directional infinite stream of data to a single receiver connected by a reliable link with unlimited capacity. As parameters, we assume a fixed maximal buffer size S for the sender and R for the receiver. Finally, the size of each packet is limited by the Maximum Segment Size (MSS) set by the network administrator.

Since we are not interested in the exact values of the transmitted data bytes, we can model the state of the protocol using the number of bytes in each protocol phase. This abstraction leads to the following five state variables:

- `W` – the number of bytes in the send buffer waiting to be sent;
- `D` – the list of data packet sizes in transit;
- `U` – the number of bytes in the receive buffer waiting to be acknowledged;
- `A` – the list of acknowledgement packets in transit;
- `ACK` – the out-of-order acknowledgement flag.

Furthermore, we use `outstanding` to denote the number of unacknowledged bytes (`U` plus the sum of all elements in `D` and `A`). Since the protocol is not limited by the link capacity, we assume the available `window` is always equal to $min(S, R)$ minus `outstanding` bytes. Notice that all the bytes considered by the model variables must be stored in the send buffer (the sender must keep the data until acknowledgement arrives), whereas only the bytes waiting to be acknowledged are stored in the receive buffer.

The dynamics of the model is governed by a set of discrete asynchronous events. Each event can be only executed when its preconditions are met. As our parametrised graph, we consider the graph of the protocol states reachable from the initial configuration where all channels are empty, and all variables are zero. The model consists of the following discrete events:

Copy data from the application: Before sending, the data needs to be copied from the application to the kernel memory where the networking layer operates. This occurs in 1024-byte chunks such that at least for every four chunks, the copying is interrupted to send available data right away [28] if possible:

$$\begin{aligned}\mathtt{W} = \mathtt{W} + k \cdot 1024;\ \text{where } k \in [1..4] \text{ is maximal}\\ \text{such that } (k \cdot 1024 + \mathtt{W} + \mathtt{outstanding} \leq S)\end{aligned}$$

Send full packet: When MSS unsent bytes are available in the send buffer and the `window` capacity is sufficient, a full packet can be constructed and sent:

$$\mathtt{W} = \mathtt{W} - \text{MSS};\ \mathtt{D} = \mathit{append}(\mathtt{D}, \text{MSS});\ \text{when } (\mathtt{window} \geq \text{MSS} \wedge \mathtt{W} \geq \text{MSS})$$

Send partial packet: When less than MSS unsent bytes are available, or the `window` is not large enough, the protocol can decide to send a partial packet. This decision is governed by Nagle's algorithm which dictates that a partial packet can be sent only when there are no outstanding bytes. This criterion prevents the sender from sending unnecessary small packets in an unbuffered stream of data:

$$\mathtt{W} = \mathtt{W} - packet;\ \mathtt{D} = append(\mathtt{D}, packet);\ \text{where}$$
$$(packet = min(\mathtt{window}, \text{MSS}, \mathtt{W}) \wedge \mathtt{outstanding} = 0)$$

Receive and acknowledge packet: The receiver can process and acknowledge any data packet (we assume the data is immediately handed over to the application). However, to avoid a large number of small acknowledgement packets, the packet acknowledgement is often delayed until a sufficient amount of data is received (RFC 813). In our case, we use the threshold specified in [28] – 35% of R. In RFC 1122, this rule is further augmented to send an acknowledgement packet whenever two full segments are received:

$$\mathtt{A} = append(\mathtt{A}, \mathtt{U} + head(\mathtt{D}));\ \mathtt{D} = tail(\mathtt{D});\ \mathtt{U} = 0;\ \text{when}$$
$$(|\mathtt{D}| > 0 \wedge \mathtt{U} + head(\mathtt{D}) \geq min(0.35 \cdot R, 2 \cdot \text{MSS}))$$

Receive without acknowledgement: When the rules of delayed acknowledgement are not met, the data bytes are transferred to the receive buffer instead:

$$\mathtt{U} = \mathtt{U} + head(\mathtt{D});\ \mathtt{D} = tail(\mathtt{D});\ \text{when}$$
$$(|\mathtt{D}| > 0 \wedge \mathtt{U} + head(\mathtt{D}) < min(0.35 \cdot R, 2 \cdot \text{MSS}))$$

Out-of-order acknowledgement: According to RFC 813, when data is received without immediate acknowledgement, a 200 ms timer should be started to acknowledge the data if no acknowledgement packet is generated in the meantime. However, as discussed in [28], regularly rescheduling such a timer can be an expensive operation. Therefore a cyclic timer acknowledging all received data every 200 ms is often used instead. In our model, we include this design decision by allowing one non-deterministic out-of-order acknowledgement packet to occur:

$$\mathtt{A} = append(\mathtt{A}, \mathtt{U});\ \mathtt{U} = 0;\ \mathtt{ACK} = 1\ \text{when}\ (\mathtt{U} > 0 \wedge \mathtt{ACK} = 0)$$

Process acknowledgement: The data cannot be removed from the send buffer until they are acknowledged. Thus whenever there is an acknowledgement packet in transit, the packet can be processed by the receiver:

$$\mathtt{A} = tail(\mathtt{A});\ \text{when}\ |\mathtt{A}| > 0$$

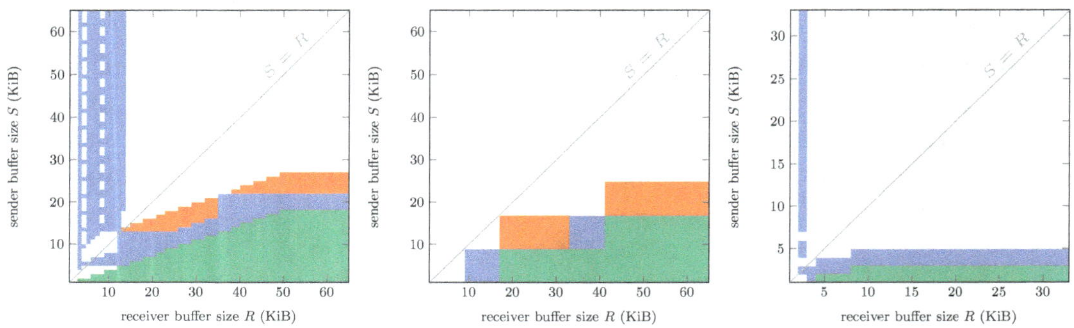

(a) (b) (c)

Fig. 5. The bifurcation diagrams showing the character of tSCCs depending on the model parameters in the TCP model. The white space indicates a single large tSCC; the other colours indicate the regions displaying various types of single state tSCCs. (a) MSS = 9204, 1 KiB increments of S and R; (b) MSS = 9204, 8 KiB increments of S and R; (c) MSS = 1460, 1 KiB increments of S and R. (Color figure online)

Analysis Results. In our analysis, we assume the buffer sizes S and R ranging from 1 KiB to 64 KiB in 1 KiB increments. First, we consider MSS to be 9204, as in [28]. This MSS configuration corresponds to a specific high-performance network and is not used in typical Ethernet configurations.

The complete results of our analysis are presented in Fig. 5a. In contrary to the previous case study, we consider the presence of a single large terminal tSCC as the desired behaviour (depicted in white). In this case, the situation indicates that the protocol is functioning properly. On the other hand, the presence of a small, single state tSCC means that the protocol cannot continue transmitting and is waiting for a time-out to resolve the problematic situation.

Additionally, based on enabling and disabling various extensions of the protocol model, we can distinguish between different bifurcation causes:

- *Delayed acknowledgement (DA):* With the delayed acknowledgement employed exclusively, the parametrisations satisfying $S < 0.35 \cdot R \wedge S < 2 \cdot \mathrm{MSS}$ can never trigger the automatic acknowledgement and thus rely on the acknowledgement time-out instead. The corresponding regions are depicted in green in Fig. 5.
- *Combination of DA and Nagle's algorithm:* A single state tSCC emerges whenever the amount of data necessary to trigger the next automatic acknowledgement cannot be sent due to Nagle's condition. The corresponding regions are depicted in blue in Fig. 5.
- *Combination of DA, Nagle's algorithm, and cyclic timer:* The regions depicted in red in Fig. 5 correspond to single state tSCCs appearing only when all the three extensions are enabled. The reason is that while delayed acknowledgement and Nagle's algorithm can coexist well under these parametrisations, the cyclic timer can cause transmissions of small packets which is not possible in the cases above.

In the case of $S < R$, the achieved results are in line with the findings of [28]. However, in the $R > S$ area, we observe a bifurcation caused by the interplay of delayed acknowledgement and Nagle's algorithm which has not been considered in the original paper. This bifurcation is caused by small packets sent right after an acknowledgement is received. The small packet is transmitted after the acknowledgement clears the outstanding bytes (so Nagle's condition holds), but before more data is copied into the send buffer (before the acknowledgement was received, the send buffer was full).

In [28], the situation might have been avoided by some undisclosed implementation or timing aspects. However, another possible explanation is that this behaviour has been overlooked because such issues never occurred during the experiments. In Fig. 5b, we present our reconstruction of the same results, but in 8 KiB increments. It corresponds exactly to the experimental evaluation presented in [28]. The described behaviour is absent in this case, since the 8 KiB increments avoid the problematic region entirely.

Finally, in Fig. 5c, we present the same analysis for the maximal buffer size of 32 KiB and MSS of 1460 bytes, which is the typical setting on an Ethernet network. In this case, the red region is completely absent, and while other bifurcations are still present, the problematic regions are much smaller due to the smaller MSS. This puts into perspective the drastic behavioural changes present for larger MSS values and shows how bifurcations can emerge in unexpected situations.

4 Discussion and Conclusion

In this paper, we have presented two case studies demonstrating a promising application of the digital bifurcation analysis in the domain of network protocols. To that end, we have utilised the methodology developed in our previous work.

The key aspects of the method as applied in this paper are the following. First, it gives rigorous results concerning the given models of the studied protocol. Second, it can be performed fully automatically. In general, the only tasks that have to be done manually are to acquire a suitable model and to post-process the results (incl. visualisation and interpretation). The crucial step to be done within the latter task is to classify the studied protocol properties in terms of attractors. However, this can be easily automated since the interest of a network administrator (or a designer) is primarily focused on parameter values for which the stable behaviour (a single simple attractor) disappears.

Both case studies show that the digital bifurcation analysis provides a methodologically different view on the protocol analysis than formal verification or testing. This is allowed by providing a global view of the protocol behaviour with respect to parameters. Due to the global approach, in the second case study, we have revealed regions in bifurcation diagrams that were omitted in previous studies.

The push-button characteristics of the digital bifurcation analysis allow making the results easily reproducible. All steps necessary to reconstruct both case studies are publicly available[1].

For future work, our primary intention is to target similar, but not yet fully explored, problems in network protocols using digital bifurcation analysis that will allow further fine-tuning (and generalisation) of the presented workflow.

References

1. Barnat, J., et al.: Detecting attractors in biological models with uncertain parameters. In: Feret, J., Koeppl, H. (eds.) CMSB 2017. LNCS, vol. 10545, pp. 40–56. Springer, Cham (2017). https://doi.org/10.1007/978-3-319-67471-1_3
2. Barnat, J., Chaloupka, J., Van De Pol, J.: Distributed algorithms for SCC decomposition. J. Logic Comput. **21**(1), 23–44 (2011)
3. Beneš, N., Brim, L., Demko, M., Pastva, S., Šafránek, D.: Parallel SMT-based parameter synthesis with application to piecewise multi-affine systems. In: Artho, C., Legay, A., Peled, D. (eds.) ATVA 2016. LNCS, vol. 9938, pp. 192–208. Springer, Cham (2016). https://doi.org/10.1007/978-3-319-46520-3_13
4. Beneš, N., et al.: Fully automated attractor analysis of cyanobacteria models. In: 2018 22nd International Conference on System Theory, Control and Computing, ICSTCC, pp. 354–359, October 2018
5. Beneš, N., Brim, L., Demko, M., Hajnal, M., Pastva, S., Šafránek, D.: Discrete bifurcation analysis with Pithya. In: Feret, J., Koeppl, H. (eds.) CMSB 2017. LNBI, vol. 10545, pp. 319–320. Springer, Heidelberg (2017)
6. Beneš, N., Brim, L., Demko, M., Pastva, S., Šafránek, D.: A model checking approach to discrete bifurcation analysis. In: Fitzgerald, J., Heitmeyer, C., Gnesi, S., Philippou, A. (eds.) FM 2016. LNCS, vol. 9995, pp. 85–101. Springer, Cham (2016). https://doi.org/10.1007/978-3-319-48989-6_6
7. Beneš, N., Brim, L., Demko, M., Pastva, S., Šafránek, D.: Pithya: a parallel tool for parameter synthesis of piecewise multi-affine dynamical systems. In: Majumdar, R., Kunčak, V. (eds.) CAV 2017. LNCS, vol. 10426, pp. 591–598. Springer, Cham (2017). https://doi.org/10.1007/978-3-319-63387-9_29
8. Bishop, S., Fairbairn, M., Norrish, M., Sewell, P., Smith, M., Wansbrough, K.: Rigorous specification and conformance testing techniques for network protocols, as applied to TCP, UDP, and sockets. SIGCOMM Comput. Commun. Rev. **35**(4), 265–276 (2005)
9. Braden, R.: Requirements for Internet Hosts - Communication Layers. RFC 1122, RFC Editor, October 1989. https://www.rfc-editor.org/rfc/rfc1122.txt
10. Brim, L., Češka, M., Demko, M., Pastva, S., Šafránek, D.: Parameter synthesis by parallel coloured CTL model checking. In: Roux, O., Bourdon, J. (eds.) CMSB 2015. LNCS, vol. 9308, pp. 251–263. Springer, Cham (2015). https://doi.org/10.1007/978-3-319-23401-4_21
11. Brim, L., Demko, M., Pastva, S., Šafránek, D.: High-performance discrete bifurcation analysis for piecewise-affine dynamical systems. In: Abate, A., Šafránek, D. (eds.) HSB 2015. LNCS, vol. 9271, pp. 58–74. Springer, Cham (2015). https://doi.org/10.1007/978-3-319-26916-0_4

[1] https://github.com/sybila/tcp-bifurcation.

12. Clark, D.D.: Window and Acknowledgement Strategy in TCP. RFC 813, RFC Editor, July 1982. https://www.rfc-editor.org/rfc/rfc813.txt
13. Fiterău-Broştean, P., Janssen, R., Vaandrager, F.: Combining model learning and model checking to analyze TCP implementations. In: Chaudhuri, S., Farzan, A. (eds.) CAV 2016. LNCS, vol. 9780, pp. 454–471. Springer, Cham (2016). https://doi.org/10.1007/978-3-319-41540-6_25
14. Floyd, S., Jacobson, V.: Random early detection gateways for congestion avoidance. IEEE/ACM Trans. Netw. **1**(4), 397–413 (1993)
15. Gallasch, G.E., Billington, J.: A parametric state space for the analysis of the infinite class of stop-and-wait protocols. In: Valmari, A. (ed.) SPIN 2006. LNCS, vol. 3925, pp. 201–218. Springer, Heidelberg (2006). https://doi.org/10.1007/11691617_12
16. Ghosh, D., Jagannathan, K., Raina, G.: Local stability and Hopf bifurcation analysis for Compound TCP. IEEE Trans. Control Netw. Syst. **5**(4), 1668–1681 (2018). (Early Access)
17. GitHub: TCP flow deadlock: receive window closes and never opens again (2017). https://github.com/mirage/mirage-tcpip/issues/340
18. Han, B., Billington, J.: Termination properties of TCP's connection management procedures. In: Ciardo, G., Darondeau, P. (eds.) ICATPN 2005. LNCS, vol. 3536, pp. 228–249. Springer, Heidelberg (2005). https://doi.org/10.1007/11494744_14
19. Hune, T., Romijn, J., Stoelinga, M., Vaandrager, F.: Linear parametric model checking of timed automata. In: Margaria, T., Yi, W. (eds.) TACAS 2001. LNCS, vol. 2031, pp. 189–203. Springer, Heidelberg (2001). https://doi.org/10.1007/3-540-45319-9_14
20. Islam, M.A., et al.: Bifurcation analysis of cardiac alternans using δ-decidability. In: Bartocci, E., Lio, P., Paoletti, N. (eds.) CMSB 2016. LNCS, vol. 9859, pp. 132–146. Springer, Cham (2016). https://doi.org/10.1007/978-3-319-45177-0_9
21. Islam, M.A., Cleaveland, R., Fenton, F.H., Grosu, R., Jones, P.L., Smolka, S.A.: Probabilistic reachability for multi-parameter bifurcation analysis of cardiac alternans. Theoret. Comput. Sci. (2018, in press)
22. Kuznetsov, Y.A.: Elements of Applied Bifurcation Theory, 2nd edn. Springer, Heidelberg (1998)
23. Lockefeer, L., Williams, D.M., Fokkink, W.: Formal specification and verification of TCP extended with the Window Scale Option. Sci. Comput. Program. **118**, 3–23 (2016)
24. Makino, K., Berz, M.: Verified computations using Taylor models and their applications. In: Abate, A., Boldo, S. (eds.) NSV 2017. LNCS, vol. 10381, pp. 3–13. Springer, Cham (2017). https://doi.org/10.1007/978-3-319-63501-9_1
25. Manjunath, S., Raina, G.: FAST TCP: some fluid models, stability and Hopf bifurcation. Perform. Eval. **110**, 48–66 (2017)
26. McLendon III, W., Hendrickson, B., Plimpton, S.J., Rauchwerger, L.: Finding strongly connected components in distributed graphs. J. Parallel Distrib. Comput. **65**(8), 901–910 (2005)
27. Milnor, J.: On the concept of attractor. Commun. Math. Phys. **99**(2), 177–195 (1985)
28. Moldeklev, K., Gunningberg, P.: Deadlock situations in TCP over ATM. In: Neufield, G., Ito, M. (eds.) Protocols for High Speed Networks IV. IAICT, pp. 243–259. Springer, Boston, MA (1995). https://doi.org/10.1007/978-0-387-34885-8_15
29. Nagle, J.: Congestion Control in IP/TCP Internetworks. RFC 896, RFC Editor, January 1984. https://www.rfc-editor.org/rfc/rfc896.txt

30. Nga, J., Iu, H., Ling, B., Lam, H.: Analysis and control of bifurcation and chaos in average queue length in TCP/RED model. Int. J. Bifurc. Chaos **18**(8), 2449–2459 (2008)
31. Postel, J.: Transmission Control Protocol. RFC 793, RFC Editor, September 1981. https://www.rfc-editor.org/rfc/rfc793.txt
32. Raman, S., Mohan, A., Raina, G.: TCP Reno and queue management: local stability and Hopf bifurcation analysis. In: CDC 2013, pp. 3299–3305. IEEE (2013)
33. Ranjan, P., Abed, E.H., La, R.J.: Nonlinear instabilities in TCP-RED. IEEE/ACM Trans. Netw. **12**(6), 1079–1092 (2004)
34. Reif, J.H.: Depth-first search is inherently sequential. Inf. Process. Lett. **20**(5), 229–234 (1985)
35. Schieferdecker, I.: Abruptly terminated connections in TCP - a verification example. In: Brezočnik, Z., Kapus, T. (eds.) Proceedings of the COST 247 International Workshop on Applied Formal Methods in System Design, pp. 136–145. University of Maribor (1996)
36. Smith, M.A., Ramakrishnan, K.K.: Formal specification and verification of safety and performance of TCP selective acknowledgment. IEEE/ACM Trans. Netw. **10**(2), 193–207 (2002)
37. Smith, M.A.S.: Formal verification of communication protocols. In: Gotzhein, R., Bredereke, J. (eds.) Formal Description Techniques IX. IFIPAICT, pp. 129–144. Springer, Boston (1996). https://doi.org/10.1007/978-0-387-35079-0_8
38. Sullivan, D., Williams, R.: On the homology of attractors. Topology **15**(3), 259–262 (1976)
39. Tarjan, R.E.: Depth-first search and linear graph algorithms. SIAM J. Comput. **1**(2), 146–160 (1972)
40. Xu, C., Tang, X., Liao, M.: Local Hopf bifurcation and global existence of periodic solutions in TCP system. Appl. Math. Mech. **31**(6), 775–786 (2010)
41. Xu, C., Li, P.: Dynamical analysis in exponential RED algorithm with communication delay. Adv. Differ. Equ. **2016**(1), 40 (2016)

Verifying Safety of Synchronous Fault-Tolerant Algorithms by Bounded Model Checking

Ilina Stoilkovska[1(✉)], Igor Konnov[2], Josef Widder[1], and Florian Zuleger[1]

[1] TU Wien, Vienna, Austria
{stoilkov,widder,zuleger}@forsyte.at
[2] University of Lorraine, CNRS, Inria, LORIA, Nancy, France
igor.konnov@inria.fr

Abstract. Many fault-tolerant distributed algorithms are designed for synchronous or round-based semantics. In this paper, we introduce the synchronous variant of threshold automata, and study their applicability and limitations for the verification of synchronous distributed algorithms. We show that in general, the reachability problem is undecidable for synchronous threshold automata. Still, we show that many synchronous fault-tolerant distributed algorithms have a bounded diameter, although the algorithms are parameterized by the number of processes. Hence, we use bounded model checking for verifying these algorithms.

The existence of bounded diameters is the main conceptual insight in this paper. We compute the diameter of several algorithms and check their safety properties, using SMT queries that contain quantifiers for dealing with the parameters symbolically. Surprisingly, performance of the SMT solvers on these queries is very good, reflecting the recent progress in dealing with quantified queries. We found that the diameter bounds of synchronous algorithms in the literature are tiny (from 1 to 4), which makes our approach applicable in practice. For a specific class of algorithms we also establish a theoretical result on the existence of a diameter, providing a first explanation for our experimental results. The encodings of our benchmarks and instructions on how to run the experiments are available at: [33].

1 Introduction

Fault-tolerant distributed algorithms are hard to design and verify. Recently, threshold automata were introduced to model, verify and synthesize asynchronous fault-tolerant distributed algorithms [19,21,24]. Owing to the well-known impossibility result [18] many distributed computing problems, including

Partially supported by: Austrian Science Fund (FWF) via NFN RiSE (S11403, S11405), project PRAVDA (P27722), and doctoral college LogiCS W1255; Vienna Science and Technology Fund (WWTF) grant APALACHE (ICT15-103).

T. Vojnar and L. Zhang (Eds.): TACAS 2019, Part II, LNCS 11428, pp. 357–374, 2019.
https://doi.org/10.1007/978-3-030-17465-1_20

```
1  int v:=input({0, 1})
2  bool accept:=false
3  while (true) do { // in one synchronous step
4    if (v = 1) then broadcast <ECHO>;
5    receive messages from other processes;
6    if received <ECHO> from ≥ t + 1 processes
7      then v:=1;
8    if received <ECHO> from ≥ n − t processes
9      then accept:=true;
10 }
```

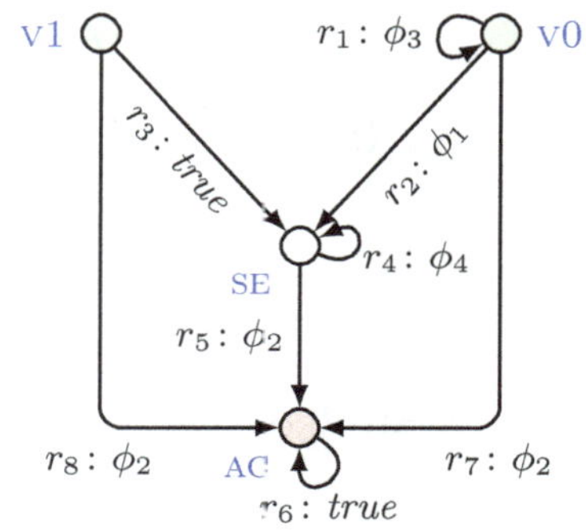

Fig. 1. Pseudo code of synchronous reliable broadcast à la [32], and its STA, with guards: $\phi_1 \equiv \#\{\text{v1}, \text{SE}, \text{AC}\} \geq t + 1 - f$ and $\phi_2 \equiv \#\{\text{v1}, \text{SE}, \text{AC}\} \geq n - t - f$ and $\phi_3 \equiv \#\{\text{v1}, \text{SE}, \text{AC}\} < t + 1$ and $\phi_4 \equiv \#\{\text{v1}, \text{SE}, \text{AC}\} < n - t$.

consensus, are not solvable in purely asynchronous systems. Thus, synchronous distributed algorithms have been extensively studied [5,26]. In this paper, we introduce *synchronous* threshold automata, and investigate their applicability and limitations for verification of synchronous fault-tolerant distributed algorithms.

An example of such a synchronous threshold automaton is given in Fig. 1 on the right; it encodes the synchronous reliable broadcast algorithm from [32]. (The pseudo code is in Fig. 1 on the left.) Its semantics is defined in terms of a counter system. For each location $\ell_i \in \{\text{v0}, \text{v1}, \text{SE}, \text{AC}\}$ (a node in the graph), we have a counter κ_i that stores the number of processes that are in ℓ_i. The system is parameterized in two ways: (i) in the number of processes n, the number of faults f, and the upper bound on the number of faults t, (ii) the expressions in the guards contain n, t, and f. Every transition moves all processes simultaneously; potentially using a different rule for each process (depicted by an edge in the figure), provided that the rule guards evaluate to true. The guards compare a sum of counters to a linear combination of parameters. For example, the guard $\phi_1 \equiv \#\{\text{v1}, \text{SE}, \text{AC}\} \geq t + 1 - f$ evaluates to true if the number of processes that are either in location v1, SE, or AC is greater than or equal to $t + 1 - f$.

Synchronous Threshold Automata (STA) model synchronous fault-tolerant distributed algorithms as follows. As processes send messages based on their current locations, we use the number of processes in given locations to test how many messages of a certain type have been sent. However, the pseudo code in Fig. 1 is predicated by received messages rather than by sent messages. This algorithm is designed to tolerate Byzantine-faulty processes, which may send spurious messages to some correct processes. Thus, the number of received messages may deviate from the number of correct processes that sent a message. For example, if the guard in line 7 evaluates to true, the $t + 1$ received messages may contain up to f messages from faulty processes. If i correct processes send `<ECHO>`, for $1 \leq i \leq t$, the faulty processes may "help" some correct processes to pass over the $t + 1$ threshold. In the STA, this is modeled by both the rules r_1 and r_2 being enabled. Thus, the assignment `v:=1` in line 7 is modeled by the rule

Table 1. A long execution of reliable broadcast and the short representative

Process	σ_0	σ_1	σ_2	...	σ_{t+1}	σ_{t+2}	σ_{t+3}
1	V1	SE	SE	...	SE	SE	AC
2	V0	V0	SE	...	SE	SE	AC
...				...			
$t+1$	V0	V0	V0	...	SE	SE	AC
...				...			
$n-f$	V0	V0	V0	...	V0	SE	AC

Process	σ'_0	σ'_1	σ'_2
1	V1	SE	AC
2	V0	SE	AC
...		...	
$t+1$	V0	SE	AC
...		...	
$n-f$	V0	SE	AC

r_2, guarded by ϕ_2. The implicit "else" branch between lines 7 and 8 is modeled by the rule r_1, guarded by ϕ_3. As the effect of the f faulty processes on the correct processes is captured by the guards, we model only the correct processes explicitly, so that a system consists of $n-f$ copies of the STA.

Contributions. We start by introducing synchronous threshold automata (STA) and the counter systems they define.

1. We show that parameterized reachability checking of STA is undecidable.
2. We introduce an SMT-based procedure for finding the diameter of the counter system associated with an STA, i.e., the number of steps in which every configuration of the counter system is reachable. By knowing the diameter, we use bounded model checking as a complete verification method [11,14,22].
3. For a class of STA that captures several algorithms such as the broadcast algorithm in Fig. 1, we prove that a diameter is always bounded. The diameter is a function of the number of guard expressions and the longest path in the automaton, that is, it is independent of the parameters.
4. We implemented our technique, by running Z3 [29] and CVC4 [7] as back-end SMT solvers, and evaluated it by applying it to several distributed algorithms from the literature: Benchmarks that tolerate Byzantine faults from [8–10, 32], benchmarks that tolerate crashes from [13,26,30], and benchmarks that tolerate send omissions from [10,30].
5. We are the first to automatically verify the Byzantine and send omission benchmarks. For the crash benchmarks, our method performs significantly better than the abstraction-based method in [3]. By tweaking the constraints on the parameters n, t, f, we introduce configurations with more faults than expected, for which our technique automatically finds a counterexample.

2 Overview of Our Approach

Bounded Diameter. Consider Fig. 1: the processes execute the send, receive, and local computation steps in lock-step. One iteration of the loop is expressed as an STA edge that connects the locations before and after an iteration (i.e., the STA models the loop body of the pseudo code). The location SE encodes that $\mathtt{v} = 1$ and `accept` is false. That is, SE is the location in which processes send

<ECHO> in every round. If a process sets accept to true, it goes to location AC. The location where v is 1 is encoded by V1, and the where v is 0 by V0.

An example execution is depicted in Table 1 on the left. We run $n - f$ copies of the STA in Fig. 1. Observe that the guards of the rules r_1 and r_2 are both enabled in the configuration σ_0. One STA uses r_2 to go to SE while the others use the self-loop r_1 to stay in V0. As both rules remain enabled, in every round one more automaton can go to SE. Hence, configuration σ_{t+1} has $t + 1$ correct STA in location SE and rule r_1 becomes disabled. Then, all remaining STA go to SE and then finally to AC. This execution depends on the parameter t, which implies that the length of this execution is unbounded for increasing values of the parameter t. (We note that we can obtain longer executions, if some STA use rule r_4). On the right, we see an execution where all STA take r_2 immediately. That is, while configuration σ_{t+3} is reached by a long execution on the left, it is reached in just two steps on the right (observe $\sigma'_2 = \sigma_{t+3}$). We are interested in whether there is a natural number k (which does not depend on the parameters n, t and f) such that we can always shorten executions to executions of length $\leq k$. (By length, we mean the number of transitions in an execution.) In such a case we say that the STA has *bounded diameter*. In Sect. 5.1 we introduce an SMT-based procedure that enumerates candidates for the diameter bound and checks if the candidate is indeed the diameter; if it finds such a bound, it terminates. For the STA in Fig. 1, this procedure computes the diameter 2.

Threshold Automata with Traps. In Sect. 5.2, we define a fragment of STA for which we theoretically guarantee a bounded diameter. For example, the STA in Fig. 1 falls in this fragment, and we obtain a guaranteed diameter of ≤ 8. The fragment is defined by two conditions: (i) The STA has a structure that implies monotonicity of the guards: the set of locations that are used in the guards (e.g., {V1, SE, AC}) is closed under the rules, i.e., from each location within the set, the STA can reach only a location in the set. We call guards that have this property *trapped.* (ii) The STA has no cycles, except possibly self-loops.

Bounded Model Checking, Completeness and (Un-)Decidability. The existence of a bounded diameter motivates the use of bounded model checking for verifying safety properties. In Sect. 6 we give an SMT encoding for checking the violation of a safety property by executions with length up to the diameter. Crucially, this approach is complete because if an execution reaches a bad configuration, this bad configuration is already reached by an execution of bounded length. We observe that for the STA defined in this paper (with linear guards and linear constraints on the parameters), the SMT encoding results in a Presburger arithmetic formula (with one quantifier alternation). Hence, checking safety properties (that can be expressed in Presburger arithmetic) is decidable for STA with bounded diameter. We also experimentally demonstrate in Sect. 7 that current SMT solvers can handle these quantified formulae well. On the contrary, we show in Sect. 4 that the parameterized reachability problem is undecidable for general STA. This implies that there are STA with unbounded diameter.

```
best := input_value
for each round 1 through ⌊t/k⌋+1 do {
  broadcast best;
  receive values b_1, ... b_ℓ from others;
  best := min {b_1, ... b_ℓ};
}
choose best
```

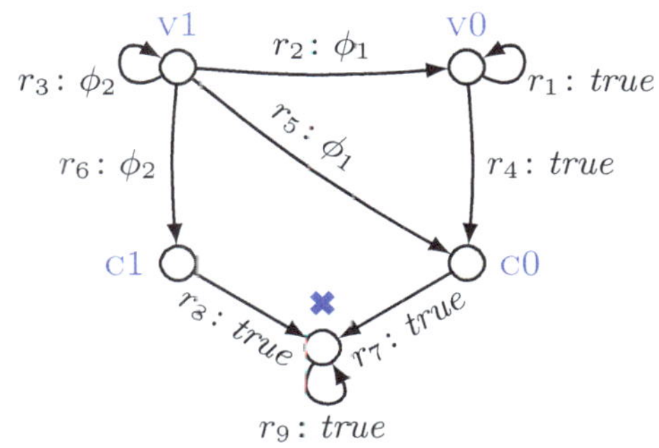

Fig. 2. Pseudo code of *FloodMin* from [13], and STA encoding its loop body, for $k = 1$, with guards: $\phi_1 \equiv \#\{\mathrm{v0}, \mathrm{c0}\} > 0$ and $\phi_2 \equiv \#\{\mathrm{v0}\} = 0$.

Threshold Automata with Untrapped Guards. The *FloodMin* algorithm in Fig. 2 solves the k-set agreement problem. This algorithm is ran by n replicated processes, up to t of which may fail by crashing. For simplicity of presentation, we consider the case when $k = 1$, which turns k-set agreement into consensus. In Fig. 2, on the right, we have the STA that captures the loop body. The locations c0 and c1 correspond to the case when a process is crashing in the current round and may manage to send the value 0 and 1 respectively; the process remains in the crashed location "✖" and does not send any messages starting with the next round. We observe that the guard $\#\{\mathrm{v0}, \mathrm{c0}\} > 0$ is not trapped, and our result about trapped guards does not apply. Nevertheless, our SMT-based procedure can find a diameter of 2. In the same way, we automatically found a bound on the diameter for several benchmarks from the literature. It is remarkable that the diameter for the transition relation of the loop body (without the loop condition) is bounded by a constant, independent of the parameters.

Bounded Model Checking of Algorithms with Clean Rounds. The number of loop iterations $\lfloor t/k \rfloor + 1$ of the *FloodMin* algorithm has been designed such that it ensures (together with the environment assumption of at most t crashes) that there is at least one *clean* round in which at most $k - 1$ processes crashed. The correctness of the *FloodMin* algorithm relies on the occurrence of such a clean round. We make use of the existence of clean rounds by employing the following two-step methodology for the verification of safety properties: (i) we find all reachable clean-round configurations, and (ii) check if a bad configuration is reachable from those configurations. Detailed description of this methodology can be found in Sect. 6. Our method requires the encoding of a clean round as input (e.g., for Fig. 2 that no STA are in c0 and c1). We leave detecting and encoding clean rounds automatically from the fault environment for future work.

3 Synchronous Threshold Automata

We introduce the syntax of synchronous threshold automata and give some intuition of the semantics, which we will formalize as counter systems below.

A *synchronous threshold automaton* is the tuple $STA = (\mathcal{L}, \mathcal{I}, \Pi, \mathcal{R}, RC, \chi)$, where $\mathcal{L}$ is a finite set of locations, $\mathcal{I} \subseteq \mathcal{L}$ is a non-empty set of initial locations, Π is a finite set of parameters, $\mathcal{R}$ is a finite set of rules, RC is a resilience condition, and χ is a counter invariant, defined in the following. We assume that the set Π of parameters contains at least the parameter n, denoting the number of processes. We call the vector $\boldsymbol{\pi} = \langle \pi_1, \ldots, \pi_{|\Pi|} \rangle$ the *parameter vector*, and a vector $\mathbf{p} = \langle p_1, \ldots, p_{|\Pi|} \rangle$ is an *instance of* $\boldsymbol{\pi}$, where $\pi_i \in \Pi$ is a parameter, and $p_i \in \mathbb{N}$ is a natural number, for $1 \leq i \leq |\Pi|$, such that $\mathbf{p}[\pi_i] = p_i$ is the value assigned to the parameter π_i in the instance $\mathbf{p}$ of $\boldsymbol{\pi}$. The set of *admissible instances of* $\boldsymbol{\pi}$ is defined as $P_{RC} = \{\mathbf{p} \in \mathbb{N}^{|\Pi|} \mid \mathbf{p}$ is an instance of $\boldsymbol{\pi}$ and $\mathbf{p}$ satisfies $RC\}$. The mapping $N : P_{RC} \to \mathbb{N}$ maps an admissible instance $\mathbf{p} \in P_{RC}$ to the number $N(\mathbf{p})$ of processes that participate in the algorithm, such that $N(\mathbf{p})$ is a linear combination of the parameter values in $\mathbf{p}$.

For example, for the STA in Fig. 1, $RC \equiv n > 3t \wedge t \geq f$, hence a vector $\mathbf{p} \in \mathbb{N}^{|\Pi|}$ is an admissible instance of the parameter vector $\boldsymbol{\pi} = \langle n, t, f \rangle$, if $\mathbf{p}[n] > 3\mathbf{p}[t] \wedge \mathbf{p}[t] \geq \mathbf{p}[f]$. Furthermore, for this STA, $N(\mathbf{p}) = \mathbf{p}[n] - \mathbf{p}[f]$. For the STA in Fig. 2, $RC \equiv n > t \wedge t \geq f$, hence the admissible instances satisfy $\mathbf{p}[n] > \mathbf{p}[t] \wedge \mathbf{p}[t] \geq \mathbf{p}[f]$, and we have $N(\mathbf{p}) = \mathbf{p}[n]$.

We introduce *counter atoms* of the form $\psi \equiv \#L \geq \boldsymbol{a} \cdot \boldsymbol{\pi} + b$, where $L \subseteq \mathcal{L}$ is a set of locations, $\#L$ denotes the total number of processes currently in the locations $\ell \in L$, $\boldsymbol{a} \in \mathbb{Z}^{|\Pi|}$ is a vector of coefficients, $\boldsymbol{\pi}$ is the parameter vector, and $b \in \mathbb{Z}$. We will use the counter atoms for expressing guards and predicates in the verification problem. In the following, we will use two abbreviations: $\#L = \boldsymbol{a} \cdot \boldsymbol{\pi} + b$ for the formula $(\#L \geq \boldsymbol{a} \cdot \boldsymbol{\pi} + b) \wedge \neg(\#L \geq \boldsymbol{a} \cdot \boldsymbol{\pi} + b + 1)$, and $\#L > \boldsymbol{a} \cdot \boldsymbol{\pi} + b$ for the formula $\#L \geq \boldsymbol{a} \cdot \boldsymbol{\pi} + b + 1$.

A *rule* $r \in \mathcal{R}$ is the tuple $(\mathit{from}, \mathit{to}, \varphi)$, where $\mathit{from}, \mathit{to} \in \mathcal{L}$ are locations, and φ is a guard whose truth value determines if the rule r is executed. The guard φ is a Boolean combination of counter atoms. We denote by Ψ the set of counter atoms occurring in the guards of the rules $r \in \mathcal{R}$.

The *counter invariant* χ is a Boolean combination of counter atoms $\#L \geq \boldsymbol{a} \cdot \boldsymbol{\pi} + b$, where each atom occurring in χ restricts the number of processes allowed to populate the locations in $L \subseteq \mathcal{L}$.

Counter Systems. The counter atoms are evaluated over tuples $(\kappa, \mathbf{p})$, where $\kappa \in \mathbb{N}^{|\mathcal{L}|}$ is a vector of *counters*, and $\mathbf{p} \in P_{RC}$ is an admissible instance of $\boldsymbol{\pi}$. For a location $\ell \in \mathcal{L}$, the counter $\kappa[\ell]$ denotes the number of processes that are currently in the location ℓ. A counter atom $\psi \equiv \#L \geq \boldsymbol{a} \cdot \boldsymbol{\pi} + b$ is *satisfied* in the tuple $(\kappa, \mathbf{p})$, that is $(\kappa, \mathbf{p}) \models \psi$, iff $\sum_{\ell \in L} \kappa[\ell] \geq \boldsymbol{a} \cdot \mathbf{p} + b$. The semantics of the Boolean connectives is standard.

A *transition* is a function $t : \mathcal{R} \to \mathbb{N}$ that maps a rule $r \in \mathcal{R}$ to a factor $t(r) \in \mathbb{N}$, denoting the number of processes that act upon this rule. Given an instance $\mathbf{p}$ of $\boldsymbol{\pi}$, we denote by $T(\mathbf{p})$ the set $\{t \mid \sum_{r \in \mathcal{R}} t(r) = N(\mathbf{p})\}$ of transitions whose rule factors sum up to $N(\mathbf{p})$.

Given a tuple $(\kappa, \mathbf{p})$ and a transition t, we say that t is *enabled* in $(\kappa, \mathbf{p})$, if

1. for every $r \in \mathcal{R}$, such that $t(r) > 0$, it holds that $(\kappa, \mathbf{p}) \models r.\varphi$, and
2. for every $\ell \in \mathcal{L}$, it holds that $\kappa[\ell] = \sum_{r \in \mathcal{R} \wedge r.\mathit{from} = \ell} t(r)$.

The first condition ensures that processes only use rules whose guards are satisfied, and the second that every process moves in an enabled transition.

Observe that each transition $t \in T(\mathbf{p})$ defines a unique tuple $(\kappa, \mathbf{p})$ in which it is enabled. We call the *origin* of a transition $t \in T(\mathbf{p})$ the tuple $o(t) = (\kappa, \mathbf{p})$, such that for every $\ell \in \mathcal{L}$, we have $o(t).\kappa[\ell] = \sum_{r \in \mathcal{R} \wedge r.from=\ell} t(r)$. Similarly, each transition defines a unique tuple $(\kappa, \mathbf{p})$ that is the result of applying the transition in its origin. We call the *goal* of a transition $t \in T(\mathbf{p})$ the tuple $g(t) = (\kappa, \mathbf{p})$, such that for every $\ell \in \mathcal{L}$, we have $g(t).\kappa[\ell] = \sum_{r \in \mathcal{R} \wedge r.to=\ell} t(r)$.

We now define a counter system, for a given $STA = (\mathcal{L}, \mathcal{I}, \Pi, \mathcal{R}, RC, \chi)$, and an admissible instance $\mathbf{p} \in P_{RC}$ of the parameter vector $\boldsymbol{\pi}$.

Definition 1. *A* counter system *w.r.t.* $STA = (\mathcal{L}, \mathcal{I}, \Pi, \mathcal{R}, RC, \chi)$ *and an admissible instance* $\mathbf{p} \in P_{RC}$ *is the tuple* $\mathsf{CS}(STA, \mathbf{p}) = (\Sigma(\mathbf{p}), I(\mathbf{p}), R(\mathbf{p}))$, *where*

- $\Sigma(\mathbf{p}) = \{\sigma = (\kappa, \mathbf{p}) \mid \sum_{\ell \in \mathcal{L}} \sigma.\kappa[\ell] = N(\mathbf{p})$ *and* $\sigma \models \chi\}$ *are the configurations;*
- $I(\mathbf{p}) = \{\sigma \in \Sigma(\mathbf{p}) \mid \sum_{\ell \in \mathcal{I}} \sigma.\kappa[\ell] = N(\mathbf{p})\}$ *are the initial configurations;*
- $R(\mathbf{p}) \subseteq \Sigma(\mathbf{p}) \times T(\mathbf{p}) \times \Sigma(\mathbf{p})$ *is the transition relation, with* $\langle \sigma, t, \sigma' \rangle \in R(\mathbf{p})$, *if* σ *is the origin and* σ' *the goal of* t. *We write* $\sigma \xrightarrow{t} \sigma'$, *if* $\langle \sigma, t, \sigma' \rangle \in R(\mathbf{p})$.

We restrict ourselves to deadlock-free counter systems, i.e., counter systems where the transition relation is total (every configuration has a successor). A sufficient condition for deadlock-freedom is that for every location $\ell \in \mathcal{L}$, it holds that $\chi \rightarrow \bigvee_{r \in \mathcal{R} \wedge r.from=\ell} r.\varphi$. This ensures that it is always possible to move out of every location, as there is at least one outgoing rule per location whose guard is satisfied.

To simplify the notation, in the following we write $\sigma[\ell]$ to denote $\sigma.\kappa[\ell]$.

Paths and Schedules in a Counter System. We now define paths and schedules of a counter system, as sequences of configurations and transitions, respectively.

Definition 2. *A* path *in the counter system* $\mathsf{CS}(STA, \mathbf{p}) = (\Sigma(\mathbf{p}), I(\mathbf{p}), R(\mathbf{p}))$ *is a finite sequence* $\{\sigma_i\}_{i=0}^k$ *of configurations, such that for every two consecutive configurations* σ_{i-1}, σ_i, *for* $0 < i \leq k$, *there exists a transition* $t_i \in T(\mathbf{p})$ *such that* $\sigma_{i-1} \xrightarrow{t_i} \sigma_i$. *A path* $\{\sigma_i\}_{i=0}^k$ *is called an* execution *if* $\sigma_0 \in I(\mathbf{p})$.

Definition 3. *A* schedule *is a finite sequence* $\tau = \{t_i\}_{i=1}^k$ *of transitions* $t_i \in T(\mathbf{p})$, *for* $0 < i \leq k$. *We denote by* $|\tau| = k$ *the length of the schedule* τ.

A schedule $\tau = \{t_i\}_{i=1}^k$ *is* feasible *if there is a path* $\{\sigma_i\}_{i=0}^k$ *such that* $\sigma_{i-1} \xrightarrow{t_i} \sigma_i$, *for* $0 < i \leq k$. *We call* σ_0 *the* origin, *and* σ_k *the* goal *of* τ, *and write* $\sigma_0 \xrightarrow{\tau} \sigma_k$.

4 Parameterized Reachability and Its Undecidability

We show that the following problem is undecidable in general, by reduction from the halting problem of a two-counter machine (2CM) [28]. Such reductions are common in parameterized verification, e.g., see [12].

Definition 4 (Parameterized Reachability). *Given a formula φ, that is, a Boolean combination of counter atoms, and $STA = (\mathcal{L}, \mathcal{I}, \Pi, \mathcal{R}, RC, \chi)$, the* parameterized reachability *problem is to decide whether there exists an admissible instance $\mathbf{p} \in P_{RC}$, such that in the counter system $\mathsf{CS}(STA, \mathbf{p})$, there is an initial configuration $\sigma \in I(\mathbf{p})$, and a feasible schedule τ, with $\sigma \xrightarrow{\tau} \sigma'$ and $\sigma' \models \varphi$.*

To prove undecidability, we construct a synchronous threshold automaton $STA_{\mathcal{M}}$, such that every counter system induced by it simulates the steps of a 2CM executing a program P. The STA has a single parameter – the number n of processes, and the invariant $\chi = true$. The idea is that each process plays one of two roles: either it is used to encode the control flow of the program P (*controller* role), or to encode the values of the registers in unary, as in [17] (*storage* role). Thus, $STA_{\mathcal{M}}$ consists of two parts – one per each role.

Our construction allows multiple processes to act as controllers. Since we assume that 2CM is deterministic, all the controllers behave the same. For each instruction of the program P, in the controller part of $STA_{\mathcal{M}}$, there is a single location (for 'jump if zero' and 'halt') or a pair of locations (for 'increment' and 'decrement'), and a special *stuck* location. In the storage part of $STA_{\mathcal{M}}$, there is a location for each register, a store location, and auxiliary locations. The number of processes in a register location encodes the value of the register in 2CM.

An increment (resp. decrement) of a register is modeled by moving one process from (resp. to) the store location to (resp. from) the register location. The guards on the rules in the controller part check if the storage processes made a transition that truly models a step of 2CM; in this case, the controllers move on to the next location, otherwise they move to the stuck location. For example, to model a 'jump if zero' for register A, the controllers check if $\#\{\ell_A\} = 0$, where ℓ_A is the storage location corresponding to register A. The main invariant which ensures correctness is that every transition in every counter system induced by $STA_{\mathcal{M}}$ either faithfully simulates a step of the 2CM, or moves all of the controllers to the stuck location.

Let ℓ_{halt} be the halting location in the controller part of $STA_{\mathcal{M}}$. The formula $\varphi \equiv \neg(\#\{\ell_{halt}\} = 0)$ states that the controllers have reached the halting location. Thus, the answer to the parameterized reachability question given the formula φ and $STA_{\mathcal{M}}$ is positive iff 2CM halts, which gives us undecidability.

5 Bounded Diameter Oracle

5.1 Computing the Diameter Using SMT

Given an STA, the diameter is the maximal number of transitions needed to reach all possible configurations in every counter system induced by the STA, and an admissible instance $\mathbf{p} \in P_{RC}$. We adapt the definition of diameter from [11].

Definition 5 (Diameter). *Given an $STA = (\mathcal{L}, \mathcal{I}, \Pi, \mathcal{R}, RC, \chi)$, the* diameter *is the smallest number d such that for every $\mathbf{p} \in P_{RC}$ and every path $\{\sigma_i\}_{i=0}^{d+1}$*

of length $d+1$ *in* $\mathsf{CS}(STA, \mathbf{p})$*, there exists a path* $\{\sigma'_j\}_{j=0}^{e}$ *of length* $e \le d$ *in* $\mathsf{CS}(STA, \mathbf{p})$*, such that* $\sigma_0 = \sigma'_0$ *and* $\sigma_{d+1} = \sigma'_e$*.*

Thus, the diameter is the smallest number d that satisfies the formula:

$$\forall \mathbf{p} \in P_{RC}. \forall \sigma_0, \ldots, \sigma_{d+1}. \forall t_1, \ldots, t_{d+1}. \exists \sigma'_0, \ldots, \sigma'_d. \exists t'_1, \ldots, t'_d.$$
$$Path(\sigma_0, \sigma_{d+1}, d+1) \rightarrow (\sigma_0 = \sigma'_0) \wedge Path(\sigma'_0, \sigma'_d, d) \wedge \bigvee_{i=0}^{d} \sigma'_i = \sigma_{d+1} \quad (1)$$

where $Path(\sigma_0, \sigma_d, d)$ is a shorthand for the formula $\bigwedge_{i=0}^{d-1} R(\sigma_i, t_{i+1}, \sigma_{i+1})$, and $R(\sigma, t, \sigma')$ is a predicate which evaluates to true whenever $\sigma \xrightarrow{t} \sigma'$. Since we assume deadlock-freedom, we are able to encode the path $Path(\sigma'_0, \sigma'_d, d)$ of length d, even if the disjunction $\bigvee_{i=0}^{d} \sigma'_i = \sigma_{d+1}$ holds for some $i \le d$.

Formula (1) gives us the following procedure to determine the diameter:

1. initialize the candidate diameter d to 1;
2. check if the negation of the formula (1) is unsatisfiable;
3. if yes, then output d and terminate;
4. if not, then increment d and jump to step 2.

If the procedure terminates, it outputs the diameter, which can be used as completeness threshold for bounded model checking. We implemented this procedure, and used a back-end SMT solver to automate the test in step 2.

5.2 Bounded Diameter for a Fragment of STA

In this section, we show that for a specific fragment of STA, we are able to give a theoretical bound on the diameter, similar to the asynchronous case [20,21].

The STA that fall in this fragment are *monotonic* and *1-cyclic*. An STA is monotonic iff every counter atom changes its truth value at most once in every path of a counter system induced by the STA and an admissible instance $\mathbf{p} \in P_{RC}$. This implies that every schedule can be partitioned into finitely many sub-schedules, that satisfy a property we call *steadiness*. We call a schedule *steady* if the set of rules whose guards are satisfied does not change in all of its transitions. We also give a sufficient condition for monotonicity, using *trapped* counter atoms, defined below. In a 1-cyclic STA, the only cycles that can be formed by its rules are self-loops. Under these two conditions, we guarantee that for every steady schedule, there exists a steady schedule of bounded length, that has the same origin and goal. We show that this bound depends on the counter atoms Ψ occurring in the guards of the STA, and the length of the longest path in the STA, denoted by c. The main result of this section is stated by the theorem:

Theorem 1. *For every feasible schedule* τ *in a counter system* $\mathsf{CS}(STA, \mathbf{p})$*, where STA is monotonic and 1-cyclic, and* $\mathbf{p} \in P_{RC}$*, there exists a feasible schedule* τ' *of length* $O(|\Psi|c)$*, such that* τ *and* τ' *have the same origin and goal.*

To prove Theorem 1, we start by defining monotonic STA.

Definition 6 (Monotonic STA). *An automaton* $STA = (\mathcal{L}, \mathcal{I}, \Pi, \mathcal{R}, RC, \chi)$ *is monotonic iff for every path* $\{\sigma_i\}_{i=0}^k$ *in the counter system* $\mathsf{CS}(STA, \mathbf{p})$*, for* $\mathbf{p} \in P_{RC}$*, and every counter atom* $\psi \in \Psi$*, we have* $\sigma_i \models \psi$ *implies* $\sigma_j \models \psi$*, for* $0 \le i < j < k$.

To show that we can partition a schedule into finitely many sub-schedules, we need the notion of a context. A *context* of a transition $t \in T(\mathbf{p})$ is the set $\mathcal{C}_t = \{\psi \in \Psi \mid o(t) \models \psi\}$ of counter atoms ψ satisfied in the origin $o(t)$ of the transition t. Given a feasible schedule τ, the point i is a *context switch*, if $\mathcal{C}_{t_{i-1}} \neq \mathcal{C}_{t_i}$, for $1 < i \le |\tau|$.

Lemma 1. *Every feasible schedule* τ *in a counter system induced by a monotonic STA has at most* $|\Psi|$ *context switches.*

Proof. Let $\tau = \{t_i\}_{i=1}^k$ be a feasible schedule and Ψ the set of counter atoms appearing on the rules of the monotonic STA. For every $\psi \in \Psi$, there is at most one context switch i, for $0 < i \le k$, such that $\psi \notin \mathcal{C}_{t_{i-1}}$ and $\psi \in \mathcal{C}_{t_i}$. □

Sufficient Condition for Monotonicity. We introduce trapped counter atoms.

Definition 7. *A set* $L \subseteq \mathcal{L}$ *of locations is called a* trap*, iff for every* $\ell \in L$ *and every* $r \in \mathcal{R}$ *such that* $\ell = r.from$*, it holds that* $r.to \in L$.

A counter atom $\psi \equiv \#L \ge \boldsymbol{a} \cdot \boldsymbol{\pi} + b$ *is* trapped *iff the set* L *is a trap.*

Lemma 2. *Let* $\psi \equiv \#L \ge \boldsymbol{a} \cdot \boldsymbol{\pi} + b$ *be a trapped counter atom,* σ *a configuration such that* $\sigma \models \psi$*, and* t *a transition enabled in* σ*. If* $\sigma \xrightarrow{t} \sigma'$*, then* $\sigma' \models \psi$.

Corollary 1. *Let* $STA = (\mathcal{L}, \mathcal{I}, \Pi, \mathcal{R}, RC, \chi)$ *be an automaton such that all its counter atoms are trapped. Then STA is monotonic.*

Steady Schedules. We define the notion of steadiness, similarly to [20].

Definition 8. *A schedule* $\tau = \{t_i\}_{i=1}^k$ *is* steady*, if* $\mathcal{C}_{t_i} = \mathcal{C}_{t_j}$*, for* $0 < i < j \le k$.

We now focus on shortening steady schedules. That is, given a steady schedule, we construct a schedule of bounded length with the same origin and goal.

Observe that $STA = (\mathcal{L}, \mathcal{I}, \Pi, \mathcal{R}, RC, \chi)$ can be seen as a directed graph G_{STA}, with vertices corresponding to the locations $\ell \in \mathcal{L}$, and edges corresponding to the rules $r \in \mathcal{R}$. We denote by c the length of the longest path between two nodes in the graph G_{STA}, and call it the *longest chain* of STA. If G_{STA} contains only cycles of length one, then STA is called *1-cyclic*.

To shorten steady schedules, in addition to monotonicity, we require that the STA are also 1-cyclic. In the following, we assume that the schedules we shorten come from counter systems induced by monotonic and 1-cyclic STA. Intuitively, if a given schedule is longer than the longest chain of the STA, then in some transition of the schedule some processes followed a rule which is a self-loop. As processes may follow self-loops at different transitions, we cannot shorten the given schedule by eliminating transitions as a whole. Instead, we deconstruct the original schedule into sequences of process steps, which we call *runs*, shorten the runs, and reconstruct a new shorter schedule from the shortened runs. The main challenge is to show that the newly obtained schedule is feasible and steady.

Schedules as Multisets of Runs. We proceed by defining runs and showing that each schedule can be represented by a multiset of runs.

We call a *run* the sequence $\varrho = \{r_i\}_{i=1}^{k}$ of rules, for $r_i \in \mathcal{R}$, such that $r_i.to = r_{i+1}.from$, for $0 < i < k$. We denote by $\varrho[i] = r_i$ the i-th rule in the run ϱ, and by $|\varrho|$ the length of the run. The following lemma shows that a feasible schedule can be deconstructed into a multiset of runs.

Lemma 3. *For every feasible schedule* $\tau = \{t_i\}_{i=1}^{k}$, *there exists a multiset* $(\mathcal{P}, m)$, *where*

1. $\mathcal{P}$ *is a set of runs* ϱ *of length* k, *and*
2. $m : \mathcal{P} \to \mathbb{N}$ *is a multiplicity function, such that for every location* $\ell \in \mathcal{L}$, *it holds that* $\sum_{r.from=\ell} t_i(r) = \sum_{\varrho[i].from=\ell} m(\varrho)$, *for* $0 < i \leq k$.

A multiset $(\mathcal{P}, m)$ of runs of length k defines a schedule $\tau = \{t_i\}_{i=1}^{k}$ of length k, and we have $t_i(r) = \sum_{\varrho[i]=r} m(\varrho)$, for every rule $r \in \mathcal{R}$ and $0 < i \leq k$.

For the counter systems of STA, which are both monotonic and 1-cyclic, we show that their steady schedules can be shortened, so that their length does not exceed the longest chain c (that is, the length of the longest path in the STA).

Lemma 4. *Let* τ *be a steady feasible schedule in a counter system induced by a monotonic and 1-cyclic STA. If* $|\tau| > c + 1$, *then there exists a steady feasible schedule* τ' *such such that* $|\tau'| = |\tau| - 1$, *and* τ, τ' *have the same origin and goal.*

Proof (Sketch). If $\tau = \{t_i\}_{i=1}^{k+1}$, with $|\tau| = k + 1 > c + 1$, is a steady schedule, then $\mathcal{C}_{t_1} = \mathcal{C}_{t_k}$, and its prefix $\theta = \{t_i\}_{i=1}^{k}$ is a steady and feasible schedule, with $k > c$. By Lemma 3, there is a multiset $(\mathcal{P}, m)$ of runs of length k describing θ. Since $k > c$, and c is the longest chain in the STA, which is 1-cyclic, it must be the case that every run in $\mathcal{P}$ contains at least one self-loop. Construct a new multiset $(\mathcal{P}', m')$ of runs of length $k - 1$, such that each $\varrho' \in \mathcal{P}'$ is obtained by some $\varrho \in \mathcal{P}$ by removing one occurrence of a self-loop rule. The multiset $(\mathcal{P}', m')$ defines the schedule $\theta' = \{t'_1\}_{i=1}^{k-1}$. Because of the monotonicity and steadiness of θ, and because we only remove self-loops (which go from and to the same location) when we build θ' from θ, the feasibility is preserved, that is, it holds that $g(t'_{i-1}) = o(t'_i)$, for $1 < i < k$, and that no guards false in θ become true in θ'. Furthermore, it is easy to check that θ' has the same origin and goal as θ. As the goal of θ' is the origin of t_{k+1}, construct a schedule $\tau' = \{t'_i\}_{i=1}^{k}$, where $t'_k = t_{k+1}$. As τ is steady, the transitions t_1 and t_{k+1} have the same contexts. From $o(t_1) = o(t'_1)$ and $o(t_{k+1}) = o(t'_k)$, we get that t'_1 and t'_k have the same contexts, which, together with the monotonicity, implies that τ' is steady. □

As a consequence of Lemmas 1 and 4, we obtain Theorem 1, which tells us that for any feasible schedule, there exists a feasible schedule of length $O(|\Psi|c)$. This bound does not depend on the parameters, but on the number of context switches and the longest chain c, which are properties of the STA.

6 Bounded Model Checking of Safety Properties

Once we obtain the diameter bound d (either using the procedure from Sect. 5.1, or by Theorem 1), we use it as a completeness threshold for bounded model checking. For the algorithms that we verify, we express the violations of their safety properties as reachability queries on bounded executions. The length of the bounded executions depends on d, and on whether the algorithm was designed such that it is assumed that there is a clean round in every execution.

Checking Safety for Algorithms that do not Assume a Clean Round. Here, we search for violations of safety properties in executions of length $e \leq d$, by checking satisfiability of the formula:

$$\exists \mathbf{p} \in P_{RC}. \exists \sigma_0, \ldots, \sigma_e. \exists t_1, \ldots, t_e.\ \mathit{Init}(\sigma_0) \wedge \mathit{Path}(\sigma_0, \sigma_e, e) \wedge \mathit{Bad}(\sigma_e) \quad (2)$$

where the predicate $\mathit{Init}(\sigma)$ encodes that σ is an initial configuration, together with the constraints imposed on the initial configuration by the safety property, and $\mathit{Bad}(\sigma)$ encodes the bad configuration, which, if reachable, violates safety.

For example, the algorithm in Fig. 1 has to satisfy the safety property *unforgeability*: If no process sets `v` to 1 initially, then no process ever sets `accept` to true. In our encoding, we check executions of length $e \leq d$, whose initial configuration has the counter $\kappa[\text{V1}] = 0$. In a bad configuration, the counter $\kappa[\text{AC}] > 0$. Thus, to find violations of unforgeability, in formula (2), we set:

$$\begin{aligned} \mathit{Init}(\sigma_0) &\equiv \sigma_0[\text{V0}] + \sigma_0[\text{V1}] = N(\mathbf{p}) \wedge \sigma_0[\text{V1}] = 0 \\ \mathit{Bad}(\sigma_e) &\equiv \sigma_e[\text{AC}] > 0 \end{aligned}$$

Checking Safety for Algorithms with a Clean Round. We check for violations of safety in executions of length $e \leq 2d$, where $e = e_1 + e_2$ such that: (i) we find all reachable clean-round configurations in an execution of length e_1, for $e_1 \leq d$, such that the last configuration σ_{e_1} satisfies the clean round condition, and (ii) we check if a bad configuration is reachable from σ_{e_1} by a path of length $e_2 \leq d$. That is, we check satisfiability of the formula:

$$\begin{aligned} \exists \mathbf{p} \in P_{RC}. \exists \sigma_0, \ldots, \sigma_e. \exists t_1, \ldots, t_e.\ & \mathit{Init}(\sigma_0) \wedge \mathit{Path}(\sigma_0, \sigma_{e_1}, e_1) \\ & \wedge \mathit{Clean}(\sigma_{e_1}) \wedge \mathit{Path}(\sigma_{e_1}, \sigma_e, e_2) \wedge \mathit{Bad}(\sigma_e) \quad (3) \end{aligned}$$

where the predicate $\mathit{Clean}(\sigma)$ encodes the clean round condition.

For example, one of the safety properties that the *FloodMin* algorithm for $k = 1$ (Fig. 2) has to satisfy, is *k-agreement*, which requires that at most k different values are decided. In the original algorithm, the processes decide after $\lfloor t/k \rfloor + 1$ rounds, such that at least one of them is the clean round, in which at most $k - 1$ processes crash. In our encoding, we check paths of length $e \leq 2d$. We enforce the clean round condition by asserting that the sum of counters of the locations $\text{C0}, \text{C1}$ are $k - 1 = 0$ in the configuration σ_{e_1}. The property

1-agreement is violated if in the last configuration both the counters $\kappa[\text{V0}]$ and $\kappa[\text{V1}]$ are non-zero. That is, to check 1-agreement, in formula (3) we set:

$$\begin{aligned} Init(\sigma_0) &\equiv \sigma_0[\text{V0}] + \sigma_0[\text{V1}] + \sigma_0[\text{C0}] + \sigma_0[\text{C1}] = N(\mathbf{p}) \\ Clean(\sigma_{e_1}) &\equiv \sigma_{e_1}[\text{C0}] + \sigma_{e_1}[\text{C1}] = 0 \\ Bad(\sigma_e) &\equiv \sigma_e[\text{V0}] > 0 \wedge \sigma_e[\text{V1}] > 0 \end{aligned}$$

7 Experimental Evaluation

The algorithms that we model using STA and verify by bounded model checking are designed for different fault models, which in our case are crashes, send omissions or Byzantine faults. We now proceed by introducing our benchmarks. Their encodings, together with the implementations of the procedures for finding the diameter and applying bounded model checking are available at [1].

Algorithms without a Clean Round Assumption. We consider three variants of the synchronous reliable broadcast algorithm, whose STA are monotonic and 1-cyclic (i.e., Theorem 1 applies). These algorithms assume different fault models:

- `rb`, [31] (Fig. 1): reliable broadcast with at most t Byzantine faults;
- `rb_hybrid`, [10]: reliable broadcast with at most t hybrid faults: at most b Byzantine and at most s send omissions, with $t = b + s$;
- `rb_omit`, [10]: reliable broadcast with at most t send omissions.

Algorithms with a Clean Round. We encode several algorithms from this class, that solve the consensus or k-set agreement problem:

- `fair_cons` [30], `floodset` [26]: consensus with crash faults;
- `floodmin`, for $k \in \{1, 2\}$ [26] (Fig. 2): k-set agreement with crash faults;
- `kset_omit`, for $k \in \{1, 2\}$ [30]: k-set agreement with send omission faults;
- `phase_king` [8,9], `phase_queen` [8]: consensus with Byzantine faults.

These algorithms have a structure similar to the one depicted in Fig. 2, with the exception of `phase_king` and `phase_queen`. Their loop body consists of several message exchange steps, which correspond to multiple rounds, grouped in a *phase*. In each phase, a designated process acts as a coordinator.

Computing the Diameter. We implemented the procedure from Sect. 5.1 in Python. The implementation uses a back-end SMT solver (currently, `z3` and `cvc4`). Our tool computed diameter bounds for all of our benchmarks, even for those for which we do not have a theoretical guarantee. Our experiments reveal extremely low values for the diameter, that range between 1 and 4. The values for the diameter and the time needed to compute them are presented in Table 2.

Table 2. Results for our benchmarks, available at [1]: $|\mathcal{L}|$, $|\mathcal{R}|$, $|\Psi|$, *RC* are the number of locations, rules, atomic guards, and resilience condition in each STA; d is the diameter computed using SMT, c is the longest chain of the algorithms whose STA are monotonic and 1-cyclic; τ is the time (in seconds) to compute the diameter using SMT; T, *SMT* is the time to check reachability using the diameter computed using the SMT procedure from Sect. 5.1; T, *Theorem* 1 the time to check reachability using the bound obtained by Theorem 1. For the cases where Theorem 1 is not applicable, we write (–). The experiments were run on a machine with Intel(R) Core(TM) i5-4210U CPU and 4GB of RAM, using `z3-4.8.1` and `cvc4-1.6`.

algorithm	$\|\mathcal{L}\|$	$\|\mathcal{R}\|$	$\|\Psi\|$	*RC*	d	τ		T, *SMT*		c	T, *Thm. 1*	
						`z3`	`cvc4`	`z3`	`cvc4`		`z3`	`cvc4`
`rb`	4	8	4	$n > 3t$	2	0.27	0.99	0.08	0.08	2	0.42	0.86
`rb_hybrid`	8	16	4	$n > 3b + 2s$	2	1.16	37.6	0.09	0.15	2	0.67	1.73
`rb_omit`	8	16	4	$n > 2t$	2	0.43	2.47	0.09	0.14	2	0.58	1.43
`fair_cons`	11	20	2	$n > t$	2	0.97	10.9	0.27	0.47	–	–	–
`floodmin`, $k = 1$	5	9	2	$n > t$	2	0.21	0.86	0.18	0.29	–	–	–
`floodmin`, $k = 2$	7	16	4	$n > t$	2	0.53	7.43	0.22	0.52	–	–	–
`floodset`	7	14	4	$n > t$	2	0.36	3.01	0.21	0.49	–	–	–
`kset_omit`, $k = 1$	4	6	2	$n > t$	1	0.08	0.09	0.04	0.03	–	–	–
`kset_omit`, $k = 2$	6	12	4	$n > t$	1	0.17	0.27	0.04	0.07	–	–	–
`phase_king`	34	72	12	$n > 3t$	4	12.9	50.5	1.41	5.12	–	–	–
`phase_queen`	24	42	8	$n > 4t$	3	1.78	17.7	0.36	1.92	–	–	–

Checking the Algorithms. We have implemented another Python function which encodes violations of the safety properties as reachability properties on paths of bounded length, as described in Sect. 6, and uses a back-end SMT solver to check their satisfiability. Table 2 contains the results that we obtained by checking reachability for our benchmarks, using the diameter bound computed using the procedure from Sect. 5.1, and diameter bound from Theorem 1, for algorithms whose STA are monotonic and 1-cyclic.

To our knowledge, we are the first to verify the listed algorithms that work with send omission, Byzantine and hybrid faults. For the algorithms with crash faults, our approach is a significant improvement to the results obtained using the abstraction-based method from [3].

Counterexamples. Our tool found a bug in the version of the `phase_king` algorithm that was given in [8], which was corrected in the version of the algorithm in [9]. The version from [8] had the wrong threshold '$> n - t$' in one guard, while the one in [9] had '$\geq n - t$' for the same guard. To test our tool, we produced erroneous encodings for our benchmarks, and checked them. For `rb`, `rb_hybrid`, `rb_omit`, `phase_king`, and `phase_queen`, we tweaked the resilience condition, and introduced more faults than expected by the algorithm, e.g., by setting $f > t$ (instead of $f \leq t$) in the STA in Fig. 1. For `fair_cons`, `floodmin`, `floodset`, and `kset_omit`, we checked executions without a clean round. For all of the erroneous encodings, our tool produces counterexamples in seconds.

8 Discussion and Related Work

Parameterized verification of synchronous and partially synchronous distributed algorithms has recently gained attention. Both models have in common that distributed computations are organized in rounds and processes (conceptually) move in lock-step. For partially synchronous consensus algorithms, the authors of [15] introduced a consensus logic and (semi-)decision procedures. Later, the authors of [27] introduced a language for partially synchronous consensus algorithms, and proved cut-off theorems specialized to the properties of consensus: agreement, validity, and termination. Concerning synchronous algorithms, the authors of [3] introduced an abstraction-based model checking technique for crash-tolerant synchronous algorithms with existential guards. In contrast to their work, we allow more general guards that contain linear expressions over the parameters, e.g., $n - t$. Our method offers more automation, and our experimental evaluation shows that our technique is faster than the technique [3].

We introduce a *synchronous* variant of threshold automata, which were proposed in [21] for asynchronous algorithms. Several extensions of this model were recently studied in [23], but the synchronous case was not considered. STA extend the guarded protocols by [16], in which a process can check only if a sum of counters is different from 0 or n. Generalizing the results from [16] to STA is not straightforward. In [2], safety of finite-state transition systems over infinite data domains was reduced to backwards reachability checking using a fixpoint computation, as long as the transition systems are well-structured. It would be interesting to put our results in this context. A decidability result for liveness properties of parameterized timed networks was obtained in [4], employing linear programming for the analysis of vector addition systems with a parametric initial state. We plan to investigate the use of similar ideas for analyzing liveness properties of STA.

The 1-cyclicity condition is reminiscent of flat counter automata [25]. In Fig. 3, we show a possible translation of an STA to a counter automaton (similar to the translation for asynchronous threshold automata from [23]). We note

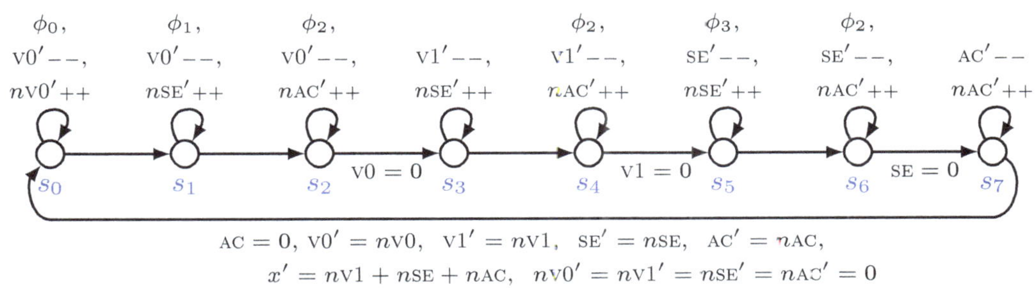

Fig. 3. A counter automaton for the STA in Fig. 1, with $\phi_0 \equiv x < t+1$, $\phi_1 \equiv x + f \geq t+1$, $\phi_2 \equiv x + f \geq n - t$, $\phi_3 \equiv x < n - t$, where x counts the number of processes in locations $\text{V1}, \text{SE}, \text{AC}$; and n, t, f are counters for the parameters. On a path from s_0 to s_7, the counters $\ell \in \{\text{V0}, \text{V1}, \text{SE}, \text{AC}\}$ are emptied, while the counters $n\ell$ are populated. This models the transitions from one location to another in the current round.

that the counter automaton is not flat, due to the presence of the outer loop, which models a transition to the next round. By knowing a bound d on the diameter (e.g., by Theorem 1), one can flatten the counter automaton by unfolding the outer loop d times. We also experimented with FAST [6] on two of our benchmarks: `rb` and `floodmin` for $k = 1$, depicted in Figs. 1 and 2 respectively. FAST terminated on `rb`, but took significantly longer than our tool on the same machine (i.e., hours rather than seconds). FAST ran out of memory when checking `floodmin`.

Our experiments show that STA that are neither monotonic, nor 1-cyclic still may have bounded diameters. Finding other classes of STA for which one could derive the diameter bounds is a subject of future work. Although we considered only reachability properties in this work—which happened to be challenging—we are going to investigate completeness thresholds for liveness in the future.

References

1. Experiments. https://github.com/istoilkovska/syncTA
2. Abdulla, P.A., Cerans, K., Jonsson, B., Tsay, Y.: General decidability theorems for infinite-state systems. In: LICS, pp. 313–321 (1996)
3. Aminof, B., Rubin, S., Stoilkovska, I., Widder, J., Zuleger, F.: Parameterized model checking of synchronous distributed algorithms by abstraction. In: Dillig, I., Palsberg, J. (eds.) Verification, Model Checking, and Abstract Interpretation. LNCS, vol. 10747, pp. 1–24. Springer, Cham (2018). https://doi.org/10.1007/978-3-319-73721-8_1
4. Aminof, B., Rubin, S., Zuleger, F., Spegni, F.: Liveness of parameterized timed networks. In: Halldórsson, M.M., Iwama, K., Kobayashi, N., Speckmann, B. (eds.) ICALP 2015. LNCS, vol. 9135, pp. 375–387. Springer, Heidelberg (2015). https://doi.org/10.1007/978-3-662-47666-6_30
5. Attiya, H., Welch, J.: Distributed Computing, 2nd edn. Wiley, Hoboken (2004)
6. Bardin, S., Leroux, J., Point, G.: FAST extended release. In: Ball, T., Jones, R.B. (eds.) CAV 2006. LNCS, vol. 4144, pp. 63–66. Springer, Heidelberg (2006). https://doi.org/10.1007/11817963_9
7. Barrett, C., et al.: CVC4. In: Gopalakrishnan, G., Qadeer, S. (eds.) CAV 2011. LNCS, vol. 6806, pp. 171–177. Springer, Heidelberg (2011). https://doi.org/10.1007/978-3-642-22110-1_14
8. Berman, P., Garay, J.A., Perry, K.J.: Asymptotically optimal distributed consensus. Technical report, Bell Labs (1989). http://plan9.bell-labs.co/who/garay/asopt.ps
9. Berman, P., Garay, J.A., Perry, K.J.: Towards optimal distributed consensus (extended abstract). In: FOCS, pp. 410–415 (1989)
10. Biely, M., Schmid, U., Weiss, B.: Synchronous consensus under hybrid process and link failures. Theor. Comput. Sci. **412**(40), 5602–5630 (2011)
11. Biere, A., Cimatti, A., Clarke, E.M., Zhu, Y.: Symbolic model checking without BDDs. In: Cleaveland, W.R. (ed.) TACAS 1999. LNCS, vol. 1579, pp. 193–207. Springer, Heidelberg (1999). https://doi.org/10.1007/3-540-49059-0_14
12. Bloem, R., et al.: Decidability of Parameterized Verification. Synthesis Lectures on Distributed Computing Theory. Morgan & Claypool Publishers (2015)

13. Chaudhuri, S., Herlihy, M., Lynch, N.A., Tuttle, M.R.: Tight bounds for k-set agreement. J. ACM **47**(5), 912–943 (2000)
14. Clarke, E.M., Kroening, D., Ouaknine, J., Strichman, O.: Completeness and complexity of bounded model checking. In: Steffen, B., Levi, G. (eds.) VMCAI 2004. LNCS, vol. 2937, pp. 85–96. Springer, Heidelberg (2004). https://doi.org/10.1007/978-3-540-24622-0_9
15. Drăgoi, C., Henzinger, T.A., Veith, H., Widder, J., Zufferey, D.: A logic-based framework for verifying consensus algorithms. In: McMillan, K.L., Rival, X. (eds.) VMCAI 2014. LNCS, vol. 8318, pp. 161–181. Springer, Heidelberg (2014). https://doi.org/10.1007/978-3-642-54013-4_10
16. Emerson, E.A., Namjoshi, K.S.: Automatic verification of parameterized synchronous systems. In: Alur, R., Henzinger, T.A. (eds.) CAV 1996. LNCS, vol. 1102, pp. 87–98. Springer, Heidelberg (1996). https://doi.org/10.1007/3-540-61474-5_60
17. Emerson, E.A., Namjoshi, K.S.: On reasoning about rings. Int. J. Found. Comput. Sci. **14**(4), 527–550 (2003)
18. Fischer, M.J., Lynch, N.A., Paterson, M.S.: Impossibility of distributed consensus with one faulty process. J. ACM **32**(2), 374–382 (1985)
19. Konnov, I., Lazić, M., Veith, H., Widder, J.: A short counterexample property for safety and liveness verification of fault-tolerant distributed algorithms. In: POPL, pp. 719–734 (2017)
20. Konnov, I., Veith, H., Widder, J.: SMT and POR beat counter abstraction: parameterized model checking of threshold-based distributed algorithms. In: Kroening, D., Păsăreanu, C.S. (eds.) CAV 2015. LNCS, vol. 9206, pp. 85–102. Springer, Cham (2015). https://doi.org/10.1007/978-3-319-21690-4_6
21. Konnov, I.V., Veith, H., Widder, J.: On the completeness of bounded model checking for threshold-based distributed algorithms: reachability. Inf. Comput. **252**, 95–109 (2017)
22. Kroening, D., Strichman, O.: Efficient computation of recurrence diameters. In: Zuck, L.D., Attie, P.C., Cortesi, A., Mukhopadhyay, S. (eds.) VMCAI 2003. LNCS, vol. 2575, pp. 298–309. Springer, Heidelberg (2003). https://doi.org/10.1007/3-540-36384-X_24
23. Kukovec, J., Konnov, I., Widder, J.: Reachability in parameterized systems: all flavors of threshold automata. In: CONCUR, pp. 19:1–19:17 (2018)
24. Lazić, M., Konnov, I., Widder, J., Bloem, R.: Synthesis of distributed algorithms with parameterized threshold guards. In: OPODIS. LIPIcs, vol. 95, pp. 32:1–32:20 (2017)
25. Leroux, J., Sutre, G.: Flat counter automata almost everywhere!. In: Peled, D.A., Tsay, Y.-K. (eds.) ATVA 2005. LNCS, vol. 3707, pp. 489–503. Springer, Heidelberg (2005). https://doi.org/10.1007/11562948_36
26. Lynch, N.: Distributed Algorithms. Morgan Kaufman, Burlington (1996)
27. Marić, O., Sprenger, C., Basin, D.A.: Cutoff bounds for consensus algorithms. In: Majumdar, R., Kunčak, V. (eds.) CAV 2017. LNCS, vol. 10427, pp. 217–237. Springer, Cham (2017). https://doi.org/10.1007/978-3-319-63390-9_12
28. Minsky, M.L.: Computation: Finite and Infinite Machines. Prentice-Hall Inc., Upper Saddle River (1967)
29. de Moura, L., Bjørner, N.: Z3: an efficient SMT solver. In: Ramakrishnan, C.R., Rehof, J. (eds.) TACAS 2008. LNCS, vol. 4963, pp. 337–340. Springer, Heidelberg (2008). https://doi.org/10.1007/978-3-540-78800-3_24
30. Raynal, M.: Fault-Tolerant Agreement in Synchronous Message-Passing Systems. Synthesis Lectures on Distributed Computing Theory. Morgan & Claypool Publishers (2010)

31. Srikanth, T.K., Toueg, S.: Optimal clock synchronization. J. ACM **34**(3), 626–645 (1987)
32. Srikanth, T., Toueg, S.: Simulating authenticated broadcasts to derive simple fault-tolerant algorithms. Distrib. Comput. **2**, 80–94 (1987)
33. Stoilkovska, I., Konnov, I., Widder, J., Zuleger, F.: Artifact and instructions to generate experimental results for TACAS 2019 paper: Verifying Safety of Synchronous Fault-Tolerant Algorithms by Bounded Model Checking (artifact). Figshare (2019). https://doi.org/10.6084/m9.figshare.7824929.v1

Measuring Masking Fault-Tolerance

Pablo F. Castro[1,3](✉), Pedro R. D'Argenio[2,3,4], Ramiro Demasi[2,3], and Luciano Putruele[1,3]

[1] Departamento de Computación, FCEFQyN, Universidad Nacional de Río Cuarto, Río Cuarto, Córdoba, Argentina
{pcastro,lputruele}@dc.exa.unrc.edu.ar

[2] FaMAF, Universidad Nacional de Córdoba, Córdoba, Argentina
{dargenio,rdemasi}@famaf.unc.edu.ar

[3] Consejo Nacional de Investigaciones Científicas y Técnicas (CONICET), Buenos Aires, Argentina

[4] Saarland University, Saarbrücken, Germany

Abstract. In this paper we introduce a notion of fault-tolerance distance between labeled transition systems. Intuitively, this notion of distance measures the degree of fault-tolerance exhibited by a candidate system. In practice, there are different kinds of fault-tolerance, here we restrict ourselves to the analysis of masking fault-tolerance because it is often a highly desirable goal for critical systems. Roughly speaking, a system is masking fault-tolerant when it is able to completely mask the faults, not allowing these faults to have any observable consequences for the users. We capture masking fault-tolerance via a simulation relation, which is accompanied by a corresponding game characterization. We enrich the resulting games with quantitative objectives to define the notion of masking fault-tolerance distance. Furthermore, we investigate the basic properties of this notion of masking distance, and we prove that it is a directed semimetric. We have implemented our approach in a prototype tool that automatically computes the masking distance between a nominal system and a fault-tolerant version of it. We have used this tool to measure the masking tolerance of multiple instances of several case studies.

1 Introduction

Fault-tolerance allows for the construction of systems that are able to overcome the occurrence of faults during their execution. Examples of fault-tolerant systems can be found everywhere: communication protocols, hardware circuits, avionic systems, cryptographic currencies, etc. So, the increasing relevance of critical software in everyday life has led to a renewed interest in the automatic

This work was supported by grants ANPCyT PICT-2017-3894 (RAFTSys), ANPCyT PICT 2016-1384, SeCyT-UNC 33620180100354CB (ARES), and the ERC Advanced Grant 695614 (POWVER).

T. Vojnar and L. Zhang (Eds.): TACAS 2019, Part II, LNCS 11428, pp. 375–392, 2019.
https://doi.org/10.1007/978-3-030-17465-1_21

verification of fault-tolerant properties. However, one of the main difficulties when reasoning about these kinds of properties is given by their quantitative nature, which is true even for non-probabilistic systems. A simple example is given by the introduction of redundancy in critical systems. This is, by far, one of the most used techniques in fault-tolerance. In practice, it is well-known that adding more redundancy to a system increases its reliability. Measuring this increment is a central issue for evaluating fault-tolerant software, protocols, etc. On the other hand, the formal characterization of fault-tolerant properties could be an involving task, usually these properties are encoded using *ad-hoc* mechanisms as part of a general design.

The usual flow for the design and verification of fault-tolerant systems consists in defining a nominal model (i.e., the "fault-free" or "ideal" program) and afterwards extending it with faulty behaviors that deviate from the normal behavior prescribed by the nominal model. This extended model represents the way in which the system operates under the occurrence of faults. There are different ways of extending the nominal model, the typical approach is *fault injection* [20,21], that is, the automatic introduction of faults into the model. An important property that any extended model has to satisfy is the preservation of the normal behavior under the absence of faults. In [11], we proposed an alternative formal approach for dealing with the analysis of fault-tolerance. This approach allows for a fully automated analysis and appropriately distinguishes faulty behaviors from normal ones. Moreover, this framework is amenable to fault-injection. In that work, three notions of simulation relations are defined to characterize *masking*, *nonmasking*, and *failsafe* fault-tolerance, as originally defined in [15].

During the last decade, significant progress has been made towards defining suitable metrics or distances for diverse types of quantitative models including real-time systems [19], probabilistic models [12], and metrics for linear and branching systems [6,8,18,23,29]. Some authors have already pointed out that these metrics can be useful to reason about the robustness of a system, a notion related to fault-tolerance. Particularly, in [6] the traditional notion of simulation relation is generalized and three different simulation distances between systems are introduced, namely *correctness*, *coverage*, and *robustness*. These are defined using quantitative games with *discounted-sum* and *mean-payoff* objectives.

In this paper we introduce a notion of fault-tolerance distance between labelled transition systems. Intuitively, this distance measures the degree of fault-tolerance exhibited by a candidate system. As it was mentioned above, there exist different levels of fault-tolerance, we restrict ourselves to the analysis of *masking fault-tolerance* because it is often classified as the most benign kind of fault-tolerance and it is a highly desirable property for critical systems. Roughly speaking, a system is masking fault-tolerant when it is able to completely mask the faults, not allowing these faults to have any observable consequences for the users. Formally, the system must preserve both the safety and liveness properties of the nominal model [15]. In contrast to the robustness distance defined in [6], which measures how many unexpected errors are tolerated by the implementation, we consider a specific collection of faults given in the implementation and measure how many faults are tolerated by the implementation in such a way that they can be masked by the states. We also require that the normal behavior of the specification has to be preserved by the implementation when no faults are present. In this case, we have a bisimulation between the specification and the non-faulty behavior of the implementation. Otherwise, the distance is 1. That is, $\delta_m(N, I) = 1$ if and only if the nominal model N and $I \backslash F$ are not bisimilar, where $I \backslash F$ behaves like the implementation I where all actions in F are forbidden ($\backslash$ is Milner's restriction operator). Thus, we effectively distinguish between the nominal model and its fault-tolerant version and the set of faults taken into account.

In order to measure the degree of masking fault-tolerance of a given system, we start characterizing masking fault-tolerance via simulation relations between two systems as defined in [11]. The first one acting as a specification of the intended behavior (i.e., nominal model) and the second one as the fault-tolerant implementation (i.e., the extended model with faulty behavior). The existence of a masking relation implies that the implementation masks the faults. Afterwards, we introduce a game characterization of masking simulation and we enrich the resulting games with quantitative objectives to define the notion of *masking fault-tolerance distance*, where the possible values of the game belong to the interval $[0, 1]$. The fault-tolerant implementation is masking fault-tolerant if the value of the game is 0. Furthermore, the bigger the number, the farther the masking distance between the fault-tolerant implementation and the specification. Accordingly, a bigger distance remarkably decreases fault-tolerance. Thus, for a given nominal model N and two different fault-tolerant implementations I_1 and I_2, our distance ensures that $\delta_m(N, I_1) < \delta_m(N, I_2)$ whenever I_1 tolerates more faults than I_2. We also provide a weak version of masking simulation, which makes it possible to deal with complex systems composed of several interacting components. We prove that masking distance is a directed semimetric, that is, it satisfies two basic properties of any distance, reflexivity and the triangle inequality.

Finally, we have implemented our approach in a tool that takes as input a nominal model and its fault-tolerant implementation and automatically compute the masking distance between them. We have used this tool to measure the masking tolerance of multiple instances of several case studies such as a redundant cell memory, a variation of the dining philosophers problem, the bounded retransmission protocol, N-Modular-Redundancy, and the Byzantine generals problem. These are typical examples of fault-tolerant systems.

The remainder of the paper is structured as follows. In Sect. 2, we introduce preliminaries notions used throughout this paper. We present in Sect. 3 the formal definition of masking distance build on quantitative simulation games and we also prove its basic properties. We describe in Sect. 4 the experimental evaluation on some well-known case studies. In Sect. 5 we discuss the related work. Finally, we discuss in Sect. 6 some conclusions and directions for further work. Full details and proofs can be found in [5].

2 Preliminaries

Let us introduce some basic definitions and results on game theory that will be necessary across the paper, the interested reader is referred to [2].

A *transition system* (TS) is a tuple $A = \langle S, \Sigma, E, s_0 \rangle$, where S is a finite set of states, Σ is a finite alphabet, $E \subseteq S \times \Sigma \times S$ is a set of labelled transitions, and s_0 is the initial state. In the following we use $s \xrightarrow{e} s' \in E$ to denote $(s, e, s') \in E$. Let $|S|$ and $|E|$ denote the number of states and edges, respectively. We define $post(s) = \{s' \in S \mid s \xrightarrow{e} s' \in E\}$ as the set of successors of s. Similarly, $pre(s') = \{s \in S \mid s \xrightarrow{e} s' \in E\}$ as the set of predecessors of s'. Moreover, $post^*(s)$ denotes the states which are reachable from s. Without loss of generality, we require that every state s has a successor, i.e., $\forall s \in S : post(s) \neq \emptyset$. A run in a transition system A is an infinite path $\rho = \rho_0 \sigma_0 \rho_1 \sigma_1 \rho_2 \sigma_2 \cdots \in (S \cdot \Sigma)^w$ where $\rho_0 = s_0$ and for all i, $\rho_i \xrightarrow{\sigma_i} \rho_{i+1} \in E$. From now on, given a tuple $(x_0, \ldots, x_n)$, we denote x_i by $\mathrm{pr}_i((x_0, \ldots, x_n))$.

A *game graph* G is a tuple $G = \langle S, S_1, S_2, \Sigma, E, s_0 \rangle$ where S, Σ, E and s_0 are as in transition systems and (S_1, S_2) is a partition of S. The choice of the next state is made by Player 1 (Player 2) when the current state is in S_1 (respectively, S_2). A weighted game graph is a game graph along with a weight function v^G from E to $\mathbb{Q}$. A run in the game graph G is called a *play*. The set of all plays is denoted by Ω.

Given a game graph G, a *strategy* for Player 1 is a function $\pi : (S \cdot \Sigma)^* S_1 \to \Sigma \times S$ such that for all $\rho_0 \sigma_0 \rho_1 \sigma_1 \ldots \rho_i \in (S \cdot \Sigma)^* S_1$, we have that if $\pi(\rho_0 \sigma_0 \rho_1 \sigma_1 \ldots \rho_i) = (\sigma, \rho)$, then $\rho_i \xrightarrow{\sigma} \rho \in E$. A strategy for Player 2 is defined in a similar way. The set of all strategies for Player p is denoted by Π_p. A strategy for player p is said to be memoryless (or positional) if it can be defined by a mapping $f : S_p \to E$ such that for all $s \in S_p$ we have that $\mathrm{pr}_0(f(s)) = s$, that is, these strategies do not need memory of the past history. Furthermore, a play $\rho_0 \sigma_0 \rho_1 \sigma_1 \rho_2 \sigma_2 \ldots$ conforms to a player p strategy π if $\forall i \geq 0 : (\rho_i \in S_p) \Rightarrow (\sigma_i, \rho_{i+1}) = \pi(\rho_0 \sigma_0 \rho_1 \sigma_1 \ldots \rho_i)$. The *outcome* of a Player 1 strategy π_1 and a Player 2 strategy π_2 is the unique play, named $out(\pi_1, \pi_2)$, that conforms to both π_1 and π_2.

A *game* is made of a game graph and a boolean or quantitative objective. A *boolean objective* is a function $\Phi : \Omega \to \{0, 1\}$ and the goal of Player 1 in a game with objective Φ is to select a strategy so that the outcome maps to 1, independently what Player 2 does. On the contrary, the goal of Player 2 is to ensure that the outcome maps to 0. Given a boolean objective Φ, a play ρ is *winning* for Player 1 (resp. Player 2) if $\Phi(\rho) = 1$ (resp. $\Phi(\rho) = 0$). A strategy π is a *winning strategy* for Player p if every play conforming to π is winning for Player p. We say that a game with boolean objective is *determined* if some player has a winning strategy, and we say that it is memoryless determined if that winning strategy is memoryless. Reachability games are those games whose objective functions are defined as $\Phi(\rho_0 \sigma_0 \rho_1 \sigma_1 \rho_2 \sigma_2 \ldots) = (\exists i : \rho_i \in V)$ for some set $V \subseteq S$, a standard result is that reachability games are memoryless determined.

A *quantitative objective* is given by a *payoff* function $f : \Omega \to \mathbb{R}$ and the goal of Player 1 is to maximize the value f of the play, whereas the goal of Player 2 is to minimize it. For a quantitative objective f, the value of the game for a Player 1 strategy π_1, denoted by $v_1(\pi_1)$, is defined as the infimum over all the values resulting from Player 2 strategies, i.e., $v_1(\pi_1) = \inf_{\pi_2 \in \Pi_2} f(out(\pi_1, \pi_2))$. The value of the game for Player 1 is defined as the supremum of the values of all Player 1 strategies, i.e., $\sup_{\pi_1 \in \Pi_1} v_1(\pi_1)$. Analogously, the value of the game for a Player 2 strategy π_2 and the value of the game for Player 2 are defined as $v_2(\pi_2) = \sup_{\pi_1 \in \Pi_1} f(out(\pi_1, \pi_2))$ and $\inf_{\pi_2 \in \Pi_2} v_2(\pi_2)$, respectively. We say that a game is determined if both values are equal, that is: $\sup_{\pi_1 \in \Pi_1} v_1(\pi_1) = \inf_{\pi_2 \in \Pi_2} v_2(\pi_2)$. In this case we denote by $val(\mathcal{G})$ the value of game $\mathcal{G}$. The following result from [24] characterizes a large set of determined games.

Theorem 1. *Any game with a quantitative function f that is bounded and Borel measurable is determined.*

3 Masking Distance

We start by defining masking simulation. In [11], we have defined a state-based simulation for masking fault-tolerance, here we recast this definition using labelled transition systems. First, let us introduce some concepts needed for defining masking fault-tolerance. For any vocabulary Σ, and set of labels $\mathcal{F} = \{F_0, \dots, F_n\}$ not belonging to Σ, we consider $\Sigma_{\mathcal{F}} = \Sigma \cup \mathcal{F}$, where $\mathcal{F} \cap \Sigma = \emptyset$. Intuitively, the elements of $\mathcal{F}$ indicate the occurrence of a fault in a faulty implementation. Furthermore, sometimes it will be useful to consider the set $\Sigma^i = \{e^i \mid e \in \Sigma\}$, containing the elements of Σ indexed with superscript i. Moreover, for any vocabulary Σ we consider $\Sigma_M = \Sigma \cup \{M\}$, where $M \notin \Sigma$, intuitively, this label is used to identify masking transitions.

Given a transition system $A = \langle S, \Sigma, E, s_0 \rangle$ over a vocabulary Σ, we denote $A^M = \langle S, \Sigma_M, E^M, s_0 \rangle$ where $E^M = E \cup \{s \xrightarrow{M} s \mid s \in S\}$.

3.1 Strong Masking Simulation

Definition 1. *Let $A = \langle S, \Sigma, E, s_0 \rangle$ and $A' = \langle S', \Sigma_{\mathcal{F}}, E', s'_0 \rangle$ be two transition systems. A' is* strong masking fault-tolerant *with respect to A if there exists a relation $\mathbf{M} \subseteq S \times S'$ between A^M and A' such that:*

(A) $s_0 \,\mathbf{M}\, s'_0$, and
(B) for all $s \in S, s' \in S'$ with $s \,\mathbf{M}\, s'$ and all $e \in \Sigma$ the following holds:
(1) if $(s \xrightarrow{e} t) \in E$ then $\exists\, t' \in S' : (s' \xrightarrow{e} t' \wedge t \,\mathbf{M}\, t')$;
(2) if $(s' \xrightarrow{e} t') \in E'$ then $\exists\, t \in S : (s \xrightarrow{e} t \wedge t \,\mathbf{M}\, t')$;
(3) if $(s' \xrightarrow{F} t')$ for some $F \in \mathcal{F}$ then $\exists\, t \in S : (s \xrightarrow{M} t \wedge t \,\mathbf{M}\, t')$.

If such relation exists we say that A' is a strong masking fault-tolerant implementation *of A, denoted by $A \preceq_m A'$.*

We say that state s' is masking fault-tolerant for s when $s \;\mathbf{M}\; s'$. Intuitively, the definition states that, starting in s', faults can be masked in such a way that the behavior exhibited is the same as that observed when starting from s and executing transitions without faults. In other words, a masking relation ensures that every faulty behavior in the implementation can be simulated by the specification. Let us explain in more detail the above definition. First, note that conditions A, B.1, and B.2 imply that we have a bisimulation when A and A' do not exhibit faulty behavior. Particularly, condition B.1 says that the normal execution of A can be simulated by an execution of A'. On the other hand, condition B.2 says that the implementation does not add normal (non-faulty) behavior. Finally, condition B.3 states that every outgoing faulty transition (F) from s' must be matched to an outgoing masking transition (M) from s.

3.2 Weak Masking Simulation

For analysing nontrivial systems a weak version of masking simulation relation is needed, the main idea is that a weak masking simulation abstracts away from internal behaviour, which is modeled by a special action τ. Note that internal transitions are common in fault-tolerance: the actions performed as part of a fault-tolerant procedure in a component are usually not observable by the rest of the system.

The *weak transition relations* $\Rightarrow \subseteq S \times (\Sigma \cup \{\tau\} \cup \{M\} \cup \mathcal{F}) \times S$, also denoted as E_W, considers the *silent* step τ and is defined as follows:

$$\stackrel{e}{\Rightarrow} = \begin{cases} (\xrightarrow{\tau})^* \circ \xrightarrow{e} \circ (\xrightarrow{\tau})^* & \text{if } e \in \Sigma, \\ (\xrightarrow{e})^* & \text{if } e = \tau, \\ \xrightarrow{e} & \text{if } e \in \{M\} \cup \mathcal{F}. \end{cases}$$

The symbol $\circ$ stands for composition of binary relations and $(\xrightarrow{\tau})^*$ is the reflexive and transitive closure of the binary relation $\xrightarrow{\tau}$.

Intuitively, if $e \notin \{\tau, M\} \cup \mathcal{F}$, then $s \stackrel{e}{\Rightarrow} s'$ means that there is a sequence of zero or more τ transitions starting in s, followed by one transition labelled by e, followed again by zero or more τ transitions eventually reaching s'. $s \stackrel{\tau}{\Rightarrow} s'$ states that s can transition to s' via zero or more τ transitions. In particular, $s \stackrel{\tau}{\Rightarrow} s$ for every s. For the case in which $e \in \{M\} \cup \mathcal{F}$, $s \stackrel{e}{\Rightarrow} s'$is equivalent to $s \xrightarrow{e} s'$ and hence no τ step is allowed before or after the e transition.

Definition 2. *Let $A = \langle S, \Sigma, E, s_0\rangle$ and $A' = \langle S', \Sigma_{\mathcal{F}}, E', s'_0\rangle$ be two transition systems with Σ possibly containing τ. A' is* weak masking fault-tolerant *with respect to A if there is a relation $\mathbf{M} \subseteq S \times S'$ between A^M and A' such that:*

(A) $s_0 \;\mathbf{M}\; s'_0$
(B) for all $s \in S, s' \in S'$ with $s \;\mathbf{M}\; s'$ and all $e \in \Sigma \cup \{\tau\}$ the following holds:
  (1) if $(s \xrightarrow{e} t) \in E$ then $\exists\, t' \in S' : (s' \stackrel{e}{\Rightarrow} t' \in E'_W \wedge t \;\mathbf{M}\; t')$;
  (2) if $(s' \xrightarrow{e} t') \in E'$ then $\exists\, t \in S : (s \stackrel{e}{\Rightarrow} t \in E_W \wedge t \;\mathbf{M}\; t')$;
  (3) if $(s' \xrightarrow{F} t') \in E'$ for some $F \in \mathcal{F}$ then $\exists\, t \in S : (s \xrightarrow{M} t \in E \wedge t \;\mathbf{M}\; t')$.

If such relation exists, we say that A' is a weak masking fault-tolerant implementation *of A, denoted by $A \preceq_m^w A'$.*

The following theorem makes a strong connection between strong and weak masking simulation. It states that weak masking simulation becomes strong masking simulation whenever transition $\rightarrow$ is replaced by $\Rightarrow$ in the original automata.

Theorem 2. *Let $A = \langle S, \Sigma, E, s_0 \rangle$ and $A' = \langle S', \Sigma_{\mathcal{F}}, E', s_0' \rangle$. $\mathbf{M} \subseteq S \times S'$ between A^M and A' is a weak masking simulation if and only if:*

(A) $s_0 \, \mathbf{M} \, s_0'$, and
(B) for all $s \in S, s' \in S'$ with $s \, \mathbf{M} \, s'$ and all $e \in \Sigma \cup \{\tau\}$ the following holds:
(1) if $(s \stackrel{e}{\Rightarrow} t) \in E_W$ then $\exists\, t' \in S' : (s' \stackrel{e}{\Rightarrow} t' \in E'_W \wedge t \, \mathbf{M} \, t')$;
(2) if $(s' \stackrel{e}{\Rightarrow} t') \in E'_W$ then $\exists\, t \in S : (s \stackrel{e}{\Rightarrow} t \in E_W \wedge t \, \mathbf{M} \, t')$;
(3) if $(s' \stackrel{F}{\Rightarrow} t') \in E'_W$ for some $F \in \mathcal{F}$ then $\exists\, t \in S : (s \stackrel{M}{\Longrightarrow} t \in E_W \wedge t \, \mathbf{M} \, t')$

The proof of this is straightforward following the same ideas of Milner in [25].

A natural way to check weak bisimilarity is to *saturate* the transition system [14,25] and then check strong bisimilarity on the saturated transition system. Similarly, Theorem 2 allows us to compute weak masking simulation by reducing this problem to compute strong masking simulation. Note that $\stackrel{e}{\Rightarrow}$ can be alternatively defined by:

$$\frac{p \stackrel{e}{\rightarrow} q}{p \stackrel{e}{\Rightarrow} q} \qquad \frac{}{p \stackrel{\tau}{\Rightarrow} p} \qquad \frac{p \stackrel{\tau}{\Rightarrow} p_1 \stackrel{e}{\Rightarrow} q_1 \stackrel{\tau}{\Rightarrow} q}{p \stackrel{e}{\Rightarrow} q} \ (e \notin \{M\} \cup \mathcal{F})$$

As a running example, we consider a memory cell that stores a bit of information and supports reading and writing operations, presented in a state-based form in [11]. A state in this system maintains the current value of the memory cell ($m = i$, for $i = 0, 1$), writing allows one to change this value, and reading returns the stored value. Obviously, in this system the result of a reading depends on the value stored in the cell. Thus, a property that one might associate with this model is that the value read from the cell coincides with that of the last writing performed in the system.

A potential fault in this scenario occurs when a cell unexpectedly loses its charge, and its stored value turns into another one (e.g., it changes from 1 to 0 due to charge loss). A typical technique to deal with this situation is *redundancy*: use three memory bits instead of one. Writing operations are performed simultaneously on the three bits. Reading, on the other hand, returns the value that is repeated at least twice in the memory bits; this is known as *voting*.

We take the following approach to model this system. Labels $\mathrm{W}_0, \mathrm{W}_1, \mathrm{R}_0$, and R_1 represent writing and reading operations. Specifically, W_0 (resp. W_1): writes a zero (resp. one) in the memory. R_0 (resp. R_1): reads a zero (resp. one) from the memory. Figure 1 depicts four transition systems. The leftmost one represents the nominal system for this example (denoted as A). The second one from the left characterizes the nominal transition system augmented with masking

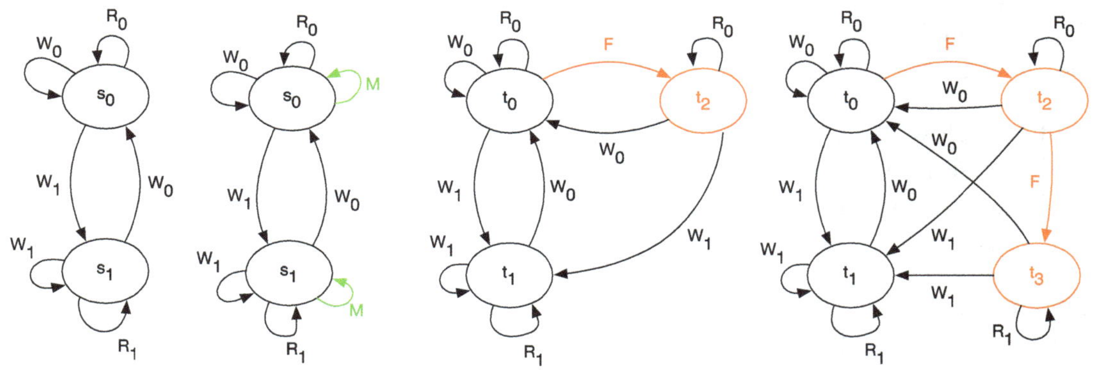

Fig. 1. Transition systems for the memory cell.

transitions, i.e., A^M. The third and fourth transition systems are fault-tolerant implementations of A, named A' and A'', respectively. Note that A' contains one fault, while A'' considers two faults. Both implementations use triple redundancy; intuitively, state t_0 contains the three bits with value zero and t_1 contains the three bits with value one. Moreover, state t_2 is reached when one of the bits was flipped (either 001, 010 or 100). In A'', state t_3 is reached after a second bit is flipped (either 011 or 101 or 110) starting from state t_0. It is straightforward to see that there exists a relation of masking fault-tolerance between A^M and A', as it is witnessed by the relation $\mathbf{M} = \{(s_0, t_0), (s_1, t_1), (s_0, t_2)\}$. It is a routine to check that $\mathbf{M}$ satisfies the conditions of Definition 1. On the other hand, there does not exist a masking relation between A^M and A'' because state t_3 needs to be related to state s_0 in any masking relation. This state can only be reached by executing faults, which are necessarily masked with M-transitions. However, note that, in state t_3, we can read a 1 (transition $t_3 \xrightarrow{R_1} t_3$) whereas, in state s_0, we can only read a 0.

3.3 Masking Simulation Game

We define a masking simulation game for two transition systems (the specification of the nominal system and its fault-tolerant implementation) that captures masking fault-tolerance. We first define the masking game graph where we have two players named by convenience the *refuter* (R) and the *verifier* (V).

Definition 3. *Let* $A = \langle S, \Sigma, E, s_0 \rangle$ *and* $A' = \langle S', \Sigma_{\mathcal{F}}, E'_W, s'_0 \rangle$. *The* strong masking game graph $\mathcal{G}_{A^M, A'} = \langle S^G, S_R, S_V, \Sigma^G, E^G, {s_0}^G \rangle$ *for two players is defined as follows:*

- $\Sigma^G = \Sigma_M \cup \Sigma_{\mathcal{F}}$
- $S^G = (S \times (\Sigma^1_M \cup \Sigma^2_{\mathcal{F}} \cup \{\#\}) \times S' \times \{R, V\}) \cup \{s_{err}\}$
- *The initial state is* $s_0^G = \langle s_0, \#, s'_0, R \rangle$, *where the refuter starts playing*
- *The refuter's states are* $S_R = \{(s, \#, s', R) \mid s \in S \wedge s' \in S'\} \cup \{s_{err}\}$
- *The verifier's states are* $S_V = \{(s, \sigma, s', V) \mid s \in S \wedge s' \in S' \wedge \sigma \in \Sigma^G \setminus \{M\}\}$

and E^G is the minimal set satisfying:

- $\{(s, \#, s', R) \xrightarrow{\sigma} (t, \sigma^1, s', V) \mid \exists\, \sigma \in \Sigma : s \xrightarrow{\sigma} t \in E\} \subseteq E^G$,
- $\{(s, \#, s', R) \xrightarrow{\sigma} (s, \sigma^2, t', V) \mid \exists\, \sigma \in \Sigma_{\mathcal{F}} : s' \xrightarrow{\sigma} t' \in E'\} \subseteq E^G$,
- $\{(s, \sigma^2, s', V) \xrightarrow{\sigma} (t, \#, s', R) \mid \exists\, \sigma \in \Sigma : s \xrightarrow{\sigma} t \in E\} \subseteq E^G$,
- $\{(s, \sigma^1, s', V) \xrightarrow{\sigma} (s, \#, t', R) \mid \exists\, \sigma \in \Sigma : s' \xrightarrow{\sigma} t' \in E'\} \subseteq E^G$,
- $\{(s, F^2, s', V) \xrightarrow{M} (t, \#, s', R) \mid \exists\, s \xrightarrow{M} t \in E^M\} \subseteq E^G$, *for any* $F \in \mathcal{F}$
- *If there is no outgoing transition from some state s then transitions $s \xrightarrow{\sigma} s_{err}$ and $s_{err} \xrightarrow{\sigma} s_{err}$ for every $\sigma \in \Sigma$, are added.*

The intuition of this game is as follows. The refuter chooses transitions of either the specification or the implementation to play, and the verifier tries to match her choice, this is similar to the bisimulation game [28]. However, when the refuter chooses a fault, the verifier must match it with a masking transition (M). The intuitive reading of this is that the fault-tolerant implementation masked the fault in such a way that the occurrence of this fault cannot be noticed from the users' side. R wins if the game reaches the error state, i.e., s_{err}. On the other hand, V wins when s_{err} is not reached during the game. (This is basically a reachability game [26]).

A *weak masking game graph* $\mathcal{G}^W_{A^M, A'}$ is defined in the same way as the strong masking game graph in Definition 3, with the exception that Σ_M and $\Sigma_{\mathcal{F}}$ may contain τ, and the set of labelled transitions (denoted as E^G_W) is now defined using the weak transition relations (i.e., E_W and E'_W) from the respective transition systems.

Figure 2 shows a part of the strong masking game graph for the running example considering the transition systems A^M and A''. We can clearly observe on the game graph that the verifier cannot mimic the transition $(s_0, \#, t_3, R) \xrightarrow{R_1^2} (s_0, R_1^2, t_3, V)$ selected by the refuter which reads a 1 at state t_3 on the fault-tolerant implementation. This is because the verifier can only read a 0 at state s_0. Then, the s_{err} is reached and the refuter wins.

As expected, there is a strong masking simulation between A and A' if and only if the verifier has a winning strategy in $\mathcal{G}_{A^M, A'}$.

Theorem 3. *Let $A = \langle S, \Sigma, E, s_0 \rangle$ and $A' = \langle S', \Sigma_{\mathcal{F}}, E', s'_0 \rangle$. $A \preceq_m A'$ iff the verifier has a winning strategy for the strong masking game graph $\mathcal{G}_{A^M, A'}$.*

By Theorems 2 and 3, the result replicates for weak masking game.

Theorem 4. *Let $A = \langle S, \Sigma \cup \{\tau\}, E, s_0 \rangle$ and $A' = \langle S', \Sigma_{\mathcal{F}} \cup \{\tau\}, E', s'_0 \rangle$. $A \preceq^w_m A'$ iff the verifier has a winning strategy for the weak masking game graph $\mathcal{G}^W_{A^M, A'}$.*

Using the standard properties of reachability games we get the following property.

Theorem 5. *For any A and A', the strong (resp. weak) masking game graph $\mathcal{G}_{A^M, A'}$ (resp. $\mathcal{G}^W_{A^M, A'}$) can be determined in time $O(|E^G|)$ (resp. $O(|E^G_W|)$).*

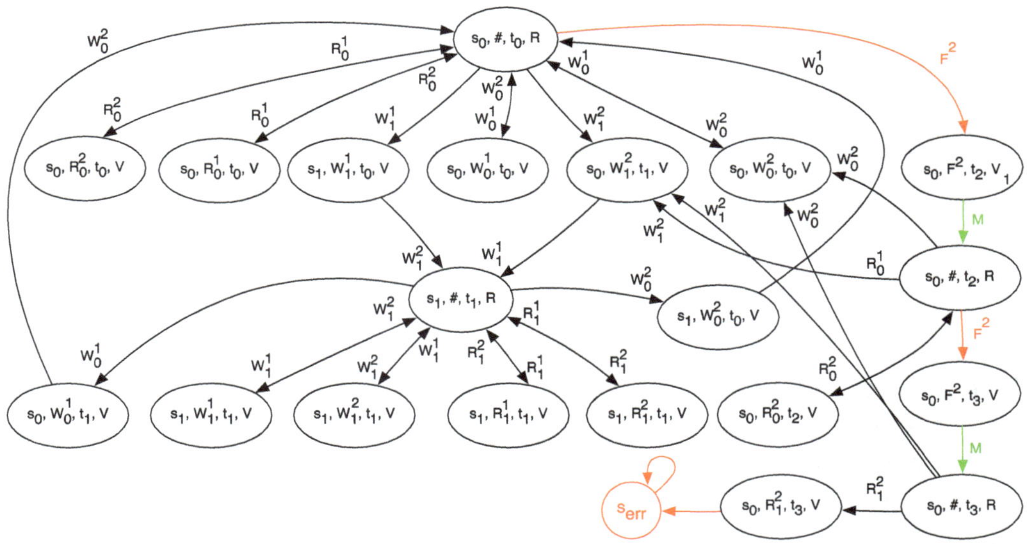

Fig. 2. Part of the masking game graph for memory cell model with two faults

The set of winning states for the refuter can be defined in a standard way from the error state [26]. We adapt ideas in [26] to our setting. For $i, j \geq 0$, sets U_i^j are defined as follows:

$$\begin{aligned} U_i^0 =& U_0^j = \emptyset, \\ U_1^1 =& \{s_{err}\}, \\ U_{i+1}^{j+1} &= \{v' \mid v' \in S_R \wedge post(v') \cap U_{i+1}^j \neq \emptyset\} \\ &\cup \{v' \mid v' \in S_V \wedge post(v') \subseteq \textstyle\bigcup_{j' \leq j} U_{i+1}^{j'} \wedge post(v') \cap U_{i+1}^j \neq \emptyset \wedge \pi_2(v') \notin \mathcal{F}\} \\ &\cup \{v' \mid v' \in S_V \wedge post(v') \subseteq \textstyle\bigcup_{i' \leq i, j' \leq j} U_{i'}^{j'} \wedge post(v') \cap U_i^j \neq \emptyset \wedge \pi_2(v') \in \mathcal{F}\} \end{aligned} \tag{1}$$

then $U^k = \bigcup_{i \geq 0} U_i^k$ and $U = \bigcup_{k \geq 0} U^k$. Intuitively, the subindex i in U_i^k indicates that s_{err} is reach after at most $i - 1$ faults occurred. The following lemma is straightforwardly proven using standard techniques of reachability games [9].

Lemma 1. *The refuter has a winning strategy in $\mathcal{G}_{A^M,A'}$ (or $\mathcal{G}^W_{A^M,A'}$) iff $s_{init} \in U^k$, for some k.*

3.4 Quantitative Masking

In this section, we extend the strong masking simulation game introduced above with quantitative objectives to define the notion of masking fault-tolerance distance. Note that we use the attribute "quantitative" in a non-probabilistic sense.

Definition 4. *For transition systems A and A', the* quantitative strong masking game graph *$\mathcal{Q}_{A^M,A'} = \langle S^G, S_R, S_V, \Sigma^G, E^G, s_0^G, v^G \rangle$ is defined as follows:*

– $\mathcal{G}_{A^M,A'} = \langle S^G, S_R, S_V, \Sigma^G, E^G, s_0^G \rangle$ *is defined as in Definition* 3,
– $v^G(s \xrightarrow{e} s') = (\chi_{\mathcal{F}}(e), \chi_{s_{err}}(s'))$

where $\chi_{\mathcal{F}}$ *is the characteristic function over set* $\mathcal{F}$, *returning* 1 *if* $e \in \mathcal{F}$ *and* 0 *otherwise, and* $\chi_{s_{err}}$ *is the characteristic function over the singleton set* $\{s_{err}\}$.

Note that the cost function returns a pair of numbers instead of a single number. It is direct to codify this pair into a number, but we do not do it here for the sake of clarity. We remark that the *quantitative weak masking game graph* $\mathcal{Q}^W_{A^M,A'}$ is defined in the same way as the game graph defined above but using the weak masking game graph $\mathcal{G}^W_{A^M,A'}$ instead of $\mathcal{G}_{A^M,A'}$.

Given a quantitative strong masking game graph with the weight function v^G and a play $\rho = \rho_0\sigma_0\rho_1\sigma_1\rho_2, \ldots$, for all $i \geq 0$, let $v_i = v^G(\rho_i \xrightarrow{\sigma_i} \rho_{i+1})$. We define the *masking payoff function* as follows:

$$f_m(\rho) = \lim_{n\to\infty} \frac{\mathrm{pr}_1(v_n)}{1 + \sum_{i=0}^{n} \mathrm{pr}_0(v_i)},$$

which is proportional to the inverse of the number of masking movements made by the verifier. To see this, note that the numerator of $\frac{\mathrm{pr}_1(v_n)}{1+\sum_{i=0}^{n} \mathrm{pr}_0(v_i)}$ will be 1 when we reach the error state, that is, in those paths not reaching the error state this formula returns 0. Furthermore, if the error state is reached, then the denominator will count the number of fault transitions taken until the error state. All of them, except the last one, were masked successfully. The last fault, instead, while attempted to be masked by the verifier, eventually leads to the error state. That is, the transitions with value $(1, \_)$ are those corresponding to faults. The others are mapped to $(0, \_)$. Notice also that if s_{err} is reached in v_n without the occurrence of any fault, the nominal part of the implementation does not match the nominal specification, in which case $\frac{\mathrm{pr}_1(v_n)}{1+\sum_{i=0}^{n} \mathrm{pr}_0(v_i)} = 1$. Then, the refuter wants to maximize the value of any run, that is, she will try to execute faults leading to the state s_{err}. In contrast, the verifier wants to avoid s_{err} and then she will try to mask faults with actions that take her away from the error state. More precisely, the value of the quantitative strong masking game for the refuter is defined as $val_R(\mathcal{Q}_{A^M,A'}) = \sup_{\pi_R \in \Pi_R} \inf_{\pi_V \in \Pi_V} f_m(out(\pi_R, \pi_V))$. Analogously, the value of the game for the verifier is defined as $val_V(\mathcal{Q}_{A^M,A'}) = \inf_{\pi_V \in \Pi_V} \sup_{\pi_R \in \Pi_R} f_m(out(\pi_R, \pi_V))$. Then, we define the value of the quantitative strong masking game, denoted by $\mathrm{val}(\mathcal{Q}_{A^M,A'})$, as the value of the game either for the refuter or the verifier, i.e., $\mathrm{val}(\mathcal{Q}_{A^M,A'}) = val_R(\mathcal{Q}_{A^M,A'}) = val_V(\mathcal{Q}_{A^M,A'})$. This can be done because quantitative strong masking games are determined as we prove below in Theorem 6.

Definition 5. *Let* A *and* A' *be transition systems. The* strong masking distance *between* A *and* A', *denoted by* $\delta_m(A, A')$ *is defined as:* $\delta_m(A, A') = \mathrm{val}(\mathcal{Q}_{A^M,A'})$.

We would like to remark that the *weak masking distance* δ^W_m is defined in the same way for the quantitative weak masking game graph $\mathcal{Q}^W_{A^M,A'}$. Roughly speaking, we are interesting on measuring the number of faults that can be masked. The value of the game is essentially determined by the faulty and masking labels on the game graph and how the players can find a strategy that leads (or avoids) the state s_{err}, independently if there are or not silent actions.

In the following, we state some basic properties of this kind of games. As already anticipated, quantitative strong masking games are determined:

Theorem 6. *For any quantitative strong masking game $\mathcal{Q}_{A^M,A'}$ with payoff function f_m:*

$$\inf_{\pi_V \in \Pi_V} \sup_{\pi_R \in \Pi_R} f_m(out(\pi_R, \pi_V)) = \sup_{\pi_R \in \Pi_R} \inf_{\pi_V \in \Pi_V} f_m(out(\pi_R, \pi_V))$$

The value of the quantitative strong masking game can be calculated as stated below.

Theorem 7. *Let $\mathcal{Q}_{A^M,A'}$ be a quantitative strong masking game. Then, $\mathrm{val}(\mathcal{Q}_{A^M,A'}) = \frac{1}{w}$, with $w = \min\{i \mid \exists j : s_{init} \in U_i^j\}$, whenever $s_{init} \in U$, and $\mathrm{val}(\mathcal{Q}_{A^M,A'}) = 0$ otherwise, where sets U_i^j and U are defined in Eq. (1).*

Note that the sets U_i^j can be calculated using a bottom-up breadth-first search from the error state. Thus, the strategies for the refuter and the verifier can be defined using these sets, without taking into account the history of the play. That is, we have the following theorems:

Theorem 8. *Players R and V have memoryless winning strategies for $\mathcal{Q}_{A^M,A'}$.*

Theorems 6, 7, and 8 apply as well to $\mathcal{Q}^W_{A^M,A'}$. The following theorem states the complexity of determining the value of the two types of games.

Theorem 9. *The quantitative strong (weak) masking game can be determined in time $O(|S^G| + |E^G|)$ (resp. $O(|S^G| + |E^G_W|)$).*

Theorems 5 and 9 describe the complexity of solving the quantitative and standard masking games. However, in practice, one needs to bear in mind that $|S^G| = |S| * |S'|$ and $|E^G| = |E| + |E'|$, so constructing the game takes $O(|S|^2 * |S'|^2)$ steps in the worst case. Additionally, for the weak games, the transitive closure of the original model needs to be computed, which for the best known algorithm yields $O(\max(|S|, |S'|)^{2.3727})$ [30].

By using $\mathcal{Q}^W_{A^M,A'}$ instead of $\mathcal{Q}_{A^M,A'}$ in Definition 5, we can define the *weak masking distance* δ^W_m. The next theorem states that, if A and A' are at distance 0, there is a strong (or weak) masking simulation between them.

Theorem 10. *For any transition systems A and A', then (i) $\delta_m(A, A') = 0$ iff $A \preceq_m A'$, and (ii) $\delta^W_m(A, A') = 0$ iff $A \preceq^w_m A'$.*

This follows from Theorem 7. Noting that $A \preceq_m A$ (and $A \preceq^w_m A$) for any transition system A, we obtain that $\delta_m(A, A) = 0$ (resp. $\delta^W_m(A, A) = 0$) by Theorem 10, i.e., both distance are reflexive.

For our running example, the masking distance is 1/3 with a redundancy of 3 bits and considering two faults. This means that only one fault can be masked by this implementation. We can prove a version of the triangle inequality for our notion of distance.

Theorem 11. *Let* $A = \langle S, \Sigma, E, s_0 \rangle$, $A' = \langle S', \Sigma_{\mathcal{F}'}, E', s_0' \rangle$, *and* $A'' = \langle S'', \Sigma_{\mathcal{F}''}, E'', s_0'' \rangle$ *be transition systems such that* $\mathcal{F}' \subseteq \mathcal{F}''$. *Then* $\delta_m(A, A'') \leq \delta_m(A, A') + \delta_m(A', A'')$ *and* $\delta_m^W(A, A'') \leq \delta_m^W(A, A') + \delta_m^W(A', A'')$.

Reflexivity and the triangle inequality imply that both masking distances are directed semi-metrics [7,10]. Moreover, it is interesting to note that the triangle inequality property has practical applications. When developing critical software is quite common to develop a first version of the software taking into account some possible anticipated faults. Later, after testing and running of the system, more plausible faults could be observed. Consequently, the system is modified with additional fault-tolerant capabilities to be able to overcome them. Theorem 11 states that incrementally measuring the masking distance between these different versions of the software provides an upper bound to the actual distance between the nominal system and its last fault-tolerant version. That is, if the sum of the distances obtained between the different versions is a small number, then we can ensure that the final system will exhibit an acceptable masking tolerance to faults w.r.t. the nominal system.

4 Experimental Evaluation

The approach described in this paper has been implemented in a tool in Java called MaskD: Masking Distance Tool [1]. MaskD takes as input a nominal model and its fault-tolerant implementation, and produces as output the masking distance between them. The input models are specified using the guarded command language introduced in [3], a simple programming language common for describing fault-tolerant algorithms. More precisely, a program is a collection of processes, where each process is composed of a collection of actions of the style: *Guard* $\rightarrow$ *Command*, where *Guard* is a boolean condition over the actual state of the program and *Command* is a collection of basic assignments. These syntactical constructions are called actions. The language also allows user to label an action as internal (i.e., τ actions). Moreover, usually some actions are used to represent faults. The tool has several additional features, for instance it can print the traces to the error state or start a simulation from the initial state.

We report on Table 1 the results of the masking distance for multiple instances of several case studies. These are: a Redundant Cell Memory (our running example), N-Modular Redundancy (a standard example of fault-tolerant system [27]), a variation of the Dining Philosophers problem [13], the Byzantine Generals problem introduced by Lamport et al. [22], and the Bounded Retransmission Protocol (a well-known example of fault-tolerant protocol [16]).

Some words are useful to interpret the results. For the case of a 3 bit memory the masking distance is 0.333, the main reason for this is that the faulty model in the worst case is only able to mask 2 faults (in this example, a fault is an unexpected change of a bit value) before failing to replicate the nominal behaviour (i.e. reading the majority value), thus the result comes from the definition of masking distance and taking into account the occurrence of two faults. The situation is similar for the other instances of this problem with more redundancy.

N-Modular-Redundancy consists of N systems, in which these perform a process and that results are processed by a majority-voting system to produce a single output. Assuming a single perfect voter, we have evaluated this case study for different numbers of modules. Note that the distance measures for this case study are similar to the memory example.

For the dining philosophers problem we have adopted the odd/even philosophers implementation (it prevents from deadlock), i.e., there are $n-1$ *even* philosophers that pick the right fork first, and 1 *odd* philosopher that picks the left fork first. The fault we consider in this case occurs when an even philosopher behaves as an odd one, this could be the case of a byzantine fault. For two philosophers the masking distance is 0.5 since a single fault leads to a deadlock, when more philosophers are added this distance becomes smaller.

Another interesting example of a fault-tolerant system is the Byzantine generals problem, introduced originally by Lamport et al. [22]. This is a consensus problem, where we have a general with $n-1$ lieutenants. The communication between the general and his lieutenants is performed through messengers. The general may decide to attack an enemy city or to retreat; then, he sends the order to his lieutenants. Some of the lieutenants might be traitors. We assume that the messages are delivered correctly and all the lieutenants can communicate directly with each other. In this scenario they can recognize who is sending a message. Faults can convert loyal lieutenants into traitors (byzantines faults). As a consequence, traitors might deliver false messages or perhaps they avoid sending a message that they received. The loyal lieutenants must agree on attacking or retreating after $m+1$ rounds of communication, where m is the maximum numbers of traitors.

The Bounded Retransmission Protocol (BRP) is a well-known industrial case study in software verification. While all the other case studies were treated as toy

Table 1. Results of the masking distance for the case studies.

Case Study	Redundancy	Masking Distance	Time
Memory	3 bits	0.333	$0.7s$
	5 bits	0.25	$1.5s$
	7 bits	0.2	$27s$
	9 bits	0.167	$34m33s$
N-Modular Redundancy	3 modules	0.333	$0.3s$
	5 modules	0.25	$0.5s$
	7 modules	0.2	$31.7s$
	9 modules	0.167	$115m$
Philosophers	2 phils	0.5	$0.3s$
	3 phils	0.333	$0.6s$
	4 phils	0.25	$7.1s$
	5 phils	0.2	$13m.53s$
Byzantines	3 generals	0.5	$0.5s$
	4 generals	0.333	$2s$

Case Study	Redundancy	Masking Distance	Time
BRP(1)	1 retransm.	0.333	$1.2s$
	3 retransm.	0.2	$1.4s$
	5 retransm.	0.143	$1.5s$
	7 retransm.	0.111	$2.1s$
BRP(3)	1 retransm.	0.333	$5.5s$
	3 retransm.	0.2	$14.9s$
	5 retransm.	0.143	$1m28s$
	7 retransm.	0.111	$4m40s$
BRP(5)	1 retransm.	0.333	$6.7s$
	3 retransm.	0.2	$32s$
	5 retransm.	0.143	$1m51s$
	7 retransm.	0.111	$6m35s$

examples and analyzed with δ_m, the BRP was modeled closer to the implementation following [16], considering the different components (sender, receiver, and models of the channels). To analyze such a complex model we have used instead the weak masking distance δ_m^W. We have calculated the masking distance for the bounded retransmission protocol with 1, 3 and 5 chunks, denoted BRP(1), BRP(3) and BRP(5), respectively. We observe that the distance values are not affected by the number of chunks to be sent by the protocol. This is expected because the masking distance depends on the redundancy added to mask the faults, which in this case, depends on the number of retransmissions.

We have run our experiments on a MacBook Air with Processor 1.3 GHz Intel Core i5 and a memory of 4 Gb. The tool and case studies for reproducing the results are available in the tool repository.

5 Related Work

In recent years, there has been a growing interest in the quantitative generalizations of the boolean notion of correctness and the corresponding quantitative verification questions [4,6,17,18]. The framework described in [6] is the closest related work to our approach. The authors generalize the traditional notion of simulation relation to three different versions of simulation distance: *correctness*, *coverage*, and *robustness*. These are defined using quantitative games with *discounted-sum* and *mean-payoff* objectives, two well-known cost functions. Similarly to that work, we also consider distances between purely discrete (non-probabilistic, untimed) systems. Correctness and coverage distances are concerned with the nominal part of the systems, and so faults play no role on them. On the other hand, robustness distance measures how many unexpected errors can be performed by the implementation in such a way that the resulting behavior is tolerated by the specification. So, it can be used to analyze the resilience of the implementation. Note that, robustness distance can only be applied to correct implementations, that is, implementations that preserve the behavior of the specification but perhaps do not cover all its behavior. As noted in [6], bisimilarity sometimes implies a distance of 1. In this sense a greater grade of robustness (as defined in [6]) is achieved by pruning critical points from the specification. Furthermore, the errors considered in that work are transitions mimicking the original ones but with different labels. In contrast to this, in our approach we consider that faults are injected into the fault-tolerant implementation, where their behaviors are not restricted by the nominal system. This follows the idea of model extension in fault-tolerance where faulty behavior is added to the nominal system. Further, note that when no faults are present, the masking distance between the specification and the implementation is 0 when they are bisimilar, and it is 1 otherwise. It is useful to note that robustness distance of [6] is not reflexive. We believe that all these definitions of distance between systems capture different notions useful for software development, and they can be used together, in a complementary way, to obtain an in-depth evaluation of fault-tolerant implementations.

6 Conclusions and Future Work

In this paper, we presented a notion of masking fault-tolerance distance between systems built on a characterization of masking tolerance via simulation relations and a corresponding game representation with quantitative objectives. Our framework is well-suited to support engineers for the analysis and design of fault-tolerant systems. More precisely, we have defined a computable masking distance function such that an engineer can measure the masking tolerance of a given fault-tolerant implementation, i.e., the number of faults that can be masked. Thereby, the engineer can measure and compare the masking fault-tolerance distance of alternative fault-tolerant implementations, and select one that fits best to her preferences.

There are many directions for future work. We have only defined a notion of fault-tolerance distance for masking fault-tolerance, similar notions of distance can be defined for other levels of fault-tolerance like failsafe and non-masking. Also, we have focused on non-quantitative models. However, metrics defined on probabilistic models, where the rate of fault occurrences is explicitly represented, could give a more accurate notion of fault tolerance.

References

1. MaskD: Masking distance tool. https://github.com/lputruele/MaskD
2. Apt, K.R., Grädel, E.: Lectures in Game Theory for Computer Scientists, 1st edn. Cambridge University Press, New York (2011)
3. Arora, A., Gouda, M.: Closure and convergence: a foundation of fault-tolerant computing. IEEE Trans. Softw. Eng. **19**(11), 1015–1027 (1993)
4. Boker, U., Chatterjee, K., Henzinger, T.A., Kupferman, O.: Temporal specifications with accumulative values. ACM Trans. Comput. Log. **15**(4), 27:1–27:25 (2014)
5. Castro, P.F., D'Argenio, P.R., Demasi, R., Putruele, L.: Measuring masking fault-tolerance. CoRR, abs/1811.05548 (2018)
6. Cerný, P., Henzinger, T.A., Radhakrishna, A.: Simulation distances. Theor. Comput. Sci. **413**(1), 21–35 (2012)
7. Charikar, M., Makarychev, K., Makarychev, Y.: Directed metrics and directed graph partitioning problems. In: Proceedings of the Seventeenth Annual ACM-SIAM Symposium on Discrete Algorithms, SODA 2006, Miami, Florida, USA, 22–26 January 2006, pp. 51–60 (2006)
8. de Alfaro, L., Faella, M., Stoelinga, M.: Linear and branching system metrics. IEEE Trans. Softw. Eng. **35**(2), 258–273 (2009)
9. de Alfaro, L., Henzinger, T.A., Kupferman, O.: Concurrent reachability games. Theor. Comput. Sci. **386**(3), 188–217 (2007)
10. de Alfaro, L., Majumdar, R., Raman, V., Stoelinga, M.: Game refinement relations and metrics. Log. Methods Comput. Sci. **4**(3:7) (2008)
11. Demasi, R., Castro, P.F., Maibaum, T.S.E., Aguirre, N.: Simulation relations for fault-tolerance. Formal Aspects Comput. **29**(6), 1013–1050 (2017)
12. Desharnais, J., Gupta, V., Jagadeesan, R., Panangaden, P.: Metrics for labelled Markov processes. Theor. Comput. Sci. **318**(3), 323–354 (2004)

13. Dijkstra, E.W.: Hierarchical ordering of sequential processes. Acta Informatica **1**(2), 115–138 (1971)
14. Fernandez, J.-C., Mounier, L.: "On the fly" verification of behavioural equivalences and preorders. In: Larsen, K.G., Skou, A. (eds.) CAV 1991. LNCS, vol. 575, pp. 181–191. Springer, Heidelberg (1992). https://doi.org/10.1007/3-540-55179-4_18
15. Gärtner, F.C.: Fundamentals of fault-tolerant distributed computing in asynchronous environments. ACM Comput. Surv. **31**, 1–26 (1999)
16. Groote, J.F., van de Pol, J.: A bounded retransmission protocol for large data packets. In: Wirsing, M., Nivat, M. (eds.) AMAST 1996. LNCS, vol. 1101, pp. 536–550. Springer, Heidelberg (1996). https://doi.org/10.1007/BFb0014338
17. Henzinger, T.A.: From Boolean to quantitative notions of correctness. In: Proceedings of the 37th ACM SIGPLAN-SIGACT Symposium on Principles of Programming Languages, POPL 2010, Madrid, Spain, 17–23 January 2010, pp. 157–158 (2010)
18. Henzinger, T.A.: Quantitative reactive modeling and verification. Comput. Sci. - R&D **28**(4), 331–344 (2013)
19. Henzinger, T.A., Majumdar, R., Prabhu, V.S.: Quantifying similarities between timed systems. In: Pettersson, P., Yi, W. (eds.) FORMATS 2005. LNCS, vol. 3829, pp. 226–241. Springer, Heidelberg (2005). https://doi.org/10.1007/11603009_18
20. Hsueh, M.-C., Tsai, T.K., Iyer, R.K.: Fault injection techniques and tools. Computer **30**(4), 75–82 (1997)
21. Iyer, R.K., Nakka, N., Gu, W., Kalbarczyk, Z.: Fault injection. In: Encyclopedia of Software Engineering, pp. 287–299 (2010)
22. Lamport, L., Shostak, R.E., Pease, M.C.: The Byzantine generals problem. ACM Trans. Program. Lang. Syst. **4**(3), 382–401 (1982)
23. Larsen, K.G., Fahrenberg, U., Thrane, C.R.: Metrics for weighted transition systems: axiomatization and complexity. Theor. Comput. Sci. **412**(28), 3358–3369 (2011)
24. Martin, D.A.: The determinacy of blackwell games. J. Symb. Log. **63**(4), 1565–1581 (1998)
25. Milner, R.: Communication and Concurrency. Prentice-Hall Inc., Upper Saddle River (1989)
26. Jurdziński, M.: Algorithms for solving parity games. In: Apt, K.R., Grädel, E. (eds.) Lectures in Game Theory for Computer Scientist, chap. 3, pp. 74–95. Cambridge University Press, New York (2011)
27. Shooman, M.L.: Reliability of Computer Systems and Networks: Fault Tolerance, Analysis, and Design. Wiley, Hoboken (2002)
28. Stirling, C.: Bisimulation, modal logic and model checking games. Log. J. IGPL **7**(1), 103–124 (1999)
29. Thrane, C.R., Fahrenberg, U., Larsen, K.G.: Quantitative analysis of weighted transition systems. J. Log. Algebraic Program. **79**(7), 689–703 (2010)
30. Williams, V.V.: Multiplying matrices faster than Coppersmith-Winograd. In: Proceedings of the 44th Symposium on Theory of Computing Conference, STOC 2012, New York, NY, USA, 19–22 May 2012 (2012)

PhASAR: An Inter-procedural Static Analysis Framework for C/C++

Philipp Dominik Schubert[1(✉)], Ben Hermann[1(✉)], and Eric Bodden[1,2(✉)]

[1] Heinz Nixdorf Institute, Paderborn University, 33102 Paderborn, Germany
{philipp.schubert,ben.hermann,eric.bodden}@upb.de
[2] Fraunhofer IEM, 33102 Paderborn, Germany

Abstract. Static program analysis is used to automatically determine program properties, or to detect bugs or security vulnerabilities in programs. It can be used as a stand-alone tool or to aid compiler optimization as an intermediary step. Developing precise, inter-procedural static analyses, however, is a challenging task, due to the algorithmic complexity, implementation effort, and the threat of state explosion which leads to unsatisfactory performance. Software written in C and C++ is notoriously hard to analyze because of the deliberately unsafe type system, unrestricted use of pointers, and (for C++) virtual dispatch. In this work, we describe the design and implementation of the LLVM-based static analysis framework PhASAR for C/C++ code. PhASAR allows data-flow problems to be solved in a fully automated manner. It provides class hierarchy, call-graph, points-to, and data-flow information, hence requiring analysis developers only to specify a definition of the data-flow problem. PhASAR thus hides the complexity of static analysis behind a high-level API, making static program analysis more accessible and easy to use. PhASAR is available as an open-source project. We evaluate PhASAR's scalability during whole-program analysis. Analyzing 12 real-world programs using a taint analysis written in PhASAR, we found PhASAR's abstractions and their implementations to provide a whole-program analysis that scales well to real-world programs. Furthermore, we peek into the details of analysis runs, discuss our experience in developing static analyses for C/C++, and present possible future improvements. Data or code related to this paper is available at: [34].

Keywords: Inter-procedural static analysis · LLVM · C/C++

1 Introduction

Programming languages from the C/C++ family are chosen as the implementation language in a multitude of projects especially in cases where a direct interface with the operating system or hardware components is of importance. Large portions of any operating system and virtual machine (such as the Java

T. Vojnar and L. Zhang (Eds.): TACAS 2019, Part II, LNCS 11428, pp. 393–410, 2019.
https://doi.org/10.1007/978-3-030-17465-1_22

VM) are written in C or C++. The reason for this is oftentimes the amount of control the programmer has over many aspects that allow for the creation of very efficient programs—but also comes with the obligation to use these features correctly to avoid introducing bugs or opening the program to security vulnerabilities.

To aid developers in creating correct and secure software, a multitude of checks have been included into compilers such as GCC [4] and Clang [2]. Various additional tools such as Cppcheck [12], clang-tidy [9], or the Clang Static Analyzer [8] provide additional means to check for unwanted behavior. Compiler-check passes and additional checkers both use static program analysis to provide warnings to their users. However, to create warnings in a timely fashion, these tools use comparatively simple analyses that provide either only checks for simple properties, or suffer from a large number of false or missed warnings, due to the imprecision or unsoundness of the used analysis.

For programs written in Java, program-analysis frameworks like Soot [16], WALA [33], and Doop [13] are available which allow for a more precise data-flow analysis to determine more intricate program problems. Furthermore, algorithmic frameworks such as *Interprocedural Finite Subset (IFDS)* [24], *Interprocedural Distributive Environments (IDE)* [26], or *Weighted Pushdown Systems (WPDS)* [25] can be used to describe dataflow problems and efficiently compute their possible solutions.

So far, such implementations have not been openly available for programs written in C/C++. This work thus presents the novel program-analysis framework PhASAR, an extension to the LLVM compiler infrastructure [17]. In its inception, we used our experience in developing previous such frameworks for JVM-based languages, namely Soot [16] and OPAL [14], to design a flexible framework that can be adapted to several different types of client analyses. Besides solving data-flow problems, PhASAR can be used to achieve other related goals as well, for instance, call-graph construction, or the computation of points-to information. Its features can be used independently and be included into other software. PhASAR's implementation is written entirely in C++ and is available as open source under the permissive MIT license [23].

PhASAR is intended to be used as a static analyzer. Therefore, it does not substitute but complement features from the LLVM toolchain and provides also for analyses which during compilation would be prohibitively expensive.

This paper makes the following contributions:

- It provides a user-centric description of PhASAR's architecture, its infrastructure, and data-flow solvers,
- it presents a case-study that shows PhASAR's overall scalability as well as the precise runtimes of a concrete static analysis, and
- it discusses our experience in developing static analyses for C/C++.

2 Related Work

There are several established and well-maintained tools and frameworks for the Java ecosystems. Frameworks from academia include Soot [16], which is a static analysis framework that allows call-graph construction, computation of points-to information and solving of data-flow problems for Java and Android. Soot does not support inter-procedural data-flow analyses directly. However, a user can solve such problems using the Heros [7] extension that implements an IFDS/IDE solver. The WALA [33] framework provides similar functionalities for Java bytecode, JavaScript and Python. OPAL [14] allows for the implementation of abstract interpretations of Java bytecode. Also the manipulation of bytecode is supported. A declarative approach is implemented by the Doop framework [13]. Doop uses a declarative rule set to encode an analysis and solves it using the logic-based Datalog solver. The framework allows for pointer analysis of Java programs and implements a range of algorithms that can be used for context insensitive, call-site and object sensitive analyses.

Tooling for C/C++ includes Cppcheck [12] which aims for a result without false positives and allows to encode simple rules as well as the development of more powerful add-ons. The clang-tidy tool [9] provides built-in checks for style validation, detection of interface misuse as well as bug-finding using simple rules, but can be extended by a user. Checks can be written on preprocessor level using callbacks or on AST level using AST matchers that can be specified using an embedded domain specific language (EDSL). The Clang Static Analyzer [8] uses symbolic execution and allows custom checks to be written. The SVF [31] framework computes points-to information for constructing sparse value flow and memory static single assignment (SSA). Hence, it can be used for analyses that rely on those information such as memory leak detection or null pointer analysis. Additionally, more precise pointer analysis can be build on top of SVF's results. However, as the computation of memory SSA does require a significant amount of computation, using SVF may not pay off for problems that can be encoded using distributive frameworks, which allow fast, summary-based solutions.

There are also commercial, closed-source tools for static analysis such as CodeSonar [10] and Coverity [11], both of which support analyses for C, C++, Java and other languages. Whereas these products are attractive to industry as they provide polished user interfaces, they are not usable for evaluating novel algorithms and ideas in static-analysis research.

3 Data-Flow Analysis

Data-flow analysis is a form of static analysis which works by propagating information about the property of interest—the data-flow facts—through a model of the program, typically a control-flow graph, and captures the interactions of the flow facts with the program. The interaction of a single statement s with a data-flow fact is described by a flow function. There are two orthogonal approaches [27] that can be used in order to solve inter-procedural (whole program) data-flow problems: the call-strings and functional approach. For the call-strings approach we refer the reader to related work [15,27]. In the following we briefly present the functional approach using a linear constant propagation that we apply to a small program shown in Listing 1.1. A linear constant propagation is a data-flow analysis that precisely tracks variables with constant values and variables that linearly ($c = a \cdot x + b$, with a, b constant values) depend on constant values through the program. Non-linear dependencies are over-approximated. In our example, we restrict the analysis to keep track of integer constants only. Such an analysis can be used to perform program optimizations by replacing variables with their constant values, and folding expressions that use constant values, eventually possibly also removing dead code. The analysis would be able to optimize the program shown in Listing 1.1 to `int main() {return 12; }`.

```
int inc(int p) { return ++p; }
int main() {
  int a = 1;
  int b = 2;
  int c = 3;
  a = inc(a); // cs1
  b = inc(b); // cs2
  c = b * 4;
  return c;
}
```

Listing 1.1. Program `P`

If the flow functions of the problem to be solved are monotone and distributive over the merge operator, it can be encoded using *Inter-procedural Finite Distributive Subset* (IFDS) or *Inter-procedural Distributive Environments* (IDE). Unlike the call-string approach which is limited to a certain level of context-sensitivity (commonly denoted as k), IFDS and IDE are fully context-sensitive, i.e., $k = \infty$. In IFDS [24] and its generalization IDE [26], a data-flow problem is transformed into a graph reachability problem. The reachability is computed using the so called exploded super-graph (ESG). If a node (s_i, d_i) in the ESG is reachable from a special tautological node Λ, the data-flow fact represented by d_i holds at statement s_i. The ESG is built according to the flow functions which can be represented as bipartite graphs. Functions for generating (`Gen`) and destroying (`Kill`) data-flow facts can be encoded into flow functions making the framework compatible to more traditional approaches to data-flow analysis. The composition $f \circ g$ of two functions can be computed by composing their corresponding bipartite graphs, i.e., merging the nodes of g with the corresponding nodes of the domain of f. The ESG for the complete program is constructed by replacing every node of the inter-procedural control-flow graph (ICFG) with the graph representation of the corresponding flow function. Scalability issues due to context-sensitivity are mitigated through summaries that are computed by composition of all bipartite graphs of a function for a given input. These summaries are reused for subsequent calls to an already summarized function.

The complexity of the IFDS algorithm is $\mathcal{O}(|N| \cdot |D|^3)$ where $|N|$ is the number of nodes on the ICFG (or number of program statements) and $|D|$ the size of the data-flow domain that is used. To make the analysis scale, the domain D should thus be kept small.

In IDE, a generalization of the IFDS framework, the edges of the ESG are additionally annotated with so-called *edge functions.* With the help of those edge functions, an additional value-computation problem can be encoded, which is solved while performing the reachability computation. The complexity of the

IDE algorithm is the same as for the IFDS algorithm. Many problems can be solved more efficiently by encoding them with IDE rather than IFDS, because IDE uses two domains to solve a given problem. In addition to the domain D of the data-flow facts, the value computation problem is formulated over a second value domain V, which can be large, even infinite. Crucially, for a given fixed-size program, the complexity of both IFDS and IDE depends only on the size of D.

Let us consider a linear constant propagation to be performed on the example program shown in Listing 1.1. Using IFDS, the data-flow domain can be encoded by using pairs of $\mathcal{V} \times \mathbb{Z}$ program variables and integer values. However, this strategy leads to a huge domain D and prevents the generation of effective summaries. For each call to `inc()` in Listing 1.1 with a different input value `a`, a new summary must be generated. In the example, we would obtain summaries $\{(\texttt{p}, 1) \mapsto (\texttt{<ret>}, 2)\}$ for call site *cs1* and $\{(\texttt{p}, 2) \mapsto (\texttt{<ret>}, 3)\}$ for *cs2*.

With IDE, the problem can be encoded in a more elegant and efficient way, by using $\mathcal{V}$ as the data-flow domain and $\mathbb{Z}$ as the value domain. The ESG for a linear constant propagation performed on Listing 1.1 using IDE is shown in Fig. 1. As the context-dependent part of the analysis is encoded using the edge functions, only one summary is generated for the `inc()` function, $\lambda x.\ x + 1$.

Performing a reachability check on the ESG for variable `c` at line 9, one finds that `c` can be replaced by the literal `12`. Because the return statement is the program's only observable effect, all other statements can be safely removed.

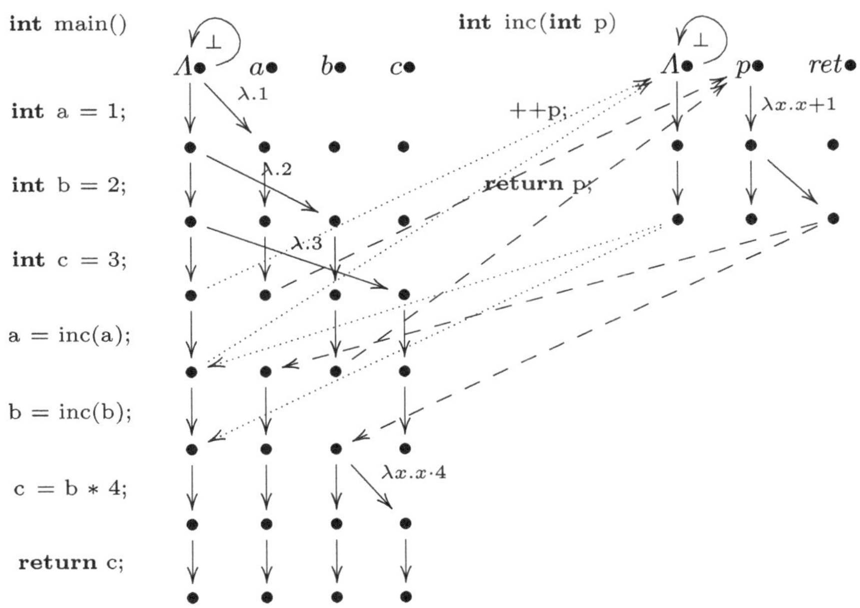

Fig. 1. Exploded super graph for the program P in Listing 1.1

4 Architecture

Precise data-flow analysis requires information from multiple supporting analyses which are typically run earlier, such as class-hierarchy, call-graph, and points-to analysis. Algorithmic frameworks like IFDS provide a generalized algorithm that is then parameterized for each individual data-flow problem. The infrastructure provided by these basic analyses and algorithmic frameworks is necessary to allow analysis designers to efficiently concentrate on the goal of a data-flow analysis. PhASAR is the first framework to provide such infrastructure for programs written in the C/C++ language family. Its infrastructure is designed modularly, such that analysis developers can choose the components necessary for their individual goals. In Fig. 2 we present the high-level architecture of the framework.

We allow PhASAR to be used in multiple ways. The first (and easiest) way is through its command-line interface. Its implementation can be seen as a blueprint to create other tools which use PhASAR. The command-line interface provides a means to execute basic analyses such as call-graph construction or pointer analysis or run pre-defined IFDS/IDE-based analyses. The output of these analyses can then be processed using other tooling or presented to the user directly.

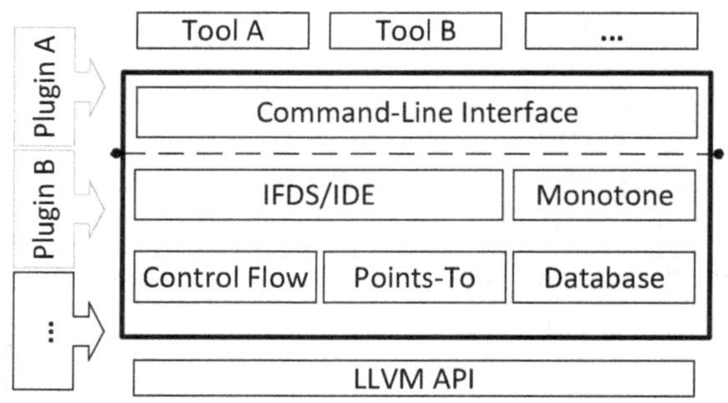

Fig. 2. PhASAR's high-level architecture

The command-line interface can also be extended with custom analyses, provided as separately compiled plugins. Currently, custom control-flow or call-graph analyses and custom data-flow analyses can be packaged in this way. The command-line interface acts as the runtime for these plugins and delegates control to the plugin at the appropriate times providing necessary information. Plugin providers need to create an implementation of a pre-defined C++ class wrapping their analysis code. The plugin is compiled separately and then provided to PhASAR in form of a shared object library.

PhASAR can also be included into other tools by using it as a library. This way of using PhASAR provides the most flexibility as developers can freely select the components that should be part of an analysis and can reuse even parts of the components provided by the framework.

PhASAR allows analysis developers to specify arbitrary data-flow problems, which are then solved in a fully-automated manner on the specified LLVM IR target code. Solving a static analysis problem on the IR rather than the source language makes the analysis generally easier. This is because it removes the dependency on the concrete source language, as the IR is usually simpler since the IR involves no nesting and has fewer instructions. Various compiler front-ends for a wide range of languages targeting LLVM IR exist. Hence, PhASAR is able to analyze programs written in languages other than C/C++, too. The framework computes all required information to perform an analysis such as points-to, call-graph, type-hierarchy as well as additional parameterizable taint and typestate analyses.

PhASAR provides various capabilities and interfaces to compute data-flow problems or aid other types of analyses. First, the framework contains interfaces and implementations for the computation of an ICFG; we provide some parameterizable implementations for the LLVM IR.

Next, PhASAR currently supports the computation of function-wise points-to information using LLVM's implementations of the *Andersen*-style [6] or *Steensgard*-style [30] algorithms. Points-to information and ICFG computation can be combined to obtain more precise results. We discuss the quality of points-to information and our current efforts to improve their quality in Sect. 8.

To resolve virtual function calls in C++, we provide means to construct a type hierarchy. We construct the type hierarchy for composite types and reconstruct the virtual-method tables from the IR, which together with the hierarchy information allow PhASAR to resolve potential call targets at a given call-site.

PhASAR provides implementations of IDE and IFDS solvers as described by Reps et al. [24] including the extensions of Naeem et al. [20]. We implemented IFDS as a specialization of IDE using a binary lattice only using a top and a bottom element much alike the Heros implementation [7]. Both solvers are accompanied by a corresponding interface for problem definition. To solve a data-flow problem using the IDE or IFDS solver, the data-flow problem must be encoded by implementing this interface. We present this in detail in Sect. 5.

For non-distributive data-flow problems PhASAR provides an implementation of the traditional monotone framework which allows one to solve intra-procedural problems. The framework provides an inter-procedural version as well that uses a user-specified context in order to differentiate calling-contexts. PhASAR provides a context interface and implementations of this interface that realize the call-strings and value-based approach VASCO [22], in which context-sensitivity is achieved by reusing information that has been computed for previous calls under the same context. The framework also implements a version of the context class to represent a *null context*. This context has the same effect as applying the monotone framework directly in an inter-procedural setting. Both solvers are accompanied by corresponding interfaces for problem descriptions which must be implemented to encode the data-flow problem. The details are provided in Sect. 5.

All of PhASAR's data-flow solvers are implemented in a fully generic manner and heavily make use of templates and interfaces. For instance, a solver follows a target program's control-flow that is specified through an implementation of either the `CFG` or the `ICFG` interface. Analysis developers can parameterize a solver with an existing implementation or they can provide their own custom implementation. They can run a forward or backward analysis depending on the direction of the chosen control-flow graph. Moreover, all data-flow related functionality is hidden behind interfaces. A solver queries the required functionality such as flow functions or merge operations for the underlying lattice whenever necessary. We have specified problem interfaces on which the corresponding solver operates. Thus, analysis developers encode their data-flow problem by providing an implementation for the problem interface and provide this implementation to the accompanying solver. PhASAR is able to solve a problem on other IRs when suitable implementations for the IR specific parts such as the control-flow graphs and problem descriptions are provided by the analysis developer.

5 Implementation

Our goal with PhASAR is easing the formulation of a data-flow analysis such that an analysis developer only needs to focus on the implementation of the problem description rather than providing details how the problem is solved.

PhASAR achieves parts of its generalizability through template parameters. These template parameters include, among others, `N`, `D`, `M`. They are consistently used throughout the implementation of PhASAR. `N` denotes the type of a node in the ICFG, i.e., typically an IR statement, `D` denotes the domain of the data-flow facts, and `M` is a placeholder for the type of a method/function. When analyzing LLVM IR, `N` is always of type `const llvm::Instruction*` and `M` is of type `const llvm::Function*`, whereas `D` depends on the specific data-flow analysis that the developer wants to encode. For our example using linear constant propagation described in Sect. 3, `D = pair<const llvm::Value *, int>` could be used to capture the property of interest. LLVM's `Value` type is quite useful as it is a super-type that is located high in the type hierarchy. This allows an analysis developer to use values of all of `Value`'s subtypes in the value domain, which makes it highly flexible.

5.1 Encoding an IFDS Analysis

Listing 1.2 shows the interface for an IFDS problem. An analysis developer has to define a new type—the problem description—implementing the `FlowFunctions` interface.

```
template <typename N, typename D, typename M> struct FlowFunctions {
  virtual ~FlowFunctions() = default;
  virtual FlowFunction<D> *getNormalFlowFunction(N curr, N succ) = 0;
  virtual FlowFunction<D> *getCallFlowFunction(N callStmt,
                                               M destMthd) = 0;
  virtual FlowFunction<D> *getRetFlowFunction(N callSite,
                                              M calleeMthd,
                                              N exitStmt,
                                              N retSite) = 0;
  virtual FlowFunction<D> *
  getCallToRetFlowFunction(N callSite, N retSite, set<M> callees) = 0;
};
```

Listing 1.2. Interface for specifying flow functions in IFDS/IDE

The flow function factories shown in Listing 1.2 handle the different types of flows. The four factory functions each have an individual purpose:

- `getNormalFlowFunction` handles all intra-procedural flows.
- `getCallFlowFunction` handles inter-procedural flows at a call-site. Usually, the task of this flow function factory is to map the data-flow facts that hold at a given call-site into the callee method's scope.
- `getRetFlowFunction` handles inter-procedural flows at an exit statement (e.g. a return statement). This maps the callee's return value, as well as data-flow facts that may leave the function by reference or pointer parameters, back into the caller's context/scope.
- `getCallToRetFlowFunction` propagates all data-flow facts that are not involved in a call along-side the call-site, typically stack-local data not referenced by parameters.

These flow function factories are automatically queried by the solver, based on the inter-procedural control-flow graph.

The functions in Listing 1.2 are factories since they have to return small function objects of type `FlowFunction` which is shown in Listing 1.3. As a `FlowFunction` is itself an interface, an analysis developer has to provide a suitable implementation. The member function `computeTargets()` takes a value of a dataflow fact of type `D` and computes a set of new dataflow facts of the same type. It specifies how the bipartite graph for the statement that represents the flow function is constructed and can be thought of an answer to the question "What edges must be drawn?".

```
template <typename D> struct FlowFunction {
  virtual ~FlowFunction() = default;
  virtual set<D> computeTargets(D source) = 0;
};
```

Listing 1.3. Interface for a flow function in IFDS/IDE

As flow function implementations often follow certain patterns, we provide implementations for the most common patterns as template classes. Many useful flow functions like `Gen`, `GenIf`, `Kill`, `KillAll`, and `Identity` are already implemented and can be directly used. Any number of flow functions can be easily combined using our implementations of the `Compose` and `Union` flow functions. We also provide `MapFactsToCallee` and `MapFactsToCaller` flow functions that automatically map parameters into a callee and back to a caller, since this behavior is frequently desired. Flow functions which are stateless, e.g. `Identity` or `KillAll`, are implemented as a singleton.

5.2 Encoding an IDE Analysis

If an analysis developer wishes to encode their problem within IDE, they have to additionally provide implementations for the edge functions. With help of the edge functions, an analysis developer is able to specify a computation which is performed along the edges of the exploded super-graph leading to the queried node (c.f. Fig. 1). The interface for the edge function factories and their responsibilities are analogous to the flow function factories in Listing 1.2.

Each edge function factory must return an edge function implementation: a small function object similar to a flow function which has a `computeTarget()` function, a compose, a merge, and an equality-check operation. The `EdgeFunction` interface is shown in Listing 1.4.

```
template <typename V> class EdgeFunction {
public:
  virtual ~EdgeFunction() = default;
  virtual V computeTarget(V source) = 0;
  virtual EdgeFunction<V> *
  composeWith(EdgeFunction<V> *secondFunction) = 0;
  virtual EdgeFunction<V> *
  joinWith(EdgeFunction<V> *otherFunction) = 0;
  virtual bool equal_to(EdgeFunction<V> *other) const = 0;
};
```

Listing 1.4. Interface for an edge function in IDE

As this interface is more complex than the flow function interface, we explain the purpose of each function. The `computeTarget()` function describes a computation over the value domain `V` in terms of lambda calculus.

The `composeWith()` function encodes how to compose two edge functions. In most scenarios, this function can be implemented as $(f \circ g)(x) = f(g(x))$. To avoid additional boilerplate code, we provide an `EdgeFunctionComposer` class that performs this job and can be used as a super class.

`joinWith()` encodes how to join two edge functions at statements where two control-flow edges lead to the same successor statement. Depending if a may or a must-analysis is performed, implementations of this function typically check which edge function computes a value that is higher up in the lattice, i.e., a more approximate value, and returns the corresponding edge function. For our linear constant propagation from Sect. 3, this function would return one of the edge functions if both describe the same value computation, the bottom edge function if both of them encode the $\perp$ value and the edge function encoding the top element otherwise. The intuition here is to always pick the element that is higher in the lattice as it represents more information.

The `equal_to()` interface function has to be implemented to return true if both edge functions describe the same value computation, false otherwise.

A complete implementation of the IDE linear constant propagation can be found along with PhASAR's other examples at our website [23].

5.3 Encoding a Monotone Analysis

If an analysis developer wishes to encode a problem that does not satisfy the distributivity property, they have to make use of the monotone-framework implementation or its inter-procedural variant. The interface for specifying an inter-procedural monotone problem is shown in Listing 1.5. Similar to an IFDS/IDE problem, an analysis developer has to specify flow functions for intra- and inter-procedural flows. But in contrast to IFDS/IDE, these flow functions do not operate on single, distributive data-flow facts, but on sets of data-flow facts instead. The solver calls the flow functions and provides the set of data-flow facts which hold right before the current statement. The return value to be computed in the flow function is a set of data-flow facts that hold after the effects of the current statement. The `join()` function specifies how information is merged when two branches join at a common successor statement. This is typically implemented as set-union or set-intersection depending on whether a may or must-analysis has to be solved. Algorithms from C++'s STL may be used here. Finally, the `sqSubSetEqual()` function must be implemented to determine if the amount of information between two sets has increased in order to check if a fixpoint is reached. The context that is used for the inter-procedural analysis can be specified by the analysis developer using the template parameter. An analysis developer can provide a pre-defined context class in order to parameterize the analysis to be a call-strings approach, a value-based approach, or they can define their own context to be used.

```
template <typename N, typename D, typename M, typename I>
struct InterMonotoneProblem {
  InterMonotoneProblem(I Icfg) : ICFG(Icfg) {}
  virtual ~InterMonotoneProblem() = default;
  virtual set<D> join(const set<D> &Lhs, const set<D> &Rhs) = 0;
  virtual bool sqSubSetEqual(const set<D> &Lhs,
                             const set<D> &Rhs) = 0;
  virtual set<D> normalFlow(N Stmt, const set<D> &In) = 0;
  virtual set<D> callFlow(N CallSite, M Callee, const set<D> &In) = 0;
  virtual set<D> returnFlow(N CallSite, M Callee, N RetStmt,
                           N RetSite, const set<D> &In) = 0;
  virtual set<D> callToRetFlow(N CallSite, N RetSite,
                               const set<D> &In) = 0;
};
```

Listing 1.5. Interface for describing an interprocedural problem for the monotone framework

5.4 Handling of Intrinsic and Libc Function Calls

LLVM currently has approximately 130 intrinsic functions. These functions are used to describe semantics in the analysis and optimization phase and do not have an actual implementation. Later-on in the compiler pipeline, the back-end is free to replace a call to an intrinsic function with a software or a hardware implementation – if one exists for the target architecture. Introducing new intrinsic functions is preferred over introducing novel instructions to LLVM since, when introducing a new instruction, all optimizations, analyses, and tools built on top of LLVM have to be revisited to make them aware of the new instruction. A call to an intrinsic function can be handled as an ordinary function call.

The functions contained in the libc standard library represent special targets as well as these functions are used by virtually all practical C and C++[1] programs. Moreover, the functions contained in the standard library cannot be analyzed themselves as they are mostly very thin wrappers around system calls and are often not available for the analysis. In many cases, however, it is not necessary to analyze these functions when performing a data-flow analysis. PhASAR

[1] The compiler translates many of C++'s features into ordinary calls to libc.

models all of them as the identity function. An analysis developer can change the default behavior and model different effects by using special summary functions. The `SpecialSummaries` class can be used to register flow and edge functions other than identity. This class is aware of all intrinsic and libc functions.

5.5 A Note on Soundness

Livshits et al. have introduced the notion *soundy* analyses [18]. Soundy analyses use sensible underapproximations to cope with certain language features that would otherwise make an analysis impractically imprecise. Analyses in PhASAR are currently *soundy*. For instance, PhASAR's ICFG misses one control-flow edge in the presence of `setjmp()/longjmp()`. Functions that are loaded dynamically from shared object libraries using `dlsym()` cannot be handled either. PhASAR's data-flow solvers treat calls to dynamically loaded libraries and libraries for which function definitions are missing as identity, unless the analysis developer specifies otherwise. A sound handling would be to set all variables involved in such calls to $\top$, which again, may lead to large imprecision.

6 Scalability

In this section, we present the runtime measurements for two concrete static analyses – `IFDSSolverTest` we name $\mathbb{I}$ and `IFDSTaintAnalysis` we name $\mathbb{T}$ – that are both implemented in PhASAR. $\mathbb{I}$ is a trivial IFDS analysis which passes the tautological data-flow fact Λ through the program. The analysis acts as a baseline as it is the most efficient IFDS/IDE analysis that can possibly be implemented. $\mathbb{T}$ implements a taint analysis. A taint analysis tracks values that have been tainted by one or more sources through the program and reports whenever one of the tainted values reaches a sink, which can be functions or instructions. Our taint analysis treats the command-line parameters `argc` and `argv` that are passed into the `main()` function as tainted. Functions that read values from the outside (e.g. `fread()`) are interpreted as sources. Functions that can leak tainted variables to the outside such as `printf()` or `fwrite()` are considered sinks. As a potentially large amount of tainted values have to be tracked through the program, analysis $\mathbb{T}$ will provide insights into the scalability of PhASAR's IFDS/IDE solver implementation.

Table 1 shows the programs that we analyzed. For each program, the IR's lines of code, number of statements, pointers, and allocation sites have been measured with PhASAR. The LLVM IR has been compiled with the Clang compiler using production flags. The figures give an intuition for the program's complexity. The programs that we analyzed comprise some C programs like some of the coreutils [3] as well as two C++ programs like PhASAR itself and a PhASAR-based tool MPT. In addition, it shows the runtimes of the analyses $\mathbb{I}$ and $\mathbb{T}$ separated into different phases (in the format runtime $\mathbb{I}$/runtime $\mathbb{T}$). We measured the runtimes for the construction of points-to information (PT), class hierarchy (CH), call-graph (CG), data-flow information (DF), and the total runtime (Σ). We also measured the number of function summaries $\psi(f)$ that could be reused while solving the analysis. The latter one is a good indicator for the quality of the data-flow domain D, as higher reuse indicates a more efficient analysis. #G and #K denote the number of facts that have been generated or killed in the taint analysis, respectively.

We measured the runtimes by performing 15 runs for each analysis on a virtual machine running on an Intel(R) Xeon(R) CPU E5-2695 v3 @ 2.30 GHz machine with 128 GB memory. We removed the minimum and maximum values and computed the average of the remaining 13 values for each of the four analysis steps and the total runtime. We used an on-the-fly call-graph algorithm that uses points-to information for the coreutils. For PhASAR and MPT, we used a declared type-analysis (DTA) call-graph algorithm in order to reduce the amount of memory required to reproduce our results. In addition, we found that DTA performed well enough on our C++ target programs.

With one exception, PhASAR is able to analyze a program from coreutils within a few seconds. Analyzing cp using $\mathbb{T}$ takes around 13 min. This is because a large amount of facts is generated which must then be propagated by the solver. This result shows the cubic impact of the number of data-flow facts on IFDS/IDE's complexity. Analyzing the million-line programs PhASAR and MPT ranges from 7 to 18 min. As one can observe for PhASAR, an analysis may destroy data-flow facts more often than it generates them. This is caused by C++'s exceptional control-flow where the same fact is destroyed during normal and exceptional flow.

We observed that the DF part of $\mathbb{T}$ actually runs faster than $\mathbb{I}$ for our C++ target programs. This is because $\mathbb{T}$ should behave very similar to the solvertest for the C++ target programs, as only very few facts are actually generated. Furthermore, $\mathbb{T}$ will take shortcuts whenever it plugs in the desired effects at call-sites of source and sink functions. $\mathbb{I}$ in contrast, follows these calls making it slower than $\mathbb{T}$.

Table 1. Program's characteristics and performance figures for analyses $\mathbb{I}/\mathbb{T}$

Program	kLOC	Stmts	Ptrs	Allocs	CH [ms]	PT [s]	CG [s]	DF [s]	Σ [s]	$\#\psi(f)$	#G	#K
wc	132	63166	10644	396	24/24	1.0/1.0	0.1/0.1	0.2/11	2/13	119/125	10202	6830
ls	152	71712	13200	438	27/27	1.4/1.4	1.1/1.2	0.6/1.0	4/5	836/839	79	74
cat	130	62588	10584	391	24/24	1.0/1.0	0.0/0.0	0.1/1.3	2/3	21/22	2525	1262
cp	141	67097	11722	443	32/30	1.3/1.3	0.6/0.6	0.4/789	3/792	547/737	16999	12839
whoami	129	61860	10433	389	24/23	1.0/1.0	0.0/0.0	0.1/0.3	2/2	8/11	97	92
dd	137	65287	11150	408	25/25	1.1/1.0	0.2/0.2	0.2/37	2/40	164/176	14711	11058
fold	130	62201	10509	390	24/23	1.0/1.0	0.0/0.0	0.1/0.3	2/2	17/22	107	102
join	134	64196	11042	402	24/24	1.0/1.0	0.0/0.0	0.1/0.5	2/3	91/95	104	94
kill	130	62304	10527	394	24/24	1.0/1.0	0.0/0.0	0.1/0.1	2/2	24/24	22	4
uniq	131	62663	10650	396	24/24	1.0/1.0	0.0/0.0	0.1/0.4	2/2	50/53	96	90
MPT	3514	1351735	755567	176540	906/903	22/22	8.8/8.8	458/379	519/439	12531/12532	20	9
PhASAR	3554	1368297	763796	178486	962/946	23/23	24/24	987/917	1064/993	25778/25782	56	77

Analyzing all of the 97 coreutils, PhASAR, and MPT requires a total analysis time of of 30 min for $\mathbb{I}$ and 1 h and 31 min for $\mathbb{T}$. These measurements show that PhASAR is capable of analyzing even a million-line program within minutes, even though PhASAR's algorithms and data structures have not yet undergone manual optimization.

7 Guidelines for the Analysis on Real-World Code

In this section, we share our experience in analyzing real-world C/C++ programs. Although the LLVM IR is expressive enough to capture arbitrary source languages, we found that the characteristics and complexity of the source language propagate into the IR. Observe the following call-site in LLVM IR: `%retval = call i32 %fptr(%class.S* dereferenceable(4) %ptr, i32 5)`, assuming C to be the source language, a plain function pointer is called. If C++ is the source language, we cannot be sure whether a function pointer or a virtual member function of class `S` is called. This is the reason why we observed that the analysis runtime for C++ target programs is usually much higher than for C programs.

For more complex languages like C++ we have to keep track of special member functions. These functions are mapped into ordinary LLVM IR functions that Clang places in a well-defined order in the generated IR. For some analyses like the declared-type analysis (DTA) call-graph algorithm, we need to be aware of these special member functions in order to preserve high precision.

We also found that even a well-debugged analysis that has been hardened on a large variety of test programs may still fail on production code as some corner cases have not been thought of. The large amount of information available to an analysis run makes debugging errors hard. A standard debugger does not suffice because an analysis writer has to step through a lot of code that is not relevant for them. For Java, a special dedicated debugger for static analysis has been developed [21] which shows the relevance of the problem.

Depending on the optimization passes that have been applied to code in LLVM IR before it is handed over to the analysis, it may have very different characteristics. Although optimization passes are required to have no impact on the semantics, the structure of the IR code changes. In our experience, it is helpful to start developing an analysis on small test programs that are translated into IR without optimization passes, and cover as many cases as the analysis should find. Once an analysis handles these test cases correctly or with the desired precision, optimization passes should be applied to the test cases. After rerunning the analysis the results should be checked against their unoptimized version. When applying an analysis to production code, the code should be compiled using production flags in order to analyze code that is as close as possible to what actually runs on the machine.

We found that the usage of debug symbols is helpful. The Clang compiler's `-g` flag can be added to propagate the debug symbols into the IR. Those can then be queried using LLVM's corresponding API. However, the debug symbols may not always present, which is why an analysis should not rely on them.

8 Future Work

In this section we briefly summarize our plans for future improvements.

It would be interesting to evaluate the use of PhASAR for analyzing a different IR. One type of IR might advantages over others for different analysis problems. We plan to additionally support the GENERIC, GIMPLE and RTL [5,19] IR from the GCC project.

Another interesting framework for data-flow analysis is *Weighted Pushdown Systems* (WPDS) [25,28]. WPDS is able to compute an analysis within a stack automaton. WPDS allows for more compact data structures, the generation of witnesses, as well as precise queries specifying paths of interest using regular expressions. We plan to support WPDS is a future version of PhASAR using the weighted/nested-word automaton library [32].

Checking the correctness of an IFDS/IDE analysis is complex since checking the correctness of the underlying ESG is tedious and time consuming. A high quality visualization may help reduce the amount of time spent debugging an analysis. A graphical user interface will reduce the amount of knowledge that is required to use the framework.

Since the flow and edge functions have to be implemented in a general purpose programming language, they require some amount of boilerplate code. It remains an open question if one could design a non-Turing-complete EDSL with a library like `boost::proto` [1] which simplifies the task of encoding analysis problems.

PhASAR currently uses LLVM's points-to information which is rather imprecise. We plan to integrate a more precise pointer analysis into PhASAR to support more precise call-graph construction and client analyses by adapting the demand-driven Boomerang approach presented in [29] to PhASAR.

9 Conclusion

In this paper, we presented our implementation of a static analysis framework for programs written in C/C++ named PhASAR. We presented its architecture and implementation from a user's perspective to make practical static analysis more accessible. We presented experiments which have shown PhASAR's scalability and discussed the runtimes of the key parts of two concrete client analyses.

With PhASAR we strive toward the goals of providing a framework for static analysis targeting (but not limited to) C/C++, a base for quickly evaluating novel ideas and applications, and a suitable way of handling the complexity. PhASAR is open-source and available online [23] under the permissive MIT licence, and therefore, open for contributions, feedback and use. PhASAR has already received tremendous support in the research community and from practitioners as 223 stars and 26 forks on GitHub show.[2]

[2] As of 8am February 07, 2019.

Acknowledgments. This work was partially supported by the German Research Foundation (DFG) within the Collaborative Research Centre "On-The-Fly Computing" (SFB 901) and the Heinz Nixdorf Foundation. We would also like to thank Richard Leer for his assistance in developing and improving the framework.

References

1. Boost.proto, August 2018. https://www.boost.org/doc/libs/1_68_0/doc/html/proto.html
2. Clang: a C Language Family Frontend for LLVM, July 2018. http://clang.llvm.org/
3. CoreUtils, July 2018. https://www.gnu.org/software/coreutils/coreutils.html
4. GCC, the GNU Compiler Collection, July 2018. https://gcc.gnu.org/
5. GNU Compiler Collection (GCC) Internals, July 2018. https://gcc.gnu.org/onlinedocs/gccint/
6. Andersen, L.O.: Program analysis and specialization for the C programming language. Technical report (1994)
7. Bodden, E.: Inter-procedural data-flow analysis with IFDS/IDE and Soot. In: Proceedings of the ACM SIGPLAN International Workshop on State of the Art in Java Program Analysis, SOAP 2012, pp. 3–8. ACM, New York (2012). https://doi.org/10.1145/2259051.2259052
8. Clang Static Analyzer, August 2018. https://clang-analyzer.llvm.org/
9. Clang-Tidy, August 2018. http://clang.llvm.org/extra/clang-tidy/
10. CodeSonar, August 2018. https://www.grammatech.com/products/codesonar/
11. Coverity, August 2018. https://scan.coverity.com/
12. Cppcheck, August 2018. http://cppcheck.sourceforge.net/
13. Doop, August 2018. http://doop.program-analysis.org/
14. Eichberg, M., Hermann, B.: A software product line for static analyses: the OPAL framework. In: Proceedings of the 3rd ACM SIGPLAN International Workshop on the State of the Art in Java Program Analysis, SOAP 2014, pp. 1–6. ACM, New York (2014). https://doi.org/10.1145/2614628.2614630
15. Kam, J.B., Ullman, J.D.: Monotone data flow analysis frameworks. Acta Informatica **7**(3), 305–317 (1977). https://doi.org/10.1007/BF00290339
16. Lam, P., Bodden, E., Lhoták, O., Hendren, L.: The Soot framework for Java program analysis: a retrospective, October 2011
17. Lattner, C., Adve, V.: LLVM: a compilation framework for lifelong program analysis & transformation. In: Proceedings of the International Symposium on Code Generation and Optimization: Feedback-Directed and Runtime Optimization, CGO 2004, p. 75. IEEE Computer Society, Washington, DC (2004). http://dl.acm.org/citation.cfm?id=977395.977673
18. Livshits, B., et al.: In defense of soundiness: a manifesto. Commun. ACM **58**(2), 44–46 (2015). https://doi.org/10.1145/2644805
19. Merrill, J.: GENERIC and GIMPLE: a new tree representation for entire functions. In: Proceedings of the GCC Developers Summit, pp. 171–180 (2003)
20. Naeem, N.A., Lhoták, O., Rodriguez, J.: Practical extensions to the IFDS algorithm. In: Gupta, R. (ed.) CC 2010. LNCS, vol. 6011, pp. 124–144. Springer, Heidelberg (2010). https://doi.org/10.1007/978-3-642-11970-5_8
21. Nguyen, L., Krüger, S., Hill, P., Ali, K., Bodden, E.: VisuFlow, a debugging environment for static analyses. In: International Conference for Software Engineering (ICSE), Tool Demonstrations Track, 1 January 2018

22. Padhye, R., Khedker, U.P.: Interprocedural data flow analysis in soot using value contexts. In: Proceedings of the 2nd ACM SIGPLAN International Workshop on State of the Art in Java Program Analysis, SOAP 2013, pp. 31–36. ACM, New York (2013). https://doi.org/10.1145/2487568.2487569
23. Phasar, July 2018. https://phasar.org
24. Reps, T., Horwitz, S., Sagiv, M.: Precise interprocedural dataflow analysis via graph reachability. In: Proceedings of the 22nd ACM SIGPLAN-SIGACT Symposium on Principles of Programming Languages, POPL 1995, pp. 49–61. ACM, New York (1995). https://doi.org/10.1145/199448.199462
25. Reps, T., Schwoon, S., Jha, S.: Weighted pushdown systems and their application to interprocedural dataflow analysis. In: Cousot, R. (ed.) SAS 2003. LNCS, vol. 2694, pp. 189–213. Springer, Heidelberg (2003). https://doi.org/10.1007/3-540-44898-5_11. http://dl.acm.org/citation.cfm?id=1760267.1760283
26. Sagiv, M., Reps, T., Horwitz, S.: Precise interprocedural dataflow analysis with applications to constant propagation. Theor. Comput. Sci. **167**(1–2), 131–170 (1996). https://doi.org/10.1016/0304-3975(96)00072-2
27. Sharir, M., Pnueli, A.: Two approaches to interprocedural data flow analysis. New York University, Computer Science Department, New York (1978). https://cds.cern.ch/record/120118
28. Späth, J., Ali, K., Bodden, E.: Context-, flow- and field-sensitive data-flow analysis using synchronized pushdown systems. In: ACM SIGPLAN Symposium on Principles of Programming Languages (POPL 2019), 13–19 January 2019 (to appear)
29. Späth, J., Nguyen, L., Ali, K., Bodden, E.: Boomerang: demand-driven flow- and context-sensitive pointer analysis for Java. In: European Conference on Object-Oriented Programming (ECOOP), 17–22 July 2016
30. Steensgaard, B.: Points-to analysis in almost linear time. In: Proceedings of the 23rd ACM SIGPLAN-SIGACT Symposium on Principles of Programming Languages, POPL 1996, pp. 32–41. ACM, New York (1996). https://doi.org/10.1145/237721.237727
31. SVF, August 2018. https://github.com/SVF-tools/SVF/
32. WALi-OpenNWA, July 2018. https://github.com/WaliDev/WALi-OpenNWA
33. WALA, August 2018. http://wala.sourceforge.net/wiki/index.php/Main_Page
34. Schubert, P.D., Hermann, B., Bodden, E.: Artifact and instructions to generate experimental results for TACAS 2019 paper: PhASAR: An Inter-procedural Static Analysis Framework for C/C++ (artifact). Figshare (2019). https://doi.org/10.6084/m9.figshare.7824851.v1

Author Index

www.ingramcontent.com/pod-product-compliance
Lightning Source LLC
LaVergne TN
LVHW082110200926
348484LV00008B/1935

* 9 7 8 1 0 1 3 2 7 1 2 3 6 *